Lecture Notes in Artificial Intelli

Edited by J. G. Carbonell and J. Siekmann

Subseries of Lecture Notes in Computer Science

Gérard Chollet   Anna Esposito
Marcos Faundez-Zanuy   Maria Marinaro (Eds.)

Nonlinear Speech Modeling and Applications

Advanced Lectures and Revised Selected Papers

 Springer

Series Editors

Jaime G. Carbonell, Carnegie Mellon University, Pittsburgh, PA, USA
Jörg Siekmann, University of Saarland, Saarbrücken, Germany

Volume Editors

Gérard Chollet
CNRS URA-820, ENST, Dept. TSI
46 rue Barrault, 75634 Paris cedex 13, France
E-mail: chollet@tsi.enst.fr

Anna Esposito
Second University of Naples, Department of Psychology
and
IIASS, International Institute for Advanced Scientific Studies
Via Pellegrino 19, Vietri sul Mare (SA), Italy
E-mail: iiass.annaesp@tin.it

Marcos Faundez-Zanuy
Escola Universitaria Politecnica de Mataro
Avda. Puig i Cadafalch 101-111, 08303 Mataro (Barcelona), Spain
E-mail: faundez@eupmt.es

Maria Marinaro
University of Salerno "E.R.Caianiello", Dept. of Physics
Via Salvatore Allende, Baronissi, 84081 Salerno, Italy
and
IIASS, International Institute for Advanced Scientific Studies
Via Pellegrino 19, Vietri sul Mare (SA), Italy
E-mail: iiass.vietri@tin.it

Library of Congress Control Number: 2005928448

CR Subject Classification (1998): I.2.7, J.5, C.3

ISSN   0302-9743
ISBN-10   3-540-27441-3 Springer Berlin Heidelberg New York
ISBN-13   978-3-540-27441-4 Springer Berlin Heidelberg New York

Springer is a part of Springer Science+Business Media

springeronline.com

© Springer-Verlag Berlin Heidelberg 2005
Printed in Germany

Typesetting: Camera-ready by author, data conversion by Olgun Computergrafik
Printed on acid-free paper   SPIN: 11520153   06/3142   5 4 3 2 1 0

Preface

This volume contains invited and contributed papers presented at the 9th International Summer School "*Neural Nets E.R. Caianiello*" on Nonlinear Speech Processing: Algorithms and Analysis, held in Vietri sul Mare, Salerno, Italy, during September 13–18, 2004.

The aim of this book is to provide primarily high-level tutorial coverage of the fields related to nonlinear methods for speech processing and analysis, including new approaches aimed at improving speech applications.

Fourteen surveys are offered by specialists in the field. Consequently, the volume may be used as a reference book on nonlinear methods for speech processing and analysis. Also included are fifteen papers that present original contributions in the field and complete the tutorials.

The volume is divided into five sections: Dealing with Nonlinearities in Speech Signal, Acoustic-to-Articulatory Modeling of Speech Phenomena, Data Driven and Speech Processing Algorithms, Algorithms and Models Based on Speech Perception Mechanisms, and Task-Oriented Speech Applications.

Dealing with Nonlinearities in Speech Signals is an introductory section where nonlinear aspects of the speech signal are introduced from three different points of view. The section includes three papers. The first paper, authored by Anna Esposito and Maria Marinaro, is an attempt to introduce the concept of nonlinearity revising several nonlinear phenomena observed in the acoustics, the production and the perception of speech. Also discussed is the engineering endeavor to model these phenomena.

The second paper, by Marcos Faundez-Zanuy, gives an overview of nonlinear predictive models, with special emphasis on neural nets, and discusses several well-known nonlinear strategies, such as multistart random weights initialization, regularization, early stop with validation, committees of neural nets, and neural net architectures.

The third paper, by Simon Haykin, faces the problem of processing nonlinear, non-Gaussian, and nonstationary signals describing the mathematical implications derived by these assumptions. The topic has important practical implications of its own, not only in speech but also in the field of signal processing.

Acoustic-to-Articulatory Modeling of Speech Phenomena deals with problems related to the acoustic-phonetic theory in which basic speech sounds are characterized according to both their articulatory features and the associated acoustic measurements. Fundamental and innovative ideas in speech production are covered. This section contains three papers. The first paper, authored by Eric Keller, discusses voice quality within a large predictive and methodological framework. Voice quality phenomena are reviewed at two levels: (1) at the level of independent variables, topic-, affective-, attitude-, emotion-, gender-, articulation-, language-, sociolect-, gender-, age- and speaker-related predictors; and (2) at the level of dependent variables, where the empirical identification of voice quality parameters in the speech signal are summarized. Specifically, Fant's original and revised source-filter models are reviewed.

The second paper, by Gernot Kubin, Claudia Lainscsek, and Erhard Rank, discusses the identification of nonlinear oscillator models for speech analysis and synthesis. The paper, starting from the first successful application of a nonlinear oscillator model to high-quality speech signal processing, reviews the numerous developments that have been initiated to turn nonlinear oscillators into a standard tool for speech technology, and compares several of these attempts with a special emphasis on adaptive model identification from data.

The third paper, by Jean Schoentgen, revises speech modeling based on acoustic-to-articulatory mapping. The acoustic-articulatory mapping is the inference of acoustic equivalents of a speaker's vocal tract. This mapping involves the computation of models of the vocal tract whose eigenfrequencies are identical to the speaker's formant frequencies. The usefulness of such a transformation is in the idea that formant data may be interpreted and manipulated more easily in the transform domain (i.e., the geometric domain) and therefore acoustic-to-geometric mapping would be of great use in the framework of automatic speech and speaker recognition.

Data Driven and Speech Processing Algorithms deals with new and standard techniques used to provide speech features valuable for related speech applications. This section contains five papers.

The first, by Alessandro Bastari, Stefano Squartini, and Francesco Piazza, reports on the problem of separating a speech signal from a set of observables when the mixing system is undetermined. A common way to face this task is to see it as a Blind Source Separation (BSS) problem. The paper revises several approaches to solve different formulations of the blind source separation problem and also suggests the use of alternative time-frequency transforms such as the discrete wavelet transform (DWT) and the Stockwell transform (ST). The second paper, by Gerard Chollet, Kevin McTait, and Dijana Petrovska-Delacretaz, reviews experiments exploiting the automatic language independent speech processing (ALISP) approach to the development of speech processing applications driven by data, and how this strategy could be particularly useful for low-rate speech coding, recognition, translation and speaker verification.

The third and the fifth papers, by Peter Murphy and Olatunji Akande, and Yannis Stylianou, respectively, describe time-domain and frequency-domain techniques to estimate the harmonic-to-noise ratio as an indicator of the aperiodicity of a voice signal. New algorithms are proposed and applications to continuous speech recognition are also envisaged.

The fourth paper, on a predictive connectionist approach to speech recognition, by Bojan Petek, describes a context-dependent hidden control neural network (HCNN) architecture for large-vocabulary continuous-speech recognition. The basic building element of the proposed architecture, the context-dependent HCNN model, is a connectionist network trained to capture the dynamics of speech sub-word units. The HCNN model belongs to a family of Hidden Markov model/multi-layer perceptron (HMM/MLP) hybrids, usually referred to as predictive neural networks.

Algorithms and Models Based on Speech Perception Mechanisms includes three papers. The first, by Anna Esposito and Guido Aversano, discusses speech segmentation methods that do not use linguistic information and proposes a new segmentation algorithm based on perceptually processed speech features. A performance study is also reported through performance comparisons with standard speech segmentation methods such as temporal decomposition, Kullback–Leibler distances, and spectral variation functions.

The second paper, by Amir Hussain, Tariq Durrani, John Soraghan, Ali Aikulaibi, and Nhamo Mterwa, reports on nonlinear adaptive speech enhancement schemes inspired by features of early auditory processing, which allows for the manipulation of several factors that may influence the intelligibility and perceived quality of the processed speech. In this context it is shown that stochastic resonance might be a general strategy employed by the central nervous system for the improved detection of weak signals and that the effects of stochastic resonance in sensory processing might extend past an improvement in signal detection.

The last paper, by Jean Rouat, Ramin Pichevar, and Stéphanie Loiselle, presents potential solutions to the problem of sound separation based on computational auditory scene analysis (CASA), by using nonlinear speech processing and spiking neural Networks. The paper also introduces the reader to the potential use of spiking neurons in signal and spatiotemporal processing.

Task Oriented Speech Applications includes the papers of 15 contributors which propose original and seminal works on speech applications and suggest new principles by means of which task oriented applications may be successful.

The editors would like to thank first of all the COST European Cooperation in the field of Scientific and Technical Research, the oldest and most widely used system for research networking in Europe. COST provided full financial support for a significant number of attendants plus some financial contributions for two outstanding speakers (Simon Haykin and José Príncipe), for which we are very grateful. COST 277 set up the first summer school on the a COST framework in the last 33 years. Thus, this work can be considered historic, and we hope to repeat this successful event in the near future. COST is based on an inter-governmental framework for cooperation research agreed following a ministerial conference in 1971. The mission of COST is to strengthen Europe in scientific and technical research through the support of European cooperation and interaction between European researchers. Its aims are to strengthen noncompetitive and prenormative research in order to maximize European synergy and added value.

The keynote presentations reported in this book are mostly from speakers who are part of the Management Committee of COST Action 277, "Nonlinear Speech Processing," which has acted as a catalyst for research on nonlinear speech processing since June 2001.

The editors are extremely grateful to the International Society of Phonetic Sciences (ISPHS), and in particular Prof. Ruth Bahr, the International Institute for Advanced Scientific Studies "E.R. Caianiello," the Università di Salerno, Dipartimento di Fisica, the Seconda Università di Napoli, in particular the Dean of the Facoltà di Psicologia, Prof. Maria Sbandi, the Regione Campania, and the Provincia di Salerno for their support in sponsoring, financing, and organizing the school. Special thanks are due to Tina Nappi and Michele Donnarumma for their editorial and technical support, and to Guido Aversano, Marinella Arnone, Antonietta M. Esposito, Antonio Natale, Luca Pugliese, and Silvia Scarpetta for their help in the local organization of the school.

In addition, the editors are grateful to the contributors of this volume and the keynote speakers whose work stimulated an extremely interesting interaction with the attendees, who in turn shall not be forgotten – they are highly motivated and bright.

This book is dedicated to those who recognize the nonsense of wars, and to children's curiosity. Both are needed to motivate our research.

September 2004

Gerard Chollet
Anna Esposito
Marcos Faundez-Zanuy
Maria Marinaro

Table of Contents

Dealing with Nonlinearities in Speech Signals

Acoustic-to-Articulatory Modeling of Speech Phenomena

Data Driven and Speech Processing Algorithms

Algorithms and Models Based on Speech Perception Mechanisms

Task Oriented Speech Applications

Some Notes on Nonlinearities of Speech

Anna Esposito[1,2] and Maria Marinaro[2,3]

[1] Seconda Università di Napoli, Dipartimento di Psicologia, Via Vivaldi 43, Caserta, Italy
anna.esposito@unina2.it, iiass.annaesp@tin.it
[2] IIASS, Via Pellegrino 19, 84019, Vietri sul Mare, Italy, INFM Salerno, Italy
[3] Università di Salerno, Via S. Allende, Baronissi, Salerno, Italy
marinaro@sa.infn.it

Abstract. Speech is exceedingly nonlinear. Efforts to propose non-linear models of its dynamics are worth to be made but difficult to implement since nonlinearity is not easily handled from an engineering and mathematical point of view. This paper is an attempt to make accessible to untrained people the notion of nonlinearity in speech, revising several nonlinear speech phenomena and the engineering endeavour for modeling them.

1 Introduction

Understanding speech is basic for facing a very broad class of challenging problems including language acquisition, speech disorders, and speech communication technologies. Verbal communication appears to be the most common, or at the least, the easiest method for conveying information and meanings among humans. Successful verbal communication is possible only if the addresser and the addressee use the same language but more importantly are provided with the same language building blocks which are constituted by the phonemes (or speech sounds), the lexicon (words), and the syntax (the rules for linking words together).

The implementation of the communication process requires a set of steps that could be summarized as follow:

1. A communicative intention of the addresser;
2. A code that assembles the communicative intention into words (the language);
3. A motor program that controls the movements of speech articulators and allows the transformation of air that emerges from the lungs into speech sounds (the code) through the appropriate configuration assumed by the vocal tract;
4. A physical channel (the air medium that conveys the produced sound to the addressee);
5. A transducer (the auditory apparatus) that converts the produced sound into the firing of the auditory neurons;
6. The addressee's understanding of the message.

The communication process could be exemplified through the ***Stimulus-Response*** model of behavioural psychology [44]. In this model there is a *sender* that encodes the communicative intention into a *message*. The message is sent out through a channel. A receiver is supposed to receive, decode, and provide feedback to the transmitted message. The communication will be considered successful if it results in a *transfer of meaning*.

G. Chollet et al. (Eds.): Nonlinear Speech Modeling, LNAI 3445, pp. 1–14, 2005.
© Springer-Verlag Berlin Heidelberg 2005

The most influential schema of such a model, was proposed by Shannon and Weaver [75] and is reported in Figure 1.

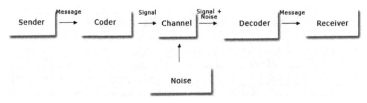

Fig. 1. An exemplification of the transmission model proposed by Shannon and Weaver [75]

The above model has several limitations, among those the most significant are: 1) it does not account for the effectiveness of the interaction between the sender and the receiver, since it assumes that communication is implemented by just carefully packaging the message to be transmitted; 2) feedback is not taken into account since it is problematic to implement it. However, some blocks in the above schema and in particular the *sender*, the *channel* and the *receiver* could be interpreted as an oversimplified description of the speech production system, the speech signal, and the speech perception system respectively. Each block has several nonlinear features and in the following sections we shall highlight some of them, in the attempt to clarify the notion of speech nonlinearities.

2 Nonlinearities in Speech Production

Speaking is a motor ability that consists of controlled and coordinated movements, performed primarily by the organs of the vocal tract (glottis, velum, tongue, lips) acting on the air in the respiratory passages (trachea, larynx, pharynx, mouth, nose) to produce speech sounds. The vocal organs generate a local disturbance of the air molecule at several positions in the vocal tract creating the sources for speech sound generation. The most common speech sources are: 1) the quasi-periodic vibration of the vocal cords – *voiced source*; 2) the turbulent noise generated by the passage the air through a quasi-narrow constriction (generally shaped by the tongue) in the oral cavity – *turbulent source*; 3) the plosive noise that follows the release of air compressed behind a complete obstruction of the oral cavity – *transient source*. However, the complex structure of speech sounds is not only due to the source generation features, but primarily to the response characteristics of the vocal tract that depends on the vocal tract configuration. The vocal tract configuration changes according to the motion of the vocal organs which modify its length, cross-sectional areas and response characteristics. The structure of speech sounds is generated by the combined effect of sound sources and vocal tract characteristics.

In absence of sounds, the vocal tract could be modeled as a single tube and the air molecules in it can be thought as a linear oscillator which responds to a disturbance with small displacements from the rest position. The conditions are extremely more complex when speech sounds are produced, since the motion of the vocal organs changes the vocal tract shape. A coarse model of the vocal tract in these conditions is a set of overlapping tubes of different lengths and cross-sectional areas. Due to its length and section area, each tube is subject to a different air pressure, which in turn, generates different forces acting on the air molecules, causing their very complicated motion. In this case, a linear description fails to describe this complex dynamics and a non-linear approach should be used. However, nonlinearities introduce uncertainty and multiple solutions to several speech problems. As an example, let us report the problem known as the *"acoustic-to-articulatory mapping"*. It consists in identifying, for a chosen vocal tract model constituted by a set of overlapping tubes, a set of parameters so that the resonances of the model correspond to the formants observed in a given produced speech sound. As is has been observed in [69], distinct vocal tract shapes can produce the same set of formant frequencies and therefore, a given set of formant values cannot univocally identify the vocal tract shape that has generated them (inverse problem). There are infinite solutions for the inverse problem. Even when functional constraints are imposed (such as minimal deformation, or minimal deformation rate of the vocal tract about a reference shape, or minimal deformation jerk) the inverse mapping does not fix the model, i.e., the real vocal tract shape that has produced that sound. To highlight the problems involved in the implementation of the acoustic-to-articulatory mapping, Schoentgen [69] reports a series of experiments where formant frequencies measured from sustained American English sounds are used to identify the corresponding vocal tract shapes. This is done taking three aspects into account: a) the accuracy of the vocal tract shapes estimate via formant-to-area mapping in comparison to the real vocal shapes; b) the underlying vocal tract models used; c) the numerical stability. Results shown that a good approximation is guaranteed only for speech sounds that are produced with a simple vocal tract configuration *"single cavity, single constriction, convex tongue, as well as constrained in the laryngo-pharynx, and, possibly, at the lips"* [69]; models based on a small number of conical tubelets with continuously varying cross area sections are preferred to exponential tubelets and cylindrical tubelets; the convergence to the desired format frequency values could be obtained with a precision greater than 1 Hz, even though the estimated vocal tract shapes could quantitatively and qualitatively differ from those built via the observed formant frequencies.

Another open problem is in the approximation of the glottal cycle waveform, i.e. the shape of the airflow produced at the glottis, before the signal is modified by the effects of the vocal tract configuration. The glottal waveform plays an important role in determining voice quality, which is defined as: *"the characteristic auditory coloring of an individual's voice, derived from a variety of laryngeal and supralaryngeal features and running continuously through the individual's speech"* [82]. An effective speech synthesizer should be able to adequately control the voice quality such that the synthesized speech sounds have a natural and distinctive tone. Several attempts have been made to model the glottal cycle waveform with the aim to identify the features of the glottal wave in accord to varying voice quality, and a *"conceptual framework"* of this research field is discussed in depth in this volume by Keller [40]. The most direct and automatic method, that does not involves invasive measurements is the inverse filtering technique [60], [61], that requires the recording (through a mask) of the glottal airflow at the mouth and its processing with a filtering system that separates the vocal tract characteristics from those of the glottal source. However, due to of the nonlinearities inside the transfer function of the vocal tract, this separation is not straightforward and the resulting glottal waveform models cannot account for several voice quality features. Nonlinearities are due to several factors, among these the interaction of the vocal tract with the nasal tract (for nasalized speech sounds), the presence of other sources of acoustic energy within the vocal tract (such as constrictions at certain locations), the degree at which the vocal folds attain a complete closure during the oscillatory cycle (as in the case of abnormal or breathy voices), the drop of sub-glottal pressure due to the sub-glottal resistance, the differences in vocal fold configurations during the opening and closing phases of the vibratory cycle, and many others. The above reported nonlinearities (together with the need to properly adjust the inverse filter parameters for each subject during the recording of the airflow) cause several errors in the glottal waveform approximation mostly due to the inadequateness of the underlying mathematical model (generally based on a linear-time invariant filter) which is not able to take into account all the phenomena mentioned above and therefore, accurately reproduces the acoustic characteristics of the real glottal waveform. Several attempts in modelling such non-linear phenomena and automating the inverse filtering procedure have been proposed requiring the introduction of non-linear transformations at different stages of the inverse filtering procedure [23], [27], [37], [60], [61], [62], [63]. However, schemes that avoid an accurate manual setting of the filter parameters and are robust under a wide variety of voice conditions are yet to be developed, even though advances in computerized methods to automate the process have been recently proposed [63].

3   Nonlinearities in Speech Acoustics

Like most of the real signals, speech sounds are complex in their form and, for applicative and basic research, there is an immense amount of investigations aimed to find an appropriate digital description for them. From an applicative point of view, a suitable digital description of speech sounds would solve speech synthesis and recognition problems, allowing an easy human-machine interaction. Moreover, in basic research, understanding speech processes holds considerable promises as well as challenges, for speech communication scientists.

The simplest digital representation of speech is directly related to the speech waveform and is based on Nyquist's sampling theorem showing that any band limited signal can be exactly reconstructed from samples taken periodically in time if the sampling rate is at least twice as high as the frequency of the signal. Based on the above idea are coding schemes like PCM (Pulse Code Modulation), DM (Delta Modulation), and DPCM (Differential Pulse Code Modulation) [14], [38]. However, in many speech applications the interest is not to reconstruct an acoustic signal but rather represent it in terms of a set of features or parameters that encode some of its invariant and descriptive attributes. All parametric representations of speech are based on the idea of short-time analysis, i.e. over a short-time interval (of about 10 to 30 ms duration), it is assumed that the properties of the speech waveform remain invariant. Figure 2 illustrates this idea. On the left side of Figure 2 is reported a waveform with windows covering small pieces of it. These small pieces are the short time intervals over which it is assumed that the signal is not affected by variations. Acoustic features are extracted from each short time interval as is shown on the right side of Figure 2. The white boxes represent a (among many) speech encoding algorithm. The choice of the encoding algorithm heavily depends on the applications.

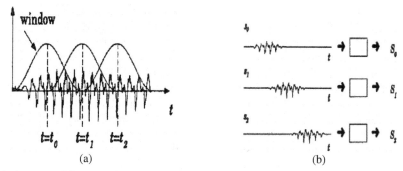

Fig. 2. An exemplification of the short time analysis idea. In (*a*) the speech signal is segmented by the sliding short-time window. In (*b*) processing is applied to each window to yield a vector S_i, of acoustic features r_j; $S_i = r_0, r_1, ..., r_k, i=1, ...,N; j=1,...k$

Short time analysis of speech allows to identify useful speech parameters derived by simple measurements of waveform characteristics (time domain analysis methods) such as peaks, energy, zero crossing measurements, and by short time autocorrelation analysis [28], [29], [58], [66], [79]. There are also frequency-domain analysis methods, essentially based on the Fourier Transform which is commonly implemented either using a bank of band-pass digital filters or through the Fast Fourier Transform (FFT) algorithm. The resulting short-time spectrum can be used as a direct representation of the speech signal in several speech related applications [25], [31], [48], [71]. However, in many cases, it is computed as an intermediate step in the estimation of one or more complex time-varying parameters of speech [6], [50], [51], [53], [67], [68], [72], [76] as in the case of homomorphic speech processing systems. Homomorphic filtering methods are based on the assumption that the time varying process speech production can be viewed on a short-time basis as the convolution of an excitation source (random noise for turbulent and transient sources or quasi-periodic impulse train for voiced source) with the vocal tract impulse response [30], [55], [56]. The result of this processing is called *cepstrum* and consists of an additive combination of the vocal tract and the source excitation components that essentially do not overlap and could be easily separated since the low-time samples contain information about the vocal tract transfer function, and the high-time samples provide information about the source excitation [52], [54].

Other useful methods of speech coding and analysis are those based on Linear Prediction [2], [34], [47]. The basic idea behind this coding is that speech samples are assumed to be the output of a time-varying digital filter whose transfer function approximates the spectral properties of both the vocal tract and the glottal pulse.

The wide variety of digital representations of speech can be applied in many speech processing applications including speech recognition, speech synthesis, speaker adaptation, and speaker verification. However, while these methods have led to great advances in speech technologies during the past 30 years, they neglect nonlinear structure known to be present in the speech signal. In practical applications, the assumption that the speech signal is basically linear causes an increase in the bit rate in speech transmission applications, a less natural synthetic speech in synthesis, and poorer discriminating ability of speech sounds and speakers in speech recognition systems.

Nonlinearities in the speech signal are present at least in two descriptive domains: the phonetic and the supra-segmental domain. In the phonetic realm, the rapid dynamic of transient and turbulent sources (as in the production of consonants), the rapid variation of formant frequency values (usually observed in vowels because of the adjacent phonetic context), confusable sounds, and segmental phenomena such as elision, assimilation, etc., cannot be accounted by the stationary and linear assumption. In the supra-segmental realm, rapid variations in speaking rate, speech energy, and fundamental frequency value (due to the speakers' emotional and health state) as well as variability in the acoustic realization of utterances from different speakers, homophone words, and the intrinsic nonlinearities of the speech production system (discussed in the previous section) cannot be encoded through a processing algorithm that can only extract linear features. To this aim, several non linear speech processing techniques have been proposed, such as non linear parametric and non parametric autoregressive models, speech fluid dynamics, modulation, and fractal methods. Some of these methods are theoretically discussed in this volume by Bastari et al.[3], Chollet et al. [7], Faundez-Zanuy [24], Haykin [33], Kubin et al. [43], Murphy and Akande [46], Petek [57], and Stylianou [81]. The results are very encouraging, showing that nonlinear speech processing methods offers a good alternative to conventional speech encoding techniques.

4 Nonlinearities in Speech Perception

The human auditory apparatus is an optimal system for speech signal recognition, even in hostile environmental conditions. Even though communication develops from the simultaneous processing of several signals detected through vision, gesticulation, and the context in which the sound information is collocated, it is evident that auditory processing offers a remarkable contribution to the understanding of a speech message. The ear is a naturally evolved device for measuring sounds, showing some highly astonishing features such as threshold sensitivity, dynamical range localization, frequency discrimination, amplification and noise suppression mechanisms [4], [5], [26], [84]. The machinery that implements such features is both mechanical and neural.

There is evidence that the human auditory apparatus implements nonlinear signal processing procedures, extracting features that are different from those obtained through the classical short-time analysis. There is interest in developing algorithms simulating the auditory processing, since it has been shown that the use of auditory features can improve the performance of both speech recognition and speech segmentation applications [8-13], [22], [34], [36], [64]. To this aim, several models of the human auditory apparatus have been proposed, that rise from the current knowledge on how the peripheral auditory system processes signals as well as on how brain mechanisms utilize information contained in the firing rates of the nervous fibers, in order to recognize sounds [11], [12], [20], [21], [34], [36], [45], [64], [73], [74]. A schematic representation of the ear is illustrated in Figure 3.

The mathematical modeling of the hearing mechanisms is generally made through four stages each realizing a particular behavior. The first and second stage simulate the mechanical ear behavior, which includes the cochlear processing. The third stage models some non-linear processes, such as half-wave rectification, short-term adapta-

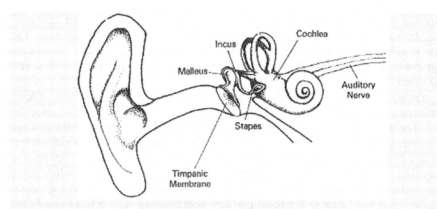

Fig. 3. A schematic representation of the ear: the ear lobe, the pinna, and the auditory canal form the outer ear; the ear ossicles (malleus, incus, and stapes) and the timpanic membrane form the middle ear; the inner ear is constituted by the cochlea

tion, and high-frequency synchrony reduction, which take place when the movements of the basilar membrane are transformed into nervous fiber activity. Finally, the last stage accomplishes the extraction of signal parameters and their interpretation through higher cognitive processes [15-19], [49], [65], [77], [78].

4.1 The Mechanical Behavior of the Ear

The physiological data on the ear performance are astonishing. The minimum audible sound intensity that we can perceive is around 10^{-6} W/cm^2, which is only slightly above the thermal noise power density at the eardrum in the audible frequency range. Hearing intensity perception extends from 0 to 120 dB, covering a 12 order range of magnitude that suggests effective mechanisms of reduction as well as amplification for high and low level signals respectively. Moreover, as a spectrum analyzer, the ear has an amazing resolving power, exhibiting a very demanding frequency resolution ($\delta f = 1$Hz) in the low frequency range (<500Hz) and a constant relative frequency resolution ($\delta f/f \approx 0.0035$) in the high frequency range (>1kHz). These features are largely implemented in the mechanical part of the ear. A prerequisite of such a high threshold sensitivity, for example, is the assumption that no energy of the incoming signal should be lost in the following processing stages. This requires an impedance matching procedure performed by the middle ear, that avoids to couple directly the sound wave with the ear sensory cells. Many biological studies [80] show that the tympanic membrane, with the malleus, the incus, and stapes, performs on the ear's incoming signal a particular transformation that enhances a low intensity signal and lowers a high one. Commonly, in a mathematical model this behavior is implemented by a linear filter, usually covering a frequency range from 100Hz to 7000Hz, i.e. a filter particularly tuned on the speech frequencies [20], [45], [74]. However, the filter alone does not explain the ear's threshold sensitivity feature since other processes performed by the cochlea should be considered.

The cochlea, a snail shaped bony canal about 3 ½ cm long, constituted of 2 and 1/2 turns of spiral, is separated by the middle ear through the oval window. It has thin rigid walls and is filled with incompressible fluid. The cochlea is divided, along its length, by two flexible membranes, Reissner's membrane and the basilar one. The basilar membrane extends for 35 mm dividing the cochlear canal along the middle and grows in thickness from the basal part of the cochlea to the apex at the inner end of the spiral.

In sensing an incoming signal, the sound wave passes down the ear canal, striking and vibrating the drum, which in turn vibrates the incus, which in turn vibrates the stapes. The footplate of the stapes covers the oval window of the cochlea and the movements of the stapes initiate in the cochlear fluid a pressure wave, which propagates in a dissipative manner along the cochlear partition [4]. Within the cochlea, the compression wave originated in the cochlear fluid is transformed into a surface wave along the basilar membrane. Because of the variable thickness of the basilar membrane, waves travel faster in the basal part and continuously slow down towards the apical region. As the velocity decreases moving to the apex, the wave amplitude must increases according to the energy conservation principle. However, the damping effects of the surrounding cochlear fluid prevents an unlimited increase of the wave peaks, that reach a maximum and then disappear. The location of the maximum depends on the driving frequency: the response to high frequencies being dominant at the basal (stiff) end and at the apex for low frequencies. Thus the basilar membrane performs a frequency analysis of the incoming signal transforming its frequency components to positions of maximum vibrations on the basilar membrane. This analysis mode maps the linear frequency scale (Hz) into a logarithmic frequency due to the high frequency scaling ratio ($\delta f/f \approx 0.0035$) mentioned above.

The mechanical analysis of sounds by traveling waves is closely related to the Fourier analysis which represents a linear and passive paradigm for signal analysis. Therefore, realistic models of the auditory apparatus implement the inner ear behavior by means of a filter bank. The filter bank frequency responses are made similar to the basilar membrane responses allowing the filter bandwidths to overlap. Moreover, due to the nonlinear scaling in frequency of the basilar membrane responses, the calculation of the filter bandwidths is commonly made using a biological measure: the Bark scale [85]. However, the behavior of a purely mechanical filter is not sufficient to explain the frequency discrimination power of the ear, and therefore it is hypothesized the intervention of other mechanisms interacting with the basilar membrane to enhance and sharpen the traveling waves. We shall see below that outer hair cells seem to play a role.

4.2 The Neural Auditory Processing

Attached to the basilar membrane is the Corti organ, a complex organ which contains the inner and outer hair cells, the apexes of cells (each composed of two to four rows of hair like structures called stereocilia) lay between the basilar and the tectorial membrane, and the bases are connected to nerve fibers of the auditory nerve. The inner hair cells are primarily connected through afferent neurons, which deliver signals to the brain. The outer hair cells are innervated by efferent neurons, which receive neural signals from the brain. The inner hair cells act as mechanoelectric transducers, converting the displacements of the hair bundles (originated by the shearing motion created between the basilar and tectorial membrane) into action potentials.

The outer hair cells act as electromechanic transducers by converting voltages across their cell membranes into length changes. The auditory neurons originating at the hair cells feed into the 8th cranial auditory nerve and terminate in the cochlear nucleus. The projection of the auditory nerve to the cochlear nucleus is geometrically ordered, preserving the signal's representation at the cochlear locations at all levels of the auditory system. Experimental results show that a given sound elicits responses in the auditory neurons that are a function of its frequency, i.e. fiber responses are selective and each neuron has a maximum response (a high firing rate) at a specific frequency, called Characteristic Frequency (CF). The CF is due to cochlear mechanisms, and the cochlea itself provides a frequency analysis of the acoustical stimulus, since each portion of the basilar membrane, when excited at the CF, generates a high firing rate of the tuned neurons.

The two type of hair cells contribute differently to the processing of the incoming signal. In fact, while the inner cells act as carriers of the signal parameters to the brain, the outer cells seem to implement a feedback mechanism that sharpen the excitation patterns of the nerve fibers, so that two perceptually different neighboring tones can be discriminated despite of the strong dissipation involved in the frequency-place transformation performed by the basilar membrane.

The way the inner hair cells stimulate the auditory neurons is highly nonlinear since neurons can transmit impulses of an *all-or-none* nature. Thus several non-linear phenomena arise when the basilar membrane motions generate the firing patterns of the auditory neurons.

Among the several nonlinear mechanisms that are part of the acoustic nerve activity there is the suppression of the firing rate during negative portions of the incoming signal. This mechanism is known as half wave rectification and occurs because hair cells show a high level distinct directional sensitivity since they tend to respond to only one direction of the displacement of the stimulating waveform. The exact shape of the half-wave nonlinearity is not obvious; mathematical models of the auditory systems implement this feature through a half-wave rectifier based on a saturating nonlinearity [41], [42], [70].

Physiological experimental data show that spikes of the auditory fibers last for about 0.2 ms and occur also without acoustic stimulation. During acoustical stimulations the firing rate reaches a maximum of 1000 spikes per second. Higher firing rates are not possible because of the refractory period of the neurons. For continued acoustical stimulations the instantaneous discharge rate of the auditory nerve decreases until it reaches a steady-state level. Goldor [32] and Zwilosky [86] have experimentally measured the decay time of the transmitter flow in the cleft and the natural decay time in which the transmitter quantum decays to the spontaneous concentration level giving a mathematical description of the variation of the transmitter quanta in the cleft. Decays in the firing rate of the auditory neurons also happen immediately after the stimulus onset generating what is called short term adaptation.

Another feature of the neural coding is the phase looking characteristic of the neural spikes. It is based on the fact that the neural output, under low-frequency periodic stimulations is phase-locked, i.e. the intervals between firing tend to cluster near multiples of the stimulus period. For example, a 500 Hz wave will have a period of 2 ms and therefore the intervals between successive neuron firings will be approximately 2 ms, or 4 ms, or 6 ms, etc. However, phase locking does not occur at frequencies higher than 4-5kHz [59] due to the loss of precision between the initiation of a nerve spike and the phase of incoming stimulus. There is, in fact, a variability in the exact instant of initiation of the neuron spike. At high frequencies this variability becomes comparables with the incoming stimulus period, and therefore above a certain frequency, the spikes will be smeared over the whole stimulus period.

The processes described above and the large amount of data gathered by studies devoted to characterize the auditory transformations [1], [15-19], [39], [49], [65], [77], [78], [83], [85], [86], suggest that the aural representations of the speech signals are significantly different from the spectral and temporal representation obtained using the standard processing techniques reported in section 3.

Speech signal parameters may be better coded by using features derived by the nonlinear discharge patterns of the auditory neurons and by exploiting the mechanisms that allow the nerve fibers to be selective in space, time, and frequency. These features could be able to overcome the limitations of the short-term analysis paradigm since they implicitly retain information on the speech production and speech perception nonlinear dynamics.

Evidences on the validity of this approach and details on the processing and modeling techniques inspired to the auditory processing mechanisms and implemented for speech analysis and speech recognition applications can be found in this volume and other works proposed in literature [11-13], [22], [34], [64].

5   Conclusions

The present paper reports an overview of nonlinearities that can be observed in speech signals at different stages of the speech chain, highlighting the need to exploit nonlinear features to improve the performance of speech related applications.

Acknowledgements

Acknowledgment goes to Tina Nappi and Marinella Arnone for their editorial help.

References

1. Albrecht, D.G.,Geisler, W.S.: Motion Selectivity and the Contrast Response Function of Simple Cells in the Visual Cortex. Visual Neuroscience, Vol. 7(6) (1991) 531–546
2. Atal, B.S., Hanauer, S.L.: Speech Analysis and Synthesis by Linear Prediction of Speech Wave. J. Acoustic. Soc. Amer., Vol.. 50(2) (1971) 637–655
3. Bastari, A., Squartini, S., Piazza, F.: Underdetermined Blind Separation of Speech Signals with Delays in Different Time-Frequency Domain. In Chollet, G., Esposito, A., Faundez-Zauny, M., Marinaro, M. (eds.): Advances in Nonlinear Speech Modeling and Applications. Lecture Notes in Computer Science, Springer-Verlag, Berlin Heidelberg New York (2005) To be Published
4. Bekesy, G. V.: Experiments in Hearing. McGRaw-Hill, New York (1960)
5. Bekesy, G. V.: Sensory Inhibition. Princeton University Press, Princeton (1967)

6. Bell, C.G., Fujisaki, H., Heinz, J.M., Stevens, K.N., House, A.S.: Reduction of Speech Spectra by Analysis–by–Synthesis Techniques. J. Acoustic. Soc. Amer.,Vol. 33 (1961) 1725–1736

7. Chollet, G., McTait, K., Petrovska-Delacretaz, D.: Data Driven Approaches to Speech and Languages Processing. In Chollet, G., Esposito, A., Faundez-Zauny, M., Marinaro, M. (eds.): Advances in Nonlinear Speech Modeling and Applications. Lecture Notes in Computer Science, Springer-Verlag, Berlin Heidelberg New York (2005) To be Published

8. Cosi, P., De Mori, R., Vagges, K.: A Neural Network Architecture for Italian Vowel Recognition. In Proceedings of VERBA90, Rome, Italy (1990) 22-24

9. Cosi, P., Bengio, Y., De Mori, R.: Phonetically-Based Multi-Layered Neural Networks for Vowel Classification. Speech Comm., Vol. 9(1) (1990) 15-29

10. Cosi, P., Ferrero, F.: Applicazione di un Modello del Sistema Uditivo Periferico alla Segmentazione Automatica del Segnale Vocale. In AIA Proceedings, Atti del XX Convegno Nazionale di Acustica, Roma, April (1992)

11. Cosi, P., Frasconi, P., Gori, M., Griggio, N.: Phonetic Recognition Experiments with Recurrent Neural Networks. Proc. ICSLP (1992) 1335-1338

12. Cosi P.: Auditory Modelling for Speech Analysis and Recognition. In M. Cooke, S. Beet, M.Crawford (eds.): Visual Representation of Speech Signals. Wiley & Sons Chichester (1993) 205-212

13. Cosi, P.: Auditory Modeling and Neural Networks. In Chollet, G., Di Benedetto, M. G., Esposito, A., Marinaro, M. (eds.): Speech Processing, Recognition, and Artificial Neural Networks. Springer-Verlag, Berlin Heidelberg New York (1999) 54–84

14. Cummiskey, P., Jayant, N.S., Flanagan, J. L: Adaptive Quantization in Differential PCM Coding of Speech. Bell Syst. Tech. J. (1973) 1105–1118

15. Delgutte, B.: Representation of Speech-like Sounds in the Discharge Patterns of Auditory-nerve Fibers. J. Acoustic. Soc. Amer. Vol.68 (1980) 843-857

16. Delgutte, B., Kiang, N.Y.S.: Speech Coding in the Auditory Nerve: I Vowel-like Sounds. J. Acoustic. Soc. Amer. Vol. 75 (1984) 866-878

17. Delgutte, B., Kiang, N.Y.S.: Speech Coding in the Auditory Nerve: II Processing Schemes for Vowel-like Sounds. J. Acoustic. Soc. Amer. Vol. 75 (1984) 879-886

18. Delgutte, B.,Kiang, N.Y.S.: Speech Coding in the Auditory Nerve: III Voiceless Fricative Consonants. J. Acoustic. Soc. Amer. Vol. 75 (1984) 887-896

19. Delgutte, B.,Kiang, N.Y.S.: Speech Coding in the Auditory Nerve: IV Sounds with Consonant-Like Dynamic Characteristics. J. Acoustic. Soc. Amer. Vol. 75 (1984) 897-907.

20. Esposito, A., Rampone, S., Stanzione, C., Tagliaferri R.: A Mathematical Model for Speech Processing. In Proceedings of IEEE on Neural Networks for Signal Processing (1992) 194-203

21. Esposito, A., Rampone, S., Stanzione, C., Tagliaferri R.: Experimental Results on a Model of the Peripheral Auditory Apparatus. In Proceedings of International Workshop on Neural Networks for Speech Recognition, Lint, Trieste (1992) 163-177

22. Esposito, A., Aversano, G.: Text Independent Methods for Speech Segmentation. In Chollet, G., Esposito, A., Faundez-Zauny, M., Marinaro, M. (eds.): Advances in Nonlinear Speech Modeling and Applications. Lecture Notes in Computer Science, Springer-Verlag, Berlin Heidelberg New York (2005) To be Published

23. Fant, G.: Preliminaries to Analysis of the Human Voice Source. Speech Communication Group Working Papers, Vol. 3, Research Laboratory of Electronics, Massachusetts Institute of Technology (1983)

24. Faundez-Zanuy, M.: Nonlinear Speech Processing: Overview and Possibilities in Speech Coding. In Chollet, G., Esposito, A., Faundez-Zanuy, M., Marinaro, M. (eds.): Advances in Nonlinear Speech Modeling and Applications. Lecture Notes in Computer Science, Springer-Verlag, Berlin Heidelberg New York (2005) To be Published

25. Flanagan, J. L., Golden, R. M.: Phase Vocoder. Tech J., Vol. 45 (1966) 1493–1509

26. Fletcher, H.: Auditory Patterns. Review of Modern Physics, Vol. 13 (1940) 47-65
27. Gauffin. J., Hammarberg. B.,Imaizumi, S.: A Microcomputer Based System for Acoustic Analsyis of Voice Characteristics. In Proceedings of ICASSP86, Tokyo, Vol. 1 (1986) 681-684
28. Gold, B.: Note on Buzz–Hiss Detection. J. Acoustic. Soc. Amer., Vol. 36 (1964) 1659–1661
29. Gold, B., Rabiner, L. R.: Parallel Processing Technique for Estimating Pitch Periods of Speech in the Time Domain. J. Acoustic. Soc. Amer., Vol.. 46(2) (1969) 442–449
30. Gold, B., Rader, C. M.: Digital Processing of Signals. New–York, McGraw–Hill (1969)
31. Gold, B., Rader, C. M.: System for Compressing the Bandwidth of Speech. IEEE Trans. Audio Electroacoustic, Vol. AU–15 (1967) 131–135
32. Goldhor, R.S.: Representation of Consonants in the Peripheral Auditory System: A Modeling Study of the Correspondence between Response Properties and Phonetic Features. RLE Technical Report N. 505, MIT press, (1985)
33. Haykin, S.: Signal Processing in Nonlinear Nongaussian and Nonstationary World. In Chollet, G., Esposito, A., Faundez-Zauny, M., Marinaro, M. (eds.): Advances in Nonlinear Speech Modeling and Applications. Lecture Notes in Computer Science, Springer-Verlag, Berlin Heidelberg New York (2005) To be Published
34. Hussain, A., Durrani, T.S., Soraghan, J.J., Aikulaibi, A., Mterwa, N.: Nonlinear Adaptive Speech Enhancement Inspired by Early Auditory Processing. In Chollet, G., Esposito, A., Faundez-Zauny, M., Marinaro, M. (eds.): Advances in Nonlinear Speech Modeling and Applications. Lecture Notes in Computer Science, Springer-Verlag, Berlin Heidelberg New York (2005) To be Published
35. Itakura, F.: Minimum Prediction Residual Principle Applied to Speech Recognition. IEEE Trans. Acoust., Speech, and Signal Process., ASSP–23 (1975) 67–72
36. Jankowski, C.R. Jr., Vo, H-D. H., Lippmann, R.P.: A Comparison of Signal Processin Front Ends for Automatic Word Recognition. IEEE Trans Speech and Audio Processing, Vol. SAP-3(3) (1995) 286-293.
37. Javkin, H.R., Antonanzas-Barroso, N., Maddieson, I.: Digital Inverse Filtering for Linguistic Research. Journal of Speech and Hearing Research. Vol. 30 (1987) 122-129
38. Jayant, N.S.: Digital Coding of Speech Waveform. Proc. IEEE Vol..62 (1964) 611–632
39. Johnson, D.H., Swami. A.: The Transmission of Signals by Auditory-Nerve Fiber Discharge Patterns. J. Acoustic. Soc. Amer., Vol. 74 (1983) 493-501.
40. Keller, E.: The Analysis of Voice Quality in Speech Processing. In Chollet, G., Esposito, A., Faundez-Zauny, M., Marinaro, M. (eds.): Advances in Nonlinear Speech Modeling and Applications. Lecture Notes in Computer Science, Springer-Verlag, Berlin Heidelberg New York (2005) To be Published
41. Kim, D.0., Molnar, C. E.: A Population Study of Cochlear Nerve Fibers: Comparison of Spatial Distributions of Average-Rate and Phase Locking Measures of Responses to Single Tones. J. of Neurophysiology Vol. 42 (1979) 16-30
42. Kim, D.0., Molnar, C.E., Matthews, J.W.: Cochlear Mechanics: Nonlinear Behaviour in Two-Tone Responses as Reflected in Cochlear-Nerve-Fiber Responses and in Ear-Canal Sound Pressure.. J. Acoustic. Soc. Amer., Vol. 67 (1980) 1704-1721
43. Kubin, G., Lainscsek, C., Rank, E.: Identification of Nonlinear Oscillator Models for Speech Analysis and Synthesis. In Chollet, G., Esposito, A., Faundez-Zauny, M., Marinaro, M. (eds.): Advances in Nonlinear Speech Modeling and Applications. Lecture Notes in Computer Science, Springer-Verlag, Berlin Heidelberg New York (2005) To be Published
44. Lakoff, G., Johnson, M.: Metaphors We Live By. Chicago: University of Chicago Press, (1980) 10-11
45. Lyon, R.F.: A Computational Model of Filtering, Detection, and Compression in the Cochlea. In Proceedings of IEEE-ICASSP (1982) 1282-1285

46. Murphy, P., Akande, O.: Cepstrum-Based Harmonics-to-Noise Ratio Measurements in Voiced Speech. In Chollet, G., Esposito, A., Faundez-Zauny, M., Marinaro, M. (eds.): Advances in Nonlinear Speech Modeling and Applications. Lecture Notes in Computer Science, Springer-Verlag, Berlin Heidelberg New York (2005) To be Published

47. Markel,, J.D., Gray, A.H., Wakita, H.: Linear Prediction of Speech Theory and Practice. Speech Communications, Santa Barbara, California, SCRL monograph. 10 (1973)

48. Martin, T.: Acoustic Recognition of a Limited Vocabulary in Continuous Speech. Ph.D Thesis, Uni. Pennsylvania, Philadelphia (1970)

49. Meddis, R.: Simulation of Mechanical to Neural Transduction in the Auditory Receptor. J. Acoustic. Soc. Amer. Vol.79 (1986) 702-711

50. Mermelstein, P.: Computer Generated Spectrogram Displays for On–Line Speech Research. IEEE Trans. Audio Electroacoustic., Vol.. AU–19 (1971) 44–47

51. Noll, A.M.: Cepstrum Pitch Determination. J. Acoustic. Soc. Amer., Vol.41 (1967) 293–309

52. Oppenheim, A.V.: A Speech Analysis–Synthesis System Based on Homomorphic Filtering. J. Acoustic. Soc. Amer., Vol. 45 (1969) 458–465

53. Oppenheim, A.V.: Speech Spectrograms Using the Fast Fourier Transform. IEEE Spectrum, Vol.7 (1970) 57–62

54. Oppenheim, A.V., Schafer, R.W.: Homomorphic Analysis of Speech. IEEE Trans. Audio Electroacoust., Vol. AU16 (1968) 221–226

55. Oppenheim, A.V., Schafer, R.W., Stochham, S.: Nonlinear Filtering of Multiplied and Convolved Signals. Proc. IEEE, Vol. 56 (1968) 1264–1291

56. Oppenheim, A.V., Schafer, R.W.: Digital Signal Processing. Englewood Cliffs, N.J. Prentice–Hall (1975)

57. Petek, B.: Predictive Connectionist Approach to Speech Recognition. In Chollet, G., Esposito, A., Faundez-Zauny, M., Marinaro, M. (eds.): Advances in Nonlinear Speech Modeling and Applications. Lecture Notes in Computer Science, Springer-Verlag, Berlin Heidelberg New York (2005) To be Published

58. Reddy, D.R.: Computer Recognition of Connected Speech. J. Acoustic. Soc. Amer., Vol.. 42(2) (1967) 329–347

59. Rose. J.E., Brugge, J.F., Anderson, D.J., Hindi, J.E.: Patterns of Activity in Single Auditory Nerve Fibers of the Squirrel Monkey. In de Reuck, A.V.S., Knight, J. (eds): Hearing Mechanisms in Vertebrate, Churchill, London (1968) 144-168

60. Rothenberg, M.: A New Inverse-Filtering Technique for Deriving the Glottal Airflow Waveform during Voicing. Journal of Acoustical Society of America, Vol. 53 (1973)1632-1645

61. Rothenberg, M.: Measurement of Airflow in Speech. Journal of Speech and Hearing Research, Vol. 20 (1977) 155-176

62. Rothenberg. M.: Acoustic Interaction between the Glottal Source and Vocal Tract. In: Stevens, K.N., Hirano, H (eds): Vocal Fold Physiology, Tokyo Press (1981) 305-328

63. Rothenberg,M.: Inverse Filtering on your Laptop. http://www.rothenberg.org/contents.htm

64. Rouat, J., Pichevar, R., Loiselle,S.: Perceptive Nonlinear Speech Processing and Spiking Neural Networks. In Chollet, G., Esposito, A., Faundez-Zauny, M., Marinaro, M. (eds.): Advances in Nonlinear Speech Modeling and Applications. Lecture Notes in Computer Science, Springer-Verlag, Berlin Heidelberg New York (2005) To be Published

65. Sachs, M.B., Young, E.D.: Encoding of Steady State Vowels in the Auditory Nerve: Representation in Terms of Discontinuities. J. Acoustic. Soc. Amer. Vol.66 (1979) 470-479

66. Schafer, R.W., Rabiner, L.R.: System for Automatic Formant Analysis of Voiced Speech. J. Acoustic. Soc. Amer., Vol. 47(2) (1970) 634–648

67. Schafer, R.W., Rabiner, L.R.: Design of Digital Filter Banks for Speech Analysis. Bell Syst. Tech. Journ., Vol.50(10) (1971) 3097–3015

68. Schafer, R.W., Rabiner, L.R.: Design and Simulation of a Speech Analysis–Synthesis System Based on Short–Time Fourier Analysis. IEEE Trans. Audio Electroacoustic., Vol. AU–21 (1973) 165–174

69. Schoentgen, J.: Speech Modeling based on Acoustic-to-Articulatory Mapping. In Chollet, G., Esposito, A., Faundez-Zauny, M., Marinaro, M. (eds.): Advances in Nonlinear Speech Modeling and Applications. Lecture Notes in Computer Science, Springer-Verlag, Berlin Heidelberg New York (2005) To be Published

70. Schroeder, M.H., Hall, J.L.: Model for Mechanical to Neural Transduction in the Auditory Receptor. J. Acoustic. Soc. Amer., Vol. 55 (1974) 1055-1060

71. Schroeder, M.R.: Vocoders, Analysis and Synthesis of Speech. Proc. IEEE, Vol.54 (1966) 720–754

72. Schroeder, M.R.: Period Histogram and Product Spectrum: New Methods for Fundamental Frequency Measurements. J. Acoustic. Soc. Amer., Vol. 43(4) (1968) 829–834

73. Seneff, S.: Pitch and Spectral Analysis of Speech Based on an Auditory Synchrony Model. Ph. D. Thesis of Speech Communication Group, MIT, Cambridge, MA (1985)

74. Seneff, S.: A Joint Synchrony/Mean-Rate Model of Auditory Speech Processing. Journal of Phonetics, Vol. 16 (1988) 55-76

75. Shannon, C.E., Weaver, W.: Mathematical Theory of Communication. US: University of Illinois Press (1949)

76. Silverman, H.R., Dixon, N.R.: A Parametrically Controlled Spectral Analysis System for Speech. IEEE Trans on Acoustic. Speech and Signal Processing, Vol. ASSP–22(2) (1974) 362–381

77. Smith, R.L., Brachman, M.L., Frisina, R.D.: Sensitivity of Auditory-Nerve Fibers to Changes in Intensity: A Dichotomy Between Decrements and Increments J. Acoustic. Soc. Amer. Vol. 78, (1985) 1310-1316

78. Smith, J.C., Zwislocki, J.J. Short-Term Adaptation and Incremental Responses of Single Auditory-Nerve Fibers. Biol. Cybernetics Vol. 17 (1975) 169-182

79. Sondhi, M.M.: New Methods of Pitch Detection. IEEE Trans. Audio Electroacoustic., Vol. AU–16(2) (1968) 262–266

80. Stewart, J.L.: The Bionic Ear. Covox Company, Santa Maria, California

81. Stylianou, Y.: Modeling Speech based on Harmonic plus Noise Models. In Chollet, G., Esposito, A., Faundez-Zauny, M., Marinaro, M. (eds.): Advances in Nonlinear Speech Modeling and Applications. Lecture Notes in Computer Science, Springer-Verlag, Berlin Heidelberg New York (2005) To be Published

82. Trask, R.L.: A Dictionary of Phonetics and Phonology. Routledge, London,UK (1996)

83. Young, E.D.,Sachs M.B.: Representation of Steady-State Vowels in the Temporal Aspects of the Discharge Pattern of Populations of Auditory Nerve Fibers. J. Acoustic. Soc. Amer., Vol. 66 (1979) 1381-1403

84. Zwicker, E.: Psychoacoustics. Springer, Berlin (1962)

85. Zwicker, E.: Suddivision of the Audible Frequency Range into Critical Bands. J. Acoustic. Soc. Amer., Vol. 88 (1961) 248–249.

86. Zwislocki, J.J.: On Intensity Characteristics of Sensory Receptors: A Generalized Function. Kybernetik Vol.12 (1973) 169-183

Nonlinear Speech Processing:
Overview and Possibilities in Speech Coding

Marcos Faundez-Zanuy

Escola Universitària Politècnica de Mataró
Avda. Puig i Cadafalch 101-111 08303 Mataro (Barcelona), Spain
faundez@eupmt.es
http://www.eupmt.es/veu

Abstract. In this paper we give a brief overview of nonlinear predictive models, with special emphasis on neural nets. Several well known strategies are discussed, such as multi-start random weights initialization, regularization, early stop with validation, committee of neural nets, different architectures, etc. Although the paper is devoted to ADPCM speech coding (scalar and vectorial schemes), this study offers a good chance to deal with nonlinear predictors, as a first step towards a more sophisticated applications. Thus, our main purpose is to state new possibilities for speech coding.

1 Introduction

Speech applications usually require the computation of a linear prediction model for the vocal tract. This model has been successfully applied during the last thirty years, but it has some drawbacks. Mainly, it is unable to model the nonlinearities involved in the speech production mechanism, and only one parameter can be fixed: the analysis order. With nonlinear models, the speech signal is better fitted, and there is more flexibility to adapt the model to the application.

The easier way to linearly predict a sample [1] is by means of a linear combination of P previous samples weighted by the prediction coefficients (a_k), according to:

$$x[n] \cong \hat{x}[n] = \sum_{k=1}^{P} a_k x[n-k]$$ (1)

Yielding a residual signal:

$$e[n] = x[n] - \hat{x}[n]$$ (2)

The general function for a predictor can be written as:

$$\hat{x}[n] = g\left(\underline{x}[n-1]\right) \cong x[n]$$ (3)

Where the input vector is:

$$\underline{x}[n-1]^{T} = \left(x[n-1], x[n-2], \cdots, x[n-P]\right)$$ (4)

For a nonlinear predictor, the function $g(\cdot)$ must be nonlinear.

In predictive speech coding using a linear predictor, we just need to fix the prediction order. Theoretically, the higher the prediction order, the higher the accuracy of the prediction, but there is saturation in performance, especially for high prediction

G. Chollet et al. (Eds.): Nonlinear Speech Modeling, LNAI 3445, pp. 15–42, 2005.

orders. This fact can be seen in the example of figure 1, which shows the segmental signal to noise ratio (SEGSNR) of a linear predictive speech coder versus prediction order, for the frame on the top of figure 1. The improvements at $P=40$ and $P=80$ prediction orders are due to the pitch periodicity of this frame, so a combined predictor with short term and pitch (long term) prediction schemes can be proposed in order to achieve similar results with a smaller number of prediction coefficients. This can be seen as a combination of linear predictors.

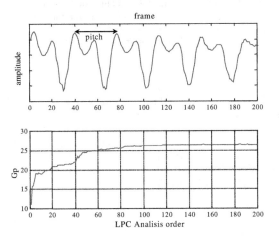

Fig. 1. Prediction Gain vs. prediction order using a linear predictor, for the frame on the top

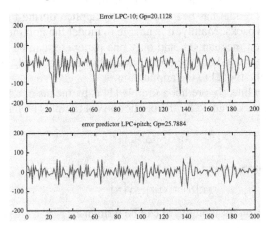

Fig. 2. Residual signal for a given frame, using short term and short term + pitch prediction

Figure 2 shows the obtained results with linear prediction analysis of order 10 and linear prediction analysis of order 10 plus pitch prediction. It can be seen that the pitch prediction can remove the peaks of the residual signal, and that the prediction gain (G_p) is improved.

One advantage of nonlinear prediction is its feasibility to remove the pitch periodicity on the residual signal without needing any pith estimation, as can be seen on figure 3. Figure 3 compares the residual error, for a given frame, obtained through:

a) Linear filtering with a prediction order of $P=10$ samples (LPC-10).
b) Linear filtering with a prediction order of $P=25$ samples (LPC-25).
c) Nonlinear filtering with a multilayer Perceptron (MLP) [2] 10x2x1 ($P=10$ input neurons. Thus, the same prediction order than LPC-10.
d) Nonlinear filtering with a multilayer Perceptron 10x4x1 ($P=10$ input neurons. Thus, the same number of prediction coefficients than LPC-25.

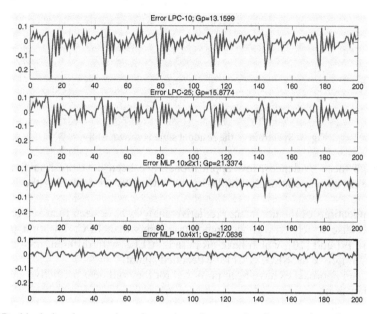

Fig. 3. Residual signal comparison for a given frame, using linear and nonlinear prediction (LPC-10, LPC-25 and MLP 10x2x1, MLP 10x4x1)

The pitch periodicity removal on the residual signal can be better seen on the spectral domain. The harmonic structure is clearly present for short-term linear prediction residual signal. Figure 4 shows the spectrum of the residual signals shown on figure 3.

Using a nonlinear predictor there is more feasibility and better results, because linear models are optimal just for gaussian signals, which is not the case of speech signals [3].

1.1 Motivation for Using Nonlinear Predictors

In the last years there has been a growing interest for nonlinear models applied to speech. This interest is based on the evidence of nonlinearities in the speech production mechanism. Several arguments justify this fact:

a) Residual signal of predictive analysis [4].
b) Correlation dimension of speech signal [5].
c) Fisiology of the speech production mechanism [6].
d) Probability density functions [7].
e) High order statistics [8].

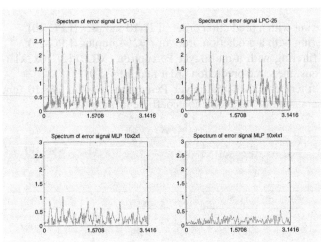

Fig. 4. Spectrum of the residual signals shown in figure 3

Although these evidences, few applications have been developed so far, mainly due to the high computational complexity and difficulty of analyzing the nonlinear systems.

The applications of the nonlinear predictive analysis have been focussed on speech coding, because it achieves greater prediction gains than LPC. The first proposed systems are [9] and [10], which have proposed a CELP with different nonlinear predictors that improve the SEGSNR of the decoded signal.

Three main approaches have been proposed for the nonlinear predictive analysis of speech. They are:

a) Nonparametric prediction: it does not assume any model for the nonlinearity. It is a quite simple method, but the improvement over linear predictive methods is lower than with nonlinear parametric models. An example of a nonparametric prediction is a codebook that tabulates several (input, output) pairs (eq. 5), and the predicted value can be computed using the nearest neighbour inside the codebook. Although this method is simple, low prediction orders must be used. Some examples of this system can be found in [11-13], [9].

$$\left(\underline{x}[n-1], \hat{x}[n]\right) \tag{5}$$

b) Parametric prediction: it assumes a model of prediction. The main approaches are Volterra series [14] and neural nets [2], [15].

The use of a nonlinear predictor based on neural networks can take advantage of some kind of combination between different nonlinear predictors (different neural networks, the same neural net architecture trained with different algorithms, or even the same architecture and training algorithm just using a different bias and weight random initialization). The possibilities are more limited using linear prediction techniques.

2   Nonlinear Predictor with Multi-layer Perceptrons

A significant number of proposals found in the literature use Volterra series [16], [17], [4] with quadratic nonlinearity (higher nonlinear functions imply a high number of coefficients and high computational burden for estimating them), and Radial Basis Function nets (RBF) [18-23], which also imply a quadratic nonlinear model.

Equation (6) shows a quadratic Volterra polynomial filter.

$$\hat{x}[n] = \sum_{i=1}^{P} h_i x[n-i] + \sum_{i=1}^{P}\sum_{j=1}^{P} h_{ij} x[n-i] x[n-j] \qquad (6)$$

We propose the use of a Multi Layer Perceptron net, because it has more flexibility in the nonlinearity. It is easy to show that an MLP with a sigmoid transfer function let to model cubic nonlinearities [24] (Taylor series expansion of sigmoid function). We believe that this is an important fact, because the nonlinearity present in the human speech prediction mechanism is probably due to saturation phenomena in the vocal chords. Figure 5 shows the possibility to model a saturation function with a cubic function. However, it is not possible with a quadratic function such as Volterra Filter.

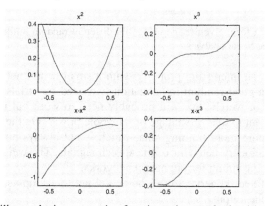

Fig. 5. The possibility to obtain a saturation function using quadratic and cubic nonlinearities

In the last decades several studies dealing with the nonlinear prediction of speech have been reported. Most part of the bibliography has been focused on parametric prediction based on neural nets, because they are the approach that offers the best improvement over LPC analysis. The following sections will be devoted to nonlinear prediction with neural networks.

2.1   Neural Net's Weight Computation

A key point for a neural net is: How do we compute the neural net weights? This can imply an initialization algorithm and a training algorithm. The weights can be randomly initialized, but it is important to take into account that the neural net performance will heavily depend on it value. Figure 6 presents an example of this problem. It consists of the representation of the prediction gain for a given frame using LPC-10, LPC-25, a 10x2x1 MLP, and a 10x4x1 MLP, for 100 different random initializations.

Obviously for linear analysis the prediction gain is always the same, because we apply a deterministic algorithm, and we always get the same set of linear coefficients. On the other hand, for nonlinear prediction, there is a high variance depending on the random initialization. Thus, one way to ensure that we get a good result is to use a multi-start algorithm [25], which consists of using several random initializations and choosing one of them, or a combination between them.

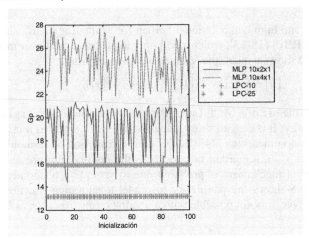

Fig. 6. Prediction gain for a given frame using 100 different random initializations for Multi-Layer Perceptrons and linear analysis

Figure 7 reveals an interesting property: with a small neural net (10x2x1) is relatively easy to get a good random initialization (we need few trials), while if we increase the number of weights we will probably need to work out more random initializations if we want to take advantage of its whole power. On the other hand, a big neural net will require more training data, which is not always possible taking into account the non-stationary behavior of the speech signals. The weight's computation will be more time consuming for big neural networks.

Thus, we have fixed the structure of the neural net to 10 inputs, 2 neurons in the hidden layer, and one output.

Figure 7 shows the histogram of the prediction gains (Gp) for 500 different random initializations, for the MLP 20x2x1 and MLP 10x4x1 architectures.

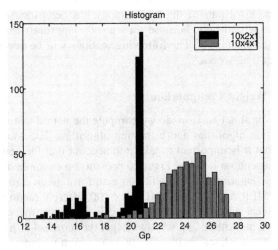

Fig. 7. Prediction gain (*Gp*) histograms for 500 random initializations for the MLP 20x2x1 and MLP 10x4x1 architectures

Another important issue is the possibility to use recurrent neural networks (like the Elman neural net), and different training algorithms. Figure 8 compares the learning performance for a given frame, in three different scenarios [26]:

a) MLP trained with a Backpropagation algorithm.
b) MLP trained with the Levenberg-Marquardt algorithm.
c) Elman recuerrent neural network.

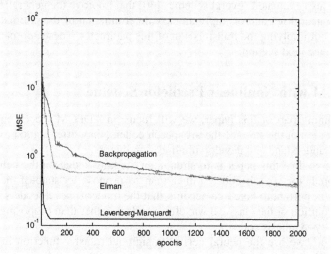

Fig. 8. Comparison of the Mean Square Error (MSE) versus number of epochs for Elman network and MLP trained with backpropagation and Levenberg-Marquardt

Our study has revealed the fast convergence and better performance of the levenberg-Marquardt algorithm. Thus, we have selected it, which computes the approximate Hessian matrix [27-28]. We also apply a multi-start algorithm [25].

Figure 9 compares the prediction gains for the whole frames of a speech sentence uttered by a female speaker in Spanish.

Figure 9 reveals that the major improvement is achieved on voiced frames.

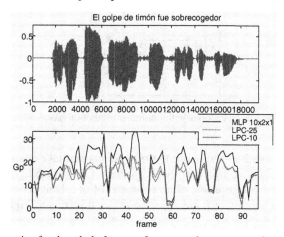

Fig. 9. Prediction gains for the whole frames of one speech sentence, using several predictors

Our experiments revealed that a critical parameter is the number of epochs. The optimal number of epochs is different for each frame. However, a variable number of epochs for each frame would imply the transmission of this number to the receiver, so we done a statistical study [29] and determined that an optimal (in average) number of epochs was 6. The main problem is that a high number of epochs implies lose of the generalization capability, and a small number a poor learning.

We have also evaluated several schemes [30] that improve the generalization capability of the neural net and/or imply an easy determination of the optimal number of epochs without implying the transmission of this parameter. These approaches will be described in the next section.

3 ADPCM with Nonlinear Predictor Scheme

In the remaining part of this paper, we will focus on ADPCM speech encoders. Although they are not the state-of-the-art speech coders, they offer a good experimentation field to understand and develop nonlinear predictors.

Thus, the goal of this paper is to strengthen the knowledge on the behaviour of a nonlinear predictor speech coder, rather than to propose a "state-of-the-art speech coder". It is important to take into account that the modern speech coders were possible as an evolution of the classical waveform coders, rather than proposing previously an analysis-by-synthesis coder.

In our work we use the neural nets with sigmoid transfer function in the hidden layers and a linear transfer function on the output layer, as a nonlinear predictor. This predictor replaces the LPC predictor in order to obtain an ADPCM scheme with nonlinear prediction. Figure 10 shows the classical ADPCM scheme, replacing the linear predictor by a nonlinear one.

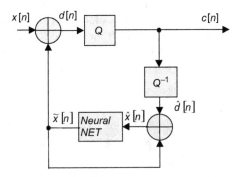

Fig. 10. ADPCM speech encoder with nonlinear prediction based on neural network

Obviously it is possible to propose hybrid systems that take advantage of the best predictor in each situation switching between them. One possibility was proposed in [24], and implies the transmission of an overhead of one 1 bit per frame, in order to inform the receiver about which has been the selected predictor. Figure 11 shows the scheme.

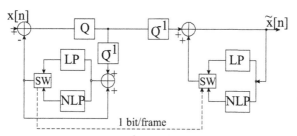

Fig. 11. Hybrid ADPCM scheme with switched predictor (Linear and Nonlinear prediction)

Classical ADPCM waveform coders with adaptive prediction work on one of two ways:

a) Sample adaptive prediction coefficients via LMS (that is, the predictor coefficients are updated for each new input sample). This system can be found in [31], [32].
b) Block adaptive prediction coefficients via Levinson Durbin recursion (that is, the predictor coefficients are updated one time for each input frame).

Block adaptive predictor coefficients update the predictor coefficients in one of two ways:

a) Backward adaptation: The coefficients are computed over the previous frame. Thus, it is not needed to transmit the coefficients of the predictor, because the receiver has already decoded the previous frame and can obtain the same set of coefficients.
b) Forward adaptation: The coefficients are computed over the same frame to be encoded. Thus, the coefficients must be quantized and transmitted to the receiver. In [29] we found that the SEGSNR of forward schemes with unquantized coefficients is similar to the classical LPC approach using one quantization bit less per sample. On the other hand with this scheme the mismatch between training and testing phases is smaller than in the previous case, so the training procedure is not as critical as in backward schemes, and the SEGSNR are greater.

We use an adaptive quantizer based on multipliers [33], using the following equation:

$$\Delta[n] = \Delta[n-1] M\left(L_{n-1}\right) \qquad (7)$$

For instance, for a three bit quantizer, the multiplying factors are shown in table 1. This set of values has been experimentally obtained for a DPCM system with linear predictor. Thus, these values could be improved taking into account the nonlinearity of the predictor.

Table 1. Multiplying factors for a $N_q=3$ bits quantizer inside an ADPCM scheme

	$L_{n-1}=0, L_{n-1}=7$	$L_{n-1}=1, L_{n-1}=6$	$L_{n-1}=2, L_{n-1}=5$	$L_{n-1}=3, L_{n-1}=4$
M	1.75	1.25	0.9	0.9

Figure 12 shows the corresponding levels (L_{n-1}) for a three bits quantizer.

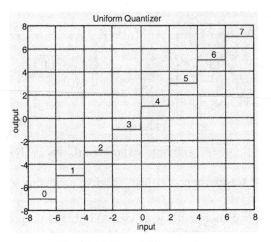

Fig. 12. Uniform 3 bits quantizer

In our experiments we have used a variable number of quantization bits between $N_q=2$ and $N_q=5$, which corresponds to 16 kbps and 40 kbps (the sampling rate of the speech signal is 8 kHz).

The initial quantization is usually chosen using equation (8):

$$\Delta[0] = \frac{1}{2^{N_q-1}} \tag{8}$$

Where the input signal $x(t)$ has been normalized using equation (9):

$$x_{normalized}(t) = \frac{x(t)}{\max|x(t)|}, \quad \in[-1,1] \tag{9}$$

However, taking into account the silent portion at the beginning of the sentences, we have experimentally chosen the 20th part of equation 8. This lets a faster quantization step track at the beginning.

We have encoded eight sentences uttered by eight different speakers (4 males and 4 females). These are the same sentences that we used in our first work related to ADPCM speech coding [29] and followings.

Computational issues and complexity of ADPCM with nonlinear prediction were addressed in [24]. Although the computational burden of the proposed system is near 30 times greater than the linear scheme, and other coding methods exist in terms of quality vs bit rate as higher complexity is allowed, some of the best results in terms of optimising both quality and bit rate are obtained from codec structures that contain some form of nonlinearity. Analysis-by-synthesis coders fall into this category. For example, in CELP coders the closed-loop selection of the vector from the codebook can be seen as a data-dependent nonlinear mechanism [7].

3.1 Proposed Schemes for Frame Basis Coefficient Update

The propositions of this paper include:

3.1.1 The Use of Regularization

The regularization involves modifying the performance function, which is normally chosen to be the sum of squares of the network errors on the training set. This technique minimizes the effect of overtraining, so more epochs can be done. The classical mean square error function (MSE) is replaced by the mean square error regularized function (MSE$_{reg}$):

$$MSE_{reg} = \gamma MSE + \left(1 - \gamma\right)\frac{1}{n}\sum_{j=1}^{n} w_j^2 \tag{10}$$

Where the last term is proportional to the modulus of the weights of the neural net, and γ is the performance ratio. In our simulations we have used $\gamma=0.9$. Using this performance function will cause the network to have smaller weights and biases, and this will force the network response to be smoother and less likely to overfit.

Figure 13 shows the evolution of the SEGSNR vs γ, for 6 and 50 epochs. This plot has been obtained with one speaker. Obviously the manual setup of this parameter is a drawback, because it can be data-dependent.

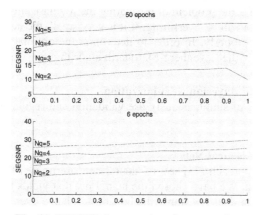

Fig. 13. SEGSNR for several performace ratios γ

3.1.2 Early Stopping with Validation

Early stopping is a technique based on dividing the data into three subsets. The first subset is the training set used for computing the gradient and updating the network weights and biases. The second one is the validation set. The error on the validation set is monitorized during the training process. The validation error will normally decrease during the initial phase of training, as does the training set error. However, when the network begins to overfit the data, the error of the validation set will typically begin to rise. When the validation error increases for a specified number of iterations, the training is stopped, and the weights and biases at the minimum of the validation error are chosen. In this paper we propose to select the training, validation and testing sets as $frame_{k-1}, frame_k, frame_{k+1}$ respectively (see figure 14). Obviously this is a good approach for stationary portions of the signal, which are the most frequent in real speech signals. With this scheme the delay of the encoder is increased in one frame.

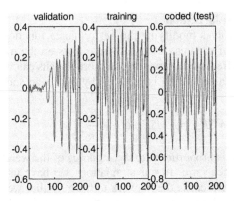

Fig. 14. Early Stopping with validation. Example of validation, training and coded sets, being them consecutive frames

3.1.3 Bayesian Regularization

The approach 3.1.1 has the problem of estimating the regularization parameter γ. If it is too large, then there will be overfitting. If it is very small, the neural net will not fit the training samples properly. In order to determine the optimal γ in an automated fashion combined with the Levenberg-Marquardt algorithm, we use [27] and [28].

3.1.4 Validation and Bayesian Regularization

This strategy consists of simultaneously use validation and regularization of sections 3.1.2 and 3.1.3.

3.1.5 Committee of Neural Nets

Using a multi-start approach [25] several neural nets are trained for each frame, and one of them is chosen. We have chosen the neural net that yields the smaller training error, but this criterion does not imply the best performance over the test frame. The main problem with a multi-start algorithm is that it is not possible to choose in advance which the best neural net is, because this implies to test all the nets over the frame we want to encode, and to transmit the index of the selected net to the receiver. Instead of using a multi-start algorithm, it is possible to use all the trained networks, combining their outputs.

In pattern recognition applications it is well known that a number of differently trained neural networks (that can be considered as "experts"), which share a common input, can produce a better result if their outputs are combined to produce an overall output. This technique is known as ensemble averaging, committee machine [34], data fusion [35], etc. The motivation for its use is twofold [34]:

1. If the combination of experts were replaced by a single neural network, the number of equivalent adjustable parameters would be large, and this implies more training time and local minima problems [2].
2. The risks of overfitting the data increases when the number of adjustable parameters is large compared to the size of the training data set.

This strategy is also suitable for improving the vulnerability of a biometric system [36], which is one of the main drawbacks of these systems [37]. This same strategy can be used in speech coding with neural network nonlinear predictors. Each trained neural network using the same training data, can be seen as an "expert", and altogether can be combined in several fashions.

It is important to see that most of the time is spent in computing the weights of the neural nets. Thus, the computational burden of a committee of neural nets is nearly the same of the multi-start algorithm. The structure is shown in figure 15. Several combinations of the neural net outputs are possible. We have studied the following:

$$\tilde{x}[n] = mean\{\tilde{x}_1[n], \tilde{x}_2[n], \cdots, \tilde{x}_N[n]\} \tag{11}$$

$$\tilde{x}[n] = median\{\tilde{x}_1[n], \tilde{x}_2[n], \cdots, \tilde{x}_N[n]\} \tag{12}$$

$$\tilde{x}[n] = nnet\{\tilde{x}_1[n], \tilde{x}_2[n], \cdots, \tilde{x}_N[n]\} \tag{13}$$

This strategy offers a great chance to improve prediction, and is more naturally related to nonlinear predictors than linear ones.

Equation (13) consists of a neural combiner, and states a situation where a neural network is used to learn the appropriate averaging weights, instead of using the formulations (11) or (12).

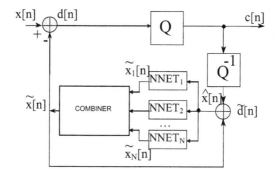

Fig. 15. ADPCM scheme with a committee of neural networks

The most relevant conclusions (looking at experimental data [30]) of these last five strategies are:
1. Without regularization, overtraining can reduce the SEGSNR up to 3 dB and increase the variance of the SEGSNR.
2. The use of regularization lets to increase the number of epochs without overfitting the training samples.
3. The use of regularization decreases the variance of the SEGSNR between frames. Thus, the quality of the reconstructed signal has less fluctuation between frames. This is, perhaps, the most relevant achievement of the proposed system.
4. Automatic selection of the regularization parameter (Bayesian regularization) must be used in order to improve the SEGSNR of the decoded speech signal. In this case, an increase of 1.2dB is achieved for $N_q=2$, and 0.8 dB in the other cases. On the other hand, for $N_q=2$ and 3 it is better to fix the number of epochs to 6 and for $N_q=4$ and 5 to 50 epochs. This is because the mismatch between training and testing is greater for small number of quantization bits (the quantization error degrades more seriously the predictor input signal).

5. The use of validation produces minor effects, and not always improves the SEGSNR or the variance of the SEGSNR.
6. The combination using the *median*{·} function yields better results than *mean*{·} function. Figure 6 shows a high variance on prediction gains for different random initializations. Thus, some random initializations can get stuck in a local minimum. This will result in a bad prediction, that can be removed with a *median*{·} filter of several networks' outputs, because for most of the speech frames, the number of "good" initializations is greater than the number of "bad" random initializations.

Thus, we will select a combination between Bayesian regularization and a committee of neural nets (being each neural net the result of training one random initialization).

4 Nonlinear Vectorial Prediction

One extension of the classical scalar linear prediction defined by equation (1) is the vectorial prediction. This can also be applied to nonlinear prediction in a more natural way.

4.1 Scalar Linear Prediction

The auto-regressive (AR) modeling of P order is given by the following relation:

$$x[n] = \sum_{i=1}^{P} a_i x[n-i] + e[n] \tag{14}$$

Where $\{a_i\}_{i=1,\ldots P}$ are the scalar prediction coefficients. Their value is usually obtained with the Levinson-durbin recursion [38].

4.2 Vectorial Linear Prediction

The AR-vector modeling of order P is given by the following relation:

$$\vec{x}[n] = \sum_{i=1}^{P} A_i \vec{x}[n-i] + \vec{e}[n] \tag{15}$$

Where $\{A_i\}_{i=1,\ldots P}$ are the $m \times m$ matrices equivalent to the prediction coefficients of the classical scalar predictor, and m is the dimension of the vectors. The prediction matrices can be estimated using the Levinson-Whittle-Robinson algorithm, which has been previously applied to speaker verification in [39].

4.3 Scalar and Vectorial Nonlinear Prediction with a MLP

Our vectorial nonlinear predictor is very close to the scalar one. It consists of a Multi Layer Perceptron (MLP) with 10 inputs, 2 neurons in the hidden layer, and N outputs, where N is the dimension of the predicted vectors. Thus, the extension from scalar to vectorial case just needs to add more output neurons, remaining the rest parts the same. Figure 16 shows the architecture of a scalar (left) and vectorial (right) nonlinear predictors based on a multilayer Perceptron. In our studies we have used $N=1,2,\cdots,6$. The selected training algorithm is the Levenberg-Marquardt, and we also apply a multi-start algorithm with five random initializations for each neural net. Thus, we have just modified the number of output neurons.

Another extension of this scheme can be the use of a vectorial quantizer [38], that lets to obtain better results than scalar quantization. Figure 17 shows this new encoder.

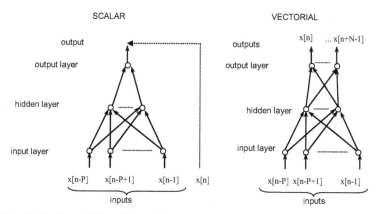

Fig. 16. Scalar and Vectorial nonlinear prediction with a Multi Layer Perceptron

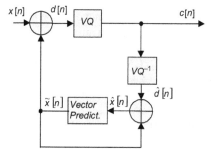

Fig. 17. ADPCM scheme with vectorial prediction and vectorial quantization

In order to evaluate the contributions of each part alone (vectorial predictor and vectorial quantizer), we have studied three different scenarios:

1. Scalar prediction and scalar quantization: this scheme is equivalent to a neural net trained with hints (N outputs are used during training phase, but only the first output is used for prediction). Thus, we train a vectorial predictor but we use it as a scalar predictor.

2. Vectorial prediction and scalar quantization: all the neural net outputs are used for prediction, but the adaptive scalar quantizer based on multipliers [33] is used consecutively in order to quantize the N output prediction errors. Although this quantizer has been tuned up for linear predictors, we have found in our previous work that it is also suitable for nonlinear prediction and it is able to remove the first order dependencies between consecutive samples [40].

3. Vectorial prediction and vector quantization: same situation than the previous scenario, but the scalar quantizer is replaced by a VQ. In [40] we obtained that this scheme with $N=2$ was unable to outperform the scalar quantizer, and that first order dependencies exist. In that paper we conclude that the system should be improved with VQ memory quantizer or increasing the vector dimension. In this paper, we have studied the results for higher vector dimensions ($N>2$) and we have improved the SEGSNR and achieved smaller bit rates.

4.4 Experiment Conditions

We have used the same database than in previous sections. The number of inputs is $P=10$, and the number of outputs is variable in the range $1 \le N \le 6$. The frame length is 200 samples. In order to obtain always the same number of training patterns, the following input/output patterns have been used:

```
For i=0:frame_length-1,
```
$$input(i) = \{x[n+i-P], \cdots, x[n+i-1],\}$$
$$output(i) = \{x[n+i], \cdots x[n+i+N-1]\}$$
```
end
```

Thus, there is a shift of one sample between consecutive input patterns during the training of the neural net (if the shift would be N samples, the number of training patters would decrease and couldn't be enough for high values of N.

Obviously we have slightly modified the frame length for $N=3$ (201 samples) and $N=6$ (204 samples), in order to achieve an exact division of *frame_length* by N.

On the other hand, the shift between consecutive input patterns when the neural net is acting as a predictor is equal to N.

This is a backward-adaptive ADPCM scheme. Thus, the coefficients are computed over the previous frame, and it is not needed to transmit the coefficients of the predictor, because the receiver has already decoded the previous frame and can obtain the same set of coefficients.

In [40] we showed that the computation of a vectorial predictor based on a MLP is not critical. This was checked using the scenario number 1 of section 4.3. In this situation the vectorial prediction training procedure can be interpreted as a particular case of neural net training with output hints. We obtained similar performance than a neural net with only one output neuron and same number of neurons on the input and hidden layers. Of course, consecutive samples are highly correlated, so really the neural net is not bounded to learn a significant amount of "new information". Thus, the generalization of the scalar NL predictor to a NL vectorial prediction does not imply a great difference with respect to the scalar predictor.

The next step is the evaluation of scenario number 2 (vectorial prediction + scalar quantization), described in section 4.3. This scheme offers worse performance than scalar prediction plus scalar quantization [40]. However, the experiments of scenario 1 revealed a good performance, with the same neural net scheme. Thus, the critical block is the quantizer, not the vectorial predictor.

It is interesting to observe that the vectorial scheme is more suitable with a vectorial quantizer. In order to check this assert we have plot the vectorial prediction errors for a two-dimensional case, on figure 18 (higher dimensional spaces cannot be represented, and they are more difficult to interpret). It is interesting to observe that the vectors to be quantized, do not lie in the whole space. Most of the vectors are around $y=x$. This means that the error vectors present the following property:

$$e_{1n} \cong e_{2n}, \quad \vec{e}[n] = (e_{1n}, e_{2n}) \tag{16}$$

Thus, a vectorial quantizer can exploit this redundancy and improve the results. Only for a uniform distribution on the whole space, the scalar quantizer would be optimum and there won't be any advantage in using a vectorial quantizer.

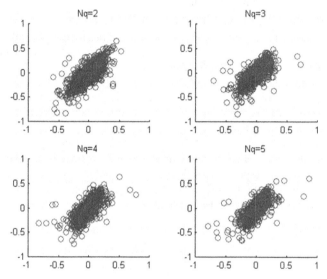

Fig. 18. Vectorial prediction errors for several quantization bits and 2-dimensional vectors

Next section will describe the situation of scenario number 3 in section 4.3.

4.5 Nonlinear Predictive Vector Quantization

A special case of vector quantization is known as predictive vector quantization (PVQ) [38]. Basically, PVQ consists on an ADPCM scheme with a vector predictor and a vectorial quantizer. Obviously, if the vector predictor is nonlinear the system is a NL-PVQ scheme. We will use the NL-vector predictor described in previous sections, and a vectorial quantizer. In order to design the vectorial quantizer we use the residual signal of the vectorial prediction and the scalar quantizer based on multipliers applied as many times as the dimension of the vectors. Thus, we have used the residual errors of the first speaker (with Nq=3) and the generalized Lloyd algorithm [38] in order to create codebooks ranging from 4 to 8 bits. The initial codebook has been obtained with the random method, and it has been improved with the Lloyd algorithm.

It is interesting to observe that the optimization procedure must be a closed loop algorithm, because there are interactions between the predictor and the quantizer. Thus, the system can be improved computing again the residual errors with the actual quantization scheme.

In order to design a vectorial quantizer (VQ) it is need a training sequence. The optimal design procedure must be iterative [41], because in a PVQ scheme the VQ is inside the loop of the ADPCM scheme. In order to achieve a "universal VQ", it should be obtained with as many speakers and sentences as possible and evaluated with a different database. In order to simplify the study (the nonlinear vectorial prediction computation is very time consuming), we have used only one speaker for VQ generation and 8 different speakers for PVQ system evaluation. We have used two different methods for codebook generation given a training sequence: random initialization plus the generalized Lloyd iteration, and the LBG algorithm [38].

We have used the following procedure:

1. A speech database is PVQ coded with a vectorial predictor and an adaptive scalar quantizer based on multipliers [33]. Although the prediction algorithm is vectorial, the residual error is scalar quantized, applying the scalar quantizer consecutively to each component of the residual vector.
2. We have used the residual signal of one sentence uttered by a female speaker (approximately 10000 vectors) and 3 quantization bits ($Nq=3$) as a training sequence. Figure 18 shows the visualization of the error sequences for several Nq.
3. A codebook is designed for several VQ sizes. Figures 19 and 20 show the obtained results with the random and the LBG method respectively.
4. The speech database is encoded and a new training sequence is computed for each VQ size. We use the respective residual errors of each VQ size (and speaker 1).
5. Go to step 3 and update the VQ using the training sequence of step 4 till a fixed number of iterations or a predefined criterion.

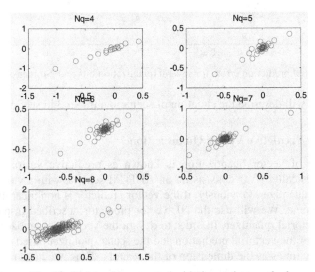

Fig. 19. Codebooks generated with the random method

We have applied this closed-loop algorithm two times. On the other hand, we believe that it is interesting the evaluation of both algorithms (random and LBG) because a very well fitted codebook to a given training sequence can be less robust when dealing with different vectors not used for training.

In a PVQ system of N-dimensional vectors, and a VQ of N_q bits, the bit rate of the speech encoder is:

$$N_q/N \quad [bits/sample] \tag{17}$$

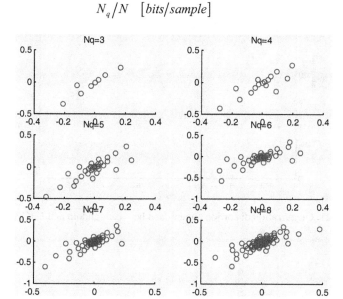

Fig. 20. Codebooks generated with the LBG algorithm

Figure 21 compares the quantization distortion of the initial training sequence using the VQ obtained with the random method and the LBG one. It is clear that the latest one is much better than the former (the quantization distortion is smaller). The obtained SEGSNR encoding the 8 speakers' database does not show significant differences between both algorithms [42].

Figure 22 summarizes the obtained results with the PVQ with non-linear prediction described in this section. These results are described with more detail in [43].

Figure 22 reveals two important achievements, related to improvement over scalar non-linear prediction:

- Vectorial nonlinear predictor outperforms a scalar nonlinear predictor for N=5. This result is analogous to the reported in [41].
- The PVQ encoder lets to extend the classical operating ranges of the ADPCM waveform speech encoder, extrapolating the behavior below 2 bits per sample (look at 4-dimensional vector results in plot 22).

5 Study of Quantizers

So far, main emphasis has been given to nonlinear prediction, as an alternative to linear prediction. However, in schemes where a predictor and a quantizer interrelate, it must be taken into account that: if the predictor can decorrelate the signal, the quantizer does not need to show any memory nor adaptation. On the other hand, if the predictor is unable to remove all the correlations between samples, some improve-

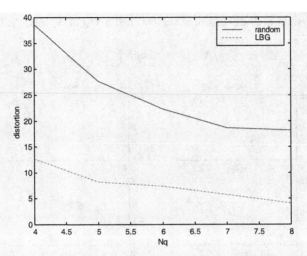

Fig. 21. Quantization distortion comparison between random and LBG VQ

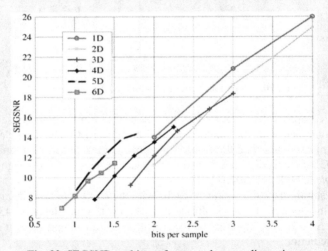

Fig. 22. SEGSNR vs. bitrate for several vector dimensions

ment can be achieved replacing a non-adaptive quantizer by an adaptive or memory quantizer.

In order to study the quantizer, we propose to evaluate the entropy of the residual signal. For a memory source, the entropy $H(X)$ can be expressed as:

$$H(X) \equiv H_\infty(X) = \lim_{N \to \infty} H_N(X) \tag{18}$$

Where:

$$H_N = \sum_{u_0=1}^{M} \cdots \sum_{u_N=1}^{M} P(u_0 u_1 \cdots u_N) \log \frac{1}{P(u_0|u_1 u_2 \cdots u_N)} \tag{19}$$

And M is the number of different states (symbols) that the source can generate.

However, the knowledge of the conditional probabilities implies a huge amount of empirical data, or the use of "academic" sources, which can be modeled with Markov models and show limited memory or are memoryless. Thus, for "real" sources, the studies are limited to what we call zero order entropy $H_0(X)$, which is identical to the source entropy for memoryless sources:

$$H_0(x) = \sum_{i=1}^{M} P_i \log_2 \frac{1}{P_i} \qquad (20)$$

Or the first order entropy (known as conditional entropy) $H_1(X)$:

$$H_1(X) = \sum_{j=1}^{M} \sum_{i=1}^{M} P(ij) \log_2 \frac{1}{P(i|j)} \qquad (21)$$

The first order entropy (21) coincides with the source entropy (18) for sources of memory just one symbol.

In order to clarify the meaning of the entropy, let us think on a binary source that emits the following symbols: $\{1,0,1,0,1,0,1,0,\cdots\}$ (It always repeats the sequence 10 periodically). If we check the zero order entropy, we will get that:

$$P(0) = P(1) = \frac{1}{2} \qquad (22)$$

And the information of this source is:

$$H_o(X) = \frac{1}{2}\log_2(2) + \frac{1}{2}\log_2(2) = 1 \quad bit / symbol \qquad (23)$$

This is in agreement with the fact that we need one bit per symbol in order to specify which the symbol emitted by the source is.

On the other hand, a deeper study reveals that:

$$P(0|0) = 0, \ P(0|1) = 1, \ P(1|0) = 1, \ P(1|1) = 0 \qquad (24)$$

Applying the conditional probability theorem we get the following probabilities:

$$P(00) = P(0|0) \times P(0) = 0, \ P(01) = P(0|1) \times P(1) = \frac{1}{2}$$
$$P(10) = P(10|0) \times P(0) = \frac{1}{2}, \ P(11) = P(1|1) \times P(1) = 0 \qquad (25)$$

And the following first-order entropy (conditional entropy):

$$H_1 = P(00) \log_2 \frac{1}{P(0|0)} + P(01) \log_2 \frac{1}{P(0|1)} + P(11) \log_2 \frac{1}{P(1|1)} +$$
$$+ P(10) \log_2 \frac{1}{P(1|0)} = 0 \qquad (26)$$

This is in agreement with the fact that the source is always emitting the same symbols $\{0,1\}$. Given one symbol, there is no uncertainty about which the next one will be. Thus, we need 0 bits per symbol to specify the outcomes of this source.

In equations (20) and (21):

- M is the number of different states (symbols) that the source can generate. In our case, we will study the entropy of the quantizer output (named codewords). Thus, if we have a N_q bits quantizer, $M = 2^{N_q}$
- P_i is the probability of the codeword i.
- $P(i|j)$ is the probability of the codeword i knowing that the previous codeword has been the codeword j.

It is important to take into account that this formulation is valid for scalar and vectorial quantization. The unique difference is that in the former case each codeword is equivalent to one sample, while in the latest one each codeword is equivalent to a vector (group of samples).

It would be interesting to study higher order entropies, but the amount of required data and the computational burden makes this evaluation unpractical.

Two important observations can be made regarding the entropy of the codewords:

1. The better designed the quantizer, the higher the entropy, because all the codewords will have the same probability of being chosen. In this case, $H_0(X) \cong N_q$.

   Otherwise, the outputs of the quantizer (codewords) can be encoded with a lossless method (for example Huffmann coding [44]) in order to reduce the data rate. Precisely, non-uniform quantizers try to balance the chance to be in each different level, producing smaller quantization errors on the most probable levels. A-law and μ-law quantizers for log PCM work in a different fashion, because they take into account perceptual information and the behavior of the human auditory system (a nearly constant SNR is desirable for this systems).

2. If $H_1(X) << H_0(X)$ means that there is a strong correlation between consecutive quantizer outputs, and two observations can be made:
   a) The outputs of the quantizer (codewords) can be encoded with a lossless method (for example Huffmann) in order to reduce the data rate.
   b) The quantizer can be improved taking into account the previous sample (using a memory quantizer). The goal is to obtain $H_1(X) \cong H_0(X) \cong N_q$ (remember that $H_1(X) \le H_0(X) \le N_q$ by definition). In this case, all the codewords are equal probable used, and $P(x[n]|x[n-1]) \cong P(x[n])$, so the predictor + quantizer have removed the first order dependencies, and no improvement on bit rate is achieved by means of a Huffmann code.

Our goal is to achieve the latest observation (2.b), rather than the former one, because the better the quantizer, the better the prediction (both systems are in a closed loop). If the entropy is smaller than Nq means that some codewords are not enough used, so the useful number of quantization bits is smaller than Nq.

[42] and [43] show experimental results using this methodology. Special care must be taken in order to obtain a good estimation of the probabilities and conditional probabilities, because the number of different codewords is 2^{Nq}, and the higher the number of different possible codewords, the higher the number of training data we need to obtain a good estimation of the probabilities of these codewords. Specially for the first order entropy, because the number of different combinations is:

$$2^{Nq} \times 2^{Nq} = 2^{2Nq} \tag{27}$$

Equation (22) takes into account that there are 2^{Nq} different codewords, and for each one, 2^{Nq} previous codewords are possible.

In [42-43] we experimentally shown than it is easy to compute the zero and first order entropies up to $Nq=5$ (a significant increase on the number of codewords used to compute the statistics did not imply a modification of the results. This lets to think that enough statistical data have been used). Thus, it is important to take into account that H_1 values are underestimated for $Nq>5$ due to the limited amount of samples used to work out $P(i|j)$.

6 Other Possibilities Extending the Input Signal

Strong efforts have been done in speech and speaker recognition for obtaining a good parameterization of the speech signal in order to improve the results and to reduce the computational burden [45-46]. However, this step is ignored in speech coding, where the parameterized signal is almost the own signal without any processing.

The relevance of feature extraction in patter recognition is twofold:

- A reduction on the number of data that must be processed, model sizes, etc., is achieved, with the consequent reduction on computational burden.
- The transformation of the original data into a new feature space can let an easier discrimination between classes.

Although at first sight it can seem that speech coding has nothing to do with speech and speaker recognition, a deeper observation shows that the problem statement is similar for both groups of applications:

Without loss of generality we will assume that the speech signal $x(t)$ is normalized in order to achieve maximum absolute value equal to 1 ($\max(|x(t)|)=1$). Otherwise, the following normalization can be done:

$$x'(t) = \frac{x(t)}{\max(|x(t)|)} \tag{28}$$

For speaker recognition applications, with a closed set of N users inside the database, the problem is: given a vector of samples $[x(1), x(2), \cdots, x(L)]$, try to guess to which speaker (i.e. $speaker_i$) it belongs, with $speaker_i \in [1, 2, \cdots, N]$. In order to achieve statistical consistency, this task is performed using several hundreds of vectors, and some kind of parameterization is performed over the signal samples, such as a bank of filters, cepstral analysis, etc.

For speech coding applications, the problem is: given a vector of previous samples $[x(1), x(2), \cdots, x(L)]$, try to guess which the next sample : $x(L+1)$, $x(L+1) \in [-1, 1]$.

Thus, the problem statement is the same with the exception that the former corresponds to a discrete set of output values, and the latter corresponds to a continuous set of output values.

Taking into account this fact, the "speech predictor" can be seen as a "classifier". This interpretation is in agreement with the committee of experts (see section 3.1.5) that we have extended from pattern recognition applications to speech prediction.

An advantage of nonlinear models for (instance neural networks) is that they can integrate different kinds of information. They can use "hints" in order to improve the accuracy, etc. For this reason we propose, in addition to the speech samples, the use of transitional information. This kind of information has certainly been useful for speaker recognition [47], where it is found that instantaneous and transitional representations are relatively uncorrelated, thus providing complementary information for speaker recognition. The computation of the transitional information is as simple as the first order finite difference. This transitional information is also known as delta parameters.

The use of delta parameters implies the replacement of the neural net architecture of figure 16 by the scheme shown in figure 23, where the delta parameters are computed with the following formulation:

Given the pair of (*inputs, output*) values used to train the neural net in the classical setting by the expression:

$$\left(\underbrace{[x(1), x(2), \cdots, x(L)]}_{inputs}, \underbrace{x(L+1)}_{output} \right) = \left(\vec{x}_1, x(L+1) \right)$$

$$\left([x(2), x(3), \cdots, x(L+1)], x(L+2) \right) = \left(\vec{x}_2, x(L+2) \right) \tag{29}$$

$$\cdots$$

$$\left([x(1+N), x(2+N), \cdots, x(L+N)], x(L+N+1) \right) = \left(\vec{x}_{1+N}, x(L+N+1) \right)$$

We propose the use of delta information computed in the following way:

$$\vec{\Delta}_i = [\Delta(i), \Delta(i+1), \cdots, \Delta(L+i-1)]$$
$$\vec{\Delta}_i = \vec{x}_i - \vec{x}_{i-1} = [x(i) - x(i-1), x(i+1) - x(i), \cdots, x(L+i-1) - x(L+i-2)] \tag{30}$$

In this case, the input-output relation is:

$$\left(\left[\underbrace{\Delta(i), \Delta(i+1), \cdots, \Delta(L+i-1)}_{\text{Transitional information}}, \underbrace{x(i), x(i+1), \cdots, x(L+i-1)}_{\text{Instantaneous information}} \right], x(L+i) \right)$$

$$(inputs, output) = \left(\underbrace{\left[\vec{\Delta}_i, \vec{x}_i \right]}_{inputs}, \underbrace{x(L+i)}_{output} \right) \tag{31}$$

That can be written in a compact notation as:

$$(inputs, output) = \left(\underbrace{\left[\vec{\Delta}_i, \vec{x}_i \right]}_{inputs}, \underbrace{x(L+i)}_{output} \right) \tag{32}$$

It is interesting to observe that this scheme just implies the addition of one more input sample, which is $x(L+i-2)$, when compared against the original system without transitional information. Thus, the predictor order is $L+1$, when using transitional information. This is due to the transitional information is obtained using a linear combination of samples already used in the instantaneous portion of the input. Obviously this will not imply an improvement in a linear predictor, but differences can be expected when entering a nonlinear predictor, because the squared value of a linear

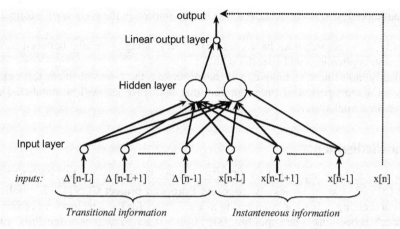

Fig. 23. Neural predictor with delta parameters

combination generates cross-product terms. Although it is supposed that the neural net is able to produce these terms by his own non-linearity; if they are explicitly entered, there is reinforcement.

[48] presents a more exhaustive explanation of this system, and experimental results.

7 Summary

In this paper, we have summarized the main non-linear predictors, with special emphasis on neural networks. We have skipped the detailed numeric results of each evaluated system, which can be found on our referenced previous work. We think that it is better to give an overview and to remember the general matters, rather than to focus on exhaustive comparisons in different scenarios, although these experiments have been really done, and can be found in the referenced documents.

The main problems that appear when dealing with neural network predictive models have been discussed, and several ways of improvement have been described:

- Regularization.
- Early stopping with validation.
- Bayesian regularization.
- Validation and Bayesian regularization.
- Committee of neural nets.

With special emphasis on the last one, which we consider that offers a great potential.

Vectorial nonlinear prediction has been proposed as a natural extension of scalar prediction, with an easier formulation than his counterpart on the linear case. This predictor has been combined with a vectorial quantizer, obtaining a new encoder that extends de operating range of the scalar schemes. This scheme is a version of the classical Predictive Vector Quantization encoder.

A methodology to study quantizers has been proposed in the context of information theory.

Finally, new research lines have been described looking at parallel between pattern recognition applications and speech coding.

Probably, non-linear techniques will never replace the classical linear techniques, at least in a short period of time, but certainly both together will be combined and improve the actual systems.

Acknowledgement

This work has been supported by FEDER and the Spanish grant MCYT TIC2003-08382-C05-02. I want to acknowledge the European project COST-277 "nonlinear speech processing", that has been acting as a catalyzer for the development of nonlinear speech processing since middle 2001. I also want to acknowledge Prof. Enric Monte-Moreno for the support and useful discussions of these years.

References

1. Makhoul, J.: Linear prediction: a tutorial review. Proceedings of the IEEE vol.63 pp.561-580, april 1975
2. Jain, A.K., Mao, J.: Artificial neural networks: a tutorial. IEEE Computer, March 1996, pp. 31-44.
3. Faundez-Zanuy, M., McLaughlin, S., Esposito, A., Hussain, A., Schoentgen, J., Kubin, G., Kleijn, W. B., Maragos,P.: Nonlinear speech processing: overview and applications. Control and intelligent systems, Vol. 30 N° 1, pp.1-10, 2002, Published by ACTA Press.
4. Thyssen, J., Nielsen, H., Hansen S.D.: Non-linear short-term prediction in speech coding. IEEE ICASSP 1994, pp.I-185 , I-188.
5. Townshend, B.: Nonlinear prediction of speech. IEEE ICASSP-1991, Vol. 1, pp.425-428.
6. Teager, H.M.: Some observations on oral air flow vocalization. IEEE trans. ASSP, vol.82 pp.559-601, October 1980
7. Kubin, G.: Nonlinear processing of speech. Chapter 16 on Speech coding and synthesis, editors W.B. Kleijn & K.K. Paliwal, Ed. Elsevier 1995.
8. Thyssen, J., Nielsen, H., Hansen, S.D.: Non-linearities in speech. Proceedings IEEE workshop Nonlinear Signal & Image Processing, NSIP'95, June 1995
9. Kumar, A., Gersho, A.: LD-CELP speech coding with nonlinear prediction. IEEE Signal Processing letters Vol. 4 N°4, April 1997, pp.89-91
10. Wu, L., Niranjan, M., Fallside, F.: Fully vector quantized neural network-based code-excited nonlinear predictive speech coding. IEEE transactions on speech and audio processing, Vol.2 n° 4, October 1994.
11. Wang, S., Paksoy E., Gersho, A.: Performance of nonlinear prediction of speech. Proceedings ICSLP-1990, pp.29-32
12. Lee Y.K., Johnson, D.H.: Nonparametric prediction of non-gaussian time series. IEEE ICASSP 1993, Vol. IV, pp.480-483
13. Ma, N., Wei, G.:Speech coding with nonlinear local prediction model. IEEE ICASSP 1998 vol. II, pp.1101-1104.
14. Pitas, I., Venetsanopoulos, A. N.: Non-linear digital filters: principles and applications. Kluwer ed. 1990
15. Lippmann, R. P.,: An introduction to computing with neural nets. IEEE trans. ASSP, 1988, Vol.3 N° 4, pp.4-22

16. Mumolo, E., Francescato, D.: Adaptive predictive coding of speech by means of Volterra predictors. Workshop on nonlinear digital signal processing. Tampere 1993, pages .2.1-4.1 to 2.1-4.4

17. Mumolo, E., Carini, A., Francescato, D.: ADPCM with nonlinear predictors. Signal Processing VII: Theories and applications EUSIPCO-1994, pp. 387-390.

18. Niranjan, M., Kadirkamanathan, V.: A nonlinear model for time series prediction and signal interpolation. IEEE ICASSP 1991, pp.1713-1716.

19. Vesin, J. M.: An alternative scheme for adaptive nonlinear prediction using radial basis functions. Signal Processing VI: Theories and applications EUSIPCO-1992, pp.1069-1072.

20. Diaz-de-Maria, F., Figueiras, A.: Nonlinear prediction for speech coding using radial basis functions. IEEE ICASSP 1995, pp. 788-791

21. Diaz-de-Maria, F., Figueiras, A.: Radial basis functions for nonlinear prediction of speech in analysis by synthesis coders. Proceedings of the IEEE Workshop on Nonlinear signal and image processing. NSIP, June 1995, pp. 66-69.

22. Yee, P., Haykin, S.: A dynamic regularized Gaussian radial basis function network for nonlinear, nonstationary time series prediction. IEEE ICASSP 1995, pp. 3419-3422.

23. Birgmeier, M.: Nonlinear prediction of speech signals using radial basis function networks. Signal Processing VIII: Theories and applications EUSIPCO-1996. Vol.1, pp.459-462.

24. Faundez-Zanuy, M.: Adaptive Hybrid Speech coding with a MLP/LPC structure". IWANN 1999, Lecture notes in computer Science, LNCS 1607 vol. II pp.814-823

25. Shang, Y., Wah, B.: Global optimization for neural network training. IEEE Computer, March 1996, pp.45-54.

26. Bishop, C.M.: Neural networks for pattern recognition. Ed. Clarendon Press. 1995

27. Foresee, F. D., Hagan, M. T.: Gauss-Newton approximation to Bayesian regularization, proceedings of the 1997 International Joint Conference on Neural Networks, pp.1930-1935, 1997.

28. Mackay, D. J. C.: Bayesian interpolation. Neural computation, Vol.4, N° 3, pp.415-447, 1992.

29. Faundez-Zanuy, M., Vallverdu, F., Monte, E.: Nonlinear prediction with neural nets in ADPCM. IEEE ICASSP-1998 .SP11.3.Seattle, USA.

30. Faundez-Zanuy, M.: Nonlinear predictive models computation in ADPCM schemes. Signal Processing X: Theories and applications EUSIPCO-2000 Vol. II, pp 813-816.

31. Faundez-Zanuy, M., Oliva, O.: ADPCM with nonlinear prediction. Signal Processing IX: Theories and applications EUSIPCO-1998. pp 1205-1208.

32. Oliva, O., Faundez-Zanuy, M: A comparative study of several ADPCM schemes with linear and nonlinear prediction" EUROSPEECH'99 , Budapest, Vol. 3, pp.1467-1470

33. Jayant, N. S., Noll, P.: Digital compression of waveforms. Ed. Prentice Hall 1984.

34. Haykin, S.: Neural nets. A comprehensive foundation, 2on edition. Ed. Prentice Hall 1999

35. Faundez-Zanuy, M.: "Data fusion in biometrics". Accepted for publication, IEEE Aerospace and Electronic Systems Magazine. In press, 2004.

36. Faundez-Zanuy M., "On the vulnerability of biometric security systems". IEEE Aerospace and Electronic Systems Magazine. Vol.19 n° 6, pp.3-8, June de 2004.

37. Faundez-Zanuy M., "Biometric recognition: why not massively adopted yet?" Accepted for publication, IEEE Aerospace and Electronic Systems Magazine. In press, 2004.

38. Gersho, A., Gray, R.M.: Vector Quantization and signal compression. Ed. Kluwer 1992.

39. Montacié, C., Le Floch, J. L.: Discriminant AR-Vector models for free-text speaker verification. EROSPEECH 1993, pp.161-164.

40. Faundez-Zanuy, M.: Vectorial Nonlinear prediction with neural nets. IWANN 2001, Lecture notes in computer Science, LNCS 2085 Vol. II, pp. 754-761. Springer Verlag.

41. Cuperman, V., Gersho, A.: Vector Predictive coding of speech at 16 kbits/s. IEEE Trans. on Comm. vol. COM-33, pp.685-696, July 1985.

42. Faundez-Zanuy, M.: Nonlinear predictive vector quantization of speech. Proceedings 7th European Conference on speech communication and technology, EUROSPEECH'2001 Vol. 3 pp. 1977-1980.

43. Faundez-Zanuy, M.: N-dimensional nonlinear prediction with MLP. Signal Processing XI: Theories and applications EUSIPCO-2002, Vol. III pp. 537-540

44. Wells R. B.: Applied coding and information theory for engineers. Ed. Prentice Hall, 1999.

45. Picone, J. W.: Signal Modeling techniques in speech recognition. Proceedings of the IEEE, Vol. 79, N° 4, April 1991, pp.1215-1247

46. Mammone, R., Zhang, X., Ramachandran R.: Robust speaker recognition. IEEE signal processing magazine, p.58-71, September 1996

47. Soong, F. K., Rosenberg, A. E.: On the use of instantaneous and transitional spectral information in speaker recognition. IEEE Trans. On ASSP, Vol. 36, N° 6, pp.871-879, June 1988.

48. Faundez-Zanuy, M.: What can predictive speech coders learn from speaker recognizers?. ISCA tutorial and research workshop on non-linear speech processing NOLISP. May, 2003. Le Croisic, France.

Signal Processing in a Nonlinear, NonGaussian, and Nonstationary World

Simon Haykin

McMaster University Hamilton, Ontario, Canada L8S 4K1
haykin@mcmaster.ca

Abstract. This article discusses three specific issues of particular interest in the study of nonlinear dynamical systems:
- Bayesian estimation, exemplified by particle filtering;
- Learning in recurrent neural networks;
- Correlative learning, exemplified by the ALOPEX algorithm.

By and large, the discussion is of a philosophical nature.

1 Introduction

Signal processing in the twenty-first century will distinguish itself from the way it was researched and practiced in the twentieth century by providing practical solutions to real-life problems where the observed signals are most likely to be nonlinear, non-Gaussian, and nonstationary. This impressive capability is being made possible through the use of new techniques or algorithms whose applications are now feasible, thanks to the ever-increasing power of digital computers.

In saying so, we do not subscribe to complete reliance on the use of computers for solving signal-processing problems. Rather, the philosophy we are advocating should embody the following ingredients:

(i) Understanding of the underlying physical or biological basis for the dynamical processes responsible for the generation of observed signals [1].
(ii) Proper statistical descriptions of the target signal and the background noise processes in question.
(iii) Learning from the environment of interest and adapting to its statistical variations with time in an efficient manner.

Simply stated, the aim should be the development of signal-processing algorithms, the mathematical formulation of which matches the physical realities of the observed signals as closely as possible, so as to minimize the loss of valuable information contained in the observed signals.

In what follows, we will focus on nonlinear dynamical systems and related issues. First, we will discuss state-space models in their most generic form. That will set the stage for the discussion of Bayesian estimation. Then we will discuss the role of learning in solving nonlinear dynamical problems. Finally, we will discuss the idea of correlative learning, exemplified by the ALOPEX algorithm.

2 Modeling of Dynamical Systems: State-Space Model

A *model* of a physical process is not expected to convey the absolute truth. Rather, the model is supposed to provide a mathematical basis for doing two things:

G. Chollet et al. (Eds.): Nonlinear Speech Modeling, LNAI 3445, pp. 43–53, 2005.

(i) Describing the dynamic behavior of the system.

(ii) Developing computational algorithms for the solution of specific control and decision-making problems.

The model that stands out in the context of dynamical systems is the so-called *state-space model*, the formulation of which revolves around the notion of state.

The state of a dynamical system is defined as the minimal set of information-bearing data that is sufficient to uniquely describe the unforced dynamic behavior of the system. In other words, the state comprises the smallest possible data on the past behavior of the system (i.e., its history) that are needed to predict future behavior of the system.

Typically, the state of the system is *hidden* from the outside world. It can only be sensed indirectly through a set of *observables* that are dependent on the state. Let the vector $\mathbf{x}_t$ denote the state of the system at discrete time t. Let the vector $\mathbf{y}_t$ denote the set of observables at time t. We may then describe the dynamic behavior of the system by the couple of equations:

(i) *Process (evolution) equation*, which defines the *updated state* $\mathbf{x}_{t+1}$ in terms of the present state $\mathbf{x}_t$ and the *dynamic noise* $\mathbf{w}_t$ as

$$\mathbf{x}_{t+1} = \mathbf{f}_t(\mathbf{x}_t) + \mathbf{w}_t \tag{1}$$

where $\mathbf{f}_t(.)$ is a vector-valued nonlinear function of its argument. The subscript t in $\mathbf{f}_t$ implies that the nonlinear function is time varying.

(ii) *Measurement (observation) equation*, which defines the *observable* $\mathbf{y}_t$ in terms of the *present state* $\mathbf{x}_t$ and *measurement noise* $\mathbf{v}_t$ as

$$\mathbf{y}_t = \mathbf{g}_t(\mathbf{x}_t) + \mathbf{v}_t \tag{2}$$

where $\mathbf{g}_t(.)$ is another time-varying, vector-valued function.

In a general setting, the dynamic noise $\mathbf{w}_t$ and measurement noise $\mathbf{v}_t$ are non-Gaussian. In such a setting, the state-space model embodying Equations (1) and (2) describes a dynamical system (environment) that is nonlinear, nonGaussian, and nonstationarity. Figure 1 shows a representation of these two equations under one flow graph.

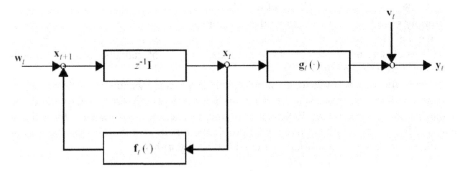

Fig. 1. Flow graph of state-space model, described by Equations (1) and (2); the symbol $\mathbf{z}^{-1}$ denotes the unit-delay operator, and I denotes the identity matrix

3 Bayesian Estimation: Particle Filtering

In much of the literature in the twentieth century, going back to the classic paper by Kalman [2], the study of sequential state-estimation focused on a special case of the state-space model that satisfies two assumptions: linearity of the dynamics, and Gaussianty of the dynamic and measurement noise processes. The fundamental premise in *Kalman filter theory* so formulated is that if the estimation-error variance is minimized, then with variance providing a quantitative measure of power, assures that the state estimate is progressively improved in a recursive manner. Indeed, under these two assumptions, the Kalman filter is not only optimal in the mean-square error sense but also the maximum-likelihood sense. In other words, the Kalman filter is a special case of the *Bayesian estimator of the state*, assuming that the state-space model is indeed linear and the noise processes in the model are Gaussian.

On the other hand, the compelling virtue of the Bayesian state estimator is that the laws of probability theory are applicable, making it possible to produce *inference* about the prediction (forecasting), filtering, and smoothing solutions of the sequential state-estimation problem. Given the entire set of the observables $\{\mathbf{y}_i\}_{i=1}^{t}$, we distinguish between these three scenarios as follows:

- In one-step prediction, the state estimate is defined by $\hat{\mathbf{x}}_{t+1}$.
- In filtering, the state-estimate is defined by $\hat{\mathbf{x}}_t$.
- In smoothing, the state estimate is defined by $\hat{\mathbf{x}}_\tau$ where $1 \le \tau < t$.

Prediction and filtering are real-time operations, whereas although smoothing is more accurate, it can only be performed in nonreal-time.

In the Bayesian approach to state estimation, the hidden state $\mathbf{x}_t$ is modelled as a Markov process, which is described by the initial distribution $p(\mathbf{x}_0)$ and the transition distribution $p(\mathbf{x}_t|\mathbf{x}_{t-1})$ for $t \ge 1$. The observable $\mathbf{y}_t$ is itself described by the marginal distribution $p(\mathbf{y}_t|\mathbf{x}_t)$. The state-estimation problem may now be stated as follows:

Given the set of observables
$$\mathbf{y}_{1:t} \overset{\Delta}{=} \{\mathbf{y}_1, \mathbf{y}_2, \ldots, \mathbf{y}_t\}$$
and defining the set of states,
$$\mathbf{x}_{0:t} \overset{\Delta}{=} \{\mathbf{x}_0, \mathbf{x}_1, \mathbf{x}_2, \ldots, \mathbf{x}_t\}$$

recursively estimate the *posterior distribution* $p(\mathbf{x}_{0:t}|\mathbf{y}_{1:t})$, the *filtering distribution* $p(\mathbf{x}_t|\mathbf{y}_{1:t})$ and all related expectations of interest.

An important step in finding the solution to the problem involves the application of Bayes' rule, which, in the context of the filtering distribution, for example, is stated as follows:

$$p(\mathbf{x}_t|\mathbf{y}_{1:t}) = \frac{p(\mathbf{y}_{1:t}|\mathbf{x}_t)p(\mathbf{x}_t)}{p(\mathbf{y}_{1:t})} \tag{3}$$

The denominator, $p(\mathbf{y}_{1:t})$ is called the *evidence*, which is defined by the joint distribution of all the observables, namely, $\mathbf{y}_1, \mathbf{y}_2, \ldots, \mathbf{y}_t$. The evidence acts merely as a *normalizing factor*. The numerator is made up of the product of two distributions:

The conditional distribution, $p(\mathbf{y}_{1:t}|\mathbf{x}_t)$ which is called the *likelihood function* or simply the *likelihood*.

The distribution $p(\mathbf{x}_t)$, which is called the *a priori distribution* or simply the *prior*.

A difficulty in applying the Bayesian approach is now apparent: Recognizing that the state $\mathbf{x}_t$ is hidden from the outside world, how do we deal with the prior for all time t?

Posing yet another question: Not knowing the prior $p(\mathbf{x}_t)$ $p(\mathbf{x}_t)$, how do we evaluate the expectation of the nonlinear function $\mathbf{f}_t(\mathbf{x}_{0:t})$ that defines the evolution of the state $\mathbf{x}_t$ with time t, except for the dynamic noise $\mathbf{w}_t$?

The answer to both of these fundamental questions lies in the so-called *proposal distribution*, which is denoted by $\pi(\mathbf{x}_{0:t}|\mathbf{y}_{1:t})$. In particular, given such a distribution, we may express the expectation of the nonlinear function $\mathbf{f}_t(\mathbf{x}_{0:t})$ as

$$
\begin{aligned}
E[\mathbf{f}_t(\mathbf{x}_{0:t})] &= \int \mathbf{f}_t(\mathbf{x}_{0:t}) p(\mathbf{x}_{0:t}|\mathbf{y}_{1:t})\, d\mathbf{x}_{0:t} \\
&= \frac{\int \mathbf{f}_t(\mathbf{x}_{0:t}) \dfrac{p(\mathbf{x}_{0:t}|\mathbf{y}_{1:t})}{\pi(\mathbf{x}_{0:t}|\mathbf{y}_{0:t})} \pi(\mathbf{x}_{0:t}|\mathbf{y}_{1:t})\, d\mathbf{x}_{0:t}}{\int \dfrac{p(\mathbf{x}_{0:t}|\mathbf{y}_{1:t})}{\pi(\mathbf{x}_{0:t}|\mathbf{y}_{0:t})} \pi(\mathbf{x}_{0:t}|\mathbf{y}_{1:t})\, d\mathbf{x}_{0:t}} \\
&= \frac{\int \mathbf{f}_t(\mathbf{x}_{0:t}) \mathbf{w}(\mathbf{x}_{0:t}) \pi(\mathbf{x}_{0:t}|\mathbf{y}_{1:t})\, d\mathbf{x}_{0:t}}{\int \mathbf{w}(\mathbf{x}_{0:t}) \pi(\mathbf{x}_{0:t}|\mathbf{y}_{1:t})\, d\mathbf{x}_{0:t}}
\end{aligned}
\tag{4}
$$

where E denotes the statistical expectation operator. The new factor $\mathbf{w}(\mathbf{x}_{0:t})$ in Equation (4) is defined by

$$
\mathbf{w}(\mathbf{x}_{0:t}) = \frac{p(\mathbf{x}_{0:t}|\mathbf{y}_{1:t})}{\pi(\mathbf{x}_{0:t}|\mathbf{y}_{1:t})}
\tag{5}
$$

Suppose next we simulate N *independent and identically distributed (iid) samples* $\{\mathbf{x}_{0:t}^{(i)}\}_{i=1}^{N}$ according to the proposal distribution $\pi(\mathbf{x}_{0:t}|\mathbf{y}_{1:t})$. Then a Monte Carlo estimate of the desired expectation of Equation (4), denoted by $\hat{I}(\mathbf{f}_t)$, is given by

$$
\begin{aligned}
\hat{I}(\mathbf{f}_t) &= \frac{\dfrac{1}{N}\sum_{i=1}^{N} \mathbf{f}_t(\mathbf{x}_{0:t}^{(i)})\, \mathbf{w}(\mathbf{x}_{0:t}^{(i)})}{\dfrac{1}{N}\sum_{j=1}^{N} \mathbf{w}(\mathbf{x}_{0:t}^{(j)})} \\
&= \sum_{i=1}^{N} \mathbf{f}_t(\mathbf{x}_{0:t}^{(i)})\, \widetilde{\mathbf{w}}(\mathbf{x}_t^{(i)})
\end{aligned}
\tag{6}
$$

where the normalized factor $\widetilde{\mathbf{w}}_t^{(i)}$ is defined by

$$\widetilde{\mathbf{w}}_t^{(i)} = \frac{\mathbf{w}\left(\mathbf{x}_{0:t}^{(i)}\right)}{\sum\limits_{j=1}^{N}\mathbf{w}\left(\mathbf{x}_{0:t}^{(j)}\right)}, \qquad i = 1,2,\ldots,N \tag{7}$$

As the number of samples, N, approaches infinity, the denominator in the first line of Equation (6) approaches unity, and so it should.

What we have been presenting in Equations (4) through (7) is basic to certain aspects of *particle filtering*[1]. The term particle stands for "sample". The idea of a proposal distribution is basic to *particle filtering theory*. In the literature on this theory, the Monte Carlo simulation procedure described herein is referred to as *importance sampling*. Correspondingly, the factor $\mathbf{w}\left(\mathbf{x}_{0:t}^{(j)}\right)$ is called an *importance weight*, and $\widetilde{\mathbf{w}}^{(i)}$ is called a *normalized importance weight*.

Particle filtering has emerged as a powerful tool for solving sequential state-estimation problems based on the generalized state-space model of Equations (1) and (2). These two equations embody nonlinearity, nonGaussianty, and nonstationarity in a general sense, hence the universal power of the particle filter as the tracker of the hidden state of a nonlinear dynamical system. Just as Kalman filtering dominated the literature on sequential state-estimation in the twentieth century, particle filtering will dominate the literature on this important and highly pervasive subject in the twenty-first century. Nevertheless, Kalman filter theory will always be an integral part of the literature on sequential-state estimation. When the dynamical model of interest is linear, the Kalman filter is the method of choice. Moreover, we frequently find that the Kalman filter or one of its variants (e.g., the extended Kalman filter) plays a significant role in the design of particle filters. The *extended Kalman filter* results from linearizations of the dynamic and measurement processes through application of Taylor series expansions of Equations (1) and (2), and then applying the Kalman filter theory [8].

4 Nonlinear Dynamical Learning Models: Recurrent Neural Networks

In 1965, Cover [9] postulated a theorem for solving complex pattern-classification tasks. In qualitative terms, *Cover's theorem on the separability of patterns* may be stated as follows [10]:

> A complex pattern-classification problem formulated nonlinearly in a high-dimensional feature (hidden) space is more likely to be linearly separable than if it is formulated in a low-dimensional space.

In other words, a nonlinearly separable pattern-classification problem may be transformed into an easier, linearly separable pattern-classification one by the combined use of a network that embodies two properties: nonlinearity, and high-dimensionality.

---

[1] Monte Carlo simulation has a long history; see the book by Robert and Caselle [3] for details. The idea of particle filtering has been discussed in the literature under different headings: bootstrap filter, condensation, etc. However, it was the paper by Gordon et al. [4] that put particle filter theory on a firm footing for the first time; for details see the books [5], [6] and the special issue [7].

Pattern-classification is a static problem. In an intuitive sense, we may formulate the dynamic *corollary to Cover's theorem* as follows[2]:

> A difficult nonlinear dynamical estimation problem formulated non-linearly in a high-dimensional recurrent (hidden) space is more likely to be solved efficiently than if it is formulated in a low-dimensional recurrent space.

In more specific terms, a conventional fully connected recurrent neural network has the potential to approximate any dynamical system, provided that a large enough number of computational units is used [9]. However, such an approach suffers from two practical difficulties:

(i) The desired approximation may not be realizable using gradient-descent learning due to a low rate of convergence and the vanishing gradient problem [13].

(ii) The rate of learning can be increased by using a second-order method of training exemplified by the extended Kalman filtering algorithm [14]. However, despite the use of annealing by purposely injecting noise of decreasing variance into the dynamic equation, there is no guarantee of reaching an optimal solution[3].

Moreover, the number of computational units (sigmoidal neurons) used in fully connected recurrent neural networks (RNNs) reported in the literature is typically on the order of 5 to 25, with the number of adjustable weights being limited to about 500.

In contrast, the echo-state network devised by Jaeger and Haas [12] and the liquid-state network devised by Maass et al. [11] provide new approaches for learning nonlinear dynamical systems that appear to overcome limitations (i) and (ii) of RNNs. The liquid-state network is neurobiologically motivated, the intention of which is to model computations in cortical microcircuits of the human brain; it does so by using spiking neurons. The echo-state network, though also biologically motivated, is developed to cater to ordinary signal-processing and control applications such as channel equalization and inverse control. Nevertheless, these two new and independently developed approaches for learning nonlinear dynamical systems do share a common approach in that they are both covered, in their own individual ways, by the dynamic corollary stated above. In what follows, we describe the echo-state network in some detail as the primary focus of this article is on signal processing.

Figure 2 depicts the block diagram of the echo-state network. The network consists of two basic functional components:

(i) *Reservoir*, which consists of a large number of sigmoidal neurons that are *randomly* connected to each other with feedback connections between them.

(ii) *Linear output neurons*, which are provided with random connections that project back into the reservoir.

---

[2] The author of this article alluded to this corollary in his book [10]. Its explicit form, as stated above, has been influenced by two recent publications [11], [12].

[3] Notwithstanding the possibility of a sub-optimal solution, RNN-based misfire-detection, based on the design procedure described in [14], has been put into commercial production. The first phase of this significant achievement has been accomplished with the release of the Aston Martin Car Model DB9 in the spring of 2004 [15]. For details see the web site http://www.astonmartin.com/thecars/db9/specification

Direct input-output connections and connections between output neurons are permitted. There are no further restrictions imposed on the network topology.

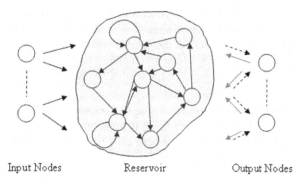

Input Nodes   Reservoir   Output Nodes

Fig. 2. The basic architecture of an echo-state network

The echo-state network derives its name from the following important property of the network. When a realization of the desired response is fed into an output neuron, the neurons inside the reservoir are excited through the feedback connections built into the reservoir. Consequently, after an initial transient period has elapsed, systematic variants of that particular exciting signal (i.e., echo functions) are exhibited by the internal neurons. This property is basic to the operation of the echo-state network. In particular, for the echo functions to be richly varied, in configuring the reservoir it is ensured that the interconnectivity within the reservoir is *sparse*, on the order of one percent. The net result is a *richly structured reservoir of excitable dynamics*. By virtue of the output layer being composed of linear neurons, the output signal produced by the network in response to an externally applied input signal is therefore a linear combination of the network's states, which are themselves governed by the echo functions. The supervised training of the network is thereby limited to the weights in the output layer, the optimization of which is achieved by performing a straightforward linear regression.

To sum up, the echo-state network provides an elegant basis for designing recurrent neural networks; in particular, the learning procedure involved in its design is computationally efficient and relatively straightforward to implement. Moreover, such recurrent networks accommodate the possible use of a large number of computational units. In so doing, they appear to overcome serious limitations of conventional fully connected recurrent neural networks.

As remarked previously, the liquid-state network works on essentially the same principle as the echo-state network. Specifically, the "liquid" component of the liquid-state network is typically made from biologically motivated spiking neurons. As with the echo-state network, the liquid part of the machine exhibits interesting excitable dynamics, which are tapped by trainable readout mechanisms; the liquid thus plays a role similar to that of the reservoir in the echo-state network.

Between them, the liquid-state network and echo-state network provide novel directions for the efficient design of recurrent neural networks. Both of them are in their early stages of development.

5 Correlative Learning: ALOPEX Algorithm

A discussion of learning would be incomplete without some attention given to the role of *correlation* in such processes. According to Eggermont [16], correlation is used in many tasks performed by the human brain, namely, the formation of topographic maps, the detection of events in the outside world, and other functions such as learning, association, pattern recognition, and memory recall.

Undoubtedly, the most influential proponent of learning as a correlative process was Donald Hebb, who postulated the following [17]:

> "When an axon of cell A is near enough to excite a cell B and repeatedly or persistently takes part in firing it, some growth process or metabolic changes take place in one or both cells such that A's efficiency as one of the cells firing B, is increased".

Stated in mathematical terms, Hebb's postulate of learning can be formulated as [10]

$$\Delta\theta_{AB,t} = \eta u_{A,t} y_{B,t} \tag{8}$$

where $u_{A,t}$ and $y_{B,t}$ represent pre-synaptic and post-synaptic signals, respectively, acting on the synapse (i.e., link) that connects neurons (cells) A and B; $\Delta\theta_{AB,t}$ denotes the change of synaptic weight, and η is a small step-size parameter. Averaged over many time steps, the synaptic weight becomes proportional to the correlation between the pre-synaptic and post-synaptic signals.

A learning algorithm that embodies correlation in a highly interesting manner is the ALOPEX (Algorithm Of Pattern EXtraction) algorithm [18]. Stated in words, *the correction term in the ALOPEX algorithm is proportional to the instantaneous cross-correlation between the weight modification $\Delta\theta_t$ in two consecutive time steps and the corresponding change $\Delta\epsilon_t$ in the objective function*, as shown by

$$\Delta\theta_{t+1} = \eta\theta_t\Delta\epsilon_t \tag{9}$$

Although, indeed, both Equations (8) and (9) embody an instantaneous form of correlation, the input and output terms in the two equations have entirely different physical meanings.

There exist several different forms of the ALOPEX algorithm [19,20]. However, these different forms of the algorithm share many common features that are attractive, as summarized here:

- The ALOPEX optimization procedure is *gradient-free*, and it is independent of the objective function and network (model) architecture.
- The optimization procedure is *synchronous* in the sense that all adjustable parameters in the network are updated in parallel, thereby sharing the features of algorithmic simplicity and ease of parallel implementation.
- The optimization procedure relies on *stochasticity* produced by the purposeful addition of noise, which is used to control the search direction and help the algorithm to escape from local minima or local maxima.
- The underlying principle in ALOPEX may be viewed as *trial and error*; it is similar in spirit to the "weight perturbation" method (a.k.a. "MIT" rule) in the control literature.

- Synaptic plasticity introduces a *feedback* mechanism into the operation of the algorithm.

In Chen's Ph.D. thesis [20], many interesting applications are investigated, using different versions of the ALOPEX algorithm. One particular application of interest discussed therein is that of neural compensation motivated by the design of an adaptive hearing system for the hearing impaired person, the idea for which was originated by Becker and Bruce [21]. The goal of the *neurocompensator* is to restore normal-hearing firing patterns in the auditory nerve in spite of damage to hair cells in the inner ear. Block diagrams of normal/impaired hearing systems as well as the compensated system are depicted in Fig. 3.

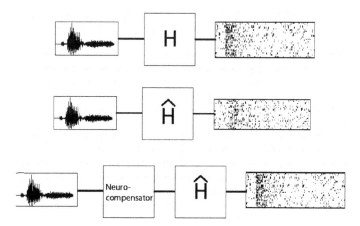

Fig. 3. Block diagrams pertaining the neurocompensation for the hearing impaired

The top part of the figure represents a normal-hearing system. The middle part represents a hearing-impaired system. The bottom part depicts the neurocompensator followed by the hearing-impaired system. The H and $\hat{H}$ in the figure denote the input-output mappings of the normal and impaired hearing models, respectively. Ideally, we would like to design the neurocompensator in such a way the top and bottom parts of the figure are indistinguishable from each other insofar as overall input-output behavior is concerned. Note that all the systems depicted in Fig. 3 exhibit nonlinear dynamical behavior, each in its own way.

The learning processes invoked in the design of the neurocompensator are twofold [20]:

- Probabilistic modeling of the auditory nerve model's spike trains, using procedures due to Bruce and collaborators [22].
- Gradient-free optimization for parameter updates, using an improved version of the ALOPEX algorithm.

Based on the preliminary results presented in [20], it has been demonstrated that neurocompensation described in Fig. 3 provides a promising adaptive approach for reducing perceptual distortion due to hearing loss. Nevertheless, more experimental work needs to be done on this novel approach to improve performance and stability of the compensated system.

6 Summary

In this article, I have presented a philosophical discussion of signal-processing issues that do arise when dealing with nonlinear dynamical systems. In particular, three important topics have been highlighted, as summarized here:

(i) *Particle filtering*, the need for which arises when, for example, the tracking of a target of interest requires a state-space model that is both nonlinear and non-Gaussian.

(ii) A new generation of recurrent neural networks, which is exemplified by the *echo-state network*.

(iii) *Neurocompensation*, which involves the use of a preprocessor in an adaptive hearing system for the hearing-impaired. The objective of the compensation is to make the overall adaptive hearing system behave in the same way as a normal-hearing model.

Each of these topics has important practical implications of its own.

Acknowledgements

First and foremost, the author would like to thank Anna Esposito for inviting him to present 3 lectures at the 2004 Summer School at Vietri, Italy, which, in turn, led to writing this article. He is grateful to the Natural Sciences and Engineering Council (NSERC), Canada, for financially supporting the research effort of the author, which has featured prominently in this article.

References

1. Haykin, S.: Signal processing: Where Physics and Mathematics Meet. IEEE Signal Processing Magazine, Vol. 18(4) (2001) 6-7 (Invited)
2. Kalman, R.E.: A New Approach to Linear Filtering and Prediction Problems. Transactions of the ASME, Journal of Basic Engineering, Vol. 82(3) (1960) 5-45
3. Robert, C.P., Casella, G.: Monte Carlo Statistical Methods. Springer, Berlin (1999)
4. Gordon, N., Salmond, D., Smith, A.F.M.: Novel Approach to Nonlinear/Non-gaussian Bayesian State Estimation. IEE Proceedings-F, Vol. 140 (1993) 107-113
5. Doucet, A., deFreitas, N., Gordon, N. (editors): Sequential Monte Carlo Methods in Practice. Springer, New York (2001)
6. Cappé, O., Moulines, E., Rydén, T.: Inference in Hidden Markov Models, Springer (2005)
7. Haykin, S., and deFreitas, N. (editors): Special Issue of the Proc. IEEE on Sequential State Estimation (2004)
8. Haykin, S.: Adaptive Filter Theory, 4th Edition, Prentice-Hall (2002)
9. Cover, T.: Geometrical and Statistical Properties of Systems of Linear Inequalities with Applications in Pattern Recognition. IEEE Trans. on Electronic Computers, Vol. EC-14 (1965) 326-334
10. Haykin, S.: Neural Networks: A Comprehensive Foundation, 2nd Edition, Prentice-Hall (1999)
11. Maass, W., Natschläger, T., and Markram, H.: Real-Time Computing without Stable States: A New Framework for Neural Computation Based on Perturbations. Neural Computation Vol. 14 (2002) 2531-2560
12. Jaegar, H. and Haas, H.: Harnessing Nonlinearity: Predicting Chaotic Systems and Saving Energy in Wireless Communication. Science, Vol. 304(5667) (2003) 78-80

13. Bengio Y., Simard, P., Frasconi, P.: Learning Long-Term Dependencies with Gradient Descent is Difficult. IEEE Transactions on Neural Networks, Vol. 5 (1994) 157-166

14. Puskorious, G.V., Feldkamp, L.: Parameter-based Kalman Filter Training: Theory and Implementation. In S. Haykin (editor), Kalman Filtering and Neural Networks. John Wiley & Son (2001) 23-67

15. Feldkamp, L.: Private Communication, Oct. 19 (2004)

16. Eggermont, J.J.: The Correlative Brain: Theory and Experiment in Neural Interaction. Springer-Verlag, New York, 1990

17. Hebb, D.: Organization of Behavior: A Neuropsychological Theory. Wiley, New York (1949)

18. Fujita, O.: Trial-and-Error Correlation Learning. IEEE Transactions on Neural Networks, Vol. 4(4) (1993) 720-722

19. Haykin, S., Chen, Z., and Becker, S.: Stochastic Correlative Learning Algorithms. IEEE Transactions on Signal Processing, Vol. 52(8) (2004) 2200-2209

20. Chen, Z.: Stochastic Optimization Approaches for Correlative-based Learning, Ph.D. Thesis, McMaster University, Hamilton, Ontario, Canada, under preparation

21. Becker, S., Bruce, I.C.: Neural Coding in The Auditory Periphery: Insights From Physiology and Modeling Lead to a Novel Hearing Compensation Algorithm. In Workshop in Neural Information Coding, Les Houches, France (2002)

22. Bruce, I.C., Sachs, M.B., Young, E.: An Auditory-Periphery Model of the Effects of Acoustic Trauma on Auditory Nerve Responses. J. of Acoustical Society of America, Vol. 113(1) (2003) 369-388

The Analysis of Voice Quality in Speech Processing

Eric Keller

Informatique et méthodes mathématiques (IMM), Faculté des Lettres,
Université de Lausanne, 1015 Lausanne, Switzerland
eric.keller@unil.ch

Abstract. Voice quality has been defined as the characteristic auditory colouring of an individual's voice, derived from a variety of laryngeal and supralaryngeal features and running continuously through the individual's speech. The distinctive tone of speech sounds produced by a particular person yields a particular voice. Voice quality is at the centre of several speech processing issues. In speech recognition, voice differences, particularly extreme divergences from the norm, are responsible for known performance degradations. In speech synthesis on the other hand, voice quality is a desirable modelling parameter, with millions of voice types that can be distinguished theoretically. This article reviews the experimental derivation of voice quality markers. Specifically, the use of perceptual judgements, the long-term averaged spectrum (LTAS) and prosodic markers is examined, as well as inverse filtering for the extraction of the glottal source waveform. This review suggests that voice quality is best investigated as a multi-dimensional parameter space involving a combination of factors involving individual prosody, temporally structured speech characteristics, spectral divergence and voice source features, and that it could profitably complement simple linguistic prosodic model processing in speech synthesis.

1 Introduction

The study of voice quality has recently gained considerable importance in speech processing. It bears a direct relationship to the naturalness of speech synthesis systems, and it is part of the natural language constraints considered in speech recognition.

Specifically, current speech synthesis systems are used in an extensive range of applications, encompassing a wide variety of individual speech styles. This brings with it a call for greater authenticity in voice quality. An automatised product description, for example, should be produced in a clearly audible and informative speech style when the context calls for an efficient transmission of factual information, e.g., by telephone. Yet in a promotional context, essentially the same information should be provided in a more "peppy", more engaging style in order to capture the client's interest. Similarly, contexts can be imagined where low, raspy voices, strong, commanding voices, or quiet, retiring voices could advantageously replace the "standard-fare", neutral and somewhat monotonous voices that are typically provided in current speech synthesis systems.

To do this, two major aspects of an individual speech style must be controlled: first, its *prosodics*, involving the timing, fundamental frequency and amplitude of various elements in the speech signal (typically syllables), and second, its *voice quality*, involving control over a whole series of further aspects of the voice signal, primarily *divergence from spectral distributions*, *voice source features* and *temporally*

G. Chollet et al. (Eds.): Nonlinear Speech Modeling, LNAI 3445, pp. 54–73, 2005.

structured features (e.g., voice on-/offsets, jitter [cycle-to-cycle durational variation]). Although it will be seen that prosodic and voice quality features interact closely, it is useful to distinguish them for historical, explanatory, and algorithmic purposes.

Since there are systematic divergences in signals produced with distinct voice types, the differentiating potential of voice quality can also be exploited for various speech recognition purposes. For example, such divergences are part of an individual biological identification pattern and can be used as one component of a larger speaker identification system for information access control. Also, acoustic properties relating to habitual articulatory configurations and to typical speech motor activity can to a large extent be obtained automatically, and can be exploited as part of a wider feature set in general speech recognition systems.

In line with this logic, this introductory review article explores the methodology of obtaining different types of voice quality from the perspectives of *articulatory determinants* and their *acoustic signal realization*. Certain *articulatory settings* in the vocal tract have been associated with particular acoustic feature sets found with specific speech styles, and thus underpin differentiations formulated at the acoustic level. At the *acoustic signal* level, a variety of signal features have been associated with various aspects of voice quality which are directly relevant to speech processing systems that must deal with *voice quality modification* in the case of synthesis systems, and with *voice quality differentiation* in the case of recognition systems. By briefly reviewing both articulatory and acoustic indicators, we wish to clarify the core of the work to be done in speech synthesis and speech recognition in the area of voice quality. In this paper, we are *not* concerned with detailed algorithmic content. We are mainly interested in understanding the *conceptual framework* of doing research on voice quality[1].

2 Laver's Articulatory and Acoustic Voice Quality Schema

We begin by examining the articulatory and acoustic correlates of voice quality in terms of an initial unified scheme. Our point of departure is the influential classification scheme proposed by Laver [2, 3], which is based on perceptual ratings of articulatorily defined voice quality modifications. This will introduce concepts and a useful initial terminology for voice quality and its acoustic measures.

In Laver's approach, the definitional process issues from a "neutral setting" of the articulatory apparatus. In this setting, the speaker is assumed to produce speech with articulatory organs that show equilibrated muscular tension throughout the vocal tract. At the supralaryngeal level, this means primarily that the jaw is neither lowered nor raised, the tongue root is neither particularly advanced nor retracted, and the lips are not protruded ([2] p. 14). At the laryngeal level, this means that "vibration of the true vocal folds is periodic, efficient and without audible friction" ([2] p. 95). This articulatory configuration produces a "neutral voice" or "modal voice" for a given speaker. Voice quality modification, or "voice modulation", can then be defined as the effect of departures from this habitual setting. This makes it possible to examine the selec-

---

[1] A reader familiar with basic information about the articulatory and acoustic aspects of speech production is supposed here. Much of the basic information not covered here, as well as many additional sources and explanations are furnished in [1].

tive modifications of labial, lingual, velar and laryngeal settings in the articulatory tract.

2.1 Summary of Laver's Voice Quality Schema

Laver's schema is summarized in the following listing. As is common, the vocal tract is divided into a supralaryngeal portion on the one hand (lips, tongue, palate, velum, pharynx), and a laryngeal portion on the other (larynx and the associated musculature). Respiration, though relevant to voice quality, is subsumed. The schema (which is based on an extensive literature review prior to 1980) summarizes articulatory settings in terms of an integrated description of active and largely independent motor components of articulatory functioning. At various points indicated in the original text, Laver's account of articulatory descriptions diverges marginally from accounts given by other authors. Settings for different articulatory structures are given in regular font, and the acoustic consequences of non-neutral ("non-modal") settings are given in italics.

1. **Supralaryngeal settings,** defined in terms of *longitudinal, latitudinal* and *velopharyngeal* settings of the vocal tract.
    a. **Longitudinal settings:** relative lengthening and shortening of vocal tract.
        i. **Raised larynx and lowered larynx voice ("high"** *vs.* **"low" voice).** *Raised: high F0, lowered: low F0, often breathy, i.e., presence of noise in all speech frequencies.*
        ii. **Labial protrusion.** *Lowers all formant frequencies, particularly higher formants.*
    b. **Latitudinal settings:** relative widening and constricting of vocal tract at various levels.
        i. **Labial settings:** constrictions and expansions of the lip opening. *Acoustic effect not specified.*
        ii. **Lingual settings:** displacement of tongue body towards the anterior, central or posterior portion of the palate or the back wall of the pharynx. *Displaces formant 1/2 vowel triangle as a whole, provides general acoustic coloring in accordance with the vowel towards which the triangle is displaced.*
        iii. **Faucal settings:** constriction of the passage between the oral and the pharyngeal cavities. *Acoustic effect not specified.*
        iv. **Pharyngeal settings:** constriction of the pharyngeal cavity. *Acoustic effect not specified.*
        v. **Mandibular settings:** close/open jaw position, protruded jaw position. *Major effect: raising of formant 1 with lowering of jaw, lowering of formant 2 with closing of jaw.*
    c. **Velopharyngeal settings:** abnormal degrees of nasality ("nasal twang") or lack of nasality ("denasality"). *With nasality, appearance of one or more nasal formants (200-300 Hz, 1 kHz and 2 kHz) and of one or more anti-formants (anti-resonances[2]), plus overall loss of acoustic power, especially in first formant and in higher frequencies, accompanied by a flattening and widening of formants.*

---

[2] Reduction of spectral amplitude at a certain resonance frequency.

2. **Laryngeal settings,** defined in terms of *adductive tension* approaching the aryte-noid cartilages, *medial compression* on the vocal processes of the arytenoid carti-lages, and *longitudinal tension* along the vocal folds ([2] pp. 108-109).

   a. **Modal voice:** moderate adductive tension, medial compression and longitudi-nal tension. *Acoustic norms for neutral or modal voice are summarized in [2], Chpt. 1. They correspond to the acoustic indicators obtainable from a standard corpus of neutral, declarative speech.*

   b. **Falsetto:** alternative to modal voice, high adductive tension, large medial com-pression and high longitudinal tension. *F0 two to three times as high as for modal voice, simplified waveform, rapid spectral falloff in high frequencies.*

   c. **Whisper:** can be combined with modal or falsetto voice; low adductive ten-sion, moderate to high medial compression, variable longitudinal tension, pro-ducing a triangular opening of vocal folds of variable size. *Addition of consid-erable noise in all frequencies, particularly in the higher ranges.*

   d. **Creak:** can be combined with modal or falsetto voice; also called "vo-cal/glottal fry"; emission of short vocal pulses at a frequency and with a degree of inter-pulse damping that permits their perception as "separate taps". *Low f0 (20-90 Hz), separate, potentially complex vocal pulses.*

   e. **Harshness:** can be combined with other voice-forms; other terms: "raspy", "rough"; due to great adductive tension and great medial compression, yet with indifferent longitudinal tension, inducing excessive approximation of vocal folds. *Aperiodicity in f0, "jitter".*

   f. **Breathiness:** can be combined with other voice-forms; low adductive tension, low longitudinal tension, in comparison with whisper, low medial compression. *Addition of moderate degrees of noise, reduction of higher frequencies.*

3. **Tension Settings.** Defined by a general tensing or laxing of the entire vocal tract musculature, giving "tense", "sharp", "shrill", "metallic" or "strident" voices on the one hand, and "lax", "soft", "dull", "guttural" or "mellow" voices on the other. *Distinguished primarily by relative amounts of energy in the upper and lower harmonics, where the limit between the two is set at about 1 kHz. Secondarily, tense voices tend to show higher overall amplitude than lax voices.*

2.2 Comments on Laver's Voice Quality Schema

A number of comments are in order with respect to Laver's approach to the analysis of voice quality. As indicated, the point of departure is the notion of *vocal tract set-ting*. Laver ([2] p. 13) says that "a preliminary way of envisaging an articulatory set-ting is to imagine a cineradiographic film being taken of the vocal apparatus in action over, say, 30 seconds. If the individual frames of the film were superimposed on top of each other, a composite picture might emerge which would represent the long-term average configuration of the vocal organs. This configuration constitutes the setting underlying the more momentary segmental articulations..." In Laver's approach, a setting is thus an average state of the vocal tract, and a given voice quality can be thought as an acoustic condition resulting from such an average articulatory configu-ration. As a reflection of this, one traditional acoustic measure of voice quality set-tings has been the long-term (average) spectrum (LTS or LTAS), a spectrum derived from a set of spectra taken over a given time period (typically 30+ seconds of speech).

The articulatory definition of a setting has a number of important implications. The first is that certain departures from a neutral setting in one part of the vocal tract can be combined with departures in another part of the speech apparatus, while other combinations are impossible because of articulatory linkage. This reduction in degrees of freedom has the effect of reducing the total number of voice quality states that can be either produced or perceived. For example, the laryngeal production of falsetto voice appears to be quite different from that used for modal voice, and a combination of falsetto and modal voice is thus impossible (although a rapid alternation between the two is). As a result, the combination of modal and falsetto is impossible, while some other combinations (such as modal and creak) are possible.

Also, some voice quality states may be articulatorily and acoustically similar to each other, such as whispered and breathy speech, while others are strongly distinctive in both respects. However since the intention behind whispered speech (typically the wish not to be heard by others) is generally different from that which leads to breathy speech (typically a secondary effect of relaxed or affective speech), it remains important to distinguish the two types of voice quality, even though in terms of an articulatory description, the two types of voice form a continuum ([2] p. 133).

A limitation of the Laver scheme is rooted in the observability of articulatory events. For example, some pathological and some less common voice styles are characterized by the prominent presence of mucus and saliva ("wet voices"). This produces audible acoustic modifications in the voice. However, such voices are not distinguished in Laver's scheme, since the presence of oral humidity was rarely measured in pre-1980 studies and even today, the degree of oral humidity is not normally assessed in voice studies.

Further, a given articulatory setting may in fact correspond to a linguistically distinctive state in a given language. For example, nasality is distinctive in French or Portuguese, and in these languages, acoustic indicators of nasality are primarily associated with the distinctive feature set of the language and not with voice quality. In English, on the other hand, nasality is common among certain speakers of U.S. English, particularly in vowels preceding nasal consonants (a "nasal twang"). In these cases, it is appropriate to speak of nasality as a type of voice quality.

Finally, there are a number of problems associated with the identification of an articulatory setting. As we have seen, this notion supposes a temporary or habitual modification of the vocal tract in a given individual. A temporary modification can be empirically verified in a given speaker. But it is difficult to do so with a habitual modification, since the vocal tract is rarely or never in a neutral setting. In such cases, the underlying norm is derived from an appropriate sample of similar speakers, which in turn introduces the difficulty of establishing what constitutes a "similar speaker". Given the small anatomical and physiological modifications that are responsible for what are often rather elusive acoustic differences, empirical verification of the notions presented here is therefore not always easy.

A related empirical difficulty resides in the fact that Laver's schema is defined in terms of a given *individual's* articulatory settings (neutral and otherwise), while voice quality as generally understood concerns the use of voice by the *generality* of speakers. The definition, distinction and classification of non-neutral voice quality, as well as its application to speech processing, usually concerns *groups* of speakers[3], yet in Laver's approach, it must be based on (sometimes only supposed) articulatory settings in individual speakers. These group associations are very difficult to verify empirically in an articulatory framework. Without suggesting that Laver's approach is ill-founded or that its schema is irrelevant to current speech processing research, it would clearly be helpful to have a set of *acoustic* features that reliably link all speakers showing a given voice quality *x* or *y*. It is with this goal in mind that we turn to a closer look at the acoustic measures used in the analysis of voice quality, to see if such features can indeed be identified in the acoustic waveform.

3   Acoustic Voice Quality Measures

Acoustic measures of voice quality must satisfy a series of requirements:

- Perceived differentiations of voice should be reflected in predictable variations in the signal waveform or in one or several of its derivatives.
- The measures should reflect states or a set of states of the vocal tract typical of a certain individual, and should be separable from states that are shared by large numbers of speakers and that are relevant to the production of phonetic segments or of prosodic features in a community of speakers ("linguistic features").
- Since perceived voice quality reflects supra-laryngeal as well as laryngeal and sublaryngeal (respiratory) vocal tract settings, measures of the acoustic speech waveform should capture all of these types of information, and should separate them if possible.

It is not easy to satisfy all of these requirements with a single measure. As will be seen, measures that satisfy one requirement tend to fail on another, and the assessment of voice quality probably ultimately requires the parallel application of a whole series of measures. Let us review the most important measures, beginning with the long-term average spectrum.

3.1   Spectral Divergence and the Long-Term Average Spectrum (LTAS)

As briefly mentioned above, one traditional measure of voice quality has been the long-term average spectrum. In this approach, power spectra are taken at a given frequency (e.g. one every *ms*) throughout a given stretch of speech, are averaged and are optionally summarized as a set of spectral bands. Average differences between spectral profiles on the same stretch of speech presumably reflect long-term settings and are ideally expected to capture the essence of voice quality differences. The LTAS typically stabilizes after about 40 seconds [4], cited in [5]. Also, the LTAS reliably identifies quasi-constant characteristics such as a singer's formant [6], cited in [5].

However, this approach is subject to four major limitations. First, long term averages mix spectral features relevant to segmental information with those more directly related to voice. This makes it difficult to compare *different* stretches of speech, or

---

[3] E.g., sportscasters, priests or ministers in a church service, mothers interacting with young children, etc.

even, stretches that are lexically the same, but pronounced somewhat differently. As a consequence, there has been a tendency to replace the simple LTAS by more localized measures recently. Klasmeyer [7] for example suggests performing LTASs on vowel nuclei only, and Keller [8] replaced LTASs by averages based on a large number of spectra obtained from the centre of vowel nuclei, as identified in a large corpus.

The second problem is that averaging neglects temporal dynamics that often contribute to the definition of a given voice quality. Creak, for example, is defined in Laver's scheme by the fact that voice pulses are clearly spaced in the temporal domain. Since fundamental frequency values between 70 and 90 Hz are common, and since spaced f0 pulses with frequencies up to 90 Hz can be perceived as creak ([2], p. 124), it is this temporal spacing, not the absolute fundamental frequency value, that is responsible for the perceptual impression of creaky voice. An LTAS neglects this type of information, just as it neglects some other prominent individual temporal features such as jitter, i.e., cycle-to-cycle variation, or particular temporal evolutions at vowel-consonant transitions.

Third, LTAS profiles obtained from high-amplitude signals show considerable divergences from LTAS profiles recorded from low-amplitude signals [5]. Increases in vocal loudness cause a larger increase of LTAS at 3 kHz than at 0.5 kHz, which complicates even comparisons of multiple recordings of the same text from a single speaker. Below 4 kHz, the difference between high- and low-amplitude LTAS profiles is predictable from overall sound level to a reasonable degree (within 2-3 dB), but above 4 kHz, the individual variation is too great to be modelled [5]. It is thus recommended to take at least three recordings at different loudness levels to calculate LTAS profiles.

Finally, distinctions obtained through averaging methods have been regrettably weak. In the Keller study just referred to ([8]) which involved the examination of some 30'000 vowel nuclei from 56 speakers of the MARSEC corpus[4], only relatively minor systematic spectral differences were identified in standardized spectra for gender and speech style (Figs. 1, 2). Attempts to use these differences to modify speech resynthesized with a harmonics-and-noise model were not successful, presumably because the averaging technique removed acoustic and temporal indices that are important for the differentiation of gender and speech style.

Altogether, while LTASs undeniably illustrate certain voice quality differences, they are apparently of insufficient power to effect voice quality modification or speaker distinctiveness in speech synthesis when used alone. It must be assumed that a number of dynamically patterned features in the acoustic waveform make further important contributions to the perception of given voice quality. We next turn to an important subgroup of such features which are the prosodic markers.

3.2 Acoustic Measures Related to Prosody

From the previous observation, it appears unlikely that voice quality can be defined solely in terms of static acoustic features such as the LTAS. As indicated in Laver's schema, several temporally structured elements enter into consideration as well, to-

---

[4] Machine-Readable Spoken English Corpus, available from
www.rdg.ac.uk/AcaDepts/ll/speechlab/marsec

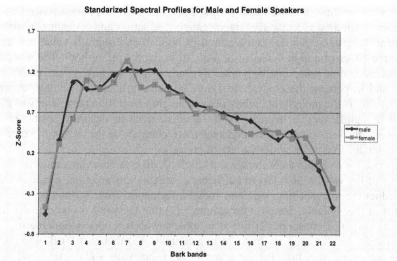

Fig. 1. Averaged and standardized *gender* profiles for some 30'000 vowel nuclei identified in the MARSEC corpus. Although all differences were significant (except for bark band 1), the only major differences occur around Bark bands 3 and 8-9

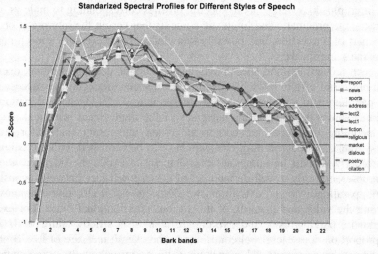

Fig. 2. Averaged and standardized *speech style* profiles for some 30'000 vowel nuclei identified in the MARSEC corpus. Although all differences were significant, the differences tend to be minor and are barely audible when resynthesized by a spectral synthesis method such as HNM (harmonics and noise modeling)

gether with static acoustic indicators, as well as several parameters that are traditionally associated with *prosody*, notably fundamental frequency (f0) for perceived pitch, intensity (dB) for perceived loudness, as well as duration (typically of vowels or syllables). Raised and lowered larynx voices, for example, were distinguished primarily on the basis of pitch in Laver's schema. Also, some voices are distinctively loud.

At the same time, it is well-known that pitch and loudness have several linguistic functions, such as the declarative/interrogative distinction and accentuation found in European languages. A local combination of high f0 and high dB value can thus be indicative either of a high voice, or of a question intonation, or both. The assignment of prosodic and/or voice quality values depends in part on how voice quality is defined, and in part on the context. In Laver's "stable articulatory setting" approach, voice quality is the underlying, relatively unchanging base for a parameter like f0, and linguistic significance is decided by different degrees of departure from this line. However, this decisional process becomes more complex as the notion of voice quality is extended to cover a wider variety of concepts.

Suppose for example a combination of high f0, dB and duration values on the first syllable of the word *really*. Given sufficient contextual information, a human listener can deduct the relevant linguistic and social information from various acoustic components of this syllable. Suppose for example (1) that the word is contextually identifiable as part of a question, (2) that it is spoken with a timbre assignable to a male voice (whatever "timbre" might be in this context), (3) that its f0, dB, and duration values are excessively high for the given speaker, language and context, and (4) that phrasal on- and offsets show a high degree of jitter. Taken together, these indicators not only suggest to another speaker of English that the word is part of a question, but also that the speaker is male and possibly anxious. This decisional process involves minimally a fairly complex and language-specific set of thresholds for f0, duration, dB and jitter, plus knowledge about spectral profiles corresponding to male vs. female vocal tracts, the pragmatic and linguistic contexts that permit the interpretation of the word as part of a question, and possibly knowledge about previous speech performances by the same speaker.

In speech recognition and speech synthesis, analogue decompositional, decisional and combinatorial efforts must be undertaken. In speech recognition, success of linguistic, paralinguistic and extralinguistic[5] interpretations of a given combination of f0, dB or jitter values depends on the adequacy of the multi-tiered statistical models to which incoming utterances are compared. When integrating such information in speech synthesis, all contributing elements have to be furnished with a credible temporal profile, and must be combined satisfactorily to evoke the intended utterance. This supposes not only a well-defined set of correspondences between acoustic and linguistic, paralinguistic and extralinguistic elements, but it also involves knowledge concerning the value and linearity of the various contributional ratios. For example, are linguistic, paralinguistic and extralinguistic models strictly additive? If not, to which proportion does each level contribute to the overall measure of f0, dB or duration? And are these proportional contributions linear throughout the usage range?

---

[5] It is useful to distinguish linguistic, paralinguistic and extralinguistic aspects of voice quality. The *linguistic* component communicates semantic and distinctive information that is part of the speaker's *language*. The *paralinguistic* component communicates the speaker's affective, attitudinal or emotional states, his/her sociolect and regional dialect, as well as aspects of turn-taking in conversation. This components is to a large degree specific to a given language or language group. The *extralinguistic* component communicates the speaker's individuality, gender and age, i.e., the characteristics of a certain speaker. It can be judged independently of the speaker's language.

Furthermore to synthesize natural-sounding speech, prosodic parameterizations must be combined with appropriate voice quality manipulations. In a study where fundamental frequency and voice quality parameters were manipulated separately in the synthesis of various types of voices[6], voice quality manipulations contributed in important fashion to the communication of affect [9]. Only the signals that included adjustments for voice quality succeeded in communicating the emotions in question reliably. By contrast, signals combining fundamental frequency manipulations with voice quality appropriate to a neutral voice (i.e., signals similar to those used in current speech synthesis systems) were judged much less expressive by comparison.

In summary, the prosodic parameters of fundamental frequency, duration and intensity are clearly of relevance in judgments of voice quality. However, in contrast to other areas of research on voice quality, particularly voice source analysis, the relationship between linguistic and individual components of prosody has been examined far less systematically. It is evident that future paralinguistic interpretation of these indicators will have to involve a parallel clarification of the speaker's linguistic and pragmatic situation. Various extralinguistic markers in the prosodic domain are also indicative of the speaker's individuality, age, sex and various psychological attributes.

Further, no study has to our knowledge systematically explored the relationship between prosodic parameters and personality style. Yet it is a common observation that speakers, apart from their voices, differ tremendously regarding their prosodic style. With respect to intonation and rhythm alone, for example, one may describe a speaker's expression as fluent, lively, constrained, relaxed, etc. Intonation, rhythm and breathing are apparently the main parameters that convey these styles, in some specific combination that still needs to be established. These are the parameters that are often imitated by impersonators, whereby the imitation of the vocal component is more difficult to perform [10, 11].

Also, studies on twins are interesting in this context because of their morphological similarity (see e.g., [12]). Loakes [13] found acoustic differences in the speech of twins, despite closeness as judged perceptually. Speech samples from twins were compared by focusing on variables which have a high degree of speaker variation (e.g. consonant sequences /stR/, /tR/ and /tS/), and also variables that show minimal variation (e.g. mid-vowels such as /E/). Within- and between-speaker differences were identified using both auditory and acoustic methods of analysis. Results indicate that *similar-sounding voices* that originated from vocal tracts with minimal differences can be discriminated acoustically in the Formant 4 region. Prosodic parameters were not explored, and one may expect that some fine prosodic differences could also be identified.

Zellner Keller is currently investigating relationships between certain prosodic styles (e.g., very expressive *vs.* barely expressive), signalled by specific combinations of acoustic parameters, and specific personality styles. The aim of the study is to examine if and to which degree some personality styles can be reliably associated with typical strategies of prosodic expression, considering that this level of expression will be more or less obfuscated, due to the other superimposed social, linguistic, emotional and attitudinal encodings. In first results, it was found that listeners can and do associate speech with personality traits [14]. These attributions are remarkably consistent

---

[6] Modal (neutral), breathy, whispery, creaky, lax-creaky, modal, tense and harsh voice.

across listeners, even when they have a different language background (French/German). The significant correlation between personality and prosody clusters can be explained by supposing that listeners attribute personality traits on the basis of prosodic features of speech.

For the assessment and the automatic processing of individual voice quality, it is thus important to examine the contribution of the three classical prosodic parameters in interaction with indicators of their linguistic and paralinguistic significance. These parameters must also be combined with appropriate voice quality parameters to effect synthesis that is natural-sounding with respect to affect. This is the issue we turn to next.

3.3 Source Modeling

While all parts of the articulatory tract contribute to some degree to voice quality, the research community largely agrees that conditions affecting the air flow at the glottis (i.e., laryngeal or *source* settings) are responsible for particularly salient aspects of this speech component[7]. Conditions relevant to voice quality can be transitory (as in the case of voice on- and offsets), short-term (e.g., over the duration of a vowel) and longer-term (i.e., affecting all voiced components on an individual's speech). Much research of the past 20 years has thus been directed at obtaining the glottal waveform reliably and automatically, with a minimum of discomfort to the speaker.

Unfortunately, the source waveform is difficult to recuperate, since even intraoral recordings performed directly above the larynx show effects of resonator coupling from the supraglottal cavities. Approximations to the "pure" glottal waveform can generally only be obtained through recordings performed with specially designed pneumotachograph mask for recording oral airflow at the mouth, the "Rothenberg mask" [15], from more indirect evidence such as glottal pulse wave trains obtained with electroglottographs[8,9] [16], or from calculations and theoretical inductions performed on the acoustic speech waveform, that is, from so-called *inverse filtering* methods. This latter approach is of particular interest to persons working in speech processing, since it can be applied to standard sound recordings performed with a microphone outside the mouth.

In inverse filtering, the glottal waveform is extracted from the speech waveform by separating the respiratory and glottal *source component* of the speech waveform from the *filter component* (corresponding to the supraglottal vocal tract resonator contribution), plus the radiation loading at the lips. This source-filter model of speech produc-

---

[7] Indeed, some researchers reserve the term "voice quality" uniquely for aspects of the sound produced by the larynx, i.e., the glottal waveform. We did not follow this tradition here, because for speech synthesis and speech recognition processing, *all* vocal tract effects on voice quality must be considered and modelled.

[8] Electroglottography is a non-invasive method of measuring vocal fold contact during the production of voiced sounds. An electroglottograph (EGG) measures the variation in impedance to a small electrical current between a pair of electrodes placed on the two sides of the neck, as the area of vocal fold contact changes during voicing.

[9] An excellent survey of empirical methods of obtaining and measuring the glottal waveform is found on the following University of Stuttgart webpages:
http://www.ims.uni-stuttgart.de/phonetik/EGG/page1.htm

tion (originally formulated by Fant in [17]) treats the glottal source and the supra-glottal filter as independent components. Although more recent research has documented various interactions between the glottal source and the vocal tract resonances [18], Fant's original theory of speech production is still a good point of departure, particularly with respect to voice quality transmitted in signal portions where the airflow is much more strongly impeded at the glottis than in the supraglottal vocal tract, a condition that characterizes most vowels. In this part of the chapter, we follow the excellent general introductions to this topic by Ní Chisaide and Gobl [20] and by Gobl [21][10].

3.3.1 Manual vs. Automatic Inverse Filtering Methods

Consider the top part of Figure 3 (adapted from [20]) showing the effects of vocal tract filtering on an idealized source spectrum. The source spectrum (representing typical mid-vowel glottal flow with a normal voice) simply reflects the harmonic components of the glottal wave with a constant slope of 12 dB fall-off for every doubling of the frequency[11]. It can be seen in the speech output spectrum that the vocal tract cavities and their resonances (formants F1-F5) in effect impose a filter on the source spectrum[12]. Inverse filtering (see middle portion of Figure 3) consists of designing a filter of *antiresonances* (opposite-valued resonances) in such a manner that the vocal-tract filtering effect is cancelled. The effect of a well-designed filter on the speech waveform is seen in the bottom portion of Figure 3. The oral airflow U(t) (essentially, the speech waveform recorded by the microphone) is transformed by inverse filtering into glottal airflow $U_g(t)$, which is generally shown in its differentiated form as the *differentiated glottal airflow* $U'_g(t)$. Various aspects of this differentiated glottal airflow have been related to voice quality (see below).

It can readily be seen that the success of the inverse filtering procedure is directly related to the nature of the input waveform. When the waveform provides insufficient digitalizable amplitude, an inverse filter is impossible. Inverse filtering methods are thus preferentially applied to voiced portions of speech with sufficient amplitude to permit a reliable identification of formants. Further, substantial problems arise when inverse filtering is performed by automatic procedures. Formants can change rapidly as a result of changes in resonator cavity size, particularly in the neighborhood of consonants, which tend to "throw off" relatively simple formant tracking mechanisms. Also, inverse filter modeling frequently suffers interference from source-filter interactions at weak glottal flows [23], or in places where a non-modal voice is used. Finally, there is the possibility of phase distortion with tape-recorded material. Ideally, inverse filtering is thus performed manually and interactively, on selected vowel nuclei with normal or high intensity, best of all with material recorded directly to computer. In 1997, Ní Chisaide and Gobl concluded that the most accurate source signal is obtained by interactively (manually) fine-tuning the formant frequencies and bandwidths of the inverse filter [20].

---

[10] See also Emir Turajlic's webpages on glottal pulse modelling at:
www.brunel.ac.uk/depts/ee/Research_Programme/COM/Home_Emir_Turajlic/index.htm

[11] The true source spectrum shows various dips and does not have a constant slope ([20], p. 427).

[12] For a recent calculation of vocal tract resonances (formants) for 18 Swedish vowel states measured with X-ray, see [19].

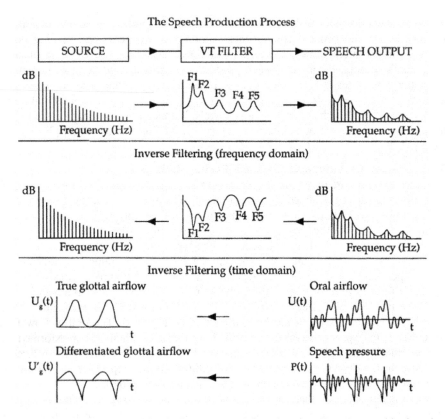

Fig. 3. Source-filter decomposition in frequency and time domains. *Top:* A smoothly decaying theoretical voice spectrum is modified by an idealized vocal tract filter to produce the measurable speech output for a vowel. *Middle:* The speech output spectrum is inverse-filtered to extract the underlying voice spectrum. *Bottom-top:* The effect of converting from oral airflow to glottal airflow. *Bottom-bottom:* The effect of the conversion from speech pressure (the differentiated oral airflow) to a differentiated glottal airflow, which is the habitual manner of representing the voice waveform in the time domain. The differentiated representation facilitates the standardized identification of voice quality markers. Figure from [20] reproduced with permission

Some more recent research suggests that at least for signal portions with sufficient amplitudes and speech falling within a reasonable range of predictability, particularly in male modal voices, automatic inverse filtering methods can show reliable performance, thus facilitating the acquisition of the considerable amount of data required in voice quality research. To understand the challenges involved in performing this type of operation for a wide variety of voices, we must examine the overall process of performing voice source analysis.

3.3.2 Voice Source Extraction: Automatic Formant Tracking

As indicated above, the extraction of the voice source involves two main steps, *inverse filtering* and *source modeling*. At the inverse filtering level, the essential difficulty consists in tracking the formant frequencies in the speech waveform, establishing their bandwidth, and assuring that classical voice parameters can be identified in the reconstituted source waveform. At the source modeling level, the challenge is to design a numeric model that captures the waveform modifications (i.e., the "classical voice parameters") that are associated with perceptible variations in voice quality.

The tracking of formants has traditionally been handled by an LPC that specifies the frequencies (and indirectly, the bandwidths) of the antiresonators required to cancel the formants. The average spacing between the poles is determined by the vocal tract length: for a typical male with a vocal tract of 17.5 cm, there is on average one formant per kHz. It is crucial to obtain the right number of poles and bandwidths, particularly in the lower frequency domain (Formant 1), while minor errors in the higher formants have less effect on the source pulse shape or the source frequency spectrum ([22], cited in [20]). LPC-type all-pole functions are adequate for many sounds such as vowels, yet for certain sounds such as nasals and laterals, the spectrum contains zeros as well as poles. While these zeros should theoretically be cancelled by the inclusion of corresponding poles in the inverse filter, they tend to be difficult to calculate and most researchers use all-pole models for all sounds.

A number of methods have been exploited for improving the reliability of formant tracking, revolving primarily around the concepts of the exploitation of contextual phonetic information, pitch-synchronous analysis, filtering and optimized voice source matching techniques.

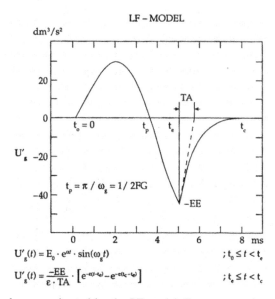

Fig. 4. A glottal pulse approximated by the LF model. Features prominently associated with voice quality are either marked in the figure or can be identified from features in the waveform: EE excitation energy (-EE), RA "return time" (TA), RG "glottal frequency" ((1/2Tp)/f0, or the inverse of twice the opening phase T_p normalized to fundamental frequency), RK "glottal asymmetry" ($t_p/(t_e-t_p)$, or the relationship between the opening and closing branches of the glottal pulses) and OQ "open quotient" (t_e/t_c, or the proportion of the glottal cycle during which the glottis is open). Figure reproduced with permission from [20]

McKenna [24] recalls that the quality of conventional fixed-frame pitch-asynchro-nous LPC (typically using the autocorrelation method) depends on the assumption that both formants and underlying articulatory movements are smooth and slow-evolving. However, the acoustic coupling of glottal and subglottal space during the open phase of the glottal period introduces momentary drops in formant frequencies that are reflected in pitch-asynchronous analysis as a general lowering of formant frequencies and an increase of formant bandwidths. By contrast, *pitch-synchronous analysis* improves the "sharpness" of formant tracking and thus contributes substan-tially to the quality of the inverse filtering process. Another benefit of pitch-synchronous analysis is that source data can be gathered specifically from the closed-glottis portions of the signal, which minimizes the effects of acoustic coupling be-tween subglottal and supraglottal space.

It is noted however that this approach implies a considerable reduction of data points available for analysis in any specific voice period. This can render it inappro-priate for female and children's voices which tend to provide a reduced number of data points, a disadvantage that can be overcome through Kalman filtering [24]. This recursive technique uses estimates based on measures of previous pitch periods to improve the modeling of relevant portions of the source waveform.

3.3.3   Voice Source Extraction: Glottal Pulse Modeling

Once the source waveform has been reconstructed through inverse filtering, it can be analyzed for voice quality features. The *differentiated* glottal waveform rather than the true glottal waveform is generally used for this purpose because of the greater ease of identifying relevant parts of the glottal cycle in the differentiated glottal pulse (see Figure 4). It also conveniently turns out that the radiation at the lips is approxi-mately 6 dB per octave in the speech midrange frequencies, which corresponds to a filter that can be approximated by a first order differentiation of the output signal. The differentiation step thus serves at the same time to cancel lip radiation. The net effect of this differentiation and the canceling of lip radiation is a boosting of the higher frequencies, which improves the modeling in this frequency range. As in the case of inverse filtering, the robustness of source modeling can be improved through optimi-zation procedures. Fu and Murphy [25] for example describe a multi-parameter nonlinear optimization procedure performed in two passes, where the first pass initial-izes the glottal source and the vocal tract models, in order to provide robust initial parameters to the subsequent joint optimization procedure, which iteratively improves the accuracy of the model estimation.

Various portions of the glottal waveform obtained in this manner have been shown to be of direct relevance to voice quality. To identify these features reliably through-out one or several databases, the source waveform is generally matched by an ap-proximate mathematical description of the waveform. Liljencrants and Fant [26] have provided the best-known such formulation, known as the LF-model[13]. Figure 4 shows a differentiated source cycle described by the LF model. The cycle is approximated

---

[13] See [20] p. 437 for a comparison and [21], p. 7, for references of other mathematical ap-proximations to the glottal cycle waveform. Alternative models share many common features with the LF model, but they can generally be described by three to five parameters, plus fun-damental frequency.

by two different equations for its two branches that extend from t_0 to t_e (the maximal excitation point) and from t_e to t_c, where t_c corresponds to point t_0 in the next cycle.

Features prominently associated with voice quality are either marked in figure 4 or can be identified from features in the waveform. They are as follows (terminology as in [21]:

EE excitation energy [shown as -EE]. This is the main source parameter, showing the overall strength of source excitation.

RA "return time" or "dynamic leakage" [shown as TA]. This parameter measures the sharpness of glottal closure, i.e., the time that the glottal folds take to accomplish closure. This in turn has a major effect on the slope of the glottal spectrum. Sharp closures are associated with increases of spectral amplitudes in the high frequencies ([20], p. 440).

RG "glottal frequency" [$(1/2T_p)/f0$, or the inverse of twice the opening phase T_p normalized to fundamental frequency]. This parameter estimates the degree of boosting found with some voices in the areas of the first and the second harmonic.

RK "glottal asymmetry" [$(t_e-t_p)/(t_p-t_0)$, or the relationship between the opening and closing branches of the glottal pulses]. In general, glottal pulses tend to be right-skewed, and increased symmetry results in a boosting of lower frequencies and a deepening of spectral dips.

OQ "open quotient" [t_e/t_c, or the proportion of the glottal cycle during which the glottis is open]. Increased degrees of OQ result in a boosting of the lowest harmonics of the voice spectrum.

AS "aspiration". This acoustically important non-periodic parameter can unfortunately not be derived from the LF model, and its algorithmic separation from periodic source information is a non-trivial challenge. However for synthesis purposes, appropriately-filtered pseudo-random noise can be generated to compensate for the absence of empirically-derived estimates of aspiration noise at the glottis.

Since some of these parameters have been found to co-vary frequently, some further simplification of this parameter list may be possible, at least in the case of some voices (see discussion in [20] pp. 441).

3.3.4 Source Parameters and Specific Voice Types

Voice quality modifications associated with variations in the described parameters have been widely examined. In this presentation, we limit ourselves to a short review of commonly occurring voice types. For this, we summarize Ní Chisaide and Gobl's observations in [20] of four key voice types defined in Laver's descriptive scheme (see above):

- *Modal voice.* In tune with the occurrence of normal, efficient and frequently complete closures at the glottis, glottal cycles take on the standard source waveform for modal voice. The spectral slope is particularly steep. Gradual or abrupt changes to other voice modes (e.g., breathy or creaky voice) are frequent.
- *Breathy voice.* It will be recalled that in Laver's scheme, glottal articulation for breathy voice was characterized as a general lack of tension. Vocal fold vibrations are inefficient and never show complete closure. Acoustically, this translates into audible aspiration and slow RA (time of "glottal return") values. High RK values demonstrate relatively greater symmetry in the glottal pulse, and high open quotient values (OQ) reflect the looseness and gradualness of the glottal gesture.

- *Whispery voice*. Like breathy voice, this type of voice is characterized by low tension in the glottis, with the exception that there is moderate to high medial compression and moderate longitudinal tension. This tension pattern creates a triangular glottal opening whose size varies inversely with the degree of medial compression. Acoustically, this inefficient mode of voice production translates into high aspiration levels and generally more extreme deviations from modal values than those seen with breathy voice. Whispery voice differs mainly from breathy voice by its lower RK values (greater pulse asymmetry due to a shorter closing branch) and a lower "open quotient" OQ, i.e., a lower proportion of cycle time spent in an open state.
- *Creaky voice*. According to Laver, creak results from high adductive tension and medial compression, but little longitudinal tension. It is generally associated with very low pitch. However, f0 and the amplitude of consecutive glottal pulses are very irregular and frequently alternate with normal, non-creaky voice. Low OQ, low RK and a relatively high RG have been observed for creaky voice [20].

4 Conclusion

In many respects, the study of voice quality represents the "ultimate frontier" for speech processing research, due to considerable complexity at both functional and signal processing levels.

At the functional level, each speaker has his or her own characteristic *individual* voice quality. In addition, the *psychological* dimension of voice quality reaches from the distinction of personality types, via the communication of affect and emotion, to the communication of delicate nuances in conversational exchanges. *Sociologically*, certain types of voice quality serve as social markers (such as markers for position in a social hierarchy, or for homosexuality). Several aspects of voice quality have also been integrated into the *linguistic* coding system of certain languages[14]. These various functional strands interact and are partially superimposed. For a successful use of parameters related to voice quality, speech processing technologies must be rendered sensitive to and/or implement structuring related to these various predictor groupings.

At the signal processing level, the multidimensional complexity of voice quality takes another form. In this review, it was seen that systematic variations relating to voice quality can be documented as *spectral divergence* in long-term spectra, in *individual prosodic parameters* and in *voice source parameters*. Certain *temporally structured parameters*, such as jitter, creak, or individually distinctive manners of producing voice on- and offsets, are also of interest for voice quality control. Further parameters, particularly *high-frequency components of the glottal waveform*, in all probability also contribute to individual voice quality [27], but have so far remained under-researched.

---

[14] See the following quote from [20]: "The contrastive use of voice quality for vowels or consonants is fairly common in South East Asian, South African, and Native American Languages, and these have been the focus of a number of studies carried out at UCLA. Although both vowels and consonants may employ voice quality contrasts in a given language, Ladefoged (1982) points out that it is very rare to find contrasts at more than one place in a syllable."

It is evident that no single parameter corresponds to that elusive propensity that is "voice quality". The challenge is to understand and to learn to manipulate the strength and interactions between the various layers of the multidimensional parameter space that emerges here. While this seems to be a formidable task, there is some reason to take heart: while the parameters reviewed in this article are unlikely to exhaust the inventory of relevant indicators of voice quality, they are likely to play a major role in any future attempt to understand the voice quality pattern of human speech.

Finally, the arguments here suggest a manner of integrating voice quality into a larger speech processing system. We can illustrate this for voice quality control in speech synthesis. The traditional structure of a speech synthesis system consists of three processing levels: text processing, prosody processing, and signal generation (Figure 5). The close articulation between linguistic and individual prosodic parameters suggest that voice quality control should probably be implemented in conjunction with prosody processing. In a model expanded to handle voice quality, processing components for linguistic prosody, individual prosody, spectral divergence, voice source parameters, plus certain temporally structured parameters would probably take the place of the single traditional prosody module. Initially, this prosody-plus-voice quality tier could be conceived as an additive model with weights assigned to each component. In time, a more complex, integrated model is conceivable, capable of handling interactions between prosodic and voice quality components.

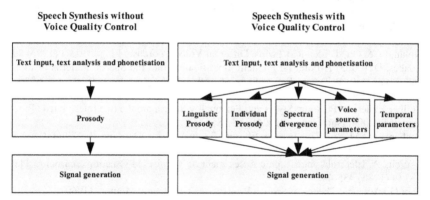

Fig. 5. Integration of voice quality control in speech synthesis. A set of processing components for linguistic prosody, individual prosody, spectral divergence, voice source parameters and temporally structured measures take the place of the single traditional prosody module. Initially, this could be conceived as an additive model with weights assigned to each component. In time, a more complex, integrated model is conceivable, capable of handling interactions between components

Acknowledgements

The present research was supported by funding obtained from the Federal Office for Education and Science (BBW/OFES), Berne, Switzerland, in the framework of the European COST 277 project entitled "Non-linear Speech Processing". Grateful acknowledgements are made to Dr. Brigitte Zellner Keller (Universities of Lausanne and Berne) for her critical reading of this contribution, and to Antonio Bonafonte (UPC Barcelona) for a number of stimulating suggestions.

References

1. Pittam, J.: Voice in Social Interaction: An Interdisciplinary Approach. Language and Language Behaviors, Volume 5. (1994)
2. Laver, J.: The Phonetic Description of Voice Quality. Cambridge University Press. (1980)
3. Laver, J.: The Description of Voice Quality in General Phonetic Theory. In: Laver, J. (eds.): The Gift of Speech. Edinburgh University Press (1991) 184-208
4. Fritzell, B., Hallén, O, Sundberg, J. Evaluation of Teflon Injection Procedures for Paralytic Dysphonia. Folia Phoniatrica, 26 (1974) 414-421.
5. Nordenberg, M., Sundberg, J. Effect on LTAS of Vocal Loudness Variation. TMH/QPSR, 1/2001. (2003). Available at: http://www.speech.kth.se/qpsr/tmh/2003/03-45-093-100.pdf.
6. Leino, T. Long-term Average Spectrum Study on Speaking Voice Quality in Male Actors. In: Friberg, A., Iwarsson, J., Jansson, E., Sundberg, J. (eds.) SMAC 93 (Proceedings of the Stockholm Music Acoustics Conference, 1993). Stockholm: Publication No. 79, Royal Swedish Academy of Music (1994) 206-210.
7. Klasmeyer, G.: An Automatic Description Tool for Time-contours and Long-term Average Voice Features in Large Emotional Speech Databases. SpeechEmotion-2000 (2000) 66-71
8. Keller, E.: Voice Characteristics of MARSEC Speakers. VOQUAL: Voice Quality: Functions, Analysis And Synthesis (2003).
9. Gobl, C., Bennet, E., Ní Chasaide, A. Expressive Synthesis: How Crucial is Voice Quality. Proceedings of the IEEE Workshop on Speech Synthesis. Santa Monica, CA (2002) Paper 52: 1-4.
10. Besacier, L. Un modèle parallèle pour la reconnaissance automatique du locuteur. Doctoral Thesis, University of Avignon, France (1998)
11. Zetterholm, E. A Comparative Survey of Phonetic Features of two Impersonators. Fonetik, 44 (2002) 129-132
12. Nolan, F., & Oh, T. Identical Twins, Different Voices. Forensic Linguistics 3 (1996) 39-49
13. Loakes, D. (2003) A Forensic Phonetic Investigation into the Speech Patterns of Identical and Non-Identical Twins. Proceedings of 15th ICPhS. Barcelona. ISBN 1-876346-48-5 (2003) 691- 694
14. Zellner Keller, B. Prosodic Styles and Personality Styles: are the two Interrelated? Proceedings of SP2004. Nara, Japan. (2004) 383-386
15. Rothenberg, M.: A New Inverse-filtering Technique for Deriving the Glottal Air Flow Waveform During Voicing. J. Acoust. Soc. Am., 53 (1973) 1632-1645.
16. Fourcin, A. Electrolaryngographic Assessment of Vocal Fold Function. Journal of Phonetics, 14 (1986) 435-442.
17. Fant G.: Acoustic Theory of Speech Production. The Hague: Mouton. (1960)
18. Fant, G.: Glottal Flow: Models and Interaction. Journal of Phonetics, 14, (1986) 393-399
19. Fant, G.: Swedish Vowels and a New Three-Parameter Model. TMH/QPSR, 1/2001. (2001). Available at: http://www.speech.kth.se/qpsr/tmh/2001/01-42-043-049.pdf
20. Ní Chasaide, A., Gobl, C.: Voice Source Variation. In W.J. Hardcastle, Laver, J. (eds.): The Handbook of Phonetic Sciences. Blackwell (1997) 427-461
21. Gobl, C.: The Voice Source in Speech Communication. Doctoral Thesis, KTH Stockholm, Sweden. (2003).
22. Gobl, C.: Speech Production. Voice Source Dynamics in Connected Speech. STL-QPSR 1/1988. (1988). 123-159.
23. Strik, H., Cranen, B., Boves, L.: Fitting a LF-model to Inverse Filter Signals. EUROSPEECH-93, Berlin, Vol. 1 (1993) 103-106
24. McKenna, J.G. Automatic Glottal Closed-Phase Location and Analysis by Kalman Filtering. 4th ISCA Tutorial and Research Workshop on Speech Synthesis, SSW4 Proceedings, Perthshire Scotland, 2001.

25. Fu, Q., & Murphy, P. A robust glottal source model estimation technique. 8th International Conference on Spoken Language Processing ICSLP, Jeju Island, Korea, 2004.
26. Fant, G., Liljencrants, J., Lin, Q.: A four-parameter model of glottal flow. STL-QPSR, No. 4/1985 (1985).
27. Plumpe, M. D., Quatieri, T. F., Reynolds D. A. Modeling of the Glottal Flow Derivative Waveform with Application to Speaker Identification. IEEE Trans. on Speech and Audio Processing, Vol. 1 (1999) 569-586.

Identification of Nonlinear Oscillator Models for Speech Analysis and Synthesis[*]

Gernot Kubin[1], Claudia Lainscsek[2], and Erhard Rank[1]

[1] Signal Processing and Speech Communication Laboratory
Graz University of Technology, Graz, Austria
{g.kubin,erank}@ieee.org
[2] Cognitive Science Department
University of California at San Diego, La Jolla (CA), USA
clainscsek@ucsd.edu

Abstract. More than ten years ago the first successful application of a nonlinear oscillator model to high-quality speech signal processing was reported (Kubin and Kleijn, 1994). Since then, numerous developments have been initiated to turn nonlinear oscillators into a standard tool for speech technology. The present contribution will review and compare several of these attempts with a special emphasis on adaptive model identification from data and the approaches to the associated machine learning problems. This includes Bayesian methods for the regularization of the parameter estimation problem (including the pruning of irrelevant parameters) and Ansatz library (Lainscsek et al., 2001) based methods (structure selection of the model). We conclude with the observation that these advanced identification methods need to be combined with a thorough background from speech science to succeed in practical modeling tasks.

1 Introduction

The introduction of nonlinear system modeling – including the system theoretic dimension up to chaos theory – has evolved as an interesting tool for speech analysis and synthesis. With speech synthesis systems based on concatenation of recorded speech segments currently yielding the highest quality at current, but being inflexible and having high storage demands, and the alternative of model based synthesis algorithms, which are more versatile, but often difficult to control, parametric nonlinear models for the speech production process are an auspicious option.

An introduction to nonlinear oscillator models and its application to speech signals can be found in [1, 2]. Applications include time-scale modification [3], adaptive-codebook pulse code modulation for speech coding [1], noise reduction [4, 5], fundamental frequency analysis (pitch extraction) [6], determination of

---

[*] This chapter corresponds to talks given at the Cost 277 summerschool at IIASS in Vietri sul Mare (IT), in Sept. 2004. We would sincerely like to thank Anna Esposito for organizing the summerschool, and for her patience editing this publication.

instants of equal phase inside the glottis cycle (epoch marking) [7], as well as new concepts for speech recognition [8].

The application to speech signal modeling and re-synthesis has been presented in a number of investigations [1, 2, 9–16], however, some common drawbacks still to be addressed are the occasional lack of *stability* of the model, the *high number of parameters*, and the missing *relation to the physical process* of speech production. Furthermore, the oscillator model is often applied for voiced speech signals only, or even only for vowels.

Here we present some attempts to improving model identification, generalization to mixed excitation speech sounds, to the reduction of model complexity, and to the application of differential equations as a model for the underlying the speech production process.

2 Bayesian Regularization for Nonlinear Oscillator Identification

In this section we will describe a learning algorithm for modeling the oscillatory part of stationary speech signals by an oscillator based on Takens' time delay embedding theorem. The Bayesian algorithm presented here was found to achieve the highest percentage of successfully re-synthesized stationary speech signals in our experiments, as compared to other methods. 'Successful re-synthesis' means the generation of an *output speech signal similar to the training signal* in the way that – for voiced or mixed-excitation speech signals used during training – a stable oscillatory signal is generated without severe deviations from the training signal in waveform shape, amplitude, and fundamental frequency. In the last subsection we briefly present a method to re-generate also the noise-like component of speech signals in addition to the oscillatory component.

2.1 Discrete-Time Oscillator Model

Nonlinear time-series prediction in discrete-time $\hat{x}(n+1) = f(x(n), x(n-1), x(n-2), \ldots)$ can be immediately used to build an oscillator by applying the prediction function $f(\cdot)$ to a vector $\boldsymbol{x}(n)$ composed of past predicted samples:

$$x(n+1) = f(\boldsymbol{x}(n)) \ . \tag{1}$$

According to Takens' embedding theorem [17] the vector $\boldsymbol{x}(n)$ is commonly built as a time delay embedding of dimension N,

$$\boldsymbol{x}(n) = [x(n), x(n-M), x(n-2M), \ldots, x(n-(N-1)M)]^T \ , \tag{2}$$

realized as a tapped delay line fed by the predicted sample and with taps every M samples. A schematic of the model is depicted in Fig. 1.

Issues for oscillator identification are the determination of the optimal embedding parameters – embedding dimension N, and embedding delay M – as well as the identification of the prediction function $f(\cdot)$ from the training signal.

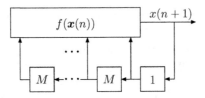

Fig. 1. Oscillator model

2.2   Embedding Parameters

Based on Takens' theorem [17] the re-construction of dynamical properties of the system of dimension D, that gave rise to a time-series $x(n)$, is possible using a time delay embedding of dimension $N \geq 2D + 1$, regardless of the choice of the embedding delay (Takens derivation is for continuous time signals; of course the embedding delay must be $M > 0$). There exists a slightly refined theorem that allows for phase space re-construction in $N > 2D_f$, with D_f being the (possibly fractal) dimension of the attractor underlying the time-series [18]. However, both embedding theorems are sufficient, but not necessary conditions for re-construction of the dynamical properties [19], so we might well find an embedding of lower dimensionality than stated by the theorems with perfect (or sufficiently good) re-construction. The dimensionality of the embedding is most often related to the complexity of the prediction function $f(\cdot)$ in our oscillator.

The search for a reasonably low-dimensional embedding with good re-construction properties is facilitated by first looking for an optimal embedding delay M. To find a good predictor, i.e., to minimize the energy of the prediction error signal $e(n) = \hat{x}(n+1) - x(n+1)$, the single components of the embedding vector $x(n), x(n - M), \ldots$ shall each contribute as much information for the prediction as possible. Hence, ideally the components should be mutually independent. For a uniform embedding[1] as in (2) the embedding delay could be chosen at the first zero crossing of the auto-correlation function of the signal $s(n)$, making two neighboring components linearly independent (uncorrelated).

Minimizing linear dependence, however, might not be optimal for the embedding of signals coming from nonlinear systems (cf. [21, App. B]). Thus, the common approach is to minimize the statistical dependence between the components in the embedding by looking at the mutual information (MI) between delayed signal samples $x(n)$ and $x(n + L)$, and choosing the embedding delay as the delay at the first minimum of MI(L). Examples for the function MI(L) for some vowel signals are depicted in Fig. 2 (a). For vowel signals a first minimum of MI(L) is commonly found in the range of $5 \leq M \leq 15$ (for a signal sampling rate of $f_s = 16\,\text{kHz}$). For mixed excitation signals, the first minimum of MI(L) – as depicted in Fig. 2 (b) – tends to be at smaller delays, or MI(L) monotonically decreases. A monotonically decreasing function MI(L) is also commonly observed for unvoiced speech signals. This raises the question of how to choose M for such signals.

---

[1] Non-uniform embeddings, as suggested in [20], are considered in section 3 below

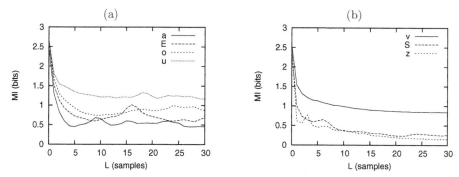

Fig. 2. Mutual information between signal samples as a function of delay L for (a) vowel signals, and (b) mixed excitation speech signals. Signals are refered to using labels from the machine-readable phonetic alphabet SAMPA. Signal sampling frequency is 16 kHz

Still, there is another aspect of setting the embedding delay for the oscillator: Besides finding an embedding delay that minimizes the error of the *predictor*, another aim for the optimization of the embedding delay for the *oscillator* is to 'unfold' the signal trajectory in phase space, thus to prevent self-intersections (cf. [18]). As an example the time signal and the two-dimensional embeddings for two choices of the embedding delay for a mixed excitation speech signal are shown in Fig. 3. For the small embedding delay $M = 2$, chosen according to the first minimum in $MI(L)$ (cf. Fig. 2 (b)), the trajectory of the signal in phase space evolves mainly on the diagonal and due to the noise-like signal component we can not identify the oscillatory component from the phase space plot in Fig. 3 (b). For a larger embedding delay $M = 13$, Fig. 3 (c), the oscillatory component becomes visible as a (still noisy) open loop of the trajectory. The identification of the signal structure by the nonlinear function in the oscillator can be considered equally difficult as the task of visually identifying the trajectory structure in the phase space plots, hence an oscillator based on an embedding with small embedding delay (and a reasonable low embedding dimension) will fail to re-produce the oscillatory signal component in this case.

Embedding delay M and embedding dimension N thus cannot always be chosen according to some fixed rule. Optimization of these parameters still may require (manual) inspection of the resulting oscillator output signal.

Our choice for the embedding parameters used throughout this section is motivated by the finding that for embeddings of *stationary* vowel signals a minimum of false neighbors [22] for $N \geq 4$ as well as a saturation of redundancy [23] for $N \geq 3$ is reached. Hence, an embedding dimension of $N = 4$ is used here. The embedding delay was chosen $M = 13$ for all signals, which represents a compromise choice based on $MI(L)$ for vowel signals (cf. Fig. 2 (a)), but also yields a sufficient unfolding of the trajectories of voiced speech signals (cf. Fig. 3). A fixed embedding delay is prefered over one optimized for each individual speech sound in our work to enable the synthesis of transitions (not described here).

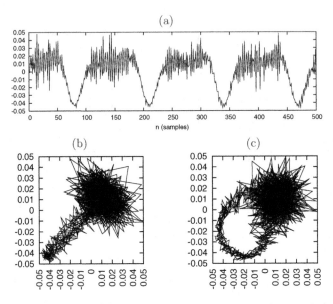

Fig. 3. Time-domain signal (a) of a mixed excitation speech sound /z/ and two-dimensional trajectories with (b) embedding delay $M = 2$ (at the first minimum of $MI(L)$), and (c) $M = 13$

2.3   Prediction Function

The prediction function $f(\cdot)$ in the oscillator is commonly realized as a trainable nonlinear mapping function, e.g., an artificial neural network (ANN) – such as a multilayer perceptron (MLP)[13], a radial basis function (RBF) network [12, 24, 15, 25, 16], or support vector machine (SVM) [26] – or by other function approximations such as multivariate adaptive regression splines (MARS) [27], classification and regression trees (CART), or lookup tables [28, 3].

All these function models have to be trained on input-output examples

$$(\boldsymbol{x}(n), x(n+1)) \ , \qquad \mathbb{R}^N \times \mathbb{R} \ , \tag{3}$$

derived from the original speech signal $x(n)$ according to a chosen embedding.

For many of the nonlinear function approximations listed above some kind of regularization has to be applied to avoid over-fitting – at least by controlling the complexity (number of parameters) of the function model – and to come up eventually with a stable oscillator for stationary speech signals. The exceptions are function realizations by lookup tables and CART, which produce a bounded output according to the range covered by the training signal. Oscillators based on lookup tables for stationary speech signals moreover entail an implicit modeling of the noise-like signal part and have been found very appropriate, e.g., for time-scale modification [3][2].

---

[2] Interactive demo at http://www.nt.tuwien.ac.at/dspgroup/tsm

MLPs with a nonlinear output layer may as well be confined to a bounded output. In our experiments, however, we found that even with a bounded output function MLP based oscillators often display no successful synthesis behavior that cannot be generally mitigated by reduction of model complexity or regularization methods such as early stopping or cross-validation. Nevertheless, more elaborate MLP structures and training algorithms (e. g., as described in [13]) may possibly yield better performance than our simple attempts.

Here, we shall focus on the realization of the nonlinear function by RBF based models, and present some methods for regularization that showed the highest number of 'successfully re-synthesized' stationary speech signals in our experiments. Particularly, we will limit the scope of our elaborations to RBF networks with a priori fixed Gaussian basis functions, i. e., RBF networks with center positions and widths of the Gaussian basis functions set to fixed values before network training. This restriction reduces the parameters of the RBF network that are optimized in the training process to the network output weights – and the training process for minimizing the squared prediction error to a problem which is linear in these parameters.

2.4   RBF Networks with Fixed Basis Functions

In an RBF network at each unit the distance of the input vector from a *center* (in input space) is computed and used as input for the according basis function. The network output is computed as the weighted sum of the basis function output values:

$$f_{\mathrm{RBF}}(\boldsymbol{x}) = \sum_{i=1}^{N_c} w_i \, \varphi_i(\|\boldsymbol{x} - \boldsymbol{c}_i\|) \;, \qquad \mathbb{R}^N \to \mathbb{R} \;. \tag{4}$$

In this equation $\boldsymbol{x}$ is the N-dimensional input vector, $\boldsymbol{c}_i$ are the center positions, $\varphi_i(\cdot)$ are the basis functions, and w_i the weighting coefficients. N_c is the number of basis functions and weights[3]. An RBF network has – as opposed to other kernel based function approximations – radially invariant basis functions. The basis functions used here are Gaussian functions,

$$\varphi_i(\|\boldsymbol{x} - \boldsymbol{c}_i\|) = \exp\left(-\frac{\|\boldsymbol{x} - \boldsymbol{c}_i\|^2}{2\sigma_i^2}\right), \tag{5}$$

centered at positions $\boldsymbol{c}_i$ in input space, and with variance σ_i^2. $\|\boldsymbol{x} - \boldsymbol{c}_i\|$ is the Euclidean vector distance between $\boldsymbol{x}$ and $\boldsymbol{c}_i$, making the basis function rotationally invariant.

If the basis functions $\varphi_i(\boldsymbol{x})$ are fixed, i. e., if the center positions $\boldsymbol{c}_i$ and the variances σ_i^2 are set to a priori chosen values, the network parameters that have

---

[3] For other applications RBF networks often comprise an additional bias term, incorporated in the network function by using a constant 'basis function' $\varphi_0(\boldsymbol{x}) = 1$ and an according weight w_0. Since our speech signals are ensured to have zero mean, we do not make use of this bias term

to be optimized in the training process are the weights w_i only. The training process becomes a linear problem: Applying the network equation (4) to all pairs of training input-output examples $(\boldsymbol{x}_k, t_k)$, $k = 1, 2, \ldots, P$ results in the following vector-matrix equation:

$$t = \boldsymbol{\Phi}\boldsymbol{w} \ , \tag{6}$$

with the training output examples ('targets') collected in vector $\boldsymbol{t} = [t_1, t_2, \ldots, t_P]^T$, the weights in vector $\boldsymbol{w} = [w_1, w_2, \ldots, w_{N_c}]^T$, and the response of the basis functions to the training input examples in matrix

$$\boldsymbol{\Phi} = \begin{bmatrix} \varphi_1(\boldsymbol{x}_1) & \cdots & \varphi_{N_c}(\boldsymbol{x}_1) \\ \vdots & \ddots & \vdots \\ \varphi_1(\boldsymbol{x}_P) & \cdots & \varphi_{N_c}(\boldsymbol{x}_P) \end{bmatrix} \ .$$

Assuming that there are more training examples than basis functions $P > N_c$, training of the RBF network relates to solving (6) for the weight vector $\boldsymbol{w}$, which is done in a minimum mean squared error (MMSE) sense using the pseudo inverse $\boldsymbol{\Phi}^\dagger = (\boldsymbol{\Phi}^T\boldsymbol{\Phi})^{-1}\boldsymbol{\Phi}^T$ of $\boldsymbol{\Phi}$,

$$\hat{\boldsymbol{w}}_{\mathrm{MMSE}} = (\boldsymbol{\Phi}^T\boldsymbol{\Phi})^{-1}\boldsymbol{\Phi}^T\boldsymbol{t} \ . \tag{7}$$

Using the weights $\hat{\boldsymbol{w}}_{\mathrm{MMSE}}$ in the RBF network (4) yields the lowest possible squared prediction error for prediction of the training data. In the case when the number of network centers is equal to the number of training examples[4], $N_c = P$, the training output examples might even be perfectly predicted by the RBF network.

Notwithstanding the optimal prediction on the *training data*, an RBF network with weights $\hat{\boldsymbol{w}}_{\mathrm{MMSE}}$ often displays bad generalization, i.e., bad prediction on unseen *test data*. Due to the aim of optimal prediction of the training data the network output function may take arbitrary output values in regions of input space between (and outside) the training data samples. In the application of modeling speech signals with the oscillator model this commonly results in the occurrence of large amplitude intermittent spikes in the oscillator generated signal, as depicted in Fig. 4. Several investigations on using RBF networks in the oscillator model indicate the necessity of using regularization for RBF network training [12, 24, 15].

2.5   Regularized RBF Networks

Regularization refers to trading prediction accuracy on the training data (leading to over-fitting, and to large amplitude spikes in the oscillator output) for some other desired property of the prediction function. In our case this desired

---

[4] For example if the network centers are chosen equal to the training input vectors: $c_i = \boldsymbol{x}_i$, $i = 1, 2, \ldots, P$

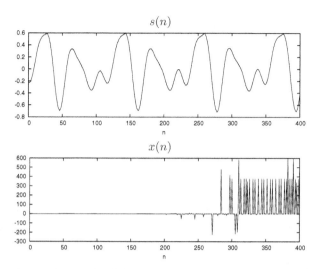

Fig. 4. Original speech signal $s(n)$, and oscillator output signal $x(n)$ using non-regularized RBF network training according to (7). Note the different scaling of the y-axes

property is *smoothness* of the RBF network output function. Two ways of modifying the weight estimation (7) of an RBF network that impose smoothness on the network function are stated in the following.

The first is regularization of matrix inversion in (7), i.e., the regularization of the linear weight estimation task without taking the nonlinear nature of the basis functions into account. The modified training equation is [29]

$$\hat{w}_{\mathrm{reg}} = (\boldsymbol{\Phi}^T\boldsymbol{\Phi} + \lambda\boldsymbol{I})^{-1}\boldsymbol{\Phi}^T\boldsymbol{t} \ , \tag{8}$$

with λ being the regularization parameter, and $\boldsymbol{I}$ the $N_c \times N_c$ identity matrix.

A method considering the nonlinear background, the Generalized Radial Basis Function (GRBF) expansion thoroughly derived in [30], arrives at a very similar equation for the RBF network weights

$$\hat{w}_{\mathrm{GRBF}} = (\boldsymbol{\Phi}^T\boldsymbol{\Phi} + \lambda\boldsymbol{\Phi}_0)^{-1}\boldsymbol{\Phi}^T\boldsymbol{t} \ , \tag{9}$$

again with λ being the regularization parameter, but the place of the identity matrix is taken by the $N_c \times N_c$ matrix $\boldsymbol{\Phi}_0$. This matrix is composed of the response of the basis functions to input vectors equal to the center positions:

$$\boldsymbol{\Phi}_0 = \begin{bmatrix} \varphi_1(\boldsymbol{c}_1) & \cdots & \varphi_{N_c}(\boldsymbol{c}_1) \\ \vdots & \ddots & \vdots \\ \varphi_1(\boldsymbol{c}_{N_c}) & \cdots & \varphi_{N_c}(\boldsymbol{c}_{N_c}) \end{bmatrix} \ .$$

For uni-modal basis functions (like Gaussians) $\boldsymbol{\Phi}_0$ has all ones on the diagonal, and smaller off-diagonal values.

Determining an optimal value for the regularization parameter λ is often based on cross-validation: The prediction error of a network is computed for an unseen validation data set for networks trained using a number of λ values of interest. The λ value yielding the minimum mean squared error on the validation set is chosen. k-fold cross-validation [31] makes best use of a small data set by partitioning the data and doing several cross-validation runs on the k partitions.

2.6   Bayesian Regularization and Pruning

The concept of Bayesian choice and training of function models has been presented in a series of papers [32–34] and refers to an iterative determination of function models (i. e., model structure and parameters) and regularization method and parameter(s) in the manner of the expectation-maximization (EM) algorithm [35]. We will here present the algorithm for Bayesian regularization for the RBF network with given fixed basis functions[5].

Bayesian Regularization of RBF Networks. In the Bayesian approach the RBF network weights $\boldsymbol{w}$ are considered random variables, with a prior probability density function (pdf) $p(\boldsymbol{w}|\alpha)$, parameterized by one parameter α. Incorporating regularization is done by stating a preference for smoother network functions by choosing the prior for the weights as a zero mean Gaussian distribution with variance α^{-1}:

$$p(\boldsymbol{w}|\alpha) = \left(\frac{\alpha}{2\pi}\right)^{-\frac{N_c}{2}} \exp\left(-\frac{\alpha}{2}\|\boldsymbol{w}\|^2\right) . \tag{10}$$

Furthermore, it is assumed that the training output samples t_k are produced by an additive noise model

$$t_k = f_{\mathrm{RBF}}(\boldsymbol{x}_k) + \epsilon_k , \qquad p(\epsilon) = \mathcal{N}(0, \sigma_n^2) , \tag{11}$$

with the function $f_{\mathrm{RBF}}(\cdot)$ from (4) and additive zero-mean Gaussian noise samples ϵ_k with variance σ_n^2. The noise variance σ_n^2 is the second additional parameter (besides α) introduced by this Bayesian formulation. As in the scope of the expectation-maximization algorithm these additional parameters are called *hidden* or *hyper-parameters*. Like the weights the hyper-parameters are unknown parameters, and have to be characterized by an a priori chosen pdf, too. Since both additional parameters are scaling parameters, proper prior distributions are, e. g., uniform distributions on a logarithmic scale.

The aim in Bayesian network training is to find the most probable values for the weights and the hyper-parameters given the training data (let $\boldsymbol{X}$ represent the collected training input vectors), i. e., to maximize $p(\boldsymbol{w}, \alpha, \sigma_n^2|\boldsymbol{X}, \boldsymbol{t})$:

$$(\boldsymbol{w}, \alpha, \sigma_n^2)_{\mathrm{bay}} = \arg\max(p(\boldsymbol{w}, \alpha, \sigma_n^2|\boldsymbol{X}, \boldsymbol{t})) . \tag{12}$$

---

[5] That means, we shall ignore the possibility of a Bayesian choice of hypothesis $\mathcal{H}$ (network complexity) and set of basis functions $\mathcal{A}$ considered in [32]. Furthermore we will restrict the derivation of the training algorithm to one specific choice of regularizer $\mathcal{R}$

Since this maximization cannot be accomplished analytically, the task is divided in two steps, maximizing the probability of the weights values for given training data and hyper-parameters, and updating the hyper-parameters, corresponding to a decomposition $p(\boldsymbol{w}, \alpha, \sigma_n^2 | \boldsymbol{X}, \boldsymbol{t}) = p(\boldsymbol{w} | \boldsymbol{X}, \boldsymbol{t}, \alpha, \sigma_n^2)\, p(\alpha, \sigma_n^2 | \boldsymbol{X}, \boldsymbol{t})$.

The first part of this decomposition can be evaluated analytically: For given hyper-parameters the resulting pdf for the weights $p(\boldsymbol{w} | \boldsymbol{X}, \boldsymbol{t}, \alpha, \sigma_n^2)$ is a product of Gaussian pdfs, and thus a multivariate Gaussian distribution itself,

$$ p(\boldsymbol{w} | \boldsymbol{X}, \boldsymbol{t}, \alpha, \sigma_n^2) = (2\pi)^{-\frac{N_c}{2}} |\boldsymbol{\Sigma}|^{-\frac{1}{2}} \exp\left(-\frac{1}{2}(\boldsymbol{w} - \boldsymbol{\mu})^T \boldsymbol{\Sigma}^{-1}(\boldsymbol{w} - \boldsymbol{\mu}) \right) , \quad (13) $$

with covariance and means, respectively:

$$ \boldsymbol{\Sigma} = (\tfrac{1}{\sigma_n^2}\boldsymbol{\Phi}^T\boldsymbol{\Phi} + \alpha\boldsymbol{I})^{-1} , $$
$$ \boldsymbol{\mu} = \tfrac{1}{\sigma_n^2}\boldsymbol{\Sigma}\boldsymbol{\Phi}^T\boldsymbol{t} . \quad (14) $$

Maximization of (13) consists of setting the weights $\boldsymbol{w}$ equal to the mean values $\boldsymbol{\mu}$:

$$ \hat{\boldsymbol{w}}_{\text{bay}} = \boldsymbol{\mu} = (\boldsymbol{\Phi}^T\boldsymbol{\Phi} + \underbrace{\alpha\,\sigma_n^2\,}_{\lambda_{\text{bay}}}\boldsymbol{I})^{-1}\boldsymbol{\Phi}^T\boldsymbol{t} . \quad (15) $$

Note, that – relating to regularization by matrix inversion (8) – the product of the hyper-parameters takes the role of the regularization parameter, $\lambda_{\text{bay}} = \alpha\,\sigma_n^2$.

The second part in the above decomposition is again split by $p(\alpha, \sigma_n^2 | \boldsymbol{X}, \boldsymbol{t}) \propto p(\boldsymbol{t} | \boldsymbol{X}, \alpha, \sigma_n^2)\, p(\alpha)\, p(\sigma_n^2)$ (where we skip the normalization by $p(\boldsymbol{t}) = \text{const.}$ and assume no conditioning of the hyper-parameters on the input training data $p(\alpha | \boldsymbol{X}) = p(\alpha), p(\sigma_n^2 | \boldsymbol{X}) = p(\sigma_n^2)$). Maximization of the right hand side terms depends on assumptions for the prior distributions of the hyper-parameters $p(\alpha)$ and $p(\sigma_n^2)$, and is treated for uniform distributions on logarithmic scale and for Gamma distributions in [32, 36]. For uniform prior distributions on a logarithmic scale the resulting update equations[6] for the hyper-parameters to maximize $p(\alpha, \sigma_n^2 | \boldsymbol{X}, \boldsymbol{t})$ are

$$ \alpha^{\text{new}} = \frac{\gamma}{\|\boldsymbol{\mu}\|^2} , $$
$$ \left(\frac{1}{\sigma_n^2}\right)^{\text{new}} = \frac{\|\boldsymbol{t} - \boldsymbol{\Phi}\boldsymbol{\mu}\|^2}{P - \gamma} , $$
$$ \gamma = N_c - \alpha\,\text{Trace}(\boldsymbol{\Sigma}) . \quad (16) $$

---

[6] Deviating from the exact Bayesian approach the following approximations are made: As already noted, the derivation of the weights from (13)-(15) assumes the hyper-parameters to be known, which corresponds to taking a delta-distribution for $p(\alpha, \sigma_n^2 | \boldsymbol{t})$. On the other hand in the update of the hyper-parameters (16) the parameters of the posterior pdf for the weights are assumed to be known. Furthermore, the update of the hyper-parameters (16) is not exactly a maximization step, since the calculation of γ involves the old value for α on the right-hand side of the equation. Hence, the Bayesian learning can only be accomplished in an iterative procedure

Bayesian optimization of weights and hyper-parameters (and thus of regularization) comprises iterating (14) and (16), in the manner of the EM algorithm:

$$\boldsymbol{\Sigma}^{(i)} = (\frac{1}{\sigma_n^{2\,(i)}}\boldsymbol{\Phi}^T\boldsymbol{\Phi} + \alpha^{(i)}\boldsymbol{I})^{-1}\ ,$$

$$\boldsymbol{\mu}^{(i)} = \frac{1}{\sigma_n^{2\,(i)}}\boldsymbol{\Sigma}^{(i)}\boldsymbol{\Phi}^T\boldsymbol{t}\ ,$$

$$\gamma^{(i)} = N_c - \alpha^{(i)}\,\mathrm{Trace}(\boldsymbol{\Sigma}^{(i)})\ ,$$

$$\alpha^{(i+1)} = \frac{\gamma^{(i)}}{\|\boldsymbol{\mu}^{(i)}\|^2}\ ,$$

$$\frac{1}{\sigma_n^{2\,(i+1)}} = \frac{\|\boldsymbol{t} - \boldsymbol{\Phi}\boldsymbol{\mu}^{(i)}\|^2}{P - \gamma^{(i)}}\ . \tag{17}$$

Here, $i = 1, 2, \ldots$ is the iteration index.

For the application in the oscillator model the iteration in (17) was found to converge in the generic case[7]. Starting with an initialization with $\sigma_n^{2\,(1)} = 10^{-4}$, $\alpha^{(1)} = 10^{-4}$, the mean number of iterations for less than $1\,\%$ variation in the hyper-parameters γ and σ_n^2 was 19.3 for signals from a database of sustained vowels and nasals, and even smaller for voiced and unvoiced fricatives. This means that the computational complexity of the Bayesian algorithm for determining the regularization factor is comparable to the computational complexity of cross-validation over a range of, e. g., $\lambda \in [10^{-12}, 10^2]$ with one λ value per decade and one validation set, and smaller by a factor of k as compared to k-fold cross-validation.

The value of the regularization parameter λ_{bay} from Bayesian training for vowel signals is, on average, four orders of magnitude higher than the value determined by cross-validation. A closer look at the error function on the validation set in the cross-validation procedure reveals that, for many vowel signals, this function displays a flat minimum with very small variation over several orders of magnitude, as in Fig. 5, due to the high signal to noise ratio (SNR) of the training signal. As a consequence, an arbitrary λ value within this large range can be chosen to yield approximately the same small prediction error on the validation set. The actual position of the minimum in the validation error highly depends on training parameters, like choice of validation set, training length, etc., as exemplified in Fig. 6. For the application in a *predictor* the actual choice of λ_{xv} does not make a big difference. However, for the *oscillator* a minimum λ value is necessary to yield stable oscillation (as indicated in Figs. 5 and 6). The Bayesian algorithm, on the other hand, always chooses a λ value at the higher end of a flat validation error function (resulting in a possibly slightly larger squared error), as shown in Figs. 5 and 6, and thus results in a significantly larger number of stably re-synthesized vowel signals.

The difference between the value of the regularization parameter found by cross-validation and by the Bayesian algorithm is less stringent for voiced and

---

[7] A 'non-generic' case encountered was the oscillator training on a strictly periodic signal, where the Bayesian algorithm did not converge

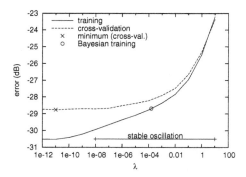

Fig. 5. Training and validation error as a function of λ for male vowel /o/, along with the choice of λ_{xv} (cross) according to cross-validation, and the value of λ_{bay} (circle) found by the Bayesian algorithm

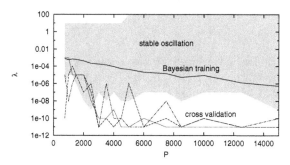

Fig. 6. Value λ for the regularization parameter as a function of training examples P found by the Bayesian algorithm (solid line), and according to cross-validation with a validation set of 10, 20, and 30% of the training data (dashed/dotted lines). The shaded region indicates λ values, where stable re-synthesis of this vowel is possible

unvoiced fricatives, which do not display a flat minimum of the validation error function.

Testing the Bayesian algorithm on artificial speech source signals according to the Liljencrants-Fant model [37] with additive noise, and artificially introduced variations in fundamental period length (jitter) and amplitude of individual fundamental cycles (shimmer), a very robust behavior is found. In Fig. 7 it can be seen that regularization is increased with increasing noise level, and, regardless of the amount of jitter and shimmer, the Bayesian algorithm yields a robust estimate of the actual noise level. A similar robust behavior has been found for the modeling of chaotic signals from the Lorenz system with the oscillator model and Bayesian regularization [16].

Pruning of Basis Functions. An extension of the Bayesian learning algorithm for kernel based function approximation, like RBF networks, is the relevance vector machine (RVM) as described in [36]. As opposed to the above approach

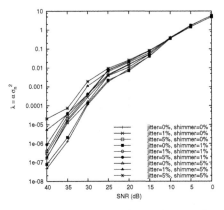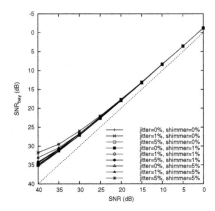

Fig. 7. Regularization factor λ_{bay} and noise variance σ_n^2 (displayed as SNR_{bay}) found by the Bayesian training as a function of training signal SNR for artificial speech source signals

where regularization is introduced by the choice of a Gaussian prior pdf for the norm of the weights vector (10), in the RVM the prior pdf for the network weights is a product of individual Gaussians for each weight:

$$p(\boldsymbol{w}|\boldsymbol{\alpha}) = \prod_{i=1}^{N_c} p(w_i|\alpha_i) \ ,$$

$$p(w_i|\alpha_i) = \left(\tfrac{\alpha_i}{2\pi}\right)^{-\frac{1}{2}} \exp\left(-\tfrac{\alpha_i}{2} w_i^2\right) \ . \tag{18}$$

Instead of the hyper-parameter α, a number of N_c hyper-parameters α_i, $i = 1 \ldots N_c$ are introduced by this model.

Again a decomposition of the pdf for the unknown parameters similar as for (12) and an iterative training algorithm can be applied (for details see [36]). During RVM learning, however, some of the hyper-parameters α_i attain large values. This means that the pdf for the according weight w_i is concentrated around zero, and that the weight value almost certainly is close to zero. Hence, the basis function φ_i does not contribute a *relevant* part to the output, and can be pruned.

When pruning basis functions for $\alpha_i > 10^6$, and stopping iterations when the number of network centers is not reduced within the last ten iterations, the mean number of iterations is 60.2 for our vowel database. The number of initial basis functions used ($N_c = 625$) is, however, significantly reduced during the RVM training iterations[8], as depicted in Fig. 8.

Using the RVM for prediction yields a prediction error not more than 1 dB higher than for Bayesian trained RBF networks without pruning. Also the oscil-

---

[8] Note, that – in spite of the higher number of iterations – the total computational complexity may be less than in the Bayesian training without pruning: The main effort is the inversion of an $N_c \times N_c$ matrix, which is of order $\mathcal{O}(N_c^3)$. Since N_c is reduced during the iterations, computational effort is also shrinking considerably

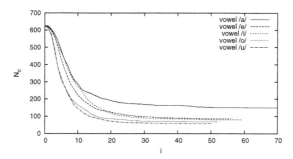

Fig. 8. Reduction of the number of basis functions N_c during iterations of RVM training for some example vowel signals

lator model with an RVM yields stable re-synthesis of almost the same number of vowel signals than without pruning. One possible reason that some signals could be re-synthesized without pruning, and cannot with the RVM, seems to be the fact that, since less basis functions are used in the RVM, the weights for these basis functions may again take larger values than without pruning.

Concerning the almost equal prediction gain and number of stably re-synthesized vowel signals the RVM can be considered a valuable tool for reducing the complexity of kernel based function models like RBF networks in applications like speech signal prediction and the oscillator model. Other applications of the RVM algorithm comprise, for example, the determination of relevant weights in adaptive filters, where the complexity of the adaptive filters is also considerably reduced without impairing performance [38].

2.7   Inverse Filtering and Oscillator Model

The application of regularization for nonlinear function learning increases the number of signals that can be stably re-synthesized with the oscillator model. However, for modeling the *full speech signal* this number is still fairly low (only 18 % for our vowel database and a fixed embedding with $N = 4$ and $M = 13$). Inspection of the structure of the signal trajectories in phase space reveals, that vowels with a simple trajectory structure, like /o/ or /u/ can be stably re-synthesized more likely than vowels with a more complicated structure, like /a/, /e/, and /i/. To gain a generally simple structure of the signals that are to be modeled by the oscillator, inverse filtering in combination with the oscillator model can be applied [13, 16]. Inverse filtering refers to the identification and compensation of the influence of the vocal tract on a glottis source signal. Here we utilize a simple inverse filtering process, since we do not aim at the identification of the source signal, but want to arrive at a simple trajectory structure only.

The inverse filtering process used for the examples here consists of identification and application of a signal dependent linear prediction (LP) inverse filter with transfer function $A(z) = 1 + a_1 z^{-1} + \ldots + a_{N_{\mathrm{LP}}} z^{-N_{\mathrm{LP}}}$, and subsequent low-pass filtering. First-order pre-emphasis filtering with a zero at $z_n = 0.75$ is used for LP analysis (but not in the signal path). For the low-pass filter $H(z)$ a first order recursive filter with a pole at $z_p = 0.95$ is applied. This low-pass filter can be stably inverted for synthesis.

Oscillator model identification is now done for the output signal $x_g(n)$ of the low-pass filter. For re-synthesis, the oscillator generated signal $y_g(n)$ is filtered by $1/H(z)$ and the LP synthesis filter $1/A(z)$ to gain the synthetic full speech signal $y(n)$. To exemplify the benefit of inverse filtering, time signals and phase space trajectories for the vowel /a/ from a female speaker are depicted in Fig. 9. This signal could not be re-synthesized in the full speech signal domain. By inverse filtering, however, the highly intermingled trajectory of the full speech signal $x(n)$ is converted to an open loop trajectory of $x_g(n)$. This simpler structure can be identified and stably re-synthesized by the oscillator model with Bayesian regularization (without pruning, in this example).

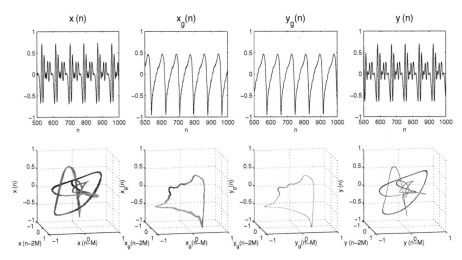

Fig. 9. Time signals (top row), phase space trajectories (bottom row) of the original full speech signal $x(n)$, the signal after inverse filtering $x_g(n)$, as well as the oscillator generated signal $y_g(n)$ and the resulting synthetic full speech signal $y(n)$ for vowel /a/ from a female speaker

By means of inverse filtering the percentage of stably re-synthesized vowel signals from our database for an embedding with $N = 4$ and $M = 13$ is increased from 18 % to 56 %. Also the spectral reproduction of speech signals is improved as compared to full speech signal modeling. However, perceptually many re-generated vowel signals still are not satisfactory, and in particular for mixed excitation speech signals, like voiced fricatives, the oscillator fails to adequately reproduce the signal quality. We attribute this to the missing modeling of *high-dimensional* or *stochastic* speech signal components by the low-dimensional and deterministic oscillator model, and present a model that accounts for a stochastic noise-like signal component in speech signals in the following.

2.8 Oscillator-Plus-Noise Model

For purely unvoiced speech signals a satisfactory synthesis system is the auto-recursive stochastic model (i. e., noise excited LP) [39]. Concerning the generation of mixed excitation speech signals it is known that a modulation of the noise-like signal component synchronized in phase with the oscillatory signal component is requisite [40–46]. To achieve this synchronized modulation for oscillator model generated speech signals we propose to use an amplitude prediction for the noise-like signal component by a second nonlinear function $f_n(\cdot)$ from the state of the oscillator model:

$$\tilde{a}(n + 1) = f_n(\boldsymbol{x}(n)) \ , \tag{19}$$

and to add a modulated noise signal to the oscillator model output signal.

Based on the assumption, that the predictor used in the oscillator model is able to capture the low-dimensional oscillatory component of speech signals, but not the high-dimensional noise-like component, the prediction function for the noise-like signal component's amplitude $f_n(\cdot)$ in (19) is trained to predict the amplitude of the prediction error signal $e(n) = \hat{x}(n) - x(n)$ of the nonlinear signal predictor (1).

For modeling general mixed excitation speech sounds we found [47] that it is also necessary to use a second LP analysis path for the noise-like signal part to achieve the spectral shaping of this signal component independent from the spectral properties of the oscillatory signal component.

A schematic of the analysis and synthesis process of the resulting *oscillator-plus-noise model* is given in Fig. 10. The upper signal path – from input signal $x(n)$ to oscillatory output component $y_{\text{osc}}(n)$ represents the model comprising inverse filtering as described in the last subsection. All additional processing is based on the above assumption that the *prediction error* of the nonlinear function $f()$ (in the oscillator) is *related to the noise-like signal component*. Hence, the predicted signal $\hat{x}_g(n)$ is considered to be the oscillatory part of the training signal. To arrive at the noise-like signal component, $\hat{x}_g(n)$ is filtered by the synthesis filters $1/H(z)$ and $1/A(z)$ and subtracted from the training signal to yield an estimate for the noise-like signal component $\hat{x}_{\text{noi}}(n)$. Synthesis filtering on $\hat{x}_g(n)$ is done to provide the means for an *individual spectral shaping* of the noise-like component independent from the oscillatory component by the LP filter $A_{\text{noi}}(z)$. From the according residual signal $x_{r\_\text{noi}}(n)$ the amplitude trajectory is extracted by rectification and moving average filtering. The function $f_n(\cdot)$ in (19) is trained to predict this amplitude trajectory $\hat{a}_{\text{noi}}(n)$ based on the trajectory of the state of the predictor $\boldsymbol{x}_g(n - 1)$.

At the bond between analysis and synthesis the speech signal is represented by parameters only, namely the coefficients for the nonlinear functions in the oscillator and the noise amplitude predictor, and the coefficients for the LP filters.

In the synthesis stage the oscillatory speech signal component is generated by autonomous synthesis as in the previous models. In addition the amplitude trajectory $\tilde{a}_{\text{noi}}(n)$ of the synthetic signal's noise-like component is predicted from the oscillator state $\boldsymbol{y}_g(n-1)$ by the function $f_n(\cdot)$. A white Gaussian noise source

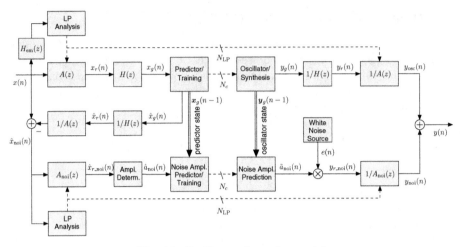

Fig. 10. Oscillator-plus-noise model

is modulated in amplitude by $\tilde{a}_{\text{noi}}(n)$ and fed to the LP synthesis filter $1/A_{\text{noi}}(z)$ to yield the noise-like signal component in the full speech signal domain $y_{\text{noi}}(n)$, which is added to the oscillatory component $y_{\text{osc}}(n)$, yielding the output signal $y(n)$.

As depicted for an example signal in Fig. 11, the oscillator-plus-noise generated signals display a spreading of the signal trajectory in phase space and a spectral noise floor, resembling the behavior of the natural signals' trajectory and spectrum, in contrary to the signals generated by the oscillator alone – which have a concentrated trajectory and a line spectrum.

Examples for the noise amplitude modulation achieved by the oscillator-plus-noise model are given in Fig. 12. For both the vowel /o/ and the voiced fricative /v/ the model achieves a *pitch-synchronous modulation* of the amplitude $\tilde{a}(n)$ for the noise-like signal component similar to the amplitude modulation $\hat{a}(n)$ of the prediction error signal. However, the two example signals display a very distinct form of the noise amplitude trajectory over the pitch cycle: Whereas the vowel signal has triangular maxima of the noise amplitude at the minima of the signal $y_g(n)$ – which is a typical behavior for vowels and often modeled using a parametric envelope [45, 48] – the noise amplitude for the voiced fricative has *minima* synchronized with the minima of $y_g(n)$.

In the oscillator-plus-noise model the envelope for the noise modulation is, for any individual training signal, identified by the prediction function $f_n(\cdot)$, in a similar manner as the oscillatory waveform is identified by the nonlinear function $f(\cdot)$ in the oscillator model.

3   ODE and DDE Models from Delay- and Differential-Embeddings

Recovery of nonlinear dynamical processes from single scalar time series observations is extremely difficult when no information on the functional form of the

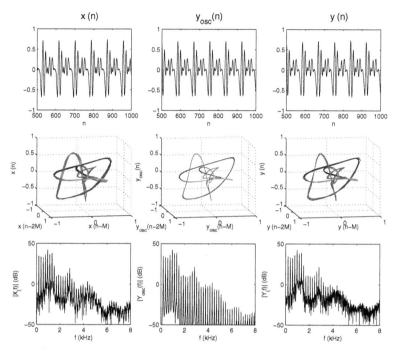

Fig. 11. Time signals (top row), phase space trajectories (middle row), and DFT spectra (bottom row) of the original full speech signal $x(n)$, the oscillator generated synthetic full speech signal $y_{osc}(n)$, and the oscillator-plus-noise generated synthetic full speech signal $y(n)$ for female /a/

underlying process is available. In this section we present the reconstruction of a dynamical process from a differential embedding using ordinary differential equations (ODEs) from an "Ansatz library", the optimization of delay differential equations (DDEs) using a genetic algorithm (GA), and some analysis results for speech characterization that can be read from the parameter values of GA optimized DDEs.

Many time series analysis methods for modeling, prediction, and classification of experimental observations rest upon nonlinear dynamical systems theory. An important analysis tool in nonlinear system theory is reconstructing phase space topological properties of a dynamical system from a single scalar time series. The embedding theorems of Takens [17], and Sauer [18] assure us that an embedding constructed from a single variable time series preserves the topological properties of the underlying dynamical system and, therefore, lays out the foundations for such reconstruction methods.

Thus, it is possible to model a multi-dimensional nonlinear process directly from the scalar data without any prior knowledge of the physical processes, such that these models reproduce the data with the original dynamical properties. Two types of models have been used. The first encompasses local models of the dynamics which allow to predict, step by step, the evolution of the system. The

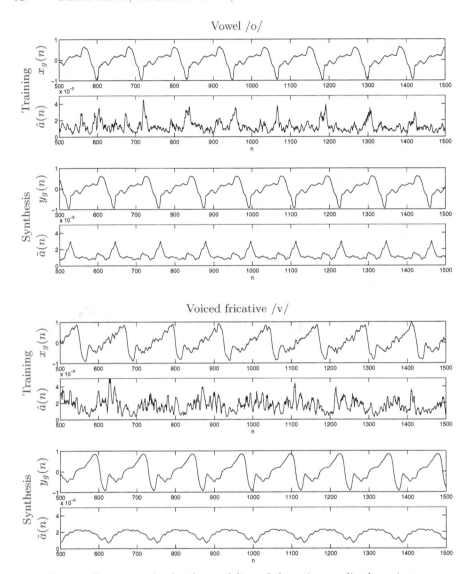

Fig. 12. Two examples for the modeling of the noise amplitude trajectory

most common model of this type is the auto-regressive moving average (ARMA) model. The second type consists of global models that attempt to characterize the global underlying dynamics of a given process. Ideally, global models can generate long time series with the same dynamical properties as the original ones.

In the simple case of noise-free observations of all original dynamical variables of a physical system, the global model can be exactly estimated if we know the precise model order, that is if we know the exact underlying structure of the original system for which we estimate the parameters. In reality, one typically does not know the proper dimensionality or functional model form of the underlying dynamical process, especially when only a scalar observation of the process is available. If this is the case, estimation of a global model can be very difficult. Any error in the assumptions made about the model dimension or its functional form may critically effect the model quality.

Here we address the problem of finding a global dynamical model in the form of a set of coupled ordinary differential equations (ODEs) from a single time series. We introduce an Ansatz library [49, 50] based method (see Fig. 13) in Sect. 3.1 and a Genetic Algorithm (GA) based method in Sect. 3.2 to find such a system of ODEs which models the entire underlying nonlinear dynamical process. In these two methods we construct from the time series either a differential embedding (Ansatz library based method) or a delay embedding (GA based method) using a non-uniform embedding [51, 20] which assumes that the given time series can have different time scales. In Sect. 3.3 we estimate DDE (delay differential equation) models from the time series. This method is here not used to find a model for synthesis of speech, but can be used to characterize certain features of the time series, e. g., for segmentation of a speech signal.

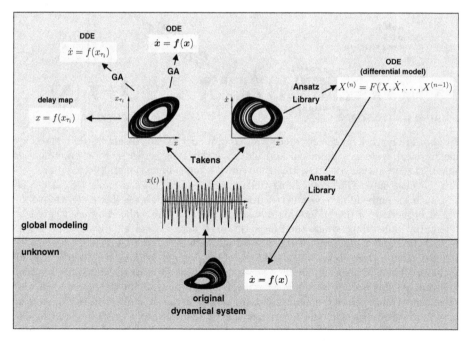

Fig. 13. Framework for global modeling from a single time series via delay- or differential- embedding: typically only a restricted set of measurements, here a single time series, is available. The underlying dynamical system is unknown. To recover information about the underlying system, following the theorems of Takens [17], either a delay- or a differential-embedding can be constructed in order to reconstruct a global model. The model form reconstructed from a delay embedding can be a delay map, a set of ODEs, or a DDE and, from a differential embedding, a set of ODEs

3.1 Differential Embedding: Ansatz Library Based Method

Ansatz Library. The framework of reconstructing an ODE model via an Ansatz library [49, 50] based method is illustrated in Fig. 14.

To obtain the general form of an ODE model in the differential embedding space, $\mathbb{R}^3(X, Y, Z)$, where $X = s(t)$ is the measured time series, $Y = \dot{X}$, and $Z = \dot{Y}$ are the successive derivatives, first consider a continuous-time system in $\mathbb{R}^3(x_1, x_2, x_3)$.

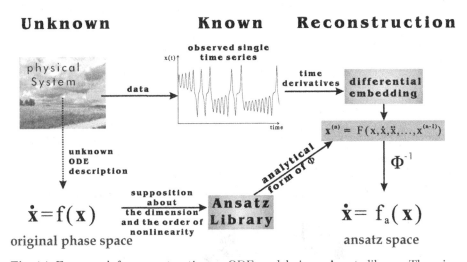

Fig. 14. Framework for reconstructing an ODE model via an Ansatz library: The original physical system is unknown and only a scalar time series (here a vowel speech signal) can be measured. From this time series a multidimensional object, an embedding, is constructed. The embedding theorems of Takens [17] and Sauer [18] assure us that such an embedding constructed from one single time series preserves the topological properties of the underlying dynamical system. The embedding used here is a differential embedding, where the time series itself and successive derivatives are used. To find the right model form of the differential model $X^{(n)} = F(X, \dot{X}, \ddot{X}, \ldots, X^{(n-1)})$ we make assumptions about the model form of the original dynamical system $\dot{x} = f(x)$ in the original phase space and then choose the model form of the differential model accordingly. This is done as follows: We make assumptions about the model form, the dimension of the original dynamical system, and the order of nonlinearities. All models $\dot{x} = f(x)$ with such a model form that can be transformed to a differential model $X^{(n)} = F(X, \dot{X}, \ddot{X}, \ldots, X^{(n-1)})$ are collected in the so-called Ansatz library [49, 50]. To use the inverse Φ^{-1} (see Fig. 13) of the transformation between the original dynamical model and the differential model, we further require that the map Φ is one-to-one. The concatenation of all possible differential models is then used as Ansatz for estimating the model from the time series. If the model falls into the class of models that were considered in the original phase space, the model can be re-transformed to an Ansatz model $\dot{x} = f_a(x)$ that is topologically equivalent to the original dynamical system and typically of 'simpler' model form than the differential model (see [50])

$$\dot{x} = f(x) \ , \qquad \text{that is} \qquad \begin{array}{l} \dot{x}_1 = f_1(x) \\ \dot{x}_2 = f_2(x) \ , \\ \dot{x}_3 = f_3(x) \end{array} \qquad (20)$$

with $x = [x_1, x_2, x_3]$, and let $s = h(x)$ be an observed scalar signal, where $h : \mathbb{R}^3 \to \mathbb{R}$ is a smooth function. The Lie derivative $L_f h(x)$ of the function $h(x)$ with respect to $f(x)$ is defined as

$$L_f h(x) = \sum_{k=1}^{3} f_k(x) \frac{\partial h(x)}{\partial x_k} \qquad (21)$$

and recursively for the higher-order derivatives $L_f^j h(x) = L_f \left(L_f^{j-1} h(x) \right)$. Using successive Lie derivatives we can build a model from the scalar signal s as follows

$$\begin{aligned} X &= s = h(x) \, , \\ Y &= L_f h(x) \, , \\ Z &= L_f^2 h(x) \, . \end{aligned} \qquad (22)$$

The phase portrait can thus be reconstructed in the differential space $\mathbb{R}^3(X, Y, Z)$. With these coordinates, a model can be obtained from the recorded scalar signal via a global modeling procedure. A *general form for a differential model* $\mathcal{D}$ is given by

$$\begin{aligned} \dot{X} &= Y \ , \\ \dot{Y} &= Z \ , \\ \dot{Z} &= F(X, Y, Z, \alpha_n) = \sum_{n=1}^{N_\alpha} \alpha_n P_n \ , \end{aligned} \qquad (23)$$

where α_n are the coefficients of the model function F to be estimated and P_n are the monomials $X^i Y^j Z^k$ [52]. The indices (i, j, k) for monomials may also be negative, yielding a model with rational monomials. System (23) is called the *differential model* [52], and its parameters can be obtained using a least square procedure, such as singular value decomposition (SVD) [53].

Here we do not choose the set of monomials P_n in (23) as truncated Taylor series expansion. Instead we use the Ansatz library approach introduced in [49, 50] where only monomials are considered that correspond to an underlying dynamical system in a three dimensional phase space $\mathbb{R}^3(x_1, x_2, x_3)$, where $x_1 = s(t)$ is the observable and $x_2 = x_2(t)$ and $x_3 = x_3(t)$ are unobserved state space variables.

The first library made of six Ansatz systems $\mathcal{A}_l$ (with indices $l = 1, 2, 3, 18, 19, 21$, cf. Table 1) for defining the structure of 3D differential models was presented in [49]. An extended Ansatz Library of systems of ODEs in a three dimensional phase space was derived in [54] for the case when the right hand sides can be written as polynomials containing up to second order non-linearities. We briefly detail how this library was built.

A three dimensional system of ODEs with the right hand sides containing polynomials with up to second order non-linearities can be written in a general form as

$$\dot{x}_1 = \sum_{i=0}^{9} a_i\, Q_i\,, \quad \dot{x}_2 = \sum_{i=0}^{9} b_i\, Q_i\,, \quad \dot{x}_3 = \sum_{i=0}^{9} c_i\, Q_i\,, \quad \text{with} \tag{24}$$

$$Q = \{1, x_1, x_2, x_3, x_1^2, x_1 x_2, x_1\, x_3, x_2^2, x_2\, x_3, x_3^2\}\,.$$

To derive the Ansatz library in [54] we restrict the terms of the differential model to the set of all monomials of the form $X^i Y^j Z^k$, where i, j and k are integers, positive or negative. Given that the order of the differential equations is interchangeable, we fix the x_1-variable as the observable in all cases, i.e. $x_1 = s$, to obtain a set of non-redundant libraries. We then find which model structures allow us to invert the maps Φ_l to express the coefficients α_n of the differential models $\mathcal{D}_l$ in (23), in terms of the coefficients a_i, b_j, c_k of the second order system equation (24). Through this process, we find which coefficients a_i, b_j, c_k in (24) must be zero for the individual differential model structures. In the end we obtain a set of ODEs containing a limited number of terms for which the coefficients a_i, b_j, c_k are non-zero. Note that we do not use data to build the library.

The library for the case of second order non-linearities consists of 26 such model structures listed in Table 1. In Table 2, the monomials involved in the

Table 1. Ansatz library for systems of ODEs with up to quadratic non-linearities. Each line represents one general system of ODEs which can be represented as a differential model in the form of (23). An '⋆' in the table indicates that the corresponding coefficient (a_i, b_j, c_k) from the general system (24) is present in the Ansatz-model. The coefficients with blank entries are zero

Ansatz	a0	a1	a2	a3	a4	a5	a6	a7	a8	a9	b0	b1	b2	b3	b4	b5	b6	b7	b8	b9	c0	c1	c2	c3	c4	c5	c6	c7	c8	c9
$\mathcal{A}_1$	⋆	⋆	⋆			⋆					⋆	⋆	⋆			⋆	⋆	⋆	⋆		⋆	⋆	⋆	⋆	⋆	⋆	⋆	⋆	⋆	⋆
$\mathcal{A}_2$	⋆	⋆	⋆			⋆					⋆	⋆	⋆	⋆	⋆	⋆		⋆			⋆	⋆	⋆	⋆	⋆	⋆	⋆	⋆	⋆	⋆
$\mathcal{A}_3$			⋆								⋆	⋆	⋆			⋆	⋆		⋆	⋆	⋆	⋆	⋆	⋆	⋆	⋆	⋆	⋆	⋆	⋆
$\mathcal{A}_4$	⋆	⋆	⋆	⋆	⋆						⋆	⋆	⋆	⋆	⋆	⋆					⋆	⋆	⋆	⋆	⋆					
$\mathcal{A}_5$	⋆	⋆	⋆	⋆	⋆						⋆	⋆				⋆					⋆	⋆				⋆		⋆		
$\mathcal{A}_6$	⋆	⋆	⋆	⋆	⋆						⋆	⋆				⋆					⋆	⋆					⋆	⋆		
$\mathcal{A}_7$	⋆	⋆	⋆	⋆	⋆		⋆				⋆	⋆				⋆					⋆	⋆				⋆				
$\mathcal{A}_8$	⋆	⋆	⋆	⋆	⋆				⋆		⋆	⋆				⋆										⋆				
$\mathcal{A}_9$	⋆	⋆	⋆	⋆	⋆				⋆		⋆	⋆				⋆							⋆							
$\mathcal{A}_{10}$	⋆	⋆		⋆			⋆							⋆		⋆	⋆							⋆		⋆				
$\mathcal{A}_{11}$	⋆	⋆		⋆			⋆						⋆	⋆		⋆								⋆		⋆				
$\mathcal{A}_{12}$	⋆	⋆		⋆			⋆				⋆		⋆			⋆								⋆		⋆				
$\mathcal{A}_{13}$	⋆	⋆		⋆	⋆		⋆				⋆		⋆											⋆		⋆				
$\mathcal{A}_{14}$	⋆	⋆		⋆	⋆											⋆								⋆		⋆				
$\mathcal{A}_{15}$	⋆	⋆		⋆	⋆										⋆									⋆		⋆				
$\mathcal{A}_{16}$	⋆	⋆		⋆	⋆								⋆											⋆		⋆				
$\mathcal{A}_{17}$						⋆							⋆			⋆								⋆		⋆				⋆
$\mathcal{A}_{18}$						⋆							⋆			⋆		⋆						⋆		⋆				
$\mathcal{A}_{19}$	⋆	⋆			⋆	⋆					⋆	⋆	⋆		⋆	⋆	⋆	⋆			⋆	⋆	⋆	⋆	⋆	⋆	⋆	⋆	⋆	⋆
$\mathcal{A}_{20}$	⋆	⋆			⋆	⋆					⋆	⋆	⋆	⋆	⋆	⋆	⋆		⋆		⋆	⋆	⋆	⋆	⋆	⋆	⋆	⋆	⋆	⋆
$\mathcal{A}_{21}$			⋆								⋆	⋆	⋆			⋆	⋆		⋆	⋆	⋆	⋆	⋆	⋆	⋆	⋆	⋆	⋆	⋆	⋆
$\mathcal{A}_{22}$	⋆	⋆			⋆	⋆	⋆				⋆	⋆				⋆					⋆	⋆				⋆	⋆			
$\mathcal{A}_{23}$	⋆	⋆			⋆	⋆	⋆				⋆	⋆				⋆					⋆	⋆					⋆	⋆		
$\mathcal{A}_{24}$	⋆	⋆			⋆	⋆	⋆				⋆	⋆				⋆					⋆	⋆			⋆	⋆				
$\mathcal{A}_{25}$	⋆	⋆			⋆	⋆	⋆				⋆	⋆				⋆					⋆	⋆	⋆			⋆				
$\mathcal{A}_{26}$	⋆	⋆		⋆	⋆	⋆	⋆				⋆	⋆				⋆					⋆	⋆				⋆				

Table 2. Monomials of the differential models corresponding to the 26 Ansatz reported in Table 1. A '★' indicates that the monomial is present in the differential model

	Ansatz monomial	1	2	3	4	5	6	7	8	9	10	11	12	13	14	15	16	17	18	19	20	21	22	23	24	25	26
1	1	★	★	★	★						★	★	★	★	★	★	★			★	★						
2	$\frac{1}{X^4}$																			★							
3	$\frac{1}{X^3}$																			★	★						
4	$\frac{1}{X^2}$																			★	★						
5	$\frac{1}{X}$	★																		★	★						
6	X	★	★	★	★	★	★				★	★	★	★	★	★	★			★	★	★			★	★	
7	X^2	★	★	★	★	★	★			★	★	★	★	★	★	★	★			★	★	★	★	★	★	★	
8	X^3	★	★	★		★	★				★	★	★	★	★	★	★			★	★	★	★	★	★	★	
9	X^4	★	★					★			★	★	★	★	★	★	★			★	★	★	★	★			
10	X^5	★	★																		★						
11	X^6	★	★																								
12	X^7	★	★																								
13	X^8		★																								
14	$\frac{1}{Y}$			★																							
15	$\frac{X}{Y}$			★																							
16	$\frac{X^2}{Y}$			★																		★					
17	$\frac{X^3}{Y}$			★																		★					
18	$\frac{X^4}{Y}$			★																		★					
19	$\frac{X^5}{Y}$																					★					
20	$\frac{X^6}{Y}$																					★					
21	Y	★	★	★	★			★	★		★	★	★	★	★	★	★	★	★	★	★	★	★	★			★
22	$\frac{Y}{X^4}$																			★							
23	$\frac{Y}{X^3}$																			★	★						
24	$\frac{Y}{X^2}$																			★	★						
25	$\frac{Y}{X}$	★				★	★		★	★	★	★			★	★	★			★	★			★			
26	XY	★	★	★	★	★	★	★			★	★	★	★	★	★	★	★	★	★	★	★			★	★	★
27	X^2Y	★	★	★		★		★			★	★	★	★	★	★	★	★	★	★	★	★	★	★	★	★	★
28	X^3Y	★	★																		★						
29	X^4Y	★	★																								
30	X^5Y	★	★																								
31	X^6Y		★																								
32	Y^2	★	★	★	★			★	★		★		★	★		★		★	★	★	★	★	★	★			★
33	$\frac{Y^2}{X^4}$																			★							
34	$\frac{Y^2}{X^3}$																			★	★						
35	$\frac{Y^2}{X^2}$																			★	★		★	★	★	★	
36	$\frac{Y^2}{X}$	★				★	★		★	★	★	★			★	★	★			★	★	★			★		
37	XY^2	★	★	★																	★						
38	X^2Y^2	★	★																								
39	X^3Y^2	★	★																								
40	X^4Y^2		★																								

Table 2. (continued)

	Ansatz monomial	1	2	3	4	5	6	7	8	9	10	11	12	13	14	15	16	17	18	19	20	21	22	23	24	25	26
41	Y^3	★	★	★																							
42	$\frac{Y^3}{X^4}$																			★							
43	$\frac{Y^3}{X^3}$																			★	★						
44	$\frac{Y^3}{X^2}$																			★	★	★	★	★	★	★	
45	$\frac{Y^3}{X}$	★																			★						
46	XY^3	★	★																								
47	X^2Y^3		★																								
48	Y^4		★																								
49	$\frac{Y^4}{X^4}$																			★							
50	$\frac{Y^4}{X^3}$																				★						
51	$\frac{Y^4}{X}$	★																									
52	Z	★	★	★	★	★	★		★	★	★	★	★	★	★	★	★	★	★	★	★	★			★		
53	$\frac{Z}{X^3}$																			★							
54	$\frac{Z}{X^2}$																			★	★						
55	$\frac{Z}{X}$	★																		★	★			★	★	★	★
56	XZ	★	★	★	★	★	★		★	★	★	★	★	★	★	★	★	★	★	★	★	★	★	★	★	★	★
57	X^2Z	★	★																		★						
58	X^3Z	★	★																								
59	X^4Z		★																								
60	$\frac{Z}{Y}$			★			★																				★
61	$\frac{XZ}{Y}$			★			★															★					★
62	$\frac{X^2Z}{Y}$			★			★															★					★
63	$\frac{X^3Z}{Y}$						★															★					★
64	YZ	★	★	★																	★						
65	$\frac{YZ}{X^3}$																			★							
66	$\frac{YZ}{X^2}$																			★	★						
67	$\frac{YZ}{X}$	★			★	★		★	★	★	★				★	★	★			★	★	★	★	★	★	★	
68	XYZ	★	★																								
69	X^2YZ		★																								
70	Y^2Z		★																								
71	$\frac{Y^2Z}{X^3}$																			★							
72	$\frac{Y^2Z}{X^2}$																				★						
73	$\frac{Y^2Z}{X}$	★																									
74	Z^2		★																								
75	$\frac{Z^2}{X^2}$																			★							
76	$\frac{Z^2}{X}$	★																			★						
77	$\frac{Z^2}{Y}$			★				★										★	★		★						★

differential models D_l corresponding to the 26 Ansatz A_l reported in Table 1 are listed. The models in Tables 1 and 2 are general forms. Systems with some of the coefficients a_i, b_j, c_k equal to zero can yield the same differential model, where some of the coefficients α_n can also be zero. To be more explicit, let us explain an example (see also [50]). The systems

$$\begin{aligned}
\dot{x}_1 &= a_0 + a_1 x_1 + a_5 x_1 x_2 \ , \\
\dot{x}_2 &= b_0 + b_1 x_1 + b_2 x_2 + b_6 x_1 x_3 \ , \\
\dot{x}_3 &= c_0 + c_2 x_2 + c_3 x_3 \ ,
\end{aligned} \tag{25}$$

and 13 sub-systems with some of the coefficients a_i, b_j, c_k of (25) equal to zero, as well as the following system

$$\begin{aligned}
\dot{x}_1 &= a_0 + a_1 x_1 + a_5 x_1 x_2 \ , \\
\dot{x}_2 &= b_0 + b_1 x_1 + b_2 x_2 + b_3 x_3 \ , \\
\dot{x}_3 &= c_0 + c_1 x_1 + c_2 x_2 + c_3 x_3 + c_5 x_1 x_2 \ ,
\end{aligned} \tag{26}$$

and 155 sub-systems with some of the coefficients a_i, b_j, c_k of (26) equal to zero yield exactly the same differential model

$$\begin{aligned}
\dot{X} &= Y \ , \\
\dot{Y} &= Z \ , \\
\dot{Z} &= \alpha_1 + \alpha_6 X + \alpha_7 X^2 + \alpha_{21} Y + \alpha_{25} \frac{Y}{X} + \alpha_{26} XY + \alpha_{35} \frac{Y^2}{X^2} \\
&\quad + \alpha_{36} \frac{Y^2}{X} + \alpha_{44} \frac{Y^3}{X^2} + \alpha_{52} Z + \alpha_{55} \frac{Z}{X} + \alpha_{67} \frac{YZ}{X} \ .
\end{aligned} \tag{27}$$

This means, that 170 possible systems with up to second order nonlinearities correspond to one and the same form of differential model (27) and therefore could have the same embedding. Only those systems of the 170 possible systems that correspond to a differential model (27) with exactly the same set and values of the coefficients α_i have the same embedding. All such systems generate the same time series and are therefore topologically equivalent. All non-equivalent systems have at least one different coefficient α_i.

Note that the equations in this library are also referred to as "jerky dynamics" in the literature. Attempts to build a complete jerky dynamics library were presented in [55], but that library was able to capture only a part of our list.

Our objective is to select the differential model $\mathcal{D}_l$ that best captures the dynamics under investigation. In order to do this, we start with the structure resulting from the concatenation of the 26 differential models $\{\mathcal{D}_l\}_{l=1}^{26}$ which reads as follows:

$$\dot{X} = Y \ ,$$
$$\dot{Y} = Z \ ,$$
$$\begin{aligned}
\dot{Z} = \ & \alpha_1 + \alpha_2 \tfrac{1}{X^4} + \alpha_3 \tfrac{1}{X^3} + \alpha_4 \tfrac{1}{X^2} + \alpha_5 \tfrac{1}{X} + \alpha_6 X + \alpha_7 X^2 + \alpha_8 X^3 + \\
& \alpha_9 X^4 + \alpha_{10} X^5 + \alpha_{11} X^6 + \alpha_{12} X^7 + \alpha_{13} X^8 + \alpha_{14} \tfrac{1}{Y} + \alpha_{15} \tfrac{X}{Y} + \\
& \alpha_{16} \tfrac{X^2}{Y} + \alpha_{17} \tfrac{X^3}{Y} + \alpha_{18} \tfrac{X^4}{Y} + \alpha_{19} \tfrac{X^5}{Y} + \alpha_{20} \tfrac{X^6}{Y} + \alpha_{21} Y + \alpha_{22} \tfrac{Y}{X^4} + \\
& \alpha_{23} \tfrac{Y}{X^3} + \alpha_{24} \tfrac{Y}{X^2} + \alpha_{25} \tfrac{Y}{X} + \alpha_{26} X Y + \alpha_{27} X^2 Y + \alpha_{28} X^3 Y + \\
& \alpha_{29} X^4 Y + \alpha_{30} X^5 Y + \alpha_{31} X^6 Y + \alpha_{32} Y^2 + \alpha_{33} \tfrac{Y^2}{X^4} + \alpha_{34} \tfrac{Y^2}{X^3} + \\
& \alpha_{35} \tfrac{Y^2}{X^2} + \alpha_{36} \tfrac{Y^2}{X} + \alpha_{37} X Y^2 + \alpha_{38} X^2 Y^2 + \alpha_{39} X^3 Y^2 + \\
& \alpha_{40} X^4 Y^2 + \alpha_{41} Y^3 + \alpha_{42} \tfrac{Y^3}{X^4} + \alpha_{43} \tfrac{Y^3}{X^3} + \alpha_{44} \tfrac{Y^3}{X^2} + \alpha_{45} \tfrac{Y^3}{X} + \\
& \alpha_{46} X Y^3 + \alpha_{47} X^2 Y^3 + \alpha_{48} Y^4 + \alpha_{49} \tfrac{Y^4}{X^4} + \alpha_{50} \tfrac{Y^4}{X^3} + \alpha_{51} \tfrac{Y^4}{X} + \\
& \alpha_{52} Z + \alpha_{53} \tfrac{Z}{X^3} + \alpha_{54} \tfrac{Z}{X^2} + \alpha_{55} \tfrac{Z}{X} + \alpha_{56} X Z + \alpha_{57} X^2 Z + \\
& \alpha_{58} X^3 Z + \alpha_{59} X^4 Z + \alpha_{60} \tfrac{Z}{Y} + \alpha_{61} \tfrac{X Z}{Y} + \alpha_{62} \tfrac{X^2 Z}{Y} + \alpha_{63} \tfrac{X^3 Z}{Y} + \\
& \alpha_{64} Y Z + \alpha_{65} \tfrac{Y Z}{X^3} + \alpha_{66} \tfrac{Y Z}{X^2} + \alpha_{67} \tfrac{Y Z}{X} + \alpha_{68} X Y Z + \\
& \alpha_{69} X^2 Y Z + \alpha_{70} Y^2 Z + \alpha_{71} \tfrac{Y^2 Z}{X^3} + \alpha_{72} \tfrac{Y^2 Z}{X^2} + \alpha_{73} \tfrac{Y^2 Z}{X} + \\
& \alpha_{74} Z^2 + \alpha_{75} \tfrac{Z^2}{X^2} + \alpha_{76} \tfrac{Z^2}{X} + \alpha_{77} \tfrac{Z^2}{Y} \ .
\end{aligned} \tag{28}$$

Because this differential model only contains terms leading to a 3D Ansatz with up to quadratic nonlinearities, the presence of spurious terms in this model structure is already greatly reduced. Note, that the Ansatz library approach does not require the knowledge of the order of the non-linearity in the system investigated. Given that our procedure can eliminate spurious model terms that we might obtain, if the order is not known, one can use a library built with an order of non-linearities higher than the one expected for the system. A library for the case of polynomials containing up to third order non-linearities was derived in [54], and libraries for 4th and higher order non-linearities can be derived analogously. Here we use the simplest case of the library obtained for the second order non-linearities. The extension to libraries that capture higher order non-linearities is postponed to future work.

Note, that involving a higher order of nonlinearities would increase the number of candidate terms considerably when the concatenation of all possible models is used as detailed here. For higher dimensions, the numerical estimation of the derivatives may also become problematic. A more favorable approach is to use candidate models $\mathcal{D}_l$ separately to reduce the number of involved terms as done in [49]. Nevertheless, since the terms used here are fractional, the number of situations which can be captured for a given order of nonlinearity is significantly increased as compared to the polynomial expansion used in [52].

Modeling of Vowels. To estimate a global model, the differential embedding from the time series $s(n)$ of the recording of the vowel /o/ (see Fig. 15a) is constructed as shown in Fig. 15b. The derivative $\dot{s}(n)$ of the time series $s(n)$ is estimated according to

$$\dot{s}(n) = \frac{1}{12 \, \delta t} \left(8 \left(s(n+1) - s(n-1) \right) - \left(s(n+2) - s(n-2) \right) \right) \ . \tag{29}$$

The second and third derivatives are then computed from the first and second derivatives, respectively. Then the model of the form (28) is estimated using

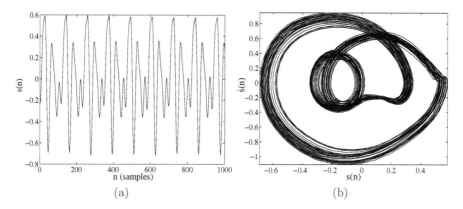

Fig. 15. (a) Time series and (b) differential embedding of the recorded signal for the vowel /o/

a least square algorithm, which here is SVD. For our present task, we set the coefficients α_i, that correspond to monomials $\frac{*}{Y}$ to zero, because such terms make numerical integration very unstable and represent only a highly restricted class of original dynamical systems. For the modeling of the vowel /o/ this yields the following differential model

$$\dot{X} = Y \; ,$$
$$\dot{Y} = Z \; ,$$
$$\begin{aligned}
\dot{Z} = &-127.7 + \frac{0.0034}{X^4} - \frac{1.35585}{X^2} - \frac{19.4471}{X} - 477.915\,X - 1100.65\,X^2- \\
&1597.75\,X^3 - 1436.2\,X^4 - 734.386\,X^5 - 154.263\,X^6 + 20.1431\,X^7+ \\
&10.8221\,X^8 - 2304.92\,Y - \frac{0.26133\,Y}{X^4} - \frac{7.45016\,Y}{X^3} - \frac{89.0811\,Y}{X^2} - \\
&\frac{583.536\,Y}{X} - 5723.88\,X\,Y - 9077.48\,X^2\,Y - 9134.39\,X^3\,Y - \\
&5627.95\,X^4\,Y - 1935.58\,X^5\,Y - 285.133\,X^6\,Y + 2044.41\,Y^2+ \\
&\frac{3.06178\,Y^2}{X^4} + \frac{52.5805\,Y^2}{X^3} + \frac{339.683\,Y^2}{X^2} + \frac{1100.29\,Y^2}{X} + 2386.52\,X\,Y^2+ \\
&1852.23\,X^2\,Y^2 + 893.248\,X^3\,Y^2 + 191.93\,X^4\,Y^2 + 6084.05\,Y^3+ \\
&\frac{28.7058\,Y^3}{X^4} + \frac{390.125\,Y^3}{X^3} + \frac{1951.32\,Y^3}{X^2} + \frac{4750.06\,Y^3}{X} + 3962.2\,X\,Y^3+ \\
&1042.75\,X^2\,Y^3 + 434.01\,Y^4 - \frac{24.9278\,Y^4}{X^4} - \frac{113.943\,Y^4}{X^3} + \frac{541.889\,Y^4}{X} + \\
&613.845\,Z + \frac{1.24638\,Z}{X^3} + \frac{23.2783\,Z}{X^2} + \frac{168.273\,Z}{X} + 1252.69\,X\,Z + \\
&1452.6\,X^2\,Z + 887.493\,X^3\,Z + 218.578\,X^4\,Z + 1148.8\,Y\,Z + \\
&\frac{3.82964\,Y\,Z}{X^3} + \frac{70.656\,Y\,Z}{X^2} + \frac{445.685\,Y\,Z}{X} + 1234.68\,X\,Y\,Z + \\
&455.848\,X^2\,Y\,Z + 1434.85\,Y^2\,Z + \frac{135.137\,Y^2\,Z}{X^3} + \frac{1035.42\,Y^2\,Z}{X^2} + \\
&\frac{2253.09\,Y^2\,Z}{X} + 55.0741\,Z^2 + \frac{3.1996\,Z^2}{X^2} + \frac{26.5625\,Z^2}{X} \; .
\end{aligned} \qquad (30)$$

The original time signal and the signal generated by integrating this model are shown in Fig. 16 (a), the according magnitude spectra are depicted in Fig. 16 (b), and the embedding of the generated signal is shown in Fig. 16 (c).

When comparing the time series of the original recording of the vowel /o/ and the integrated model in Fig. 16(a) we see a similar structure. The generated signal of the vowel /o/ sounds very unnatural, though. When looking at the

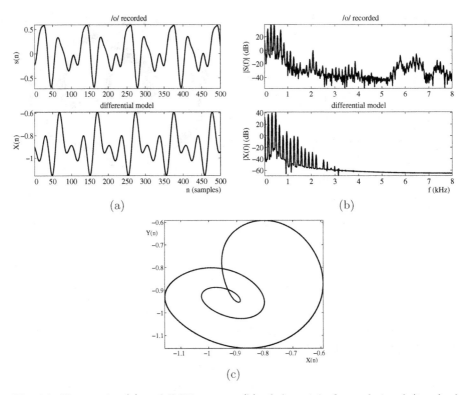

Fig. 16. Time series (a) and DFT spectra (b) of the original vowel signal (top bar) and the signal generated by the estimated differential model in (30) (bottom bar), and (c) embedding of the signal generated by the estimated differential model

power spectra in Fig. 16(b) we see, that the low frequency parts are similar, but the high frequency parts are completely missing. Also the embedding in Fig. 16(c) has only a similar structure when compared to the embedding of the original recording in Fig. 15. The embedding of the generated sound is periodic, while the original sound is not strictly periodic. A non-periodic, or even chaotic behavior of the model could be achieved by changing some of the coefficients slightly. Such a change would have to be done very carefully since this model is very sensitive to tiny changes and gets easily numerically unstable and, therefore, such investigations are postponed for future work. One way to reduce the model complexity and to enhance the quality would be to use model (30) as basis for some pruning procedure. We currently develop a Genetic Algorithm that fulfills such a task.

3.2 Delay Embedding: Genetic Algorithm Based Method

Genetic Algorithm. A genetic algorithm (GA) [56, 57] is a search algorithm that is based on natural genetics. A given problem is encoded as an array (population) of artificial strings (chromosomes). In the cases considered here, where an optimization problem has to be solved, the guesses for possible solutions are encoded. The GA is split into two parts: the first one is devoted to estimation of the time delay set and the second part is used for estimating the ODE model. In the model-selection part, different guesses for models are encoded, while in the delay-selection part, possible delay-combinations are encoded into binary strings. These chromosomes can be strings of 1's and 0's. The GA will then manipulate this representation of the solution, but not the solution itself. A GA also must have a criterion for discriminating good from bad solutions according to the fitness measure of these solutions. This criterion is used to guide the evolution towards future generations. In the case considered here, we use a complex criterion composed of different objectives that include stability of the model, topology, and, of course, similarity of the original and the generated time series.

After encoding the problem in a chromosomal manner and finding a discrimination strategy for good solutions, an initial population of encoded solutions is created. This is done by using a random number generator without any prior knowledge of possibly good solutions. For the model-selection part, it is a set of different ODE models and for the delay-selection part, it is a set of possible delay-combinations.

The evolution of this initial population towards later generations is done by applying genetic operators in an iterative process. The most common genetic operators are (a) selection, (b) recombination, and (c) mutation [56, 57]. Selection allocates greater survival to better individuals. Better solutions are preferred to worse ones. Additional new, possibly better, individuals not present in the original population have to be created. This is done via recombination and mutation. Recombination combines bits of parental solutions to form a better offspring. It combines parental traits in a novel manner. Mutation, on the other hand, modifies a single individual. It is a random walk in the neighborhood of a particular solution.

The GA proposed here is implemented in two parts to solve the given optimization problem. The algorithm is initialized by selecting a first set of delays. If no *a priori* information on the delays is available, a first set of delays can be obtained by visually inspecting the embedded attractors. The algorithm then uses the model-selection-GA to optimize a system of ODEs while the delays are kept fixed. Once the modeling error is minimized for the given delay set, the found model is fixed and the second, delay-selection-GA, is used to optimize over the delays. The process is repeated until the selected model and the delays do not change over a given number of iterations.

The flexibility of GAs allows us to design a strict and, at the same time, complex fitness criterion composed of four different objectives. The modeling error in our algorithm is defined as the least squares error weighed differentially over time to penalize later observations. The penalty for later observations is included because nonlinear systems can only be predicted within the Lyapunov time limit. Since we are working with a single time series, which is also noisy, we typically can only make predictions within the time range which are considerably less then the Lyapunov limit. We further take into account that the dynamics can be different for selected data segments. Our algorithm computes the modeling error from randomly selected data segments and the corresponding segments are integrated. A good model should also be stable when numerically integrated over long time intervals. The algorithm, therefore, automatically discards all models that do not fulfil a long-term stability criterion. Yet, the fourth optimization constraint used is the topological equivalence of the model to the original embedded data. This is implemented by comparing the topology, which we define as the density of the embedded input data with the corresponding integrated data in a two dimensional projection. The nonlinear series generated by the resulting global models not only produce the smallest point-to-point error to the original process, but also recover the topological properties of the embedded data. The GA approach allows us to implement this complex optimization criteria in a straightforward fashion.

GA for Modeling Vowel Signals. The aim here is to find the optimal ODE model for a given time series $s(n)$ and a time delay embedding, with simultaneous optimization of the embedding lags, using a GA for model selection.

We allow models with quadratic order of nonlinearity, leading to a system of three equations with a maximum of 10 coefficients in each equation:

$$\dot{x}_1 = \sum_{i=0}^{9} a_i Q_i , \quad \dot{x}_2 = \sum_{i=0}^{9} b_i Q_i , \quad \dot{x}_3 = \sum_{i=0}^{9} c_i Q_i , \quad \text{with}$$

$$Q = \{1, x_1, x_2, x_3, x_1^2, x_1 x_2, x_1 x_3, x_2^2, x_2 x_3, x_3^2\} .$$

(31)

where $x_1(n) = s(n - M_1), x_2(n) = s(n - M_2), x_3(n) = s(n - M_3)$ are delayed versions of the original input-data, and a_i, b_j, c_k are the coefficients, estimated with SVD [53]. Note, that the GA prefers models with as many coefficients a_i, b_j, c_k as possible to be equal to zero. The minimal delay is set to 0 and the maximal one is 120.

To initialize the GA an initial set of delays $M_1 = 0, M_2 = 12, M_3 = 20$ is chosen. The initial population size was set to 100. Our GA increases the population size, if for 2 generations no better individual was found and decreases the population size, if evolution was successful, but never below 100 individuals. Since the number of possible models, together with the number of possible delay combinations is huge, no absolute convergence in reasonable time can be expected. To find a reasonable model, we start the GA a couple of times and then compare the resulting models. All these models are then fed into a new GA. The best model found by the GA for the vowel signal /o/ is

$$\dot{x}_1 = 0.006 - 0.1x_2 + 0.06x_1^2 + 0.05x_1x_2 - 0.15x_1x_3 - 0.22x_2x_3 - 0.16x_3^2 ,$$
$$\dot{x}_2 = -0.011 + 0.08x_1 - 0.06x_3 + 0.05x_1^2 + 0.12x_1x_3 + 0.2x_3^2 ,$$
$$\dot{x}_3 = 0.01 + 0.15x_2 - 0.06x_3 - 0.05x_1^2 - 0.05x_2^2 .$$

(32)

This model was numerically integrated and the resulting signals for x_1, x_2 and x_3 as well as the magnitude spectra are depicted in Fig. 17, the differential embeddings are given in Fig. 18. During numerical integration the number of

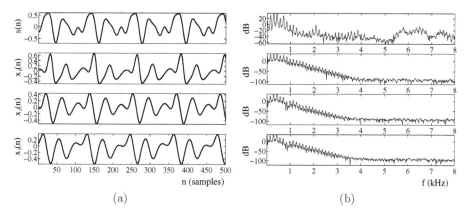

Fig. 17. Time series (a) and DFT spectra (b) of the original vowel signal $s(n)$, and the state variables $x_1(n), x_2(n)$, and $x_3(n)$ of the ODE model found by the GA

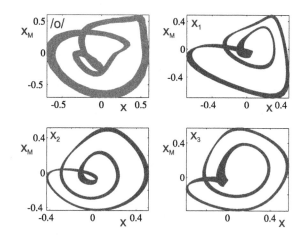

Fig. 18. Differential embeddings of the signals in Fig. 17

used digits was fixed to 6. A nonlinear dynamical system is very sensitive to small changes in the initial conditions. Trajectories with slightly different initial conditions can exponentially diverge after a few cycles. Fixing the number of used digits during numerical integration adds a random component to the system.

The reconstructed time-series as shown in Fig. 17 (a) on the lower three plots of $x_1(n)$, $x_2(n)$, and $x_3(n)$ look somehow similar to the time-series of the original recording in the upper plot. When looking at the magnitude spectra in Fig. 17 (b) missing parts in the higher frequency ranges in the lower three plots of the reconstructed signal-components can immediately be seen. The embeddings in Fig. 18 look very similar to the embedding of the original signal. To improve this model, a more general Ansatz in (31) could be used or the GA could be restricted to only models that are also part of the Ansatz library.

3.3 DDE Models

We also can use a GA to estimate a model of a given signal in form of a DDE,

$$\dot{x} = F(x_1, x_2, \dots) \ , \tag{33}$$

where $x_i = x(n - M_i)$ and $M_i \in \mathbb{N}_0$. The discrimination strategy for better models are obtained by minimizing the error of the model, i.e.,

$$f \equiv \frac{\left\langle [\dot{x} - F(x_1, x_2, \dots)]^2 \right\rangle}{\sigma_{\dot{x}}^2} \ , \tag{34}$$

where $\sigma_{\dot{x}}^2$ is the variance of the time series $\dot{x}$. The coefficients of the models are numerically estimated by a least square algorithm, which is in our case a singular value decomposition (SVD) [53]. The principal idea of minimizing a function using a GA can be found in [56].

The GA works in two steps, the delay-selection and the model-selection part, which can be described as follows: The GA depends on four modeling parameters, (i) the number of delays, n_τ, (ii) the maximal number of coefficients in the models, N_c, (iii) the order of nonlinearity, m, and (iv) the initial population size, N_p. Then a first set of delay(s) and the initial population of models are generated with a random number generator. The model-selection GA is applied and is stopped when the modeling error does not change for 5 iteration steps. The best model is selected and, starting from the initial population of delays, the delay-selection GA is applied and is stopped when the modeling error does not change for 5 iteration steps. Then the model-selection GA is applied again starting from the best models of former runs. When the modeling error does not change for 5 iteration steps again, the delay-selection GA is applied once, and so on. This alternative run of the two codes is stopped, when the modeling error remains constant for both parts of the GAs.

The choice of the population-size is a critical point for a fast convergence to the global minimum of the solution space and should be related to the number of possible combinations of solutions. After some runs of our code, we found empirically that 0.1% of all possible combinations of solutions is a good choice for the population size. Furthermore, we do not keep the population size constant, but change it dynamically during a run. For instance, when the new generation has a better winner which is the same as in the former generation, the population size can be reduced. This could mean that the solution is possibly trapped in a local minimum. With a larger population size the escape from local minima towards the global one is accelerated.

To find a good DDE model to characterize speech signals we first run this GA on a set of 1000 randomly chosen speech signal segments of 1200 data points each. Here we do not aim to find a model that can be used for synthesis of speech, but for characterizing different features of the data. We therefore restrict our search to models with up to five terms and up to three delays where smaller models are preferred in the algorithm.

Our finding is that three-delay models have on average about the same modeling error as two-delay models and therefore we choose to use only two delays for our analysis. Furthermore a three-term model seems to characterize as many features as more term models. Therefore we use the three-term model that is the statistical winner of this run. Note that this model was good for all different kinds of sounds and sound combinations since the signals for this run were randomly chosen from a set of speech signals from different speakers and sentences.

For our further analysis we use the DDE model with two delays,

$$\dot{x} = a_1 x_1 + a_2 x_2 + a_3 x_1 x_2 \ . \tag{35}$$

The delays are adjusted by a global search procedure, a GA (genetic algorithm) for windows of L_W points in the signal such that the least square error of (35) is minimal. The choice of L_W tunes if we want to look at more or less global effects. For example emotional expressions in speech can be better seen if L_W is larger and on the other hand the segmentations into phonemes requires a smaller L_W. For the optimal delays of each window the coefficients $a_{1,2,3}$ are computed directly using SVD (singular value decomposition). Our set of features for classification will then be the delays $M_{1,2}$, the coefficients $a_{1,2,3}$, and the error ρ.

In Fig. 19 the sentences "My dog and my neighbor's cat are hiding under the chair. They are extremely good friends." were analyzed by such a procedure. The window length L_W was 1200 points which corresponds to about 6 characteristic cycles.

Several things can be seen immediately:
- delays $M_{1,2}$:
  The bigger one of the two delays, M_2 has regions where it is somehow constant for some time. The mean value and its deviation of these regions is characteristic for the speaker. Female speakers have a lower mean value than male speakers. The variance around the mean is characteristic for the speaker. It expresses the melody of speech. There is a direct connection to the fundamental frequency F_0.
  The smaller one of the two delays, M_1 can sometimes jump up to the second delay. This is a characteristics for emotions.
- coefficients $a_{1,2,3}$:
  For harmonic parts of the signal the two linear coefficients have symmetric values, $a_1 \approx -a_2$ and the nonlinear coefficient is $a_3 \approx 0$. This is the case for vowels, nasals and approximants.
  In some regions of the signal one of the coefficients, a_1 has significantly smaller values, the second linear coefficient, a_2 is not correlated to a_2, and the nonlinear coefficient a_3 has nonzero values. This is the characteristics for fricatives and affricates.
- error ρ:
  The error is small for voiced sounds with a harmonic structure – such as vowels, nasals, and approximants – and large for unvoiced sounds, like fricatives and affricates.

Figure 19 shows the speech signal, the delays, the coefficients $a_{1,2,3}$, and the least square error. In the signal plot (top bar) of Fig. 19 the segments highlighted in darker grayshading denote plosives or unvoiced fricatives. They are

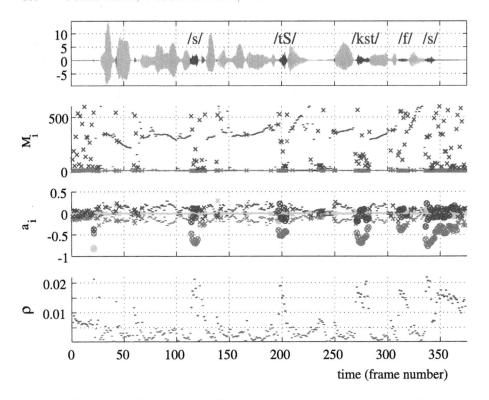

Fig. 19. Time series of the sentences "My dog and my neighbor's cat are hiding under the chair. They are extremely good friends", optimized delays $M_{1,2}$, coefficients $a_{1,2,3}$, and the least square error ρ of (35)

characterized by a coefficient $a_1 < -0.3$ and an error $\rho > 0.005$. Harmonic sounds are characterized by a low error ($\rho < 0.005$), symmetric linear coefficients ($a_1 \approx -a_2$), and delays that are around the characteristic value for the speaker.

Figure 20 shows the part of Fig. 19 where the word "extremely" is spoken. The previously discussed characteristics are very clear in these plots.

This technique can also be used to segment speech signals into phonemes. For our modeling techniques different samples of certain vowels could be selected by such a DDE model and then fed into our modeling algorithms of Secs. 3.1 and 3.2. This could yield more realistic models than starting from recordings of sustained speech sounds.

4   Summary and Conclusion

The identification of a nonlinear oscillator based on a Takens embedding for the re-generation of stationary speech signals requires – besides an adequate

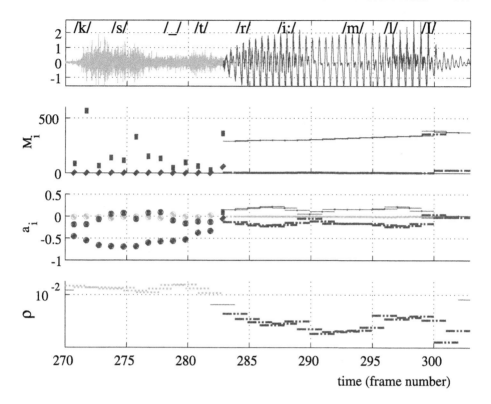

Fig. 20. Part of Fig. 19 where the word "extremely" is spoken

choice of embedding parameters – a careful modeling of the nonlinear function characterizing the dynamics of the signal trajectories in embedding phase space.

For the oscillator model based on a time delay embedding some form of regularization of the nonlinear function model used in the oscillator has to be applied. We found that the Bayesian approach to determining weights and regularization parameter of an RBF network is a computationally equivalent and more robust alternative to cross-validation. Besides the automatic determination of adequate regularization the Bayesian approach also gives an accurate estimate for the power of an additive noise-like signal component. An extension of the Bayesian algorithm, the relevance vector machine, additionally allows for pruning of RBF basis functions, thus reducing the complexity of the nonlinear function model at only minimal impairment of prediction accuracy or oscillator stability.

The number of vowel signals that can be stably re-synthesized with the oscillator model is substantially increased when the model is complemented by inverse filtering. Up to now, vowels with a complicated trajectory structure of the full speech signal often could only be stably re-synthesized using a high embedding dimension, a specific set of embedding parameters, or a specific structure of the nonlinear function model. With a simple inverse filtering approach using linear prediction and low-pass filtering and a Bayesian trained RBF network more than half of the vowel signals in our database can be stably re-synthesized using one and the same low-dimensional embedding, since an open loop trajectory is attained for all vowels.

For the additional regeneration of the noise-like component in speech signals we propose the oscillator-plus-noise model, which is able to generate a pitch-synchronous modulation and individual spectral shaping of the noise-like signal component, with the modulation envelope and spectral characteristics automatically learned from the training speech signal.

The parameterization by an RBF model (and all other nonlinear function models referenced in Sect. 2) is, however, not directly related to physical parameters of the speech production process, nor to higher level speech parameters such as fundamental frequency. This fact hinders the use of the oscillator model in a speech synthesizer, since the robust control of fundamental frequency, for example, is still an unsolved problem. Models more closely related to the physical process of speech production are lumped mass-spring-damper models like the two-mass model by Ishizaka and Flanagan [58] and its descendants, which are, however, more difficult to control in terms of higher level speech parameters.

Another step towards a parameterization of the nonlinear oscillator in a physically sensible way is the system modeling by differential equations based on a differential embedding. Here the selection of polynomial terms from an Ansatz library provides the means for a computationally traceable and robust modeling. A three-dimensional differential model for a stationary vowel signal, as given by (30), for example, captures the signal dynamics with a number of 64 parameters.

A further reduction of system complexity is achieved by the application of a genetic algorithm for model structure selection. For modeling a vowel signal the GA with fitness criteria including long-term stability and topological equivalence may choose a model with only 18 parameters, as given by (32), from all possible models based on a certain three dimensional embedding. The GA can also be used for optimizing low complexity nonlinear models for speech analysis, where, in the example given, the distinction of voiced and unvoiced speech, and the identification of an optimal embedding delay for prediction related to the fundamental frequency is demonstrated.

The benefit due to including inverse filtering, the proper re-generation of the noise-like signal part with an additional non-deterministic system, as well as the identification of different optimal model structures for voiced and unvoiced phonemes and of an optimal embedding delay related to the fundamental period point at the fact that for the application of oscillator models to general purpose speech synthesis – besides robust and elaborate nonlinear function identification methods – a broad spectrum of knowledge from phonetics and speech science is necessary. Based on such knowledge the further development of nonlinear oscillator models for speech analysis and synthesis is on a promising path to being employed as a standard tool for speech technology.

References

1. Kubin, G.: Nonlinear processing of speech. In Kleijn, W.B., Paliwal, K.K., eds.: Speech Coding and Synthesis. Elsevier, Amsterdam etc. (1995) 557–610
2. Kubin, G.: Synthesis and coding of continuous speech with the nonlinear oscillator model. In: Proceedings of the International Conference on Acoustics, Speech, and Signal Processing, Atlanta, GA (1996) 267–270
3. Kubin, G., Kleijn, W.B.: Time-scale modification of speech based on a nonlinear oscillator model. In: Proceedings of the International Conference on Acoustics, Speech, and Signal Processing. Volume 1., Adelaide, South Australia (1994) 453–456
4. Sauer, T.: A noise reduction method for signals from nonlinear systems. Physica D **52** (1992) 193–201
5. Hegger, R., Kantz, H., Matassini, L.: Noise reduction for human speech signals by local projection in embedding spaces. IEEE Transactions on Circuits and Systems **48** (2001) 1454–1461
6. Terez, D.E.: Robust pitch determination using nonlinear state-space embedding. In: Proceedings of the International Conference on Acoustics, Speech, and Signal Processing. Volume 1., Orlando (FL), USA (2002) 345–348
7. Mann, I., McLaughlin, S.: A nonlinear algorithm for epoch marking in speech signals using Poincaré maps. In: Proceedings of the European Signal Processing Conference. Volume 2. (1998) 701–704
8. Lindgren, A.C., Johnson, M.T., Povinelli, R.J.: Joint frequency domain and reconstructed phase space features for speech recognition. In: Proceedings of the International Conference on Acoustics, Speech, and Signal Processing. Volume 1., Montreal, Quebec, Canada (2004) 533–536
9. Birgmeier, M.: A fully Kalman-trained radial basis function network for nonlinear speech modeling. In: Proceedings of the IEEE International Conference on Neural Networks, Perth, Australia (1995) 259–264
10. Kubin, G.: Synthesis and coding of continuous speech with the nonlinear oscillator model. In: Proceedings of the International Conference on Acoustics, Speech, and Signal Processing. Volume 1., Atlanta (GA) (1996) 267–270
11. Haas, H., Kubin, G.: A multi-band nonlinear oscillator model for speech. In: Proceedings of the 32nd Asilomar Conference on Signals, Systems and Computers, Pacific Grove, CA (1998)
12. Mann, I., McLaughlin, S.: Stable speech synthesis using recurrent radial basis functions. In: Proceedings of the European Conference on Speech Communication and Technology. Volume 5., Budapest, Hungary (1999) 2315–2318
13. Narasimhan, K., Príncipe, J.C., Childers, D.G.: Nonlinear dynamic modeling of the voiced excitation for improved speech synthesis. In: Proceedings of the International Conference on Acoustics, Speech, and Signal Processing, Phoenix, Arizona (1999) 389–392
14. Rank, E., Kubin, G.: Nonlinear synthesis of vowels in the LP residual domain with a regularized RBF network. In Mira, J., Prieto, A., eds.: Lecture Notes in Computer Science. Volume 2085., Springer (2001) 746–753, part II
15. Mann, I., McLaughlin, S.: Synthesising natural-sounding vowels using a nonlinear dynamical model. Signal Processing **81** (2001) 1743–1756
16. Rank, E.: Application of Bayesian trained RBF networks to nonlinear time-series modeling. Signal Processing **83** (2003) 1393–1410

17. Takens, F.: Detecting strange attractors in turbulence. Lecture Notes in Mathematics **898** (1981) 366
18. Sauer, T., Yorke, J.A., Casdagli, M.: Embedology. Journal of Statistical Physics **65** (1991) 579–616
19. Haykin, S., Príncipe, J.: Making sense of a complex world. IEEE Signal Processing Magazine **15** (1998) 66–81
20. Judd, K., Mees, A.: Embedding as a modeling problem. Physica D **120** (1998) 273–286
21. Bernhard, H.P.: The Mutual Information Function and its Application to Signal Processing. PhD thesis, Vienna University of Technology (1997)
22. Hegger, R., Kantz, H., Schreiber, T.: Practical implementation of nonlinear time series methods: The TISEAN package. CHAOS **9** (1999) 413–435
23. Bernhard, H.P., Kubin, G.: Detection of chaotic behaviour in speech signals using Fraser's mutual information algorithm. In: Proc. 13th GRETSI Symp. Signal and Image Process., Juan-les-Pins, France (1991) 1301–1311
24. Mann, I.: An Investigation of Nonlinear Speech Synthesis and Pitch Modification Techniques. PhD thesis, University of Edinburgh (1999)
25. Rank, E., Kubin, G.: Nonlinear synthesis of vowels in the LP residual domain with a regularized RBF network. In Mira, J., Prieto, A., eds.: Lecture Notes in Computer Science. Volume 2085. Springer (2001) 746–753, part II
26. Li, J., Zhang, B., Lin, F.: Nonlinear speech model based on support vector machine and wavelet transform. In: Proceedings of the 15th IEEE International Conference on Tools with Artificial Intelligence (ICTAI'03), Sacramento, CA (2003) 259–264
27. Haas, H., Kubin, G.: A multi-band nonlinear oscillator model for speech. In: Proc. 32nd Asilomar Conference on Signals, Systems, and Computers, Pacific Grove, CA (1998)
28. Townshend, B.: Nonlinear prediction of speech. In: Proceedings of the International Conference on Acoustics, Speech, and Signal Processing. (1991) 425–428
29. Tikhonov, A.N., Arsenin, V.Y.: Solutions of Ill-posed Problems. W.H. Winston (1977)
30. Poggio, T., Girosi, F.: A theory of networks for approximation and learning. A.I. Memo 1140, Massachusetts Institute of Technology (1989)
31. Stone, M.: Cross-validation choice and assessment of statistical predictions. Journal of the Royal Statistical Society B **36** (1974) 111–147
32. MacKay, D.J.: Bayesian interpolation. Neural Computation **4** (1992) 415–447
33. MacKay, D.J.: A practical Bayesian framework for backprop networks. Neural Computation **4** (1992) 448–472
34. MacKay, D.J.: The evidence framework applied to classification networks. Neural Computation **4** (1992) 698–714
35. Dempster, A.P., Laird, N.M., Rubin, D.B.: Maximum likelyhood from incomplete data via the EM algorithm. Journal of the Royal Statistical Society B **39** (1977) 1–38
36. Tipping, M.E.: Sparse Bayesian learning and the relevance vector machine. Journal of Machine Learning Research **1** (2001) 211–244
37. Fant, G., Liljencrants, J., Lin, Q.G.: A four parameter model of glottal flow. Quarterly Progress Status Report 4, Speech Transmission Laboratory/Royal Institute of Technology, Stockholm, Sweden (1985)
38. Köppl, H., Kubin, G., Paoli, G.: Bayesian methods for sparse RLS adaptive filters. In: Thirty-Seventh IEEE Asilomar Conference on Signals, Systems and Computers. Volume 2. (2003) 1273–1277

39. Kubin, G., Atal, B.S., Kleijn, W.B.: Performance of noise excitation for unvoiced speech. In: Proc. IEEE Workshop on Speech Coding for Telecommunication, St.Jovite, Québec, Canada (1993) 1–2
40. Holm, S.: Automatic generation of mixed excitation in a linear predictive speech synthesizer. In: Proceedings of the International Conference on Acoustics, Speech, and Signal Processing. Volume 6., Atlanta (GA) (1981) 118–120
41. Hermes, D.J.: Synthesis of breathy vowels: Some research methods. Speech Communication **10** (1991) 497–502
42. Skoglund, J., Kleijn, W.B.: On the significance of temporal masking in speech coding. In: Proceedings of the International Conference on Spoken Language Processing. Volume 5., Sydney (1998) 1791–1794
43. Jackson, P.J., Shadle, C.H.: Aero-acoustic modelling of voiced and unvoiced fricatives based on MRI data. In: Proceedings of 5th Speech Production Seminar, Kloster Seeon, Germany (2000) 185–188
44. Jackson, P.J., Shadle, C.H.: Frication noise modulated by voicing, as revealed by pitch-scaled decomposition. Journal of the Acoustic Society of America **108** (2000) 1421–1434
45. Stylianou, Y., Laroche, J., Moulines, E.: High-quality speech modification based on a harmonic + noise model. In: Proceedings of the European Conference on Speech Communication and Technology, Madrid, Spain (1995) 451–454
46. Bailly, G.: A parametric harmonic+noise model. In Keller, E., Bailly, G., Monaghan, A., Terken, J., Huckvale, M., eds.: Improvements in Speech Synthesis. Wiley (2002) 22–38
47. Rank, E., Kubin, G.: An oscillator-plus-noise model for speech synthesis. Speech Communication (2005) Accepted for publication.
48. Lu, H.L., Smith, III, J.O.: Glottal source modeling for singing voice. In: Proc. International Computer Music Conference, Berlin, Germany (2000) 90–97
49. Lainscsek, C., Letellier, C., Schürrer, F.: Ansatz library for global modeling with a structure selection. Physical Review E **64** (2001) 016206:1–15
50. Lainscsek, C., Letellier, C., Gorodnitsky, I.: Global modeling of the Rössler system from the z-variable. Physics Letters A **314(5-6)** (2003) 409–127
51. Judd, K., Mees, A.: On selecting models for nonlinear time series. Physica D **82** (1995) 426–444
52. Gouesbet, G., Letellier, C.: Global vector-field reconstruction by using a multivariate polynomial l_2 approximation on nets. Phys. Rev. E **49** (1994) 4955
53. Press, W., Flannery, B., Teukolsky, S., Vetterling, W.: Numerical Recipes in C. Cambridge University Press (1990)
54. Lainscsek, C., Gorodnitsky, I.: Ansatz libraries for systems with quadratic and cubic non-linearities. http://cloe.ucsd.edu/claudia/poster_DD_2002.pdf (2002)
55. Eichhorn, R., Linz, S., Hänggi, P.: Transformations of nonlinear dynamical systems to jerky motion and its application to minimal chaotic flows. Physical Review E **58 (6)** (1998) 7151–7164
56. Goldberg, D.: Genetic Algorithms in Search, Optimization and Machine Learning. Addison-Wesley (1998)
57. Holland, J.H.: Adaptation in natural and artificial systems. MIT Press (1992)
58. Ishizaka, K., Flanagan, J.L.: Synthesis of voiced sounds from a two-mass model of the vocal cords. Bell Systems Technical Journal **51** (1972) 1233–1267

Speech Modelling
Based on Acoustic-to-Articulatory Mapping

Jean Schoentgen

Laboratory of Experimental Phonetics, Université Libre de Bruxelles, Brussels, Belgium
National Fund for Scientific Research, Belgium

Abstract. Acoustic-to-articulatory mapping is the determination of the parameters of a model of the vocal tract so that its first few eigenfrequencies agree with a set of observed formant frequencies. The article presents an analytical method for acoustic-to-articulatory mapping, which is generic. The plausibility of computed vocal tract shapes is examined and methodological problems as well as possible applications are considered.

Introduction

Acoustic-to-articulatory mapping refers to the determination of the parameters of a model of the vocal tract so that the first few eigenfrequencies agree with a set of observed formant frequencies. This article is a tutorial presentation of an acoustic-to-articulatory transform. It takes into account recent developments of a generic mapping that has been presented elsewhere [27]. Recent developments include the increase of the numerical stability of the inverse mapping, a generalization of the kinetic constraints to arbitrary-order rates of deformation of the vocal tract, structural constraints that force model parameters to stay within fixed intervals, as well as speaker normalisation. The results are preliminary. They concern the demonstration of the numerical stability of the inverse mapping as well as a discussion of the plausibility of the shapes inferred with the aid of several vocal tract models.

One reason for involving models in acoustic-to-articulatory transforms is that a given speech signal does not uniquely define vocal tract shape. A model with a small number of parameters, together with additional acoustic or anatomical constraints, may therefore provide a simplified framework within which the tract shape is specified and so decrease the number of possible tract shapes that are compatible with a given set of formants.

More precisely, the article is devoted to formant-to-area mapping, which is the inference, based on observed formant frequencies, of the parameters of a model of the area function. The area function relates the cross-section of the vocal tract to the distance from the glottis. Indeed, one may distinguish vocal tract models that characterize the contour of the area function from models the parameters of which are the positions of the articulators in the mid-sagittal plane. Acoustic-to-articulatory or formant-to-area transforms are hereafter also called acoustic-to-geometric mapping.

The text is organized as follows. The Introduction section gives an overview of existing approaches to acoustic-to-articulatory mapping, followed by a discussion of possible motivations for attempting the conversion of acoustic into geometric data. The Methods section presents the steps involved in one such inverse transformation. The Experiments section presents, for a same corpus of speech sounds, vocal tract

G. Chollet et al. (Eds.): Nonlinear Speech Modeling, LNAI 3445, pp. 114–135, 2005.

shapes calculated via inverse mapping for several vocal tract models. For each speech sound, the calculated shapes are compared to the original shapes observed via nuclear magnetic resonance imaging. The Discussion section concerns the numerical stability of the mapping as well as the physiological and phonetic plausibility of the inferred tract shapes.

Acoustic-to-articulatory inversion methods have been deployed in the framework of most automatic speech processing tasks, such as speech coding, speech analysis and synthesis, as well as automatic speech and speaker recognition. Often, their authors have concluded that acoustic-to-articulatory inversion methods perform well compared to competing techniques. But, acoustic-to-geometric transforms do not belong to the mainstream in automatic speech processing at present.

Table I summarizes published studies. This overview is based on Ciocea *et al.* [36] and Krstulovic [35]. They suggest classifying acoustic-to-geometric transforms according to technique: codebooks and table look-ups, constrained optimization, pattern recognition, including artificial neural nets, signal modelling, stochastic modelling and statistical inference, or analytical techniques.

Table 1. Published studies involving acoustic-to-geometric mapping; LPC: linear predictive coding; ANN: artificial neural nets; SVD: singular value decomposition

Mermelstein, 1967	Fourier exp.	Shirai et al., 1993	ANN
Schroeder, 1967	Fourier exp.	Rahim, 1993	ANN
Wakita, 1973	LPC	Yu, 1993	Codebook
Wakita et al., 1975	LPC	Jospa et al., 1994	Variationl form.
Ladefogd et al., 1978	Codebook	Deng et al., 1994	Stochastic mod.
Atal et al., 1978	Codebook	Schroeter et al., 1994	Codebook
Wakita, 1979	LPC	Ramsay, 1996	Stochastic mod.
Flanagan et al., 1980	Optimization	Erler et al., 1996	Stochastic mod.
Shirai et al., 1980	Codebook	Hodgen, 1996	Stochastic mod.
Levinson et al., 1983	Optimization	Schoentg. et al., 1997	SVD
Charpentier, 1984	Codebook	Mokhtari, 1998	Fourier exp.
Scaife, 1989	LPC	Laprie et al., 1998	Variationl form.
Atal et al., 1989	ANN	Ouni et al., 2000	Codebook
Schroeter et al., 1989	Codebook	Mokhtari et al., 2000	Fourier exp.
Rahim, 1990	ANN	Richardsn et al., 2000	Stochastic mod.
Soquet et al., 1990	ANN	Stephnsn et al., 2000	Stochastic mod.
Shirai et al., 1991	ANN	Frankel et al., 2001	Stochastic mod.
Laboissre et al., 1991	ANN	Krstulovic, 2001	LPC
Prado, 1992	Optimization		

Inversion by table look-up uses paired data that sample plausible combinations of articulatory shapes and acoustic features [5-6,9,11,14,21,30,57]. Inversion consists in looking up observed acoustic data and retaining the corresponding articulatory features as candidates for further processing that uses constraints for selecting one candidate among many possible ones. Artificial neural nets and other general-purpose pattern recognizers may be trained so that they compress codebook data into a map that outputs plausible articulatory shapes when acoustic data are input [13,15-18,20,51].

Inversion by (constrained) optimization consists in letting a general-purpose optimizer manoeuvre the parameters of a model till observed and modelled acoustic data agree to within a given tolerance. Usually, the path followed by the optimizer within the multi-parameter landscape defined by the cost function is constrained by assumptions about the plausibility of tract shapes and their movements from one target to another [8,10,19].

According to Krstulovic [35], stochastic approaches to acoustic-to-geometric mapping include mixture density networks, mixtures of dynamical systems, hidden Markov models, maximum likelihood continuity mapping, as well as Bayesian networks. These approaches have mainly been developed in the context of automatic speech recognition [23-26,32-34].

Signal models that are based on linear predictive coding take the form of linear filters, which are fitted to recorded signal samples. These filters may be transformed into matching concatenations of cylindrical acoustic tubes of equal length but unequal cross-section. Such models "explain" the delays contained in the filter as the travel in a finite time of the signal through concatenated loss-free cylinders, which may be interpreted as stylized vocal tract shapes [3-4,7,12,31,35].

Analytic methods, finally, involve the mathematical modelling of the physical relation between geometric and acoustic parameters and the transformation of these relations so that they may be inverted. Analytic methods have been based, for instance, on variational formulations, on expansions of the vocal tract shape in truncated Fourier series, or on linearization and singular value decomposition [1-2,22,27-29].

Linearization and singular value decomposition are used in the context of the present study. This approach belongs to the analytical methods because it is based on a physically motivated map that predicts formant frequency increments from vocal tract parameter increments. A reason for presenting this method in the context of a summer school devoted to nonlinear speech processing is that it may be suited not only to formant-to-area mapping, but also to other direct or inverse nonlinear problems.

The title of the chapter refers to acoustic-to-geometric mapping as a speech-modelling tool for reasons that are discussed here. Published data as well as results that are presented hereafter suggest that acoustic-to-geometric inversion is not able to infer under all circumstances vocal tract shapes that are anatomically or phonetically accurate. This raises questions about the purpose of formant-to-area or acoustic-to-articulatory inversion in general. Published studies suggest that, in an applied framework, calculated shapes are often used as geometric equivalents, that is, abstract but plausible, smoothly time-evolving shapes that represent speech properties geometrically rather than spectrally. Conditions are that the calculated shapes reproduce observed acoustic data accurately and evolve smoothly; that is, small acoustic differences are transformed into small geometric differences. The inversion method that is presented hereafter has been developed to satisfy these criteria. The precision of the agreement between observed formant frequencies and eigenfrequencies of calculated tract shapes may indeed be guaranteed to be 1 Hz at least.

Generally speaking, geometric equivalents ease the interpretation of formant data. One reason is that the outcomes of a statistical processing of formant and tract shape data are not equivalent. This is because tract geometry and eigenfrequencies are related nonlinearly. Acoustically equivalent tract shapes may therefore be better suited for statistical processing than raw formant data. Preliminary studies that illustrate such applications of formant-to-area mapping can be found in [37] and [38].

One other application that may exploit the possibilities offered by acoustic-to-geometric conversion is the fusion of articulatory with acoustic data. At present, it is possible to record acoustic as well as articulatory data; the latter being obtained non-invasively. But, more often than not, articulatory data thus obtained are incomplete or not in perfect synchrony with the acoustic data. The interpretation of the co-existing acoustic and articulatory data would therefore be easier in the framework of a common description. Geometric equivalents of the acoustic data may offer this joint framework if their acquisition is constrained by the available articulatory data. The results are tract models that optimally integrate acoustic and geometric information. Preliminary studies of the fusion of acoustic and articulatory data published by Fant [39] and Story [40] can be found in Ciocea *et al.* [36].

Methods

Generally speaking, a map is a generalized function with multiple inputs and outputs. Maps have been used to describe speech production formally. The relations between muscle lengths and articulatory positions, articulatory positions and cross-sections of the vocal tract as well as cross-sections and formant frequencies can be understood as maps, e.g. [41]. Here, these maps are called direct because their inputs may be interpreted as causes and their outputs as effects. They may therefore be postulated to exist based on the observation that speech production takes places and that the maps' input and output can be recorded.

This article is devoted to formant-to-area mapping, which is an inverse problem because the corresponding map turns cause (tract shape) into effect and effect (eigenfrequencies) into cause. The inverse map can therefore not be hypothesized to exist based on any observations about speech production. Indeed, most of the problems that are discussed hereafter only come to attention because of the ambiguity of the inverse link between formant frequencies and tract shape. A list of problems that must be solved are the following.

First, geometric and acoustic models must be chosen that enable describing the contour of the area function as well as the propagation of an acoustic wave within the vocal tract. These models implicitly relate vocal tract geometry and eigenfrequencies. Intuitively speaking, the eigenfrequencies of a vocal tract model are the frequencies of the free vibrations of the acoustic field given the boundary conditions at the glottis, vocal tract walls and lips.

Second, A direct map must be formulated that explicitly relates cross-sections and formant frequencies. This map is based on the implicit function that has been obtained at the previous step, It is defined locally in time and the direct mapping of a given area function onto the eigenfrequencies must therefore be carried out iteratively.

Third, the direct map must be inverted. At this step, the inverse map has a nominal existence only. One reason is that the number of observed formant frequencies is necessarily less than the number of parameters that describe the tract shape; infinitely many different tract shapes may therefore agree with the observed formant frequencies.

Fourth, additional constraints must consequently be found that enable the direct map to be inverted actually. This means that one tract shape must be chosen among the infinitely possible ones that agree with observed data.

Fifth, once a single-solution inverse mapping has been carried out, the agreement between modelled eigenfrequencies and observed formant frequencies is asserted. The reason is that the direct map is a local approximation of an implicitly defined function, which may cause observed formants and calculated eigenfrequencies to differ. Errors must be reduced till modelled and observed frequencies agree to within a fixed tolerance, to avoid accumulating errors during iteration.

Sixth, the inverse mapping must be initialized. The reason is that the inversion is done iteratively.

Seventh, at this stage the model parameters are free to assume arbitrary values. However, for physiological as well as physical reasons, most parameters are required to stay within plausible intervals. For instance, lengths as well as cross-sections are positive and the maximum cross-section of the laryngo-pharyngeal cavity is narrower than the maximum cross-section elsewhere in the vocal tract. One may therefore wish to insert structural constraints in the inverse map that force calculated parameters to remain within pre-defined intervals.

Eight, for reasons that are given later, the direct and inverse maps only enable determining vocal tract parameters that evolve with time. Static parameters, such as the average vocal tract length, must be determined via speaker normalisation that transforms observed formant frequencies so that length differences between a speaker's vocal tract and the tract model are compensated for.

For tutorial reasons, the most straightforward solutions to each of the listed problems are presented hereafter. The objective is to illustrate, as simply as possible, an approach to inverse mapping that is generic. Also, solutions to problems number seven and eight are omitted due to lack of space. The method can be applied without structural constraints or speaker normalisation, even though these are desirable options [27].

Model

The models are spectral. That is, they relate cross-sections and lengths of sub-sections of the tract model to the eigenfrequencies. The simplest possible sub-section consists in a single tubelet that is a right cylinder. Several may be concatenated to imitate a given vocal tract shape.

Acoustically speaking, such a cylinder is represented by a 2 by 2 transfer matrix (1) that relates acoustic pressures and velocities at the cylinder input and output. The symbols designate the following quantities: p (acoustic pressure), v (acoustic velocity), j (imaginary constant), ρ (density of air), c (speed of sound), a (tubelet cross-section), l (tubelet length) and ω (angular velocity) [51].

$$\begin{pmatrix} p_{in} \\ v_{in} \end{pmatrix} = \begin{vmatrix} \cos\dfrac{\omega l}{c} & \dfrac{j\rho c}{a}\sin\dfrac{\omega l}{c} \\ \dfrac{ja}{\rho c}\sin\dfrac{\omega l}{c} & \cos\dfrac{\omega l}{c} \end{vmatrix} \begin{pmatrix} p_{out} \\ v_{out} \end{pmatrix} \tag{1}$$

The total transfer matrix (2) of a concatenation of cylindrical tubelets that approximate a vocal tract shape can be obtained by multiplying the elementary transfer matrices (1). The result is a global 2 by 2 matrix that relates the acoustic pressures and velocities at the lips and glottis [51].

$$\begin{pmatrix} P_{glottis} \\ v_{glottis} \end{pmatrix} = \begin{bmatrix} A & B \\ C & D \end{bmatrix} \begin{pmatrix} P_{lips} \\ v_{lips} \end{pmatrix} \tag{2}$$

The eigenfrequency conditions, i.e. the physical conditions that determine the frequencies at which the tube-internal acoustic field vibrates freely, are that the acoustic velocity is zero at the glottis and the acoustic pressure zero at the lips. Inserting these conditions leads to $D = 0$. In practice, matrix element D involves physical constants such as density of air and speed of sound, vocal tract parameters such as tubelet cross-sections and lengths, as well as the eigenfrequencies that are all the values of frequency ω for which expression D is zero once the shape parameters are given.

Losses

Transfer matrix (1) is lossless. That is, losses owing to sound radiation at the lips and glottis, vocal tract wall vibration as well as to friction along the walls and heat conduction through the walls have not been considered. An earlier study has shown that the losses that affect formant frequencies most are the acoustic radiation at the lips and vocal tract wall vibration [36]. The acoustic radiation at the lips is taken into account by adding a corrective length to the total tract length and the wall vibration by adding a corrective term to the speed of sound or to the first formant [42-45].

Direct Map

Formally, relation $D = 0$ implicitly maps the vocal tract shape onto the formant frequencies. In practice, these are found by inserting lengths, cross-sections as well as physical constants, and numerically searching for all frequency values that zero expression D. This search is systematic and guarantees that all eigenfrequencies of the model are found.

The implicitly defined dependence of the model frequencies on the model parameters can be made explicit via the chain rule. Deriving $D = 0$ with respect to time yields the following set of equations, one equation per formant F_j. Symbol P_i designates model parameters that evolve in time, symbol t designates time and M the number of time-variable parameters.

$$\sum_{i=1}^{M} \left(\frac{\partial D}{\partial P_i} \right) \left(\frac{dP_i}{dt} \right) + \left(\frac{\partial D}{\partial F_j} \right) \left(\frac{dF_j}{dt} \right) = 0 \tag{3}$$

The former expression is best understood once it is rewritten in matrix form (5) and derivatives with respect to time are replaced by increments (4).

$$\Delta P_i = \frac{dP_i}{dt} \Delta t$$

$$\Delta F_j = \frac{dF_j}{dt} \Delta t \tag{4}$$

Hereafter, the number of time-variable model parameters is assumed to be equal to M and the number of observed formants equal to 3.

$$
\begin{bmatrix}
\dfrac{\frac{\partial D}{\partial P_1}}{\frac{\partial D}{\partial F_1}} & \dfrac{\frac{\partial D}{\partial P_2}}{\frac{\partial D}{\partial F_1}} & \cdots & \dfrac{\frac{\partial D}{\partial P_M}}{\frac{\partial D}{\partial F_1}} \\[3ex]
\dfrac{\frac{\partial D}{\partial P_1}}{\frac{\partial D}{\partial F_2}} & \dfrac{\frac{\partial D}{\partial P_2}}{\frac{\partial D}{\partial F_2}} & \cdots & \dfrac{\frac{\partial D}{\partial P_M}}{\frac{\partial D}{\partial F_2}} \\[3ex]
\dfrac{\frac{\partial D}{\partial P_1}}{\frac{\partial D}{\partial F_3}} & \dfrac{\frac{\partial D}{\partial P_2}}{\frac{\partial D}{\partial F_3}} & \cdots & \dfrac{\frac{\partial D}{\partial P_M}}{\frac{\partial D}{\partial F_3}}
\end{bmatrix}
\begin{pmatrix} \Delta P_1 \\ \Delta P_2 \\ \cdots \\ \Delta P_M \end{pmatrix}
= -\begin{pmatrix} \Delta F_1 \\ \Delta F_2 \\ \Delta F_3 \end{pmatrix}
\tag{5}
$$

The matrix elements may be determined by computing analytically or by estimating numerically the ratios that contain derivatives of D. An alternative consists in re-interpreting the matrix elements via implicit differentiation [55]. This enables equating the matrix elements to the partial derivatives of the formant frequencies with respect to the model parameters.

$$
\frac{\partial F_j}{\partial P_i} \approx -\frac{\frac{\partial D}{\partial P_i}}{\frac{\partial D}{\partial F_j}}
\tag{6}
$$

The numerical estimation of matrix elements (6) may be easier because it omits implicit function D and ratios of ratios. Formula (5) is however better suited for computing matrix elements analytically [27].

The local, linear, explicit, direct expression (5) maps increments of the model parameters onto increments of the formant frequencies. Map (5) rests on the Taylor expansion (4) of the movement of the model parameters over time. The map is therefore valid for short time intervals over which the matrix elements can be assumed to be constant. These must therefore be (re)estimated for each small increment ΔP of the model parameters. The smaller these increments are, the more precise are the estimates via (5) of the increments ΔF of the formant frequencies. The formant frequencies are therefore calculated iteratively with the previous formant values and the present formant increments.

$$
F_{i,t_{k+1}} = F_{i,t_k} + \Delta F_i
\tag{7}
$$

Inverse Map

In the context of inverse mapping, the formant frequency increments are observed and the model parameter increments computed. This computation formally involves inverting map (5). Mathematically speaking, this is not possible because the matrix is usually singular [46]. This is because the number of model parameters must be greater than the number of observed formants in vocal tract models that enable controlling the first few formant frequencies independently. The number of observed formants is three or four at most.

This suggests computing the pseudo-inverse of matrices (5) or (8) instead. Matrix (8) is obtained by inserting relations (6) into map (5). In matrix A, symbols F designate the model eigenfrequencies and symbols P the model parameters.

$$A = \begin{vmatrix} \dfrac{\partial F_1}{\partial P_1} & \dfrac{\partial F_1}{\partial P_2} & \cdots & \dfrac{\partial F_1}{\partial P_M} \\[2mm] \dfrac{\partial F_2}{\partial P_1} & \dfrac{\partial F_2}{\partial P_2} & \cdots & \dfrac{\partial F_2}{\partial P_M} \\[2mm] \dfrac{\partial F_3}{\partial P_1} & \dfrac{\partial F_3}{\partial P_2} & \cdots & \dfrac{\partial F_3}{\partial P_M} \end{vmatrix} \qquad (8)$$

The pseudo-inverse of matrix A is obtained via its singular value decomposition that is based on the break-up of matrix A into a product (9) of three matrices. This break-up can be carried out for any matrix.

$$A = UWV^T \qquad (9)$$

Matrices U and V are square and orthogonal, and matrix W is diagonal [46]. Matrix V^T is the transpose of V. The elements w_{ii} of W are zero for index $i > 3$, because the number of observed formant frequencies is assumed to be three. Therefore, a $(M-3)$-dimensional family of solutions of the system of equations (5) usually exists when the formant increments are given and the parameter increments are unknown.

These solutions are found via decomposition (9). The solution involves the transposes of matrices U and V^T as well as the pseudo-inverse of diagonal matrix W. Because the number of rows, 3, is less than the number of columns, M, decomposition (9) yields $M-3$ or more diagonal elements of matrix W that are zero or nearly zero. The pseudo-inverse W^I is therefore obtained by equating diagonal elements I/w_{ii} to zero if the absolute values of the original diagonal elements w_{ii} are below a small threshold. A particular solution (10) of system (5) is then obtained as follows.

$$\vec{v}_0 = VW^{-1}U^T \begin{pmatrix} \Delta F_1 \\ \Delta F_2 \\ \Delta F_3 \end{pmatrix} \qquad (10)$$

The general $(M-3)$-dimensional solution (11) is obtained from particular solution (10) as follows. The columns of V^T that correspond to zeroed diagonal elements of W^I are the basis vectors the linear combination of which, added to particular solution (9), gives general expression (11), which spans the whole solution space. Solutions (10) and (11) involve a reorganization of matrices W and V according to an algorithm based on Press *et al.* [47].

$$\begin{pmatrix} \Delta P_1 \\ \Delta P_2 \\ \cdots \\ \Delta P_M \end{pmatrix} = \vec{v}_0 + \sum_{j=1}^{M-3} \lambda_j \vec{v}_j \qquad (11)$$

$$\vec{v}_j = jth\ column\ V^T$$

$$\lambda_j = real\ parameter$$

Kinetic Constraints

The time-evolving parameter values P must be computed iteratively from the evolving formant frequencies F because system of equations (5) maps increments onto each other. Pseudo-inverting matrix A obtains infinitely many parameter increments for one set of formant increments. The number of solutions is infinite because parameters λ may assume any real value. To carry out the iteration, a single set of parameter increments must therefore be selected. The selection is carried out with additional constraints that, hereafter, are called kinetic because they contain the increments of the model parameters. The constraints consist in the request that some quantities are kept as small as possible. These quantities are squared. The squaring formally guarantees the existence of an absolute minimum that may be determined via the solution of a linear system of equations. Possible constraints are the following.

Minimal Deformation
One popular constraint used in the framework of acoustic-to-articulatory inversion is the minimal deformation of the vocal tract about a reference shape. That is, the increments are solutions of map (5) and at the same time the parameter values stay as near as possible to reference values P_{ref} that are fixed by the experimenter. Often, the reference shape is chosen to be the neutral tract shape, which is assumed to be quasi-uniform. This constraint, although popular, has no physiological basis. Whether it has a phonetic one depends on the wider phonetic/phonological context of the modelling. Relevant issues are the meaning of the "rest position" of the vocal tract, the task of this "rest position" as a default target, and the assignment or not of the schwa to this default, e.g. [50]. Formally, the quantity that must be minimized is written as follows.

$$\sum_{i=1}^{M} \left(P_{i,t_k} - P_{i,ref} \right)^2 \tag{12}$$

Minimal Rate of Deformation
A second popular constraint is the selection of the model parameter increments so that the rate of change of the vocal tract shape is as small as possible. That is, the parameter increments are chosen so that their values are solutions of map (5) and so that they are as small as possible. This principle is not based on physiology. Its phonetic relevance is a matter of debate [48]. The quantity that must be minimal is formally written as follows.

$$\sum_{i=1}^{M} \Delta P_{i,t_k}^2 \tag{13}$$

Minimal Acceleration of Deformation
The minimal acceleration of deformation is the minimal rate of change of the rate of deformation. The acceleration of deformation has not been considered before in the context of acoustic-to-articulatory inversion, as far as we know. Formally, it would rest on constraints on the forces that the vocal tract walls or articulators are subjected to, a topic that has been studied only rarely in speech production. The order of this constraint is in-between the orders of the speed and the jerk of deformation, which is

considered next. Formally, the quantity that is kept to a minimum is written as follows.

$$\sum_{i=1}^{M} \left(\Delta P_{i,t_k} - \Delta P_{i,t_{k-1}} \right)^2 \tag{14}$$

Minimal Jerk of Deformation
Jerk is the rate of change of acceleration. Physically speaking, minimizing jerk corresponds to minimizing mechanical shock. The minimization of the jerk of human limb movement has a physiological basis, which appears to apply to the movements of the articulators as well [49]. Formally, the quantity that is minimized is written as follows.

$$\sum_{i=1}^{M} \left[\left(\Delta P_{i,t_k} - \Delta P_{i,t_{k-1}} \right) - \left(\Delta P_{i,t_{k-1}} - \Delta P_{i,t_{k-2}} \right) \right]^2 \tag{15}$$

Selection of a Single Solution
Constraints (12)-(15) enable selecting a single solution among the infinitely many M-tuples ΔP that are compatible with an observed triplet ΔF. Formally, the selection consists in fixing the values of the free parameters λ in general solution (11) so that map (5) and at least one kinetic constraint are satisfied. The values of free parameters λ are obtained by solving a system of linear equations.

In practice, this system of equations is established as follows. General solution (11) is inserted into one of the constraints (12)-(15). After, the derivative is taken with respect to each free parameter and equated to zero. One equation for each parameter is thus obtained. Solving the linear system of equations yields a single solution for each free parameter. Inserting these into general solution (11) obtains the desired single solution for the parameter increments.

Hereafter, the systems of equations are given that must be solved for the constraints of minimal deformation and minimal rate of deformation, which are the most popular.

Minimal Deformation

$$\sum_{i=1}^{M} \sum_{j=1}^{M-3} v_{ij} v_{il} \lambda_j = -\sum_{i=1}^{M} \left[v_{0i} + \left(P_{i,t_k} - P_{i,ref} \right) \right] v_{i,l} \tag{16}$$

$$l = 1 ... M - 3$$

The proof that system of equations (16) yields a minimum of constraint (12) can be found in [36]. System of equations (16) is linear in the unknown free parameters λ. It contains the elements of some columns of matrix V^T obtained via singular value decomposition (9), particular solution (10), as well as the reference parameters P_{ref} that are fixed by the experimenter.

Minimal Rate of Deformation

$$\sum_{i=1}^{M} \sum_{j=1}^{M-3} v_{ij} v_{il} \lambda_j = -\sum_{i=1}^{M} v_{0i} v_{il} \tag{17}$$

$$l = 1 ... M - 3$$

The proof that system of equations (17) yields a minimum of constraint (13) can be found in [36]. System of equations (17) is linear in the unknown free parameters. It includes particular solution (11) as well as the elements of some column vectors of matrix V^T obtained via singular value decomposition (9).

Prediction – Correction

The inverse of map (5) is used to compute parameter increments from observed frequency increments. The inverse mapping does, however, not guarantee that the eigenfrequencies of the calculated vocal tract shapes perfectly agree with observed formant frequencies. On the contrary, one expects small errors to occur that would accumulate when iterating the mapping. Reasons for locally expecting small errors are that the observed increments are not infinitesimally small, the matrix elements of (8) must be estimated numerically via small increments of the eigenfrequencies and model parameters, the iteration is based on a Taylor expansion that is cut off at the linear term, and numerical singular value decomposition as well as numerical solutions of equations (16) or (17) are finite-precision only.

Frequency errors are corrected as follows. One considers that solution (11) enables the prediction of the parameters that describe the tract shape whose eigenfrequencies ideally agree with the observed frequencies at that time. Then, the eigenfrequencies of the "predicted" model are subtracted from the observed formant frequencies to give the formant error at that time.

Expressions (5) to (8) are based on a linearization that is valid locally in time. Inspecting these expressions, it appears that the formant errors together with the corresponding parameter errors also obey these relations. As a consequence, they can be used for error correction. For this, expressions ΔP and ΔF are re-interpreted as parameter and formant errors respectively. Parameter errors are predicted from observed formant errors and used to correct the model parameters so that the formant errors decrease. This correction stage is repeated until the formant error is smaller than a given threshold.

If this predictor-corrector loop fails to decrease the formant errors below a given threshold after a fixed number of iterations, the algorithm stops and emits a warning. In practice, this means that if it proceeds iteratively without stopping, the eigenfrequencies of the computed tract shapes are guaranteed to agree with the observed formant frequencies to within a fixed tolerance, which in practice may be as low as 0.01 Hz.

Iteration

Once increments ΔP of the model parameters have been obtained as a function of the observed increments of the formant frequencies, the model parameters at time t_{k+1} can be calculated via the model parameters at time t_k.

$$P_{i,t_{k+1}} = P_{i,t_k} + \Delta P_i \tag{18}$$

Initialisation

The evolving vocal tract shapes are computed via an iteration that must be initialized. In practice, initialization is done with a modelled vocal tract shape the eigenfrequencies of which are computed. A typical choice for the initial vocal tract shape is the quasi-neutral one. An interpolation is then carried out between the computed initial eigenfrequencies and the first observed formant data. The number of time steps included in the interpolation is chosen to keep the formant increments small so that the approximations that are included in map (5) apply. To sum up, initialization involves the selection of an initial tract shape as well as the inverse mapping along interpolated formant movements till observed formant data are reached from which the inversion then proceeds with observed data.

Questions

The purpose of the results that are presented hereafter is to demonstrate the feasibility of the inverse mapping, which is the determination of the parameters of a vocal tract model so that the model's first few eigenfrequencies agree with observed formant frequencies. The questions that are addressed are the following. A first pertains to the numerical stability of the iteration. In other words, what is the number of model parameters that may be included in the model the formant frequencies are converted into? This question is discussed in the framework of a model that comprises a concatenation of 32 cylindrical tubelets the cross-sections of which are determined by three measured formant frequencies. The cross-sections are unconstrained, that is, their values are free to assume any value.

A second question is whether tubelets with exponentially changing cross-sections may be concatenated to form plausible models of the vocal tract shape. Indeed, concatenations of such exponentially varying tubelets have occasionally been discussed in the literature as alternatives to right cylindrical tubelets that produce area functions that include jump discontinuities.

The problem with exponential tubelets is, however, that they comprise finite cut-off frequencies that cause spectral components that propagate in the direction of the main axis of the tract to be dampened out when their frequency is below a critical threshold. The cut-off frequency increases with the curvature of the tubelet. Mapping observed formants onto a concatenation of exponential tubelets and inspecting their curvatures might therefore discover whether exponential tubelet-based vocal tract models are able to propagate all speech-relevant frequency components.

A third issue is whether vocal tract shapes that are calculated via formant-to-area mapping are accurate estimates of the original shapes that have produced the observed formant frequencies. The experiment involves several models, including the exponential and cylindrical ones that are discussed above. The calculated tract shapes are compared to observed shapes that have been obtained via magnetic resonance imaging for several American-English speech sounds [40].

Corpus

In this study, we have used a corpus published by Story et al. that includes acoustic as well as cross-section data for one speaker sustaining American English speech sounds [40]. Table 2 gives the observed formant data.

Table 2. Formant frequencies of American English vowels and lateral [l] for one speaker [40]

	[i]	[ɪ]	[ɛ]	[æ]	[ʌ]	[ɑ]
F1(Hz)	333	518	624	692	707	754
F2(Hz)	2332	2004	1853	1873	1161	1195
F3(Hz)	2986	2605	2475	2463	2591	2685

	[ɔ]	[o]	[ʊ]	[u]	[ɜ] retro- flex	[l]
F1(Hz)	654	540	541	389	500	348
F2(Hz)	944	922	1045	987	1357	1250
F3(Hz)	2739	2584	2568	2299	2124	2785

Experiments

All results that are discussed hereafter concur with the stated objective, that is, the first three eigenfrequencies of the vocal tract shapes that have been calculated agree numerically with the first three observed formant frequencies. The acoustic accuracy has been 1 Hz at least, that is, observed and computed frequencies agree to within the specified tolerance. The displayed shapes are static because they refer to published data that concern sustained speech sounds. The inversion procedure per se is, however, time-evolving because it includes interpolated formant movements from the quasi-neutral initial tract shape to the observed formant data.

Experiment 1

A first experiment involves a concatenation of six loss-less tubelets the cross-sections of which vary exponentially. The tubelet length is a constant fixed to 2.66 cm. The constant total tract length therefore is 16 cm. The "laryngo-pharyngeal" tubelet that is adjacent to the glottis is cylindrical with a constant default section of 0.5 cm². The other tubelet cross-sections are calculated by an inverse mapping involving a minimal deformation constraint about a quasi-uniform reference shape whose cross-section equals 0.5 cm² for the "laryngo-pharyngeal" tubelet and 3 cm² elsewhere.

One purpose is to examine the suitability of exponential tubelets for modelling vocal tract shapes. A second purpose is the comparison of calculated and measured shapes to examine the accuracy with which calculated shapes represent the original ones.

Figure 1 shows the calculated and measured area functions. The speech sounds are listed in the same order as in Table 2. The displayed contours have been aligned after inversion so that their total lengths agree. Dark lines are measured and light lines computed shapes. The horizontal axis shows from the left to the right the numbered cross-sections from the glottis to the lips. The vertical axis shows the square root of the measured and calculated cross-sections. In addition, the computed cross-sections are scaled by a constant so that the volumes of the measured and computed shapes are identical. The scaling has consequences for the visual display but does not affect the correlation between observed and calculated contours.

Table 3 shows the correlation coefficients between measured and calculated tract shapes. The correlation is computed by the cross-section radii assuming that the sections are circular. The purpose of the square root is to decreases the influence of large cross-sections that contribute proportionally less to observed formant frequencies than small cross-sections. Table 3 shows that the agreement between observed and calculated shapes varies in the range between 0.94 for the not quite open front unrounded vowel and 0.12 for the high back rounded vowel [u].

Table 3. Correlation coefficients of aligned measured and calculated contours displayed in Figure 1. Coefficients marked by an (*) are statistically significant at the 0.05 level at least (two-tailed test)

[i]	[ɪ]	[ɛ]
0.51*	0.51*	0.62*
[æ]	[ʌ]	[ɑ]
0.94*	0.89*	0.82*
[ɔ]	[o]	[ʊ]
0.71*	0.50*	0.41*
[u]	[ɜ]	[l]
0.12	0.44*	0.30*

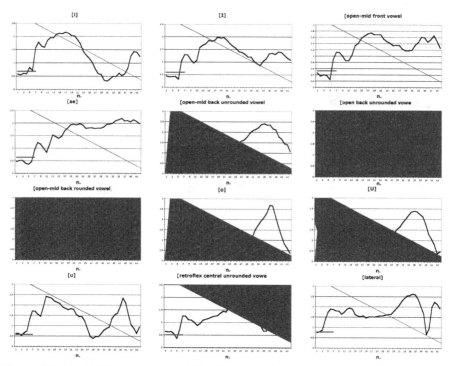

Fig. 1. Calculated (light) and measured (dark) square root values of the area functions corresponding to several American-English vowels as well as lateral [l]. The speech sounds are displayed in the same order as in Table 2 and the contours have been aligned so that they have the same length and the vocal tract volumes are identical. The glottis is to the left, the lips to the right

Experiment 2

Experiment 2 involves a concatenation of 32 right cylindrical lossy tubelets. The total length of the tract model equals 17.26 cm +/- 1 cm and includes a correction for acoustic radiation losses at the lips. The constraint on the total length is implemented via a method that enables inserting arbitrary structural constraints in direct map (5). Structural constraints on the cross-sections of the cylindrical tubelets are *deliberately* left out. The kinetic constraint is the minimal jerk constraint (15).

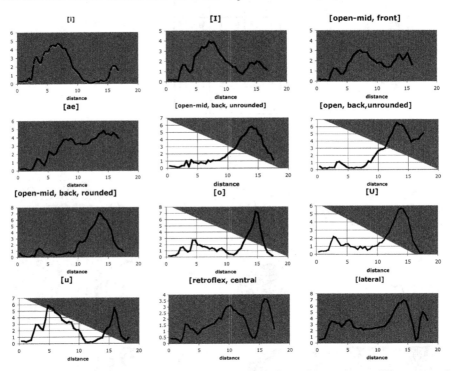

Fig. 2. Computed (light) and measured (dark) cross-section values corresponding to several American-English speech sounds. The sounds are displayed in the same order as in Table 2. The horizontal axis shows the distance from the glottis in cm and the vertical axis the cross-section area in cm-square. The glottis is to the left and the lips to the right

One objective is to test the numerical stability of the formant-to-area mapping. A second objective is to compare calculated and measured shapes when no constraints are imposed on the calculated cross-sections, including the ones in the vicinity of the glottis.

Figure 2 shows the calculated area cross-sections (light lines) overlaid on the observed area cross-sections (dark lines) for the speech sounds listed in Table 2 in that order. The horizontal axis shows the distance of the cross-sections from the glottis (left to right). The vertical axis shows the cross-sections in cm^2. All calculated cross-sections are positive and they evolve gradually from the glottis to the lips, although the cross-sections have been kept constraint-free. But, the calculated shapes occasionally differ considerably from the measured shapes. The largest differences are observed in the laryngo-pharyngeal and lip zones as well as for the position of the tongue constriction.

Table 4 shows the values of the correlation coefficients between measured and computed cross-section contours. Before computing the correlation coefficients, the contours have been aligned so that the total lengths agree. No other standardization has been carried out. Table 4 shows that the agreement between observed and calculated shapes varies in the range between 0.88 for the not quite fully open front unrounded vowel and minus 0.62 for the high back rounded vowel [u].

Table 4. Correlation coefficients of aligned measured and calculated contours displayed in Figure 2. Coefficients marked by an (*) are statistically significant at the 0.05 level at least (two-tailed test)

[i]	[ɪ]	[ɛ]
0.75*	0.51*	0.78*
[æ]	[ʌ]	[ɑ]
0.88*	0.79*	0.75*
[ɔ]	[o]	[ʊ]
0.59*	-0.13	0.49*
[u]	[ɜ]	[ɪ]
-0.62*	-0.27	-0.18

Experiment 3

The third experiment involves the concatenation of four conical lossy tubelets the lengths and cross-sections of which are free to vary. The kinetic constraint is the minimal jerk constraint. Structural constraints are imposed on the cross-sections as well as lengths of the individual tubelets. The cross-sections must be positive and not exceed 1 cm^2 at the glottis and 6 cm^2 elsewhere. The lengths of the tubelets are unequal and time-variable. The maximal length is 2 cm for the two tubelets in the vicinity of the glottis and lips respectively. The lengths of the remaining tubelets are fixed automatically so that the total length equals 17.26 +/- 1 cm.

One objective is to test the inverse mapping on conical tubelets whose lengths may vary individually. Transfer matrix (1), which bears upon cylindrical tubelets, shows that tubelet lengths are inserted into nonlinear expressions whereas the tubelet cross-sections enter the matrix elements proportionally. The same observation applies to conical tubelets. The effects of the lengths and cross-sections on the formant frequencies might therefore not to be equally well approximated in the locally linear map (5); the lengths presenting a greater challenge than the cross-sections. A second objective is to compare calculated and observed tract shapes when the cross-sections are constrained so as to remain within given intervals, especially in the laryngo-pharynx.

Figure 3 shows the calculated area cross-sections (light lines) overlaid on the observed area cross-sections (dark lines) for the speech sounds listed in Table 2 in that order. The horizontal axis shows the distance of the cross-sections from the glottis (left to right). The vertical axis shows the cross-section in cm^2. The calculated shapes approximate the measured shapes in the laryngo-pharyngeal region because of structural constraints. Also, the co-existence of time-variable cross-sections and time-variable tubelet lengths does not cause the inverse mapping to be less stable or the (computed) acoustic data to be less accurate than in models in which the lengths of the tubelets are fixed or let to evolve deterministically with the total tract length.

Table 5 shows the values of the correlation coefficients between measured and computed cross-sections. Before the calculation, the contours have been aligned so that the total lengths agree. No other standardization has been carried out. Table 5 shows that the agreement between observed and calculated shapes varies in the range between 0.90 for the not quite fully open front unrounded vowel and 0.06 for the lateral [l].

Table 5. Correlation coefficients of aligned measured and calculated contours displayed in Figure 3. Coefficients marked by an (*) are statistically significant at the 0.05 level at least (two-tailed test)

[i]	[ɪ]	[ɛ]
0.54*	0.78*	0.84*
[æ]	[ʌ]	[ɑ]
0.90*	0.76*	0.84*
[ɔ]	[o]	[ʊ]
0.78*	0.38*	0.87*
[u]	[ɜ]	[l]
0.35*	0.49*	0.06

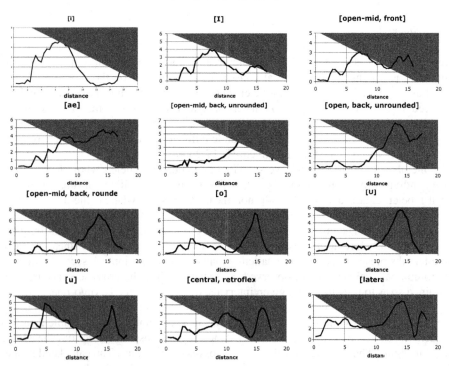

Fig. 3. Computed (light) and measured (dark) cross-section values corresponding to several American-English speech sounds. The sounds are displayed in the same order as in Table 2. The horizontal axis shows the distance from the glottis in cm and the vertical axis the cross-section area in cm-square. The glottis is to the left and the lips to the right

Discussion

Plausibility of Computed Vocal Tract Shapes

Figures 1, 2 and 3, as well as Tables 3, 4 and 5 suggest that the agreement between observed and calculated tract shapes is volatile, even though the formant-to-area mapping is mathematically neat and acoustically accurate, the selection of single solutions subject to physiologically or phonetically plausible constraints and the vocal tract model lengths are controlled.

More precisely, Figure 2 confirms that additional structural constraints are called for that incorporate in the model anatomical properties that are typical of the vocal tract, such as the feeble cross-section of the laryngo-pharynx, for instance. The qualitative mismatches in Figure 2 are indeed the result of (deliberately) letting the cross-sections in the vicinity of the glottis assume any value. As a consequence, the computed shapes are only determined by the acoustic properties of the vocal tube. As a result, the computed shapes differ qualitatively from the measured shapes because iterative inversion is able to exploit acoustic front-back mirror symmetries a speaker is unable to take advantage of, because of the narrow constriction of the vocal tract near the glottis.

Also, Figure 2 demonstrates that increasing the number of model parameters does not improve the fit of the calculated shapes to the observed ones. The computed shapes change gradually with position and capture the acoustically relevant features of the tract, but do not embrace the fine details of the area function. A possible explanation is that only the first three formants are measured the frequencies of which are fixed by the gross features of the tract shape. Tracking the fine features would require measuring more formants as well as increasing the sophistication of the tract models so as to represent longitudinal as well as transversal wave propagation.

In the framework of the corpus that has been used here, problem sounds appear to be the retroflex central unrounded vowel, the lateral [l] as well as the rounded back vowels that are high, quasi-high or high-mid. The mediocre performance of the inversion for the lateral consonant [l] as well as the retroflex vowel is possibly related to the choice of the vocal tract models. The models are best suited for representing single-cavity convex-tongue tracts. For the central retroflex unrounded vowel the tongue shape is concave, however, and the lateral consonant frontally splits the mouth cavity into two smaller sub-cavities.

The lack of agreement for high vowel [u] has been observed and discussed before. A possible explanation appears to be the following [36]. Vowel [u] is a high vowel that is rounded. Because of the highness, the jaw is high and the tongue close to the palate, and lip rounding is very marked. As a consequence, the vocal tract is equally narrow in two different positions. Since the acoustic properties of the vocal tract are mainly fixed by narrow constrictions, trade-offs appear to be possible between the constrictions at the velum and lips, and qualitatively different shapes may be characterized by similar formant values. This is a known issue, which is discussed in [56] in terms of simulated pseudo-articulatory features.

To conclude, this would suggest that acoustic-to-articulatory inversion based on the first few formants may be expected to approximate only vocal tract shapes that are single-cavity, single-constriction, convex-tongue, as well as suitably constrained in the laryngo-pharynx and, possibly, at the lips. For sounds that do not satisfy these criteria, actual and calculated shapes may differ qualitatively.

Numerical Stability
Numerical stability designates here the convergence of the predictor-corrector loop to the desired formant frequencies with a precision that is better than 1 Hz. In earlier studies, models with up to 8 cross-sections have been used, and the link between model parameters and formant frequencies has been transformed logarithmically to extend the intervals over which the linearization of these relations applies [36].

Figure 3 shows that numerical stability can be obtained with models that comprise up to 32 parameters that may vary freely. Here, inversion has been based on matrix (8), which is easier to estimate numerically. Also, linear systems that must be solved to select a single solution, e.g. (16) or (17), have been solved by *LU*-decomposition [46] rather than singular value decomposition, which has been strictly reserved for the calculation of the pseudo-inverse of direct map (8). No logarithmic transforms of the shape-frequency relations have been included. These transforms are not required to attain numerical stability. They may, however, speed up inversion because they enable larger time steps to be taken and fewer recursions to be carried out.

Discontinuous Versus Continuous Area Functions
Models that are included in Experiments 1 to 3 have deliberately been chosen to be different. In Experiments 1 and 3, the models are based on concatenations of exponential or conical tubelets that enable the area function to vary continuously with the distance from the glottis, even when the number of tubelets is small. Concatenations of right cylindrical tubelets only evolve pseudo-gradually with position when their number is fairly high, e.g. 32 in Experiment 2. In practice, a choice of 32 cross-sections is redundant and computationally too expensive for many applications.

Exponential tubelets differ from cylindrical or conical tubelets insofar that exponential tubelets cut off strictly positive frequency components in waves that propagate along the main axis of the vocal tract. The cut-off frequency depends on the tubelet curvature. Exponential tubelets have occasionally been discussed in the framework of the modeling of the vocal tract [39]. One purpose of Experiment 1 therefore has been to test whether exponential tubelets that are required to simulate vowel-typical tract shapes are characterized by cut-off frequencies that would be high enough to impede speech-relevant frequencies to propagate, which is contrary to observation.

Strictly speaking, the discussion that follows is only straightforward for semi-infinite hard-wall exponential tubelets [53]. For finite-length exponential tubelets, the reflection of the acoustic wave at the tubelet boundaries causes irregularities in the impedance characteristic. Finite-length and semi-infinite tubelets share, however, formally identical finite cut-off frequencies [54]. The formula that predicts the cut-off frequency of an exponential tubelet of semi-infinite length shows that for a length of 2.66 cm, the cut-off frequency would be approximately equal to 100 Hz if the vocal tract radius increased by 5 % over that distance. Inspecting Figure 1 therefore suggests that one might expect speech-relevant frequencies to be cut off in the tract models that have been inferred via inverse mapping. This suggests avoiding modeling with exponential tubelets, because they might intimate incorrectly that the first harmonic of the voice source does not propagate through the vocal tract. Exponential tubelets can be replaced by conical tubelets, the longitudinal cut-off frequency of which is strictly zero.

Acknowledgments

Part of this work has been carried out during a stay of the author with the Speech Group of the « Laboratoire Lorrain pour la Recherche en Informatique et ses Applications » (LORIA), Nancy, France.

References

1. Mermelstein P.: Determination of the vocal tract shape from measured formant frequencies. J. Acoust. Soc. Am. 41, 5 (1967) 1283-1294
2. Schroeder M.: Determination of the geometry of the human vocal tract by acoustic measurements. J. Acoust. Soc. Am. 41, 4 (1967) 1002-1010
3. Wakita H. : Estimation of vocal tract shape by inverse filtering of acoustic speech waveforms. IEEE Trans. Audio Electroacoustics (1973) 417-427
4. Wakita H., Gray A. H.: Numerical determination of the lip impedance and vocal tract area functions. IEEE Trans. Acoustics, Speech, Sig. Proc. 23, 6 (1975) 574-580
5. Ladefoged P., Harshman R., Goldstein L., Rice L.: Generating vocal tract shapes from formant frequencies. J. Acoust. Soc. Am. 64 (1978) 1027-1035
6. Atal B. S., Chang J. J., Mathews M. V., Tukey J. W.: Inversion of acoustic-to-articulatory transformation in the vocal tract by computer sorting technique. J. Acoust. Soc. Am. 63, 5, (1978) 1535-1555
7. Wakita H.: Estimation of vocal tract shapes from acoustical analysis of the speech wave: the state of the art. IEEE Trans. Acoustics, Speech, Sig. Proc. 27, 3 (1979) 281-285
8. Flanagan J. L., Ishizaka K., Shipley K. L.: Signal models for low bit-rate coding of speech. J. Acoust. Soc. Am. 68 (1980) 780-791
9. Shirai K., Honda M.: Estimation of articulatory motion from speech waves and its application for automatic recognition. In Simon J. C. (ed.): Spoken language generation and understanding, D. Reidel Publishing Company (1980) 87-99
10. Levinson S. E., Schmidt C. E.: Adaptive computation of articulatory parameters from the speech signal. J. Acoust. Soc. Am. 74 (1983) 1145-1154
11. Charpentier F.: Determination of the vocal tract shape from the formants by analysis of the articulatory-to-acoustics nonlinearities. Speech Communication 3 (1984) 291-308
12. Scaife: Vocal tract area estimation – extending the Wakita inverse filter. Proc. Eurospeech (1989) 648-651
13. Atal B. S., Rioul O.: Neural networks for estimating articulatory positions from speech. J. Acoust. Soc. Am., 86 (1989) 123-131
14. Schroeter J., Sondhi M. M.: Dynamic programming search of articulatory codebooks. Proc. ICASSP 1 (1989) 588-591
15. Rahim M. G., Goodyear C. C.: Estimation of vocal tract parameters using a neural net. Speech Comm. 9 (1990) 49-55
16. Soquet A., Saerens M., Jospa P.: Acoustic-to-articulatory inversion based on a neural controller of a vocal tract model. Proc. ESCA Workshop Speech Synthesis (1990) 71-74
17. Shirai K., Kobayashi T.: Estimation of articulatory motion using neural networks. J. Phonetics 19 (1991) 379-385
18. Laboissière R., Schwartz J.-L., Bailly G.: Motor control of speech skills: a connectionist approach. In Touretzky, Elman, Sejnowski, Hinton (eds) Proc. 1990 Connectionist Summer School (1990) 319-327
19. Prado P. P. L., Shiva E . H., Childers D. G.: Optimization of acoustic-to-articulatory mapping. Proc. ICASSP 2 (1992) 33-36
20. Rahim M. G., Goodyear C .C., Kleijn W. B., Schroeter J., Sondhi M. M.: On the use of neural networks in articulatory speech synthesis. J. Acoust. Soc. Am. 93, 2 (1993) 1109-1121

21. Yu J.: A method to determine the area function of speech based on perturbation theory. STL-QPSR 4 (1993) 77-95
22. Jospa P., Soquet A., Saerens M.: Variational formulation of the acoustico-articulatory link and the inverse mapping by means of a neural network. In: Levels in speech communication, relations and interactions, Elsevier, Amsterdam (1994) 103-113
23. Deng L., Sun D. X.: A statistical approach to automatic speech recognition using the atomic speech units constructed from overlapping articulatory features. J. Acoust. Soc. Am. 95, 5 (1994) 2702-2719
24. Ramsey G.: A nonlinear filtering approach to stochastic training of the acoustic-to-articulatory mapping using the EM algorithm. Proc. ICSLP (1996)
25. Erler K., Freeman G. H.: An HMM-based speech recognizer using overlapping articulatory features. J. Acoust. Soc. Am. 100, 4 (1996) 2500-2513
26. Hodgen J.: Improving on hidden Markov models: an articulatory constrained, maximum likelihood approach to speech recognition and speech coding. Technical Report LA-UR-96-3945, Los Alamos national Laboratory (1996)
27. Schoentgen J., Ciocea S.: Kinematic formant-to-area mapping. Speech Comm. 21 (1997) 227-244
28. Mokhtari P.: An acoustic-phonetic articulatory study of speech-speaker dichotomy. PhD thesis, Univ. South Wales, Canberra, Australia (1998)
29. Laprie Y., Mathieu B.: A variational approach for estimating vocal tract shapes from the speech signal. Proc. ICASSP (1998) 929-932
30. Ouni S., Laprie Y.: Improving acoustic-to-articulatory inversion by using hypercube codebooks. Proc. ICSSLP, Beijing (2000)
31. Mokhtari P., Clermont F.: New Perspectives on linear-prediction modelling of the vocal tract: uniqueness, formant-dependence and shape parameterization. Proc. 8th Austral. Int. Conf. Speech Sc. and Tech. Canberra, Australia (2000)
32. Richardson M., Bilmes J., Diorio C.: Hidden-articulator Markov models: performance improvements and robustness to noise. Proc ICSLP, Beijing, China (2000)
33. Stephenson T., Bourlard H., Bengio S., Morris A. C.: Automatic speech recognition using dynamic Bayesian networks with both acoustic and articulatory variables. Proc. ICSLP, Beijing, China (2000)
34. Frankel J., King S.: Speech recognition in the articulatory domain: investigating an alternative to acoustic HMMs. Proc. Workshop for Innov. Speech Proc. (2001)
35. Krstulovic S.: Speech analysis with production constraints. PhD Thesis, Ecole Polytechnique Fédérale, Lausanne, Suisse (2001)
36. Ciocea S., Schoentgen J.: Semi-analytic formant-to-area mapping. Etudes et Travaux, ULB-ILVP 2, Brussels (1998)
37. Ciocea S., Schoentgen J., Crevier-Buchman L.: Analysis of dysarthric speech by means of formant-to-area mapping. Proceedings "Eurospeech 97", European Speech Communication Association, Rhodes, Greece (1997) 1799-1802
38. Ciocea S., Schoentgen J.: Formant-to-area mapping as a method of acoustic and articulatory data fusion in the context of automatic speaker recognition. Proceedings "Speaker Recognition and its Commercial and Forensic Applications", Société Française d'Acoustique, European Speech Communication Association, Avignon (1998) 33-36
39. Fant G.: Acoustic theory of speech production. Mouton, The Hague, Netherlands.
40. Story B., Titze I., Hoffman E.: Vocal tract area functions from magnetic resonance imaging. J. Acoust. Soc. Am., 100 (1996) 537-554
41. Abry C, Badin P, Scully C et al Sound-to-Gesture Inversion in Speech: the Speech Maps approach ESPRIT Speech Project Workshop, Berlin (1993)
42. Fant G.: Vocal tract wall effects, losses and resonance bandwidths. STL-QPSR 2-3 (1972) 28-52

43. Fant G., Nord L., Branderud P.: A note on the vocal tract wall impedance. STL-QPSR 4 (1976) 13-20
44. Fant G.: The vocal tract in your pocket calculator. In: Linguistic Phonetics, V. Fromkin (Ed.) Springer Verlag (1985) 55-77
45. Crawford F. S.: Ondes. Berkeley: Cours de Physique. Armand Collin, Paris (1972)
46. Stevens J. L.: Linear algebra with applications. Prentice Hall, New Jersey (2001)
47. Press W. S., Teukolsky S., Vetterling W., Flannery B.: Numerical recipes – the art of scientific computing. Cambridge University Press, New York (1987)
48. Carré R.: From an acoustic tube to speech. Speech Comm., 42, 2 (2004) 227-240
49. Tasko S. M., Westbury J. R.: Speed-curvature relations for speech-related articulatory movement. J. Phonetics, 32 (2004) 65-80
50. Barry W.: Time as a factor in the acoustic variation of schwa. Proceedings Int. Conf. Spoken Lang. Proc., Sydney (1998) n. 554
51. Chaigne A.: Ondes acoustiques. Editions de l'Ecole polytechnique, Palaiseau, France (2001)
52. Shirai K.: Estimation and generation of the articulatory motion using neural networks. Speech Comm. 13 (1993) 45-51
53. Rossing T. D., Fletcher N. H.: Principles of vibration and sound. Springer Verlag, New York (1995)
54. Marshall L.: A two-port analogous circuit and SPICE model for Salmon's family of acoustic horns. J. Acoust. Soc. Am., 99, 3 (1996) 1459-1464
55. McCallum W., Hughes-Hallet D., Gleason A.: Multivariable calculus. Wyley, New York (1998)
56. Boë L.-J., Perrier P., Bailly G.: The geometric vocal tract variables controlled for vowel production: proposals for constraining acoustic-to-articulatory inversion. J. Phonetics 20 (1992) 27-38
57. Schroeter J., Sondhi M.: Techniques for estimating vocal-tract shapes from the speech signal. IEEE Transactions on Speech and Audio Proc. 2 (1994) 133-150

Underdetermined Blind Separation of Speech Signals with Delays in Different Time-Frequency Domains

Alessandro Bastari, Stefano Squartini, and Francesco Piazza

Dipartimento di Elettronica, Intelligenza Artificiale e Telecomunicazioni-Università Politecnica delle Marche Via Brecce Bianche 12, I-60121 Ancona, Italy
a.bastari@univpm.it, {sts,upf}@deit.univpm.it

Abstract. This paper is devoted to the problem of speech signal separation from a set of observables, when the mixing system is underdetermined and static with unknown delays. The approaches appeared in the literature so far have shown that algorithms based on the property of sparsity of the original signals (effectively satisfied by speech sources) can be successfully applied to such a problem, specially if implemented in the time-frequency domain. Here, a survey on the usage of different time-frequency transforms within the already available three-step procedure for the addressed separation problem is carried out. The novelty of the contribution can be seen from this perspective: Wavelet, Complex Wavelet and Stockwell Transforms are the new transforms used in our problem, in substitution of the usual Short Time Fourier Transform (STFT). Their performances are analyzed and compared to those attainable through the STFT, evaluating how much different is the influence that their sparseness and spectral disjointness properties on the algorithm behavior.

1 Introduction

Recovering information from recordings where several audio sources are mixed is a challenging problem in digital signal processing. In particular it is often required to separate speech signals from the available observables, to get a certain level of intelligibility or listening quality. A common way followed in the literature to face this task is to see it as a problem of blind source separation (BSS) [1]. Actually, there is a big interest for BSS; this is mainly justified by its large applicability in several scientific fields, like bioinformatics, communications, speech and audio processing of course, imaging, and so on. In fact in all of them we are often asked to recover unknown sources from a certain set of observables (namely *mixtures*) detected by the sensors. This is what surely happens when we think of the well-known "cocktail party problem", that is commonly used to introduce beginners to the scientific area related to BSS. In fact, in a cocktail party there are many audio sources (speech, music, various kinds of noise), contemporarily present at the sensors (the listener's ears) and the goal is to be able to focus the attention on a single talker, minimizing the disturbing effect of the other signals.

In the BSS scenario we are supposed to separate the original signals by the only means of such mixtures, that is in general more than tracking a certain source of interest. The problem is completely blind when we do not have knowledge of the original signals and the system that performs the mixing. In order to face the large variety of possible applications, different formulations of the BSS problem have been proposed and studied, in accordance with the nature of the mixing [2], [3], [4]. First of all we

G. Chollet et al. (Eds.): Nonlinear Speech Modeling, LNAI 3445, pp. 136–163, 2005.
© Springer-Verlag Berlin Heidelberg 2005

can distinguish between linear and nonlinear models. Within both these categories we can have static or convolutive mixing, mathematically represented by matrices of numbers and matrices of filters. The case of static mixing with delays (i.e. the sources are delayed, weighted and summed up to yield the mixture signals) has been considered too. Looking at the number of sources (N) or sensors (M) involved we can differentiate between overdetermined and underdetermined models, with $N \leq M$, $N > M$ respectively. Diverse techniques have been proposed to handle these formulation of BSS; they generally move from different hypotheses and exploit different characteristics of the signals involved. Therefore, they cannot be applied in all situations. In the following we shall take into account those approaches that are well suited to deal with separation of speech signals.

2 Separating Speech Signals Through BSS Models

In this section we shall describe the BSS model we are going to consider in the following for the separation of speech signals, and justify its choice in accordance with the assumptions we can make on the nature of sources. Moreover we will be able to exploit some characteristics of the signals involved to find out adequate separating techniques. Regarding speech signals, we can say that they generally superpose linearly at sensor level, like all acoustic signals. Neglecting the presence of echoes and delays (for the moment) in the model, we are allowed to consider the mixture values at time instant t as a real coefficient linear combination of the source values at the same time instant. Therefore, let $x_i(t)$, $i = 1, 2, ..., M$ be the M known signal mixtures (the *sensor signals*), yielded as the linear combination of N unknown sources $s_j(t)$, $j = 1, 2, ..., N$, through an unknown matrix A (dimensions: $M \times N$), namely mixing matrix, and eventually corrupted by the additive noise $\xi(t)$. In formula:

$$\begin{bmatrix} x_1(t) \\ \vdots \\ x_M(t) \end{bmatrix} = A \begin{bmatrix} s_1(t) \\ \vdots \\ s_N(t) \end{bmatrix} + \xi(t), \quad \forall t. \tag{1}$$

As aforementioned, the objective is to recover $s_j(t)$ by the only means of mixtures $x_i(t)$. Eq.(1) can be written in the following compact form

$$\mathbf{x}(t) = A\mathbf{s}(t) + \boldsymbol{\xi}(t) \tag{2}$$

where $\mathbf{x}(t) = [x_1(t) \ \cdots \ x_M(t)]^\mathsf{T}$ and $\mathbf{s}(t) = [s_1(t) \ \cdots \ s_N(t)]^\mathsf{T}$ are the mixture and source vectors respectively at time instant t. Assuming the involved signals to be of length T ($t = 1, 2, ..., T$), we shall denote

$$X = \begin{bmatrix} x_1(1) & x_1(2) & \cdots & x_1(T) \\ \vdots & \vdots & \ddots & \vdots \\ x_M(1) & x_M(2) & \cdots & x_M(T) \end{bmatrix} \tag{3}$$

as the $M \times T$ matrix having the i-th sensor sequence as its i-th row, and similarly:

$$S = \begin{bmatrix} s_1(1) & s_1(2) & \cdots & s_1(T) \\ \vdots & \vdots & \ddots & \vdots \\ s_N(1) & s_N(2) & \cdots & s_N(T) \end{bmatrix} \quad (4)$$

the $N \times T$ matrix having the i-th source sequence as its i-th row. Then, model in (1), assumed to be in the *noiseless case* becomes:

$$X = AS \quad (5)$$

Let us consider the different cases we can have in dependence on the M, N values. The one $M = N$ is called *quadratic*: the matrix A is square; assuming that it is known and non-singular, we are able to get a perfect source reconstruction by simply inverting the mixing system: $S = A^{-1}X$. If $M > N$ then we deal with the *overdetermined* BSS: the problem can be easily solved, e.g. as in the previous case by neglecting a suitable number of mixtures. When the number of sensors is less the number of sources ($M < N$), we are in the *underdetermined* case: even though A is known and full-rank we cannot recover our sources by simple inversion and further conditions must be introduced. This is certainly the most difficult case and the one we will address in the following.

Now, assuming that the noise contribution ξ is zero, denoting a_{ij} the generic matrix entry (i-th row, j-th column), and omitting the time variable we can rewrite (1) as:

$$\mathbf{x} = \begin{bmatrix} x_1 \\ \vdots \\ x_M \end{bmatrix} = A \begin{bmatrix} \mathbf{s}_1 \\ \vdots \\ \mathbf{s}_N \end{bmatrix} = \begin{bmatrix} \mathbf{a}_1 & \cdots & \mathbf{a}_N \end{bmatrix} \begin{bmatrix} \mathbf{s}_1 \\ \vdots \\ \mathbf{s}_N \end{bmatrix} = \sum_{j=1}^{N} s_j \mathbf{a}_j \in \mathbb{R}^M. \quad (6)$$

If A is full-rank then we can say that the M columns of $\mathbf{A}$ are linear dependent and represent generator vectors for the mixture space $\mathbb{R}^M$. In other words, the set $\{\mathbf{a}_j\}$ is an overcomplete basis: that is why the underdetermined BSS problem is also called *overcomplete* [5]. From this perspective, we can re-formulate our task in these terms: determine vectors $\mathbf{a}_1 \cdots \mathbf{a}_N \in \mathbb{R}^M$ and the representation of each data point $\mathbf{x}(t) \in \mathbb{R}^M$ as a function of those.

The BSS problem, as presented so far, does not seem to be solvable, since we just know the mixtures $x_1(t), \ldots, x_M(t)$ and we do not have any access to the mixing matrix and the sources $s_1(t), \ldots, s_N(t)$. Anyway, as we are dealing with a certain type of signals (i.e. speech), we can take advantage from this aspect and introduce a sort of a-priori knowledge to make the problem tractable. Basically, it is useful to make some assumptions on the statistics of $s_j(t)$. First, we require that sources are statistically independent at each time instant t: in this way, the BSS problem becomes equivalent to the one of Independent Component Analysis (ICA). In general, the assumption of statistically independence of two random variables means that the value of each of them does not carry any information related to the other one. Looking at the afore cited cocktail party problem, this seems to be plausible since it is not very probable that two or more speakers can produce the same speech content in a certain time interval.

It can be shown that a necessary condition to let ICA have solution is that the independent components do not have to be gaussian [6], [7]. This is widely satisfied by the majority of signals coming from the real-world; for example, as we will see later on, speech has a laplacian distribution, that is a special case of the supergaussian one. Supegaussianity can be exploited to develop suitable algorithms for BSS. Indeed signal sparsity (well modeled by a laplacian distribution) has been extensively used in the literature to determine the unknown matrix and recover the sources through geometric methods, as [8], [9], [10]. As it will be discussed in the following, they have shown to be very effective in the underdetermined case, where the standard approaches for ICA cannot be directly applied.

It has to be underlined that the addressed ICA problem does not have a unique solution, in both case considered (quadratic and underdetermined). Indeed A is not the only matrix that guarantees to get the independent components of the mixtures: any matrix of the form $A' = APL$, does it, where P is an invertible matrix with unitary row vectors, the *permutation matrix*, while L is an invertible diagonal matrix, namely the *scaling matrix*.

3   Underdetermined Blind Separation of Speech Sources

Once highlighted the speech properties that can be effectively used for separation within the BSS framework, we can move to describe how the different techniques work in relation to the specific BSS formulation. As already mentioned, ICA is perhaps the most widely used approach for separation of signals and well suited for speech too. We shall give some insights about its basic principles, and way of operating, taking into account that many algorithms have been proposed in the literature to find the independent components we are interested to. In particular we will spend the most of our efforts on the geometric approaches, that have shown to give a solution to the ICA problem both in quadratic and underdetermined case, also in presence of delays. For the sake of completeness, the quadratic case is firstly described.

3.1   The Quadratic BSS

Let the number of independent components be exactly equal to the number of observed random variables (quadratic ICA). Under these assumptions the mixing matrix A is square, and after its recovery also the sources $s_i(t)$ can be obtained simply inverting the mixing model (5). For this reason quadratic ICA has been the first model to be intensively studied, so that a lot of different techniques can be found in literature. We can distinguish two important categories: the first one comprises the geometric methods [8], [9] that are based on the analysis of the statistical properties of the mixture space, whereas in the second one we can collect all the approaches where a proper objective function is minimized or maximized. Within the latter we can cite those algorithms oriented to the minimization of the mutual information [11], maximization of non-gaussianity or maximization of likelihood [12]. This list is obviously non exhaustive and much more details can be found in [6], [13].

In the following, we shall focus on a geometric method for the quadratic BSS. Without loss of generality, we can consider $M = N = 2$ and, since the columns of the mixing matrix A can be recovered up to permutation and scaling indeterminacies, we can assume in general they have unitary norm, so that we have:

$$A = \begin{bmatrix} \cos(\alpha_1) & \cos(\alpha_2) \\ \sin(\alpha_1) & \sin(\alpha_2) \end{bmatrix} \tag{7}$$

and each column $\mathbf{a}_i$ is determined by the single parameter α_i. If we consider a particular time instant t, the mixture vector $\mathbf{x}(t)$, called *data point*, can be seen as a point in the mixture plane $x_1 x_2$, with coordinates $(x_1(t), x_2(t))$. The complete set of data points, for all values of t, is called *scatter plot* and geometric methods are well suited to solve the BSS problem. In particular, to make the recovery of mixing parameters possible by geometric methods, the sources must be independent and sparse. A signal is sparse if only a very little portion of its samples are significantly different from zero, that is its amplitude pdf $P(s)$ must be supergaussian.

Therefore let us consider two independent and sparse (for example laplacian) sources, mixed by a mixing matrix A like in(7), so that (5) becomes

$$\mathbf{x}(t) = \begin{bmatrix} \cos(\alpha_1) \\ \sin(\alpha_1) \end{bmatrix} s_1(t) + \begin{bmatrix} \cos(\alpha_2) \\ \sin(\alpha_2) \end{bmatrix} s_2(t) . \tag{8}$$

Sparseness ensures that both $s_1(t)$ and $s_2(t)$ assume very low values (nearly zero) in many time instants t, so we expect that the vector $\mathbf{x}(t)$ has correspondingly little norm too, and the scatter plot is composed of a dense cloud of data points around the origin. Conversely, when $\mathbf{x}(t)$ norm is big, we can suppose that only a single source contributes to it. It follows that:

$$\mathbf{x}(t) \approx \begin{bmatrix} \cos(\alpha_1) \\ \sin(\alpha_1) \end{bmatrix} s_1(t) . \tag{9}$$

So $\mathbf{x}(t)$ lies close to the direction related to the vector $\begin{bmatrix} \cos(\alpha_1) & \sin(\alpha_1) \end{bmatrix}^\mathsf{T}$, which is the direction that forms an angle α_1 with the x_1 axis. The same can be said if the source $s_2(t)$ assumes a significant value, but in this case the direction of the data point would lie close to the angle direction α_2.

Summarizing, under the assumptions of independent and sparse sources, from the scatter plot analysis we would find a dense cloud of data points in proximity of the origin, and clusters along two directions with a density of data point decreasing with the distance from the origin. So the BSS problem in the quadratic two-dimensional case can be solved by analyzing the scatter plot of data points and detecting the directions corresponding to a maximum density of data points. The simplest way to find the two directions is to plot the angular distribution of the data points and find its maxima, which correspond to the two desired directions.

This method can be also used for N mixtures of N sources, under the same assumptions of independence and sparsity of the sources. In this situation, however, the generic data point belongs to an N-dimensional vector space and we must use more complex clustering algorithms (for example neural learning algorithms [14], or fuzzy C-means clustering algorithms [15]).

3.2 The Underdetermined BSS

This paragraph deals with the problem of static underdetermined BSS; the algorithm proposed in [10] is the solution here analyzed. It is a generalization of the method described previously and in these terms it can still be considered a geometric ICA approach. As aforementioned, source sparsity is a fundamental assumption to let the algorithm achieve good separation performances, specially now that we have to handle more clusters than before in the same mixture space. This explains why in order to recover the mixing matrix columns from the mixture scatterplot we have to find out a way to enhance the source sparsity, that it is often not satisfying in the time domain. This represent a key point for the effectiveness of the overall algorithm and the real separation performances achievable.

The underdetermined BSS problem is hard since we cannot say to have got the solution even when we know the mixing parameters, simply because A is not square and there are more unknown variables than equations. So assuming that we know A, the linear system:

$$\mathbf{x}(t) = A \cdot \mathbf{s}(t) \tag{10}$$

has infinite solution vectors $\mathbf{s}(t)$ at each time instant (they belong to the affine space to $\mathbb{R}^V$ and of dimension $V = N - M$): we are asked to make further assumption to get a unique solution, even up to permutation and scaling indeterminacies.

The separation method proposed in [10] is a two-step procedure: in the first one, namely *Blind Mixing Model Recovery* (BMMR), the mixing matrix is recovered starting from the available mixtures, while in the second one, the *Blind Source Recovery* (BSR), the sources are reconstructed by taking advantage of the just performed estimation of the mixing matrix. This is the notation formalized in [16]. Both steps are implemented in a time-frequency domain, instead of the usual time domain which available signals originally belong to.

We shall describe the algorithm in a simple case: $M = 2$, when the mixture space is a plane and directions can be represented just by one parameter, the θ angle in polar coordinates. Then, let $\mathbf{x}(t)$ be a generic data point at time instant t, l_t and θ_t be the corresponding amplitude and phase in the mixture space and α the angle between a certain direction and θ_t; it is possible to define a local potential function around the θ_t direction as follows:

$$\phi_t(\alpha) = \begin{cases} 1 - \dfrac{|\alpha|}{\pi/4} & \text{if } |\alpha| < \dfrac{\pi}{4} \\ 0 & \text{otherwise} \end{cases} \tag{11}$$

Now we can define a global potential function Φ, that is related to the generic direction θ like:

$$\Phi(\theta, \lambda) = \sum_t l_t \phi\left(\lambda(\theta - \theta_t)\right) \tag{12}$$

where λ is needed to adjust the angular resolution of local contributions while l_t acts like a weight to enhance the contribution of most significant data points (those with highest amplitude). Such directions are calculated over a K-point grid in the interval $[-\pi/2, \pi/2]$, resulting in a potential function $\Phi(\theta_k, \lambda)$ depending on a discrete value parameter. The local maxima $(\alpha_1, \cdots, \alpha_N)$ of this function are identified as the directions of the mixing matrix to be recovered, according to the model described in (7).

Concerning the second phase (BSR), we have to recover the original sources through the knowledge of A and x, and, as said above, we need to introduce some constraints to make the problem solvable (with unique solution). According to [10], we decide to follow the principle of maximum likelihood (ML). Let us consider the system $x = As$, we can say that the generic data point is completely determined by A and s; the probability that x has a certain value is then related to the values of A and s, and it can be written as $P(x \mid s, A)$. The Bayes theorem tells us that the a-posteriori probability of the event s once A and x are known is given by:

$$P(s \mid x, A) = \frac{P(x \mid s, A) P(s)}{P(x)}. \tag{13}$$

Given a certain data point x, we want to recover s through the ML approach, that means to maximize the a-posteriori probability of s, (13), assuming that we have access to its a-priori probability $P(s)$. From another point of view, we can say that we are looking for the most probable decomposition of x in terms of overcomplete basis of $\mathbb{R}^M$ given by the A columns, with the constraint $x = As$. Our maximization problem for the estimation of s is the following:

$$s = \arg\max_{x=As} P(s \mid x, A) =$$
$$= \arg\max_{x=As} P(x \mid s, A) P(s) \tag{14}$$

Since in the noiseless case x is completely determined by A and s, (14) becomes

$$s = \arg\max_{x=As} P(s). \tag{15}$$

That does not have a unique solution in general: it depends on the formula adopted for $P(s)$. Assuming that each source s_i has a laplacian distribution, we have:

$$P(s_i) \propto \exp(-\lambda |s_i|) \tag{16}$$

The hypothesis of statistically independence let us write:

$$P(s) = \prod_{i=1}^{N} P(s_i), \tag{17}$$

A new formulation for the maximization problem in (15) follows:

$$s = \arg\max_{x=As} P(s) =$$
$$= \arg\max_{x=As} \prod_{i=1}^{N} P(s_i) =$$
$$= \arg\max_{x=As} \exp(-\lambda|s_1| - \cdots - \lambda|s_N|) = \tag{18}$$
$$= \arg\min_{x=As} |s_1| + \cdots + |s_N| =$$
$$= \arg\min_{x=As} \|s\|_1$$

where $\|s\|_1$ is the 1-norm of $s = (s_1, \cdots, s_N)$. Under these assumptions it can be shown that the solution exists and is unique.

The final formula reported in (18) tells us that our maximization problem is nothing but a problem of linear programming, that can be solved by using one of the many techniques in the literature. Taking into account that the 1-norm of a vector is the length of the path from the origin to the point fixed by the vector moving along the coordinate axis, it can be easily understood why this maximization procedure is called the Shortest Path Decomposition. Indeed, minimizing $\|s\|_1$ under the constraint $x = As$ means minimizing the path from the origin to the data point, moving along the columns a_i (i.e. minimum number of those a_i corresponding to the minimum values of s_i).

The assumption of laplacianity arisen in the BSR step confirms the importance of being sparse for the source signals. This property is not always satisfied in the time domain, so, even if we know the mixing model, the source recovery algorithm is not able to yield good results. This aspect is particularly enhanced if we have more sources than sensors. That is why some authors [10] have proposed to consider the problem in a different domain by applying a linear and invertible transform T to the signals involved, so that the new data point representation is more sparse than the original one. It operates as:

$$T(X) = A \cdot T(S) \Rightarrow \tilde{X} = A\tilde{S} \tag{19}$$

where $\tilde{X}$ and $\tilde{S}$ are the mixture and source matrices in the new domain, where the blind separation procedure is performed. Obviously, once the algorithm has given its results, the inverse transformation T^{-1} is needed to convert the signals in the original time domain.

3.3 The Underdetermined BSS with Delays

Here we introduce delays at source level in the underdetermined BSS formulation studied in the previous paragraph. It will be discussed the technique proposed in [17] by using the same notation there adopted.

As usual, let $s_j(t)$, $j = 1, \ldots, N$ be the N unknown sources, $t = 1, \ldots, T$ the discrete time variable and e $x_i(t)$, $i = 1, \ldots, M$ the M mixture, generated through the following model:

$$\begin{cases} x_1(t) = \beta_{11} s_1(t - \tau_{11}) + \ldots + \beta_{1N} s_N(t - \tau_{1N}) \\ \quad \vdots \\ x_M(t) = \beta_{M1} s_1(t - \tau_{M1}) + \ldots + \beta_{MN} s_N(t - \tau_{MN}) \end{cases} \tag{20}$$

where β_{ij} and τ_{ij} are the unknown real-valued parameters , respectively the weight and the delay relative to the contribution of source j to sensor i. According to such a formulation, the BSS problem consists in recovering the unknown parameters of the model and the original signals $s_j(t), \forall t$ by the only means of the mixture information. Again, our interest is on the underdetermined case: we shall describe a procedure to get good separation performances when $M = 2$. As for the previous algorithms studied, this one [17] is based on the fundamental assumptions of statistically independence and laplacianity (then sparsity) of sources. Also in this case, the source sparsity is enhanced by converting the basic two-step procedure for separation into the time-frequency domain through the Short Time Fourier Transform (STFT).

In particular, the new input variables for the algorithm are the STFT coefficients of the original mixture, calculated over K-samples long frames. The separation procedure is performed frame by frame. Indeed, let X_i^k denote the k-th coefficient of the Discrete Fourier Transform (DFT) of a generic frame of the i-th mixture: from this point of view, k plays the same role of t in the time domain counterpart. Now we can apply the DFT to (20), taking into account the properties of linearity and circular shifting (satisfied with a good rate of approximation) and get the following system of complex equations:

$$
\begin{cases}
X_1^k = \beta_{11} e^{-j2\pi k\tau_{11}/K} S_1^k + \dots + \beta_{1N} e^{-j2\pi k\tau_{1N}/K} S_N^k \\
\quad\vdots \\
X_M^k = \beta_{M1} e^{-j2\pi k\tau_{M1}/K} S_1^k + \dots + \beta_{MN} e^{-j2\pi k\tau_{MN}/K} S_N^k
\end{cases}
\tag{21}
$$

A more compact way to describe (21) can be achieved in terms of matrices:

$$
\mathbf{X}^k = \mathbf{Z}^k \, \mathbf{S}^k
\tag{22}
$$

where $\mathbf{X}^k$ is an M dimension complex column vector, $\mathbf{S}^k$ an N dimension complex column vector, and $\mathbf{Z}^k$ an $M \times N$ dimension complex matrix given by:

$$
\mathbf{Z}^k = \left[\beta_{ij} \, e^{-j2\pi k\tau_{ij}/K} \right]_{ij}.
\tag{23}
$$

We can identify two further matrices within (23): the *attenuation matrix* $\mathbf{B} = \left[\beta_{ij} \right]$ and the *delay matrix* $\mathbf{T} = \left[\tau_{ij} \right]$. It follows that the mixing matrix becomes:

$$
\mathbf{Z}^k = \mathbf{B} \star e^{-j2\pi k\mathbf{T}/K}
\tag{24}
$$

where $\star$ is the element-wise matrix product and it is assumed that the exponential function operates element-wise as well. We shall describe the 3-step procedure proposed in [12], starting from the first one: recovering the attenuation matrix. Therefore, we can rewrite (22) splitting the second term into the sum of N vectors, each one being the product of the j-th $\mathbf{Z}^k$ column weighted by the corresponding source:

$$
\mathbf{X}^k = \mathbf{Z}_1^k S_1^k + \dots + \mathbf{Z}_N^k S_N^k.
\tag{25}
$$

This confirms that, like in the instantaneous case, sources can be recovered up to permutation and scaling indeterminacies. Looking at the latter, it follows from (25) that a reciprocal scaling in S_j^k and $\mathbf{Z}_j^k$ does not influence the $\mathbf{X}^k$ value; so, without loss of generality, it can be assumed that the $\mathbf{Z}$ columns have unitary norm, meaning that the columns of the attenuation matrix do. Considering the amplitude of both terms in (25), we can deduce:

$$
Mag\left(\mathbf{X}^k\right) = Mag\left(\mathbf{Z}_1^k \, S_1^k + \dots + \mathbf{Z}_N^k \, S_N^k\right).
\tag{26}
$$

At this point we can exploit the hypotheses of laplacianity of the source amplitudes: there is an high probability (close to one) that, for each k, $Mag(\mathbf{X}^k)$ is influenced by only one $\mathbf{Z}_j^k S_j^k$. This is equivalent to sat that the most significant values in the observables belong to just one source.

Besides the sparsity assumption, we have to require that the used signal representation is disjoint. Assuming that only j-th source is relevant for data point $\mathbf{X}^k$ we get:

$$Mag(\mathbf{X}^k) = Mag(\mathbf{Z}_j^k) Mag(S_j^k) + \varepsilon = \mathbf{B}_j \, Mag(S_j^k) + \varepsilon \qquad (27)$$

where ε is the approximation error. This means that the direction of $Mag(\mathbf{X}^k)$ almost coincides with the one of $\mathbf{B}_j$, and its amplitude is approx $Mag(S_j^k)$. Taking into account what said in the instantaneous underdetermined case, we can conclude that the representation of $Mag(\mathbf{X}^k)$ vectors in the mixture space is dense around the origin while the most significant data points (those with the highest amplitudes) tend to cluster along certain directions corresponding to those of $\mathbf{B}_j$ vectors. Therefore, a proper clustering method can be applied on the mixture space represented by $Mag(\mathbf{X}^k)$ for the estimation of attenuation matrix columns.

In the two-dimensional case ($M = 2$), an efficient approach is the one of potential function [17]. This phase allows us to associate each data point to one source (the most relevant in its representation) and, having $\mathbf{B}_j$ unitary norm, the norm of vector $\mathbf{S}_j^k$ turns to be fixed. However, both $\mathbf{T}_j$ and $\mathbf{S}_j^k$ are still unknown, so concerning the delays, the only thing we can do is determining the differential delay between one source (taken as reference) and the other sensors. That is why we can consider that the mean value of $\mathbf{T}_j$ components, for all j are zero, without loss of generality. It follows that the mean value of the delay between such source and the other sensors is comprised in the $\mathbf{S}_j$ phase. Such an assumption (always in case $M = 2$) means to require that $\tau_{1j} = -\tau_{2j} = \delta_j / 2$, where δ_j is the differential delay. If $\delta_j = 0$, then it holds that $\mathbf{T}_j = [0 \quad 0]^\mathsf{T}$ and $e^{-\mathrm{j}2\pi k\mathbf{T}_j/K} = [1 \quad 1]^\mathsf{T}$; as done before for the amplitude values, we can derive the following from (25) for the real (or imaginary) part of $\mathbf{X}^k$:

$$\mathrm{Re}(\mathbf{X}^k) = \mathbf{B}_j \, \mathrm{Re}(S_j^k) + \varepsilon. \qquad (28)$$

Again, we are able to identify clusters in the relative scatterplot, corresponding to the $\mathbf{B}_j$ directions. However when $\delta_j \neq 0$ and $\mathbf{T}_j = [\delta_j/2 \quad -\delta_j/2]^\mathsf{T}$, it is possible to apply a phase correction term for both channels to get a differential delay ρ again. By denoting $\mathbf{R} = [\rho/2 \quad -\rho/2]^\mathsf{T}$, (28) becomes:

$$\mathbf{X}^k \star e^{-\mathrm{j}2\pi k\mathbf{R}/K} = \mathbf{B} \star e^{-\mathrm{j}2\pi k(\mathbf{T}_j+\mathbf{R})/K} S_j^k + \varepsilon. \qquad (29)$$

It follows that if $\rho = -\delta$, the phase term disappears and we get (28). The approach proposed in [17] for the estimation of the delay matrix, moves from the association data point-source resulting from the previous step and consists in adjusting iteratively the delay till to detect the cluster along the $\mathbf{B}_j$ direction (already achieved). At each iteration step we evaluate $\Phi\left(\tilde{\theta}_j\right)$, i.e. the potential function along the direction relative to j-th source. The $\tilde{\rho}$ value that maximizes $\Phi(\theta)$ is used to get an estimation of the differential delay as follows:

$$\tilde{\mathbf{T}}_j = \begin{bmatrix} \tilde{\delta}_j / 2 \\ -\tilde{\delta}_j / 2 \end{bmatrix} = \begin{bmatrix} -\tilde{\rho}_j / 2 \\ \tilde{\rho}_j / 2 \end{bmatrix} = -\tilde{\mathbf{R}} . \tag{30}$$

This can be done for all sources, yielding the final estimation of the delay matrix $\mathbf{T}$, that together with the attenuation matrix $\mathbf{B}$ allows us to recover the overall mixing model $\hat{\mathbf{Z}}^k = \tilde{\mathbf{B}} e^{-j2\pi k\tilde{\mathbf{T}}/K}$. Such a procedure can be easily extended to the case of $M > 2$ channels, by estimating the differential delays existing between each couple of channels.

The third and last step of the algorithm is the source recovering (separation). The previous ones obviously work also in the quadratic case, where the mixing model can be easily inverted to get the sources perfectly. In contrast, when $M < N$ again we have to face the problem of solving an underdetermined equation systems, that requires the presence of some constraints to be able to find a unique solution. Similarly to what described in paragraph 3.2, we follow an approach based on the likelihood maximization, under the assumptions that the source representation S_j^k are statistically independent, with equi-variance laplacian distribution of amplitudes and uniformly distributed phase. The resulting pdf of S_j^k is:

$$P\left(S_j^k\right) \propto e^{-\lambda \, Mag\left(S_j^k\right)} . \tag{31}$$

Statistically independence lets us write the following for the pdf of the source vector $\mathbf{S}^k = [S_1^k \quad \dots \quad S_N^k]^\top$:

$$P\left(\mathbf{S}^k\right) = \prod_{j=1}^{N} P\left(S_j^k\right) \propto \prod_{j=1}^{N} e^{-\lambda \, Mag\left(S_j^k\right)} \propto e^{-\lambda \sum_{j=1}^{N} Mag\left(S_j^k\right)} \tag{32}$$

As aforementioned, we have to maximize the source a-posteriori probability with respect to $\mathbf{X}^k$, by means of the mixing model estimation $\hat{\mathbf{Z}}^k$:

$$\hat{\mathbf{S}}^k = \arg\max_\mathbf{S} P\left(\mathbf{S}^k \mid \mathbf{X}^k\right) \tag{33}$$

where $\mathbf{S}$ belong to the space of solution of the underdetermined system $\mathbf{X}^k = \hat{\mathbf{Z}}^k \mathbf{S}^k$. According to the Bayes theorem, we can rewrite (33) as:

$$\hat{\mathbf{S}}^k = \arg\max_\mathbf{S} P\left(\mathbf{X}^k \mid \mathbf{S}^k\right) P\left(\mathbf{S}^k\right) . \tag{34}$$

Since in the noiseless case $\mathbf{X}^k$ is completely determined by $\mathbf{S}^k$ and by the mixing matrix (i.e. $P\left(\mathbf{X}^k \mid \mathbf{S}^k\right) = 1$), from (34) we derive:

$$\hat{\mathbf{S}}^k = \arg\max_\mathbf{S} P\left(\mathbf{S}^k\right) . \tag{35}$$

Substituting (32) into (35) we get:

$$\hat{\mathbf{S}}^k = \arg\max_{\mathbf{s}} P\left(\mathbf{S}^k\right) = \arg\max_{\mathbf{s}} e^{-\lambda \sum_{j=1}^{N} Mag\left(S_j^k\right)} = \arg\min_{\mathbf{s}} \sum_{j=1}^{N} Mag\left(S_j^k\right). \tag{36}$$

So that the final problem to solve has this form:

$$\min_{\mathbf{s}} \sum_{j=1}^{N} Mag\left(S_j^k\right) \text{ under the constraint } \mathbf{X}^k = \hat{\mathbf{Z}}^k \mathbf{S}^k. \tag{37}$$

It can be shown that (37) is a second order convex (cone) programming problem, and it can be solved by using techniques already available in the literature [18]. Once separation has been performed for all values of k parameter, the inverse Discrete Fourier Transform must be applied to the estimated recovered sources in order to get the relative signals in the time domain (on a frame by frame basis).

4 Sparsity of Speech Signals in Different Domains

In the previous sections we analyzed two geometric techniques for the solution of the underdetermined BSS problem with instantaneous and delayed mixing model and we highlighted how the improved signal sparsity achievable in a proper transformed domain leads to better results in both the BMMR and the BSR stage. Sparsity is not, however, the unique requirement: it is also important that the representations of different sources are *disjoint* [19] in the new domain, i.e. the small number of significant coefficients (carrying the most information) must occupy different positions in the vector of representation coefficients for different sources. In [10] and [17] the STFT based time-frequency representation is used, but this is not the only admissible choice since any linear and invertible transformation can be adopted. This is a key issue, in the sense that we can expect to get a relevant sparseness and spectral disjointness if we are able to yield a strong speech-oriented time-frequency representation, i.e. a suitable transform whose expansion functions would catch the information content of the speech signals in the mixtures. Of course, this attempt must be considered in relation to the usual STFT approach, widely addressed in the literature so far for the same problem. In the following we shall briefly introduce some new transforms that will be used within the algorithmic framework described above. They all differ from the STFT for one main characteristic: the time and frequency resolution are not uniform over the phase plane, that is expected to give a more adequate analysis of the spectral content of a typical speech signal rather than the STFT counterpart (uniform tiling). These transforms will be compared in the sense of degree of sparseness and disjointness, before studying the performances achievable when implemented in the three-step separation procedure.

Let us consider, the Wavelet Transform [20] first, which employs a windowing technique with variable size on the phase plane. Formally, given a continuous-time signal $f(t)$, its *Continuous Wavelet Transform* (CWT) is a two-indexed family of coefficients $C(a,b)$ computed in the following manner

$$C(a,b) = \int_{-\infty}^{\infty} f(t) \frac{1}{\sqrt{a}} \psi\left(\frac{t-b}{a}\right) dt \tag{38}$$

where $a \in \mathbb{R}^+ \setminus \{0\}$ and $b \in \mathbb{R}$, while $\psi(t)$ is a real or complex valued assigned function, called *mother wavelet*, which must satisfy some conditions to consider (38) a valid CWT [20]. Given the family of coefficients, the original signal can be reconstructed using the following synthesis formula

$$f(t) = \frac{1}{K_\psi} \int_0^{+\infty} \int_{-\infty}^{+\infty} C(a,b) \frac{1}{\sqrt{a}} \psi\left(\frac{t-b}{a}\right) \frac{da\,db}{a^2} \qquad (39)$$

where K_ψ is a constant depending on ψ.

Intuitively, the original signal is written as superimposition of *shifted* and *scaled* versions of the original mother wavelet $\psi(t)$, which is a limited duration waveform with average value of zero. The parameter a is called scale factor and determines how much the mother wavelet is stretched or compressed. Instead, the parameter b represents a translation and tells the position of the wavelet on the time axis. For this reason the representation provided by the Wavelet Transform is called *time-scale representation* of a signal.

The *Discrete Wavelet Transform* (DWT) [21] [22] is obtained from (38) choosing scales and positions based on powers of two (i.e. *dyadic* scales and positions)

$$\begin{aligned} a &= 2^j \\ b &= ka = k2^j \end{aligned} \qquad \text{where } j,k \in \mathbb{Z}. \qquad (40)$$

Note that for small j, also the scale $a = 2^j$ is small, hence the analysis is local (high frequencies); instead, for big values of j, the scale is big and the analysis is global (low frequencies). An efficient way to implement the DWT using perfect reconstruction filter banks was derived in [23], and the resulting scheme is known as *two channel subband coder* and it is realized using dyadic QMF banks.

Given a signal s of length N, the DWT consists of $\log_2 N$ stages at most. Starting from s, the first step produces two sets of coefficients: *approximation coefficients* cA_1 and *detail coefficients* cD_1. These vectors are obtained by convolving the signal s with a low pass filter Lo_D for approximation, and a high pass filter Hi_D for details, followed by dyadic decimation. In the subsequent steps the same decomposition scheme is applied to split the approximation coefficients cA_i to obtain two set of output coefficients cA_{i+1} and cD_{i+1}. So the i-level Wavelet decomposition of a signal s is a dyadic binary tree of depth i.

The Wavelet Packet Analysis [22] is a generalization of the previously described Wavelet decomposition. The generic decomposition step is identical to the classic DWT one, but in the successive step both the approximation and the detail coefficients are decomposed by the QMF banks. So at the i-th decomposition step we obtain a complete binary tree, and the dyadic DWT tree is only a part of it. A still more interesting option is given by the *Best Wavelet Packet* decomposition, which at the generic decomposition step, decides if it is convenient to further split both the approximation and the detail coefficients, using a suitable convenience rule. In this way the binary decomposition tree can assume a generic structure, and it is possible to obtain the best resolution in each different region of the phase plane. This yields more than $2^{2^{n-1}}$ different ways to encode the signal by a tree of depth n. Choosing one of all these possible encodings presents a difficult problem and usually a criterion based on the computation of an *entropy function* is used to select the most suitable decomposition of a signal. This means we look at each node of the decomposition tree and quantify the information to be gained in performing each split: the split is performed only if the information increases. The most common algorithms to choose the best decomposition are based on [24].

Another kind of transformation we propose for the BSS problem is the *Stocwell Transform* (ST) [25], which can be seen as a time-frequency representation (TFR). The ST is introduced as a reversible time-frequency spectral localization technique and combines some elements of the DWT and the STFT, exploiting several advantages and overcoming several limits of these representations. The ST has indeed a variable resolution on the phase plane, which is one of the greatest advantages of the Wavelets over the STFT, but maintains in the meantime the phase information, that is lost in the Wavelet representation. This is due to the particular expansion functions used, made by sinusoids fixed as to time axis that are used to modulate a translating Gaussian window, with amplitude and scale modified by the analyzed frequency, allowing to localize with different resolutions distinct regions of the phase plane. So, from a conceptual point of view, the ST can be considered as an hybrid between STFT and Wavelet Transform, since it contains elements of both of them, but it can not be entirely considered into neither of these two categories. For the Discrete Stockwell Transform, two equivalent formulation can be derived

$$
S\left[jT, \frac{n}{NT}\right] = \frac{|n|}{\sqrt{2\pi}N} \sum_{k=0}^{N-1} h(kT) \left(\sum_{r=-\infty}^{+\infty} e^{-\frac{(j-k-rN)^2 n^2}{2N^2}} \right) e^{-i\frac{2\pi}{N}nk}
$$

$$
S\left[jT; \frac{n}{NT}\right] = \sum_{m=-N/2}^{N/2} H\left[\frac{m+n}{NT}\right] e^{-\frac{2\pi^2 m^2}{n^2}} e^{i\frac{2\pi}{N}mj}
$$

(41)

where

$$
\begin{cases} j = 0, 1, \cdots, N-1 \\ n = -\frac{N}{2}, \cdots, 0, \cdots, \frac{N}{2} \end{cases} \quad \text{e} \quad S[jT, 0] = \frac{1}{N} \sum_{m=0}^{N-1} h[kT].
$$

(42)

The synthesis (or inverse) formula is given by

$$
h[kT] = \frac{1}{N} \sum_{n=0}^{N-1} \left\{ \sum_{j=0}^{N-1} S\left[jT; \frac{n}{NT}\right] \right\} e^{i\frac{2\pi}{N}nk}.
$$

(43)

From (41) we can see that the ST provides an highly overcomplete representation of original time series, since it associates a set of N^2 complex coefficients to N-length sequence. For this reason, using the Theory of Frames [26], we derived a reduced version of the discrete ST, a version that allows the original time sequence to be described with a smaller number of coefficients. See Appendix for further details.

The last kind of representation introduced here to deal with the BSS problem is the Dual Tree Complex Wavelet Transform (DT CWT) [27]. The DT CWT is a particular DWT, that generates complex coefficients using a dual tree of real wavelet filters to obtain the real and imaginary parts, respectively. This leads to a limited redundancy ($2^m : 1$ for m-dimensional signals), and allows the transform to provide approximate shift invariance and directionally selective filters (properties lacking in the traditional DWT), while preserving the important properties of perfect reconstruction and computational efficiency.

The decomposition tree used by the DT CWT is shown in Fig. 1, in its dyadic version. From a computational point of view, this transform has twice the cost of a traditional DWT, since a real N-length signal leads to a $2N$-length vector of real coefficients. The filters are designed so that the output of the upper tree (tree **a**) could be considered as the real part of a complex DWT coefficients, while the output of the lower tree corresponds to the imaginary parts of the same coefficients. It can be shown that the described scheme constitutes a Wavelet frame with redundancy 2; and if the filters are designed such that the analysis and the reconstruction filters have very similar frequency response (i.e. are almost orthogonal), then the frame is almost *tigh*, which means that the energy is approximately preserved in the DT CWT representation. At last it can be noted that, rather than use a dyadic decomposition like in Fig. 1, we can also use the Wavelet Packet or the Best Wavelet Packet Decompositions, formerly seen for the classic DWT. As for the DWT, for the DT CWT we will use all the three different decompositions too.

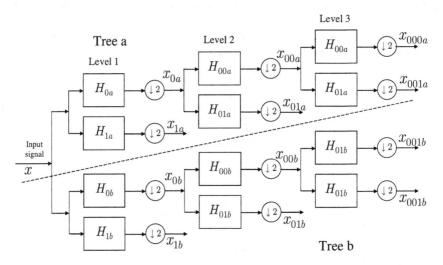

Fig. 1. DT CWT dyadic decomposition tree. Tree **a** generates the real part of complex representation coefficients; Tree **b** generates the corresponding imaginary part

To make a comparison between different kinds of sparsity possible, we will use the amplitude distributions of representation coefficients, that for speech signals are almost laplacian, as well known. A representation is more sparse if it has a higher central peak and lower lateral tails. As an example, in Fig. 2 on the left it is plotted the histogram related to the original time sequence (time representation), consisting in a 10000 sample female voice, sampled at 11025 Hz; on the right the histogram related to the STFT representation is plotted, obtained by 1024 length windowing and 512 samples of overlap between consecutive frames. We can highlight that the STFT representation is more sparse; for the other time frequency (or time-scale) representations previously described, similar increments of sparsity can be obtained too.

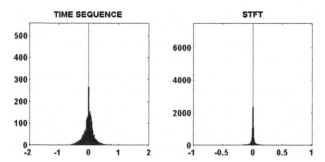

Fig. 2. Left: histogram of the amplitude distribution of a time sequence consisting of a 10000 sample female voice; Right: histogram of the STFT representation of the original time sequence, obtained by 1024 length windowing and 512 sample overlap

To study the sparseness and disjointness properties of various time-frequency representations and justify results obtained both in the BMMR and in the BSR phase, we made the following experiments. First, let us consider three 32768 sample speech signals, sampled at 11025 Hz and containing two male voices and a female voice and let us determine the time-frequency representations of all three signal separately. For each different transformation, we have calculated how many times a single source is significant in a generic position of coefficient vector, i.e. how many times the norm of a source coefficient (being the representation vectors normalized $s_i' = s_i / \max\left(\|s_i\|\right)$)

is bigger than a certain threshold M and the norms of the other two source coefficients are lower than another threshold $m \ll M$. Table 1 reports the number of these events in part per million (ppm), for different m, M values.

It can be noted that such occurrences are less frequent in the case of STFT rather than the other transforms. So we can state the STFT has a lower one-source sparsity compared to the other representations analyzed; on the contrary the ST has the higher one-source sparsity. This kind of sparsity is important in the BMMR phase, since the potential function method assigns to each coefficient a weight proportional to its norm and for the ST is more probable that a big norm coefficient in a mixture leads to a single source, lying very close to the real direction related to that source.

As second experiment we have determined how many times all three sources are present simultaneously and relevantly at a specific position of coefficient vectors, i.e. how often the norm of all three sources is higher than threshold M . Results in table 2 are shown in ppm, and we can see that for the ST this happens more frequently than for the other representations. The STFT has, instead, very disjoint representation, if compared to the others. This is a considerable advantage for the BSR step.

5   Alternative Approaches for Underdetermined BSS with Delays

Let us consider the mixing model in(20). As proved above, we are only able to recover differential delays, then we can use the following formulation for(20):

$$\begin{cases} x_1(t) = \beta_{11}\, s_1(t) + \ldots + \beta_{1N}\, s_N(t) \\ x_2(t) = \beta_{21}\, s_1(t - \tau_1) + \ldots + \beta_{2N}\, s_N(t - \tau_N) \end{cases} \tag{44}$$

Table 1. Number of occurrences (in ppm) the norm of a source coefficient is bigger than the threshold M and the norms of the other two source coefficients are lower than a threshold $m \ll M$. For the ST 1024 sample frame without overlap; for STFT 1024 sample frame with 512 sample of overlap; for DWT a db3 level6 is used

	ST	STFT	DWT	DT CWT
$M = 0,1$ e $m = 0,01$	70862	22355	47967	44174
$M = 0,1$ e $m = 0,001$	6256	1996	5580	6043
$M = 0,2$ e $m = 0,01$	28763	5987	14393	12070
$M = 0,2$ e $m = 0,001$	2701	587	1738	1679
$M = 0,4$ e $m = 0,01$	6454	1230	1616	1785
$M = 0,6$ e $m = 0,01$	1343	340	214	229

Table 2. Number of occurences (in ppm) all three sources are simultaneously and significatively present in coefficient vectors; For the ST 1024 sample frame without overlap; for STFT 1024 sample frame with 512 sample of overlap; for DWT a db3 level6 is used

	ST	STFT	DWT	DT CWT
$M = 0,01$	68573	30725	55805	45319
$M = 0,025$	18448	4889	19349	16372
$M = 0,05$	4044	665	7989	6104
$M = 0,1$	732	16	1616	1190
$M = 0,2$	107	0	61	46

with obvious notation for variables and parameters. We are still in the time domain: system (44) can be converted into a new one in the time-frequency domain through a proper transform:

$$\begin{cases} X_1^{j,n} = \beta_{11} S_1^{j,n} + \ldots + \beta_{1N} S_N^{j,n} \\ X_2^{j,n} = \beta_{21} S_1^{j-\tau_1,n} + \ldots + \beta_{2N} S_N^{j-\tau_N,n} \end{cases} \tag{45}$$

It might be underlined that the terms S_k in the second mixture depend on delays τ_k, so that, even under hypotheses of sparse and disjoint representation of sources, we cannot expect in general to detect the clusters along (β_{1k}, β_{2k}) directions in the mixture scatterplot. However, if we suppose to know one of the two mixtures, for example $x_2(t)$, in order to compensate the delay relative to the k-th source, resulting a perfect time-alignment for such source in both mixture. It follows that (45) can be written as:

$$\begin{cases} X_1^{j,n} = \beta_{11} S_1^{j,n} + \ldots + \beta_{1k} S_k^{j,n} + \beta_{1N} S_N^{j,n} \\ \tilde{X}_2^{j,n} = \beta_{21} S_1^{j-(\tau_1-\tau_j),n} + \ldots + \beta_{1k} S_k^{j,n} + \cdots + \beta_{2N} S_N^{j-(\tau_N-\tau_j),n} \end{cases} \tag{46}$$

Therefore we can expect now to identify the cluster along the direction θ_k relative to (β_{1k}, β_{2k}), that can be evaluated by calculating the maximum of the potential function, as usual, whereas the most significant coefficients of other sources, which are not aligned in the two mixture representations, do not generate any cluster, but only point clouds around 0 and $\pi/2$ directions. So, if we suppose there is a range $\left(\tau_{\min}, \tau_{\max}\right)$ of admissible values for our unknown differential delays, we can think to proceed according to the following procedure. For any τ in the range $\left(\tau_{\min}, \tau_{\max}\right)$:

1. shift the second mixture of τ;
2. evaluate the potential function for the mixture representation in the time-frequency domain;
3. store what obtained in a row vector of a proper dimensioned matrix.

In conclusion we get a matrix whose row number is equal to $\tau_{\max} - \tau_{\min}$, where each row is relative to a certain τ value, and whose column number is the number of grid points used for the evaluation of the potential function. Therefore we get a new potential function depending on two parameters θ and τ, instead of only one, and which can be depicted in a 3D graph. We expect to detect a number of peaks (evident local maxima) in such a graph equal to the number of sources and corresponding to those values $\left(\tau^*, \theta^*\right)$ of independent variables that allow to recover the unknown parameters of the mixing model (44). It can be said that the estimation of this model can be performed in one single step by evaluating the maxima of the 3D potential function $\Phi(\tau, \theta)$.

Concerning the BSR step, we are asked to solve an optimization problem with constraints described by (45), that can be seen in general as a linear or non-linear programming problem. Nevertheless, we shall deal with alternative separation techniques, that, like all geometric approaches, consist in analyzing the mixture space somehow.

It must be observed that in the majority of cases, especially when underdetermined systems are involved, such separation techniques are not able to guarantee perfect reconstruction, and loss of useful information and cross-talk usually appear in recovered sources. That is why we propose a sort of post-separation processing, based on some a-priori assumptions on the source signals, that could be very effective and yield improved (audio) quality.

First method. When mixtures are time-aligned in order to compensate one of the differential delays, as said above, we can identify one evident cluster in the mixture scatterplot, together with two point clouds (clusters that are not so evident and with lower point density) around 0 and $\pi/2$ directions. Therefore, we can think to apply the BSR technique used in the instantaneous case by using three angle directions: the one corresponding to the evident cluster, 0 and $\pi/2$. It follows that we can recover the source relative to the compensated delay and we have to repeat the algorithm for the other delays and sources.

Second method. This method represent an interesting approach for source cancellation, rather than source separation. We always start from the time-alignment of mixture respect with one differential delay. Then we can apply the usual BSR procedure to perform the separation between the cluster direction and the relative maximally distant one, i.e. the orthogonal direction. It results that the recovered source (reference) presents a sensible quantity of cross-talk, whereas the reconstructed signal along the other direction there is no mention of the reference source.

Third method. Among the alternative approaches proposed, this one seems to guarantee the best separation achievable. It is based on the simple observation that, once compensated one differential delay, the mixture coefficients that mostly represent the source relative to the cluster direction in the scatterplot tend to be very close to such direction. Consequently, instead of considering all the data points, we can take into account only those distant from the cluster direction less than an adequate threshold angle $\hat{\theta}$. So, source recovering can be performed by simple projection of these points along the privileged direction, setting to zero all the other ones. This inevitably introduces a loss of information on the reconstructed signal with respect to the original source, that is the main reason of noise in our experimental tests. Otherwise, increasing the $\hat{\theta}$ value we reduce the number of coefficients forced to zero and so we let information related to other sources influence the one to be recovered, resulting in a cross-talk effect.

Such a drawback can be partially limited by using some of the a-priori knowledge on the signals (speech) under study we have. Even in this case, the procedure must be repeated for all sources in the mixtures.

6   Experimental Results

In this section we report the experimental results obtained by applying different types of time-frequency transforms to the aforementioned approaches to the problem of underdetermined BSS with delays: STFT, ST, DWT (classic, packet and best packet), DTCWT (classic, packet and best packet). Such results are referred to the case of two mixtures and three sources. However further tests have been performed in the case of more than 3 sources, and all results allowed us to state that separation performances depend on several factors, listed as follows:

1. obviously the closer delays and attenuation parameters are the more critical the separation process is;
2. λ is a parameter involved in the calculation of potential function; empirical results confirm that, for speech signals, λ values in the range $(10, 20)$ allow to achieve the best results

Moreover, looking at the Wavelet based transforms we have to take the following into consideration:

3. *mother Wavelet* ψ : there exist several types of Wavelet families (haar, daubechies, coifflets, etc.) and many mother Wavelet with different order can be specified within them; in dependence on this choice we have different filters used for the decomposition and the reconstruction;
4. *decomposition level*: it is the maximum depth of the decomposition tree; determining the maximum frequency resolution adopted to analyze the input signal;
5. *cost function*: it is the function involved in the choice of the best tree for Wavelet Packet decomposition; different cost functions can yield significantly different selection of the optimal tree.

In order to achieve an objective evaluation of the separation quality we use the following signal to noise ratio (SNR), widely accepted in the literature:

$$S/N = 10\log\frac{\left\|\mathbf{s}_k\right\|^2}{\left\|\mathbf{s}_k - \tilde{\mathbf{s}}_k\right\|^2} \tag{47}$$

where the original and recovered signals are supposed to be unitary energy normalized. In the experiments we made, 37846 samples long sources have been used, obtained by sampling three speech signals (two male and one female) at 11025 Hz and 16 bit resolution. The attenuation matrix $\mathbf{B}$ has been chosen as follows:

$$\mathbf{B} = \begin{bmatrix} \cos(\theta_1) & \cos(\theta_2) & \cos(\theta_3) \\ \sin(\theta_1) & \sin(\theta_2) & \sin(\theta_3) \end{bmatrix} \text{ with } \theta_1 = -0,9,\ \theta_2 = 0,2 \text{ e } \theta_3 = 1,1, \tag{48}$$

while the differential delays are:

$$\tau_1 = 12,\ \tau_2 = -4 \text{ e } \tau_3 = -18. \tag{49}$$

As mentioned above, once compensated one differential delay in the two mixtures we can identify in the scatterplot the cluster whose angle direction matches the corresponding one of the relative attenuation matrix column. The graphs reported on the top of Fig.3 depict the scatterplots of mixture representation in the S-Transform domain, for each delay value compensated, whereas the relative directions inferred through the potential functions can be well recovered from the second row graphs. Looking at those graphs we can note how small peaks appear in location $\theta = 0, \pi/2$, corresponding to the spurious contributions to the compensated sources. Fig.4 reports the graph of 3D potential function, where the local maxima are well defined, whose coordinates (τ, θ) are directly related to the real values of the mixing parameters.

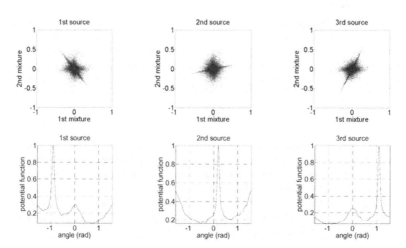

Fig. 3. Top: Scatter plot of ST coefficients obtained by time aligning the mixtures with respect to one of the three sources; Bottom: potential functions corresponding to the scatterplot depicted in the previous row graphs

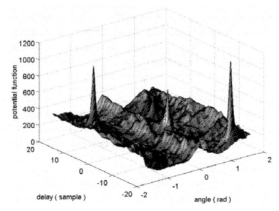

Fig. 4. 3D potential function obtained through the mixture ST coefficients

In Fig. 5 (left) the 3D potential function in the case of dyadic decomposition DWT (mother wavelet=coiflets order 5, decomposition level=6) is plotted. Two of the three sources can be well recovered, as the presence of two evident peaks confirm. However, the third peak is not evident as the other two, even though in Fig.5 (right) we are still able to detect the right local maximum corresponding to the right angle direction.

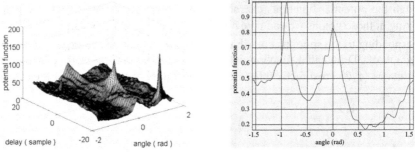

Fig. 5. Left: 3D potential function from dyadic decomposition DWT coefficients; Right: potential function obtained by time-aligning the two mixtures respect with the first source

Fig.6 is the analogue of the previous one: in this case the Best Packet DWT (coiflets order 5, level 6) is used for decomposition. It is evident that the third peak is more visible than the dyadic DWT counterpart. Even the usage of the complex wavelet transform allows us to get the same conclusion (Fig.7): the choice of the best tree (according to a certain algorithm) brings benefit to the detection of the right mixing parameters on the 3D potential function plot.

The usage of the STFT yields approximately the same results obtained with the Best Packet decompositions, with two peaks much more evident than the third one. It can be concluded that the ST allows to get the best estimation of the mixing parameters, among the transforms here considered.

Concerning the BSR step, we made several experiments, employing the same input signals above and assuming to know the mixing parameters that are:

$$\theta_1 = 0,2 , \ \theta_2 = 0,7 \ e \ \theta_3 = 1,1 ; \ \tau_1 = 10 , \tau_2 = -4 \ e \ \tau_3 = -8 . \tag{50}$$

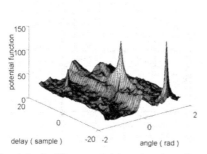
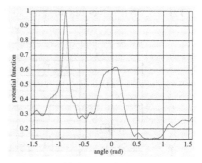

Fig. 6. Left: 3D potential function from Best Packet DWT coefficients; Right: potential function obtained by time-aligning the two mixtures respect with the first source

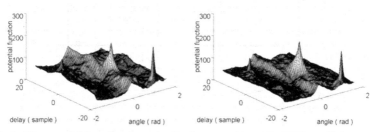

Fig. 7. Left: 3D potential function from dyadic decomposition DT-CWT coefficients; Right 3D potential function from Best Packet DT-CWT coefficients

The obtained SNR values for all three different alternative approaches dealt with are reported in Table 3 The threshold angle in the third method is $\hat{\theta} = 0,2$.

Looking at the values appearing in tables above, it can be noted that the Best versions of the Wavelet based decompositions used generally outperform their correspondent dyadic counterparts. In particular, the DT-CWT yields the highest SNRs, while those attainable in the case of ST are pretty low. From the subjective listening perspective, informal tests have allowed to conclude that the quality of separation and the amount of cross-talk present in recovered signals are not significantly different for the time-frequency transforms implemented, a part from the dyadic Wavelet based decomposition and the ST where the residual noise is relevant, as a conformal conclusion to the SNR values listed in the tables.Moreover, it must be underlined that sources recovered through the third method show a lower cross-talk level, even though the SNRs obtained do not seem to support this observation. This is due to its way of operating: forcing to zero many coefficients in mixture vectors lead to loss of information but also tends to null the noise presence.

7   Conclusions

In this work the problem of speech signal separation has been dealt with and faced as a BSS problem. It has been highlighted how the statistical properties of speech fit suitably the assumptions usually required in the algorithms proposed in the literature to face the BSS problem in different possible formulations. The one we considered

Table 3. SNR values obtained for all three different alternative approaches described

Method		SNR (dB)		
		s_1	s_2	s_3
ST	I	2.9781	2.8887	1.4739
	II	5.2639	1.3494	1.4275
	III	2.1756	1.6913	0.2670
STFT	I	5.0575	4.8242	2.8263
	II	5.2639	1.3494	1.4275
	III	6.9441	5.0444	2.4487
DWT	I	3,9943	3,1416	2,4504
	II	5,7483	0,9385	1,6949
	III	3,9084	2,7028	0,8813
BEST DWT	I	3,7024	4,0875	2,3593
	II	5,2648	1,3459	1,4309
	III	4,1547	3,9628	1,3495
DT CWT	I	4,5919	3,4386	2,7516
	II	5,7483	0,9385	1,6949
	III	4,9525	3,8446	1,7219
BEST DT CWT	I	5,2454	4,7192	3,2543
	II	5,2648	1,3459	1,4309
	III	7,7948	5,8561	3,7536

here is the underdetermined BSS with delays, that is the case when the sources are delayed, weighted and summed up to give rise to the mixture signals. The goal is to recover the original sources without having any insights on the mixing parameters. The approach followed for its solution is a three step procedure, already appeared in the literature, completely performed in the time-frequency domain, into which the available signals are converted through proper linear transformation. The statistically independence, sparsity and spectral disjointness are fundamental assumptions for the addressed algorithm and even typical characteristics of speech signals.

We have suggested the employment of alternative time-frequency transforms (ST, DWT, DT-CWT) rather than the usual STFT, used in the original version of the algorithm, Accordingly, it has been pointed out how the sparseness degree in the signal representation varies transform by transform, and how the related performances from the perspective of mixing parameter recovering and source separation are different. Concerning this, three new methods for blind source recovering (the last step of the overall procedure) have been considered and implemented to further compare how much the transform characteristics influence the separation process. As final conclusions, it can be said that ST (for which we have developed a low-redundancy discrete version, still addressable as a frame based decomposition) allows to achieve the best estimation of the delay and attenuation parameters, whereas the non-dyadic transforms seem to guarantee a superior behavior when sources are reconstructed from the mixtures and the estimated mixing model.

As further works, some of the authors are actually involved in evaluating the applicability and separation performances of different time-frequency transforms for the underdetermined convolutive BSS problem, recently addressed in the literature [28]

[29] but only employing the usual STFT. This seems to be the natural extension of the efforts made in the present paper. Moreover, we can think of implementing more performing filter banks for signal decomposition and reconstruction. Various optimization techniques could be implemented for the filter design task, even introducing a sort of a-priori knowledge about the signals involved. Indeed some spectral information (like pitch, formants, and so on) of the speech signals in the mixture could be retrieved somehow and used to develop a strong speech-oriented time-frequency transform of the available observables. Nevertheless, such information could have a strong impact on the application of suitable post-processing algorithms for speech quality enhancement.

References

1. Jutten, C., Hérault, J., Comon, P., Sorouchiary, E.: Blind Separation of Sources, Parts I, II and III, Signal Processing, Vol. 24, No. 1, July 1991, pp. 1-29
2. Haykin, S.: Unsupervised Adaptive Filtering, Volume 1: Blind Source Separation. Wiley Series on Adaptive and Learning Systems for Signal Processing, Communications and Control, Simon Haykin Series Editor 2000
3. Haykin, S.: Unsupervised Adaptive Filtering, Volume 2: Blind Deconvolution. Wiley Series on Adaptive and Learning Systems for Signal Processing, Communications and Control, Simon Haykin Series Editor 2000
4. Cichocki, A., Amari, S.: Adaptive Blind Signal and Image Processing. Learning Algorithms and Application, Wiley Ed. 2002
5. Lee, T.W., Lewicki, M.S, Girolami, M., Bell, A.J., Sejnowski, T.J.: Blind Source Separation of More Sources Using Overcomplete Representations. IEEE Signal Processing Letters, 6(4):87-90, 1999
6. Hyvärinen, A., Karhunen, J., Oja, E.: Independent Component Analysis. Wiley & Sons, New York, 2001
7. Lee, T.W., Girolami, M., Bell, A.J., Sejnowski, T.,J.: A Unifying Information Theoretic Framework for Independent Component Analysis. Computers & Mathematics with Applications, 31(11):1-21, March 2000
8. Theis, F.J., Lang, E.W.: Geometric Overcomplete ICA. Proc of ESANN 2002, pp 217-223, 2002
9. Puntonet, G.C., Prieto, A., Jutten, C., Rodrìguez-Alvarez, M., Ortega, J.: Separation of Sources: a Geometry Based Procedure for Recostruction of n-Valued Signal. Elsevier Signal Processing, vol.46, no.3, pp267-284, June 1995
10. Bofill, P., Zibulevsky, M.: Blind Separation of More Sources than Mixtures Using the Sparsity of the Short-Time Fourier Transform. International Workshop on Independent Component Analysis and Blind Signal Separation, (Helsinki, Finland), pp. 87-92, June 2000
11. Bell, A.J., Sejnovsky, T.J.: An Information-Maximization Approach to Blind Separation and Blind Deconvolution. Neural Comput. 7 (1995) 1129-1159
12. Cardoso, J.F.: Informax and Maximum Likelihood for Blind Source Separation. IEEE Sign. Process: Letters , 4:109-111, April 1997
13. Amari, S.:Natural Gradient Learning for Over- and Under-Complete Bases in ICA. Neural Computation, 11(8):1875-1883, November 1999
14. Theis, F.J., Lang, E. W., Lautenschlager, M.A., Puntonet, C.G.: A Theoretical Framework for Overcomplete Geometric BMMR. Proc. of SIP 2002, pp. 201–206, 2002.

15. Zibulevsky, M., Kisilev, P., Zeevi, Y.Y., & Pearlmutter, B. A. (2001). Blind Source Separation via Multinode Sparse Representation. In T. K. Leen, T. G. Dietterich, & V. Tresp (Eds.), Advances in Neural Information Processing Systems, 13. Cambridge, MA: MIT Press

16. 16 Theis, F.J. Lang, E.W: Formalization of the Two-Step Approach to Overcomplete BSS" SIP 2002

17. Bofill, P. : Underdetermined Blind Separation of Delayed Sound Sources in the Frequency Domain. Neurocomputing, Special Issue ICA and BSS, 2 March 2001

18. Lobo, M.S., Vandenberghe, L., Boyd, S., Lebret, H.: Applications of Second Order Cone Programming. In Linear Algebra and Its Applications, 284, pp 193-228, 1998

19. Yilmaz, O., Rickard, S.,: Blind Separation of Speech Mixtures via Time-Frequency Masking. IEEE Transaction on Signal Processing, vol.52, no.7, July 2004

20. Daubechies, I.: Ten Lectures on Wavelets. Society for Industrial and Applied Mathematics, Philadelphia, 1992

21. Vetterli, M, Kovačević, J. : Wavelets and Subband Coding, Prentice Hall, 1995

22. Mallat, S.G.: A Wavelet Tour of Signal Processing. Academic Press, London UK, 1998

23. Mallat, S.G.: A Theory for Multiresolution Signal Decomposition: The Wavelet Representation. IEEE Transactions on Pattern Analysis and Machine Intelligence, vol.11, no.7, July 1989

24. Coifman, R.R., Wickerhauser, M.V.: Entropy-Based Algorithms for Best Basis Selection. IEEE Trans. Inform. Theory, 38(2)

25. Stockwell, R.G., Mansinha, L., Lowe, R.P. : Localization of the Complex Spectrum: The S Transform. IEEE Trans. Signal Process., 44 (1996), pp. 998–1001

26. Daubechies, I.: The Wavelet Transform, Time Frequency Localization and Signal Analysis. IEEE Transactions on Information Theory, Vol. 36 No.5 September 1990

27. Kingsbury, NG. The Dual Tree Complex Wavelet Transform: a New Technique for Shift Invariance and Directional Filters. Proc th IEEE DSP Workshop Bryce Canyon Aug 1998

28. Sawada, H., Mukai, R., Araki, S., Makino, S.; Convolutive Blind Source Separation for More Than Two Sources in the Frequency Domain. ICASSP 2004

29. Winter S., Sawada, H., Araki, S., Makino, S.: Hierarchical Clustering Applied to Overcomplete BSS for Convolutive Mixtures. Workshop on Statistical and Perceptual Audio Processing SAPA-2004, 3 Oct 2004, Jeju Korea

Appendix: Dyadic Tiling in Discrete Time Stockwell Transform

The discrete time Frame theory [26] can be seen as a generalization of the principle decomposition of an N-dimension vector into orthonormal basis. Let us assume to have a redundant set of generator vectors $\{\mathbf{v}_i\}$, $i = 1,2,\cdots,M$ of a vector space of dimension N. Any vector of this space can be written in terms of $\mathbf{v}_i$ as follows:

$$\mathbf{f} = \sum_{i=1}^{M} \langle \mathbf{f}, \mathbf{v}_i \rangle \tilde{\mathbf{v}}_i = \sum_{i=1}^{M} \langle \mathbf{f}, \tilde{\mathbf{v}}_i \rangle \mathbf{v}_i \quad \text{with} \quad M > N \tag{51}$$

The $\mathbf{v}_i$ are the *members of a frame* while the set $\{\mathbf{v}_i\}$ is called *frame*. The set $\{\tilde{\mathbf{v}}_i\}$ is the *dual frame* of $\{\mathbf{v}_i\}$ and the difficult goal of the frame based description is finding out the dual frame, that is not unique. A frame $\{\tilde{\mathbf{v}}_i\}$ is a set of vectors satisfying, for any non-zero vector $\mathbf{f}$ of dimension $N \times 1$ the following:

$$A\|\mathbf{f}\|^2 \leq \sum_{i=1}^{M} |\langle \mathbf{f}, \mathbf{v}_i \rangle|^2 \leq B\|\mathbf{f}\|^2 \quad \text{with} \quad M > N \tag{52}$$

where A and B are constants, depending on $\{v_i\}$, namely the *frame bounds*, so that $0 < A \le B < +\infty$.

The inferior limit A guarantees that $\{v_i\}$ is a set of generators of the vector space, i.e. that the frame is complete. It is important that $A \ne 0$, meaning that any non-zero norm vector is always represented by a set of coefficients which are not all zeros.

Then, the fact that $B \ne \infty$ means that any finite-norm vector is represented by a set of coefficients which are all finite. A frame is said *tight* if $A = B$ and in such a case it can be shown that (51) holds with $\tilde{v}_i = v_i / A$. So, when all vectors of a tight frame have unitary norm, the A value informs us about the redundancy rate of the frame, i.e. how many further vectors we have rather than a classic basis.

Moreover, if removing one single vector from the frame set results in a non-complete frame, then the frame is said *exact*: it means that it coincides with a basis, not necessarily orthonormal. It is possible to prove that if the frame vectors have unitary norm and if $A = B = 1$, then such a frame coincides with an orthonormal basis.

As aforementioned, the main goal is often to find out the dual frame once given the original frame. Let $\mathbf{V}$ be the $N \times M$ matrix having $\{v_i\}$ as its column vectors:

$$\mathbf{V}_{N \times M} = \begin{bmatrix} \mathbf{v}_1 & \mathbf{v}_2 & \cdots & \mathbf{v}_M \end{bmatrix} \tag{53}$$

and $\tilde{\mathbf{V}}$ be the $N \times M$ matrix generated by the dual frame vectors $\{\tilde{v}_i\}$:

$$\tilde{\mathbf{V}}_{N \times M} = \begin{bmatrix} \tilde{\mathbf{v}}_1 & \tilde{\mathbf{v}}_2 & \cdots & \tilde{\mathbf{v}}_M \end{bmatrix}. \tag{54}$$

If $\{v_i\}$ is a frame, then (51) holds, and in terms of matrices it can be written as:

$$\mathbf{f} = \tilde{\mathbf{V}} \cdot \mathbf{V}^H \mathbf{f} = \mathbf{V} \cdot \tilde{\mathbf{V}}^H \mathbf{f}. \tag{55}$$

This means that $\tilde{\mathbf{V}}$ has to satisfy the following:

$$\tilde{\mathbf{V}}_{N \times M} \mathbf{V}^H_{M \times N} = \mathbf{I}_{N \times N} \tag{56}$$

where $\mathbf{I}$ is the identity matrix. Eq. (56) is a system of N^2 equations where the $M \times N$ unknowns are the entries of matrix $\tilde{\mathbf{V}}$. Since we are dealing with the over-complete case, it holds $N < M$ and the system has infinite solutions. A particular solution is the one achievable through the *pseudo-inverse*, given by:

$$\tilde{\mathbf{V}} = \left(\mathbf{V} \cdot \mathbf{V}^H \right)^{-1} \mathbf{V}. \tag{57}$$

The inverse matrix in (57) surely exists if $\{v_i\}$ is a frame, since $\mathbf{V} \cdot \mathbf{V}^H$ is a N dimension symmetric full-rank square matrix. Substituting (57) into the second member of (55) yields the identity matrix. It can be proved that such a solution is the $\|.\|_2$ minimum one. Moreover, it can be stated that any matrix $\overline{\mathbf{V}}$, assuming $\left\| \overline{\mathbf{V}} \right\| \ne 0$ and $\overline{\mathbf{V}} \cdot \mathbf{V}^H = 0$ allows to have another admissible solution of the form $\tilde{\mathbf{V}} + \overline{\mathbf{V}}$.

Now, starting from the definition of discrete S transform of a temporal series $h[kT]$ given by the first equation in (41) and, using the following notation for the hermitian product between two complex vectors $\mathbf{v}$ and $\mathbf{w}$:

$$\langle \mathbf{v}, \mathbf{w} \rangle = \mathbf{w}^H \mathbf{v} = \sum_i v_i w_i^* \tag{58}$$

the transform coefficient in (41) evaluated at discrete indexes (j, n) can be written as:

$$S_{jn}[\mathbf{h}] = S\left[jT, \frac{n}{NT}\right] = \langle \mathbf{h}, \mathbf{g}_{(j,n)} \rangle = \mathbf{g}_{(j,n)}^H \mathbf{h} \tag{59}$$

where

$$g_{(j,n)}[k] = \frac{|n|}{\sqrt{2\pi}N}\left(\sum_{r=-\infty}^{+\infty} e^{-\frac{(j-k-rN)^2 n^2}{2N^2}}\right)e^{i\frac{2\pi}{N}nk}. \tag{60}$$

Vectors $\mathbf{g}_{(j,n)}$ play the role of expansion functions and, from the Theory of Frames perspective, we can think of the ST based decomposition in the following terms:

$$\mathbf{h} = \sum_{j,n} \langle \mathbf{h}, \mathbf{g}_{(j,n)} \rangle \tilde{\mathbf{g}}_{(j,n)} = \sum_{j,n} S_{jn}[\mathbf{h}] \tilde{\mathbf{g}}_{(j,n)} \tag{61}$$

where $\{\tilde{\mathbf{g}}_{(j,n)}\}$ is one of the admissible dual frame of $\{\mathbf{g}_{(j,n)}\}$.

The N^2 elements obtained by calculating (41) for all possible parameter values constitute a complete representation of the original signal, as confirmed by the fact that it can be perfectly reconstructed by means of the inversion formula (43). However, the information carried by such a representation is redundant: N coefficients would be sufficient to get a complete description of $\mathbf{h}$ (basis decomposition). The issue is to find out how to reduce such a redundancy without compromising the representation capability of the transform. We know that the collection of vectors $\{\mathbf{g}_{(j,n)}\}$

attained for all possible values of discrete parameters j and n sets up an N^2 element frame in the vector space which the temporal series $\mathbf{h}$ belongs to. Then, we want to extract a subset of the complete original frame so that it would be still a frame whose coefficients calculated through (59) allow to re-synthesize the original series through (61). The choice of this new set of vectors is critical since we are expected to guarantee a complete tiling of time-frequency plane and this has to be performed taking the transform localization properties into account. Indeed, as depicted in Fig.8, each ST expansion function corresponds to one single area of the phase plane. Therefore it seemed to the authors that one reasonable choice was the dyadic tiling, as that one considered in the classic Wavelet decomposition.

If we assume to deal with real valued temporal series, the ST symmetries and causality of the signals allow us to limit our discussion to the portion of phase plane corresponding to positive time and frequency values. According to the dyadic grid we select those vectors from the set described by (60), so that, starting from zero, their frequency value doubles the immediate lower value, and for each frequency we consider a number of equidistant temporal instants that doubles the number relative to the immediate lower frequency. The zero frequency must be considered apart. Then we can say that we get $k = \lfloor \log_2 N/2 \rfloor$ values of the frequency n, where $\lfloor \cdot \rfloor$ is operator rounding its argument to the nearest integer towards minus infinity. This guarantees that the last value coincides to $\lfloor N/2 \rfloor$. Then a certain number of temporal instants is associated to each element of the k dimension frequency vector, according to what said above. It follows that the total amount of selected coefficients is

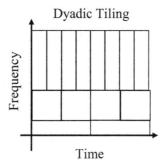

Fig. 8. Dyadic tiling of the ST based Time–Frequency domain: each ST expansion function is localized by one single sub-area of the graph

$$2^0 + 2^1 + \cdots + 2^k = K - 1$$
$$K = 2^{\lfloor \log_2 N \rfloor} = 2^{k+1} \tag{62}$$

Consequently, if we take positive and negative frequency values into account, we have $2K - 1$ complex coefficients to represent a N sample long discrete sequence. Obviously, the maximum number of coefficients is achieved when N is a power of two: the more distant from this condition we are, the bigger the reconstruction error is.

Data Driven Approaches to Speech and Language Processing

Gérard Chollet[1], Kevin McTait[1], and Dijana Petrovska-Delacrétaz[2]

[1] CNRS-LTCI, GET-ENST, 46 rue Barrault, 75634 Paris cedex 13, France
{chollet,mc-tait}@tsi.enst.fr
http://www.tsi.enst.fr/
[2] GET-INT, Institut National des Télécommunications,
9 rue Charles Fourier, F-91011 Evry cedex, France
Dijana.Petrovska@int-evry.fr
http://www-eph.int-evry.fr/∼petrovs

Abstract. Speech and language processing systems can be categorised according to whether they make use of predefined linguistic information and rules or are data driven and therefore exploit machine learning techniques to automatically extract and process relevant units of information which are then indexed and retrieved as appropriate. As an example, most state of the art automatic speech processing systems rely on a representation based on predefined phonetic symbols. The use of language dependent representations, whilst linguistically intuitive, has several drawbacks i.e. portability across languages, development time. Therefore, in this article, we review and present our recent experiments exploiting the idea inherent in the ALISP (Automatic Language Independent Speech Processing) approach, with particular respect to speech processing, where the intermediate representation between the acoustic and linguistic levels area is automatically inferred from speech data. We then present prospective directions in which the ALISP principles could be exploited by different domains such as audio, speech, text, image and video processing.

Speech and language processing systems may be divided into two categories: a) those that make use of prior linguistic knowledge and b) those that automatically derive the information they need from representative examples of the data they are to process using machine learning techniques[1] [102].

The first category represents systems that require an amount of language dependent linguistic knowledge produced manually by a team of linguists, lexicographers, phoneticians etc. While such systems may be well tuned to certain linguistic phenomena, and represent a compromise between an economy principle and the necessity to maintain sufficient discrimination between communicative elements, they suffer from several disadvantages, namely that:

---

[1] Hybrid systems exist for instance where the additional linguistic information is added in order to improve the performance of a data driven system

G. Chollet et al. (Eds.): Nonlinear Speech Modeling, LNAI 3445, pp. 164–198, 2005.
© Springer-Verlag Berlin Heidelberg 2005

- they are language dependent, therefore not portable across languages;
- they require significant human effort to acquire the knowledge base;
- the linguistic model of processing may not be the most suitable method of processing language and speech on a computer and therefore reproducing it may not prove to be the optimal solution;
- there is no underlying and unifying theory of linguistics able to represent all linguistic phenomena at all levels (phonetic, morpho-syntactic, syntactic, discourse etc.) with the required level of representativeness, accuracy and discrimination.

On the other hand, data driven (empirical) systems that automatically learn the linguistic units and information required from representative examples of data are interesting from the point of view that they do not require prior linguistic information, thus doing without the need for large teams of linguists and large amounts of annotated training data. Since raw data (audio, speech, video and text) is available in large quantities[2] and is usually inexpensive (via the WWW for example), it is possible to create systems that are portable across domains and languages (rapidly and cheaply), with some amount of fine tuning.

Currently, memory and data storage devices are becoming ever larger in capacity and cheaper. The WWW may also be viewed as an enormous data repository containing huge amounts of audio-visual and textual data which could be exploited. This capacity rapidly becomes larger and cheaper. Data driven systems are therefore attractive in that the problem of speech and language processing becomes one of efficient indexing, retrieval and processing of the available data. As the amounts of available data increase, more representative samples of speech and language are provided, returning more accurate results. The role of a data driven speech and language system would then be to efficiently store, index, retrieve then process relevant and appropriate units of speech or text. As an example, let us consider a translation system with access to a vast number of translations between two languages. The role of such a system would merely involve matching input with the translations in its database, retrieving appropriate units in the target language and possibly recombining them to generate a translation. As more data, in this case translations, are added to the database, ambiguity and the sparse data problem decrease and more accurate or bijective translation equivalents are produced with the net result that translations are more accurate.

Applications. This article reviews the general concepts of ALISP (Automatic Language Independent Speech Processing) based speech processing with particular reference to phone rate speech coding, speaker verification and forgery, spoken language acquisition and understanding and language identification. We then attempt to present a unified data driven approach by showing how this concept is equally applicable to a number of domains including not only gen-

---

[2] at least for well studied languages, such as English, Japanese, Chinese, Spanish, German, French, ...

eral audio and speech processing, but also audiovisual and textual processing systems.

This article also explores each domain where a data driven approach is applicable and presents the state of the art in data driven approaches and our recent experiments using the ALISP approach where it has been applied. Where ALISP has not yet been introduced as a solution, we show prospectively how ALISP may be used as a data driven technology in that domain.

An additional aim of this article is to show the synergy of a data driven approach between the two technologies of text and speech processing by analysing and breaking down data driven text and speech processing systems into the following stages:

- coding: learning/automatic extraction of relevant units of data or patterns from representative examples;
- indexing: efficient storage of patterns;
- decoding: retrieval and processing of patterns.

Efficient indexation and retrieval techniques are also exploited in image processing applications such as the coding of faxes [62] and the management of large document repositories [160]. Audiovisual forgery could be achieved with an indexed database of audiovisual sequences in order to animate talking heads according to the audiovisual parameters extracted from a database of a given speaker [80].

The article is organised as follows: Section 1 on classification methods presents a variety of techniques to organise, structure and analyse the important concepts or categories of information that we are processing. We go on to discuss supervised and non-supervised methods at searching for the coherent units of information in which we are interested for a given task. Of course, the information retrieved must also be organised and stored in an appropriate data structure for efficient retrieval. Section 2 presents a broad overview of the application of the ALISP approach to speech processing, in particular, phone rate speech coding and compression, speaker verification, voice forgery, spoken language acquisition and understanding for call-type classification. Section 3 presents the domain of data driven approaches to textual processing with particular reference to machine translation of natural languages. Speech translation is also presented as a prospective problem where the ALISP approach represents a promising solution. Finally, the conclusions drawn from our experiments and prospective studies are summarised in Section 4.

1   Supervised and Non-supervised Classification Techniques

Let us imagine the ideal situation where all documents (books, letters, emails, audio-visual files etc.) are available on-line. This universal digital library will serve as a reference and representative sample of all written and audiovisual material of any given language. Any new document added to this reference could be interpreted in terms of its correlations with existing ones. In addition, this reference would not only represent instances of written and spoken language (and gesture) but from this reference, certain rules or knowledge about the structure or workings of language and speech may be inferred.

In reality, it is impossible to produce a reference of all written, spoken and visual material ever produced, in which case large repositories (databases or corpora) of text, audio and audiovisual information are produced with the goal of being as representative as possible of a given language. More often than not, such references are representative of a given genre or class of written or spoken language.

In any case, and in order to be useful, the reference data needs to be analysed, organised, structured and ultimately classified in order that useful and semantically meaningful concepts can emerge and be efficiently retrieved. The scenario in which knowledge about the reference is structured, organised and retrievable is highly desirable for data driven systems which make no use of *a priori* linguistic information. Instead, such systems must process the structured and organised data already found. Therefore, the pertinent issues here are:

- what sort of information or patterns are pertinent?
- how is the information to be classified?
- what methods or algorithms are available to classify the information?
- what type of patterns (continuous vs. non-continuous, discrete vs. continuous, time-invariant vs. time varying...) are to be retrieved?

This section attempts to answer some of these questions. Here we look at supervised and non-supervised methods at classifying the information or patterns from a given reference for further processing by a data driven system. It could be argued that all pattern classification problems are data driven since a set of examples is usually needed to define the classes. The classification problem is said to be *supervised* if the examples are labeled or *unsupervised* if the classification techniques are able to infer patterns from the training data.

To exemplify the classification of patterns, let us take the example of texts. In texts, a variable length sequence of characters specifies a *word*. Words are usually (but not always) separated by a white space. Words may be further grouped into patterns such as *terms, noun-phrases, verb phrases, sentences, paragraphs* ... and also decomposed into lexemes, inflectional and derivational morphological endings etc.

Speech, audio and video sequences are time dependent, continuous and time-varying. Some time segmentation is necessary (either implicit or explicit). Handwritten texts are either time (on-line) or space (off-line) varying. In any case, *features* are extracted in order to classify the signal in some way. The most commonly used features for speech are cepstral coefficients along a logarithmic scale, which reflect the amount of energy at a given time in a given frequency band. This enables the speech signal to be classified into regions denoting certain phones or representative sounds of a language.

1.1 Selection of Reference Patterns

Pattern classification problems are said to be supervised if the training data is labeled in terms of classes to be recognized [55]. In many cases, an accurate labeling is either too costly or impossible to achieve and non-supervised techniques are a suitable alternative. A non-supervised approach consists of structuring the training data in terms of classes which are not defined a priori. A distance measure needs to be defined either in the feature space or the transformed space [135]. Self-organization, [27], [82] fits in the general approach of Machine Learning [125] to help discover structures in data. Genetic algorithms [138] and genetic programming [83] combined with information-theoretic criteria [162] could also help in this respect.

Inferring the sequential structure [108] of time-dependent data is important to reduce the perplexity [76] of the description. Language models of variable length [50] have been experimented on textual [52] and acoustic [51] data.

Retrieval of Coherent Units. In the case of speech processing, it is possible to automatically derive and classify segments of speech, that approximate the variable length phonetic units classified a priori, currently in use by the majority of systems. As in conventional speech processing techniques, the decoding aspect is solved by modeling the derived segments, usually by using Hidden Markov or Graphical Models (Bayesian Networks) [74].

For very low bit rate speech coding and decoding, the ALISP (Automatic Language Independent Speech Processing) method [39] has proved highly successful, reducing the bit rate to approximately 400 bps. This method is based on the temporal decomposition of the speech signal, vector quantization of the resulting segments, iterative Hidden Markov Modeling (HMM) and resegmentation to produce a set of acoustic segments stored in a dictionary. Coding a new speech signal consists of replacing each segment of the input by the index of a segment in the dictionary. Decoding is realized by concatenation of segments from the dictionary with an adequate control of prosody. More details and references are given in Section 2.3.

In the case of automatic speech recognition, phonetic units may be replaced by the acoustic units automatically derived by the ALISP method. It is then possible to retain the remaining system architecture since the derived acoustic units strongly (but not entirely) resemble the predefined phonetic units currently in use by the majority of systems [34].

Speech synthesis systems may also take advantage of the fact that automatically derived speaker-dependent acoustic segments may be derived using the ALISP method and subsequently concatenated using existing techniques, such as HNM (Harmonic Noise Model) [86].

Segmental approaches to speaker verification also take advantage of data driven techniques, such as ALISP, to derive meaningful units from the audio signal [58], [120].

An additional application which has received much attention is the design of forgery scenarios for challenging the robustness of biometric authentication systems. The ALISP method is useful in such scenarios where the units or segments derived from an impostor's speech signal are replaced with the equivalent units derived from the client's training set of speech signals [113]. This allows an impostor to imitate the voice of a client user.

Finally, in the case of automatic translation, an index of translation equivalents (whether on the textual or acoustic level) may also be derived from training data. In this case, translation units of variable length are derived automatically from bilingual sources using a stochastic model and the target language units are combined (decoded) using a statistical model of the target language [11], [20], [21], [22], [25], [157], [156]. While practical for textual translation, we shall show how this is also possible for the translation of speech signals where relevant and meaningful acoustic units are derived using ALISP.

1.2   Data Structures for Efficient Storage and Retrieval

Once the relevant patterns from the reference of stored textual, audio or visual documents have been retrieved, the task is to store them in an appropriate manner (data structure) for efficient search and retrieval. The following subsections present a small sample of the data structures currently in use in state of the art data driven systems for efficient storage and indexation of the data in question.

Hash Tables. Hash tables, sometimes also known as associative arrays, or scatter tables, represent a data structure that offers fast lookup, insertion, and deletion of unique $\{key, value\}$ pairs [2], [81], [73]. In a well-designed implementation of a hash table, all of these operations have a time complexity of $O(1)$, as opposed to the $O(n)$ required by linked lists, associative arrays and vectors.

Inverted File. In the field of information retrieval, large amounts of textual documents are stored off line, a subset of which is to be retrieved by means of user defined queries. Given that the size of such data repositories may be enormous (cf. WWW), efficient lexicographical indexing and retrieval schemes are required.

One popular way of indexing such information is an *inverted file*. Assuming a collection of documents, each document is assigned a list of keywords (with additional relevance weights associated to each keyword as attributes). An inverted file is then the sorted list or index of keywords with each keyword having links to the documents containing that keyword (Figure 1).

A search in an inverted file is the composition of two search algorithms: a search for a keyword returning an index and then a possible search on that index for a particular attribute value. Efficient retrieval of a document collection is enabled by one or a combination of data structures such as sorted arrays, B-trees [10], [45] [81], tries and PAT trees [64] and various hashing structures. This data structure is not limited to the field of information retrieval but is a well-used storage and retrieval mechanism suitable for database type applications.

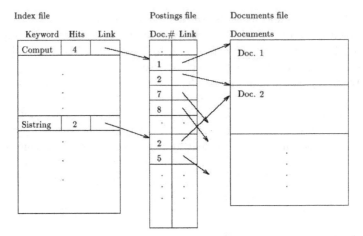

Fig. 1. Inverted File implemented using a sorted array [72]

2   ALISP Based Speech Processing

In this section we review our experiments underlying the idea of using unsupervised data classification for speech processing applications such as very low bit rate speech coding, speaker verification and audiovisual forgery, call type classification and language identification.

The common denominator of different speech processing methods is the set of speech units that is being used. The majority of current speech processing systems use phones (or related units) as an atomic representation of speech. These phonetic symbols are chosen based on a language dependent analysis of the correspondences between acoustic (speech signal) and linguistic (morphemes, words) data. Using phonetic speech units leads to efficient representation and enables various implementations for many speech processing applications.

The major problems that arise when phone based systems are being developed is the possible mismatch of the development and test data and the lack of transcribed data for new applications and new languages. For each new language and application, new transcribed databases are needed. This is a serious bottleneck for developing new applications and adapting the existing applications to new languages and new tasks. In order to avoid this tedious, error-prone and expensive step of transcribing speech data, we are focusing our research on developing systems that minimize the requirement of transcribed speech databases.

The set of speech units can also be inferred in an unsupervised manner using data driven speech segmentation methods. In [39], [40] the ALISP architecture for speech processing was introduced. The idea inherent in the ALISP approach, is that the intermediate representation between the acoustic and linguistic levels are automatically inferred from speech data rather than from a priori phonetic and linguistic knowledge. The idea of extracting meaningful units for speech encoding is further developed as we show how automatically building a memory or database of meaningful, but language independent, units from data can be used in speech processing, including translation (the concept remains the same: representative units are extracted and subsequently indexed for efficient retrieval and recombination to take place during the translation phase).

In Section 2.1, we review how speech data can be organized in an unsupervised manner into coherent speech units using the ALISP principles. These ALISP units are compared with phonetic units in Section 2.2. These units can also be used for very low bit rate speech coding, as shown in Section 2.3. Furthermore, if the speech data are organized according to the speaker, language or call type, the ALISP data driven segmentation can be used for speaker verification (Section 2.4), automated telephone call routing and language identification (Section 2.5). The advantage of using the ALISP based segmentation is that no previous linguistic knowledge is required to perform the above mentioned classification tasks and that the applications developed are completely language independent.

2.1   Automatic Acquisition of ALISP Units

The following outlines the steps required in order to acquire and model the set of data driven *ALISP* speech units [39], [40].

Temporal Decomposition. After a classic pre-processing step leading to acoustic feature vectors, temporal decomposition [6], [3], [30] is used for the initial segmentation of the speech data into quasi-stationary segments. The matrix

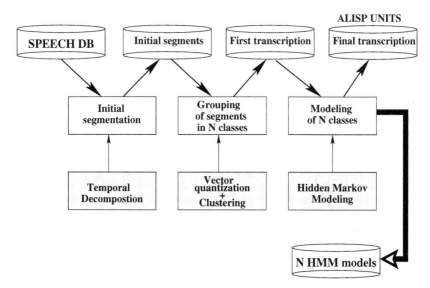

Fig. 2. Unsupervised Automatic Language Independent Speech Processing (ALISP) unit acquisition and their Hidden Markov Modeling (HMM)

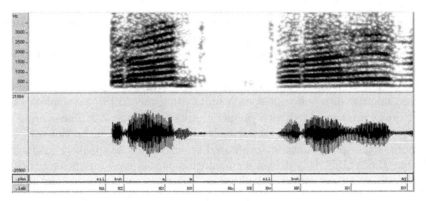

Fig. 3. Example of the ALISP segmentation, of an excerpt of a speech data, spoken by a male American speaker (from NIST 2004 speaker verification database) [120]

of spectral parameters is decomposed into a limited number of events, represented by a target and an interpolation function. Short time singular value decomposition with adaptive windowing is applied during the initial search of the interpolation functions, followed by an iterative refinement of targets and interpolation functions. At this point, the speech is segmented into spectrally stable portions and for each segment, its gravity center frame is also determined.

Vector Quantization Clustering and Segmentation. A vector quantization algorithm is used to cluster the center of gravity frames of the temporal decomposition. The training phase of the codebook is based on the K-means algorithm. The codebook size defines the number of ALISP symbols. The result of this step is the labeling of each temporal decomposition gravity center frame with the label of the nearest centroid of the codebook. The next step is realized using cumulated distances of all the vectors from the segment, leading to an initial segmentation of the speech data. These segments are used for the training of the Hidden Markov Models(HMMs) representing the ALISP units.

Hidden Markov Modeling and Speech Memory Dictionary. The Hidden Markov method is used to model efficiently the set of the automatically acquired segments. The output of this phase is a set of Hidden Markov Models that represents the set of ALISP symbols. At this point our speech memory is organized according to the data driven set of ALISP speech units. We can also use all the automatically labelled training speech segments in order to build the set of examples for each ALISP unit, denoted here as the speech memory dictionary.

2.2 Comparison of ALISP Units with Phone Units

The automatically derived speech units are the central part of the proposed method. In order to have a better understanding of these units, we have studied their correspondence with an acoustic-phonetic segmentation on the BREF corpus. This database, [85], is a large vocabulary read speech corpus for French. The texts are selected from 5 million words of the French newspaper "Le Monde". The correspondence between the ALISP segmentation and an acoustic-phonetic segmentation for the 40 male speakers from the BREF corpus is given in [118].

We have applied the same principles to acquire the ALISP units to the NIST speaker verification databases [53], [93], [124]. In Figure 3, an example of a spectrogram, the manually transcribed speech data (.phn) and the corresponding ALISP segmentation (.lab) are given [119]. Our data driven segmentation corresponds quite well to the spectrally stable segments of speech, as shown in the spectrogram.

2.3   ALISP Based Phone Rate Speech Coding and Compression

In order to achieve bit rates lower than 600 bps in speech coding, it is necessary to use recognition and synthesis techniques. By transmitting only the indexes of the recognized unit, the transmission bit rate is drastically reduced. The coder and the decoder share a dictionary of speech segments. On the decoder side speech synthesis is used in order to reconstruct the output speech, from the sequence of the transmitted symbols. The quality of the reconstructed speech data is also dependent on the choice of the synthesis method.

Current coders working at bit rates lower than 600 bps are based on segmental units related to phones (the phones being the physical realization of the corresponding phonemes). An alternative approach using automatically derived speech units based on ALISP tools was developed at ENST, ESIEE and VUT Brno [8]. These speech units are derived from a statistical analysis of a speech corpus, requiring neither phonetic nor orthographic transcriptions of the speech data as described in Section 2.1. Harmonic Noise synthesis was used in order to improve the quality of the reconstructed speech data [9].

2.4   ALISP Based Speaker Verification

Current best performing text-independent speaker verification systems are based on Gaussian Mixture Models [126]. Speech is composed of different sounds and speakers differ in their pronunciation of these sounds. These models could be interpreted as a "soft" representation of the various acoustic classes that make up the speakers' sounds. They do not take into account the temporal ordering of the feature vectors.

The main advantages of introducing a speech segmentation stage in speaker verification experiments are to exploit the different speaker discriminant power of speech sounds [57], [114], and to benefit from higher-level information resulting from the segmentation without having to use transcribed data. In [114], [115] we have already used the ALISP data-driven speech segmentation method for speaker verification. The number of classes (8) was chosen in order to have enough data for each class when dealing with 2 min of enrollment speech data used to build the speaker models. In these experiments, we studied speaker

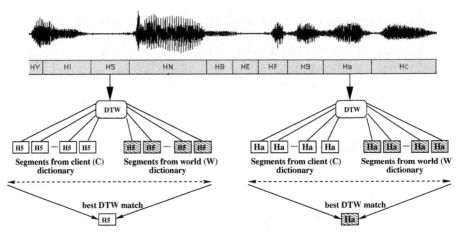

Fig. 4. Illustration of the proposed speaker verification method based on a Dynamic Time Warping (DTW) distance measure

modeling algorithms such as Multiple Layer Perceptrons and Gaussian Mixture Modeling. Classifying speech into only 8 speech classes did not lead to effective coherence of the speech classes. In [119], [120], we used a finer segmentation of the speech data into 64 speech classes and a Dynamic Time Warping distortion measure for the speaker verification step. If the two speech patterns belong to the same speech class, we could expect that the distortion measure can capture the speaker specific characteristics.

Our segmental speaker verification approach is the following: the segments found in the enrollment speech constitute the speaker specific speech memory, termed the *Client-Dictionary*. Another set of speakers is used to represent the non-speaker (world) speech memory, the *World-Dictionary*. The speaker verification step is done combining these two dictionaries. The non-linear Dynamic Time Warping distance measure is applied in order to find the similarities of an incoming test segment to the client and world dictionaries. The final client score is related to the distance measures.

A speaker verification system is composed of training and testing phases. During the training (also known as enrollment) phase the client models are constructed. We propose the use of a client's speech memory, built from the ALISP segments, to represent the client enrollment data. The world speech memory is built with segments found in the speech data representing the world speakers. During the testing phase (see Figure 4), each of the speech segments found is compared with the Dynamic Time Warping distance measure, to a set of speech segments representing the claimed speaker identity S_c and the world speakers S_W. In such a way the nearest speech segment from the *Client* or *World Dictionary* is found. This is done for all the segments of the test speech data. During the next step, the ratio of the number of times that a segment belonging to the speaker is chosen $nb(S_c)$, versus the mean value of the number of times a world segment is chosen, $mnb(S_W)$, is estimated. This ratio represents the score S of the claimed speaker:

$$score(S) = \frac{nb(S_c)}{mnb(S_W)}.$$

The final decision is taken comparing this score to a threshold found on an independent development set.

The first experimental results of the proposed method are comparable to the current state-of-the-art speaker verification results, as obtained in NIST speaker recognition evaluations. We could also benefit of combining the results of our segmental speaker verification method with a conventional Gaussian Mixture Method, in order to benefit from the higher level information resulting from the ALISP segmentation.

Voice Forgery. This section describes a data driven approach to forgery applications that is used to challenge the robustness of biometric identity verification systems. In the context of speaker verification, a typical forgery scenario includes automatic voice transformation techniques that an impostor may use to assume the identity of an authorized client. The method chosen for voice transformation depends on two factors:

- the working principle of the system targeted for intrusion;
- the amount of client data available to the impostor.

For speaker verification systems using Gaussian Mixture Models (where the temporal ordering of feature vectors is irrelevant) it may be sufficient to find a mapping function F between the impostor's feature vectors $\mathbf{x}$ and the client's features $\mathbf{y}$. Given two sequences composed by the same words, pronounced respectively by the impostor and by the client, F can be derived by minimizing the mean square error:

$$\epsilon_{mse} = E[||\mathbf{y} - F(\mathbf{x})||^2],$$

where E is the expectation. This approach may require a relatively limited amount of client data, but it has the disadvantage of being text, language and speaker dependent.

Forgery of the above kind [1], [77], [78], [26] is not so likely to be effective in the case of more sophisticated systems that exploit speech recognition in the speaker verification process. To be a real threat for such systems, the impostor should be sure that the linguistic elements present in the source voice are not altered by the voice transformation, so that they can be recognized as if they were uttered by the original voice.

For verification system designers, ALISP-based recognition and synthesis could constitute an interesting forgery tool that is able to transform any arbitrary voice into the client's voice without text or language restrictions. As in the case of very low bit rate speech coding, a codebook of ALISP units can be built by statistical analysis of a database of the client's speech that requires neither orthographic nor phonetic annotation. Subsequently, recognition of the impostor's speech in terms of ALISP units allows the replacement of the impostor's voice segments with equivalent representative units taken from the client's codebook. The speech recognition with the Hidden Markov Models representing the ALISP processing system, assures that a subsequent recognition performed by the verification system will result in a good match.

Recent experiments [113] have shown that using ALISP as a voice forgery technique returns significant results. Using the *one-side* data from the NIST 2004 speaker verification database, voice forgeries carried out using the ALISP approach were scored using the BECARS speaker verification system [17]. An increase in the Equal Error Rate of 10% indicates that significantly more successful forgeries were possible (Figure 5).

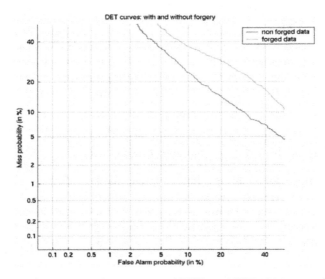

Fig. 5. Results for voice forgery using ALISP on NIST 2004 *one-side* data

Audiovisual Forgery. In the same way that acoustic units of an impostor's voice are replaced by acoustic units of a client's voice using ALISP, video segments are equally replaceable. Given an audiovisual sequence, the problem consists of extracting relevant visual (and acoustic) features that will enable the production of a speaking head resembling the subject in the audiovisual sequence. The impostor maintains a database of face and speech feature vectors of a client which are then used to drive and animate an MPEG-4 compliant face model [112]. Given the relevant features extracted from an audiovisual sequence relating to the client in question, these features may be encoded into MPEG-4 in order to produce and animate a talking head resembling the client [80].

In [80], the impostor's talking face is detected and facial features are extracted and tracked from a database of audiovisual sequences of the client. Audio-visual coding and synthesis is realized by indexing in a database containing audio-visual sequences. Stochastic models (coupled Hidden Markov Models) of characteristic segments are used to drive the search in memory. An MPEG-4 compliant talking head, *Greta*, is used for facial animation. Facial animation in MPEG-4 is controlled by the Facial Definition Parameters and Facial Animation Parameters, which describe the face shape and movement respectively.

Realistic face synthesis is one of the most difficult problems in computer graphics due to the complexity of its geometric form. Rendering and modeling the human face on a screen has proven to be an extremely challenging task. It is even more challenging to naturally animate a synthetic face, since the human brain can effortlessly notice any tiny unnatural deviation from reality. In [121] a modeling technique to generate realistic texture-mapped 3D face models from face images and videos is presented. Speech-driven facial animation has also been extensively investigated ([137], [18], [161], [145], [134], [106], [159], [4]).

2.5   Spoken Language Acquisition and Understanding

Acquisition of Acoustic Morphemes for Call Type Classification. Addressing the problem of devices which understand and act upon spoken input from people, Gorin [67] introduces the idea that in human language acquisition, the phonemes, vocabulary, grammar and semantics seem to emerge naturally during the course of interacting with the world. Research into such language acquisition devices yields insights into how to construct speech understanding systems which are trainable, adaptive and robust and that minimize the use of annotated corpora. There are several reports in the literature in this general direction. The earliest work in this field [111] demonstrates automatic acquisition of 'words' and 'grammar' from collapsed text. However, this work did not address the issues arising from non-perfect recognition of speech. In [68], it was shown how to acquire lexical units from speech alone without transcriptions and exploit them for spoken language understanding. However, that experiment was constrained to speech comprising isolated word sequences and used Dynamic Time Warping matching to decide whether an observation was a new "word" or variation of a known "word". While one can learn much about a spoken language by merely listening to it, we can progress further and faster by exploiting semantics. This has been demonstrated in both an engineering domain [67] and in an analysis of children's language acquisition [129].

Our main interest is to exploit speech plus meaning for 'learning to understand without transcriptions'. We are interested in methods for automatically acquiring salient speech parts, which we call *acoustic morphemes*. Their utility could be evaluated within an automated dialog system that is designed to infer an appropriate machine action upon the service requests made over the phone. In the majority of current systems, the man-machine interaction is typically carried out via a touch-tone system with a rigid pre-determined navigational menu. Navigating in such menus is time consuming and frustrating for the users. It is time consuming because the users have to listen to all the options, and frustrating because of the difficulty of matching the users requests to the given options. In the case where a satisfactory option is found, this option is often related to other nested menus, with the same problem. We are interested in alternatives to touch-tone menus that allow users to interact with the system with a natural spoken language dialog just as they would do with a human operator. By natural we mean that the machine recognizes and understands what people actually say, in contrast to what a system designer hoped they would say.

There are few existing systems based on the principle of using natural language as a human-machine interface modality. The system developed by Gorin and his colleagues at AT&T uses a probabilistic model with salient phrases [66], [5]. Another approach, developed at Bell Labs, is based on a vector-based information retrieval technique [42], [84]. These methods require training material in the form of transcribed calls and the classes to which they belong. The satisfactory results achieved with these systems are partly based on the transcription input of the training sentences, and also on effective performance of the automatic speech recognizer. Although current speech recognition methodology is making progress, the speech recognition systems are still language and task dependent and require collection and annotation of large speech corpora for each specific task and for each new language. Adapting the existing systems for a new task or language would require transcribing and annotating new data. The human transcription is the major problem in rapidly porting such systems to new tasks and languages.

Several recent experiments [39] [90] report attempts to automatically acquire speech units from *untranscribed* speech using sub-word methods. All of the above efforts involve learning from speech alone. The *fenonic* base forms, introduced by [76], do not presuppose any phonetic concepts either. While one can learn much about a spoken language by merely listening to it, we can progress further and faster by exploiting semantics. Semantic labels can be extracted automatically from either wizard experiments [5] or from autonomous dialogs [67]. This approach was addressed in [65] [116], where the *tabula rasa* problem was addressed: investigate how to 'learn to understand' from a database of untranscribed speech with semantic labels. In this work the *acoustic morphemes* were automatically acquired from the output of a task-independent phone recognizer. The utility of these units was experimentally evaluated for call-type classification in the '*How may I help you?*$^{(sm)}$' task. Detected occurrences of the acoustic morphemes provided the basis for the classification of the test sentences. In [116] we started with a task-independent phone recognizer, and investigated how to 'learn to understand' from a database of *un*-transcribed speech plus semantic labels. The 'understanding' module is based on automatically acquired *acoustic morphemes*. The utility of these units is experimentally evaluated for call-type classification in the '*How may I help you?*$^{(sm)}$' task. Detections of the acoustic morphemes in the Automatically Recognised Speech lattices are exploited for classification of the test sentences, achieving an operating point with 81% correct classification rate at rank 2, with 15% false rejection rate [116] .

One could even go a step further toward minimizing and even replacing the use of human transcriptions. The only annotations (needed during the training phase) are those indicating the call type of the training sentences. The set of meaningful acoustic morphemes could be acquired from the output of an ALISP recognizer. The meaningful parts of the speech will be acquired automatically from the output of the task- and language-independent ALISP recognizer. The human effort required in this case will be limited to supplying the classes of the calls, making the system task- and language- independent. This points could enable increased portability to new tasks and languages.

Acquisition of Acoustic Morphemes for Language Identification. In [119] we reported how ALISP data-driven speech segmentation methods could also be used to automatically acquire a set of salient ALISP sequences for language identification experiments. Language identification systems currently rely on the information gathered from the output of the automatic speech recognizers of the languages involved ([71], [107], [146], and [59]). The likelihoods of the recognizer outputs are used to decide on the observed language. The speech units involved are phones. In [119] the first step consisted of the automatic acquisition of a common set of acoustic segments from the training data of the languages to be identified, based on the ALISP tools. The ALISP sequences could be compared to the multi-grams defined in [51]. The next step consisted of the search of the language specific variable length ALISP sequences that characterize the languages to be identified. The final step is the definition of a classification strategy used for the language identification. The utility of our proposed method is evaluated for language identification on subsets of the Swiss French and Swiss German Polyphone databases[3]. The speech pre-processing parameters are kept identical as for the speaker verification experiments. The number of gender dependent ALISP units common to Swiss German and Swiss French is 64. To have an idea of their classification performance, we chose empirically the classification criteria (priority given to longer sequences, and to the maximal number of sequences per language). Among the 5000 test sentences belonging to female speakers (with a mean length of 3s), in 31% of cases, no language specific ALISP-sequences are detected (given the best output of the recognizer). Among the 69% of the test phrases where language specific sequences are detected, using the above mentioned classification criteria, 76% are correctly classified. These results could be improved using batter classification methods and exploiting the lattice output of the task-independent phone recognizer.

An example of an automatically acquired salient French ALISP sequence is *Hp-HH-Ht*. These units correspond to the French word *Trois*. Another example is the ALISP sequence *HG-Hp-HT* which corresponds to the French sub-word *-apa*. An example of an automatically detected and correctly classified ALISP sequence in the test data, corresponding to German sub-word from the word *Name*, is the ALISP sequence *HM-HT-HM*, represented in Figure 6.

3   Translation

Classic machine translation paradigms are based on an analysis, transfer and generation architecture. A source language input sentence is analyzed to some varying degree of abstraction (text normalization, morphological analysis, syntactic analysis, semantic analysis). Subsequently, based on a set of manually

---

[3] We thank Swisscom and Robert van Kommer for the availability of these databases

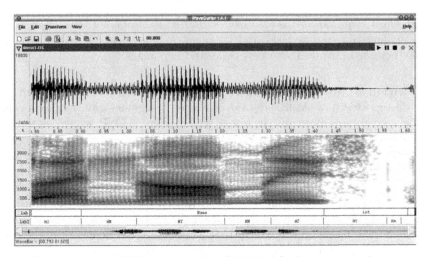

Fig. 6. Example of the ALISP segmentation (*.lab* labels) of an excerpt of a test speech segment spoken by a male speaker corresponding to the German word *Name*, leading to a correct classification result

crafted transfer rules at the appropriate level of abstraction, a target language structure is retrieved. The reverse process of analysis (generation) is then applied to the target language representation to produce the target language sentence. This general architecture is represented in Figure 7.

A *direct system* largely involves surface level i.e. word-to-word transfer with some degree of morphological analysis and target language word reordering. A *transfer based* system typically involves transfer at the level of the syntactic structure, while at the top of the pyramid, the deepest level of abstraction is represented by an interlingual system which attempts to create a language-neutral meta-language [147].

Clearly, this architecture, while linguistically motivated, requires language and language-pair dependent analysis, transfer and generation modules. To some extent, tools for analyzing language have been and are still limited to the world's major languages with most emphasis on English. Furthermore, due to the fact that there is no unifying theory of linguistics enabling a sound and comprehensive linguistic analysis of an input sentence, analysis and generation tools will be error prone. More importantly, the transfer modules are more complex in that:

– they are often uni-directional;
– given the level of abstraction, they are difficult to encode;
– rule selection at run-time is a conflicting process (which rule is applied in which order?).

In addition, given a multilingual system involving translation between more than one language pair, $n^2 - n$ uni-directional transfer modules are required given n languages, clearly an undesirable quality when considering the cost and time involved in system development.

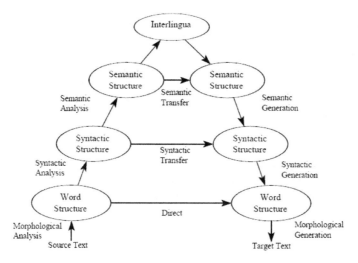

Fig. 7. Level of transfer in a classic machine translation paradigm [54]

It is for the above reasons that data driven machine translation systems were developed. Instead of using large teams of linguists and computational linguists to develop language and language-pair specific linguistic resources, the linguistic structures and the bilingual correspondences between them are learned directly from bilingual texts (corpora) and subsequently classified, structured, stored, retrieved and recombined as appropriate in order to form target language translation strings.

3.1 Example Based Machine Translation

In general terms, Example-Based Machine Translation (EBMT) provides a data driven solution to the machine translation problem where the *longest* matches between variable length segments of text in an input source language sentence and the segments in the source language side of a bilingual database of segments are sought [20], [24], [110], [109]. The corresponding target language segments are retrieved and subsequently recombined after a recombination or decoding stage in order to produce a well-formed target language sentence. Longest matches are preferred in that they reduce monolingual and translation ambiguity and boundary friction between segments. However, this reduces the rate of recall, a ratio to be carefully balanced. As Nagao [105] correctly identified in his original paper, the three main components of an Example-Based Machine Translation system are:

- matching variable length text fragments against a database of real examples;
- identifying the corresponding translation fragments;
- recombining these fragments to produce target language text.

There are many different varieties of Example-Based Machine Translation or data driven approaches to machine translation (non-symbolic [139], statistical

[11], structural [79] or case-based reasoning [44]) which have in common the fact that they all use a bilingual corpus of translations as their primary knowledge source. These approaches vary in the way in which they match source language input, form bilingual correspondences and recombine textual sequences in the target language. The availability of *a priori* linguistic knowledge sources such as part-of-speech taggers and syntactic parsers for a given language pair, also affects the choice of paradigm. As an example, Figure 8 denotes the result of a non-supervised approach at extracting surface and structural level subsentential bilingual correspondences from a corpus of unlabeled English-Japanese sentence pairs. On the other hand, Figure 9 denotes detailed structural correspondences given a syntactically annotated English-Japanese corpus. Of course, the level of linguistic preprocessing of the corpus, while intended to provided more accurate translations, has implications for the level of portability across language pairs.

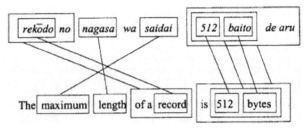

Fig. 8. String level correspondences learned between an English and Japanese sentence pair [79]

Performance of Example-Based Machine Translation Systems. A common evaluation methodology relies on partitioning the bilingual training corpus into a test set and unseen evaluation set. Given that reference translations are available in the evaluation set, the translations produced are compared to the reference translations and scored according to a distance metric, such as Levenshtein Distance [88] or the string-edit distance [91]. The approach of [97] [96] used a training corpus of 3000 English-French sentence pairs from the World Health Organisation AFI corpus[4] and tested on a further 1000 unseen English sentences from the same corpus. Figure 10 shows the accuracy of the French sentences produced using this system, and at the same time, the accuracy of the French translations produced from the same evaluation set using the on line *BabelFish* commercial translation system[5] which is largely based on the classic architecture of bilingual lexica and transfer rules.

While the rates of recall were not comparable (the commercial system uses resources of a far wider scope than the 3000 sentence pairs used for training and is thus able to produce translations for all source language input), the results clearly show the interest of data driven approaches to translation in that they

---

[4] http://www.who.int/pll/cat/cat_resources.html
[5] http://babelfish.altavista.com

generally produce more accurate translations for a given text type, genre or even language pair, since by definition, they are tuned to the data in the training corpus.

3.2   Statistical Machine Translation

One variety of data driven machine translation, based on parametric translation and language models, is termed statistical machine translation (SMT) [23] [21]. It has its foundations in information theory where a message is transmitted over a noisy channel. In this case, the task is decoding an source language sentence that was transmitted over a noisy communication channel which 'corrupted' it to a target language sentence.

Given a classic (if not the original) statistical translation system [11], a translation model is produced by computing the probabilities of the bilingual word pairings given a bilingual corpus aligned at the level of the sentence. A statistical model of the target language is also precomputed given a corpus of target language text which provides the probabilities of translation strings being well formed in the target language. Therefore, the translation process consists of a search (decoding) for the string that maximises the product of the two sets of probabilities i.e. the translation model and the model of the target language.

In mathematical terms, the task is to find the TL sentence $\hat{T}$ that is most likely given the source language sentence S:

$$\hat{T} = \arg\max_{T} p(T|S) \tag{1}$$

Using Baye's theorem, this is equivalent to finding $\hat{T}$ such that:

$$\hat{T} = \arg\max_{T} p(S|T)p(T) \tag{2}$$

An statistical system therefore has to estimate $p(T)$ i.e. the probability that a string T of words is a well formed target language sentence, using a parametric model of the target language, commonly referred to as a *language model*. The system must also estimate $p(S|T)$ i.e. the probability that a source language string S is a translation of T using a parametric bilingual model of the two languages in question. This is known as the *translation model*. The two models in combination with a search strategy, namely a Viterbi style search algorithm or $A\star$ search for finding the $\hat{T}$ that maximizes the above equation for some S, comprise the translation engine.

A thorough account of constructing translation models, or rather translation parameter estimation, is given in [22] with further bilingual statistical alignment approaches given in [24], [99], [148], [149]. In addition, a description of the decoding step is given in [157].

Traditionally, due to the enormous computational complexity of parameter estimation on very large corpora (millions of words of text), translation models are limited to word-to-word alignments. However, more recent work has highlighted the need for phrasal translation models (alignments between multiword

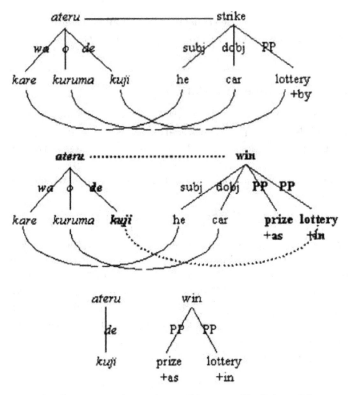

Fig. 9. Syntactic level correspondences learned between English and Japanese sentence pairs [158]

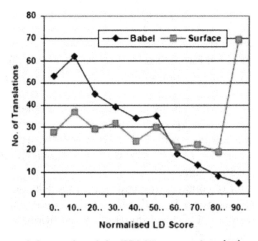

Fig. 10. Comparison of the results of the EBMT approach in [95] and a commercial MT system. Normalised LD score represents the Levenshtein Distance between translations and their references translations normalised over sentence length (maximum number of errors). Also, the curve indicated by *Surface* indicates the non-symbolic (knowledge-free) version of [95]

units) in order to reduce translation ambiguity with the aim of returning more accurate translations [156], [94].

3.3 Translation Memory

Translation Memory systems are closely related to the data driven approach to translation, but are more accurately described as computer-aided translation tools as they do not actually *translate* a document, but assist the human translator by providing close matches between a given SL input and a database of translations.

In a traditional TM system [144] [130], translation equivalents on the sentential level are stored in an associative array or any other efficient storage and retrieval mechanism. Given a SL input sentence, closely matching SL sentences in the associative array are found, returning a ranked list of their equivalent TL sentences. A user-defined similarity score is adjusted in order to define the closeness of the matches. Where there are no exact matches in the database of examples, the user is left to modify the resulting TL string so that it represents a translation of the original SL sentence. No actual translation by machine takes place. This is merely a storage and retrieval mechanism with a user-defined matching threshold, where a match is determined traditionally by criteria such as the number of words in common between the input sentence and the SL sentences in the database, with some word order information.

However, TM systems have evolved over time in that they now attempt to approach the methodology of EBMT systems where sub-sentential matches are taken into consideration and are integrated into the TL proposals output to the human translator [136], [98]. In addition, given an amount of labeling of the database of translations, more accurate matches may take place on one or more levels of analysis i.e. raw text, part-of-speech tags and document metadata such as XML tags. In [122], translation examples are stored in a multi-level data structure and a new notion of retrieving matches between SL input and SL sentences in the translation memory is proposed based on string edit distance on one or more of these levels. The authors also propose this method of extending TM towards EBMT via recombination of multiword chunks of matches with the SL input, thus bridging the gap between TM and EBMT.

3.4 Text Processing

The field of data-driven or statistical natural language processing (NLP) has received much attention recently [35] [92] given the availability of large textual corpora to estimate statistical parameters. This has allowed the development and application of a number of probabilistic and machine learning techniques to be applied to traditionally rule-based tasks. Statistical methods represent several advantages over rule-based approaches such as their need for hand-crafted linguistic resources and their development time and consequent lack of portability across languages.

The field of statistical natural language processing covers many applications and domains such as, but not limited to:

- part-of-speech (POS) tagging;
- terminology extraction;
- syntactic parsing;
- text summarisation;
- information extraction;
- statistical language modeling;
- grapheme-phoneme conversion;
- language recognition;
- word sense disambiguation;
- anaphora resolution.

However, due to the limitations of this work, this section will give a brief overview of a few of the more well-studied applications and methodologies.

Statistical POS tagging consists in finding the most probable tag sequence $t_1 \ldots t_n$ given a word sequence $w_1 \ldots w_n$, in short $max\ P(Tags|Words)$. Each word in the word sequence is assigned one POS tag from a finite set of possible tags. Due to the ambiguity of natural language, words in different contexts may be assigned different POS tags. A statistical model based on HMMs is clearly explained in [43] [46] [100]. Statistical taggers generally distinguish between lexical probabilities i.e. the probability of a particular tag conditional on the particular word, and contextual probabilities, which describe the probability of a particular tag on the surrounding tags. The latter is usually conditional on the tags of the neighbouring words and very often on the $n-1$ previous words. Thus in general, there are often two information sources:

- The probability of each tag T^i conditional on the word W that is to be tagged $P(T^i|W)$. Often the converse probability is given instead $P(W|T^i)$
- The probability of tag T^i at position k in the input string denoted T^i_k, given that tags $T_{k-n+1} \ldots T_{k-1}$ have been assigned to the previous $n-1$ words. Often n is set to 2 or 3 and thus bigram and trigram models are used. When using trigrams, this quantity is $P(T^i_k|T_{k-2}, T_{k-1})$.

These probabilities can be estimated either from a pretagged training corpus or from untagged text, a lexicon and an initial bias.

The field of data driven syntactic disambiguation or parsing also makes use of a similar statistical model where the aim is to find the most probable parse tree T given the word sequence $w_1, \ldots, w_n$ and a labeled training data set [15] [140] [36]. Another important task for text processing is that of word sense disambiguation. Approaches vary with respect to the parameters from which they estimate the disambiguation but parameters are typically estimated from corpora [63] [19] and are clustered according to their distribution in a structural context [48] or their distribution with respect to semantic category [63].

Language models (LM) have received particular attention due to their use within speech recognition, SMT systems or any other large vocabulary system, due to the fact that they do not need labeled training data. LMs known as $n-gram$ language models assign a probability to a word sequence $w_1, \ldots, w_n$ and represent n-th order Markov chains in which the probability of occurrence of a symbol (word) is conditioned upon the prior occurrence of $n-1$ other symbols. N-gram language models are typically constructed from statistics obtained from a large corpus of text using the co-occurrences of words in the corpus to determine word sequence probabilities, as given in 3:

$$P(w_{1,N}) = \prod_{i=1}^{N} P(w_i | w_{1,i-1}) \qquad (3)$$

Due to data sparseness, one cannot reliably estimate the probability distribution for contexts of arbitrary length. Therefore n-gram models provide the solution of restricting the contexts $w_{1,i-1}$ for predicting the next word, w_i, to the last $n-1$ words [75]. Many improvements to this model are reported in the literature, one of note is the use of variable length sequences as opposed to where the value n is fixed [50].

3.5   Speech to Speech Translation

The domain of speech-to-speech machine translation has largely emerged from statistical translation research groups where early initiatives include the Verb-mobil [153] [152] and JANUS projects [155], [143], [154], [89] and the ASURA speech translation system from ATR [104]. Consequently, the architecture of such speech translation systems reflects a statistical approach to translation: a (statistical) speech recognition system forms the input to a textual statistical translation system, the output of which is synthesised by a text-to-speech (TTS) module [16]. In fact, many of the statistical approaches found in textual translation were initially inspired by statistical approaches from the speech processing domain [76]. Knowledge based speech translation systems, such as the NESPOLE! interlingua-based system [101] are much rarer.

Given the somewhat general architecture of such systems where speech recognition is followed by textual translation, the output of which is in turn followed by speech synthesis, the problem of sufficient labeled data for the acoustic processing modules (recognition and synthesis) is still not resolved. In order to correctly recognise speech input and correctly synthesise the translation strings, phonetically labeled speech databases are required in order to map the acoustic phenomena to the linguistic level in the form of phones.

In this case, the ALISP approach may be useful in that the phonetic classes for a given language are learned directly from raw (unlabeled) speech data for any given language (see Section 2). This removes the requirement for phonetically transcribed speech databases, thus increasing development time and portability across languages.

However, a more ambitious and novel SSMT architecture, still involving the ALISP approach, would be one where the ALISP methodology is used for non-supervised classification of acoustic units in conjunction with traditional parametric translation models from the statistical translation domain: *acoustic* translations units and the bilingual correspondences between them are derived automatically from an *untranscribed* (and thus unlabeled) bilingual speech database. The translation units and the mapping between source and target language equivalents are efficiently indexed and the target language equivalents are recombined as appropriate in order to produce sequences of target language acoustic units which are then synthesised into speech with (minor) spectral distortion and prosodic processing if appropriate.

In more detail, let us imagine the case where we have access to a bilingual speech database where source language speech utterances are aligned with an equivalent target language speech signal (such as the recordings of the sessions of the European Parliament with simultaneous interpretation). Acoustic segments (both for the source and target language sides of the database) are derived using the ALISP methodology then clustered into longer sequences of acoustic segments using silence or low-energy distribution points in the audio signal. These 'acoustic phrases' then become the translation units for the translation process. Subsequently, classic parametric translation model parameters are estimated on the basis of the co-occurrence statistics of these acoustic phrases and translation correspondences between the acoustic phrases is produced. In the translation stage, acoustic phrases are derived from the unseen source language input in the same manner. The longest matches between acoustic segments in the source language input and the source language side of the database are computed, the target language equivalents of which are recombined using the translation model and a parametric model of the target language (trained on sequences of acoustic segments in the target language). The resulting sequence of acoustic phrases is subsequently synthesised with spectral, energy and prosodic smoothing to produce an acoustic utterance.

The advantage of this new architecture is that it removes the requirement for phonetically labeled acoustic data and even more importantly, orthographically transcribed speech data. In bypassing a classic speech recognition stage, an important source of error is removed. Of course, this approach remains prospective work, the feasibility of which remains to be seen. Further research is required, particularly in the crucial area of clustering acoustic units derived by ALISP into longer sequences representing a higher level linguistic representation resembling morphemes, words or word sequences. It is on the basis of this linguistic level that the statistical parameters of the translation models are calculated. The granularity of this level is therefore crucial for optimising the performance of the system whilst maintaining a suitable level of discrimination.

4   Conclusions and Perspectives

As more and more text, speech, audio and video data are available on line, the development of algorithms and programs to analyse, structure, compress, index and retrieve such data is necessary and offers exciting opportunities for data-driven and example-based approaches. One may imagine that as this amount of data increases, the performance of data-driven systems will also increase.

As an example, the ALISP (Automatic Language Independent Speech Processing) tools can already achieve a very high compression ratio for speech signals (down to 500 bps). This coder exploits the hypothesis that "everything has already been said!" i.e. that if enough speech data is available in memory, any new speech signal can be reconstructed (with minimal spectral distortion) by the concatenation of existing (representative) acoustic segments in memory.

If the speech examples are labelled in terms of classes (call types, language, topics,...), typical sequences of segments (*acoustic morphemes* can be found to aid the classification process. This would result in more accurate and, where appropriate, more natural speech processing systems.

Based on a similar principle, text and speech translation is achieved by searching in a memory containing many examples of high quality (bilingual and multilingual) translations for all genres, text-types and oral situations. Given unseen source language input, representative examples are subsequently retrieved and recombined by any of the methods grouped under the analogy principle (Section 3).

However, many issues remain to be studied and resolved including, but not limited to:

- Efficient indexing, classification and retrieval of terabytes (and beyond) of data, in particular the large amounts of memory required by audio and video data (as opposed to text);
- Availability of labeled data for supervised approaches or the improvement of machine learning algorithms for non-supervised approaches;
- Availability of data for minority or lesser studied languages;
- Intelligent incorporation of linguistic knowledge (where appropriate and desired) in order to produce more natural text or speech output.

The reader is invited to consult the references given at the end of this article for a more detailed discussion on ALISP and the data driven technologies discussed in this article.

Acknowledgments

The authors would like to thank Guido Aversano, Asmaa El-Hannani, Walid Karam, Patrick Perrot and Mutsuko Tomokiyo for their contributions to this article.

References

1. Abe, M., Nakamura, S., Shikano, K., Kuwabara, H.: Voice Conversion Through Vector Quantization. In Proceedings ICASSP, New-York, (1988) 565–568.
2. Aho, A. V.: Data Structures and Algorithms. Addison-Wesley (1983).
3. Ahlbom, G., Bimbot, F., Chollet, G.: Modeling Spectral Speech Transitions using Temporal Decomposition Techniques. In Proceedings IEEE-ICASSP, Dallas (1987) 13–16.

4. Aleksic, P., Williams, J., Katsaggelos A.: Speech-To-Video Synthesis Using MPEG-4 Compliant Visual Features. In IEEE Trans. Circuits and Systems for Video Technology, Vol. 14(5) (2004) 682–692.
5. Ammicht, E., Gorin A.L., Alonso T.: Knowledge Collection for Natural Spoken Dialog Systems. In Proceedings EUROSPEECH, Budapest, Hungary (1999).
6. Atal B.: Efficient Coding of LPC Parameters by Temporal Decomposition. In Proceedings ICASSP (1983) 81–84.
7. Baudoin, G., Cernocky, J., Chollet, G.: Quantization of Spectral Sequences using Variable Length Spectral Segments for Speech Coding at Very Low Bit Rate. In Proceedings EUROSPEECH, Rhodes (1997) 1295–1298.
8. Baudoin, G., Cernocky, J., Gournay P., Chollet, G.: Codage de la parole à bas et très bas débit. Annales des télécommunications, Vol. 55 (2000) 462–482.
9. Baudoin, G., Cernocky, J., El Chami, F., Charbit, M., Chollet, G., Petrovska-Delacretaz, D.: Advances in Very Low Bit Rate Speech Coding using Recognition and Synthesis Techniques. In Proceedings of the 5th Text, Speech and Dialog Workshop, Brno, Czech Republic ISBN 3-540-44129-8 (2002) 269–276.
10. Bayer, R., Unterauer, K.: Prefix B-Trees. ACM Transactions on Database Systems, Vol. 2(1) (1977) 11–26.
11. Berger, A., Brown, P., Della Pietra, S., Della Pietra, V., Gillett, J., Lafferty, J., Mercer, R., Printz, H., Ures, L.: The Candide System for Machine Translation. In Proceedings of the ARPA Workshop on Human Language Technology (1994).
12. Bimbot, F., Chollet, G., Deleglise, P., Montacié, C.: Temporal Decomposition and Acoustic-Phonetic decoding of Speech. In Proceedings IEEE-ICASSP, New York (1988) 445-448
13. Bimbot, F., Deleglise, P., Chollet, G.: Speech Synthesis by Structured Segments using Temporal Decomposition. In Proceedings EUROSPEECH, Paris (1989) 183–186.
14. Bimbot, F., Pieraccini R., Levin E., Atal B.: Variable Length Sequence Modelling: Multigrams. IEEE Signal Processing Letters Vol. 2(6) (1995) 111–113.
15. Black, E., Jelinek, F., Lafferty, J. D., Magerman, D. M., Mercer, R. L. and Roukos, S.: Towards History-Based Grammars: Using Richer Models for Probabilistic Parsing. In Proceedings DARPA Speech and Natural Language Workshop, Harriman, NY (1992) 134–139.
16. Black, A., Brown, R.D., Frederking, R., Singh, R., Moody, J., Steinbrecher, E.: TONGUES: Rapid Development of a Speech-to-Speech Translation System In Proceedings of HLT-2002: Second International Conference on Human Language Technology Research, San Diego, CA (2002) 24–27.
17. Blouet, R., Mokbel, C., Mokbel, H., Sanchez-Soto, E., Chollet, G., Greige, H.: BECARS: A Free Software for Speaker Verification. In Proceedings ODYSSEY 2004 - The Speaker and Language Recognition Workshop, Toledo, Spain (2004) 145–148.
18. Bregler, C., Covell, M., Slaney, M.: Video Rewrite: Driving Visual Speech with Audio. In Proceedings ACM SIGGRAPH 97, (1997).
19. Brown, P. F., Della Pietre, S.A., Della Pietra, V.J., Mercer, R.: Word-Sense Disambiguation using Statistical Methods. In Proceedings of the 29th Annual Meeting of the Association for Computational Linguistics, Berkeley, CA (1991) 264–270.
20. Brown, P. F., Cocke, J., Della Pietra, S.A., Della Pietra, V.J., Jelinek, F., Mercer, R., Roossin, P.: A Statistical Approach to Language Translation. In Coling Budapest: Proceedings of the 12th International Conference on Computational Linguistics, Budapest, Hungary (1998) 71–77.

21. Brown, P. F., Cocke, J., Della Pietra, S. A., Della Pietra, V. J., Jelinek, F., Lafferty, J., Mercer, R. L., Roossin, P. S.: A Statistical Approach to Machine Translation. In Computational Linguistics, Vol. 16 (1990) 79–85.

22. Brown, P. F, Della Pietra, S. A., Della Pietra, V. J., Mercer, R. L.: The Mathematics of Statistical Machine Translation : Parameter Estimation. In Computational Linguistics, Vol. 19 (1993) 263–311.

23. Brown, R. D.: Example-Based Machine Translation in the PANGLOSS System. In COLING-96: The 16th International Conference on Computational Linguistics, Copenhagen, Denmark (1996) 169–174.

24. Brown, R. D.: Automated Dictionary Extraction for Knowledge-Free Example-Based Translation. In Proceedings of the 7th International Conference on Theoretical and Methodological Issues in Machine Translation, Santa Fe, New Mexico (1997) 111–118.

25. Brown, R. D., Frederking, R. E.: Applying Statistical Language Modelling to Symbolic Machine Translation. In Proceedings of the Sixth International Conference on Theoretical and Methodological Issues in Machine Translation, Leuven, Belgium (1995) 354–372.

26. Cappe, O., Stylianou, Y., Moulines, E.: Statistical Methods For Voice Quality Transformation. In Proceedings of EUROSPEECH 95, Madrid, Spain (1995) 447–450.

27. Carpenter G., Grossberg S.: A Massively Parallel Architecture for a Self-Organizing Neural Pattern Recognition Machine. In Proceedings of Computer Vision, Graphics and Image Processing, Vol. 37 (1987) 54–115.

28. Casacuberta, F., Vidal, E., Vilar, J-M.: Architectures for Speech-to-Speech Translation using Finite-State Models In Proceedings of the Workshop on Speech-to-Speech Translation: Algorithms and Systems, Philadelphia (2002) 39–44.

29. Cernocky, J., Baudoin, G., Chollet, G.: Speech Spectrum Representation and Coding using Multigrams with Distance. In Proceedings IEEE-ICASSP, Munich (1997) 1343–1346.

30. Cernocky, J., Baudoin, G., Chollet, G.: Segmental Vocoder - Going Beyond the Phonetic Approach. In Proceedings IEEE-ICASSP, Seattle, ISBN 0-7803-4428-6 (1998) 605–608.

31. Cernocky, J., Baudoin, G., Chollet, G.: Very Low Bit Rate Segmental Speech Coding using Automatically Derived Units. In Proceedings RADIOELEKTRONIKA, Brno, Czech Republic ISBN 80-214-0983-5 (1998) 224-227

32. Cernocky, J., Petrovska-Delacretaz, D., Pigeon, S., Verlinde, P., Chollet, G.: A Segmental Approach to Text-Independent Speaker Verification. In Proceedings EUROSPEECH, Budapest Vol. 5 (1999) 2203–2206.

33. Cernocky, J., Kopecek I., Baudoin, G., Chollet, G.: Very Low Bit Rate Speech Coding: Comparison of Data-Driven Units with Syllable Segments. In Proceedings of the Text, Speech and Dialog Workshop, Pilsen, Czech Republic ISBN 3-540-66494-7 (1999) 257–262.

34. Cernocky, J., Baudoin, G., Petrovska-Delacretaz, D., Chollet, G.: Vers une analyse acoustico-phonétique de la parole indépendante de la langue, basée sur ALISP. In Revue Parole, ISSN 1373-1955, Vol. 17 (2001) 191–226.

35. Charniak E.: Statistical Language Learning. MIT Press (1993).

36. Charniak, E.: Statistical Parsing with a Context-Free Grammar and Word Statistics. In Proceedings of the 14th National Conference on Artificial Intelligence (AAAI-97), Menlo Park, CA (1997) 598–603.

37. Chollet, G., Galliano, J-F., Lefevre, J-P., Viara, E.: On the Generation and Use of a Segment Dictionary for Speech Coding, Synthesis and Recognition. In Proceedings IEEE-ICASSP, Boston (1983) 1328–1331.
38. Chollet, G., Grenier, Y., Marcus, S.: Segmentation and Non-Stationary Modeling of Speech. In Proceedings EUSIPCO, The Hague (1986).
39. Chollet, G., Cernocky, J., Constantinescu, A., Deligne, S., Bimbot, F.: Toward ALISP: Automatic Language Independent Speech Processing. In K. Ponting and R. Moore (eds.): Computational Models for Speech Pattern Processing. Springer Verlag, ISBN 3-540-65478-X (1999) 375–387.
40. Chollet, G., Cernocky, J., Gravier, G., Hennebert, J., Petrovska-Delacretaz, D., Yvon, F.: Toward Fully Automatic Speech Processing Techniques for Interactive Voice Servers. In G. Chollet, M-G. Di Benedetto, A. Esposito, M. Marinaro (eds.): Speech Processing, Recognition and Artificial Neural Networks. Springer Verlag (1999).
41. Chollet, G., Cernocky, J., Baudoin, G.: Unsupervised Learning for Very Low Bit Rate Coding. In Proceedings of SCI-ISAS 2000, Orlando (2000).
42. Chu-Carroll J., Carpenter B.: Vector-based Natural Language Call Routing. Computational Linguistcs, Vol. 25(3) (1999) 361–388.
43. Church, K.: A Stochastic Parts Program and Noun Phrase Parser for Unrestricted Text. In Proceedings Second Conference on Applied Natural Language Processing, ACL, Austin, Texas (1988) 136–143.
44. Collins, B., Cunningham, P.: Adaptation Guided Retrieval in EBMT: A Case-Based Approach to Machine Translation. In I. Smith and B. Faltings (eds.): Advances in Case-Based Reasoning: Third European Workshop, EWCBR-1996 (Lecture Notes in Computer Science 1168), Berlin. Springer (1996) 91–104.
45. Cutting, D., Pedersen, J.: Optimizations for Dynamic Inverted Index Maintenance. In Proceedings 13th International Conference on Research and Development in Information Retrieval, Brussels, Belgium (1990) 405–411.
46. Cutting, D., Kupiec, J., Pedersen, J. and Sibun, P.: A Practical Part-of-Speech Tagger. In Third Conference on Applied Natural Language Processing, Trento, Italy (1992) 133–140.
47. Daelemans, W., Zavrel, J., Berck, S.: MBT: A Memory Based Part of Speech Tagger-Generator. In Proceedings of the 4th Workshop on Very Large Corpora, Copenhagen, Denmark (1996) 14–27.
48. Dagan, I., Perreira, F., Lee, L.: Similarity Based Estimation of Word Co-occurence Probabilities. In Proceedings of the 32nd Annual Meeting of the Association for Computational Linguistics, Las Cruces, New Mexico (1994) 272–278.
49. Damper, R.I. (ed.): Data-Driven Techniques in Speech Synthesis. Kluwer (2001).
50. Deligne, S., Bimbot, F.: Language Modeling by Variable Length Sequences: Theoretical Formulation and Evaluation of Multigrams. In Proceedings ICASSP, Munich (1997) 1731–1734.
51. Deligne, S., Bimbot, F.: Inference of Variable-length Linguistic and Acoustic Units by Multigrams. In Speech Communication Vol. 23 (1997) 223–241.
52. Deligne, S., Yvon, F., Bimbot, F.: Introducing Statistical Dependencies and Structural Constraints in Variable-Length Sequence Models. In Proceedings of the 3rd International Colloquium on Grammatical Inference: Learning Syntax from Sentences, Montpellier, France (1996) 156–167.
53. Doddington, G., Martin, A., Przybocki, M., Reynolds, D.: The NIST Speaker Recognition Evaluation - Overview, Methodology, Systems, Results, Perspectives. Speech Communications, Vol. 31(2-3) (2000) 225–254.

54. Dorr, B. J., Jordan, P. W., Benoit, J. W.: A Survey of Current Paradigms in Machine Translation. Technical Report: LAMP-TR-027, UMIACS-TR-98-72, CS-TR-3961, University of Maryland, College Park, December 1998.
55. Duda R.O., Hart P.E., Stork D.G.: Pattern Classification. John Wiley and Sons, 2nd edition (2001).
56. Du Jeu, C., Charbit, M., Chollet, G.: Very Low Rate Speech Compression by Indexation of Polyphones. In Proceedings of EUROSPEECH, Geneva (2003) 1085-1088.
57. Eatock J.P., Mason J.S.: A Quantitative Assessment of the Relative Speaker Discriminant Properties of Phonemes. In Proceedings ICASSP, Vol. 1 (1994) 133–136.
58. El Hannani, A., Petrovska-Delacretaz, D., Chollet, G.: Linear and Non-linear Fusion of ALISP- and GMM-Based Systems for Text-Independent Speaker Verification. In Proceedings of ISCA Workshop: A Speaker Odyssey, Toledo, Spain, (2004) 111–116.
59. Farinas, J., Obrecht, R.A.: Modélisation phonotactique de grandes classes phonétiques en vue d'une approche différenciée en identification automatique des langues. In Proceedings 18ème colloque GRETSI sur le traitement du signal et des images, Toulouse, France (2001).
60. Frakes, W. B., Baeza-Yates, R.: Information Retrieval: Data Structures and Algorithms. Prentice Hall (1992).
61. Fukunaga K.: Statistical Pattern Recognition. Academic Press, 2nd edition (1990).
62. Gailly, J-L., Nelson, M.: The Data Compression Book. John Wiley and Sons (1995).
63. Gale, W., Church, K. W., Yarowsky, D.: Work on Statistical Methods for Word Sense Disambiguation. In Proceedings of the AAAI Fall Symposium: Probabilistic Approaches to Natural Language, Cambridge, MA (1992) 54–60.
64. Gonnet, G.H., Baeza-Yates, R.: Handbook of Algorithms and Data Structures (2nd edition). Addison-Wesley (1991).
65. Gorin, A.L., Petrovska-Delacrétaz, D., Riccardi, G., Wright J.H.: Learning Spoken Language without Transcriptions. In Proceedings IEEE Workshop on Automatic Speech Recognition and Understanding, (1999).
66. Gorin A.L.: How May I Help You?. Speech Communication, Vol. 23 (1997) 113–127.
67. Gorin A,L.: On Automated Language Acquisition. Journal of the Acoustical Society of America-JASA, Vol. 97(6) (1995) 3441–3461.
68. Gorin, A.L., Levinson, S., Sankar A.: An Experiment in Spoken Language Acquisition. In Proceedings IEEE Transactions on Speech and Audio, Vol. 2 (1994) 224–240.
69. Haines, D., Croft, W.B.: Relevance Feedback and Inference Networks. In Proceedings of the ACM SIGIR Conference on Research and Development in Information Retrieval, Pittsburg, Penn. (1993) 2–11.
70. Hankerson, D., Harris, G.A., Johnson P.D.: Introduction to Information Theory and Data Compression. CRC Press (2003).
71. Harbeck, S., Ohler U.: Multigrams for Language Identification. In Proceedings EUROSPEECH, Budapest, Hungary (1999).
72. Harman, D., Baeza-Yates, R., Fox, E., Lee, W.: Inverted Files. In W.B. Frakes and R. Baeza-Yates (eds.): Information Retrieval: Data Structures and Algorithms. Prentice Hall (1992).
73. Ho, Y.: Application of Minimal Perfect Hashing in Main Memory Indexing. MIT-LCS-TM-508 (1994).

74. Jensen F.V.: Bayesian Networks and Decision Graphs. Springer (2001).
75. Jelinek, F.: Self-Organized Language Modeling for Speech Recognition. In A. Waibel and K. F. Lee (eds.): Readings in Speech Recognition. Morgan Kaufmann Publishers, San Mateo, CA (1990) 450–506.
76. Jelinek F.: Statistical Methods for Speech Recognition. MIT press (1999).
77. Kain, A., Macon, M. W.: Spectral Voice Conversion for Text to Speech Synthesis. In Proceedings ICASSP 88, New-York, Vol. 1 (1998) 285–288.
78. Kain, A., Macon, M. W.: Design and Evaluation of a Voice Conversion Algorithm Based on Spectral Envelope Mapping and Residual Prediction. In Proceedingsd ICASSP 01, Salt Lake City, USA (2001).
79. Kaji, H., Kida, Y., Morimoto, Y.: Learning Translation Templates from Bilingual Text. In Proceedings of the 14th Conference on Computational Linguistics, Nantes, France, Vol. 2 (1992) 672–678.
80. Karam, W., Mokbel, C., Aversano, G., Pelachaud, C., Chollet, G.: An Audiovisual Imposture Scenario by Talking Face Animation. In G. Chollet, A. Esposito, M. Faundez, M. Marinaro (eds.): Nonlinear Speech Processing: Algorithms and Analysis. Springer-Verlag (2005) (in this volume).
81. Knuth, D.E.: The Art of Computer Programming. Addison-Wesley (1973).
82. Kohonen T.: Self Organizing Maps. Springer Verlag (1995).
83. Koza J.R.: Genetic Programming. MIT Press (1992).
84. Kuo H.-K.J., Lee, C.-H.: A Portability Study on Natural Language Call Steering. In Proceedings EUROSPEECH, Aalborg, Denmark (2001).
85. Lamel, L.F, Gauvain, J.-L., Eskénazi, M.: BREF, A Large Vocabulary Spoken Corpus for French. In Proceedings of the European Conference on Speech Technology, EUROSPEECH (1991) 505–508.
86. Laroche, J., Stylianou, Y., Moulines, E.: HNM: A Simple, Efficient Harmonic Plus Noise Model for Speech. In Proceedings of IEEE ASSP Workshop on Applications of Signal Processing to Audio and Acoustics (1993).
87. Lee K-S., Cox R.V.: A Segmental Speech Coder Based on a Concatenative TTS. Speech Communication, Vol. 38(1) (2002) 89–100.
88. Levenshtein, V.I.: Binary Codes Capable of Correcting Deletions, Insertions and Reversals. Cybernetics and Control Theory, Vol. 10 (1966) 707–710.
89. Levin, L., Lavie, A., Woszczyna, M., Gates, D., Gavaldá, M., Koll, D., Waibel, A.: The Janus-III Translation System: Speech-to-Speech Translation in Multiple Domains. In Machine Translation Archive, Vol. 15(1-2) (2000) 3–25.
90. Lloyd-Thomas H., Parris E., Wright J.W.: Recurrent Substrings and Data Fusion for Language Recognition. In Proceedings ICSLP, Sydney, Australia (1998).
91. Lowrance, R., Wagner, R.A.: An Extension of the String-to-String Correction Problem. In Journal of the Association of Computing Machinery, Vol. 22(2) (1975) 177–183.
92. Manning, C.D., Schutze, H.: Foundations of Statistical Natural Language Processing. MIT Press (1999).
93. Martin, A., Przybocki, M.: The NIST Speaker Recognition Evaluations: 1996-2001. In Proceedings Odyssey 2001, Crete, Greece (2001) 39–42.
94. Marcu, D., Wong, W.: A Phrase-Based, Joint Probability Model for Statistical Machine Translation. In Proceedings of the Conference on Empirical Methods in Natural Language Processing, Philadelphia, PA (2002) 133–139.
95. Mc-Tait K.: Translation Patterns, Linguistic Knowledge and Complexity in an Approach to EBMT. In M. Carl, A. Way (eds.): Recent Advances in Example-Based Machine Translation. Amsterdam: Kluwer Academic Press (2003).

96. McTait, K.: Translation Pattern Extraction and Recombination for Example-Based Machine Translation. Ph.D. Thesis, University of Manchester Institute of Science and Technology, Manchester, UK (2001).
97. McTait, K., Trujillo, A.: A Language-Neutral Sparse-Data Algorithm for Extracting Translation Patterns. In Proceedings of the 8th International Conference on Theoretical and Methodological Issues in Machine Translation TMI-99, Chester, UK (1999) 98–108.
98. McTait, K., Olohan, M., Trujillo, A.: A Building Blocks Approach to Translation Memory. In Proceedings of the 21st ASLIB International Conference on Translating and the Computer, London, UK (1999).
99. Melamed, I. D.: A Word-To-Word Model of Translation Equivalence. In 35th Annual Meeting of the Association for Computational Linguistics and 8th Conference of the European Chapter of the Association for Computational Linguistics, Madrid, Spain (1997) 490–497.
100. Merialdo, B.: Tagging English Text with a Probabilistic Model. In Computational Linguistics, Vol. 20(2) (1994) 155–172.
101. Metze, F., McDonough, J., Soltau, H., Waibel, A., Lavie, A., Burger, S., Langley, C., Levin, L., Schultz, T., Pianesi, F., Cattoni, R., Lazzari, G., Mana, N, Pianta, E.: The NESPOLE! Speech-to-Speech Translation System. In Proceedings of HLT-2002 Human Language Technology Conference, San Diego, CA (2002).
102. Mitchell, T.M.: Machine Learning. McGraw-Hill (1997).
103. Mitchell, T.M.: Machine Learning and Data Mining. In Communications of the ACM, Vol. 42(11) (1999) 30–36.
104. Morimoto, T., Takezawa, T., Yato, F., Sagayama, S., Tashiro, M., Nagata, M., Kurematsu, A.: ATR's Speech Translation System: ASURA. In Proceedings EUROSPEECH 1993, 1291–1295.
105. Nagao, M.: A Framework of a Mechanical Translation between Japenese and English by Analogy Principle. In A. Elithorn and R. Banerji (eds.): Artificial and Human Intelligence. NATO Publications (1984) 173–180.
106. Nakamura, S.: Fusion of Audio-Visual Information for Integrated Speech Processing. In Proceedings Audio- and Video-Based Biometric Person Authentication (AVBPA), Halmstad, Sweden (2001) 127–143.
107. Navrátil, J.: Spoken Language Recognition: A Step Towards Multilinguality. In IEEE Trans. Audio and Speech Processing, Vol. 9(6) (2001) 678–685.
108. Nevill-Manning, C.G.: Inferring Sequential Structure. PhD Thesis, Univ. of Waikato (1996).
109. Nirenburg, S., Beale, S., Domashnev, C.: A Full-Text Experiment in Example-Based Machine Translation. In Proceedings of the International Conference on New Methods in Language Processing (NeMLaP), Manchester, UK (1994) 78–87.
110. Nirenburg, S., Domashnev, C., Grannes, D. J.: Two Approaches to Matching in Example-Based Machine Translation. In Proceedings of the Fifth International Conference on Theoretical and Methodological Issues in Machine Translation, TMI-93: MT in the Next Generation, Kyoto, Japan, (1993) 47-57.
111. Olivier, D.C.: Stochastic Grammars and Language Acquisition Mechanism. Ph.D. Thesis, Harvard University (1968).
112. Pasquariello, S., Pelachaud, C.: Greta: A Simple Facial Animation Engine. In 6th Online World Conference on Soft Computing in Industrial Applications, Session on Soft Computing for Intelligent 3D Agents, September 2001.
113. Perrot, P., Aversano, G., Chollet, G., Charbit, M.: Voice Forgery Using ALISP: Indexation in a Client Memory. to appear in proc. of ICASSP 2005.

114. Petrovska-Delacrétaz, D., Černocký, J., Hennebert, J., Chollet G.: Text-Independent Speaker Verification Using Automatically Labeled Acoustic Segments. In ICLSP, Sydney, Australia, 1998.
115. Petrovska-Delacretaz, D., Cernocky, J., Hennebert, J., Chollet, G.: Segmental Approaches to Automatic Speaker Verification. In Digital Signal Processing: A Review Journal, Vol. 10, (1/2/3), Academic Press, ISSN 1052-2004 (2000) 198–212.
116. Petrovska-Delacrétaz D., Gorin, A.L., Wright, J.H., Riccardi G.: Detecting Acoustic Morphemes in Lattices for Spoken Language Understanding. In Proceedings ICSLP, Beijing, China (2000).
117. Petrovska-Delacretaz, D., Gorin, A.L., Riccardi, G., Wright, J.H.: Detecting Acoustic Morphemes in Lattices for Spoken Language Understanding. In Proceedings of ICASSP, Beijing, China (2000).
118. Petrovska-Delacretaz, D., Chollet, G.: Searching Through a Speech Memory for Efficient Coding, Recognition and Synthesis. In A. Braun and H. Masthoff (eds.): Phonetics and its Applications. Franz Steiner Verlag, ISBN 8094-5 (2002) 453–464.
119. Petrovska-Delacretaz, D., Abalo, M., El Hannani, A., Chollet, G.: Data-Driven Speech Segmentation for Speaker Verification and Language Identification. In Proceedings of NOLISP, Le Croisic, (2003).
120. Petrovska-Delacretaz, D., El Hannani, A., Chollet, G.: Searching through a Speech Memory for Text-Independent Speaker Verification. In Proceedings of AVBPA, Guilford, paper 84 (2003).
121. Pighin, F., Szeliski, R., Salesin, D.: Modeling and Animating Realistic Faces from Images. In International Journal of Computer Vision, Vol. 50(2) (2002) 143–169.
122. Planas, E., Furuse, O.: Formalizing Translation Memory. In M. Carl A. Way (eds.): Recent Advances in Example-Based Machine Translation. Amsterdam: Kluwer Academic Press (2003).
123. Prudon, R., d'Alessandro, C.: A Selection/Concatenation Text-to-Speech Synthesis System: Database Development, System Design, Comparative Evaluation. In Proceedings of the 4th Speech Synthesis Workshop, Pitlochy, Scotland (2001)
124. Przybocki, M., Martin, A.: NIST's Assessment of Text Independent Speaker Recognition Performance 2002. The Advent of Biometrics on the Internet, A COST 275 Workshop in Rome, Italy, Nov. 7-8 2002.
125. Quinlan J.R.: C4.5 : Programs for Machine Learning. Morgan Kaufmann, San Mateo, CA (1993).
126. Reynolds, D.A., Quatieri, T.F., Dunn R.B.: Speaker Verification Using Adapted Gaussian Mixture Models. DSP, Special Issue on the NIST'99 Evaluations, Vol. 10(1-3) (2000) 19–41.
127. Ribeiro, C.M., Trancoso, I.M.: Improving Speaker Recognisability in Phonetic Vocoders. In Proceedings of ICSLP, Sydney (1998).
128. Ribeiro, C.M., Trancoso, I.M.: Phonetic Vocoder Assessment. In Proceedings ICSLP, Beijing, Vol 3 (2000) 830-833.
129. Roy D.: Learning Words from Sights and Sounds: A Computational Model. Ph.D. Thesis, MIT (1999).
130. Sadler, V., Vendelmans, R.: Pilot Implementation of a Bilingual Knowledge Bank. In Proceedings of the 13th International Conference on Computational Linguistics, Helsinki, Vol. 3 (1990) 449–451.
131. Salton, G., McGill, M.S.: Introduction to Modern Information Retrieval. McGraw-Hill, NY (1983).

132. Sayood, K.: Introduction to Data Compression. Morgan Kaufmann (2000).
133. Shiraki, Y., Honda, M.: LPC Speech Coding based on VLSQ. In Proceedings IEEE Trans. on ASSP, Vol 3(9) (1988).
134. Schroeter, J., Graf, H.P., Beutnagel, M., Cosatto, E., Syrdal, A., Conkie, A., Stylianou, Y.: Multimodal Speech Synthesis. In Proceedings IEEE International Conference on Multimedia and Expo, NY (2000) 571–578.
135. Simard, P.Y., Le Cun, Y., Denker, J.S.: Memory Based Character Recognition using a Transformation Invariant Metric. In Proceedings of ICPR, Jerusalem (1994) 262–267.
136. Simard, M., Langlais, P.: Sub-Sentential Exploitation of Translation Memories. In MT Summit VIII: Machine Translation in the Information Age, Santiago de Compostela, Spain (2001) 335–339.
137. Simons, A., Cox, S.: Generation of Mouth Shapes for a Synthetic Talking Head. In Proceedings Inst. Acoust., Vol. 12 (1990) 475–482.
138. Smith, T.C., Witten, I.H.: Learning Language using Genetic Algorithms. In S. Wermter, E. Riloff, G. Scheler (eds.): Connectionist, Statistical and Symbolic Approaches to Learning for Natural Language Processing. Springer Verlag, NY (1996) 132–145.
139. Somers, H., McLean, I., Jones, D.: Experiments in Multilingual Example-Based Generation. In Proceedings CSNLP 1994: 3rd Conference on the Cognitive Science of Natural Language Processing, Dublin, Ireland.
140. Stolcke, A.: An Efficient Probabilistic Context-Free Parsing Algorithm that Computes Prefix Probabilities. In Computational Linguistics 21(2) (1995) 165–201.
141. Stylianou, Y., Cappé, O., Moulines, E.: Statistical Methods for Voice Quality Transformation. In Proceedings of EUROSPEECH, Madrid (1995) 447–450.
142. Stylianou, Y., Cappé, O., Moulines, E.: Continuous Probabilistic Transform for Voice Conversion. In Proceedings IEEE Transactions on SAP, Vol. 6(2) (1998) 131–142.
143. Suhm, B., Geutner, P., Kemp, T., Lavie, A., Mayfield, L., McNair, A.E., Rogina, I., Schultz, T., Sloboda, T., Ward, W., Woszczyna, M, Waibel, A.: JANUS: Towards Multilingual Spoken Language Translation. In Proceedings ARPA Spoken Language Technology Workshop , Austin, TX (1995).
144. Sumita, E., Tsutsumi, Y.: A Translation Aid System Using Flexible Text Retrieval Based on Syntax-Matching. In TMI 1988 Proceedings Supplement, Pittsburgh (1988) [pages not numbered].
145. Tamura, M., Masuko, T., Kobayashi, T., Tokuda, K.: Visual Speech Synthesis Based on Parameter Generation from HMM: Speech-Driven and Text-and-Speech-Driven Approaches. In Proceedings Auditory-Visual Speech Processing (1998).
146. Thomas, H.L., Parris, E., Wright, J.: Reccurent Substrings and Data Fusion for Language Recognition. In Proceedings ICASSP 2000, Instanbul, Turkey, Vol. 2 (2000) 169–173.
147. Tomokiyo, M., Chollet, G.: A Proposal to Represent Speech Control Mechanisms within the Universal Networking Digital Language. In Proceedings of the International Conference on the Convergence of Knowledge, Culture, Language and Information Technologies, Alexandria, Egypt (2003).
148. Turcato, D.: Automatically Creating Bilingual Lexicons for Machine Translation from Bilingual Text. In Proceedings COLING-ACL 98: 36th Annual Meeting of the Association for Computational Linguistics and 17th International Conference on Computational Linguistics, Montreal, Canada, (1998) 1299-1305.

149. Utsuro, T., Matsumoto, Y., Nagao, M.: Lexical Knowledge Acquisition from Bilingual Corpora. In Proceedings of the fifteenth [sic] International Conference on Computational Linguistics, COLING-92, Nantes, France (1992) 581–587.
150. Valbret, H., Moulines, E., Tubach, J-P.: Voice Transformation using PSOLA Technique. In Proceedings ICASSP 92, San Francisco, CA, Vol. 1 (1992) 145–148.
151. Valiant, L.G.: A Theory of the Learnable. In Communications of the ACM, Vol. 27(11) (1984) 1134-1142.
152. Vogel, S., Och, F., J., Tillmann, C., Nießen, S., Sawaf, H., Ney, H.: Statistical Methods for Machine Translation. In W. Wahlster (ed.): Verbmobil: Foundations of Speech-to-Speech Translation. Springer Verlag, Berlin (2000).
153. Wahlster, W.: First Results of Verbmobil: Translation Assistance for Spontaneous Dialogues. In Proceedings ATR International Workshop on Speech Translation, Kyoto, Japan (1993).
154. Waibel, A., Finke, M., Gates, D., Gavaldà, M., Kemp, T., Lavie, A., Maier, M., Mayfield, M., McNair, A., Rogina, I., Shima, K., Sloboda, T., Woszczyna, M., Zhan, P., Zeppenfeld, T.: Janus II - Advances in Spontaneous Speech Translation. In Internatational Conference on Acoustics, Speech and Signal Processing, Atlanta, Georgia (1996).
155. Waibel, A., Jain, A, M., McNair, A. E., Saito, H., Hauptmann, A. G., Tebelskis, J.: JANUS: A Speech-To-Speech Translation System Using Connectionist and Symbolic Processing Strategies. In ICASSP 1991, Toronto, Canada, Vol. 2 (1991) 793–796.
156. Wang, Y-Y., Waibel, A.: Modeling with Structures in Statistical Machine Translation. In Proceedings of the 36th Annual Meeting of the Association for Computational Linguistics and 17th International Conference on Computational Linguistics, Montreal, Canada (1998) 1357–1363.
157. Wang, Y., Waibel, A.: Decoding Algorithm in Statistical Machine Translation. In Proceedings of the 35th Annual Meeting of the Association for Computational Linguistics and 8th Conference of the European Chapter of the Association for Computational Linguistics ACL/EACL 97, Madrid, Spain 366–372.
158. Watanabe, H.: A Method for Extracting Translation Patterns from Translation Examples. In Proceedings of the 5th International Conference on Theoretical and Methodological Issues in Machine Translation (TMI 93): MT in the Next Generation, Kyoto, Japan (1993) 292–301.
159. Williams, J., Katsaggelos, A.: An HMM-Based Speech-to-Video Synthesizer. In Proceedings IEEE Transactions on Neural Networks, Vol. 13(4) (2002) 900–915.
160. Witten, I.H., Moffat, A., Bell, T.C: Managing Gigabytes: Compressing and Indexing Documents and Images.. Morgan Kaufmann, San Francisco, 2nd ed. (1999).
161. Yamamoto, E., Nakamura, S., Shikano, K.: Lip Movement Synthesis from Speech Based on Hidden Markov Models. Speech Communication, Vol. 26(12) (1998) 105–115.
162. Yi, J., Glass, J.: Information-Theoretic Criteria for Unit Selection Synthesis. In Proceedings of ICSLP, Denver, Colorado (2002) 2617–2620.
163. Yvon, F.: Paradigmatic Cascades: A Linguistically Sound Model of Pronunciation by Analogy. In Proceedings of the 35th Annual Meeting of the Association for Computational Linguistics, Somerset, NJ (1997) 428–435.

Cepstrum-Based Harmonics-to-Noise Ratio Measurement in Voiced Speech

Peter Murphy and Olatunji Akande

Department of Electronic and Computer Engineering,
University of Limerick, Limerick, Ireland
{peter.murphy,olatunji.akande}@ul.ie

Abstract. The estimation of the harmonics-to-noise ratio (HNR) in voiced speech provides an indication of the ratio between the periodic to aperiodic components of the signal. Time-domain methods for HNR estimation are problematic because of the difficulty of estimating the period markers for (pathological) voiced speech. Frequency-domain methods encounter the problem of estimating the noise level at harmonic locations. Cepstral techniques have been introduced to supply noise estimates at all frequency locations in the spectrum. A detailed description of cepstral processing is provided in order to motivate its use as a HNR estimator. The action of cepstral low-pass liftering and subsequent Fourier transformation is shown to be analogous to the action of a moving average filter. Based on this description, short-comings of two existing cepstral-based HNRs are illustrated and a new approach is introduced and shown to provide accurate HNR measurements for synthesised glottal and voiced speech waveforms.

1 Introduction

Aperiodicity in voice may be due to any one of, or a combination of, acoustic properties such as jitter, shimmer, aspiration noise and inter-period glottal waveshape differences. The harmonics-to-noise ratio in voiced speech provides an indication of the overall aperiodicity of the speech signal i.e. it quantifies the ratio between the periodic and aperiodic components of the signal. The estimation of the harmonics-to-noise ratio (HNR) has been shown to provide a useful index for non-invasive analysis of voice disorders. A valid and reliable method for estimating the HNR in human voice is important for effective evaluation and management of voice pathology. Many methods have been proposed for measuring the harmonics-to-noise ratio (HNR) in voiced speech. The different methodologies can be broadly classified as time, frequency and cepstral domain techniques. Most of these methods, however, are not validated for accuracy; at best they represent the general HNR trend i.e. they show a decrease or increase in HNR values with a corresponding decrease or increase in input noise values. Accurate estimation of the HNR requires the use of a calibrated measurement technique that correlates the estimated HNR values against known HNR values. Pitch synchronous time-domain methods for HNR estimation are problematic because of the difficulty of estimating the period markers for (pathological) voiced speech. Frequency-domain methods encounter the problem of estimating the noise level at harmonic locations. Cepstral techniques have been introduced to supply noise estimates at all frequency locations in the spectrum. In this chapter, two existing cesp-

G. Chollet et al. (Eds.): Nonlinear Speech Modeling, LNAI 3445, pp. 199–218, 2005.

tral-based HNR estimation techniques are evaluated systematically for the first time using synthetically generated glottal flow and voiced speech signals, with *a priori* knowledge of the HNR. Moreover, detailed elucidation and illustrations are provided to improve the understanding of the rationale underlying the use of liftered low-quefrency cepstral coefficients for estimating the HNR in speech signals. In light of this development, a new cepstrum-based technique is proposed and implemented for accurate estimation of the HNR. The method improves the noise floor estimation procedure. A selective pre-emphasis technique is introduced to reduce the contaminating influence of the glottal source on the noise baseline. The HNR is calculated as the ratio of the harmonic energy (without pre-emphasis) to the liftered noise energy. The accuracy of the new technique is compared with that of two existing cepstral-based methods using synthetically generated voice signals with a set of predetermined additive noise levels.

2   Existing Methods for HNR Estimation

Initial attempts at estimating noise levels in voiced speech have followed perceptual and spectrographic based approaches [c.f. [1]]. Although perceptual and spectrographic methods show promise in clinical analysis and management of pathological voice, the methods are somewhat subjective. In recent years research has aimed at developing objective procedures for quantifying the noise level in voiced speech. Such procedures may also be used for broader applications, such as speech quality enhancement and speech synthesis. Objective and quantitative evaluation of signal-to-noise levels is now possible through estimation of the HNR (harmonics-to-noise ratio). This quantity (HNR) is a function of the additive noise and other factors such as jitter and shimmer, which are responsible for the aperiodic component in voiced speech. The many methods that have been proposed for HNR estimation can be broadly classified into (a) time domain, (b) frequency domain and (c) cepstral-based techniques. Time domain techniques are described in [2-9]. Frequency domain methods include the work of [10-20] while cepstral-based techniques include [21-23].

2.1   Time-Domain Methods

Representative time domain HNR estimation techniques are reported in, for example, [2] and [8]. In general, these methods calculate the harmonics-to-noise ratio by first computing the average waveform of a single period of speech though calculating the mean of successive periods. The noise energy is then calculated as the mean squared difference between the average waveform and the individual periods. The ratio of the energy of the average waveform to the average variance gives the HNR. Though very simple and less computationally intensive as compared to frequency and cepstral based approaches, time domain HNR estimation requires accurate estimation of the beginning and end of individual pitch periods in the underlying speech waveform. This requires the use of complex signal processing algorithms. Moreover, the pitch boundaries are very sensitive to phase distortion, hence a high quality recording device with good amplitude and phase response is required for collecting the speech data.

2.2 Frequency-Domain HNR Methods

Frequency domain approaches to HNR estimation may overcome, to a certain degree, the necessity for accurate fundamental period estimation. The periodic component is approximated by extracting from the spectrum the summed energy at harmonic locations. The noise energy is estimated by summing the between-harmonic estimates. The noise at harmonic locations is typically estimated as the average of the noise estimates either side of the harmonic locations (c.f. [12]). The final harmonics-to-noise ratio is expressed in dBs. A further advantage of HNR estimation in the frequency domain is the ability to estimate HNR over a desired frequency band.

2.3 Cepstrum-Based Methods

Before outlining the basis of the procedure underlying the cepstral-based HNR estimators a brief introduction to the cepstrum of voiced speech is provided.

2.3.1 Cesptral Analysis of Voiced Speech

Cesptral processing of speech was introduced in [24]. Cepstrum analysis belongs to the class of homomorphic filtering developed as a general method of separating signals, which have been non-additively combined. It has been used in general speech analysis for pitch [24] and vocal-tract transfer function estimation [25-27]. A brief review of Noll's interpretation [24] is given.

The cepstrum is defined as the square of the Fourier transform of the power spectrum of the speech signal. Voiced speech, s(t) is considered as a periodic source component, e(t) convolved by the impulse response of the vocal tract, v(t).

$$s(t)=e(t)*v(t) \tag{1}$$

Taking the Fourier transform magnitude gives

$$|S(f)|=|E(f) \times V(f)| \tag{2}$$

Taking the logarithm changes the multiplicative components into additive components.

$$\log|S(f)|=\log|E(f)|+\log|V(f)| \tag{3}$$

It is noted (Fig.1(a)) that the vocal tract contributes a slow variation, while the periodicity of the source manifests itself as a fast variation in the log spectrum. Taking the Fourier transform of the logarithmic power spectrum yields a prominent peak corresponding to the high frequency source component and a broader peak corresponding to the low frequency formant structure. To distinguish between the frequency components in a temporal waveform and the frequency in the log spectrum the term quefrency is used to describe the log spectrum "frequency", while the first prominent cepstral peak is termed the first rahmonic (Fig.1(b)). In present day processing the inverse Fourier transform of the log magnitude spectrum is generally taken to represent the cepstrum of voiced speech. The *real cepstrum* is defined as the inverse Fourier transform of the log of the magnitude spectrum:

$$\hat{C}(t) = \int_{-\infty}^{\infty} \log |S(f)| e^{j2\pi ft} df . \tag{4}$$

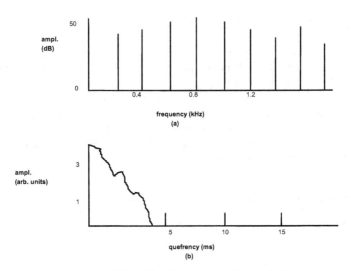

Fig. 1. Schematic representation of (a) a Fourier spectrum of a periodic speech waveform, and (b) its corresponding cepstrum with rahmonics spaced at integer multiples of T, the fundamental period

2.3.2 Cepstral-Based HNR Estimation

A cepstrum technique for estimating the HNR in voiced speech was introduced in [21]. The potential advantage of the cepstral approach lies in the fact that it supplies a noise estimate at all frequencies in the spectrum. In this approach, the cepstrum is applied to a segment of voiced speech and the Fourier transform of the liftered cepstral coefficients approximates a noise baseline from which the harmonics-to-noise ratio is estimated. The ratio (expressed in dB) of the energy of the original speech spectrum at harmonic locations to the energy of the Fourier transformed liftered noise baseline is taken as the HNR estimate. The basic procedure presented in [21] is as follows; the cepstrum is produced for a windowed segment of voiced speech, the rahmonics are zeroed and the resulting liftered cepstrum is Fourier transformed to provide a noise spectrum. After performing a baseline correction procedure on this spectrum (the original noise estimate is high), the summed energy of the modified noise spectrum (in dB) is subtracted from the summed energy of the original harmonic spectrum (in dB) in order to provide the harmonics-to-noise ratio estimate. A modification to the de Krom technique [21] is presented in [22]. Problems with the baseline fitting procedure are highlighted and a way to avoid these problems by calculating the energy and noise estimates at harmonic locations only is proposed. In addition, rather than comb-liftering the rahmonics, the cepstrum is low-passed filtered to provide a smoother baseline.

An alternative cepstral-based approach for extracting a HNR from speech signals is estimated in [23]. This technique involves directly estimating the magnitude of the cepstral rahmonic peaks, leading to a geometric-mean harmonics-to-noise ratio (i.e. an average of the dB harmonics-to-noise ratios at a specific frequency locations). This is quite a distinct measurement from a traditional harmonics-to-noise ratio estimator, which reflects the average signal energy divided by the average noise energy, expressed in dB. Hence, this technique is not considered further in the current analysis.

In the present study the basis behind, and the accuracies of the cepstral-based HNR estimation techniques in [21] and [22] are evaluated, and a new cepstral-based HNR method is proposed and tested. Before proceeding into the methodological details of these techniques, a more detailed description of the cepstrum of voiced speech is given in order to motive its use as a HNR estimator.

3 Cepstrum-Based Harmonic and Noise Estimation

The introduction to cepstral processing given in [24] provides an insightful and practical approach for applying the technique for speech processing applications. As noted previously, as the slow variation due to the vocal tract and the fast variation due the pitch period can usually be separated by taking the inverse Fourier transform of the log spectrum the technique has been used for pitch and formant estimation. However, for a more complete understanding of the application of the technique for use as a harmonics-to-noise estimator it is necessary to go beyond the simple representation of voiced speech as a periodic source and a vocal tract filter. In the introduction to the cepstrum three important aspects (for the present purpose) have been neglected; (i) aspiration noise, (ii) the influence of the glottal source and (iii) the window function.

A voiced speech waveform, $s_{en}(t)$, including aspiration noise, $n(t)$ at the glottal source, can be approximated as

$$s_{en}(t)=[e(t)*g(t)+n(t)]*v(t)*r(t) \tag{5}$$

where $e(t)$ is a periodic impulse train, $g(t)$ is a single glottal pulse, $v(t)$ is the impulse response of the vocal tract and $r(t)$ represents the radiation load.

Applying a Hanning window, (w)

$$s_{en}^{w}(t)= \{[e(t)*g(t)+n(t)]*v(t)*r(t)\}\times w(t) \tag{6}$$

Provided the window length is sufficiently long the window function can be moved inside the convolution [27] to give

$$s_{en}^{w}(t) = [(e_w(t)*g(t))+n_w(t)]*v(t)*r(t) \tag{7}$$

Taking the Fourier transform gives

$$S_{en}^{w}(f)=[E_w(f)\times G(f)+N_w(f)]\times V(f)\times R(f) \tag{8}$$

Taking the logarithm of the magnitude squared values and approximating the signal energy at harmonic locations, $\log|S_{en}^{w}(f)|_h^2$ and at between-harmonic locations, $\log|S_{en}^{w}(f)|_{bh}^2$, gives

$$\log|S_{en}^{w}(f)|_h^2=\log|E_w(f)\times G(f)|^2+\log|V_R(f)|^2 \tag{9}$$

$$\log|S_{en}^{w}(f)|_{bh}^2=\log|N_w(f)|^2+\log|V_R(f)|^2 \tag{10}$$

where $V_R(f)$ is the Fourier transform of $v(t)$ and $r(t)$ combined.

Although the noise spectrum is broadband, its estimation in the presence of a harmonic signal can be concentrated at between-harmonic locations i.e. in the spectrum of voiced speech, signal energy dominates at harmonic locations and noise energy dominates at between-harmonic locations. This approximation becomes more exact if the spectra are averaged in which case the harmonics approach the true harmonic values and the between-harmonics approach the true noise variance [28], Fig.2.

The cepstral technique is described with reference to Fig.3. The spectrum of voiced speech can now be seen to consist of (a) two slowly varying spectral envelopes, one due to the glottal flow excited vocal tract $|G(f) \times V(f)|$, and the other due to the noise excited vocal tract, $|N(f) \times V(f)|$ and (b) a rapidly varying periodic structure due to $|E(f)|$. The noise excited vocal tract, $|N(f) \times V(f)|$ constitutes the spectral envelope at the bottom of speech spectrum, while the spectral envelope due to the glottal source excited vocal tract, $|G(f) \times V(f)|$ constitutes the spectral envelope at the top, as depicted in Fig. 3(a). The two spectral envelopes are lumped together in the low quefrency part of the speech.

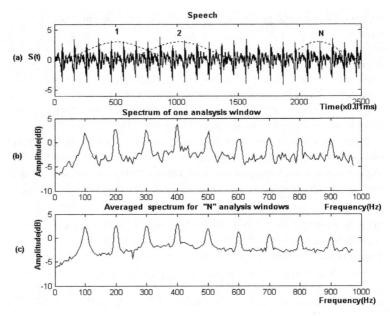

Fig. 2. Illustrating spectral averaging (a) Synthesized speech signal including aspiration noise (b) Spectrum of speech without averaging (c) Spectrum of speech with averaging cepstrum (highlighted in green in Fig.3(b))

In addition, the DC component of $|E(f)|$ resides at zero quefrency in the cepstrum. The periodic structure due to $|E(f)|$ translates to high amplitude peaks (rahmonics) at periodic locations in the cepstrum. If the low quefrency cepstral coefficients are low-pass liftered (filtering in the cepstral domain) below the first rahmonic, the Fourier transformed result represents the average of the spectral envelopes due to $|G(f) \times V(f)|$ and $|N(f) \times V(f)|$ as illustrated in Fig.3(a) (dotted blue line).

This Fourier transformed liftered cepstrum provides a noise baseline estimate which forms the basis for the HNR estimation techniques presented in [21] and [22]. However, the noise baseline estimate essentially behaves like a moving average (MA) filter and hence is dependent on both glottal and noise contributions (eqtn.5 and eqtn.6, Fig.3).

3.1 Influence of the Glottal Source, Window Length and Noise on the Cepstrum

Although the cepstrum was initially introduced as a method for separating the source and filter components of voiced speech it has been shown above that the spectral tilt

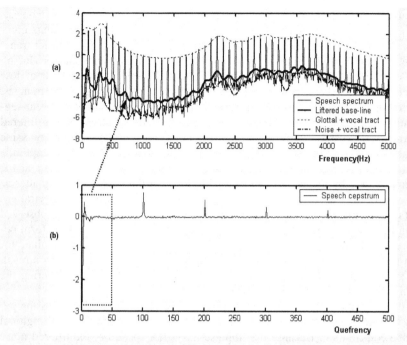

Fig. 3. (a) Spectrum of voiced speech showing spectral envelopes and harmonic structure (b) Cepstrum of voiced speech, illustrating low quefrencies due to the vocal tract, and periodically spaced rahmonics due the harmonic structure

information due to the glottal source, in fact remains within the low quefrency coefficients along with the vocal tract influence. The periodicity due to the source is reflected at rahmonic locations. Moreover, the cepstrum technique can be applied directly to the spectrum of a periodic glottal source signal to separate the periodicity and glottal spectral tilt characteristics. A noise-free, windowed, periodic glottal source is analysed to highlight the fact that the spectral tilt due to the glottal source is the primary contributor to the skewing of the noise baseline estimate in the speech spectrum. In addition, it simplifies the illustration of the effect of the window length on the cepstral analysis.

A periodic glottal source, $g_e(t)$ can be written as

$$g_e(t) = e(t)*g(t) \tag{11}$$

where $e(t)$ is a periodic impulse train and $g(t)$ is a single glottal pulse.

Windowing and applying the same analysis applied to the voiced speech waveform gives

$$g_e^w(t) = e_w(t)*g(t) \tag{12}$$

Taking the Fourier transform gives

$$G_e^w(f) = E_w(f) \times G(f) \tag{13}$$

Taking the logarithm of the magnitude squared values gives

$$\log|G_e^w(f)|^2 = \log|E_w(f) \times G(f)|^2 \tag{14}$$

The logarithm of the product in eqtn.14 turns the multiplicative components consisting of the periodic pulse train and the glottal source into additive components comprised of $(\log|G(f)|)$ and a periodic pulse train $(\log|E_w(f)|)$. The inverse Fourier transform (i.e. the cepstrum) operates separately on these additive components, producing cepstral coefficients that contain information about the source spectral tilt at low quefrencies and periodic structure representing the pulse train at higher quefrencies. An illustration of cepstral analysis of a periodic glottal source signal of different segment lengths, is given in Fig.4(a)-(c). The log magnitude spectrum of the liftered cepstrum (first 40 rhamonics, representing the source spectral tilt) is plotted on same axes as the original source spectrum (512-point log magnitude FFT). The amplitude at zero quefrency represents the DC contributions from the two additive components, and is conditioned by the window length. The DC contributions become smaller as the analysis window length increases, and as a consequence, the liftered spectral envelope (spectral tilt) approaches the baseline of the source spectrum. The observed trend can be explained by noting that the spectral peaks of the Fourier transform become more resolved (approaching an impulse), while more estimates are obtained for between harmonic locations as the analysis window length increases and as a result the DC average drops. This highlights the MA filter effect of low-pass liftering the cepstrum with subsequent Fourier transformation.

Conversely, examination of a periodic impulse train with noise, illustrates the periodicity and noise contributions to the cepstral baseline, independent of the glottal waveshape contribution. Because the impulse has a flat spectrum, the liftered noise floor is not skewed due to the harmonic peaks (as per the spectrum of the periodic glottal source) and provides a close fit to contour of the actual noise floor and will reside close to the noise floor provided the window length is sufficiently long.

Combining the periodic glottal source with additive noise, $g_{en}(t)$ and windowing gives

$$g_{en}^{w}(t)=e_w(t)*g(t)+n_w(t) \tag{15}$$

Taking the Fourier transform gives

$$G_{en}^{w}(f)=E_w(f)\times G(f)+N_w(f) \tag{16}$$

Taking the logarithm of the magnitude squared values and, as stated previously, approximating the signal energy at harmonic locations, $\log|G_{en}^{w}(f)|_h^2$ and at between-harmonic locations, $\log|G_{en}^{w}(f)|_{bh}^2$, gives

$$\log|G_{en}^{w}(f)|_h^2=\log|E_w(f)\times G(f)|^2 \tag{17}$$

$$\log|G_{en}^{w}(f)|_{bh}^2=\log|N_w(f)|^2 \tag{18}$$

Applying the cepstrum to such a signal and obtaining the baseline as previously, it can be seen that the baseline is influenced by the noise source and by the glottal spectral tilt. It interpolates between these values. As the window length increases the baseline approximates the noise floor more accurately (because more estimates are available for the between harmonics as opposed to the harmonics and the Fourier transform of the liftered cepstrum behaves like a moving average filter applied to the logarithmic spectrum) but the influence of the spectral tilt remains. The interpretation of the existing cepstral-based HNR estimators and the development of a new estimator follows directly from the present development.

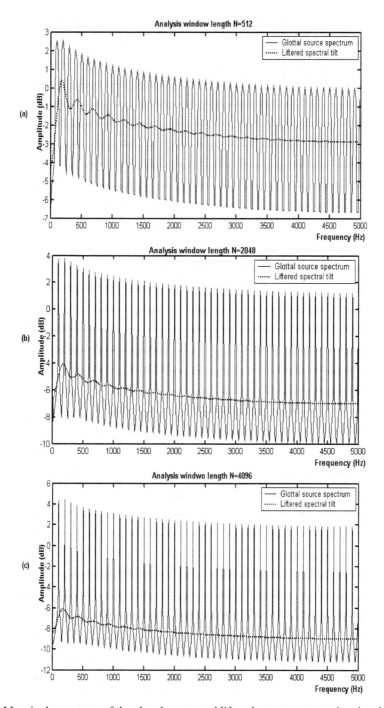

Fig. 4. Magnitude spectrum of the glottal source and liftered spectrum approximating the spectral tilt for different analysis window lengths (a) $N = 512$ sample points, (b) $N = 2048$ sample points and (c) $N = 4096$ sample points

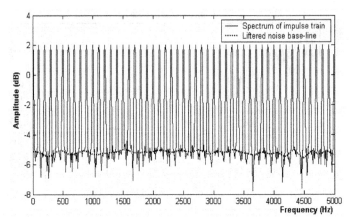

Fig. 5. Spectrum of an impulse train with 1% additive noise and liftered noise baseline (window length 4096 points)

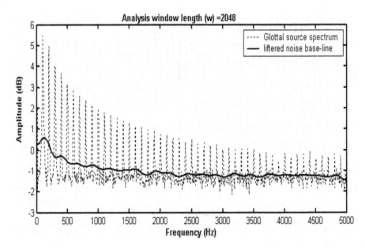

Fig. 6. Spectrum of a glottal source with aspiration noise and liftered noise baseline. The spectrum is calculated with an analysis window length of 2048 points

4   Evaluation of Existing HNR Estimation Methods

In order to evaluate the performance of the existing cepstral-based HNR estimation techniques, synthesized glottal source and vowel /AH/ waveforms are generated at five fundamental frequencies, beginning at 80 Hz and increasing in four steps of 60 Hz up to 320 Hz. The model, described in [29] is adopted to synthesise the glottal flow waveform, while the vocal tract impulse response is modelled with a set of poles [30]. Lip radiation is modelled by a first order difference operator $R(z)=1-z^{-1}$. A sampling rate of 10 kHz is used for the synthesis. Noise is introduced by adding pseudo-random noise to the glottal pulse via a random noise generator, arranged to give additive noise of a user-specified variance (seven levels from std. dev. 0.125%, doubling in steps up to 8 %). The corresponding HNRs for the glottal flow waveform are 58 dB to 22 dB, decreasing in steps of 6 dB. The HNR for the corresponding speech signals are different to those for the glottal source because the source signal receives different resonant contributions depending on the fundamental frequency [19]. However, *a priori* knowledge of the HNR for synthesized speech signals can be obtained by comparing noise-free synthesised speech with synthesised speech obtained from exciting the vocal tract with glottal plus noise signals. The HNR estimation procedures in [21] and [22] are systematically evaluated for the first time.

4.1 de Krom Algorithm

The cepstrum-based method for estimating the HNR in speech signals presented in [21] is evaluated. In this approach, the rahmonics, representing the prominent peaks at integer multiples of the reciprocal of the pitch period (1/T) in the cepstrum of voiced speech are removed through comb-liftering. The resulting comb-liftered cepstrum is Fourier transformed to obtain a noise spectrum (log power spectrum in dB) $N_{ap}(f)$, which is subtracted from the log (power) spectrum, $O(f)$, of the original signal. This gives a source related spectrum (log power spectrum) $H_{ap}(f)$. A baseline correction factor $B_d(f)$, defined as the deviance of harmonic peaks from the zero dB line, is determined. This factor is subtracted from the estimated noise spectrum to yield a modified noise spectrum. The modified noise spectrum $N(f)$ is now subtracted from the original log-spectrum, in order to estimate the harmonics-to-noise ratio

$$H_{ap}(f) = O(f) - N_{ap}(f) \qquad (19)$$

$$N(f) = N_{ap}(f) - B_d(f) \qquad (20)$$

$$HNR = \sum_{k=1}^{p} O(f_k) - \sum_{k=1}^{p} N(f_k) \qquad (21)$$

Analysis parameters, consisting of a variable window length (1024, 2048, 4096) and a fixed overlap of 256 sample points for each window length are used to compute the Fourier transform of synthesized glottal sources and vowel sounds /AH/ (1.6 second duration). For each analysis window, a set of HNRs is calculated. The arithmetic mean of the estimated HNR values is taken as the representative HNR value for a given signal. The input signal is preconditioned with a Hanning window. In this case, the analysis window length is the control variable that is adjusted to evaluate the accuracy of the HNR estimate. Fig.7 shows the estimated HNR for the glottal signals, while Fig.8 showed the HNR estimates for the vowel /AH/, at different frequencies and noise levels.

4.1.1 Discussion of Results
The estimated HNR values deviate from their actual values for this method. The method overestimates the true values of the HNR with errors ranging between 22%-38% (about 3-5 dB). The inaccuracies of the estimated HNR values are as a result of a biased noise floor estimate. As discussed in previous sections, the low frequency components of the glottal source (spectral tilt) and DC part of the harmonic structure reside in the low quefrency part of the speech cepstrum, hence, the liftered noise baseline, which consists of low quefrency cepstral coefficients, is influenced by the glottal source component. Although the baseline correction procedure (eqtn.19, i.e.

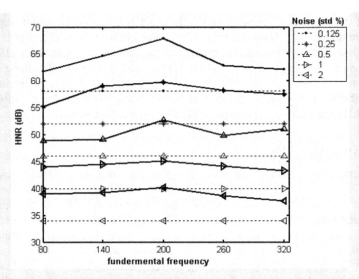

Fig. 7. Estimated HNR (de Krom, [21]) for synthetic glottal source signal for different input frequencies and aspiration noise levels

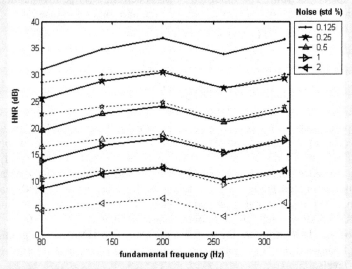

Fig. 8. Estimated HNR (de Krom, [21]) for synthesised vowel /AH/ for different input frequencies and aspiration noise levels

equivalent to moving the noise baseline at between-harmonic locations to the minima of the spectral noise estimates at these locations) tends to compensate for this effect, however this leads to underestimates in the noise baselines and hence overestimates of the HNR. A sample plot of the liftered noise baseline overlaid on the original speech spectrum is shown in Fig.9 to illustrate this effect. As can be seen in the figure, the liftered noise baseline does not provide an exact match to the true noise floor.

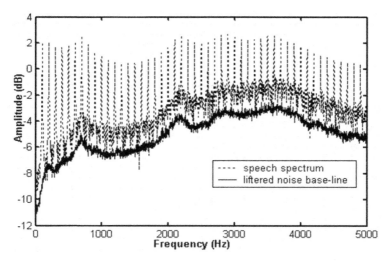

Fig. 9. HNR estimation using de Krom [21] cepstral baseline technique using 1024, 2048, 4096 window lengths (1024 shown)

4.2   Qi and Hillman Algorithm

In the Qi and Hillman implementation [21], the HNR is computed by calculating a 3200 point DFT for the input signal. Harmonic peaks are identified using a frequency delayed, peak peaking algorithm. The frequency delay is introduced to ensure that each peak located is global within a given frequency range of the spectrum. The spectrum of the same signal segment is then computed and a cepstral window is applied to lifter out a high-quefrency part of the cepstrum. Through Fourier transform of the liftered cepstrum, a smoothed reference noise level is obtained. Finally, HNR is computed as the mean difference between the harmonic peaks and the reference levels of noise at these peak frequencies. The results of estimating the synthesised glottal source and vowel /AH/ HNRs, using an implementation of the technique presented in [21], are shown in Fig.10 and Fig.11.

4.2.1   Discussion of Results

The estimated HNR values fall below the actual HNR values for this method. The method grossly underestimates the true values of the HNRs, with errors ranging between 30%-40% (about 4-6dB). As per the de Krom technique [20], the inaccuracy of the estimated HNR values is also linked to incorrect estimation of the noise floor. The technique uses a long analysis window length, which provides for more resolved harmonics. The effect of low frequency components of the glottal source (spectral tilt) are diminished, though not completely removed, and still influence the liftered noise baseline. This problem is exemplified in Fig.12, where a 3200 point DFT of the synthesised vowel /AH/ is plotted together with the liftered noise baseline. From the figure it can be seen that the liftered noise baseline matches the true noise floor at high frequencies reasonably well. However the baseline does not provide a good match at low frequencies. The observed trend can be explained as due to the influence of the glottal source on the low frequency details on the liftered noise cepstrum.

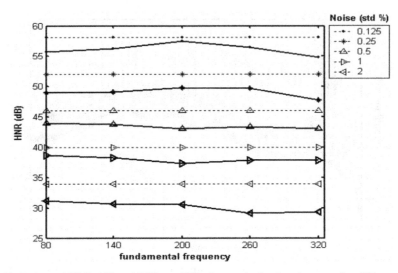

Fig. 10. Estimated HNR (Qi and Hillman [22]) for synthetic glottal source for different input frequencies and aspiration noise levels

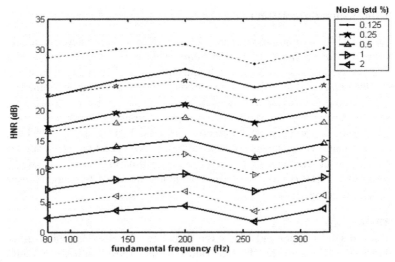

Fig. 11. Estimated HNR (Qi and Hillman [22]) for synthesised vowel /AH/ for different input frequencies and aspiration noise levels

5 New Cepstrum Technique for HNR Estimation

In this section, a new cepstral–based HNR method is presented. The new technique addresses the short-comings of the existing cepstral-based methods and provides a more accurate estimate of the noise floor. Performance evaluations of the new method are performed using the synthetic input signals with *a priori* knowledge of noise input, as per the testing of the existing techniques.

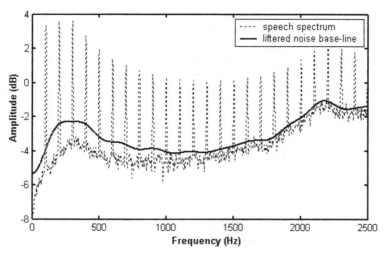

Fig. 12. HNR estimation (Qi and Hillman [22]) cepstral baseline technique (window length 3200 points)

5.1 Harmonic Pre-emphasis Method

As illustrated in the preceding sections, the noise baseline estimate essentially behaves like a moving average (MA) filter and, hence, is dependent on both glottal and noise contributions (eqtn.17 and eqtn.18, Fig.13).

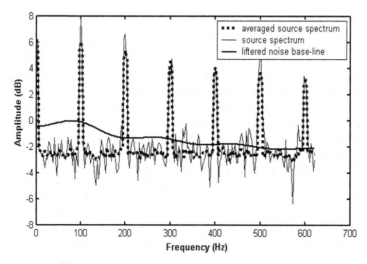

Fig. 13. Spectrum of glottal source with 1% additive noise. The solid line represents a single spectral estimate. The dashed line represents an average of n spectral estimates. The liftered noise baseline is also shown

The noise baseline (which is equivalent to a traditional vocal tract transfer function estimate via the cepstrum) is influenced by the glottal source excited vocal tract and by the noise excited vocal tract. It is the interpretation of the noise baseline as a MA filter that explains the need for the baseline fitting in [21]. The liftered spectral baseline does not rest on the actual noise level but interpolates the harmonic and between harmonic estimates and, hence, resides somewhere between the noise and harmonic levels. As the window length increases, the contribution of harmonic frequencies to the MA cepstral baseline estimate decreases. However, the glottal source still provides a bias in the estimate. To remove the influence of the source, pre-emphasis is applied to the glottal source, $g_e^w(t)$ for the glottal signals and to $s_e^w(t)$ for the voiced speech signals (i.e. noiseless signals). $|G_e^w(f)|_h$ and $|S_e^w(f)|_h$ are estimated using periodogram averaging ([28], Fig.13).

A pre-emphasis filter,

$$h(z) = 1 - 0.97z^{-1} \tag{22}$$

is applied to these estimates in the frequency domain by multiplying each harmonic value by the appropriate pre-emphasis factor. The HNR is computed as

$$HNR = 10 \log 10 \left\{ \frac{\sum_{i}^{N/2} |S_i|^2}{\sum_{i=1}^{N/2} |N_i|^2} \right\} \tag{23}$$

where $|S_i|$ represents harmonic amplitudes, and $|N_i|$ noise estimate.

5.1.1 Implementation

In the proposed approach, the spectrum (2048-point FFT) of the test signal is computed using an analysis window (Hanning) of 2048 points overlapped by 1024 points. The analysis is applied to a 1.6 second segment of synthesized speech, providing 14 spectral estimates. The resulting power spectra are averaged (in order to reduce the noise variance at harmonic locations) to give a single 2048-point FFT. Harmonic peaks and bandwidths in the averaged spectrum are identified, and are modified using a pre-emphasis filter. The between-harmonics, which are not pre-emphasized, approach the noise variance in the averaged spectrum. The cepstrum is applied to the log spectrum of the pre-emphasized harmonics with the non pre-emphasized between-harmonics. The noise floor is extracted using a rectangular, low-pass liftering window to select the first forty cepstral coefficients. In order to calculate the noise energy, the extracted baseline is transformed back to a linear power spectrum and summed at the harmonic points. A sum, representing the signal energy, is taken of the harmonic peaks in the power spectrum of the signal (without pre-emphasis). The HNR is calculated as per eqtn.23.

In order to illustrate the improvement offered by the new method over the existing cepstrum-based techniques, the liftered noise baseline (using pre-emphasis) is plotted together with the spectrum of the glottal source signal (with 1% additive noise). It can be seen that without pre-emphasis (Fig.6) the estimated noise baseline deviates from the true noise floor as a result of the source influence on the liftered noise baseline. The result of removing the source influence before extracting the noise baseline from the cepstrum is depicted in Fig.14 where the estimated noise baseline provides a much improved fit to the actual noise floor.

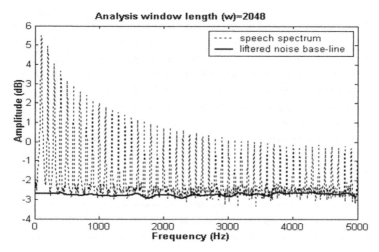

Fig. 14. Spectrum of the glottal source and liftered noise baseline, where pre-emphasis (not shown) is applied in the baseline estimation procedure. The spectrum is calculated with an analysis window length of 2048 points

5.1.2 Performance Evaluation
The results of the HNR measurement for the synthesized glottal source and vowel /AH/ are shown in Fig.15 and Fig.16. In order to evaluate the performance of the method, the estimated HNR is compared to the original HNR (dotted curve).

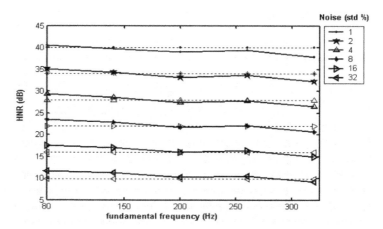

Fig. 15. Estimated HNR (solid line, with the new method) versus for synthesized glottal source waveform (dotted line – actual HNR)

5.1.3 Discussion of Results
A combination of appropriate window length and pre-emphasis is shown to remove the bias due to the glottal source, providing an accurate noise baseline from which to estimate the HNR. The estimated HNR values with the new method tracks the corresponding input HNRs with marginal error; less than 10% (about 1.5dB). The method

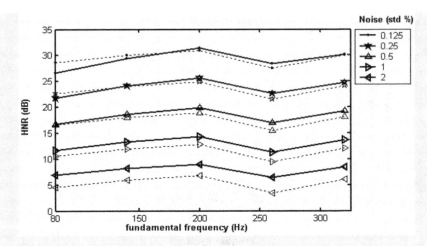

Fig. 16. Estimated HNR (solid line, with the new method) versus f0 for synthesized vowel /AH/ (dotted line – actual HNR)

provides a more accurate measure of the HNR when compared with the techniques presented in [21] and [22]. The new technique, however, requires that analysis window length should not fall below a minimum value. This is important because the DC offset, due to the MA filtering effect becomes significant as the window length decreases. The DC content, which translates to zero quefrency in the cepstrum, influences the accuracy of liftered noise baseline. A recommended minimum analysis window length is 2048 points.

6   Summary and Conclusion

The harmonics-to-noise ratio provides a global indicator of the aperiodicity of a voice signal. Reliable and accurate estimation procedures for HNR estimation are required for voice quality assessment. It is noted that time-domain techniques are compromised by the need for accurate period estimation while frequency domain techniques are problematic for estimating noise at harmonic locations. The cepstrum has been proposed and used as an alternative to overcome these problems. The cepstral technique is described as per its original introduction for speech analysis; as a technique capable of changing multiplicative components into additive components and hence being capable of separating source periodicity from the vocal tract. Additional interpretations of the cepstrum are provided to motivate the use of the cepstrum as a HNR estimator. Considerations include the effect of the glottal source, the window length, the impulse train and additive noise. The baseline estimate (or traditional vocal tract estimate) via the cesptrum technique, is shown to be influenced by both the glottal source excited vocal tract and the noise excited vocal tract. The DC bias and the influence of the glottal source excited vocal tract are reduced as the window length increases. In this sense the baseline estimation via the cepstrum is equivalent to the action of a MA filter applied to the logarithmic spectrum. Pre-emphasis is suggested to remove the source influence. The new technique is shown to provide more accurate

HNR estimates than two existing techniques. The proposed technique required a relatively long analysis window length (2048 points, sampled at 10 kHz). Further development of the technique will investigate an adaptation to include a shorter window length for application to continuous speech.

Acknowledgements

This work is supported through Enterprise Ireland research grants STR/2000/100 and RIF/2002/037.

References

1. Yanaghihara, N.: Significance of harmonic changes and noise components in hoarseness, J. Speech Hear. Res. 10, (1967) 531–541.
2. Yumoto, E., Gould, W. J., and Baer, T.: Harmonics-to-noise ratio as an index of the degree of hoarseness, J. Acoust. Soc. Am. 71, (1982) 1544–1549.
3. Kasuya, Y.: An adaptive comb filtering method as applied to acoustic analysis of pathological voice, ICASSP Tokyo, IEEE, (1986) pp. 669–672.
4. Kasuya, H., and Ando, Y.: Analysis, synthesis and perception of breathy voice, in Vocal Fold Physiology: Acoustic, Perceptual and Physiologic Aspects of Voice Mechanisms, edited by Jan Gauffin and Britta Hammarberg (Singular Publishing Group, San Diego), (1991) pp. 251-258.
5. Imaizumi, S.: Acoustic measurement of pathological voice qualities for medical purposes, ICASSP, Tokyo, IEEE, (1986) pp. 677–680.
6. Klatt, D., Klatt, L.: Analysis, synthesis, and perception of voice quality variations among female and male talkers, J. Acoust. Soc. Amer., Vol. 87, (1990) pp. 820-857.
7. Hillenbrand, J., Cleveland, R. A., and Erickson, R. L.: Acoustical correlates of breathy vocal quality, J. Speech Hear. Res. 37, (1994) 769–778.
8. Qi, Y.: Time normalization in voice analysis, J. Acoust. Soc. Am.92, (1992) 1569–1576.
9. Ladefoged, P., and Antonanzas-Barroso, N.: Computer measures of breathy voice quality, UCLA Working Papers in Phonetics 61, (1985) 79–86.
10. Kitajima, K.: Quantitative evaluation of the noise level in the pathologic voice, Folia Phoniatr, Vol. 3, (1981) pp. 145–148.
11. Klingholtz, M., and Martin, F.: Quantitative spectral evaluation of shimmer and jitter, J. Speech Hear. Res. 28, (1985) 169–174.
12. Kasuya, H., Ogawa, S., Mashima, K., and Ebihara, S.: Normalized noise energy as an acoustic measure to evaluate pathologic voice, J. Acoust. Soc. Am. 80, (1986) 1329–1334.
13. Kasuya, H., and Endo, Y.: Acoustic analysis, conversion, and synthesisof the pathological voice, in Vocal Fold Physiology: Voice Quality Control, edited by Osamu Fujimura and Minoru Hirano (Singular PublishingGroup, San Diego), (1995) pp. 305–320.
14. Kojima, H., Gould, W. J., Lambiase, A., and Isshiki, N.: Computer analysis of hoarseness, Acta Oto-Laryngol. 89, (1980) 547–554.
15. Muta, H., Baer, T., Wagatsuma, K., Muraoka, T., and Fukuda, H.: A pitch synchronous analysis of hoarseness in running speech, J. Acoust. Soc. Am. 84, (1998) 1292–1301
16. Hiraoka, N., Kitazoe, Y., Ueta, H., Tanaka, S., and Tanabe, M.: Harmonic intensity analysis of normal and hoarse voices, J. Acoust. Soc. Am. 76, (1984) 1648–1651.
17. Qi, Y., Weinberg, B., Bi, N., and Hess, W. J.: Minimizing the effect of period determination on the computation of amplitude perturbation in voice, J. Acoust. Soc. Am. 97, (1995) 2525–2532.
18. Michaelis, D., Gramss, T., and Strube, H. W.: Glottal to noise excitation ratio-a new measure for describing pathological voices, Acust. Acta Acust. 83, (1997) 700–706.

19. Murphy, P.J.: Perturbation-free measurement of the harmonics-to-noise ratio in speech signals using pitch-synchronous harmonic analysis, *J. Acoust. Soc. Amer.* 105(5): (1999) 2866:2881.
20. Manfredi, C., Iadanza, E., Dori, F. and Dubini, S.: Hoarse voice denoising for real-time DSP implementation: continuous speech assessment, Models and analysis of vocal emissions for biomedical applications:3rd International workshop, Firenze Italy (2003).
21. de Krom, G.: A cepstrum based technique for determining a harmonics-to-noise ratio in speech signals, J. Speech Hear. Res. 36(2): (1993) 254-266.
22. Qi, Y. and Hillman, R.E.: Temporal and spectral estimations of harmonics-to-noise ratio in human voice signals, J. Acoust. Soc. Amer. 102(1): (1997) 537-543.
23. Murphy, P.J.: A cepstrum-based harmonics-to-noise ratio in voice signals, Proceedings International Conference on Spoken Language Processing, Beijing, China, (2000) 672-675.
24. Noll, AM.: Cepstrum pitch determination, J. Acoust. Soc. Am. 41, (1967) 293-309.
25. Oppenheim, A. V. and Schafer, R.W.: Homomorphic analysis of speech," IEEE Trans. Audio Electroacoust., Vol. AU-16, (1968) 221-226.
26. Oppenheim , A. V.: Speech analysis-synthesis system based on homomorphic filtering, J. Acoust. Soc. Amer., Vol. 45, (1969) 459-462.
27. Schafer, R. W and Rabiner, L. R.: System for automatic analysis of voiced speech, J. Acoust. Soc. Amer. Vol. 47, pt. 2, (1970) 634-648.
28. Murphy, P.J.: Averaged modified periodogram analysis of aperiodic voice signals, Proceedings Irish Signals and Systems Conference, Dublin, (2000) 266-271.
29. Fant, G., Liljencrants, J. and Lin, Q. G.: A four parameter model of glottal flow, STL-QPSR 4, (1985) 1-12.
30. Childers, D.G.: Speech processing and synthesis toolboxes, John Wiley & Sons, Inc., New York (1999)

Predictive Connectionist Approach to Speech Recognition

Bojan Petek

Interactive Systems Laboratory, University of Ljubljana
Snežniška 5, 1000 Ljubljana, Slovenia
Bojan.Petek@Uni-Lj.si

Abstract. This tutorial describes a context-dependent Hidden Control Neural Network (HCNN) architecture for large vocabulary continuous speech recognition. Its basic building element, the context-dependent HCNN model, is connectionist network trained to capture dynamics of sub-word units of speech. The described HCNN model belongs to a family of Hidden Markov Model/Multi-Layer Perceptron (HMM/MLP) hybrids, usually referred to as Predictive Neural Networks [1]. The model is trained to generate continuous real-valued output vector predictions as opposed to estimate maximum a posteriori probabilities (MAP) when performing pattern classification. Explicit context-dependent modeling is introduced to refine the baseline HCNN model for continuous speech recognition. The extended HCNN system was initially evaluated on the Conference Registration Database of CMU. On the same task, the HCNN modeling yielded better generalization performance than the Linked Predictive Neural Networks (LPNN). Additionally, several optimizations were possible when implementing the HCNN system. The tutorial concludes with the discussion of future research in the area of predictive connectionist approach to speech recognition.

1 Introduction

Speech is a complex biological signal. It can be regarded as a result of semantic, linguistic, articulatory and acoustic series of transformations. As signal it exhibits high non-linearity and non-stationarity. The way how phonetic information is encoded in the acoustic speech signal and how a human listener understands speech are still partially understood problems and remain open challenges for future research in the area of speech production and processing [28].

When considering spoken language the following remarks can be given:

- *Naturalness.* Speech is the most natural means of human-human communication.
- *Flexibility.* Speech leaves the eyes and hands free for other tasks.
- *Efficiency.* Speech enables more efficient information transfer than typing, handwriting, graphical pointing devices, or menu-driven user selections.
- *Economy.* Speech transmission is rather inexpensive with modern communication devices and digital media.

Human-human (or human-machine) communication can be inefficient when both entities do not speak the same language. Speech recognition system, as part of a multimodal interactive system, is expected to bridge the gap between different human languages and to enable efficient information transfer in modern information-communication technologies [29].

G. Chollet et al. (Eds.): Nonlinear Speech Modeling, LNAI 3445, pp. 219–243, 2005.
© Springer-Verlag Berlin Heidelberg 2005

Some important applications in spoken language processing are:

- *Interactive problem solving.* Multimodal interactive systems require full integration of speech recognition and natural language understanding for the input, as well as natural language generation with speech synthesis for the output communication modalities.
- *Automatic translation.* The ultimate goal is to be able to deal with unlimited vocabulary and to transcribe spontaneous speech in real time.
- *Robustness, portability and multilinguality.* The systems should be portable to different tasks and languages, i.e., to exhibit robust performance and enable expandable multilingual solutions at minimal development costs.

These issues represent the long-term research goals. Their successful solution is expected to significantly change the way of life and to present a strong economic impact. Many fundamental problems still need to be addressed in order to achieve these goals, including:

- *Advanced modeling of speech.* Research is expected to provide novel techniques for information extraction in order to achieve robust speech recognition and synthesis. Speech modeling is expected to address important phonetic and linguistic phenomena, including inter- and intra-speaker variability, as well as robustness to environmental variability.
- *Automatic acquisition and modeling of linguistic phenomena.* Research is needed to address the efficient domain-dependent and domain-independent knowledge acquisition (lexicon, task structure; semantics, discourse, pragmatics).
- *Addition of human-factors to address user-friendliness.* Research is expected to study various aspects of spoken language interface design (e.g., ways to integrate audio-visual spoken language processing with gesture and emotions).

Hidden Markov Model (HMM) technology dominates the area of spoken language processing. These statistical methods have sound theoretical background and are capable of modeling variability in speech despite their assumptions about the nature of speech do not hold. The HMM performance, however, is frequently still inferior when compared to the human one. Additionally, robustness and gradual degradation in performance in non-ideal communication channels remains to be one of the main research challenges.

The resurgence of interest in connectionist models, also called "artificial neural networks" or "parallel distributed processing models", opened new avenues of research and studies of their potential advantages in the area of Automatic Speech Recognition (ASR). Expected benefits rely on the following set of their properties:

- *Massive parallelism.* The connectionist models consist of many simple interconnected computing elements, called units. Computation can be performed in parallel. The model operation is fast, uniform and fault tolerant.
- *Automatic learning algorithms.* Powerful learning algorithms allow applications of artificial neural networks to various tasks.
- *Non-linear modeling.* Connectionist networks are in general non-linear models. Their ability to learn complex input-output relationships form the basis for classification and non-linear prediction, where sample distributions with complex relationships need to be inferred from the training data.

- *Distributed modeling.* The connectionist models do not assume specific type of statistical distributions of the input data.

While decades of research have been spent on refining and developing the statistical modeling techniques like HMMs, the connectionist approaches to many real-world problems are still not exhaustively researched. Specifically, some hybrid connectionist/HMM approaches have already shown improved systems performance in comparison with the traditional techniques [1].

2 Predictive Connectionist Approach to ASR

Early connectionist approach to automatic speech recognition predominantly used connectionist models as classifiers of either full words (e.g., digits), or sub-word units of speech (e.g., syllables, phones, phonemes).

Early work where connectionist models were applied beyond classification is described in [2]. It was shown for two topics in signal processing (signal prediction and system modeling) that the connectionist techniques can outperform the traditional approaches.

In early 1990s, several predictive approaches were proposed in the area of ASR, e.g., "Neural Prediction Model", NPM, by Iso [2], Iso and Watanabe [4, 5, 6], "Hidden Control Neural Network", HCNN, by Levin [7, 8, 9] and "Linked Predictive Neural Networks", LPNN, by Tebelskis and Waibel [10], Tebelskis et al., [11, 12], Tebelskis [13]. The common idea in this work was to apply the connectionist networks as acoustic models of speech. These models performed non-linear function approximation, prediction or interpolation, and generated real-valued output speech vectors. Successive speech frames were presented to the input and output of the network. Therefore, this approach attempts to model the causal relationships between the parametrized speech frames and can therefore be seen as dynamical systems approach to speech processing [14].

The basic idea of NPM, HCNN, and LPNN predictive modeling is shown in Figure 1. A P-frame window, $P = P_f + P_b$, of speech vectors is presented to the multilayer feed-forward network. The network is trained to generate the speech vector at time t as closely as possible. Prediction error, defined as Euclidean (or Mahalanobis) distance between the predicted and observed speech frames, is used as an error criterion for the backpropagation training. During the training phase, a pool of canonical models learns to become specialized predictors in parts of speech utterance, while developing the lowest prediction errors in those regions. Word is typically represented as a sequence of predictors that best predict the observed parts of speech. The problem of applying each predictor optimally and sequentially over time in order to explain the observed speech signal with the lowest cumulative prediction error is addressed by the Dynamic Programming algorithm.

Initial evaluations of these models were performed on small vocabulary recognition tasks, such as speaker-independent digit recognition experiments [4, 7, 8, 9], yielding high recognition performances, as well as large vocabulary and continuous speech recognition experiments [5, 6, 11, 12], uncovering some problems in the predictive approach on the English database [12].

In the following, the architectures of NPM, LPNN, and HCNN systems and their performance results are described and discussed.

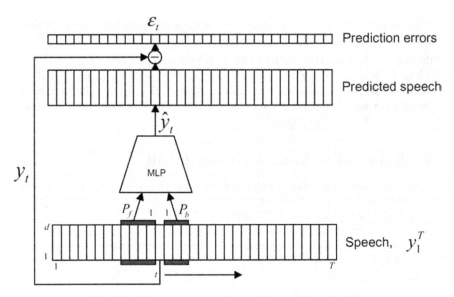

Fig. 1. Predictive connectionist modeling principle in ASR

2.1 Neural Prediction Model

One of the earliest proposals to use the Multi-Layer Perceptron (MLP) as predictor in ASR was formulated by Iso [3]. The "Neural Prediction Model" (NPM) was initially evaluated in speaker-independent isolated Japanese digit word recognition experiments [4]. The NPM model was later improved by introduction of "backward prediction" and variance modeling [5, 6], and applied to large vocabulary speaker-dependent Japanese isolated word recognition.

The baseline NPM model configuration is given in Figure 2 [5]. The basic NPM building block is a feed-forward MLP. On input, the predictor receives two groups of speech feature vectors, i.e., P_f feature vectors $y_{t-P_f}^{t-1}$, used for "forward prediction", and P_b feature vectors $y_{t+1}^{t+P_b}$, used for "backward prediction". The latter feature vectors have been introduced as improvement to the original NPM formulation in order to increase the prediction accuracy for voiceless stop consonants, characterized by a closure interval and followed by a sudden release.

The MLP output, $\hat{y}_t$, is used as predicted feature vector to the observed speech frame y_t. The difference between the input speech vector y_t and the predicted speech vector $\hat{y}_t$ is defined as the prediction error, and is used as error measure for the MLP back-propagation training, and as local prediction error during testing.

Each recognition class (e.g., demi-syllable, word) is constructed as a state transition network, where each state has its own MLP. The NPM model is therefore similar to the Hidden Markov Model, in which each state has a vector emission probability distribution.

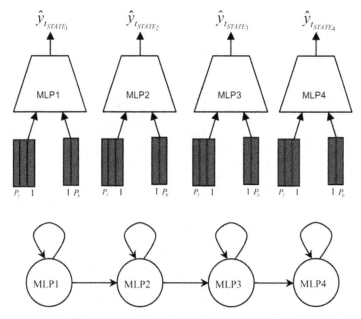

Fig. 2. The Neural Prediction Model (NPM) [5]

Speaker-independent recognition accuracy of 99.8% was obtained using the NPM word model for 10-digit vocabulary recognition, spoken over the telephone lines [4]. The number of MLP predictors per digit token was determined as half the average training sample duration (in frames), and ranged from 9 to 14. Every MLP predictor had 11 input and output units (10 mel-scaled cepstral parameters (excluding the 0-th order) and changing ratio parameter for the speech amplitude was used as the feature vector). Every MLP predictor had three layers and 9 units in the hidden layer. The P_f was 2 and the P_b was 0.

Speaker-dependent recognition accuracy of 97.6% was reported on the large vocabulary task including 5000 words. The system consisted of 241 demi-syllable NPMs, each having 4 MLP predictors, and used 10 mel-scaled cepstral and 10 mel-scaled delta cepstral parameters with the amplitude ratio parameter as the feature vector. Each MLP predictor had 20 hidden units. The P_f and P_b were 2 and 1, respectively. The introduction of covariance matrix in the local prediction error measures was introduced as an additional improvement of the NPM model.

2.2 Linked Predictive Neural Networks

One of the first large vocabulary extensions of predictive connectionist approach to ASR is described in work of Tebelskis & Waibel [10]. Their system, called Linked Predictive Neural Networks (LPNN), achieved large vocabulary speech recognition by linking phonemic predictive networks. The system was initially evaluated on a confusable set of Japanese isolated word recognition experiments [10], and later extended by Tebelskis et al., to the continuous speech recognition task using an English database collected at CMU [11, 12].

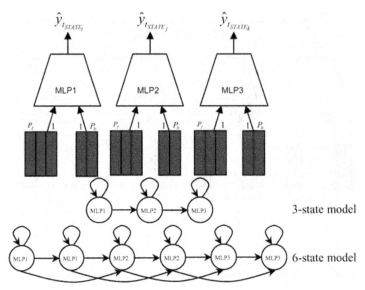

Fig. 3. The Linked Predictive Neural Network (LPNN) [10]

The baseline LPNN model is shown in Figure 3 [10]. As in the NPM case, a sub-word unit (e.g., phoneme) is represented by a sequence of MLPs (typically, 3 networks are used). The sequential application of the neural networks is enforced by the LPNN system implementation. Words are represented as the sequence of models corresponding to the phonetic spelling of the word. Multiple occurrences of the same phonetic symbol are tied. These links cause the LPNN's phoneme models to be trained on various contexts, thus enabling the system to perform vocabulary independent speech recognition, i.e., the system is expected to recognize words that were not present in the training set vocabulary.

Initial evaluation of the LPNN system in the 234 Japanese isolated word recognition test yielded 94% recognition accuracy. On larger vocabulary of 924 words, 90% recognition accuracy was obtained. In the tests, 8 and 14 canonical phoneme models were used, respectively. Each canonical phoneme model consisted of 3 MLPs, coding for the 3-state phoneme model [10]. Several extensions were added to the baseline LPNN system, such as the alternate phoneme models (to better represent different pronunciations and context dependencies) and heuristic addition of the duration constraints.

Continuous speech recognition LPNN system yielded 95%, 58%, and 39% word accuracies on tasks with perplexities 7, 111, and 402, respectively, averaged over the two speakers [11, 12]. Although the LPNN system outperformed some simple HMMs on the same database, the system was observed to exhibit the discriminatory problem among predictive models of the system (40 canonical phoneme models were used).

2.3 Hidden Control Neural Network

Another predictive approach to ASR was proposed by Levin [7, 8, 9]. The baseline model, called the Hidden Control Neural Network (HCNN), is depicted in Figure 4.

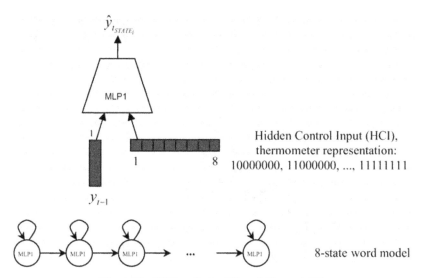

$\hat{y}_{t_{STATE_i}}$

MLP1

Hidden Control Input (HCI), thermometer representation: 10000000, 11000000, ..., 11111111

y_{t-1}

8-state word model

Fig. 4. The Hidden Control Neural Network [7]

The HCNN approach was initially evaluated on small vocabulary recognition task (i.e., TI digits) in speaker-dependent, multi-speaker and speaker-independent experiments. Unlike in the NPM or LPNN modeling, where each state is typically represented by a separate MLP, the HCNN uses only one MLP per sub-word model. Since single MLP with fixed weights cannot model the temporal variability of speech efficiently, additional input, called the Hidden Control Input (HCI), is added to the MLP. With the MLP parameters (i.e., weights) fixed, the HCI modulates the input-output mapping function, thus enabling the network to model sequence of states in a unit of speech. The binary "thermometer" representation is composed of two blocks. In the first block all bits are 1, and in the second one, all bits are set to 0. The HCI transition during recognition is hidden, and must be determined by the Viterbi alignment.

The HCNN model is more compact than the NPM or LPNN models (i.e., only one MLP is used), thus the generalization performance and resource requirements to implement the model are expected to be advantageous for this type of model.

Each HCNN-word model in [7] used 12 cepstral and 12 delta cepstral coefficients representing the observed speech y_{t-1} and the predicted speech $\hat{y}_t$, 8 HCIs coding for eight states within a word. HCNNs had 30 hidden units. Each digit was modeled by the left-to-right state transition diagram. In speaker dependent tests, 99.3% word recognition accuracy was obtained. For multi-speaker and speaker-independent evaluation, 99.3% and 98.75% word accuracies were reported. In the later experiments, the mean and covariance of the driving noise were additionally modeled [7].

3 The Hidden Control Neural Network (HCNN-CDF) Architecture

The Hidden Control Neural Network (HCNN) architecture described in this section represents a large vocabulary continuous speech recognition extension of the small vocabulary word level based HCNN system originally proposed by Levin [7, 8, 9].

After formal definition of the HCNN model [7], two contributions are described, i.e., the HCNN context-dependent phone model and a natural extension of it, the HCNN context-dependent function-word model.

The main component of the Hidden Control Neural Network is multi-layer perceptron (MLP) depicted in Figure 5.

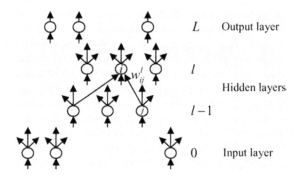

Fig. 5. The Multi Layer Perceptron (MLP)

The MLP is connectionist model that implements nonlinear mappings from the input space to the output space. This model can be successfully applied for approximation of nonlinear multivariate functions. Cybenko [15], Funahashi [16] and Hornik [17, 18] showed that the MLP with one hidden layer of sigmoid units can approximate arbitrarily well any continuous function. Since the MLP represents a static model, its applicability to model signals with inherent variability remains limited.

The MLP with $L + 1$ layers of processing units is shown in Figure 5. Its architecture is fixed and consists of $N_l, 0 \leq l \leq L$ units per layer. Units in the *l-th* layer are connected to any number of units in the previous layer and their output activations $u_i^l, 1 \leq i \leq N_l$ are given by

$$a_i^l = \sum_{j=1}^{N_{l-1}} w_{ij}^l u_j^{l-1} + \Theta_i^l$$

$$u_i^l = F(a_i^l), 1 \leq i \leq N_l$$

(1)

where

$$F(x) = \frac{1}{1 + e^{-x}}$$

(2)

The output activation u_i^l of the *i-th* unit in the *l-th* layer is determined by total input activation of the unit a_i^l, mapped through a sigmoid nonlinearity $F(x)$.

The parameter set of the MLP Λ consists of the network connection weights w and biases Θ

$$\Lambda : w_{ij}^l, \Theta_i^l, 1 \leq i \leq N_l, 1 \leq j \leq N_{l-1}, 1 \leq l \leq L$$

(3)

Therefore, the MLP is a realization of a mapping from an N_0-dimensional input space x to the N_L-dimensional output space y.

The Hidden Control Neural Network model is defined by an addition of mechanism that allows the mapping to change with time, while keeping the network parameter fixed [7]. To achieve this, the input layer is divided into the two distinct groups. The first group represents the observable input to the network (i.e., speech) and the second represents the control signal (thermometer representation) that controls the mapping function between the observable input x and the network output y.

Output of the HCNN network y is therefore

$$y = F_\Lambda(x, c) \qquad (4)$$

where (x, c) denotes concatenation of the two inputs. Mapping between the network input x and output y is now modulated by the control input c, i.e., for x fixed and the different values of c, the network generates different outputs. Furthermore, for c fixed, the network implements a fixed input-output mapping, but when the control input changes, the network's mapping changes as well, modifying the characteristics of the observed signal

$$y = F_\Lambda(x, c) \stackrel{\Delta}{=} F_{\Lambda,c}(x) \qquad (5)$$

If the control signal c is known for $\forall t$ there would be no point in distinguishing between the x and c. The interesting case is when the control signal is unknown, i.e., the hidden control case, which is considered throughout this work.

The HCNN model [7] described above can be used for prediction and modeling of non-stationary signals generated by time-varying sources. If the control signal c is restricted to take its values from a finite set

$$c \in \{C_1, ..., C_{N_c}\} \qquad (6)$$

then the HCNN is a finite state network, where in each state it implements a fixed input-output mapping $F_{\Lambda,C_i}(x)$. According to [15, 16, 17, 18], the HCNN with $L \geq 2$ can arbitrarily closely approximate any set of continuous functions of the observable input x

$$\{F_1, ..., F_{N_c}\}. \qquad (7)$$

3.1 The Baseline Model

Levin [7-9] used the described HCNN model for word modeling in the TI-digit recognition task. The model used in her experiments was an 8-state, left-to-right state transition model, where the control signal c was restricted to take value C_i only if in the previous time step it had a value of C_i or C_{i-1}. Each state of this model represents a part of the modeled word.

A natural extension towards the large vocabulary continuous ASR represents the introduction of sub-word unit, e.g., a phone-level HCNN model, considered in this work. The limitation of such model is its context-independence. Initial experiments also uncovered the discriminatory problem among predictive models, i.e., trained models were good predictors for each others data.

To address this problem, the next two sections introduce the HCNN context-dependent phone model and the HCNN context-dependent function-word model. Evaluations of the proposed solutions confirmed that these modeling principles increased the discrimination among the predictive models of the HCNN system. This resulted in an increased word accuracy of the HCNN system.

3.2 Context Dependent Phone Model

One of the strengths of connectionist models is their ability to successfully combine information from several input information sources (e.g., in the case of predictor, acoustics (real valued vectors) with linguistic information (binary representation)). This capability has also been exploited in context-dependent HCNN modeling principle for large vocabulary ASR described here.

Since the coverage of left and right contexts of the database used in this work was rather small, the predictor model implemented only the right-context information. The binary pattern of contextual information represented coding of the linguistic features of the right-hand phoneme, as described in [19].

10 bits were used for input representation of the context, coding each phoneme along four dimensions. The first dimension (three bits) was used to divide the phonemes into interrupted consonants (stops and nasals), continuous consonants (fricatives, liquids and semivowels), and vowels. The second dimension (two bits) was used to subdivide these classes. The third dimension (three bits) classified the phonemes by places of articulation (front, middle, back). Finally, the fourth dimension (two bits) divided the consonants into voiced and unvoiced, and vowels into long and short.

As can be seen in Figure 6, separate first hidden layers for the speech/state and the context information were used. Activations in the context part in the first hidden layer after training phase can be saved to a lookup table, thus providing additional computational savings. Given the context, previously saved hidden unit activations are input to the first hidden layer instead of the context input vector representation to the input layer.

Mapping function of the HCNN model is now state (HCI) as well as context dependent (Figure 6), $p \in P$, where P represents the set of contexts (e.g, phone mod-

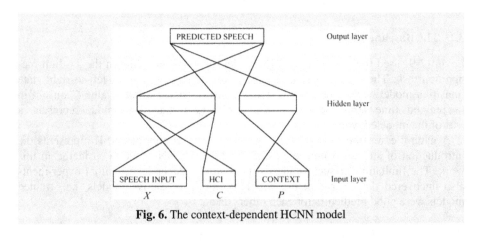

Fig. 6. The context-dependent HCNN model

els) modeled by the system. Therefore, the baseline HCNN equation can be rewritten as

$$y = F_\Lambda(x,c,p) \overset{\Delta}{=} F_{\Lambda,c,p}(x) \tag{8}$$

The hidden control input enables the connectionist model to handle temporal variability, i. e., state transitions within in a phone. The contextual input permits more context-specific predictions, thus potentially increasing discrimination among the predictive models of the system.

3.3 Context Dependent Function Word Model

Function word modeling for continuous speech recognition was shown to be an important issue in ASR [20]. Function words have strong co-articulation effects, are very frequent in continuous speech, and are often poorly articulated by the speaker. Poor modeling of these words can considerably degrade the overall word accuracy of the ASR system.

Initially, the HCNN system consisted of the 40 canonical phone models. Preliminary analysis of the recognition results showed that most recognition errors occur on short words and/or function words. To address this problem, additional resources were added to the system in order to achieve their better modeling and improved recognition accuracy for these words.

Function word models have been added to the system by introducing context-dependent HCNN word models (previously, every word was modeled by a sequence of one or more general purpose phone models). The hidden control input now codes for the states within a word, as in the word-level HCNN system of [7], but the word model here is explicitly context-dependent.

The context input code of the word model was chosen to be the same as the first code in the standard phonetic spelling of the function word.

An important issue when adding additional resources to the predictive system described here is the fact that the existing resources (i.e., phone models) need not to be retrained. If the system was classification-based, however, all models would have to be retrained to insure proper learning of the discrimination hyperplanes for the increased number of decision classes.

3.4 The HCNN-CDF System

The HCNN-CDF system consisted of N context-dependent phone models and M context-dependent function-word models. The $N=40$ phone models used in this work are given in Table 1.

Word models are defined by concatenation of phone models, as defined in the systems dictionary. Given that any word can be described by concatenation of canonical phone models, large vocabulary speech recognition can be achieved. Each phone or function-word model used transition diagram as depicted in Figure 7.

3.5 Implementation Advantages of the HCNN-CDF System

When comparing the LPNN and HCNN modeling principles (Figure 8), advantages unique to the HCNN modeling principle can be observed when implementing the system on a non-parallel computer.

Table 1. Canonical models of the HCNN system

HCNN Model							
SIL	(silence)	IH	bit	F	fluff	Q	(garbage)
AA	father	IY	beet	G	gig	R	roar
AE	bat	OW	coat	HH	how	S	see
AH	but	UH	book	JH	fudge	SH	ship
AO	hot	UW	boot	K	key	T	time
AW	cow	B	bib	L	lull	TH	thin
AY	bite	CH	chip	M	main	V	valve
EH	bet	D	dime	N	Anna	W	one
ER	bird	DH	the	NG	bang	Y	you
EY	bait	DX	at	P	ship	Z	zoos

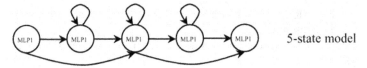

5-state model

Fig. 7. The state transition diagram implemented by the HCNN-CDF system

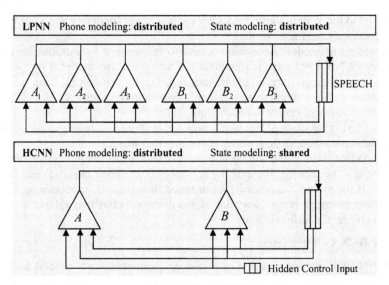

Fig. 8. Comparison of the LPNN and HCNN modeling principles

For sake of comparison the same number of input, hidden and output units of the prototype MLP network will be assumed for the LPNN and HCNN model (see Figures 3 to 5).

- Comparison of the resource requirements R_i when implementing the LPNN and HCNN models yields

$$R_{HCNN} \approx \frac{R_{LPNN}}{C_N} \qquad (9)$$

where C_N represents the total number of states implemented in the LPNN or HCNN model. Given the assumption of equal MLP size, a lower memory requirement advantage of the HCNN model can be observed.

- Considering compactness issue of the LPNN and HCNN models, one can conclude that:
  - The HCNN model is computationally more efficient (Figure 9).
  - The HCNN model has shared modeling ability, i.e., single network can be used to model different speech units (e.g., syllables, words).
  - Given the finite training database size, the MLP in HCNN model receives more training examples than in the LPNN model, since the HCNN state modeling is shared.

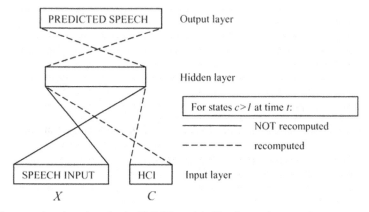

Fig. 9. Computational savings in the HCNN model. The forward passes for states $c>1$ require fewer (weight*activation) computations, since partial activations can be saved in the lookup table

Implementation of the context-dependent HCNN model (Figure 6) can be optimized as well. After the training phase is completed the hidden layer activations, instead of input layer unit activations, can be input to the network. This saves unnecessary computation of the contextual internal representation patterns and optimizes the HCNN implementation.

3.6 Training the HCNN-CDF System

The training goal is to determine HCNN predictor parameters, i.e., weights and biases, given by Equation 2, that minimize the accumulated prediction errors for utterances in the training set. The objective function for this minimization is defined as the average value of accumulated prediction errors for the entire training set

$$\overline{d} = \frac{1}{N}\sum_{n=1}^{N}d(n) \tag{10}$$

where N is the number of the utterances in the training set and $d(n)$ is the accumulated prediction error of the *n-th* training set utterance. The iterative minimization procedure is combination of the Dynamic Programming (DP) and Back Propagation (BP) algorithms:

```
1. Initialize all HCNN parameters by random values
2. n=1
3. repeat
   a. Compute the accumulated prediction errors d(n)
   b. Determine the optimal alignment path a*(t)
   c. do
         i. using the model found on the optimal alignment path,
            calculate the local prediction error between the ob-
            served speech and its prediction
```

$$\text{ii.} \quad \varepsilon_t = \left\| s_t - \hat{s}_t \right\|^2$$

```
        iii. backpropagate  s_t - ŝ_t  to update the HCNN predictor pa-
             rameters
```

$$\text{iv.} \quad n = n+1$$

```
   d. while  n ≤ N
4. until convergence
```

Convergence proof of the training procedure is elaborated in [4]. Let $\overline{d}_k$ be the value of the objective function, given by Equation 10, at the k-th iteration

$$\overline{d}_k = \frac{1}{N} \sum_{n=1}^{N} d_k(n) \tag{11}$$

where

$$d_k(n) = \min_{\{a_k(t)\}} \sum_{t=1}^{T_n} \left\| s_t(n) - \hat{s}_t(n,k) \right\|^2 \tag{12}$$

and $\hat{s}_t(n,k)$ is the HCNN predictor output at time t for the n-th utterance at k-th iteration. At the k-th iteration, the weight correction by the BP algorithm is done along the optimal alignment path $\{a_k^*(t)\}$. Since BP is a gradient descent optimization procedure, the value $\overline{d}_k$ after the weight update $\overline{d}_{k,BP}$ is decreased

$$\overline{d}_{k,BP} \le \overline{d}_k \tag{13}$$

After the weight correction by BP, optimality of the alignment path $\{a_k^*(t)\}$ is lost. Therefore, the DP at $(k+1)$-th iteration finds a new optimal alignment path, such that

$$\overline{d}_{k+1} \le \overline{d}_{k,BP} \tag{14}$$

Combining Equations 13 and 14, the successive values of the objective function gives

$$\overline{d}_{k+1} \le \overline{d}_k \tag{15}$$

which yields the convergence of the HCNN training algorithm[1].

---

[1] Infinitesimal learning rate of the BP algorithm is assumed

The training algorithm can also be described as a sequence of three steps [10]:

1. Forward pass.
2. Alignment step.
3. Backward pass.

These steps are described more in detail in order to additionally clarify the training algorithm used in this work.

3.6.1 The Forward Pass

The first step of training algorithm is shown in Figure 10.

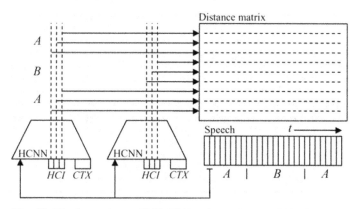

Fig. 10. The forward pass (HCI: Hidden Control Input, CTX: Context)

For every frame of speech at time t, s_t, each HCNN model in the phonetic spelling of the training token (phoneme, word, sentence) outputs its context dependent predictions.

The local prediction errors, defined by

$$\varepsilon_t(c_i, p) = \left\| s_t - \hat{s}_t(c_i, p) \right\|^2 \tag{16}$$

are then stored in the prediction error matrix where $c_i \in \{C_1, ..., C_{N_c}\}$ represents the N_c states defined for the HCNN model and p represents the context information.

3.6.2 The Alignment Step

The second step applies the Dynamic Programing (DP) algorithm to the prediction error matrix in order to optimally align the observed speech s_t with its predicted vector $\hat{s}_t(c_i, p)$. The DP algorithm minimizes the accumulated prediction errors

$$d = \min_{\{a(t)\}} \sum_{t=1}^{T_n} \left\| s_t - \hat{s}_t(c_i, p) \right\|^2 \tag{17}$$

The resulting path through the prediction error matrix defines the optimal segmentation $\{a^*(t)\}$ of speech which is used for BP procedure, as described in the next section. An illustrative example of the optimal alignment is given in Figure 11.

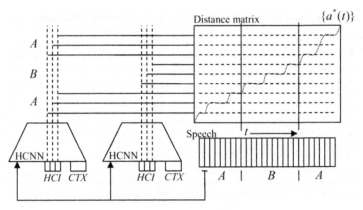

Fig. 11. The alignment step

3.6.3 The Backward Pass

Given the optimal segmentation {a*(t)} determined in the previous step, the Back Propagation algorithm is used to propagate errors into the HCNN networks, as shown in the Figure 12.

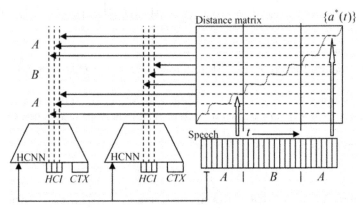

Fig. 12. The backward pass

The errors are accumulated until the last frame of the training token. Parameters of the HCNN model are typically updated after the end of the training utterance.

3.7 Testing the HCNN-CDF System

The HCNN system can be evaluated in two speech recognition modes, i.e., isolated word recognition and continuous speech recognition, as described in the following.

3.7.1 Isolated Word Recognition

Isolated word recognition is possible by performing the first two steps: the Forward pass and the Alignment step. Word boundaries in speech utterance in this case are known a priori.

After matching all vocabulary words to the testing token, the word with the lowest cumulative score d_{min}, thus the lowest distortion is considered as the recognition result. By comparing d_{min} with the score of the second-best word candidate, a rough estimate of the discrimination power among predictive models of the system can be obtained.

3.7.2 Continuous Speech Recognition

Continuous speech recognition is performed by the One-Stage algorithm [21] which solves the problem of finding word boundaries in a continuous speech utterance while matching words within these boundaries. The segmentation and word matching is considered as a joint optimization process which yields the sentence hypothesis.

The basic idea of the One-Stage algorithm [21] is depicted in Figure 13. The time frames i of the test utterance and the j time frames of the reference axis (In case of the HCNN system, the reference axis is multidimensional.) for each vocabulary entry k define a set of grid points (i,j,k). Each grid point has the value of a local distance $d(i,j,k)$, defined as a distance measure between the input frame and the reference frame.

The continuous speech recognition problem can thus be regarded as one of finding the optimal path W^* through the set of the grid points (i,j,k), giving the best match between the test pattern and the unknown sequence of templates

$$W = \{\, w(1), w(2), ..., w(m), ..., w(L)\,\} \tag{18}$$

where $m \equiv path\_parameter$ and

$$w(m) = (i(m), j(m), k(m)) \tag{19}$$

The optimal path W^* is the one which minimizes the global distance

$$\min_{W} \sum_{m} d(w(m)) \tag{20}$$

and from this path, the associated sequence of templates can be uniquely recovered (Figure 13).

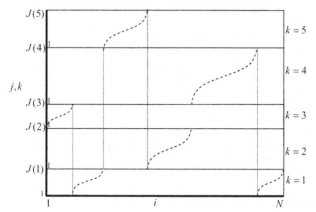

Fig. 13. The optimal path W^* in continuous speech recognition

Every time the warping path has to satisfy the constraints given by a set of transition rules that specify for any path point (i,j,k) a list of legal predecessor points. When considering transition rules in view of composing a "super" reference pattern out of vocabulary words, two types of transition rules can be defined – within-word and between-word transition rules.For the former case, i.e.,

$$w(m) = (i, j, k), j > 1 \qquad (21)$$

the following rule applies

$$w(m-1) \in trans_t \{(i_t, j_t, k)\} \qquad (22)$$

i.e., the point *(i,j,k)* can be reached from one of the within-word points defined by a list of backward transitions *trans_t*.

The between-word transition case, when

$$w(m) = (i, 1, k) \qquad (23)$$

the following rule applies

$$w(m-1) \in \{(i-1, J(k^*), k^*) : k^* = 1, ..., K\} \qquad (24)$$

where *J(k*)* denotes the template boundary at *j=J(k)* of the *k-th* vocabulary word.

In order to apply the Dynamic Programming algorithm to minimize Equation 20, a minimum accumulated distance *D (i,j,k)* is defined along any path to the grid point *(i,j,k)* that is simply a sum of local distances *d (i,j,k)* found on the path to that point.

For selection of the best path, predecessor with the minimum total distance should be considered. Thus for the within-word transitions

$$D(i, j, k) = d(i, j, k) + \min_{trans_t} \{D(i_t, j_t, k)\} \qquad (25)$$

and for the between-word transitions

$$D(i, 1, k) = d(i, 1, k) + \min\{D(i-1, J(k^*), k^*) : k^* = 1, ..., K\} \qquad (26)$$

Equations 25 and 26 define recurrence relations from which the accumulated distances *D (i,j,k)* can be recursively evaluated on a point by point basis.

In summary, the One-Stage algorithm can be described as follows [21]:

1. Initialize $D(1, j, k) = \sum_{n=1}^{j} d(1, n, k)$
2. (a) **For** $i=2, ..., N$, do steps 2b-2e.
   (b) **For** $k=1, ..., K$, do steps 2c-2e.
   (c) $D(i, 1, k) = d(i, 1, k) + \min\{D(i-1, J(k^*), k^* : k^* = 1, ..., K\}$
   (d) **For** $j=2, ..., J(k)$, do step 2e.
   (e) $D(i, j, k) = d(i, j, k) + \min_{trans_t} \{D(i_t, j_t, k)\}$.
3. Trace back the best path from the grid point at a template ending frame with the minimum total distance using the array D (i,j,k) of accumulated distances.

The sentence hypothesis is derived in the Step 3 of this algorithm by tracing back the optimal alignment path.

4   The Task and the Database

Early HCNN system performance evaluation was done on the Conference Registration Database (CRD) developed at CMU in the framework of the Speech-to-Speech translation project.

The CRD database consisted of 12 dialogs with 204 utterances in the conference registration domain. When no grammar constraints are used, the perplexity of the CRD task was given by its 402 unique words of the database. Two dialog sessions per speaker were recorded and used as the training and test sets for system evaluations. In speaker-dependent tests described in this work, two speakers ("mblw" and "mjmt") were used in the evaluation experiments. The speech signal was digitized with the sample frequency of 16 kHz. Every 5 ms, frame of speech, multiplied by Hamming window, was taken to yield 16 mel-scaled power spectrum coefficients. Pairs of consecutive speech frames were averaged, yielding the final 10 ms frame rate of the speech signal. Finally, the coefficient values were normalized between [0.0,1.0].

Brief summary of the task is given in Table 2.

Table 2. The Conference Registration Database (CRD) of CMU

Dialog	Sentences	Words	Unique words
1	13	89	60
2	15	96	65
3	13	101	69
4	16	145	93
5	11	97	66
6	19	166	98
7	16	138	89
8	19	150	102
9	19	154	92
10	18	183	95
11	13	115	61
12	32	300	136

5 Experimental Results

Evaluations of the HCNN and other systems were carried out using the CRD database described in the previous section. The most important comparative results among the conducted experiments are:

- Comparison between the context-independent LPNN and HCNN modeling evaluated at full perplexity of the task (i.e., P=402), and
- Evaluation of the context-dependent HCNN system with and without function-word modeling and the comparison to the standard version of the LPNN system.

For additional comparative analysis, several performance results of other non-predictive systems evaluated on the same database are also reported.

5.1 Context-Independent and Context-Dependent HCNN Results

In order to evaluate the LPNN and HCNN modeling principles, a careful comparative performance analysis was carried out. In these series of experiments, the training/testing conditions for both systems were made as similar as possible.

The testing performance differences in word recognition accuracies, evaluated after every 20 epochs of training, are given in Table 3. The performance scores of both systems were analyzed twice, starting from different initial conditions, to average for the sensitivity to random initialization of the systems parameters prior to training. The maximum word accuracy of the HCNN system obtained during these tests was 20%.

The "mblw" speaker and a 2-state model topology were used in evaluations.

Table 3. Difference in word recognition accuracies between the context-*independent* LPNN and HCNN systems, i.e., Word accuracy$_{HCNN}$-Word accuracy$_{LPNN}$, at task perplexity of 402

Epoch	20	40	60	80	100	120	140	160	180	200
Diff.	33%	25%	13%	11%	6%	9%	11%	9%	12%	14%

Results of the evaluation of context-dependent modeling and function word modeling are given in Table 4. The word recognition accuracy of the standard version of the LPNN system is also included in the table.

Speaker "mjmt" and a 5-state model topology were used during the evaluation experiments.

Table 4. Speaker-dependent word recognition accuracy of LPNN and HCNN systems (speaker „mjmt", perplexity 111)

System	LPNN	HCNN-CD	HCNN-CDF
Substitutions	28%	20%	18%
Deletions	8%	6%	3%
Insertions	4%	2%	4%
Word Accuracy	60%	72%	75%

The HCNN-CD denotes the system with 40 context-dependent canonical phone models (i.e., no function word models), and the HCNN-CDF system additionally models three function words (a, the, you).

The results summarized in the Table 4 show that the speaker-dependent performance evaluation of the developed versions of the LPNN and HCNN systems on the same task with perplexity 111 yield 60% and 75% word recognition accuracies, respectively.

Typical recognition example by the HCNN-CDF system is illustrated in Figure 14. Note that the optimal segmentation in this case includes two function words (i.e., a, you) integrated with the phone models describing words as defined in the HCNN-CDF system dictionary. The figure also illustrates that the human and the HCNN-CDF recognition segmentations differ.

Major tick marks denote transitions between the predictive models. Minor tick marks denote the state changes within the models and the horizontal bars over the major tick marks denote the alternate model index. Up to two alternates per phone or function word models were introduced to enable additional context-dependent clustering of the HCNN models. This typically retained good generalization performance of predictive models while taking into account the finite training set size.

Figure 15 gives an illustrative example of the context dependent HCNN function word modeling. Function word "the" is indeed quite often strongly co-articulated. Therefore, judicious addition of the word-level models improves the overall modeling and recognition accuracy of the HCNN-CDF system.

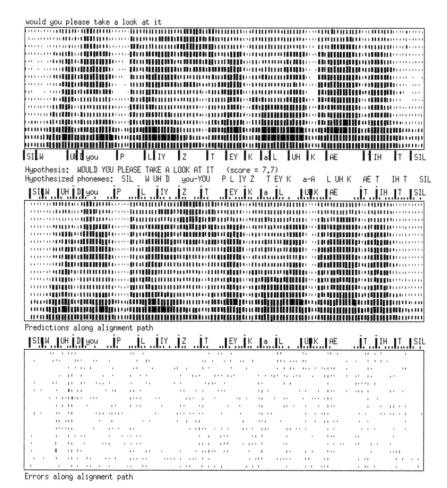

Fig. 14. Illustrative example of the HCNN-CDF continuous speech recognition. Upper trace: Observed speech test utterance. Middle trace: Predictions along the optimal alignment path. Lower trace: Prediction errors

5.2 Comparison to Other Systems

Several non-predictive approaches were evaluated on the same database as well [22]. The results are summarized in Table 5.

Table 5. Word recognition accuracies of non-predictive ASR approaches on the CRD database (after [22])

| System | Perplexity | | | Self test |
	7	111	402	111
HMM-1		55%		
HMM-5	96%	71%	58%	76%
HMM-10	97%	75%	66%	82%
LVQ	98%	77%		83%
tied-LVQ	98%	83%		

Fig. 15. The HCNN-CDF system function word modeling. Upper trace: observed signal; middle trace: predicted speech using the word-level HCNN model; lower trace: prediction errors

The HMM-Ns in Table 5 denote continuous density Hidden Markov Models using 1, 5, and 10 mixtures per state. The LVQ denotes a system trained using the Learning Vector Quantization algorithm [23]. The implemented LVQ system had 3 separate networks per model, each serving two consecutive HMM states and the tied-LVQ system used only one network per phoneme model [22].

6 Conclusion and Discussion

The tutorial presented the continuous speech recognition HCNN connectionist system based on the idea of dynamical systems approach to automatic speech recognition.

The developed system can be seen as large vocabulary extension of the word-based HCNN system described in [9]. While addressing the problem of applying the HCNN model to the large vocabulary task, two solutions in the framework of predictive connectionist approach have been presented and evaluated, i.e, the HCNN context-dependent phone model and the HCNN context-dependent function-word model.

Recognition performance of the extended HCNN system when evaluated on the same task compares favorably with the LPNN system [12], but still has lower performance when compared to the classification based approach, like LVQ. Note, however, that in contrast to the HCNN training algorithm, the LVQ training is discriminative. The expected advantages of the context-dependent HCNN modeling, and the context-dependent HCNN function word modeling, have indeed been observed in series of speaker-dependent experiments.

Additional advantages of the HCNN modeling, such as improvements in execution speed, the amount of resources used, and slightly improved generalization, were also discussed.

In conclusion, initial step towards continuous speech recognition system based on prediction has been demonstrated. Several important and promising research issues, however, remain open. Some possible future research directions are discussed in the final section of this tutorial.

7 Summary

The most significant extensions described in this tutorial are:

- Demonstration of the connectionist large vocabulary HCNN continuous speech recognition system, based on the idea of nonlinear prediction.
- Comparative evaluation of context-independent LPNN and HCNN modeling principles.
- Analysis of implementation advantages of the HCNN modeling principle given by the shared modeling ability and compactness of the HCNN model.
- Extension towards the context-dependent modeling in the connectionist framework, by introducing the context-dependent HCNN model.
- Extension towards context-dependent function word modeling in the predictive connectionist framework.
- Evaluation of the proposed extensions implemented in the large vocabulary context-dependent HCNN continuous speech recognition system on the Conference Registration Database.

8 Future Research

One of the remaining drawbacks of the system was found to be the insufficient discrimination among predictive models of the system. Main reasons for this could be the following:

→ *The lack of corrective training.* As the models get trained only on "positive" examples along the optimal alignment path, no explicit mechanism enforces them to behave discriminantly among each other. The consequence is that predictors have undefined regions, on which no training examples were given to define more controlled, i.e., non-confusable, response when compared to the other models of the system. Mellouk and Galinari have already studied discriminative training within the predictive neural network framework [24, 25, 26, 27].

→ *The problem of identity mappings.* Described system implementation aims to predict successive speech frames in the utterance. Some sub-word speech units, e.g., vowels, exhibit very small change between successive speech frames, thus enforcing the model to learn very similar (i.e., identity) mappings. The response of the model trained in this manner increases the confusability among the predictive models of the system, since it predicts fairly well also the data of the other models.

One possibility to address this problem is to develop efficient corrective training procedure. This should enable training on examples outside the optimal alignment path, thus enforcing the discriminant behavior of predictive models outside the regions of "positive" training examples.

Research issues that merit further investigation include:

→ *Adaptive network and system architecture.* Addition of the predictor resources in an adaptive way could be studied. The addition of resources to the individual network and adaptive adjustment of the number of networks in the system during training could yield to the increased discrimination among predictive models and to improved performance of the system.

→ *The framework of the dynamical systems approach to ASR.* Specifically, the ideas developed in other research fields, e.g., in nonlinear control theory (the combination of vector fields to model speech dynamics) could be explored in the context of speech processing and recognition.

→ *Novel speech modeling techniques.* Recently, a mathematical approach derived from quantum physics has been proposed to model speech. This model uses small amount of parameters to efficiently represent relatively large amount of acoustical information. Its application to robust speech coding, synthesis and recognition currently represent open research issues [30]. Speech recognition by modeling the dynamics of model parameters could become an interesting avenue for future research.

References

1. Bourlard, H.A., Morgan, N.: Connectionist Speech Recognition: a Hybrid Approach. Kluwer Academic Publishers (1994)
2. Lapedes, A., & Farber, R.: Nonlinear Signal Processing Using Neural Networks: Prediction and System Modelling. Technical Report LA-UR-87-2662, Los Alamos National Laboratory, (1987)
3. Iso, K.: Speech Recognition Using Neural Prediction Model. IEICE Technical Report SP89-23 (1989) 81-87
4. Iso, K., & Watanabe, T.: Speaker-Independent Word Recognition Using a Neural Prediction Model. Proc. IEEE Int. Conf. on ASSP (1990) 441-444
5. Iso, K., & Watanabe, T.: Speech Recognition Using Demi-Syllable Neural Prediction Model. Advances in Neural Information Processing Systems 3 (1991) 227-233
6. Iso, K., & Watanabe, T.: Large Vocabulary Speech Recognition Using Neural Prediction Model. Proc. IEEE Int. Conf. on ASSP (1991) 57-60
7. Levin, E.: Word Recognition Using Hidden Control Neural Architecture. Proc. Speech-Tech'90 (1990) 20-25
8. Levin, E.: Word Recognition Using Hidden Control Neural Architecture. Proc. IEEE Int. Conf. on ASSP (1990) 433-436

9. Levin, E.: Modeling Time Varying Systems Using a Hidden Control Neural Network Architecture. Advances in Neural Information Processing Systems 3 (1991) 147-154
10. Tebelskis, J. &Waibel, A.: Large Vocabulary Recognition Using Linked Predictive Neural Networks. Proc. IEEE Int. Conf. on ASSP (1990) 437-440
11. Tebelskis, J., Waibel, A., Petek, B., and Schmidbauer, O.: Continuous Speech Recognition by Linked Predictive Neural Networks. Advances in Neural Information Processing Systems 3 (1991) 199-205
12. Tebelskis, J., Waibel, A., Petek, B., and O. Schmidbauer: Continuous Speech Recognition Using Linked Predictive Neural Networks. Proc. IEEE Int. Conf. on ASSP (1991) 61-64
13. Tebelskis, J.: Speech Recognition using Neural Networks. PhD thesis, School of Computer Science, Pittsburgh, PA (1995)
14. Tishby, N.:A Dynamical Systems Approach to Speech Processing. Proc. IEEE Int. Conf. on ASSP (1990) 365-368
15. Cybenko, G.: Approximation by Superpositions of a Sigmoidal Function. Technical report CSRD 856, University of Illinois, (1989)
16. Funahashi, K: On the Approximate Realization of Continuous Mappings by Neural Networks. Neural Networks Vol. 2, (1989) 183-192
17. Hornik, K., Stinchcombe, M., White, H.: Multi-Layer Feedforward Networks are Universal Approximators. Technical Report USCD, (1989)
18. Hornik, K.: Approximation Capabilities of Multilayer Feedforward Networks. Neural Networks Vol. 4, (1991) 251-257
19. McClelland, J. L., Rumelhardt, D. E., and the PDP research group: Parallel Distributed Processing. MIT Press, Vol. 2, Chapter 18 (1986) 217-268
20. Lee, K. F.: Large Vocabulary Speaker Independent Continuous Speech Recognition: the SPHINX System. PhD dissertation, Computer Science Department, Carnegie Mellon University (1988)
21. Ney, H.: The Use of a One-Stage Dynamic Programing Algorithm for Connected Word Recognition. IEEE Trans. on ASSP Vol. 32, No. 2 (1984) 263-271
22. Schmidbauer, O., Tebelskis, J.: An LVQ Based Reference Model for Speaker-Adaptive Speech Recognition. IEEE Int. Conf. on ASSP (1992) 1: 441-445
23. Kohonen, T., Barna, G., and Chrisley, R.: Statistical Pattern Recognition with Neural Networks: Benchmarking Studies. Proc. IEEE Int. Conf. on Neural Networks (1988) 61-66
24. Mellouk, A., Gallinari, P.: A Discriminative Neural Prediction System for Speech Recognition. Proc. IEEE Int. Conf. on ASSP (1993) 533-536
25. Mellouk, A., Gallinari, P.: Discriminative Training for Improved Neural Prediction Systems. Proc. IEEE Int. Conf. on ASSP (1994) I 233-236
26. Mellouk, A., Gallinari, P.: Global Discrimination for Neural Predictive Systems based on N-best algorithm. Proc. IEEE Int. Conf. on ASSP (1995) 465-468
27. Gallinari, P.: Predictive Models for Sequence Modelling, Application to Speech and Character Recognition. http://citeseer.ist.psu.edu/28957.html (accessed Oct 2004)
28. NATO ASI on Dynamics of Speech Production and Perception. Kluwer Academic Publishers (2002)
29. Deng, L., Huang, X.: Challenges in Adopting Speech Recognition. Comm. of the ACM, 47(1) (2004) 69-75
30. Forbes, B.J., Pike, E.R.: Acoustical Klein-Gordon Equation: A Time-Independent Perturbation Analysis. Phys. Rev. Lett. 93, 054301 (2004)

Modeling Speech
Based on Harmonic Plus Noise Models

Yannis Stylianou

Computer Science Dept. University of Crete, Heraklion, Crete, Greece
yannis@csd.uoc.gr

Abstract. Hybrid models of speech have received increasing interest from the speech processing community. Splitting the speech signal into a periodic and a non-periodic part increases the quality of prosodic modifications necessary in concatenative speech synthesis systems. This paper focuses on the decomposition of the speech signal into a periodic and a non-periodic part based on a Harmonic plus Noise Model, HNM; three versions of HNM are discussed with respect to their effectiveness in decomposing the speech signal into a periodic and a non-periodic part. While the harmonic part is modeled explicitely, the non-periodic part (or noise part) is obtained by subtracting in the time domain the harmonic part from the original speech signal. Three versions of HNM are discussed. The objective of the discussion is to determine which of these versions could be useful for prosodic modifications and synthesis of speech.

1 Introduction

Speech decomposition into a periodic and a non-periodic part is a subject of considerable importance with applications in speech synthesis, speech coding, psychoacoustic research and pathological voice detection. Because the signal is decomposed into two parts, different modification methods can be applied to each part, yielding, for example, more natural sounding pitch and time-scale modifications. The naturalness of the prosodic modified speech signal is very important for high-quality text-to-speech synthesis based on acoustical units concatenation. For speech coding different coding schemes can be applied to each part [1].

A number of techniques have been proposed for the decomposition of the speech signal. The approach developed by Griffin and Lim [1] is referred to as the Multiband Excitation Model (MBE) and it is used for speech coding and speech synthesis[2]. Smith and Serra [3], and Serra [4], have developed a system for sound analysis/transformation/synthesis based on a deterministic part (sum of sinusoids) and a residual or a stochastic part. This model has been developed initially for musical use. X. Rodet and P. Depalle proposed decomposing audio signals in order to obtain high-quality synthesis and modifications [5]. Recently a novel iterative algorithm for decomposition of the speech signal into a periodic

G. Chollet et al. (Eds.): Nonlinear Speech Modeling, LNAI 3445, pp. 244–260, 2005.

and an aperiodic part has been proposed in [6][7]. The method aims at decomposing the excitation signal (linear prediction residual) rather than the original speech signal.

In this paper we describe and compare three versions of a Harmonic plus Noise Model, HNM, for speech decomposition. The periodic (or quasi-periodic) part is supposed to be harmonic. For the first version of HNM, denoted by HNM_1, the harmonic part designates sums of harmonically related sinusoidal components with constant amplitudes within each analysis frame. The phase is modeled by a first-order polynomial (i.e., is assumed to be linear). For the second version, denoted by HNM_2, the periodic part is also a sum of harmonically related sinusoidal components, however, with *piece-wise linearly varying complex amplitudes*. The third version, denoted by HNM_3, makes use of a p-th order polynomial with *real* coefficients for the harmonic amplitudes, and the phase is assumed to be linear. Given the harmonic part, the non-periodic part is obtained by subtracting the harmonic part from the original speech signal. The non-periodic part (or *residual signal*) thus accounts for everything in the signal that is not described by harmonic components. It includes the friction noise, the period-to-period fluctuations produced by the turbulences of the glottal airflow, etc [8].

The paper is organized as follows. The development and description of the three versions of HNM is given first. The second part is devoted to estimating parameters for the harmonic part of the three models, followed by a comparison of the three harmonic models. The comparison will be done on the variance of the residual signal obtained from the three models, the spectral content of the residual signal and the error modeling. Although the paper focuses on the harmonic part modeling, some models for the noise part are also proposed. Finally, the paper concludes with a discussion of the usefulness of the proposed models for prosodic modifications of speech.

2   Description of the Three Models

The basic approaches to speech analysis proposed in this paper are to approximate a discrete-time sequence $s[n]$ using three versions of HNM[9][10]. The sequence $s[n]$ represents the sampling version of the continuous speech signal $s(t)$ sampled at a rate of F_s samples per second. HNM assumes the speech signal to be composed of a periodic component $h[n]$ and a non-periodic component $r[n]$. The periodic component are designated as sums of harmonically related sinusoids

– HNM_1: Sum of exponential functions without slope

$$h_1[n] = \sum_{k=-L(n_a^i)}^{L(n_a^i)} a_k(n_a^i) e^{j2\pi k f_0(n_a^i)(n-n_a^i)} \tag{1}$$

– HNM$_2$: Sum of exponential function with complex slope

$$h_2[n] = \Re \left\{ \sum_{k=1}^{L(n_a^i)} A_k(n) \exp^{j2\pi k f_0(n_a^i)(n-n_a^i)} \right\} \tag{2}$$

where

$$A_k(n) = a_k(n_a^i) + (n - n_a^i) b_k(n_a^i) \tag{3}$$

with $a_k(n_a^i), b_k(n_a^i)$ to be complex numbers (amplitude and slope respectively). $\Re$ denotes taking the real part.

– HNM$_3$: Sum of sinusoids with time-varying real amplitudes

$$h_3[n] = \sum_{k=0}^{L(n_a^i)} a_k(n) cos(\varphi_k(n)) \tag{4}$$

where

$$\begin{aligned} a_k(n) &= c_{k0} + c_{k1}(n - n_a^i)^1 + \cdots + c_{kp}(n - n_a^i)^{p(n)} \\ \varphi_k(n) &= \epsilon_k + 2\pi k\zeta(n - n_a^i) \end{aligned} \tag{5}$$

where $p(n)$ is the order of the amplitude polynomial, which is, in general, a time-varying parameter.

The parameters of the three models are updated at specific time-instants denoted by n_a^i. $f_0(n)$ and $L(n)$[1] represent the fundamental frequency and the number of pitch-harmonics included in the harmonic part, respectively. These two parameters are held constant within each analysis frame, and they equal the values at the center of the analysis window, n_a^i.

The non-periodic part is just the *residual* signal obtained by subtracting the periodic-part (harmonic part) from the original speech signal in the time-domain

$$r[n] = s[n] - h[n] \tag{6}$$

where $h[n]$ is either $h_1[n], h_2[n]$, or $h_3[n]$.

3   Estimation of Model Parameters

3.1   Pitch and Maximum Voiced Frequency Estimation

Assuming voiced speech, the first step of the analysis process consists of estimating the fundamental frequency and the number of harmonics to be included in the harmonic part. In a first step, an initial pitch estimation is obtained by using a standard time-domain pitch detector based on a normalized cross-correlation function [11]. Then, this initial pitch estimate is used to separate voiced from unvoiced frames based on an analysis-by-synthesis method.

The voiced/unvoiced estimation has also to be based on a criterion which takes into account how close the harmonic model will be to the original speech

---

[1] For convenience, the index "n_a^i" will be omitted from the number of harmonics, L

signal. Thus, using the initial fundamental frequency, we generate a synthetic signal, $\tilde{s}[n]$ as the sum of harmonically related sinusoids with amplitudes and phases estimated by the DFT algorithm. Denoting $\tilde{S}(f)$ to be the synthetic spectrum and $S(f)$ to be the original spectrum, the voiced/unvoiced decision is made by comparing the normalized error over the first four harmonics of the estimated fundamental frequency to a given threshold (-15 dB is typical).

$$E = \frac{\int_{0.7f_0}^{4.3f_0} (|S(f)| - |\tilde{S}(f)|)^2}{\int_{0.7f_0}^{4.3f_0} |S(f)|^2} \tag{7}$$

where f_0 is the initial fundamental frequency estimate. If the error E is below the threshold, this frame is marked as voiced. Otherwise, it is marked as unvoiced.

The next step of the process is the estimation of the maximum voiced frequency, F_m. The largest sine-wave amplitude (peak) in the frequency range $[f_0/2, 3f_0/2]$ is found. For this peak, two amplitudes and a frequency location are determined. The location is defined simply as the frequency at which the actual peak occurs and it is denoted here by f_c. The first amplitude is defined as the magnitude of the sample at the peak, while the second amplitude is defined as the non-normalized sum of the amplitudes of all of the samples from the previous valley to the following valley. (see Fig.1). This second amplitude is called cumulative amplitude and it is denoted by Amc in contrast to the simple amplitude : Am. Using the cumulative amplitudes also resulted in a better

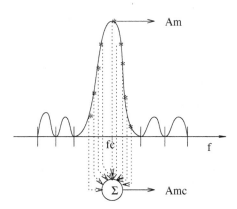

Fig. 1. Cumulative amplitude definition

separation between true peaks and spurious peaks compared to using just the simple amplitude at the peak [12]. The peaks which are in the frequency range $[f_c - f_0/2, f_c + f_0/2]$ are also considered and the two types of the amplitudes are calculated for each peak. Denote the frequencies of these neighboring peaks and the mean value of their cumulative amplitudes, by f_i and $\overline{Amc}(f_i)$ respectively, the following "harmonic tests" are applied to the largest peak:

if

$$\frac{Amc(f_c)}{\overline{Amc(f_i)}} > 2 \tag{8}$$

or

$$Am(f_c) - max\{Am(f_i)\} > 13db \tag{9}$$

then, if

$$\frac{|f_c - l\hat{f}_0|}{l\hat{f}_0} < 10\% \tag{10}$$

the frequency f_c is declared voiced; otherwise this frequency is declared unvoiced. l is the number of the nearest harmonic to the f_c. Having classified frequency f_c as voiced or as unvoiced, then the interval $[f_c + \frac{f_0}{2}, f_c + 3\frac{f_0}{2}]$ is searched for its largest peak and the same "harmonic tests" are applied. The process is continued throughout the speech band. In many cases the voiced regions of the spectrum are not clearly separated from the unvoiced ones. To counter this, a vector of binary decisions is formed adopting the convention that the frequencies declared as voiced will be noted as 1 and the others as 0. Filtering this vector by a three-point median smoothing filter, the two regions are separated. Then, the highest entry in the filtered vector that is 1 provides the maximum voiced frequency.

As the pitch values estimated by the pitch detection algorithm will be used in the harmonic modelling of the speech, an accurate pitch estimation is necessary. Using the initial pitch estimation, f_0 and the frequencies f_i classified as voiced from the previous step, the refined pitch, $\hat{f}_0$, is defined as the value which minimizes the error:

$$E(\hat{f}_0) = \sum_{i=1}^{L_n} |f_i - i \cdot \hat{f}_0|^2 \tag{11}$$

where L_n is the number of the voiced frequencies f_i.

The number of harmonics, the index L in (1), (2) and (4), included in the harmonic part is completely determined by the chosen maximum voiced frequency and the final estimate of the fundamental frequency.

3.2   Harmonic Amplitudes and Phases Estimation

Using the stream of the estimated pitch values, the position of the analysis time-instants, n_a^i, are set at *a pitch-synchronous rate*[2].

The second step of the analysis process for voiced frames of speech consists of estimating the harmonic amplitudes and phases. This is done using a weighted least-squares method aiming at minimizing the following criterion with respect to $a_k(n_a^i)$ for HNM$_1$, to $a_k(n_a^i)$ and $b_k(n_a^i)$ for HNM$_2$ and to unknown coefficients of the amplitude and phase polynomial for HNM$_3$:

---

[2] One can use a non pitch-synchronous analysis. However, as our goal is to use these models for prosodic modifications, we prefer to work in a pitch-synchronous context

$$\epsilon = \sum_{n=n_a^i-N}^{n_a^i+N} w^2[n](s[n] - \hat{h}[n])^2 \tag{12}$$

in which $\hat{h}[n]$ is defined as in (1), (2) or (4) for HNM$_1$, HNM$_2$ or HNM$_3$ respectively. $w[n]$ is a weighting window and N is the integer closest to the local pitch period $T(n_a^i)$. The above criterion has a quadratic form for the parameters in HNM$_1$ and HNM$_2$, and is solved by inverting an over-determined system of linear equations [13]. For HNM$_3$, a non-linear system of equations has to be solved.

At this point in the analysis, we find it convenient to switch to matrix notation. In particular we may write the harmonic parts of the three models as

$$\begin{aligned}
\text{for HNM}_1 &: \mathbf{P}_1\mathbf{x}_1 = \mathbf{h}_1 \\
\text{for HNM}_2 &: \mathbf{P}_2\mathbf{x}_2 = \mathbf{h}_2 \\
\text{for HNM}_3 &: \mathbf{P}_3\mathbf{x}_3 = \mathbf{h}_3
\end{aligned} \tag{13}$$

where $\mathbf{P}_1$ is a $(2N+1)$-by-$(2L+1)$ matrix, $\mathbf{P}_2$ is a $(2N+1)$-by-$(2L+2)$ matrix (the dc components for amplitudes and slope have been added) and $\mathbf{P}_3$ is a $(2N+1)$- by-$((p+1)(L+1))$ matrix. We recall that N is the integer closest to the local pitch period and L represents the number of harmonics included in the harmonic part. Then $\mathbf{P}_1$ is defined by

$$\mathbf{P}_1 = \left[\mathbf{b}_{-L} \vdots \mathbf{b}_{-L+1} \vdots \mathbf{b}_{-L+2} \vdots \cdots \vdots \mathbf{b}_L \right] \tag{14}$$

where $\mathbf{b}_k$ is a $(2N+1)$-by-1 vector corresponding to k-th harmonic and it is defined by :

$$\mathbf{b}_k = \left[e^{j2\pi k f_0(t_a^i-N)} \; e^{j2\pi k f_0(t_a^i-N+1)} \; e^{j2\pi k f_0(t_a^i-N+2)} \; \cdots \; e^{j2\pi k f_0(t_a^i+N)} \right]^T \tag{15}$$

where the superscript "T" denotes the transpose operator.

The matrix $\mathbf{P}_2$ is formed by concatenating the following matrices

$$\mathbf{P}_2 = [\mathbf{B}_1|\mathbf{B}_2] \tag{16}$$

with

$$\begin{aligned}
(\mathbf{B}_1)_{nk} &= E^{(n-N)(k)} \\
(\mathbf{B}_2)_{nk} &= (n-N)(\mathbf{B}_1)_{nk}
\end{aligned} \tag{17}$$

where $E = exp(j2\pi f_0(n_a^i))$ and $0 \le n \le 2N$, $0 \le k \le L$.

The matrix $\mathbf{P}_3$ is defined by

$$\mathbf{P}_3 = \left[\mathbf{B}_1 \vdots diag(\mathbf{n})\mathbf{B}_1 \vdots diag(\mathbf{n})^2\mathbf{B}_1 \vdots \cdots \vdots diag(\mathbf{n})^p\mathbf{B}_1 \right] \tag{18}$$

where $\mathbf{n} = [-N, -N+1, \cdots, N]^T$ denotes the $(2N+1)$-by-1 time vector, $diag(\mathbf{n})$ denotes a $(2N+1)$-by-$(2N+1)$ diagonal matrix with $\mathbf{n}$ the diagonal entries of this matrix and $\mathbf{B}_1$ is a $(2N+1)$- by-$(L+1)$ matrix given by

$$\mathbf{B}_1 = \left[\mathbf{b}_1 \vdots \mathbf{b}_2 \vdots \cdots \vdots \mathbf{b}_L \vdots 1 \right] \tag{19}$$

$\mathbf{b_k}$ is a $(2N + 1)$-by-1 vector defined by

$$\mathbf{b_k} = [cos(\varphi_k[-N]) \, cos(\varphi_k[-N+1]) \, \cdots \, cos(\varphi_k[N])]^T \quad \text{for } k = 1 \cdots L \quad (20)$$

and $\mathbf{1}$ denotes the $(N + 1)$-by-1 unit vector : $\mathbf{1} = [1\,1\,1\cdots 1]^T$. In (20), $\varphi_k[n]$ represents the first order polynomial of the phase.

The vector, $\mathbf{x}$, for each of the harmonic models is defined by

– HNM$_1$:
$$\mathbf{x_1} = \begin{bmatrix} a^*_{-L} \, a^*_{-L+1} \, a^*_{-L+2} \cdots a_L \end{bmatrix}^T \quad (21)$$

a $(2L + 1)$-by-1 vector,
– HNM$_2$:
$$\mathbf{x_2} = [\Re\{a_0\} \, a_1 \, a_2 ... a_L \, \Re\{b_0\} \, b_1 \, b_2 ... b_L] \quad (22)$$

a $(2L + 2)$-by-1 vector,
– HNM$_3$:

$$\mathbf{x_3} = \begin{bmatrix} c_{10} \, c_{20} \, \cdots \, c_{L0} \, c_{00} \, \vdots \, c_{11} \, c_{21} \, \cdots \, c_{L1} \, c_{01} \, \vdots \, \cdots \, \vdots \, c_{1p} \, c_{2p} \, \cdots \, c_{Lp} \, c_{0p} \end{bmatrix}^T \quad (23)$$

a $((p + 1)(L + 1))$-by-1 vector.

For the two first models, the criterion in (12) leads to a linear set of equations. The solution to the least-squares problem is then

– HNM$_1$:
$$\mathbf{x_1} = \left(\mathbf{P_1}^h \mathbf{W}^T \mathbf{W} \mathbf{P_1}\right)^{-1} \mathbf{P_1}^h \mathbf{W}^T \mathbf{W} \mathbf{s} \quad (24)$$

– HNM$_2$:
$$\mathbf{x_2} = \left(\mathbf{P_2}^h \mathbf{W}^T \mathbf{W} \mathbf{P_2}\right)^{-1} \mathbf{P_2}^h \mathbf{W}^T \mathbf{W} \mathbf{s} \quad (25)$$

where $\mathbf{s}$ denotes the $(2N + 1)$-by-1 vector of the original speech samples of the current frame
$$\mathbf{s} = [s[-N] \, s[-N+1] \cdots s[N]]^T \quad (26)$$

and $\mathbf{W}$ denotes the $(2N + 1)$-by-$(2N + 1)$ diagonal matrix with diagonal entries the weight vector
$$\mathbf{w} = [w[-N] \, w[-N+1] \cdots w[N]]^T \quad (27)$$

which is typically a Hamming window. Note that the choice of the weighting window $w[n]$ is important in order to control the variance of the residual signal. An extended discussion of the importance of the choice of the window can be found in [10] [8]. The superscript "h" denotes the transpose and conjugate operation whereas the superscript "T" denotes just the transpose operator.

It can be shown[10] that for HNM$_1$ the matrix to invert in (24) is Toeplitz which means that fast algorithms can be used to solve the respective linear set of equations.

The solution for the third model can not be obtained so easily. Specifically, as the coefficients ϵ_k and ζ are unknown and the amplitude polynomial has an order greater than zero, the above error criterion leads to nonlinear equations for HNM$_3$ and then, the solution must be calculated using iterative methods. We have found that using only one iteration was sufficient and so the following analysis scheme was adapted. As the instanteneous frequency, $f_0(n)$, has been already calculated during the first step of the analysis and given that within the analysis frame $|n - n_a^i| \leq N$ we suppose that $f_0(n) = f_0(n_a^i)$, it is straightforward to show that the parameter ζ of the phase polynomial is equal to $f_0(n_a^i)$. Denoting by ϕ_k^i the phase value of the k-th harmonic at the time-instant n_a^i, and evaluating the phase polynomial at n_a^i, using (5), the coefficients ϵ_k are given by

$$\epsilon_k = \phi_k^i \text{ for } k = 1, \cdots, L \tag{28}$$

Note that ϕ_k^i can be efficiently estimated using the HNM$_1$ analysis process, presented above. In fact, HNM$_1$ makes use of a zero order polynomial for the harmonic amplitudes and a first order polynomial for the phase. Hence, using the HNM$_1$ analysis step we estimate the phase ϕ_k^i and then by (28) the coefficients ϵ_k. Having determined all the coefficients of the phase polynomial, the next step consists of estimating the coefficients of the amplitude polynomial. As $\varphi(t)$ is known for each $n \in [n_a^i - N \quad n_a^i + N]$, it turns out that the solution to the least-squares error is given by

$$\mathbf{x_3} = \left(\mathbf{P_3}^T \mathbf{W}^T \mathbf{W} \mathbf{P_3}\right)^{-1} \mathbf{P_3}^T \mathbf{W}^T \mathbf{W} \mathbf{s} \tag{29}$$

Unfortunately, the matrix to invert in HNM$_3$ does not have such an attractive structure (like in HNM$_1$ and HNM$_2$). However, it is symmetric and positive definite. One method that could be used is the Cholesky decomposition[14] for solving this linear set of equations. Note that this method is about a factor of two faster than alternative methods for solving linear equations[14].

Lastly, the harmonic part is readily obtained by

$$\hat{\mathbf{h}}_i = \mathbf{W}^{-1} \mathbf{P_i} \mathbf{x_i} \tag{30}$$

The residual signal $r_i[n]$ is obtained by

$$r_i[n] = s[t] - \hat{h}_i[t] \tag{31}$$

Note that the subscript "i" in (31) denotes the model that we use.

4   Analysis Window Size Problem

Given that the analysis frame is always two local pitch periods long, $2T(n_a^i)$ (see Eq.12), to avoid conditioning problems during the analysis, the number of parameters that must be estimated should be less than $2T(n_a^i)$. In order to take into account harmonics up to $F_s/2$ (the maximum number of harmonics), where

F_s denotes the sampling frequency, one would choose $L(n_a^i) = T(n_a^i)/2$, meaning that the maximum number of harmonics should be less (in theory, equal) to half of the local pitch period, $T(n_a^i)/2$. For HNM$_1$, $2L(n_a^i)$ *complex* parameters must be estimated so the analysis frame should be $4L(n_a^i)$ long, or $2T(n_a^i)$. For HNM$_2$, $2L(n_a^i)$ *complex* parameters must be estimated, meaning that the analysis frame should be as long as for HNM$_1$. Finally, for HNM$_3$, $(p+2)L(n_a^i)$ *real* parameters must be estimated, where p is the order of the amplitude polynomial. The length of the analysis frame constrains the maximum order, p_{max} that can be used. For example, if we choose the analysis frame to be two local pitch periods long, it turns out that the order p has an upper bound $p_{max} = 2$.

We have found that the maximum voiced frequency seldom exceeds the threshold of $6500Hz$ (a sampling frequency of $16kHz$ was used). Thus, taking as upper bound for the maximum voiced frequency of $6500Hz$, and respecting $p \leq 2$, the analysis frame could be as short as $1.6\,T(n_a^i)$. This means that as the analysis frame is always equal to twice the local pitch period, we avoid in practice the ill-conditioning of matrix $\mathbf{P_i}^T\mathbf{W}^T\mathbf{W}\mathbf{P_i}$, where the subscript "$i$" denotes the model that we use.

5   Properties of the Residual Signals

Before addressing modeling of the noise part, some properties of the residual signals obtained from the proposed HNM versions using (31) should be discussed. In the following, we will assume that the order p of the amplitude polynomial of HNM$_3$ is fixed: $p = 2$.

5.1   Variance of the Residual Signal

It can be shown [10] [8] that if the input signal, $s[n]$, is a white noise with unit variance then the covariance matrix is given by[3]:

$$E(\mathbf{rr}^h) = \mathbf{I} - \mathbf{WP}(\mathbf{P}^h\mathbf{W}^h\mathbf{WP})^{-1}\mathbf{P}^h\mathbf{W}^h \tag{32}$$

and the variance of the residual signal, $r[n]$, is the diagonal of the above matrix. Using the same weighting window $w(t)$, typically a Hamming window, the variance of the residual signal from each of the harmonic models has been computed. The three variances are depicted in the Fig.2. The variance of the HNM$_1$ residual signal is represented by a solid line, the variance of the HNM$_2$ residual by a dashed line, and finally the variance of the HNM$_3$ residual signal by a dash-dotted line. As is made clear by Fig.2 the variance of the HNM$_1$ residual signal is not evenly distributed across the analysis frame (as it ideally should be) in contrast to the variance of the residual signal obtained from the two other models. The variance of the HNM$_2$ residual error is comparable with the variance

---

[3] To simplify the notation the the subscript "i" which represents the model version has been omitted and the upscript "h" denotes conjugate and/or transpose depending on the case

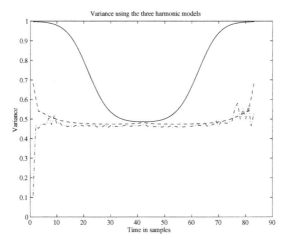

Fig. 2. Variance of the least-squares residual signals from: HNM$_1$ (solid line), HNM$_2$ (dashed line) and HNM$_3$ (dash dotted line). The weighting window was a typical hamming window

of the residual from HNM$_3$. Furthermore, it can be seen that the variance from HNM$_3$ is closest to the ideal least-squares variance for most of the analysis time than the variance of the HNM$_2$ residual signal. However, at the boundaries of the analysis frame the variance of the HNM$_3$ residual is irregular.

5.2   Time Domain Comparison of the Residual Signal

In this section we compare the residual signals in the time-domain. From the discussion presented in previous sections, we recall that HNM$_1$ makes use of a stationary model for the estimation of the harmonic amplitudes and phases. The amplitudes and the phases estimated by this model correspond at the center of each analysis frame and there is, therefore, no information about the parameters variation within the analysis frame. This causes low frequencies to appear in the HNM$_1$ residual signal. To demonstrate this characteristic of the HNM$_1$ residual signal, a voiced fricative frame from a speech signal sampled at $16kHz$ was selected. Data of this frame is plotted in Fig.3(a); the length of the analysis frame is twice the local pitch period. Harmonic peaks have been found up to $4000Hz$. To synthesize this frame, the harmonic parameters from the frame vicinity (one frame before and one next) have been used and then the overlap-add approach has been applied. This means that we postulate a linear model for the harmonic amplitudes (approximately the case of HNM$_3$ when $p = 1$).

Fig.3(b) shows the residual signal from HNM$_1$. This figure clearly shows the behavior of the HNM$_1$ residual signal indicated above. For the same frame the residual signals for HNM$_2$ and HNM$_3$ are presented in Fig.3(c) and (d), respectively. At first glance in Fig.3, it seems that information about the periodicity of the original speech signal is not detectable in the residual signals of HNM$_2$

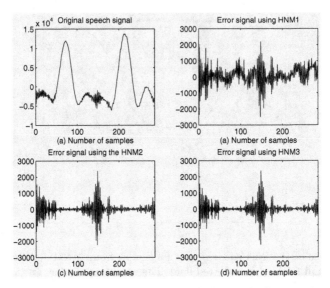

Fig. 3. (a) a voiced fricative speech signal and the residual error signals from (b) HNM$_1$, (c) HNM$_2$ and (d) HNM$_3$

and HNM$_3$ (they appear to be noisy). Also, based on the same figure we are tempted to say that the residual errors from HNM$_2$ and HNM$_3$ are very similar. As we will see later, when the magnitude spectrum of the residual signals will be compared, this is not really true.

To measure the similarity between the harmonic part and the original speech signal the following expression for the error has been used:

$$E = 10 log_{10} \frac{\sigma^2_{r(t)}}{\sigma^2_{s(t)}} \tag{33}$$

where $\sigma^2_{r(t)}$ denotes the variance of the residual signal $r(t)$ and $\sigma^2_{s(t)}$ denotes the variance of the original speech signal $s(t)$. For example, the error produced by the three models for the original speech frame in Fig.3 was : $-15.8dB$ for HNM$_1$, $-25.56dB$ for HNM$_2$ and $-25.58dB$ for HNM$_3$. Fig.4(a) shows a segment of a speech signal ('$wazi\,waza$') and in (b) the modeling error in dB produced from the three models is plotted. The modeling error of HNM$_1$ is presented by a solid line, the error of HNM$_2$ by a dashed line, and the error of HNM$_3$ by a dash-dotted line. It is clear by this figure that the modeling error using HNM$_1$ is greater than those produced by the two other models. As the full frequency band (from $0Hz$ up to half of the sampling frequency) of the residual signal is used in the definition of the modeling error, the error is large on voiced fricative regions (for example, between the 0.25 and 0.35 sec.). To give an acoustic notion to the modeling error, note that if the modeling error is less than $-25dB$, the synthetic speech signal produced from the model is *indistinguishable* from the original speech signal.

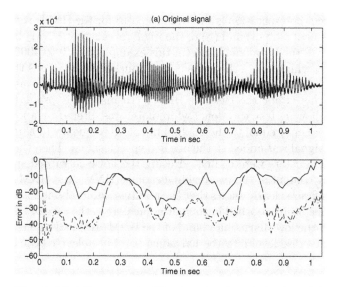

Fig. 4. Modeling error in dB using the three hybrid models

5.3   Frequency Domain Comparison of the Residual Signal

As was mentioned above, although the HNM_2 and the HNM_3 residual signals
seem to be similar in the time domain, in the frequency domain they do not
have the same properties. This can be seen in the next figure.

Fig.5(a) shows, for the same voiced frame as before (Fig.3), the magnitude (in
dB) of the HNM_2 residual signal (solid line) and of the original speech (dashed

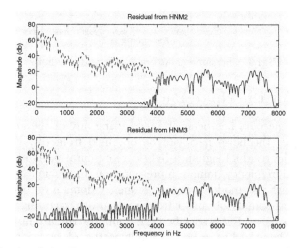

Fig. 5. Magnitude of the Fourier transform of the residual signal (solid line) of (a)
HNM_2 and (b) HNM_3. The magnitude of the Fourier transform of the original speech
signal has also been included (dashed line)

line). The same representation is shown in Fig.5(b) for the HNM$_3$ residual signal. The comparison of part (a) and (b) of the Fig.5 reveals that HNM$_2$ has cancelled the noise part in the harmonic band (in this example from 0 to $4000Hz$) in contrast to HNM$_3$ which leaves the noise part untouched. This means that this part of the noise signal was passed on into the harmonic part in the case of HNM$_2$. Fortunately, this is not the case for HNM$_3$. To make this property of HNM$_3$ clearer, the following test was done: white noise was filtered by a low pass filter with cutoff frequency equal to the maximum voiced frequency ($4000Hz$). The resulting noise signal was added to the original speech signal. Then the HNM$_2$ and the HNM$_3$ parameters were estimated using the noise-corrupted speech signal. The frequency content of the two residual signals (HNM$_2$ and HNM$_3$) are shown in Fig.6. This figure clearly shows that the additive noise (about $25dB$) below the speech level has been absorbed in the harmonic part in the case of HNM$_2$, as it is not present in the low (harmonic) band of the HNM$_2$ residual signal. In contrast, for HNM$_3$, the noise level into the harmonic band has clearly been augmented.

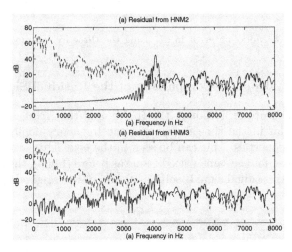

Fig. 6. The same as in Fig.5 with additive noise

6   Models for the Noise Part

Once the harmonic part has been obtained using any of the above mentioned harmonic models, the noise part can be obtained from (6). For high-quality re-synthesis of the residual signal, a hybrid representation is necessary: a joint time-domain and frequency-domain representation. In previously reported work, the stochastic part was modeled in the frequency-domain exclusively [1, 3, 15]. However, residual signals obtained from real speech recordings (voiced fricatives, plosives etc...) exhibit a specific time-domain structure in terms of energy localization[9]. The model proposed here follows this observation: the frequency contents of the stochastic part is described by a time-varying AR envelope; its time-domain structure is represented by a time-domain energy-envelope function. In each time-frame, the residual signal's spectral density function is modeled by fitting an lth-order all-pole filter by use of a standard autocorrelation-based LPC method. Finally, the temporal energy distribution-function $d(t)$ is calculated by squaring the residual signal, low-pass filtering it with a positive impulse-response filter and decimating it by a factor R. In practice, for a signal sampled at $16kHz$, the AR model order is set to 15, and the decimating factor to 10.

Note that the above noise model can be applied only to HNM_2 and to HNM_3 residual signals; the HNM_1 residual signal contains low frequencies which would bias the AR model. For HNM_1, it is better to fit an lth-order AR model to *the original signal's spectral density function*. Then, during the synthesis step, a high-pass filter with cutoff frequency equal to the local maximum voiced frequency can be used to eliminate the low frequencies. Obviously, in that case temporal energy distribution function can not be estimated as before. Some deterministic envelopes can be used instead. Fig.7 shows the envelopes that have been tested. It was found that they are speaker-dependent. However, the envelope in Fig.7(a) was found to be more consistent for the most part of our database speakers and it was the envelope finally used.

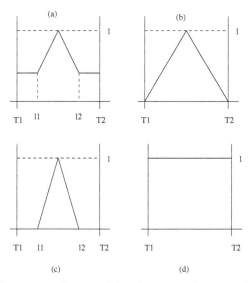

Fig. 7. The time-domain envelope used for the time-behaviour of the noise part from HNM_1. The T1 and T2 represent two successive analysis time-instants. Typical values for l1 and l2 are : l1 = 0.15 (T2-T1) and l2 = 0.85 (T2-T1)

7   Synthesis

The synthesis of the speech signal can be performed in two different ways using either a pitch-synchronous overlap-add technique, or a time-domain sinusoidal synthesis. In this paper we will only present the first alternative while for the second one the interested reader may check in [10]. The harmonic and the noise components are synthesized separately and then added together.

The deterministic part is simply obtained by overlap-adding a stream of short-time signals $s_i(t)$ at the specific time-instants t_i in pitch synchronous manner. Here, the short-time signals are obtained from the harmonic parameters using a synthesis equation depending on the model that is used (e.g., 1), (2), or (4)and applying a Hamming window centered at t_i. The length of the synthesis window is twice the local pitch-period, and the overlap between successive short-term signals is one pitch-period.

The noise component is obtained by filtering a unit-variance white Gaussian noise through a time-varying normalized lattice filter whose coefficients $k_i(t)$ are derived from the stream of $A(t_i, z)$ using a linear interpolation of the model coefficients on a sample-by-sample basis. Note that, since the lattice is normalized, the energy of the output signal is constant in time (and equal to unity). The time-domain energy envelope-function is then applied directly on this synthetic signal.

8   Discussion and Conclusion

This paper concentrated on the harmonic modeling of speech, based on a Harmonic plus Noise Model. The analysis has been concentrated on the harmonic part development; the noise part is assumed to be obtained from the substraction of the harmonic part from the original speech signal. Some directions have been given for the modeling of the noise part. Three versions have been proposed for modeling periodic speech aimed at text-to-speech synthesis based on acoustical units concatenation. From the three models presented in this paper, HNM_1 is the simplest one. HNM_1 has been found to have the largest modeling error among the proposed models. This was expected, as HNM_1 does not include any information about the variation of the harmonic amplitudes; only during the synthesis step these parameters are changed linearly. HNM_1 seems to be an acceptable model for "strongly" voiced speech frames where the period does not change quickly from one frame to another. The analysis step in HNM_1 is faster than in the other two models. The noise model proposed for HNM_1 is very simple and it can be easily manipulated during prosodic modifications. The output speech signal produced by HNM_1 is *almost* indistinguishable from the original one; some slight distortions are observed in transitional voiced speech frames where pitch changes quickly, or in voiced/unvoiced to unvoiced/voiced passages.

HNM_2 has low modeling error but it cancels completely the noise part in the harmonic band (from $0Hz$ up to the maximum voiced frequency), absorbing it in the harmonic part. Thus, during prosodic modifications the noise part of the harmonic band will be repeated (if, for example, a time scaling by factor 2 is applied) producing an artificial long-term autocorrelation in the output signal that is perceived as some sort of periodicity [10]. This is also a problem of the PSOLA approach for prosodic modifications[16]. The signal produced by HNM_2

is indistinguishable from the original one, when no prosodic changes are made. We use a large number of parameters to model speech, and taking into account that this model it is not useful for speech modifications, it tend to be excluded from further analysis.

HNM_3 also has a small modeling error and, in contrast to HNM_2, does not cancel the noise part of the harmonic band. Original speech signals are indistinguishable from their synthetic version produced by HNM_3. Using a second order amplitude polynomial quasi-periodicity and fast transitions are efficiently modeled. A nice property of the amplitude polynomial coefficients, c_{k1} and c_{k2}, is that they exhibit a strong peak during transitions from one phoneme to another inside a voiced island. During steady regions of voiced speech they have almost constant values. This can be useful in two ways. First, one could combine HNM_1 and HNM_3 using a time-dependent order p, thus reducing the number of parameters of HNM_3, and second, HNM_3 could be used for automatic speech segmentation or detection of steady speech regions.

Comparing the noise models proposed in this paper, HNM_2 and HNM_3 are not as flexible as HNM_1, but are more accurate; the temporal energy distribution function that they use is estimated in the analysis step and it is not imposed as for the HNM_1 noise model. However, in HNM_1, a parametric energy distribution function is simple to stretch in the case of pitch and time-scale modifications. A disadvantage of this approach is that the same envelope is used for all speakers.

Further developments will aim at combining HNM_1 and HNM_3 for high-quality speech synthesis and prosodic modifications. Also, a speaker-dependent parametric temporal energy envelope needs to be explored in further research, as this is an important factor for high-quality speech reproduction.

Acknowledgment

The author would like to thank J. Laroche, and E. Moulines for their valuable remarks during this work.

References

1. Griffin, D., Lim, J.: Multiband-excitation vocoder. IEEE Trans. Acoust., Speech, Signal Processing **ASSP-36** (1988) 236–243
2. Dutoit, T., Leich, H.: Text-To-Speech synthesis based on a MBE re-synthesis of the segments database. Speech Communication **13** (1993) 435–440
3. Serra, X., Smith, J.: Spectral modeling synthesis: A sound analysis/synthesis system based on a deterministic plus stochastic decomposition. Computer Music J. **14** (1990) 12–24
4. Serra, X.: A System for Sound Analysis/Transformation/Synthesis Based on a Deterministic Plus Stochastic Decomposition. PhD thesis, Stanford University, Stanford, CA (1989) STAN-M-58.
5. Rodet, X., Depalle, P., Poirot, G.: Speech Analysis and Synthesis Methods Based on Spectral Envelopes nad Voiced/Unvoiced Functions. In: Proc. EUROSPEECH, Edinburgh, U.K. (1987)

6. d'Alessandro, C., B.Yegnanarayana, Darsinos, V.: Decomposition of speech signals into deterministic and stochastic components. In: Proc. IEEE Int. Conf. Acoust., Speech, Signal Processing. (1995) 760–763

7. B.Yegnanarayana, d'Alessandro, C., Darsinos, V.: An iterative algorithm for decomposition of speech signals into periodic and aperiodic components. Proc. IEEE **6** (1998)

8. Laroche, J., Stylianou, Y., Moulines, E.: HNS: Speech modification based on a harmonic + noise model. Proc. IEEE ICASSP-93, Minneapolis (1993) 550–553

9. Stylianou, Y., Laroche, J., Moulines, E.: High-Quality Speech Modification based on a Harmonic + Noise Model. Proc. EUROSPEECH (1995) 451–454

10. Stylianou, Y.: Harmonic plus Noise Models for Speech, combined with Statistical Methods, for Speech and Speaker Modification. PhD thesis, Ecole Nationale Supèrieure des Télécommunications (1996)

11. Hess, W.: Pitch determination of Speech Signals: Algorithmes and Devices. Springer, Berlin (1983)

12. Seneff, S.: Real-time harmonic pitch detector. IEEE Trans. Acoust., Speech, Signal Processing **ASSP-26** (1978) 358–365

13. Lawson, C.L., Hanson, R.J.: Solving Least–Squares Problems. Prentice Hall, Englewood Cliffs, New Jersey (1974)

14. Press, W., Teukolsky, S., Vettering, W., Flannery, B.: Numerical Recipes in C, Second Edition. Cambridge University Press (1994)

15. Poirot, G., Rodet, X., Depalle, P.: Diphone sound synthesis based on spectral envelopes and harmonic /noise excitation functions. Proc. Internat. Computer Music Conf. (1988) 364–373

16. Moulines, E., Laroche, J.: Techniques for pitch-scale and time-scale transformation of speech. part I. non parametric methods. Speech Communication **16** (1995)

Text Independent Methods for Speech Segmentation

Anna Esposito[1,2] and Guido Aversano[2,3]

[1] Seconda Università di Napoli, Dipartimento di Psicologia, Via Vivaldi 43, Caserta Italy
anna.esposito@unina2.it, iiass.annaesp@tin.it
[2] IIASS, Via Pellegrino 19, 84019, Vietri sul Mare, Italy, INFM Salerno, Italy
[3] École Nationale Supérieure des Télécommunications (ENST), 46 rue Barrault,
75634 Paris cedex 13, France
aversano@tsi.enst.fr

Abstract. This paper describes several text independent speech segmentation methods. State-of-the-art applications and the prospected use of automatic speech segmentation techniques are presented, including the direct applicability of automatic segmentation in recognition, coding and speech corpora annotation, which is a central issue in today's speech technology. Moreover, a novel parametric segmentation algorithm will be presented and performance will be evaluated by comparing its effectiveness against other text independent speech segmentation methods proposed in literature.

1 Introduction

The present work is situated in the context of non linear speech processing algorithms and in particular, it aims to present an overview of the proposed speech segmentation techniques. The main goal is to present a new algorithm, capable of performing phonetic segmentation of speech without prior knowledge of the phoneme sequence contained in the waveform.

Automatic segmentation of speech is such a difficult task that current-generation speech dictation and recognition systems avoid to deal with it directly; in such applications instead, statistical modeling of transitions between phonetic units seems to be preferable to an explicit, a priori fixed, segmentation.

Nevertheless, automatic language-independent segmentation is still an important challenge in speech research, playing a central role in today's speech technology, for applications like automatic speech recognition, coding, text to speech synthesis and corpora annotation.

Reliable automatic speech segmentation is of fundamental importance for Automatic Speech Recognition (ASR). In some way, the sequence of speech frames resulting from short-term analysis should be organized into homogeneous segments that are to be associated with a set of symbols representing phones, words, syllables, or other specific acoustic units. From this point of view, automatic speech segmentation could be highly useful, allowing to first segment the speech wave into a set of symbols and then implement the algorithms that recognize them. However, a technical solution to the segmentation problem that is completely satisfying (from the recognition point of view) has not been found yet [41]. This is one of the main reasons why the current state-of-the-art ASR systems do not operate in a bottom-up way, i.e. starting from an explicit segmentation. They instead adopt a generative, top-down approach, estimating the likelihood of top-level linguistic hypotheses, modeled as sto-

G. Chollet et al. (Eds.): Nonlinear Speech Modeling, LNAI 3445, pp. 261–290, 2005.

chastic processes, on the basis of the observed sequence of speech frames. Hidden Markov Models (HMMs) [74] are the most common implementation of the generative paradigm, and are widely used in both research and commercial applications of ASR systems. Nevertheless, the above approach tends to privilege lexical constraints over phonetic reality where known phonetic transcriptions are used to constrain the recognition of the speech signal into a forced alignment. A more balanced approach could be realized by including phonetic information into the generative decoding process. A possible step in this direction is to define a transition probability between speech units based on explicit segmentation and acoustic-phonetic cues [4].

The aim of speech coding applications is to generate a compressed representation of the speech signal for its efficient transmission or storage [43], [44]. Digital speech coding technologies are widely used in everyday-life applications, and in some of them, like cellular telephony, are of crucial importance.

Analysis methods are often shared between the ASR and coding areas. However, speech preprocessing and modeling for coding purposes must satisfy specific needs that are different from those of the ASR case. Actually, the speech signal has to be reconstructed from the coded information in all its variability and richness in order to preserve not only the linguistic message, but also many other physical features of the signal (that the listener can perceive).

Several speech coders are explicitly based on segmentation concepts such as the temporal decomposition segmentation method proposed by [3]. Moreover language-independent segmentation is essential to those techniques that realize very-low bit rate speech coding by indexing in a memory of speech segments [10], [24]. For these techniques, the segmentation of speech signals into phonetic units is crucial, since the incorrect detection of phone boundaries may significantly degrade the overall system performance. Therefore the development of more efficient speech segmentation techniques can largely help to improve speech coding techniques.

In speech research, the availability of large, annotated speech corpora is a fundamental issue. Such corpora are needed to train automatic speech recognition systems, and huge training data sets usually imply higher recognition accuracy [21]. Large quantities of labeled speech materials are also needed to obtain high-quality speech synthesis in text-to-speech (TTS) and coding applications. Collecting and manually annotating a speech corpus (either at word or phonetic level) is a complex and expensive task, especially for spontaneous speech recordings. As a consequence, reliable quantities of annotated speech data are available only for relatively few languages [41]. To overcome these difficulties several automatic techniques for phonetic transcription/annotation have been developed, regularly based on top-down ASR methods, like text-dependent Viterbi alignment with modeling of pronunciation variants (e.g. see [11], [12], [13],],[16], [76], [92). However, the above mentioned automatic annotation methods have good performances only if an accurate modeling is done of pronunciation variants and other phonetic phenomena like cross-word assimilation, elision, de-gemination, or dialectal variation, that are frequent in spontaneous speech. Hesitations, false-starts and other dysfluencies are another source of problem for these methods. In addition, the segmentation accuracy requirements for TTS applications are higher than those required for ASR applications, since ASR systems, being focused on the correct identification of the speech sequence, do not require, as the TTS systems, an accurate placement of phone boundaries. Text-independent segmentation of speech could be a useful means for defeating these problems. Moreover, in absence of a word transcript, or when a precise phonetic modeling is not available (they both require too much time and high financial resources), a bottom-up language-independent automatic phonetic labeler, potentially based on automatic phone-level segmentation, can be a very desirable tool [20], [41].

Besides the applications discussed above, there are other areas of speech research that could benefit from a reliable phone-level segmentation algorithm. For example, Time Scale Modification applications [29], [52], could benefit of appropriate speech segmentation to produce phoneme alterations, as well as a computer-aided system for segmentation (possibly including the visualization of acoustic features and different annotation tiers) could be a valid research tool for studies in linguistics and phonetics.

2   Overview on Speech Segmentation Techniques

Automatic speech segmentation has been faced through several strategies based on different speech features; some of them incorporate linguistic knowledge, others are based on reference templates [65], [86]. Linguistically constrained segmentation methods rely on an externally supplied transcription of the sentence for determining phoneme boundaries. The sentence transcription may be generated manually or automatically derived from orthographic transcription. Linguistically constrained speech segmentation methods typically take both speech and information about its contents (either the phonemic transcription, or a probabilistic model derived through a learning procedure based on a set of manual segmented training data) as input to output a reliable segmentation of the speech signal. Several procedures have been proposed along these lines, most of them based on Dynamic Time Warping (DTW) [80] and Forward-Backward algorithms [70] always coupled with Hidden Markov Models and/or Artificial Neural Networks [73]. Interesting results have been reported by several authors [7], [14], [15], [18], [31], [33], [35], [36], [38], [47], [49], [53], [55], [59], [60], [64], [67], [78], [85], among others.

The underlying strategy of the above mentioned procedures is to consider all the boundaries of the speech segments of interest (since segmentation could be done at level of phones, syllables, sub-words, words, or other specific acoustic units) and to choose the best one based on an efficient parsing algorithm. However, this strategy tries to perform only an accurate acoustic matching avoiding the problem of detecting of transitions either because some may have not been observed in the training corpus or they rarely occur and therefore their estimation model is poorly descriptive. As a consequence of this poor modeling many insertion errors are produced affecting the performance of the next processing step which could be the recognition or the synthesis of the speech segment detected. To overcome this problem many different context modeling methods, developed mostly for ASR and TTS applications, have been proposed, based either on deterministic rules [84] or statistics algorithms [50], [77], [82], [94]. These devices seem to work very well, increasing the recognition rate of about 10% more than context-independent methods. The drawback is an increased computational load. However, the problem of the inadequate modeling of the transition regions, producing many insertion errors, still remains, even though some researchers propose to include a transition detection stage as front end of speech segmentation applications [49].

In the present work, our attention is devoted to linguistically unconstrained segmentation methods, i.e. methods that do not use any prior knowledge about the linguistic content and only exploit acoustic information (such as the spectral changes from one frame to the next) contained in the speech signal in order to detect phone transitions. It should be pointed out that some text dependent segmentation procedures combine explicit information about the linguistic content of the signal with frame to frame spectral changes and therefore, the performance of the resulting systems benefit of both the acoustic and linguistic information [14], [15], [18], [38], [47], [49], [59], [67], [78], [85].

The text-independent approach can be useful in all those applications that require or that may benefit from explicit speech segmentation, when a phonetic transcription is unavailable (as for speech recognition) or inaccurate (as in speech annotation improvement tasks). Text-independent segmentation seems particularly suited for multilingual applications, even though it should be noted that text-independent does not necessarily mean language independent, since language-specific cues could nevertheless be used to perform segmentation.

Many text independent methods have already been suggested in literature. Gibson [57] suggested to classify them into two broad categories, i.e. model-based and model-free methods (see [8], [86] for a review). Both methods are essentially based on distance measures of the spectral changes among consecutive speech frames. The underlying difference between the two methods is the front-end processing of the speech signal that precedes the computation of the distance measures.

Model-based methods mostly depend on Linear Predictive Coding (LPC [61]) modeling and they have been successfully employed in the segmentation of continuous speech signals by the sequential detection of spectral changes [2], [19], [30], [32], [63], [68], [79]. Due to their simplicity and their computational efficiency, they are largely used to clean speech applications, although they are not quite suitable for modeling consonantal sounds such as nasals, fricatives, and stops, due to the fact that LPC spectral estimates are always biased toward the F0 harmonics.

The general idea behind these methods is to accomplish the segmentation of the speech signal through sequential detection of model changes. Once fixed the signal model, there are two hypothesis running: one is that no change has been detected in a given frame against the alternative hypothesis that a change has been detected at a certain frame n. When the LPC model is used, the Gaussian likelihood function is evaluated under both hypotheses and the likelihood ratio $LR(n)$ is calculated for each n. If at a certain frame n^*, $LR(n^*)$ overcomes a fixed threshold, a change is detected. LPC models are also used to estimate the spectrum of the speech signal when other spectral distortion measures (such as change functions, and spectral variation functions) are exploited for spectral change detection [8], [39], [86]. Two of these change functions, the Delta Cepstral Function (DCF) proposed in literature by Mitchell et al. [63] and the Spectral Variation Function (SVF) proposed by [19], were selected for comparing the proposed algorithm vs. model-based methods performance. Their mathematical expressions are reported by the equations (1) and (2) respectively:

$$DCF_k(n) = C_k(n+1) - C_k(n-1) \quad k = 1,\ldots,Q \tag{1}$$

Where $C_k(n)$ is the kth cepstral coefficient for the frame n and Q is the number of cepstral coefficients extracted from that frame. $DCF_k(n)$ is then used to compute a cost function which should be able to detect spectral changes associated with phoneme transitions (see [63] for further details).

$$SVF(n) = \frac{\hat{C}(n-1) \bullet \hat{C}(n+1)}{\left\|\hat{C}(n-1)\right\| \cdot \left\|\hat{C}(n+1)\right\|} \qquad (2)$$

Where $\hat{C}(n)$ is the difference between the nth cepstral vector and the time average of the cepstral vectors that lie within a window centered at n; the "$\bullet$" indicates the scalar product (see [18], [63] for further details).

Model-free methods provide a means to overcome these problems exploiting different processing algorithms such as parametric filtering [57], [58]. These methods, try to identify spectral changes in the speech signal, directly considering the speech spectrum coupled with several spectral distortion measures. This means that, if S1(ω) and S2(ω) are the spectral distribution functions estimated for two neighboring frames of the signal, a change will be detected if the distance between them exceeds a given threshold. Along these lines, several spectral distances have been suggested [9], [23] [39], [54], among them the Kullback-Leibler (KL) spectral divergence [66] defined as:

$$KL = \int_{-\pi}^{\pi} K\left(\frac{S_1(\omega)}{S_2(\omega)}\right)\partial\omega \qquad (3)$$

Where $K(x) := x - log\ x - 1$, and $S_1(\omega)$ and $S_2(\omega)$ are the spectral densities (or a parametric representation of the spectral densities) of the speech signal in two neighboring frames (the indexes denote two consecutive overlapping frames, the current and the previous one).

The drawback of these model-free distortion measures is that they are strongly dependent on the spectral densities. When mixed-type spectra are present in the signal, large distortion values obtained from these measures may not necessarily correspond to significant changes in the signal [8], [57], [58].

Once a distortion measure has been determined, the speech segmentation process can be implemented in different ways [86]. Besides the methods discussed above, other implicit speech segmentation schemes include the cumulative sum and localized smoothing of distortion measures for boundary estimation [79], [83], multiscale segmentation by varying the bandwidth [1], frequency domain logarithmic distortion measures [51], wavelet transform [90], minimum phase group delay [71], entropy rate estimation [93], convex hull [56], temporal decomposition [3], some variations of the parametric filtering techniques [28], and more [37], [95]. A new spectral distance measure, called DAPCOSH has been recently proposed by Wei and Gibson [88], who also compared the steady-state error for different spectral distance measures [89].

A common drawback to both model-based and model-free methods is that, together with the correct segmentation points, they also insert into the speech signal a high number of false segmentation points. Therefore, there are two problems that should be faced when the goal is to perform an automatic speech segmentation of an utterance without a previous linguistic knowledge: 1) which kind of acoustic features are able to give robust information on the acoustic transitions from one phone to another? and, 2) how can we reduce the number of false insertions so that the percentage of correct detection is not affected by the number of false insertions? To solve both of these problems we carried out the segmentation task in two steps: we used several encoding schemes and tested the performance of a new segmentation algorithm on the different acoustic features they encoded. We systematically evaluated the effectiveness of the proposed algorithm comparing its performance with those obtained by the segmentation methods mentioned above, that are commonly adopted in speech segmentation tasks. The main judging criterion used in this comparison was the ability of the segmentation algorithms under test to reproduce a high-quality exemplar segmentation (manual annotation of speech performed by expert phoneticians). Other important criteria were the computational efficiency and the possibility to integrate them into more complex speech applications.

3   A Novel Speech Segmentation Algorithm

The proposed algorithm performs the segmentation task working on an arbitrary number of time-varying features obtained through a short-term analysis of the speech signal. The automatic procedure tries to catch sharp transitions in the evolution of these parameters, i.e. speech frames where the value of a parameter changes significantly and quickly. Fundamental in the algorithm is the step that takes care of combining different sharp transition events, detected by distinct features, into a single indication of phone boundary, since it has been observed that sharp transitions do not occur simultaneously for each parameter, even though they occur in a close time interval. For this reason, the segmentation algorithm uses a *Fitting Procedure*, which places the segmentation boundary into what we called the barycentre of each group of quasi-simultaneous sharp transitions, combining the sharp transitions detected in the neighboring of the same frame n into a unique indication of phone boundary. The segmentation algorithm is regulated by three operational parameters. The first two parameters a and b are related to the individuation of abrupt changes occurring in the values of the acoustic features that encode the speech signal during its temporal evolution. Parameter a identifies how many consecutive frames, in the temporal evolution of the signal, are needed to estimate the height (or the intensity) of an abrupt change. When this height exceeds a certain threshold b, a possible transition (from one phone to another) is accounted by the following fitting procedure. The parameter c is used in the fitting procedure to identify the width of the neighborhood where the barycentre is individuated. The algorithm can be described by the following pseudo-code:

```
program Segmentation (Output)
    {Assume as input a set of k time-sequence x_i[n]_{i=1}^{k} n=1,...,N, N is
    the # of frames in the sentence};
        begin
        for every sentence in the data set;
            for every time-sequence x_i[n] in the sentence:

                computes the function J_i^a[n];

            end for;
        detect peaks in J_i^a[n] according the threshold b;
        Store the detected peaks in a matrix S(i,n);
```

```
% Fitting Procedure
    for every frame n=a TO N-a-c
        computes the function f[n] and its minimum in
        the frame interval [n,n+c];
        set nwin = n', where f[n'] is the minimum of f[n];
        set acc[nwin] = acc[nwin]+1;
        set n=n+1;
        end for;
        set a boundary in the frame n corresponding to
        a peak of acc[n];
    end for;
end.
```

In the above pseudo code the functions $J_i^a[n]$, $f[n]$, $f[n']$ are defined by the following formulas:

$$J_i^a[n] = \left| \sum_{m=n-a}^{n-1} \frac{x_i[m]}{a} - \sum_{m=n+1}^{n+a} \frac{x_i[m]}{a} \right| \tag{4}$$

$$f[n'] = \min_{n\in[p,q]} f[n] \tag{5}$$

$$f[n] = \sum_{m=p}^{q} \sum_{i=1}^{k} S(m.i)|n-m| \quad \forall n \in [p,q] \tag{6}$$

Where a represents the width of the frame interval over which equation (4) is computed; b is a relative threshold identifying peaks in equation (4); c is the width of the frame interval where the *Fitting Procedure* searches for exemplar segmentation boundaries; and S is a binary matrix where $S(n,i)$ is equal to 1 if a valid sharp transition has been detected for the time-sequence i at the frame n, and 0 otherwise. Figure 1 exemplifies for a given sequence $x_i[n]_{i=1}^k$, (where k is the number of time-sequences obtained processing the speech waveform and also the number of coefficients used to encode each speech frame) the corresponding function in equation (4).

The relative thresholding procedure[1] used to identify the frame $n' \in [p,q]$ where an appropriate peak for equation (4) could be identified according to the parameter b is described by the following mathematical formulation:

$$\forall \; [p,q] \in [a, N-a] \; \; select \; \; n' \in [p,q] \; \; so \; \; that:$$

$$J_i^a[n'] > J_i^a[n'-1] > ... > J_i^a[p] < J_i^a[p-1]$$
$$J_i^a[n'] \geq J_i^a[n'+1] \geq ... \geq J_i^a[q] < J_i^a[q+1] \tag{7}$$

compute $h = min \left[J_i^a[n'] - J_i^a[p] \; , \; J_i^a[n'] - J_i^a[q] \right]$

According to equation (7) n' is a peak for equation (4) - normalized within the interval [0,1] - if h exceeds the threshold b. Generally, the peaks computed according to

---

[1] It is worth emphasizing that the thresholding is accomplished on the relative height of each peak and not on the absolute amplitude of the peaks in equation (4)

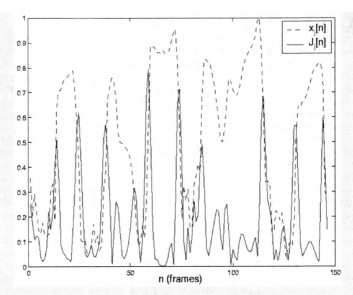

Fig. 1. An example of a sequence $x_i[n]$ (*dashed lines*) and its corresponding function $J_i^a[n]$ (*solid lines*) for $a=5$

equation (7) do not occur simultaneously but in close frames. The *Fitting Procedure* takes care of combining such peaks into a unique indication of phone boundary that is placed in the middle of a cluster of quasi-simultaneous peaks in a frame window of length c. The accumulation function, *acc[n]*, implements the clustering procedure identifying, in its temporal evolution, a phone boundary in each frame n' that clusters together – along a window of length c – the highest number of peaks in the k coefficients' encoding of the speech frame. An exemplification of the temporal behavior of the function *acc[n]* is given in Figure 2.

The accumulation function produces a sequence of transition frames. The exact timing for these transitions (useful for comparing automatic and manual speech labeling that is expressed in samples or milliseconds) is obtained positioning the detected segmentation point in the central sample of each transition frame.

3.1 Performance Evaluation

The output of the proposed algorithm depends on the three parameters a, b and c. However, also the choice of the speech coding scheme, as well as the thresholding procedure, can strongly influence the segmentation results. Thus, a coherent evaluation of the efficacy of the proposed segmentation is necessary in order to identify the best performing parameters, and the most suitable coding and thresholding procedures. Well-defined performance indexes are also needed in order to compare the algorithm's segmentation results with other automatic segmentation procedures (either text-dependent or text-independent). For all the above reasons, we decided to test our algorithm on a set of speech data (the TIMIT and NTIMIT corpora [34],[48]) that provide a reliable phonetic annotation, manually performed by expert phoneticians.

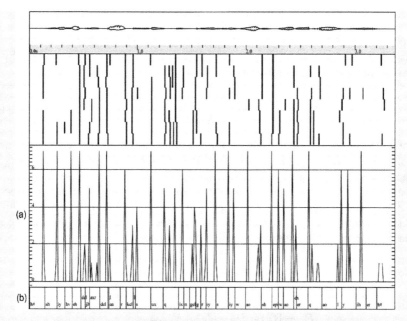

Fig. 2. An exemplification of the temporal behavior of the function *acc[n]*. In (*a*) is reported a typical *acc[n]* sequence generated from the *Fitting Procedure*. Its peaks correspond to a detected frame transition point. In (*b*) the phonetic transcription of the speech wave is reported

We also defined some performance indexes relative to a generic exemplar segmentation. Obviously, if the exemplar segmentation is particularly accurate we are allowed to use these indexes to assess the segmentation efficacy; otherwise, the indexes will simply express the agreement between the two compared segmentation procedures.

The exemplar segmentation consists, in our case, of labeled speech files that record the position of all the phone boundaries (usually expressed in milliseconds or samples). The overall number of phone boundaries contained in the prototype database will be indicated with the symbol S_t. The first index defined to express the performance of the algorithm is the *percentage of correctly detected phone boundaries*. In our treatment, an exemplar segmentation point is correctly detected if a corresponding boundary is found by the algorithm, with a tolerance of ±20 ms. If we indicate with S_c the number of correctly detected boundaries, the above-mentioned percentage is defined as follows:

$$P_c = 100 \cdot \frac{S_c}{S_t} \qquad (8)$$

It should be noted that such an index alone is not adequate to assess the accord between the automatic and the exemplar segmentation, since it does not take into account the number of phone boundaries erroneously detected. These erroneously detected segmentation points generate an *over-segmentation*, quantified by the difference S_{ins}, between the whole number of segmentation points detected by the algorithm S_d, and the number of exemplar segmentation points S_t:

$$S_{ins} = S_d - S_t \tag{9}$$

The percentage of erroneously inserted points S_{ins} over the number of exemplar segmentation points S_t is called *over-segmentation rate (D)* [68] and is expressed by the following mathematical formulation:

$$D = 100 \cdot \left(\frac{S_d}{S_t} - 1 \right) \tag{10}$$

Performance indexes similar to those defined above but mathematically more accurate are devised from the theory of signal detectability [69]. In this framework, an exemplar segmentation point can be considered as the target of a detection task. The segmentation points automatically detected can be either accepted as *hit targets* if they match an exemplar segmentation point or as *missed targets* otherwise. This allows the definition of two performance indexes, the *hit rate* P_h and the *missing rate* P_m according to the following mathematical formulations:

$$P_h = P_c = 100 \cdot \frac{S_c}{S_t} \tag{11}$$

$$P_m = 100 - P_c = 100 \cdot \left(1 - \frac{S_c}{S_t} \right) \tag{12}$$

Again, to take into account the number of non-targets segmentation frames identified as targets S_{nt}, we need to consider the *false alarm rate* P_{fa}, i.e. the percentage of non-targets that have been erroneously hit. Equation (11) gives the mathematical formulation of such index, where $S_{nt} = S_f - S_t$, and S_f is the full number of speech frames contained in the speech corpus under test.

$$P_{fa} = 100 \cdot \left(\frac{S_d - S_c}{S_{nt}} \right) = 100 \cdot \left(\frac{S_d - S_c}{S_f - S_t} \right) = \frac{(D + P_m) \cdot S_t}{S_f - S_t} \tag{13}$$

It should be observed that the *over-segmentation D* is negative when the number of segmentation boundaries detected by the algorithm is lower than the number of segmentation boundaries contained in the exemplar segmentation. The *false alarm rate* P_{fa} is always positive and its values are defined in the range [0, 100].

3.2 Choice of the Algorithm Parameters *a*, *b*, and *c*

The proposed algorithm operates on a speech signal encoded in the form of time sequence vectors. Therefore, every short time representation, i.e. any encoding performed on small time windows, could be used. Ideally, the encoded data should only retain the portion of informational content which is useful to the segmentation task, whilst every useless information should be discarded. The choice of the encoding scheme can strongly influence the overall system performance [27]. This is a well-known issue, at least from a theoretical point of view, and it is often addressed in literature as the "data processing theorem" [17]. However, the effectiveness of the segmentation performed by the algorithm is also affected by the values attributed to the three free parameters, a, b, and c that regulate its functioning. Parameters a and c are integers representing the number of frames taken into account in the computation of equation (4) and the *Fitting Procedure* respectively. Parameter b is a threshold used to reject frames that are candidates to the role of phonemic boundaries. The fine tuning of the above parameters is not only desirable for granting optimal perform-ance, but it also plays a role in the choice of the encoding technique that underlies the entire segmentation process.

Table 1. Correct detection (P_c) and over-segmentation (D) rates obtained fixing $a=2$, $b=0.2$, and $c=6$ using PCBF and MELBANK as encoding schemes

Encoding	P_c	D
5-PCBF	71.4%	3%
8-PCBF	77.2%	14%
5- MelBank	74.4%	-3%
8- MelBank	79.3%	9%

To make the above discussion clear, it is worth investigating the experimental re-sults reported in Table 1 showing the P_c and D rates obtained for fixed values of the a, b, and c parameters, and for two different encoding schemes: the Perceptual Criti-cal Band Filters (PCBF) and the MelBank [5], [6].

It should be noticed that the name of the encoding scheme is preceded by a nu-meral indicating the number of frequency bands (coefficients) in which the signal full spectral range is partitioned. Several partitionings have been tested in order to assess the minimum number of coefficients needed to represent a speech frame that gives the best segmentation performance for the proposed algorithm. More details on such a partitioning will be given below.

The above results have been obtained running the algorithm on a set of 480 sen-tences (24 male and 24 female speakers) extracted from the *Train* directory of the TIMIT corpus. The P_c rates were computed using as exemplar segmentation the man-ual labeling of TIMIT. A quick inspection of such results, clearly shows that it is difficult to assess which encoding scheme, between 5-PCBF and 8-PCBF (i.e using 5 or 8 coefficients for each speech frame) or between 5-MelBank and 8-MelBank pro-vides better performance. As a matter of fact, 8-PCBF gave a higher correct detection rate than 5-PCBF, but it also resulted in a higher number of erroneously inserted points. The same considerations can be made comparing the performance obtained with the 5-MelBank and 8-MelBank encoding schemes. Moreover, it is worth to notice that the negative D value for the 5-MelBank encoding, indicates that the num-ber of segmentation points detected by the algorithm is lower than the number of real segmentation points contained in the database. Furthermore, the optimality of a par-ticular triple of a, b, and c values cannot be caught at a glance, due to the correlation between P_c and D (as noted before, a higher over-segmentation rate corresponds to a higher correct detection rate). Table 2 makes the above considerations clear, showing how different values of c parameter affect both P_c and D, in a way that does not un-veil what should be an optimal value for c.

It would be easier to evaluate the performance of the algorithm if in the above ta-bles, either P_c or D, always showed the same numeric value. A situation of this kind could be experimentally induced by making several trials, in which two of the three

Table 2. Correct detection (P_c) and over-segmentation (D) rates for $a=2$, $b=0.2$, and $c=4,5,6$, obtained with the 8-MelBank encoding

c	P_c	D
4	80.8%	14%
5	80.1%	11%
6	79.3%	9%

parameters are fixed and the other is "moved around" until a configuration is found where D, for example, has the same value for every encoding scheme considered. In this way P_c remains the sole significant index for judging the performance of both the algorithm and the encoding scheme. Such an approach, however, has two weak points. The first is that the process needed to find the desired common value for D is highly time consuming, since it consists in hypothesizing the values for the varying parameters, getting the results of the current experiment, changing the initial hypothesis at the light of these results, and starting a new trial. Then the process should be repeated for every encoding scheme under test, and for every pair of values that can be taken by the two remaining parameters until an optimal value for c is identified. The other problem is related to the choice of the reference level: it would be better, for instance, if the common value chosen for D had some particular properties which could justify its adoption.

To overcome the first of the above limitations an automatic procedure is proposed, which finds (given a particular encoding scheme) the value of parameters a, b, and c maximizing the correct detection rate and satisfying the condition $D=0$. For every fixed a and c, the proposed procedure looks for the exact value of b that gives as over-segmentation value $D=0$. The choice of b as the "varying" parameter and that of $D=0$ as the reference level can be motivated as follows. It has already been said that b plays the role of a threshold. Actually b, which is a real number falling within the interval $[0, 1]$ almost directly regulates the amount of segmentation points detected by the algorithm and consequently the over-segmentation D. Moreover, having fixed $a=a^*$, $c=c^*$, D becomes a decreasing monotonic function of b^2, i.e. $D(a^*, b, c^*)=D(b)$. When $b=1$, D reaches its minimum value, $D=-S_t$, which is a negative number. When $b=0$ no preliminary thresholding procedure is performed by the algorithm and the D value depends on a^*, c^* and the current encoding scheme. $D(0)$ is supposed to be greater or equal to zero[3]. Based on the above considerations, the choice of $D(b)=0$ as constraint for the optimization of P_c appears the most natural one. An additional support to this choice comes from the fact that for text-dependent speech segmentation algorithms (which rely on an externally supplied transcription) $D=0$ by definition [68].

---

[2] More precisely, the way b is defined implies a "large-scale" monotonic behaviour of the function $D(b)$. However the same definition may allow small non-monotonic fluctuations of D for small variations of b ($\Delta b \ll 10^{-4}$)

[3] Having $D(0)<0$ means that, for every b, the algorithm always detects a number of segmentation points lower than the number of real segmentation points. Such an "under-segmentation" leads to change either the current encoding scheme or the a^* and c^* values. Note that when $D(0)=0$ there would be no need to perform the thresholding procedure

The procedure that looks for the exact value of b that gives as over-segmentation $D=0$ for fixed a, and c and a selected coding scheme is summarized in the following steps:

1. Set a and c to some integer values, $a*$ and $c*$, using an external control mechanism (see step 9);
2. Run a few trials on the whole data set using different values of $b \in (0,1)$;
3. Compute for such trials D and P_c obtaining a set of sampling points for the functions $D(b)$ and $P_c(b)$;
4. Identify a function $\beta(b)$ (e.g. a polynomial) that fits the obtained sampling points approximating the behavior of $D(b)$. The choice of $\beta(b)$ is essentially dictated by empirical considerations on the distribution of the sampling points;
5. Compute the analytic zeros of $\beta(b)$ and select as the zero of interest the one belonging to the decreasing monotonic region of $\beta(b)$ (e.g. if $\beta(b)$ is a parabola then only the zero associated to the descending branch should be considered, since the function to be approximated, $D(b)$, is decreasing monotonic). The selected zero gives an estimate value for b, let it be $b*$ such that $\beta(b*) \cong 0$;
6. Identify, as for D, a function $\rho(b)$ approximating the behavior of $P_c(b)$. This makes it possible to express the estimated detection rate as $\rho* = \rho(b*)$;
7. Run the segmentation algorithm again using $b=b*$ as threshold;
8. If $D(b*) \neq 0$ restart from step 4 using as additional sample points $D(b*)$ and $\rho(b*)$. Otherwise assume that $\rho* = P_c(b*)$ is the detection rate corresponding to a zero over-segmentation value;
9. $P_c(a*,c*)=\rho*$ is returned to the external mechanism which cares of finding the maximum of $P_c(a, c)$. This control routine will eventually restart the whole procedure using a new $(a*, c*)$ pair.

The procedure converges to an exact zero of $D(b)$ typically after a low number (< 10) of iterations even when a simple 2-order polynomial is used to approximate the over-segmentation function. However, if $D(b*)$ does not vary from one iteration to the next, it is advisable to increase the order of the approximation function. In addition, it is also possible to stop the procedure at step 6; in this case the declared performance would be the estimated detection rate $\rho*$, with an error bounded by the two experimental P_c values that are immediately lower and higher than $\rho*$.

Figure 3 shows, for several values of c and $a=2$, how the over-segmentation D (top) and the correct detection rate P_c (bottom) vary as a function of the threshold b. Figure 3 also shows a maximum for P_c at $c=7$.

Figure 4 shows in turn, the over-segmentation D (top) and the correct detection rate P_c (bottom) as a function of the threshold b, for several values of a and $c=7$. Figure 4 also shows a maximum for P_c at $a=3$.

4   Phone Segmentation Experiments

The data processed by the proposed algorithm result from a standard short-term parameterization of speech. Conventional short-term analysis encodes the speech signal into a time-sequence of feature vectors. The width of the analysis window has been fixed to 20 ms with an overlap of 10 ms between adjacent frames. The window samples have been weighted by a Hamming function to avoid spectral distortions

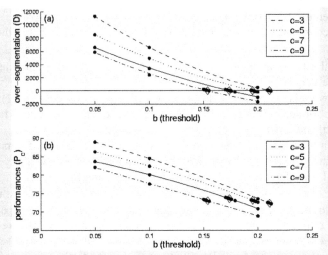

Fig. 3. Over-segmentation D (*top*) and correct detection rate P_c (*bottom*) as a function of the threshold b, for $a=2$ and different values of c. Note that P_c is maximized at $c=7$

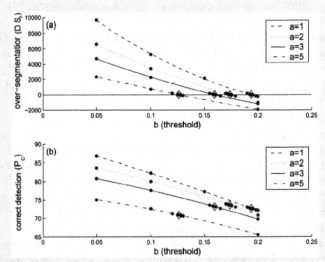

Fig. 4. Over-segmentation D (*top*) and correct detection rate P_c (*bottom*) as a function of the threshold b, for $c=7$ and different values of a. Note that the P_c is maximized at $a=3$

[73]. If not explicitly stated, the speech signal is assumed to be sampled at 16 kHz, thus each frame contains 320 samples and overlaps with the next of 160 samples.

4.1 The Speech Corpora

To test and compare the performances of the proposed algorithm with respect to those obtained using others text-independent techniques proposed in literature, all the experiments reported below have been performed using both the TIMIT and NTIMIT corpora [34], [48].

The TIMIT database is a reference American English speech corpus, most commonly adopted for phone recognition and segmentation experiments on read speech. The corpus consists of 6300 sentences (630 speakers, 10 sentences per speaker) representing 8 different US dialectal regions. The data are divided into *dialect sentences* (whose file name begins with SA), *phonetically-compact sentences* (beginning with SX) and *phonetically-diverse* sentences (beginning with SI). The dialect sentences are two and are produced by all the 630 speakers; they are designed to show the dialectal origin of the speaker. The phonetically-compact sentences (450 in all) are explicitly meant to provide a good coverage of all the American English phone pairs; each speaker reads 5 phonetically compact sentences. Finally, the phonetically-diverse sentences are defined with the aim to maximize the variety of allophonic contexts; there are 1890 in all (3 sentences per speaker).

The NTIMIT corpus, on the other hand, is a telephone bandwidth version of TIMIT. It was constructed transmitting the TIMIT sentences over telephone channels, through either local or long-distance calls. This database is a precious resource for studying the effect of the telephone bandwidth noise on the performance of speech technology applications. Manual phonetic transcription is provided for both the TIMIT and NTIMIT speech corpora.

The conventional *Train* and *Test* subsets of TIMIT and NTIMIT are made up of 462 and 168 speakers respectively, without overlap of text (excluding the SA sentences). In our experiments we used both of these sets, including the SA sentences; they will be indicated in the following with the acronyms TTRAIN, TTEST in the case of TIMIT, and with NTRAIN, NTEST for the NTIMIT corpus.

Table 3. List of the datasets used in experiments. For each dataset we report the number of sentences, phone boundaries S_t, and frames S_f

Acronym	# sentences	# phone boundary - S_t	# frames - S_f
SmallTRAIN	480	17930	145271
SmallTEST	320	11947	97639
TTRAIN	4620	172460	1412467
TTEST	1680	62465	516165
NTRAIN	4620	172460	1412230
NTEST	1680	62465	516079

In the preliminary experiments reported above we also used two smaller datasets, extracting 48 speakers (24 females and 24 males) from the *Train* directory of TIMIT and 32 different speakers (16 females and 16 males) for the *Test* directory of TIMIT. These two sets are indicated with the acronyms SmallTRAIN and SmallTEST respectively. Table 3 reports the whole number of sentences, the number of exemplar segmentation points and frames contained in each of the speech corpora that were used in our experiments.

4.2 The Choice of the Encoding Scheme

It is worthwhile to notice that, once the operational parameters have been fixed through the procedure described in the previous section, the performance of the proposed segmentation algorithm is a function of the selected encoding schemes. Therefore, among the problems that should be faced when the goal is to perform an automatic speech segmentation of an utterance (without a previous linguistic knowledge) there is the identification of the encoding scheme able to provide acoustic features whose informational content is explicitly related to the transitions from one phone to another.

The input of our segmentation algorithm (described in the previous sections) consists in a sequence of N arbitrary k-dimensional feature vectors, where N is the length of the sequence, corresponding to the total number of speech frames in a short-term analysis framework.

As previously stated, the development of our segmentation technique took moves from a multi-band representation of speech. The term multi-band is used here to designate those parameterizations of speech, like PCBF and MelBank [81], for which each component of the feature vectors represents a particular frequency band. In a broader sense, the multi-band approach is distinguished from the traditional full-band paradigm by the fact that, in the former, the full frequency range is divided into multiple, either overlapping or non-overlapping, regions for further processing [62]. In our case, we only consider one feature per frequency band (a measure of spectral power), but it is possible to have a whole set of features (like Mel Frequency Cepstral Coefficients, MFCCs) extracted from each sub-band.

Recently there is a growing interest in speech community on multi-band models for speech recognition (e.g. recognition using multi-stream Dynamic Bayesian Networks [22]). Among all the possible motivations for such an approach, there is a property of the speech signal that is particularly relevant to speech segmentation. In fact, it has been evidenced that phone transitions do not occur simultaneously in the different sub-bands; band-selective phone alignment experiments, carried out by Mirghafori [62], showed significant timing deviations between transitions determined in sub-bands and full-band alignments. Thus, we expect that performing phone segmentation separately in different frequency intervals gives better results than operating on the whole frequency range. In this sense, PCBF and Melbank features are particularly suitable front-ends for our multi-stream algorithm.

The above considerations are supported by experimental results. Figure 5 shows the performance of the proposed algorithm for Melbank, MFCCs, and Log-area Ratios[4] [72] encoding schemes. To better assess the effects of the encoding schemes, the results are plotted in terms of false alarms and miss rates for several b values.

The graph in Figure 5 and those that follow should be read as Receiver Operating Characteristic (ROC) curves. The closer the curve is to the bottom and to the left axes, the more accurate is the detection.

To help the reader understand the following graphs, it is worth noticing that a reliable automatic segmentation procedure produces about 12 phones per second, corresponding to a very low over-segmentation rate of $D \approx 0$, and a false alarm rate around $P_{fa} \approx 0.05$. A false alarm rate of $P_{fa} \approx 0.15$ is generated by an automatic segmentation

---

[4] The Log Area Ratio (LAR) encoding is another LPC-based technique, which uses PARCOR (partial correlation) coefficients [61], [72]. The PARCOR coefficients form a set of parameters derived from the short-time LPC representation of the speech signal. The area ratio functions of these coefficients give the Log-area ratios coefficients.

procedure that outputs about 24 phones per second, corresponding to an over-segmentation rate of $D \approx 100\%$. Furthermore, the values of $P_{fa} \approx 0.3$ and $D \approx 200\%$ are obtained by a segmentation procedure that generates about 36 phones per second. More details on how to interpret ROC curves and their properties can be found in [40], [69].

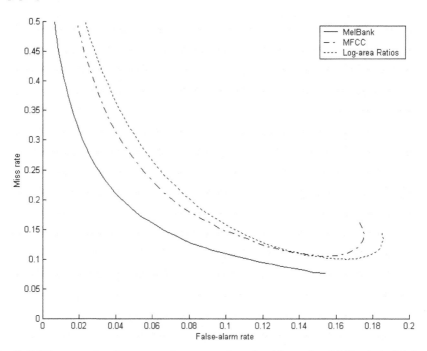

Fig. 5. ROC curves for the proposed segmentation algorithm using MelBank (*solid lines*), MFCC (*dotted and dashed lines*), and Log Area Ratios (*dotted lines*) encodings. The threshold b varies from 0 (the bottom-right end of the curves) to 1 and the remaining parameters are fixed at $a = 2$, $c = 5$. Only the significant part of the graph corresponding to a miss rate <50% is shown

The curves in Figure 5 are obtained with $a=2$ and $c=5$. Threshold b varies from 0 (which corresponds to the bottom-right end of the curve) to 1 with an increment $\Delta b=0.01$. Only the most significant part of the graph, corresponding to a miss rate <50%, is shown.

Figure 5 shows that the proposed algorithm achieves the best performance using an 8-coefficients representation of the Melbank encoding scheme. The encoding schemes were also tested for several dimensions of the frame representation. The results reported in Figure 5 correspond (for each encoding) to the number of coefficients that give the best performance. Melbank (8 coefficients) outperforms significantly not only MFCC (13 coefficients) and Log Area Ratio (12 coefficients) but also other encoding schemes such as Linear Predictive Coding (LPC), Perceptual Linear Prediction (PLP), RASTA-PLP and Perceptual Critical Band Feature (PCBF) [5], [6], [45], [46], [61]. Details on these experiments can be found in [4].

4.3   Comparison with Other Text Independent Segmentation Techniques

The effectiveness of the proposed algorithm was tested comparing its performances with respect to several segmentation procedures proposed in literature. The methods selected for the comparison were the Delta Change Function (DCF), the Spectral Variation Function (SVF), the Kullback-Leibler distance (KL), and the Temporal Decomposition (already discussed in section 2).

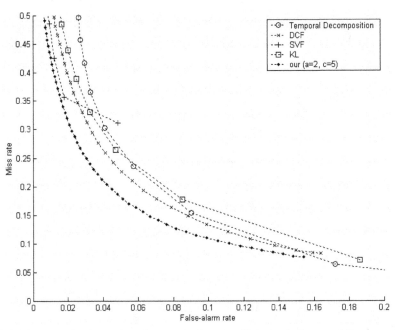

Fig. 6. ROC curves for the proposed segmentation algorithm (*our*), Temporal Decomposition, DCF, SVF, and Kullback-Leibler (*KL*) distance obtained using Melbank and the *Test* directory of TIMIT as experimental dataset. Each point corresponds to a different threshold (or sensitivity in the case of Temporal Decomposition) which varies in the [0,1] interval with an increment Δb=0.01. For the Temporal Decomposition the first visible point (bottom-right end) corresponds to sensitivity s=200, and Δs=200

Figure 6 shows the performance of these techniques against the proposed algorithm using a Melbank encoding for each of them. The experiments reported in Figure 6 were performed on the *Test* directory of the TIMIT corpus (if not explicitly stated, all the following graphs were obtained using the *Test* directory of TIMIT as experimental dataset) and the evaluation of the false alarm and miss rate values were computed assuming as exemplar segmentation the manual labeling on TIMIT. The curves in Figure 6 were obtained using Merlbank encoding for all the tested segmentation procedures, and fixing to a=2 and c=5 the parameters of our algorithm. Each point corresponds to a different threshold (or sensitivity in the case of Temporal Decomposition) which varies in the [0,1] interval with a increment Δb=0.01. For the Temporal Decomposition the first visible point (bottom-right end) corresponds to sensitivity s=200, and Δs=200. Figure 6 shows that, under the Melbank encoding scheme, the proposed algorithm outperforms significantly all the other segmentation techniques under test when the false alarm rate has a value around 0.05, corresponding roughly to a D=0 over-segmentation rate and to a correct detection rate P_c=82%.

Figure 6 also shows that, under the Melbank encoding, and for the same false alarm and over segmentation rates, DCF gives a correct detection rate of roughly P_c=76%, Temporal Decomposition gives a P_c=70%, KL gives a P_c=73%, and SVF performs very poorly giving a correct detection rate of roughly P_c=67%.

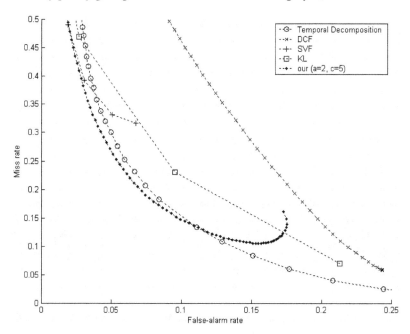

Fig. 7. ROC curves for the proposed segmentation algorithm (*our*), Temporal Decomposition, DCF, SVF, and Kullback-Leibler (*KL*) distance obtained using MFCC and the *Test* directory of TIMIT as experimental dataset. Each point corresponds to a different threshold (or sensitivity in the case of Temporal Decomposition) which varies in the [0,1] interval with Δb=0.01. For the Temporal Decomposition the first visible point (bottom-right end) corresponds to a sensitivity s=600 and $\Delta s = 200$

Since it has been shown (see Figure 5) that the optimal performance for the proposed segmentation method is obtained under the Melbank encoding, the results reported in Figure 6 may not appear surprising. For a fair comparison, it would be necessary to test our segmentation method when other encoding schemes are exploited. To this aim, several encoding schemes were tested (see [4]). In the following however, we only report the results obtained using MFCC and Log-area Ratios encoding schemes (the curves in Figures 7 and 8 respectively) since they are used as front-end for several speech segmentation techniques (in particular Log-area Ratios is commonly used as a front-end for the Temporal Decomposition [10]).

Each data point in Figures 7 and 8 corresponds to a different threshold (or sensitivity in the case of Temporal Decomposition) which varies in the [0,1] interval with

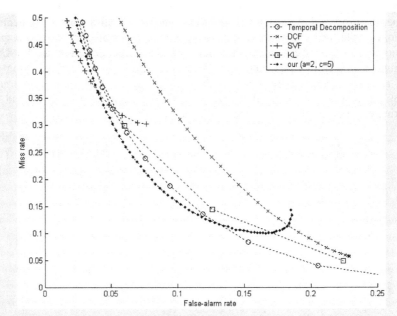

Fig. 8. ROC curves for the proposed segmentation algorithm (*our*), Temporal Decomposition, DCF, SVF, and Kullback-Leibler (*KL*) distance obtained using Log-area Ratios and the *Test* directory of TIMIT as experimental dataset. Each point corresponds to a different threshold (or sensitivity in the case of Temporal Decomposition) which varies in the [0,1] interval with Δb=0.01. For the Temporal Decomposition the first visible point (bottom-right end) corresponds to a sensitivity s=1200 and Δs = 200

Δb=0.01 [5]. For the Temporal Decomposition the first visible point (bottom-right end) corresponds to a sensitivity s=600 and s=1200 for MFCC and Log-area Ratios respectively. The sensitivity increment is always Δs=200. The curves in Figures 7 and 8 show that also for different encoding schemes the proposed algorithm still performs better than the other segmentation techniques under examination. However, its performance is significantly affected by the encoding scheme since, for the same false alarm and over-segmentation rates (P_{fa}=0.05, D=0) discussed in Figure 6, the correct detection rate is P_c=76% and P_c=70% under MFCC and Log-area Ratios encodings respectively. The choice of the encoding scheme also affects the performance of the other tested segmentation techniques. Considering always the same ROC curve regions (i.e. P_{fa}=0.05, D=0) it could be seen (from Figures 7 and 8) that the Temporal Decomposition correct detection rates are P_c=74% and P_c=67% under MFCC and Log-area Ratios respectively, suggesting that, for such a segmentation technique, MFCC is the most appropriate encoding scheme. SVF and KL instead are not affected, since the correct detection rate is almost the same (i.e. P_c is roughly around

---

[5] It should be noted that the behavior of the ROC curves is clearly visible even with lower experimental data points, corresponding to higher increments of the threshold. Different increment values are generally used to improve the visual representation of the ROC curves and do not affect the performance of the segmentation procedures

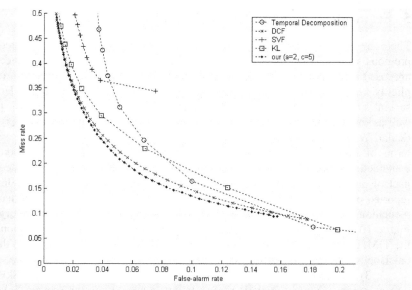

Fig. 9. ROC curves for the proposed segmentation algorithm (*our*), Temporal Decomposition, DCF, SVF, and Kullback-Leibler (*KL*) distance obtained using Melbank and the *Test* directory of NTIMIT as experimental dataset. Each point corresponds to a different threshold (or sensitivity in the case of Temporal Decomposition) which varies in the [0,1] interval with Δb=0.01 for our algorithm, DCF and KL, and Δb=0.001 for SVF. For the Temporal Decomposition the first visible point (bottom-right end) corresponds to a sensitivity s=200 and Δs = 200

67% and 60% respectively) for the two tested encodings. Surprisingly DCF perform very poorly, either under MFCC or Log-area Ratios since in the ROC regions of interest the correct detection rate is outside the most significant part of the graph, corresponding to a miss rate <50%.

In order to test the robustness of the proposed algorithm on noisy speech, we also tested its performance and that of the other segmentation procedures on the *Test* directory of the NTIMIT corpus using a Melbank encoding of a speech signal resampled at 8kHz. The re-sampling was required since sentences in NTIMIT were recorded over the restricted frequency bandwidth of the telephone channels which varies approximately in the (0, 4kHz) frequency range. The ROC curves for this experiment are reported in Figure 9. Each data point in Figure 9 corresponds to a different threshold (or sensitivity in the case of Temporal Decomposition) which varies in the [0,1] interval with Δb=0.01 for our algorithm, KL and DCF, and Δb=0.001 for SVF. For the Temporal Decomposition the first visible point (bottom-right end) corresponds to a sensitivity s=200 with an increment Δs=200. Figure 9 shows that the proposed segmentation technique maintains its performance even in a noisy environment, giving a correct detection rate P_c=80% that outperforms all the other segmentation procedures. Only DCF, with a P_c =77%, gives comparable performance, whereas Temporal Decomposition, SVF and KL perform relatively poorly with a correct detection rate of 67%, 67%, 60% respectively. It is worth to note that for all the above results the accepted over-segmentation rate is close to zero.

5 Segmentation Examples and Main Error Sources

There are several considerations that should be made on the results reported in the previous section. The first one is that, in the assessment of the performance of the proposed algorithm and the segmentation techniques tested for comparison, it is implicitly assumed that the TIMIT manual segmentation is 100% accurate. However, several studies showed that manual annotations for read speech [25], [26], [91], as well as for spontaneous speech [42], [75], may also produce inconsistencies. In particular, Wesenick and Kipp [91] report that different human transcribers disagreed in terms of alignment (with a tolerance of 20 ms) for 4% of the segment boundaries contained in a dataset of read speech. Since it is difficult to exactly estimate the impact of ambiguous annotations on the previously defined performance indexes the reported percentages could slightly underestimate the efficacy of the automatic segmentation. An accurate inspection of Figure 10 can help clarify the above argument. Figure 10 shows, from top to bottom: 1) a portion of speech wave corresponding to the TIMIT sentence *"Her wardrobe consists of only skirts and blouses"*; 2) the manual labeling of such a portion (corresponding to the text: *"Her wardrobe consists of...."*); 3) its MelBank encoding (8 frequency bands spanned in the (0, 8kHz) frequency range); 4) two automatic segmentations generated by the proposed algorithm fixing $a=2$, $c=7$ and $b=0.25$ or $b=0.20$ for the upper and lower segmentation plot respectively; and 5) a wide band spectrogram of this part of the sentence (in the 0-

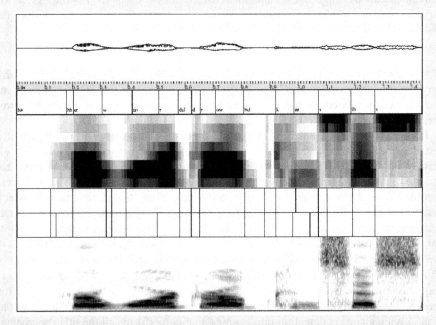

Fig. 10. Automatic segmentation for a part of the TIMIT sentence *"Her wardrobe consists of..."*. The different panels show from top to bottom: 1) the speech signal, 2) the TIMIT manual labeling, 3) the Melbank representation, 4) two different automatic segmentations obtained fixing $a=2$, $c=7$, $b= 0.25$ (*upper panel*) and $b= 0.20$ (*lower panel*), 5) the wide-band spectrogram in the (0, 8kHz) frequency range

8000 Hz frequency range). Both the automatic segmentations are based on the displayed Melbank parameterization, and the "relative thresholding" methods. This particular sentence allows to individuate two kinds of inconsistencies between manual labeling and automatic segmentation. The first one is a segmentation error, that could be either a false alarm or a missed boundary or a misplaced phone transition. In this case, it is assumed that the TIMIT labeling reflects the acoustic reality better than the automatic segmentation. In Figure 10, in the first part of the word "*wardrobe*", false boundaries are inserted between the phones [w] and [ao], whereas the phone transitions from [ao] to [r] as well as from the second [r] to [ow] are missed by both the two automatic performed segmentation.

The second inconsistency concerns the position, at the beginning of the speech signal, of the transition from the silence [h#] to the phone [hh]. An inspection of the spectrogram in Figure 10 suggests that the manual labeling may have missed this transition that instead is correctly detected by the algorithm. Furthermore, the manual labeling also misses the transition from the [b] closure [bcl] to the [k] release at the end of the word "*wardrobe*" and the beginning of the word "*consists*" that is detected both by the algorithm and the spectrogram. This is a case where the manual labeling of TIMIT is incorrect, evidencing that manual annotations can be arbitrary to a certain extent and an automatic segmentation may appear more coherent. Other examples of TIMIT incorrect or questionable labeling are reported in [87].

Beside the inconsistencies in the TIMIT manual labeling discussed above, it should be interesting to investigate on which class of phone transitions is generally missed by the automatic segmentation. To this aim, we performed an analysis on the SmallTRAIN dataset computing the frequency of occurrence for all the allowed transitions from one phone to another. We grouped these transitions in 6 classes according to their frequency of occurrence and evaluated the correct detection rate of the proposed algorithm on them. The results of this evaluation, reported in Table 4, showed that there are 1695 allowed classes of phone transitions in the SmallTRAIN dataset and that the proposed segmentation procedure is very effective in detecting the most frequent phone transitions (P_c=86%) and less effective in detecting very rare (P_c=67.6%) phone transitions. Also this analysis showed that, grouping the phones

Table 4. List of allowed phone-to-phone transitions in the SmallTRAIN dataset, grouped in classes according to their frequency of occurrence. Also reported is the total number of transitions for each class and the corresponding correct detection rate obtained running the proposed algorithm on a Melbank encoding fixing a=2, c=7, b=0.2

#Allowed phone transitions	Frequency of occurrence	Total #of transitions	Correct detection rate
12	100< n<500	2562	(2205) 86.06%
51	50<n<=99	3180	(2443) 76.82%
368	10<n<=50	7923	(6201) 78.27%
473	3<n<=10	2917	(2278) 78.09%
162	n=3	486	(388) 79.84%
232	n=2	464	(352) 75.86%
398	n=1	398	(269) 67.59%
Total 1695		17930	(14136) 78.84%

into phonetic categories according to their manner of articulation, there are specific transitions from one category to another that are not effectively detected.

Table 5 reports those transitions between phonetic categories whose correct detection rate is lower than 50%. The data are always referred to the SmallTRAIN dataset.

Table 5. List of transitions between phonetic categories whose correct detection rate is lower than 50%. Also reported, between parentheses, is the number of transitions correctly detected (second column) and the number of occurrences of each transition (third column)

1 phone category	2 phone category	Correct detection rate
nasal	semi-vowel (37)	(78) 47.44%
semi-vowel	vowel (687)	(1449) 47.41%
vowel	semi-vowel (413)	(888) 46.51%
nasal	silence (40)	(99) 40.40%
Stop	fricative (68)	(196) 34.69%
Stop	silence (29)	(91) 31.87%
Vowel	vowel (116)	(394) 29.44%
Stop closure	silence (14)	(81) 17.28%
Nasal	nasal (3)	(20) 15.00%
Total	1407	(3296) 42.68%

It is interesting to note that, among the phone transitions that are not effectively detected, there are transitions from vowel to vowel, from vowel to semi-vowel and vice-versa, transitions from stop to fricative, and from nasal to vowel. These transitions are difficult to be identified even by expert phoneticians and generally it is a matter of convention to establish when, for example, a given vowel ends and a new vowel starts. The above considerations rise a more general question on the essence of the segmentation process since, implicitly it assumes that during phone transitions there are enough discontinuities (or sharp changes) to make their detection possible. This assumption does not take into account that speech articulators vary continuously and smoothly during speech production and that the changes from one vocal tract configuration to another happen along a temporal continuum and not at precise time instants. These dynamics produce limitations on any segmentation procedure based on the above assumption and the only way to overcome these limitations is to identify a speech segmentation algorithm that models these continuously varying dynamics (Principe, personal communication).

6   Conclusions

Speech phonetic segmentation is a challenging task, that finds application in speech recognition, coding and synthesis. This task can be performed either in a bottom-up fashion, exploiting acoustic properties of the speech signal, or can be a "secondary product" of the recognition process carried out by top-down generative systems, like Hidden Markov Models.

This work proposes an original segmentation algorithm, that carries out the phonetic segmentation using a bottom-up approach based on the detection of spectral instability in multiple frequency bands. According to the results reported in section 3, the algorithm gives better performance than other methods of the same class, being able to reproduce the reference segmentation of the TIMIT and NTIMIT corpus with a correct detection rate of 82% and 80% respectively and an over-segmentation rate close to zero. The results on NTIMIT also showed a good robustness of the algorithm to additive noise and telephone bandwidth distortions.

Part of our work has been devoted to the analysis of the relationships between segmentation performance indexes and their dependence from the algorithm's parameters. Using concepts and methods borrowed from the theory of signal detectability, the segmentation results have been displayed as ROC curves that offer a better understanding of the statistic properties and performance of segmentation systems.

It has also shown that the processing algorithm and the acoustic information that such processing is able to encode play an important role on the final performance of all the examined segmentation procedures. Results showed that Melbank is the best encoding scheme for the proposed segmentation algorithm.

Compared to generative models, the proposed bottom-up segmentation method has the advantage of being computationally less expensive, independent from the language and the linguistic context, and more robust to mismatches between training and testing conditions. These properties make it preferable to Hidden Markov Models – whose accuracy is highly dependent on the quality of the training data annotation – since only HMMs trained on carefully annotated data can achieve comparable performance in either phonetic decoding or alignment tasks.

From all the above investigations, we gained the belief that phonetic segmentation based on the bottom-up acoustic analysis of speech has not been yet exploited in all its potentialities. The proposed method is still open to improvements, especially in the detection of smooth transitions that occur between particular classes of phones.

Acknowledgements

Acknowledgment goes to Antonietta Esposito and Maria Marinaro for their collaboration in some of the reported experiments. Mrs. Tina Nappi is acknowledged for her editorial help.

References

1. Altosaar, T., Karjalainen, M.: Event-Based Multiple Resolution Analysis of Speech Signals. In Proceedings of International Conference on Acoustics, Speech, and Signal Processing, New-York (1988) 327 – 330
2. Andre-Obrecht R.: A New Statistical Approach for the Automatic Segmentation of Continuous Speech Signals. IEEE Transactions on Acoustics, Speech Signal Processing, Vol. 36 (1988) 29 – 40
3. Atal, B. S.: Efficient Coding of LPC Parameters by Temporal Decomposition. In Proceedings of International Conference on Acoustics, Speech, and Signal Processing (1983) 81 – 84
4. Aversano, G.: Phone Level Automatic Speech Segmentation. A Text-Independent Segmentation Algorithm and a Software Tool for Speech Annotation and Analysis. Ph.D. Thesis, Università di Salerno – Italy (2004)
5. Aversano, G., Esposito, A: Automatic Parameter Estimation for a Context-Independent Speech Segmentation Algorithm. In Sojka, P., Kopecek, I., Pala, K. (eds.): Text Speech and Dialogue, 5th International Conference, Lecture Notes in Artificial Intelligence. Springer-Verlag, (2002) 293 – 300

6. Aversano G., Esposito A., Esposito A., Marinaro M.: A New Text-Independent Method for Phoneme Segmentation. In R. L.Ewing et al. (eds): Proceedings of the IEEE International Workshop on Circuits and Systems, Vol.2 (2001) 516 – 519

7. Backfried, G., Rainoldi, R., Riedler, J.: Automatic Language Identification in Broadcast News. In Proceedings of International Joint Conference on Neural Networks, Vol.2 (2002) 1406 – 1410

8. Basseville M., Nikiforov I. V.: Detection of Abrupt Changes: Theory and Applications. Englewood Cliffs, NJ, Prentice Hall (1993)

9. Basseville, M.: Distance Measures for Signal Processing and Pattern Recognition. Signal Processing, Vol. 18 (1989) 349 – 369

10. Baudoin, G., Capman F., Cernocky, J., El Chami, F., Charbit, M., Chollet, G., Petrovska-Delacretaz, D.: Advances in Very Low Bit-rate Speech Coding using Recognition and Synthesis. In: Sojka, P., Kopecek, I., Pala, K. (eds.): Text Speech and Dialogue, 5th International Conference. Lecture Notes in Artificial Intelligence. Springer-Verlag, Berlin Heidelberg New York (2002) 269 – 276

11. Beringer, N., Neff, M.: Regional Pronunciation Variants for Automatic Segmentation. In Proceedings of the 2nd International Conference on Language Resources and Evaluation. Athens, Greece (2000)

12. Beringer, N., Schiel, F.: The Quality of Multilingual Automatic Segmentation Using German MAUS. In Proceedings of the 6th Int. Conference on Spoken Language Processing. Beijing, China (2000) 728 – 731

13. Beringer, N., Schiel, F.: Independent Automatic Segmentation of Speech by Pronunciation Modeling. In Proceedings of the 14th Int. Congress of Phonetic Sciences. San Francisco (1999) 1653 – 1656

14. Beulen, K., Ney, H.: Automatic Question Generation for Decision Tree Based State Tying. In Proceedings of IEEE International Conference on Acoustics, Speech and Signal Processing (1998) 805 – 808

15. Beulen, K., Bransch, E., Ney, H.: State Tying for Context Dependent Phoneme Models. In Proceedings of European Conference on Speech Communication and Technology (1997) 1179 – 1182

16. Binnenpoorte, D., Goddijn, S., Cucchiarini, C.: How to Improve Human and Machine Transcriptions of Spontaneous Speech. ISCA/IEEE Workshop on Spontaneous Speech Processing and Recognition. Tokyo (2003) 147 – 150

17. Bishop, C. M.: Neural Networks for Pattern Recognition, Clarendon Press (1995)

18. Brugnara F., Falavigna, D., Omologo, M.: Automatic Segmentation and Labeling of Speech Based on Hidden Markov Models. Speech Communication, Vol. 12 (1993) 357–370

19. Brugnara F., De Mori A., Giuliani D., Omologo M.: Improved Connected Digit Recognition Using Spectral Variation Functions. In Proceedings of International Conference on Spoken Language Processing (1992) 627 – 630

20. Chang, S., Shastri, L., Greenberg, S.: Automatic Phonetic Transcription of Spontaneous Speech (American English). Proceedings of the 6th International Conference on Spoken Language Processing. Beijing, China (2000) 330 – 333

21. Church, K. W.: Speech and Language Processing: Where Have We Been and Where Are We Going? Proceedings of the 8th European Conference on Speech Communication and Technology - Eurospeech '03. Geneva, Switzerland (2003) 1– 4

22. Daoudi, K., Fohr, D., Antoine, C.: Continuous Multi-Band Speech Recognition using Bayesian Networks. Proceedings of IEEE Automatic Speech Recognition and Understanding Workshop, Trento, Italy (2001)

23. Deshayes, J., Picard, D.: Off-line Statistical Analysis in Change-point Models Using Nonparametric and Likelihood Methods". In M. Basseville, A. Beneviste (eds): Detection of Abrupt Changes in Signals and Dynamical Systems, Springer-Verlag, New-York (1986)

24. du Jeu, C., Charbit, M., Chollet, G.: Very-low-rate Speech Compression by Indexation of Polyphones. Proceedings of the 8th European Conference on Speech Communication and Technology - Eurospeech '03. Geneva, Switzerland (2003) 1085 – 1088

25. Eisen, B., Tillman, H. G.: Consistency of Judgments in Manual Labeling of Phonetic Segments: The Distinction between Clear and Nnclear Cases. Proceedings of ICSLP '92. Banf, Canada (1992) 871– 874

26. Eisen, B.: Reliability of Speech Segmentation and Labeling at Different Levels of Transcription. Proceedings of the 3rd European Conference on Speech Communication and Technology. Eurospeech '93. Berlin, Germany (1991) 673 – 676

27. Esposito, A.: The Importance of Data for Training Intelligent Devices. In B. Apolloni, F. Kurfess (eds.): From Synapses to Rules: Discovering Symbolic Rules from Neural Processed Data. Kluwer Academic/Plenum Publishers (2002) 229 – 250

28. Esposito, A., Pannacci, L., Perfetti, R., Russo, R.C.: Speech Segmentation by Parametric Filtering: Two New Distortion Measures and Experimental Evaluation, Technical Report n. IIASS-1-00, International Institute for Advanced Scientific Studies, Vietri sul Mare (SA), Italy (2000)

29. 29.Fairbanks, G., Everitt, W. and Jaeger, R.: Method for Time or Frequency Compression Expansion of Speech. IEEE Transactions on Audio and Electro-acoustics, AU-2 (1954) 7 –12

30. Faundez-Zanuy, M., Vallverdù-Bayes, F.: Speech Segmentation Using Multilevel Hybrid Filters. In Proceedings of European Signal Processing Conference (EUSIPCO) (1996) 1003 – 1006

31. Finster, H.: Automatic speech segmentation using neural network and phonetic transcription. In Proceedings of International Conference on Neural Networks, Vol.4 (1992) 734 – 736

32. Flammia, G., Dalsgaard, P., Andersen, O., Lindberg, B.: Segment Based Variable Frame Rate Speech Analysis and Recognition Using Spectral Variation Function. In Proceedings of International Conference on Spoken Language Processing (1992) 983 – 986

33. Furuichi, C., Aizawa, K., Inoue, K.: Speech Recognition Using Stochastic Phonemic Segment Model Based on Phoneme Segmentation. Systems and Computers in Japan, Vol. 31(10) (2000) 1111 – 1119

34. Garofolo, J. S., Lamel, L. F., Fisher, W. M., Fiscus, J. G., Pallett, D. S., Dahlgren, N. L.: The DARPA TIMIT Acoustic-Phonetic Continuous Speech Corpus. CDROM (1992) NTIS order number PB91-100354

35. Gemello, R., Albesano, D., Mana, F.: CSELT Hybrid HMM/Neural Networks Technology for Continuous Speech Recognition. In Proceedings of IEEE-INNS-ENNS International Joint Conference on Neural Networks, Vol. 5 (2000) 103 – 108

36. Glass, J. R.: A Probabilistic Framework for Segment -Based Speech Recognition. Computer Speech and Language, Vol. 17 (2003) 137 – 152

37. Glass, J. R., Zue, V.W.: Multilevel Acoustic Segmentation of Continuous Speech". In Proceedings of International Conference on Acoustics, Speech, and Signal Processing (1988) 429 – 432

38. Gómez, J.A., Castro, M. J.: Automatic Segmentation of Speech at the Phonetic Level. In T. Caell et al. (eds): Lecture Notes in Computer Science, Vol. 2396 (2002) 672 – 680

39. Gray, R.M., Buzo, A., Gray, A., Matsuyama, Y.: Distortion Measures for Speech Processing. IEEE Transactions on Acoustics, Speech Signal Processing, Vol. 28 (1980) 367 – 376

40. Green, D., Swets, J.: Signal Detection Theory and Psychophysics. John Wiley and Sons (1996)

41. Greenberg, S.: Strategies for Automatic Multi-Tier Annotation of Spoken Language Corpora. In Proceedings of the 8th European Conference on Speech Communication and Technology - Eurospeech '03. Geneva, Switzerland (2003) 45 – 48

42. Greenberg, S.: The Switchboard Transcription Project. Technical Report # 24, Center for Language and Speech Processing, Johns Hopkins University, Baltimore USA (1997)
43. Hermansky, H.: Analysis in Automatic Recognition of Speech. In: Chollet, G., Di Benedetto M., Esposito, A., Marinaro M. (eds.): Speech Processing, Recognition and Artificial Neural Networks, 3rd International School on Neural Nets "Eduardo R. Caianiello". Springer-Verlag, Berlin Heidelberg New York (1999) 115 – 137
44. Hermansky, H.: Auditory Modeling in Automatic Recognition of Speech. Proceedings of the ESCA Workshop on the Auditory Basis of Speech Perception. Keele, Sweden (1996)
45. Hermansky H., Morgan N.: RASTA Processing of Speech. IEEE Transactions. Speech and Audio Processing, Vol. 2(4) (1994) 578 – 589
46. Hermansky H.: Perceptual Linear Predictive (PLP) Analysis of Speech. Journal of Acoustical Society of America, Vol. 87(4) (1990) 1738 – 1752
47. Horak, P.: Automatic Speech Segmentation Based on DTW with the Application of the Czech TTS System. In E. Keller, G.Bailly, A, Monaghan, J. Terken, M. Huckwale (eds.): Improvements in Speech Synthesis. John Wiley and Sons Ltd. (2001) 331 – 340
48. Jankowski, C., Kalyanswamy, A., Basson, S., Spitz, J.: NTIMIT: A Phonetically Balanced, Continuous Speech, Telephone Bandwidth Speech Database. Proceedings of ICASSP (1990) 109 – 112
49. Jeong, C. G., Jeong, H.: Automatic Phone Segmentation and Labeling of Continuous Speech. Speech Communication, Vol. 20 (1997) 291 – 311
50. Kanthak, S., Ney:, H.: Multilingual Acoustic Modeling Using Graphemes. In Proceedings of European Conference on Speech Communication and Technology, Vol.2 (2003) 1145 – 1148
51. Kolokolov, A.S.: Preprocessing and Segmentation of the Speech Signal in the Frequency Domain for Speech Recognition. Automation and Remote Control, Vol.64(6) (2003) 985 – 994
52. Laroche, J.: Time and Pitch Scale Modification of Audio Signals. In M. Kahrs, K. Brandenburg (eds.): Applications of Digital Signal Processing to Audio and Acoustics. Kluwer Academic Publishers (1998)
53. Laureys, T., K. Demuynck, J. Duchateau, Wambacq, P.: An Improved Algorithm for the Automatic Segmentation of Speech Corpora. In M. González Rodriguez, C. Paz Suárez Araujo (eds.): Proceedings of Third International Conference on Language Resources and Evaluation (2002) 1564 – 1567
54. Lavielle, M.: Detection of Changes in the Spectrum of Multidimensional Process. IEEE Transactions on Signal Processing, Vol. 41(1993) 742 – 749
55. Le Cerf, P., Demuynck, K., Duchateau, J., Van Compernolle, D.: Pseudo-Segment Based Speech Recognition Using Neural Recurrent Whole-Word Recognizers. In Proceedings of International Conference on Acoustics, Speech and Signal Processing, Vol.1 (1994) 609 – 612
56. Li, B. N.L., Liu, J.N.K.: A Comparative Study of Speech Segmentation for Automatic Multi-Lingual Recognition. In Proceedings of Second ACM Hong Kong Postgraduate Research Conference (1999) http://www.cse.cuhk.edu.hk/~acm-hk/activity/pg/polyu-nlli.pdf
57. Li T. H., Gibson J. D.: Speech Analysis and Segmentation by Parametric Filtering. IEEE Transactions on Speech and Audio Processing, Vol. 4(3)(1996) 203 – 213
58. Li T. H., Gibson J. D.: Time-Correlation Analysis of Non-stationary Signals with Application to Speech Processing. In Proceedings of International Symposium on Time- Frequency &Time-Scale Analysis, Paris, France (1996) 449 – 452
59. Lin, M.-T., Lee, C.-K., Lin, §C.-Y. : Consonant/Vowel Segmentation for Mandarin Syllable Recognition. Computer Speech and Language, Vol. 23 (1999) 207 – 222

60. Malfrère, F., Deroo, O., Dutoit, T., Ris, C.: Phonetic Alignment: Speech Synthesis-Based vs. Viterbi-Based. Speech Communication, Vol. 40(4) (2003) 503 – 515

61. Makhoul, J.: Spectral Linear Prediction: Properties and Applications. IEEE Transactions ASSP, Vol. 23(5) (1975) 283 – 296

62. Mirghafori, N.: A Multi-Band Approach to Automatic Speech Recognition. Ph.D. thesis, University of California, Berkeley, December 1988, chap. 4. Reprinted as ICSI Technical Report, TR-99-04, Berkeley, CA (1999)

63. Mitchell C. D., Harper M. P., Jamieson L. H.: Using Explicit Segmentation to Improve HMM Phone Recognition. In Proceedings of International Conference on Acoustic, Speech and Signal Processing (I995) 229 – 232

64. Park E.-Y.; Kim, S.-H, Chung, J.-H.: Automatic Speech Synthesis Unit Generation with MLP Based Postprocessor against Auto-segmented Phoneme Errors. In Proceedings of International Joint Conference on Neural Networks, Vol.5 (1999) 2985 – 2990

65. Parson, T.: Voice and Speech Processing. McGraw-Hill, New-York (1986)

66. Parzen, E.: Time Series, Statistics and Information. In D. Brillinger, P. Caines, J. Geweke, E. Parzen, M. Rosenblatt, M.S. Taqqu (eds): New Directions in Time Series Analysis, Part I,. The IMA Volumes in Mathematics and its Applications. Series. Vol. 45, Springer Verlag, New York (1992)

67. Pellom B. L., Hansen J. H. L.: Automatic Segmentation of Speech Recorded in UnknownNoisy Channel Characteristics. Speech Communication, Vol. 25 (1998) 97 – 116

68. Petek B., Andersen O., Dalsgaard P.: On the Robust Automatic Segmentation of Spontaneous Speech. In Proceedings of International Conference on Spoken Language Processing (1996) 913 – 916

69. Peterson, W., Birdsall, T., Fox, W.: The Theory of Signal Detectability. IEEE Transactions on Information Theory, Vol. 4(4) (1954) 171 – 212

70. Picone J.: Continuous Speech Recognition Using Hidden Markov Models. IEEE ASSP Magazine (1990) 26 – 41

71. Prasad, V. K., Nagarajan, T., Mutrhy, H. A.: Automatic Segmentation of Continuous Speech Using Phase Group Delay Functions. Speech Communication, Vol.42 (2004) 429 – 446

72. Quackenbush, S. R., Barnwell, T. P., Clements, M. A.: Objective Measures of Speech Quality, Prentice Hall, Englewood Cliffs (1988)

73. Rabiner L., Juang B.-H.: Fundamentals of Speech Recognition. Prentice-Hall, Inc. Upper Saddle River, NJ (1993)

74. Rabiner, L.R., Juang, B. H.: An Introduction to Hidden Markov Models. IEEE ASSP Magazine (1986) 4 – 16

75. Raymond W. D. et al.: An Analysis of Transcription Consistency in Spontaneous Speech from the Buckeye Corpus. Proceedings of ICSLP '02. Denver, USA (2002).

76. Schiel, F.: Automatic Phonetic Transcription of Non-Prompted Speech. Proceedings of the 14th International Congress on Phonetic Sciences. San Francisco (1999) 607 – 610

77. Schillo, C., Fink, G. A., Kummert, F.: Grapheme Based Recognition for Large Vocabularies. In Procceedings of International Conference on Spoken Processing (2000) 129 – 132

78. Sharma, M., Mammone, R.: Automatic Speech Segmentation Using Neural Tree Networks. In Proceedings of IEEE Workshop on Neural Networks for Signal Processing (1995) 282 – 290

79. Segura-Luna J. C., Soler J. M., Peinado A. M., Sanchez V., Rubio A.: Signal Segmentation into Spectral Homogeneous Units. In Proceedings of European Signal Processing Conference (1990) 1251 – 1254

80. Silverman, H. F., Morgan, D. P.: The Application of Dynamic Programming to Connected Speech Recognition. IEEE ASSP Magazine (1990) 6-25

81. Stephens S. S., Volkman, J.: The Relation of Pitch to Frequency. American Journal of Psychology, Vol. 53(3) (1940) 329 – 353

82. Suontasuta, J., Hakkinen, J.: Decision Tree Based Text-to-Mapping for Speech Recognition. In Procceedings of International Conference on Spoken Processing (2000) 199 – 202

83. Svendsen, T., Soong, F. K.: On Automatic Segmentation of Speech Signals. In Proceedings of International Conference on Acoustics, Speech, and Signal Processing, Dallas (1987) 77 – 80

84. Torkolla, K.: An Efficient Way to Learn English Grapheme-to-Phoneme Rules Automatically. In Proceedings of International Conference on Acoustics, Speech and Signal Processing, Vol. 2 (1993) 199 – 202

85. van Hemert, J.P.: Automatic Segmentation of Speech. IEEE Transactions on Signal Processing, Vol. 39 (4) (1991) 1008 – 1012

86. Vidal, E., Marzal, A.: A Review and New Approaches for Automatic Segmentation of Continuous Speech Signals. In L. Torress et al. (eds): Signal Processing V: Theories and Applications, Elsevier Publisher, New-York (1990) 43 – 53

87. Vorstermans, A., Martens, J.P., Van Coile, B.: Automatic Segmentation and Labeling of Multi-lingual Speech Data. Speech Communication, Vol.19(4) (1996) 271 – 293

88. Wei, B., Gibson, J.D.: A New Discrete Spectral Modeling Method and an Application to CELP Coding. IEEE Signals Processing Letters, Vol. 10(4) (2003) 101 – 103

89. Wei, B., Gibson, J.D.: Comparison of Distance Measure in Discrete Spectral Modeling. In Proceedings of IEEE Digital Signal Processing Workshop (2000) 1 – 4

90. Wendt, C., Petropulu, A.P.: Pitch Determination and Speech Segmentation Using the Discrete Wavelet Transform. In Procceddings of IEEE International Symposium on Circuits and Systems, Vol. 2 (1996) 45 – 48

91. Wesenick, M.B., Kipp, A.:Estimating the Quality of Phonetic Transcriptions and Segmentations of Speech Signals. Proceedings of ICSLP'96. Philadelphia, USA (1996) 129 – 132

92. Wester, M., Kessens, J. M., Cucchiarini, C., Strik, H.: Comparison between Expert Listeners and Continuous Speech Recognizers in Selecting Pronunciation Variants. Proceedings of the 14th Int. Congress of Phonetic Sciences. San Francisco (1999) 723 – 726

93. Wokurek, W.: Corpus Based Evaluation of Entropy Rate Speech Segmentation. In Proceedings of 14th International Congress of Phonetic Sciences (I999) 1217 – 1220

94. Young., S. J., Woodland, P. C.: State Clustering in Hidden Markov Model-Based Continuous Speech Recognition. Computer Speech and Language, Vol.8 (1994) 369 – 383

95. Zue, V.W., Glass, J. R., Philips, M., Seneff, S.: Acoustic Segmentation and Phonetic Classification in the Summit System". In Proceedings of International Conference on Acoustics, Speech, and Signal Processing (1989) 389 – 392

Nonlinear Adaptive Speech Enhancement Inspired by Early Auditory Processing

Amir Hussain[1], Tariq S. Durrani[2], John J. Soraghan[2],
Ali Alkulaibi[3], and Nhamo Mtetwa[1]

[1] Centre for Cognitive and Computational Neuroscience,
University of Stirling, Stirling FK9 4LA, Scotland, UK
ahu@cs.stir.ac.uk
http://www.cs.stir.ac.uk/~ahu/
[2] Institute of Communications & Signal Processing,
University of Strathclyde, Glasgow G1 1XW, Scotland, UK
t.durrani@eee.strath.ac.uk
[3] P.O. Box 4822, Jeddah 21412, Saudi Arabia

Abstract. This paper presents non-linear adaptive speech enhancement schemes inspired by features of early auditory processing. A generic multi-microphone sub-band adaptive (MMSBA) framework is described which allows for the manipulation of several factors that may influence the intelligibility and perceived quality of the processed speech. The proposed framework supports inclusion of: non-linear distribution of sub-bands (as in humans), cross-band effects such as lateral inhibition, and robust adaptive metrics for selecting an appropriate coherent or incoherent noise canceller for each sub-band, based on identified features of the band-limited signals from multiple-sensors during silence periods. An efficient higher order statistics (HOS) based speech/non-speech detector is proposed for enabling effective adaptive control of MMSBA filtering against the environment. New hybrid extensions of the MMSBA scheme incorporating neural networks and post-Weiner filtering are also described and their comparative performance assessed in real reverberant environments. Finally, some future research directions for MMSBA based speech enhancement are proposed including possible alternative strategies based on stochastic resonance.

1 Introduction

Speech enhancement is motivated by the need to improve the performance of voice communications systems in noisy conditions. The goal is either to improve the perceived quality of the speech, or to increase its intelligibility.

In much speech enhancement research, new ideas are often based on the human auditory process. This is because of the fact that humans can detect and understand speech at very low Signal to Noise Ratios (SNR); and this too, without any a priori knowledge of the actual speech, the noise or the surrounding environment. It would therefore seem logical to model the characteristics of desired speech enhancement and recognition systems on the human ear [1].

In this paper, we first briefly review features of the human auditory system and aspects of sensori-neural hearing loss (SHL) that support the suspicion of a multi-microphone sub-band adaptive (MMSBA) processing approach to enhancement of speech in noisy environments. Next we present the background of the MMSBA

G. Chollet et al. (Eds.): Nonlinear Speech Modeling, LNAI 3445, pp. 291–316, 2005.
© Springer-Verlag Berlin Heidelberg 2005

framework and discuss the various factors whose manipulation it allows for, in order to influence the intelligibility and perceived quality of the processed speech.

The two-sensor acoustic model employed in the MMSBA scheme is shown to be less restrictive (and hence more practically realizable) than the conventional two-sensor noise-cancellation approach of Widrow, thereby extending the range of applications for which the MMSBA framework can be employed. A new computationally-efficient adaptive Higher Order Statistics (HOS) technique for implementation within the MMSBA scheme is proposed in order to achieve effective speech detection (for determining the required noise-alone periods). A human cochlear model resulting in a non-linear distribution of the sub-band filters (as in humans) is described and the choice of possible sub-band processing options for handling coherent and incoherent noises are discussed. An adaptive metric based on the coherence function is described for selecting the appropriate coherent/incoherent noise-cancellation SBP option.

New hybrid extensions of the MMSBA scheme incorporating neural networks and post-Weiner filtering are presented which aim to conceptually model cochlear mechanical filtering (in the auditory periphery) with a form of non-linear SBP to approximate the neural circuits in the auditory brainstem. Preliminary comparative results achieved in simulation experiments using anechoic speech corrupted with real automobile noise are used to show that the proposed hybrid MMSBA structures are capable of significantly outperforming the conventional MMSBA scheme (without WF) as well as the conventional wide-band noise cancellation schemes. Finally, some future research directions for MMSBA based speech enhancement are proposed including some alternative schemes based on stochastic resonance.

1.1 Aspects of Human Hearing

From the outer ear to the auditory nerve leaving the cochlea, the various processing functions are known to include: transduction, filtering, amplification, non-linear compression, impedance matching and cochlear operation of spectral analysis. The processing centres of the auditory brainstem are known to receive from the cochlea, a two-channel (binaural) set of time-domain signals in contiguous non-linearly spaced frequency (sub) bands. Popular interpretations of experimental evidence [1] have also identified the separation of: left from right ear signals, low from high-frequency signals, timing from intensity information; and their re-integration at various processing centres and levels in the hierarchy.

The masked threshold of intelligibility has been found by Plomp [2] to be about 3dB lower for competing connected speech than for continuous speech-noise. It has been suggested that the windows in either the desired or competing signal could be used to view and estimate the other for interference reduction [3]. Experimental evidence has also suggested that the auditory system is able to model a communications channel [4]. Thus enhancement and source location may be aided by the estimation of the acoustic path transfer function between the interference and the desired signal [5].

1.2 Aspects of Sensori-Neural Hearing Loss (SHL)

Over 8.5 million people in the UK suffer some degree of deafness [5]. Probably the most common cause of hearing loss is damage to the cochlea. This sensorineural hearing loss (SHL) may arise from infection, the toxic effects of certain drugs, or long term exposure to sound and is at present irreversible. A major cause of SHL is age related cochlear degeneration (presbyacusis) which usually reveals itself by the sixth decade.

Many persons with a degree of SHL find that one-to-one conversations in quiet, low reverberation surroundings can become unintelligible as background noise or reverberation levels increase [6]. Under these conditions, sufferers of SHL often employ signal reinforcement by lip reading, but otherwise there seems to be little advantage in knowing the desired speaker's location. Presbyacusis tends to present as a progressively increasing loss towards the higher frequencies, but in practice the major speech-formants are often detectable by SHL sufferers even at the SNRs which cause intelligibility problems. It is around these formant frequencies that lateralization has been shown to depend more on interaural time difference (ITD) than interaural level difference (ILD), with ITD being more the dominant lateralization cue when both are available [7]. This suggests that failure to lateralize acoustically is not the main culprit in depressing intelligibility [5]. Carhart et al [8] also demonstrated for normal hearing subjects that the "capacity to recognize a sound and attribute an azimuth location ... is distinct from the capacity to achieve intelligibility for speech under various interaural conditions.

SHL is typically manifested in experiments as a broadening of the auditory bandpass filters which can be viewed as reducing spectral contrast. However results of processing that attempt to improve spectral contrast [9] tend to support an earlier study's conclusion "that speech selectivity, by itself, is not a major factor for speech recognition in background noise with hearing impaired subjects".

1.3 Binaural Processing: Lateralization and Unmasking

Binaural information can be used to deemphasize an undesired signal dependent on its binaural correlation properties, as demonstrated by the binaural unmasking effect, which can lower the hearing threshold. This noise cancellation by contralateral inhibition appears located at the auditory brainstem and there is evidence to suggest it may operate in sub-bands [10].

Binaural hearing has been found superior to monaural at maintaining the intelligibility of speech in the presence of reverberation, continuous speech shaped noise, or competing connected speech.

Several researchers (e.g. [10]) have confirmed the involvement of interaural correlation in binaural unmasking. However, the masking release has been found to be independent of the pattern of interaural correlations across frequency, and masking release may not be supported by source segregation through grouping of frequency components with common ITD [11].

To summarize, unilateral or bilateral SHL can seriously degrade the intelligibility of speech in the everyday complex acoustic-environment containing noise, particularly competing speakers, and medium to high reverberation. This is in spite of considerable redundancy in speech, the presence of many contextual cues, knowledge of the location of the speaker from residual hearing, vision or other means; and in those with a unilateral hearing deficiency, the ability to exploit monaurally the full spectral content of the signals [5]. In addition, there also exists the absence of a link between the ability to lateralize sources and the ability to reject undesired signals.

Since lateralization is not necessary for effective binaural masking release, an obvious question arises: how can correlation aid binaural unmasking if not used for grouping ITD? According to Campbell [5], one possibility could be that sub-band signals are grouped for selective processing dependent on their *degree* of interaural correlation rather than their ITD value. This suggests that the main enhancement advantage of binaural unmasking may be in the ability to perform binaural unmasking possibly as an adaptive noise cancellation process operating in frequency sub-bands.

Adaptive noise cancellation (ANC) is an operation at least superficially analogous to binaural unmasking. It has structural similarities to the sub-band and cancellation (EC) model proposed by Durlach [12] to explain binaural unmasking. The performance of noise cancellation schemes improves with the accuracy of the noise estimate, and thus tends to yield greater improvements at low SNR. Speech signal energy is low in the high frequency range (such as unvoiced speech) and a noise cancellation. An engineering implementation sub-band adaptive noise cancellation offers the possibility of performing "binaural unmasking" out with the human body, providing signals of improved SNR to the better ear, a conventional aid or a cochlear implant processor. It is likely that the ability to exploit adaption, intermittency, channel modeling, and lateral inhibition will be necessary features.

2 Multi-microphone Sub-band Adaptive (MMSBA) Processing

Over the past two decades, numerous researchers have looked to the human-auditory system as a source of engineering-models for the speech enhancement problem, e.g. Ghitza [13] modelling the cochlea and Cheng and O'Shaughnessy [14] modeling lateral-inhibition effects. A recurring feature in this growing body of work is the accepted model of the cochlea as a spectrum-analyser, which splits incoming signals into a large number of band-limited (sub-band) signals prior to further processing. In reverberant environments, it is also expected that some spectral components of the received signal will be boosted more than others due to constructive and destructive interference caused by changes in phase between the ears [5]. It is therefore possible that that there may be some frequency bands which contain no signal power or noise power. Thus, it would seem advantageous to split any incoming signals into a number of band-limited components prior to processing, as this will enable the use of parallel, diverse sub-processing. If it can be determined that one particular band-limited signal contains no intelligible speech information, then that particular frequency component can simply be blocked. On the other hand, if a particular band-limited signal contains little or no noise that could significantly degrade the intelligibility of the speech signal, then that particular component can be passed through without any processing. If both speech and noise are present, then a decision can be made based on for example, the signal-to-noise ratio, the correlation, coherence information or some other criteria, as to which particular noise cancellation scheme will prove most effective for that particular frequency sub-band.

In engineering systems, sub-band approaches combined with multi-microphone methods have been found to be useful in compensating for reverberation, and speech/noise spectral overlap especially due to interfering speech. Sub-band based speech-recognizers have also been shown to offer a number of practical advantages over classical speech recognizers [15][16]. Smith [17] suggests that spike-based systems may have additional advantages for grouping sounds across frequency bands, and such spike-based systems have received considerable interest recently.

It is well-known that the non-stationarity of many everyday sound sources and the effects of room acoustics further complicates the enhancement problem. Humans may invoke short-term adaptation (Darwin et al. [4]), to compensate for these. Thus an effective speech enhancement processing system should incorporate adaptation to compensate for changing noise-fields due e.g., to non-Gaussian sources, source/sensor motion, or time-varying acoustic-paths.

Environmental reflections of acoustic-energy are dependent on the geometry and materials of the reflecting structures and the relative locations of the sound sources and receivers [18], and a high-correlation exists between the acoustic transfer-function of the environment and -speech intelligibility. Correlation between signals from two-microphones within an average echoic room varies with frequency [19], and studies using automobile noise [20][21] have found that the long-term correlation of the noise signal at two-microphone locations was high for frequencies below 500Hz, and decreased gradually with virtually 0 above 2kHz. The adaptive system used by Wallace and Goubran [22] applied the Widrow's classical (wide-band) multi-sensor linear Finite-Impulse Response (FIR) filter (also sometimes known as the Least Mean Squares (LMS) filter) as a correlated noise-canceller to recorded automobile noise and obtained significant noise-reduction in the low-frequency range, but at high frequencies where both the correlation and noise energy were low, the noise increased, implying that processing appropriate in one sub-band may not be so in another. We therefore propose an adaptive-approach using diverse processing in frequency (sub)-bands, with the required sub-band processing being identified from features of the sub-band signals from the multiple-sensors. We call this a multi-microphone sub-band adaptive (MMSBA) system.

The assessment of a speech-enhancement scheme should place emphasis on a quantitative analysis of the improvement in terms of intelligibility, rather than on SNR improvement or speech-transmission index [21]. In the everyday complex noisy environment, simple linear or adaptive filtering approaches, and monophonic approaches such as spectral subtraction and spectral contrast enhancement have had only limited success in demonstrating improved intelligibility. For example, an evaluation of processing based on spectral-subtraction [23] was unable to demonstrate any benefit to normal or hearing-impaired listeners. Kollmeier et al [24] reported a binaural frequency-domain processing technique related to spectral subtraction and beamforming approaches, however the subjective-assessment by hearing-impaired listeners did not demonstrate an unequivocal improvement in speech-intelligibility in reverberant surroundings. Processing that attempts to improve spectral-contrast [9] has also not resulted in unequivocal benefit and has been criticized as being at odds with the action of amplitude compression. A recent study by Moore et al [25] using elderly subjects with moderate to severe cochlear hearing loss, has concluded that fast-acting multi-channel compression amplification can improve the ability to understand speech in background sounds with spectral and temporal dips, but it does not restore performance to normal. Altered spectra (e.g. spectral tilt, coloration) and processing artifacts (e.g. musical tones, misadjustment noise) are limitations of many of the present methods.

Signal-processing research into improving intelligibility of noisy-speech has taken various approaches e.g. beamforming, spectral-modification, or binaural noise-reduction [26-29]. These methods have had various degrees of success e.g. Soede et al [26] demonstrated an overall SNR improvement of 7dB, Le Bouquin et al [28] obtained a 10-12dB improvement, and Abutalebi et al. [29] employed sub-band Weiner filtering for the monaural case to achieve some SNR improvements. An important point to note is that all of these reported improvements were verified using informal listening tests. Dabis et al. [30] also used closely spaced microphones in a full-band adaptive noise cancellation scheme involving the identification of a differential acoustic path transfer-function during a noise only period in intermittent speech. A Multi-Microphone Sub-Band Adaptive (MMSBA) speech enhancement system inspired by certain features of early auditory processing modeling, such as cochlear mechanical filtering and binaural 'unmasking', has been described which extends this method by applying it within a set of linearly or non-linearly spaced sub-bands provided by a filter-bank [21][31][32]. In pilot studies, this non-optimised *linear* MMSBA scheme incorporating linear Finite Impulse Response (FIR) based sub-band filters, has shown the potential to yield up to 20dB signal-to-noise ratio (SNR) improvements over conventional wide-band (linear FIR filtering based) methods in real-reverberant room & automobile environments. Recent pilot experiments using normal and hearing-impaired human-listeners and real-noisy reverberated speech have demonstrated statistically-significant improvements in intelligibility & perceived-quality [21][31][32].

Preliminary experiments [33][34] with a similar structure but incorporating relatively low-complexity artificial neural networks (ANN) as novel non-linear sub-band processing elements (the overall structure termed *non-linear* MMSBA processing scheme) show significantly improved relative SNR performance (verified by informal listening tests) over the conventional linear MMSBA and wide-band schemes in a real reverberant automobile-environment. The superior performance of the non-linear MMSBA scheme is attributed to the incorporated ANN based sub-band filters which are better capable of taking account of the non-Gaussian nature of speech and non-linear distortions in electro-acoustic transmission systems. The non-linear MMSBA framework attempts to conceptually combine cochlear mechanical filtering (performed in the auditory periphery), with a form of neural-network sub-band processing to approximate the neural-circuits in the auditory brainstem. Additionally, the proposed non-linear MMSBA structure is capable of supporting more complex cross-band & cross-channel interactions, which mimic human lateral-inhibition effects, which need investigation. Note that, whilst the preliminary reported results to-date on the non-linear MMSBA scheme must be taken with care, they do give interesting information on the capabilities of such methods, as well as the enhancement brought about by the new scheme. Further development and extensive testing through formal subjective assessment using listening and intelligibility tests with additional real data is now proposed, as is a detailed theoretical analysis for defining the attainable performance.

Also note that the developed MMSBA schemes assume noisy speech input to both (or all) system sensors, in contrast to the practically restrictive 'classical' full-band multi-microphone speech enhancement schemes, where speech signal occurs only at the primary input sensor [33]. This makes the MMSBA based solutions more attractive for practical realization and extends the range of applications in which it can be employed. However an effective method for detecting noise-only periods is assumed available within the MMSBA schemes. In this paper, we propose the use of a recently developed fast and robust three-level binary Higher Order Statistics (HOS)-based VAD algorithm within the MMSBA schemes [35]. The proposed scheme can give not just voiced/unvoiced detection but also simultaneous pitch estimation of speech signals using the normalized autocorrelation of the one-dimensional (1D) slice of the third-order cumulants that can work satisfactorily in low SNR environments

Also, in this paper, the novel use of post-Wiener filtering (WF) within the non-linear MMSBA scheme is also investigated, in order to more effectively deal with residual incoherent noise components that may result from application of the conventional non-linear MMSBA scheme (without WF). This preliminary work also extends that recently reported in [29] where a *linear* sub-band adaptive noise-cancellation scheme utilizing WF was developed for the *monaural* case. Performance of the two proposed *hybrid* non-linear MMSBA (incorporating post-WF) schemes is compared with the stand-alone non-linear MMSBA scheme (without WF) both quantitatively and qualitatively using informal subjective listening tests, for the case of a real anechoic speech signal corrupted with simulated noise, and initial results appear promising.

The rest of this paper is organized as follows: the proposed HOS based VAD is presented in section 2.1. The non-linear MMSBA schemes incorporating WF are then described in section 2.2, including the choice of neural-network based Sub-band Processing (SBP), post-Weiner Filtering theory, details of the diverse SBP options available to the designer, and the adaptive correlation metric (CM) developed for selecting the appropriate SBP option. In section 3, preliminary simulation results are used to demonstrate the effectiveness of the proposed approach. Finally, some future work directions are presented in section 4.

2.1 New HOS-Based Identification of Noise-Alone/Silence Periods for MMSBA Schemes

Accurate and reliable voiced/unvoiced detection of a speech signal and associated pitch period estimation for the voiced part are crucial preprocessing steps in many speech-processing applications such as adaptive speech enhancement (e.g. MMSBA schemes [21]) and are essential in most analysis and synthesis (vocoder) systems. These include automatic detection of the beginning and ending of an utterance in a long recording, speech segmentation, and automatic isolated word recognition (AIWR) [35]. The effect of wrongly selecting a pitch period is very significant in coders where no memory is used in pitch modelling. Many algorithms have been reported in the literature for separately solving the voiced/unvoiced detection and pitch estimation using second-order statistics such as autocorrelation, cepstrum, and average magnitude difference function (AMDF).

A common problem with these second-order based algorithms is that they are sensitive to various noises. In addition, traditional voiced/unvoiced speech detectors have used other criteria, such as periodicity, coherence function, energy and zero crossing, or a mixture of techniques [35]. These criteria, however, only work well with certain types of noises. There has been increasing interest in using higher order statistics (HOS) in speech analysis, due to this method's immunity to various noises. The growing demand for digital signal processing of speech in noisy environments such as rotating machine environments and mobile communication environments requires the use of powerful algorithms to combat such noises from various environments. Third-order statistics have superior performance in suppressing various noises and are particularly insensitive to all Gaussian noises and sinusoidal and car noise due to their symmetrical probability density function. Hence, the problem of degradation in processing the speech signal due to noise is greatly minimized. Third-order statistics of a voice speech signal has been shown to have nonzero value due to the presence of quadratic harmonic coupling produced by the vocal tract. These results suggest the use of the third-order statistics speech signal rather than the more computationally demanding fourth-order statistics for the speech signal.

A main concern in using HOS in practice is the excessive computation involved in its estimation. HOS has been applied to speech signals for pitch determination using autocorrelation of the third-order cumulants. This algorithm requires a preprocessing stage to eliminate the unvoiced part and keep only the voiced part. Also, it suffers from pitch period error such as pitch doubling or pitch halving. A new fast and robust three-level binary HOS-based algorithm for simultaneous voiced/unvoiced detection and pitch estimation of speech signals has recently been described in [35] using the normalized autocorrelation of the one-dimensional (1D) slice of the third-order cumulants that can work satisfactorily in low SNR environments.

2.1.1 The Three-Level Binary NACC Algorithm

The three-level binary HOS-based detection and estimation system is now described. The noisy speech signal $s_1(n)$ is segmented into overlapping frames. The system uses centre clipping and infinite peak clipping as a nonlinear spectrum flattening on the speech signal to remove the spectral shaping in the waveform due to the formants [35]. This will have the effect of destroying the formant information associated with the vocal tract and retaining only the information on periodicity. This process makes the periodicity of the speech signal much easier to measure, and hence eliminates the chance of erroneous decision. Centre clipping suppresses the signal between certain levels, and what is not suppressed starts from zero level. For each frame a clipping threshold is computed as follows:

$$Cl = K \min[Cl_1, Cl_2] \tag{1}$$

High-level clipping enhances the periodicity of the speech signal; however, it may result in much of the signal being lost when the amplitude signal varies considerably during the speech segment. Hence, clipping threshold has a key roll in the NACC, as it determines the parts of the speech signal used in the algorithm, and should be chosen carefully to prevent loss of waveform information during a transition from voiced to unvoiced and vice versa, or when a low voiced part is present. From computer simulations an appropriate value for K is found to be 0.2; Cl_1 and Cl_2 are the maximum amplitude in the first and last third of the frame, respectively. The speech signal is centre clipped and infinite peak clipped to produce a three-level binary signal of -1, 0, +1 depending on the relation of the original speech sample to the clipping thresholds as follows:

$$\chi(n) = \begin{cases} 1 & if \quad s_1(n) \geq Cl \\ -1 & if \quad s_1(n) \leq -Cl \\ 0 & otherwise \end{cases} \tag{2}$$

where $s_1(n)$ is a frame of the speech signal $s(n)$. As the 1D slice of the third-order cumulants is defined as:

$$c_3(\tau_1) = E[x(n)x(n)x(n + \tau_1)] \tag{3}$$

each combination in (3) can assume the following three-level binary values:

$$x(n)x(n + \tau_1)x(n + \tau_1) = \begin{cases} 0 & if \quad \{x(n) = 0, \\ & or \quad if \quad x(n + \tau_1) = 0\} \\ 1 & if \quad x(n) = 1 \\ -1 & if \quad x(n) = -1 \end{cases} \tag{4}$$

Thus, a simple combinatorial logic circuit is required only in computing each term in the third-order cumulant and an up-down counter to accumulate the actual third-order cumulant value of (3). The three-level binary HOS-based detection and estimation system uses a normalized autocorrelation function of the 1D slice of the third-order cumulants NACC defined as:

$$N\ ACC(\tau_2) = \left[\frac{\sum_{n=0}^{N-1} c_3(n)c_3(n + \tau_2)}{\sqrt{\sum_{n=0}^{N-1} c_3^2(n + \tau_2)}} \right]^2 \tag{5}$$

The system carries out simultaneous voiced/unvoiced detection and pitch period estimation for the voiced part. For each frame the peak value of the NACC is extracted and compared to a threshold. If the NACC peak value exceeds the threshold level the frame is classified as a voiced frame; otherwise the frame is classified as unvoiced. The pitch is estimated from the voiced frame directly from the positions where the NACC has its maximum peak value in its first half. Any peak picking algorithm can be used for this purpose [35].

To summarize, a fast and robust three-level binary higher order statistics (HOS) based algorithm has been presented in this section for simultaneous voiced/unvoiced detection and pitch estimation of speech signals in colored noise environments with low SNR. The use of the three-level binary speech signals dramatically reduces the computational effort required in evaluating the higher order cumulants. The superior performance of the new algorithm over the conventional autocorrelation method using real speech signals has been demonstrated by Soraghan and Hussain et al. recently using a range of real-world signals in [35]. The proposed algorithm can easily be implemented in digital hardware using simple combinatorial logic.

2.2 Distribution of Sub-bands in New Hybrid MMSBA Schemes Incorporating Weiner Filtering

Two or more relatively closely spaced microphones may be used in an adaptive noise cancellation scheme [31] to identify a differential acoustic-path transfer function during a noise only period in intermittent speech. The extension of this work, termed the Multi-Microphone sub-band Adaptive (MMSBA) speech enhancement system, applies the method within a set of sub-bands provided by a filter bank. The filter bank can be implemented using various orthogonal transforms or by a parallel filter bank approach. In this work, the sub-bands are distributed non-linearly according to a co-chlear distribution, as in humans, following the Greenwood [36] model, in which the spacing of the sub-band filters is given by:

$$F(x) = A(10^{ax} - k) \text{ Hz} \qquad (6)$$

where x is the proportional distance from 0 to 1 along the cochlear membrane and $F(x)$ are the upper and lower cut-off frequencies for each filter obtained by the limit-ing value of x. For the human cochlea, values of $A=165.4$, $a=2.1$ and $k=0.88$ are rec-ommended and chosen here.

The conventional *linear* MMSBA approach has been shown to considerably im-prove the mean squared error (MSE) convergence rate of an adaptive multi-band linear FIR filter compared to both the conventional wideband time-domain and fre-quency domain FIR filters [21][31][32]. The use of a cochlear distribution of the sub-band filters as above, has also been shown to result in an equalized power distribution across the sub-bands (for the case of speech signals), resulting in further improved sub-band filter convergence compared to the case of linearly distributed sub-band filters [21,31]. The recently developed *non-linear* MMSBA scheme incorporating neural network based non-linear FIR (NLFIR) sub-band filtering is depicted in Figure 1, which is a further extension of the linear MMSBA approach, and has been shown to offer further performance benefits in preliminary studies [33,34].

Note that as depicted in Figure 1, it is again assumed in this work that: the speaker is close enough to the microphones so that room acoustic effects on the speech are insignificant, that the noise signal at the microphones may be modelled as a point source modified by two different acoustic path transfer functions H_1, H_2, and that an effective HOS based voice activity detector (VAD) is available (as in Figure 1).

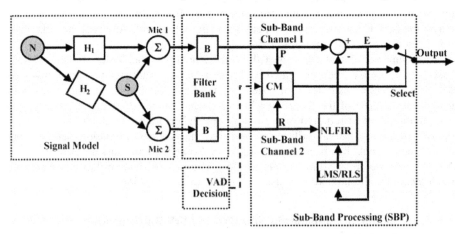

Fig. 1. Non-linear MMSBA scheme without WF

In the proposed *hybrid* non-linear MMSBA architecture shown in Figure 2, post-Weiner Filtering (WF) operation can be applied in two different ways: at the output of each sub-band processor (SBP), as shown in Figure 2a(i), or at the global output of the non-linear MMSBA scheme as shown in Figure 2a(ii). In the rest of this paper, the new non-linear MMSBA scheme employing WF in the sub-bands is termed *MMSBA-WF*, whereas the proposed non-linear MMSBA scheme employing wide-band (WB) WF is termed *MMSBA-WBWF* respectively.

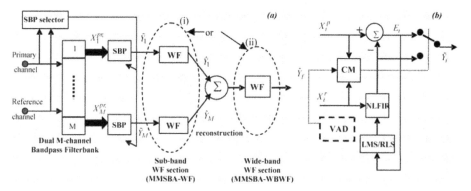

Fig. 2. (a): New hybrid non-linear MMSBA systems incorporating post-Weiner Filtering (WF) in the form of: (i) MMSBA-WF, or, (ii) MMSBA-WBWF configuration, (b): Sub-band Processing (SBP) configurations

In both the proposed hybrid architectures illustrated in Figure 2, the role of post-WF is to further mitigate the residual noise effects on the original signal to be recovered, following application of conventional non-linear MMSBA noise-cancellation processing. The next sub-sections discuss: the non-linear Artificial Neural Network (ANN) based NLFIR filters used in SBP together with the new post-WF extensions, the choice of diverse SBP options and finally the Correlation Metric (CM) used for selecting the appropriate SBP option.

2.3   Artificial Neural Network (ANN) Based Nonlinear SBP

A class of general adaptive non-linear FIR (NLFIR) type filters based on single hidden-layered linear-in-the-parameters ANNs is described in [33][34] for processing the band-limited signals in a multi-band speech enhancement system.

The general structure of the NLFIR type filter is based on single-hidden layered, linear-in-the-parameters feedforward ANNs, as shown in Figure 3. It employs an input expander which transforms the n inputs $[x_1,..., x_n]$ (representing lagged values of the sub-band input signal x passed through a tapped delay line of order $(n$-$1))$ into a non-linear intermediate (hidden) space of increased dimension N. The expanded input terms (termed the basis functions) are then weighted and linearly combined to form the adaptive filter output y. The overall mapping of the adaptive NLFIR is thus $R^n \rightarrow R^N \rightarrow R$.

The advantage of this particular non-linear filter structure is that linear adaptive filter theory can be readily applied for on-line adaptation [34]. The non-linear expansion model is completely general and can employ any of the non-linear basis functions commonly employed in e.g. the Radial Basis Function (RBF) neural networks, such as the thin-plate spline basis functions, multi-quadratic activation functions, the inverse multi-quadratic functions, or indeed the widely used Gaussian basis functions.

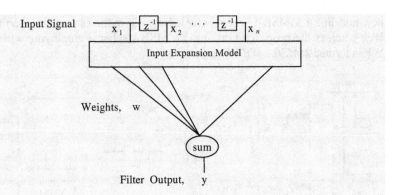

Fig. 3. General structure of the proposed neural-network based adaptive non-linear FIR (NLFIR) type Filter used in SBP (Figure 2.b above)

Alternatively, the sigmoidal basis functions employed in Multi-Layered Perceptron (MLP) networks, or the Volterra (polynomial) expansion employed in the hidden layer of the conventional Volterra Neural Network (VNN) can also be employed. Another possibility described in [33] includes the *hybrid* functional-expansion employed in a recently developed Functionally-Expanded Neural Network (FENN), which is a variant of the conventional Functional-Link Neural-Network. The FENN expansion model comprises a *combination* of sigmoidal-shaped, Gaussian-shaped and polynomial-subset activation (basis) functions, and an additional benefit of this approach (like the VNN's polynomial-expansion) is that the use of the original network inputs within the expansion model, also enables efficient modeling of linear dynamical transfer-functions.

As discussed in [34], the choice of an appropriate non-linear expansion-model is, in general, problem dependent. For example, it has been shown that some problems such as functional approximation can be solved more efficiently with the sigmoidal-type basis functions employed in the MLP; while others such as classification problems are more amenable to localized (e.g. Gaussian-type) basis functions employed in the RBF. However, all the above expansion-models are known to be *universal approximators* as they can approximate any non-linear function to an arbitrary degree of accuracy.

Further details on the choice of an appropriate expansion model can be found in [33][34] where it has been argued that the relative performance-complexity trade-off for the non-linear models needs to be determined for each specific problem. However in practice, the simple polynomial expansion-model employed in the VNN is attractive since it requires relatively low-complexity hardware for implementation. In this paper, we shall restrict our choice of the NLFIR filter's expansion-model to be polynomial, that is:

$$\mathbf{f(x)} = [1 \, , x_{i1} \, , x_{i1} \, x_{i2} \, , \ldots , x_{i1} \, x_{i2}...x_{ik}] \qquad (7)$$

where $i\gamma = 1,..., n$ for $\gamma=1,...,k$ with k representing a k-th order polynomial expansion of the n (sub-band) filter inputs; and $\mathbf{f}(.)=[f_1 ... f_N]$ are the N non-linear basis functions.

Once the full expansion-model $\mathbf{f(x)}$ at the single hidden-layer of the ANN based NLFIR filter has been specified, conventional stochastic-gradient or least-squares based adaptation algorithms (such as the LMS, RLS or their robust versions) can then be used to provide an efficient means for real-time adaptation of the filter weights $\mathbf{W}$, as shown in Figures 2.b and 3 This will give these non-linear FIR filters a significant advantage over multi-layered (MLP type) neural-network based filters in recursive applications. Further details on the choice of adaptation algorithms for the ANN based NLFIR sub-band filters can be found in [33][34].

For the derivation of the post-WF theory in the next section, we now define $\tilde{X}_j, \tilde{S}_j, \tilde{N}_j$ as the global output, the reconstructed signal and the residual noise component at the j-th SBP output (or, equivalently, the adaptive NLFIR noise-canceller output of j band) respectively, as shown in Figure 2a. The following relationship can be assumed to hold due to noise and the desired signal at each band being uncorrelated:

$$\tilde{X}_j = \tilde{S}_j + \tilde{N}_j \tag{8}$$

In the original non-linear MMSBA (without WF), all $\tilde{x}_j$ sub-band NLFIR noise canceller outputs are summed (at the reconstruction section) to yield the global MMSBA output $\tilde{y}$, which can be expressed in the frequency domain as:

$$\tilde{Y} = \sum_j \tilde{S}_j + \sum_j \tilde{N}_j = \tilde{S} + \tilde{N} \tag{9}$$

2.4 Post-Wiener Filtering (WF)

The coefficients of a Wiener filter (WF) [37] are calculated to minimise the average squared distance between the filter output and a desired signal, assuming stationarity of the involved signals. This can be easily achieved in the frequency domain yielding:

$$W(f) = \left(P_{DY}(f) / P_{YY}(f) \right) \tag{10}$$

where $D(f)$ is the desired signal, $\hat{S}(f) = W(f)Y(f)$ is the Wiener filter output, $Y(f)$ the Wiener filter input and $P_{YY}(f)$, $P_{DY}(f)$ are the power spectrum of $Y(f)$ and the cross power spectrum of $Y(f)$, $D(f)$ respectively. If we apply such a solution to the case where the global signal is given by addition of noise and signal (to be recovered), and moving from the assumption that noise, signal are uncorrelated (as $\tilde{S}_j, \tilde{N}_j$ are) we can derive the following:

$$W_j(f) = \left(P_{\tilde{S}_j \tilde{S}_j}(f) / P_{\tilde{S}_j \tilde{S}_j}(f) + P_{\tilde{N}_j \tilde{N}_j}(f) \right) \tag{11}$$

where $P_{\tilde{S}_j \tilde{S}_j}(f)$, $P_{\tilde{N}_j \tilde{N}_j}(f)$ are the signal and noise power spectra. Note that, in this task, the desired signal is $\tilde{S}_j$. It must be observed that such a formulation can be easily extended to the case when involved signals are not stationary, by simply periodically recalculating the filter coefficients for every block l of N_s signal samples. In this way the filter adapts itself to the average characteristics of the signals within the blocks and becomes block-adaptive.

Moreover, the presence of a VAD (in the MMSBA) is a pre-requisite to making the Wiener filtering operation effective: in noise alone period, a precise estimation of noise power spectrum can be performed and then used in (11), assuming that its properties are still the same when the signal power spectrum is calculated during the noisy speech period. The former approximation is carried out iteratively by using the power spectrum of the Wiener filter global output $\hat{S}_j(f)$.

Note that the above WF derivations are readily applicable to the hybrid MMSBA-WF architecture as follows. Similar to (8) and (9), the following holds at the j-th band Wiener filter output:

$$\hat{X}_j = \hat{S}_j + \hat{N}_j$$
$$\hat{Y} = \sum_j \hat{S}_j + \sum_j \hat{N}_j = \hat{S} + \hat{N} \qquad (12)$$

where $\hat{y}$ is the new global output resulting from the reconstruction section.

Finally, the same considerations can be made when the hybrid MMSBA-WBWF structure is dealt with, simply adapting the above equations to the new situation where WF occurs after the reconstruction section. Specifically, taking (9) into account, implies:

$$\hat{Y}_f = W_f \tilde{Y} = \hat{S}_f + \hat{N}_f \qquad (13)$$

where f indicates full-band processing, since WF operation is applied directly to non-linear MMSBA output $\tilde{y}$ to form the new Wiener filtered output $\hat{y}_f$. Next, the choice of various non-linear SBP options available to the MMSBA designer, are discussed.

2.5 Diverse SBP Options

A significant advantage of using SBP for non-linear MMSBA speech enhancement is that it allows independent processing in each sub-band in an attempt to cancel the dominant noise components, coherent or non-coherent, present in each sub-band. The SBP can be accomplished in a number of ways (as depicted in Figure 2b), for example:

1. *No Processing:* Examine the noise power in a sub-band and if below (or the SNR above) some arbitrary threshold, then the signal in that band need not be modified.

2. *Intermittent Coherent Noise Canceller:* If the noise power is significant and the noise between the two channels is significantly correlated in a sub-band, then perform adaptive intermittent noise cancellation, wherein the adaptive NLFIR filter may be determined which models the differential acoustic-path transfer function between the microphones during the "noise-alone" period. This can then be used in a noise cancellation format during the speech plus noise period (assuming short term constancy) to process the noisy speech signal. This scheme (illustrated in Figure 1) can be described mathematically as follows:

Assuming N, S, P, R represent the z-transforms of the noise signal, speech signal, primary signal and reference signal, respectively. The primary and reference signals in each sub-band are thus:

$$P = B(S + H_1 N) \; ; \; R = B(S + H_2 N) \tag{14}$$

The transformed error signal is thus,

$$E = B[(1 - H_3)S + (H_1 - H_3 H_2)N] \tag{15}$$

which is a frequency domain error, weighted by the band-limiting transfer function B, and H_3 represents the sub-band NLFIR adaptive filter. The Mean Squared Error function is:

$$J_E = (2\pi j)^{-1} \oint_{|z|=1} E.E^* z^{-1} dz \tag{16}$$

The sub-band noise cancellation problem is thus, to find an H_3 such that within the sub-band defined by B, the variance of J_E is minimised. During a noise only period $S = 0$, defining the noise spectral density Φ_{nn}, then

$$J_E = (2\pi j)^{-1} \oint_{|z|=1} B(H_1 - H_3 H_2)\Phi_{nn}(H_1 - H_3 H_2)^* B^* z^{-1} dz \tag{17}$$

which is minimised in the least squares sense when

$$H_3 = (BH_1)(BH_2)^{-1} \tag{18}$$

That is, H_3 is (an NLFIR estimated) band-limited transfer function that minimises the noise power in E. Now using H_3 as a fixed non-linear processing filter when speech and noise are present ideally gives:

$$E = B(1 - H_3)S \tag{19}$$

where the (sub-band intermittent coherent noise-canceller) output E is a noise reduced, filtered version of the sub-band speech signal S. This approach will fail if: $H_1 = H_2$, however in practical situations such acoustic path balancing is difficult to achieve.

3. Non-coherent Noise Canceller: If the noise power is significant but not highly correlated between the two channels in a sub-band, then the non-coherent noise cancellation approach of Ferrara and Widrow (FW) [38] may be applied here during the noisy speech period. Since in this case, the primary signal noise component $BH_1 N$ is uncorrelated with the reference signal noise component $BH_2 N$, the filtered reference (output of NLFIR) is now an estimate of the sub-band speech signal S.

In this paper, we employ the above three SBP options and implement the adaptive sub-band processing using neural network based NLFIR type filters together with post-WF as described earlier. In the next section, we describe a metric for selecting the appropriate type of SBP option.

2.6 Correlation Metric (CM) for Selecting SBP

The Magnitude Squared Coherence (MSC) has been used by Bouquin and Faucon [39] who have applied it for the reduction of noise in speech signals and have also employed it as a Voice Activity Detector (VAD) for the case of spatially uncorrelated noises. In this work, we employ the MSC within a Correlation Metric (CM), as a part of a system for selecting an appropriate SBP option in the non-linear MMSBA speech enhancement system. Assuming that the speech and noise signals are independent, the observations received by the two microphones, as shown in Figure 2, may be written as:

Assuming that the speech and noise signals are independent, the observations received by the two microphones are:

$$x_p = s_p + n_p \quad primary; \qquad x_r = s_r + n_r \quad reference \qquad (20)$$

where $s_{p,r}$, $n_{p,r}$ represent the clean speech signal and the additive noise, respectively. For each block l and frequency bin f_k, the coherence function is given by:

$$\rho(f_k,l) = \frac{P_{X_p X_r}(f_k,l)}{\sqrt{P_{X_p X_p}(f_k,l)P_{X_r X_r}(f_k,l)}} \qquad (21)$$

where $P_{X_p X_r}(f_k,l)$ is the cross-power spectral density, $P_{X_p X_p}(f_k,l)$ and $P_{X_r X_r}(f_k,l)$ are the auto-power spectral densities; which can be estimated by:

$$P_{X_p X_r}(f_k,l) = \beta P_{X_p X_r}(f_k,l-1) + (1-\beta)X_p(f_k,l)X_r^*(f_k,l) \qquad (22)$$

where β is a forgetting factor. During the noise alone period, for each overlapped and Hanning windowed block l we compute the Magnitude Squared Coherence (MSC) averaged over all the overlapped blocks (at each frequency bin) as:

$$\overline{MSC}(f_k) = \frac{1}{l}\sum_{i=1}^{l}\left[\rho(f_k,i)\right]^2 \qquad (23)$$

Finally the correlation metric (CM) is estimated for each linear or cochlear spaced sub-band s (over the appropriate frequency range f_p to f_q Hz) as:

$$CM(s) = \sum_{k=p}^{q} \overline{MSC}(f_k) \qquad (24)$$

The above CM can thus be used as a means for determining the level of correlation between the disturbing noise sources within each sub-band during the "noise-alone" period in intermittent speech. On the basis of this CM, the subsequent form of NLFIR and post-Weiner filtering based processing in each respective frequency band can be selected as either the intermittent-coherent noise canceller or the non-coherent FW type noise canceller, provided the absolute and relative sub-band noise powers are above an experimentally determined threshold.

3 Simulation Results

In this section the two new hybrid non-linear MMSBA-based WF approaches are compared to the original non-linear MMSBA approach (without WF) in order to investigate their relative effectiveness. For experimental purposes, a real anechoic speech signal $s(k)$ is used as the desired signal, whilst the noise signals $n_1(k), n_2(k)$ are chosen to be real stereo car noise sequences recorded in a Ferrari Mondial T (1991

Model), using an Audio Technica AT9450 stereo microphone mounted on a SONY DCR-PC3-NTSC video camera and a sampling frequency of 44.1 kHz. The noise sequences were manually added to the anechoic speech sentence to manufacture different SNR cases.

The value of the initial SNR, namely SNR_i, is used as a reference for the three SNR improvements calculated at the output of each of the speech enhancement structures under study, namely: the original non-linear MMSBA without WF (Figure 1), the new hybrid MMSBA-WF (Figure 2a(i)) and the hybrid MMSBA-WBWF (Figure 2a(ii)). Taking into account the non-correlation between noise and signal on the same channel, we can define the SNR at the output level as:

$$SNR_o(f) = \begin{cases} \left[P_{\tilde{Y}\tilde{Y}}(f) - P_{\tilde{N}\tilde{N}}(f)\right] \Big/ P_{\tilde{N}\tilde{N}}(f) \\ \left[P_{\hat{Y}\hat{Y}}(f) - P_{\hat{N}\hat{N}}(f)\right] \Big/ P_{\hat{N}\hat{N}}(f) \\ \left[P_{\hat{Y}_f\hat{Y}_f}(f) - P_{\hat{N}_f\hat{N}_f}(f)\right] \Big/ P_{\hat{N}_f\hat{N}_f}(f) \end{cases} \tag{25}$$

where all involved power spectra are related to signals described by (9), (12), and (13).

Moreover it has to be said that $P_{\tilde{N}\tilde{N}}(f)$ is calculated over a sub-range of the noise alone period where noise cancellers are assumed to have converged, since this is the noise power spectrum expected to occur when the desired signal is present. On this basis, $P_{\hat{N}\hat{N}}(f)$ and $P_{\hat{N}_f\hat{N}_f}(f)$ are obtained from Wiener filtered versions for the two new hybrid schemes addressed (MMSBA-WF and MMSBA-WBWF).

In this work, the sub-bands are achieved by modifying the spectra of the FFT of the input signals, and the number of filters is therefore limited by the size of the FFT. The processing in each sub-band is performed using the ANN-based adaptive non-linear FIR-type filters.

Choices for various experimental parameter values were selected on a trial and error basis as: speech-signal number of samples corresponding to a 2s long speech sentence; noise signal number of samples (in the manually defined noise alone period) corresponding to 0.2s of car noise recording; number of iterations of WF operation: 5; number of cochlear-spaced sub-bands: 4; number of taps (order) of VNN-based NLFIR adaptive sub-band filters: 32. A truncated 2nd order polynomial expansion of the sub-band NLFIR filter inputs was employed comprising the actual sub-band filter inputs and their square terms which resulted in a total of 64 terms (basis functions) in each sub-band NLFIR filter.

The following SBP options were compared for each of the three non-linear MMSBA schemes.

3.1 Case (A): Intermittent only SBP

In the first experimental case study, the intermittent coherent noise-canceller approach is employed as the only SBP option in each band. Table 1 summarizes the results obtained using the three non-linear MMSBA approaches: from which it can be seen that the hybrid MMSBA-WF and the hybrid MMSBA-WBWF both deliver an improved SNR performance over the original non-linear MMSBA approach (without WF).

3.2   Case (B): Diverse (Intermittent/FW) SBP

In this case the value of the adaptive CM is used to employ both intermittent and non-coherent (FW) SBP options, with the former option used in the first sub-band (with a high CM) and the latter in the other three bands (with a low CM). This is justified by the coherence characteristics of available stereo noise signal. It can be seen from Table 2 that the choice of sub-band WF (within the hybrid MMSBA-WF scheme) gives the best results in this case, due to its operation in the sub-bands, resulting in more effective noise cancellation in the frequency domain, compared to the hybrid MMSBA-WBWF scheme (employing wide-band WF processing) as well as the conventional non-linear MMSBA (without WF).

Table 1. Case (A): Comparison of various Non-linear MMSBA approaches (all adapted using intermittent SBP only). Relative average SNR improvements for all architectures involved (over 10 runs).Standard deviation values are directly depicted on bars

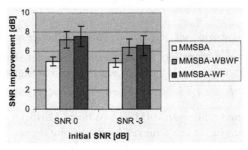

Table 2. Case (B): Comparison of various Non-linear MMSBA approaches all employing diverse (intermittent and non-coherent FW based) SBP. Relative average SNR improvements for all architectures involved (over 10 runs). Standard deviation values are directly depicted on the bars

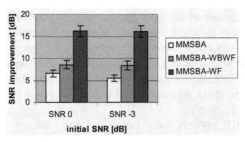

Note that application of the classical linear wide-band noise cancellation approach, namely the MMSBA with number of bands set to one and a wideband linear FIR filter order of 256 (of comparable complexity to the non-linear MMSBA) was actually found to degrade the speech quality resulting in a negative SNR improvement value, which is hence not shown in the Table 1. This finding of the inability of classical wideband processing to enhance the speech in real automobile environments is consistent with the previous results reported in [21][33][34].

Finally, informal listening tests using random presentation of the processed and unprocessed signals to three young male adults of normal hearing, also confirmed the MMSBA-WF processed speech to be both enhanced in SNR and of significantly better perceived quality than that obtained by all the other conventional wide-band and sub-band (non-linear MMSBA) methods.

4   Some Possible Future Research Directions

4.1   MMSBA Factor: Cross-Band and Cross-Channel Interaction Strategies

This is virgin territory requiring fundamental engineering research. Both cross-band and cross-channel interactions are major influences on human-hearing abilities, cross-band effects supporting *spectral sharpening* operations and cross-channel (binaural) effects invoking lateralisation and noise-cancellation to separate desired from unwanted undesired signals. Some investigators [9][14][40] have attempted to employ single-channel/sensor or monaural cross-band spectral sharpening, including the use of neural networks, to mimic the human "lateral inhibition" effects. The results so far are equivocal and this work will investigate cross-band effects with new two-sensor or binaural systems to mimic human lateral inhibition.

One possibility seems to extend the recently reported promising work of [41], who have shown that non-linear masking of a time-space representation of speech can be used to achieve simulated noise suppression for the monaural case, by discarding or masking the undesired (noise) signals and retaining the desired (speech) signals. They have demonstrated that this non-linear masking can enhance single-sensor or monaurally recorded speech by performing non-linear filtering with adaptive thresholding (based on the Teager Energy operator [42]) on a time-frequency (multi-band) representation of the noisy signal. One could extend this non-linear masking to the two-sensor or binaural case within the MMSBA framework, by replacing the FFT/DCT with a Wavelet Transform to achieve a multi-band (multi-scale) decomposition for subsequent non-linear ANN based filtering of the representation, along with adaptive sub-band thresholding. The resulting speech enhancement improvements in real noisy environments could be assessed using formal listening & intelligibility tests on human subjects & results compared with monaural cross-band & binaural MMSBA (without cross-band processing) schemes

4.2   MMSBA Factor: Metrics for Selecting SBP Options

Work towards this important factor of the MMSBA approach can include the use of a theoretical and simulation search for practical metrics and thresholds for automatically selecting the appropriate form of sub-band processing (SBP). Initial possibilities such as the correlation and coherence between sub-band stereo channels have been investigated and reported in this paper. For future work, adaptive HOS metrics (such as based on the bicoherency measure [43]) for detecting linear/non-linear sub-band features may also be used. The development of effective metrics could result in a novel generic MMSBA scheme which would operate effectively in any acoustic-environment, by automatically selecting the appropriate (linear or non-linear) SBP option, the required SBP being identified from features of the sub-band signals from multiple sensors. The developed sub-band features may include a combination of coherence, noise power, relative SNR and bicoherency.

Self-structuring LMS type algorithms [44] for pruning conventional linear FIR filters can also be applied to non-linear MMSBA schemes for adaptively pruning their non-linear FIR type (linearly weighted neural network) filters in real acoustic environments. A range of linear-in-parameters (linearly weighted) ANN functional-models (e.g. Radial-Basis Function (RBF), Functional-Link (FL) and Volterra Network (VN) models) will need to be employed within the non-linear filters, and their relative qualitative and quantitative performance/complexity trade-offs investigated when processing acoustic-signals from real reverberant-noisy environments. The aim would be to determine an optimal ANN functional-model (with the best performance-complexity trade-off) for incorporation in the MMSBA non-linear filters. Since the choice of ANN models can be restricted to single-layered linear-in-parameters type networks, on-line adaptation using computationally-efficient stochastic-gradient (e.g. LMS) or numerically robust Square-Root (or UD factorization) based least squares algorithms could be employed for training the ANN based non-linear FIR-type filters [34]. A new detailed theoretical analysis extending the preliminary analysis reported in this paper also needs to be carried out for defining the attainable (minimum mean squared error) performance of these non-linear MMSBA based noise cancellers.

4.3   Alternative Speech Enhancement Possibilities: Stochastic Resonance

Periodically modulated stochastic processes have been studied intensely over the last two decades under the paradigm of stochastic resonance (SR). Stochastic resonance (SR) is said to occur when a bi-stable nonlinear system is driven by a weak periodic signal, and provision of additional noise improves the system's detection of the periodic signal (see [45] for a review). Here "weak" means that the input signal is so small that when applied alone it is undetected [46]. Experimentally, SR was first demonstrated with a noise driven circuit known as a Schmitt trigger [48]. It took several years before the interest of physicists (who have done most of the theoretical analysis) ignited, sparked by the demonstration of SR in a bi-stable ring-laser experiment [49]. Now SR has crossed disciplinary boundaries: its role in sensory biology has been explored in experiments on single crayfish neurons [47], cat visual cortex [51], cricket cercal sensory system [52], human memory retrieval [53], human visual perception [54] and human hearing [55].

Since its introduction, SR has been shown to occur under many different circumstances, with various types of signals, nonlinear processes, and measures of performance [56]. Most of the literature on SR involves a signal which is it self too weak to elicit a strong response from the nonlinear system. For larger (suprathreshold) signals, SR induced by a single nonlinearity disappears [52]. However it has recently been shown that suprathreshold SR can occur in an array of parallel nonlinear units with independent noise injection where their outputs are summed [57]. Like subthreshold SR, there is an optimal nonzero noise level. The increase in output entropy improves the independence in information transmitted by individual units, giving rise to a net increase in transmitted information, under optimal noise conditions. However, suprathreshold SR cannot be measured using SNR [58].

Stochastic resonance should not be confused with 'dithering' also known as stochastic linearisation, a technique where in periodic or random forcing, noise is intentionally introduced to overcome regions of 'dead' dynamical behaviour in self regulating systems [59]. Dithering is also used in electronic circuits, e.g. CD-players: the digital-analog converter should produce a smooth analog output from a digital "staircase" input. To this end, a little bit of noise is added to the output to smear out the steps.

4.3.1 Measuring Stochastic Resonance

Stochastic resonance can be demonstrated using almost any method of detecting or reconstructing a subthreshold signal from information contained in the crossings of the threshold of a detector by the signal plus noise. SR metrics are chosen according to the nature of the input signals and of the transmission system itself. If the signal is periodic and observed over a relatively long time interval, then it is common to do a Fourier analysis of the crossing times and to measure the information thus gained about the signal as the ratio of the power spectral density (PSD) at the signal frequency to that generated by noise at the nearby frequencies (the signal-to-noise ratio SNR [49]).

Another way to quantify the SR effect, related to the way neural activity is analysed, is to investigate the (empirical) residence-time probability distribution, or interspike interval histogram [60]. If an aperiodic signal is observed over a relatively long time interval, then goodness of signal reconstruction or the coherence between the signal and the output has been measured by a correlation measure [61] and entropy based methods [45].

SR is characterised by improving the measure of dependence of the output on the input by means of an increase in the level of noise. The standard measure of SR has been the SNR of the power spectrum [49]. All spectral quantities, including the SNR, are based on averages over long times. A feature present on average, however, is not necessarily present in a limited sample, such as the record of a single neuron's spike train over the first few hundred milliseconds of its response. Thus the SNR does not in any way address whether the system can reliably perform signal detection based on the spike output of a single neuron over a short duration. More appropriate measures that explicitly depend on the sampling time are ones based on information theory [62]. Recent work on the use of information theoretic measures to characterise stochastic resonance in a neural arrays can be found in the work of [58].

4.3.2 Tools and Techniques of Modeling Stochastic Resonance

The seminal paper by [63] provoked no immediate reaction in the literature. Apart from a few early theoretical studies by [64] and [65], only one experimental paper [48] addressed the phenomenon of stochastic resonance. One reason may be that the simulations required needed faster machines than were easily available to researchers at the time. The experimental article by [66] marked a renaissance of SR, which has developed and flourished ever since in different directions. The present knowledge of SR has been reached through a variety of investigation tools. Here we will outline the most popular ones.

4.3.3 Digital Simulation

The first demonstration of SR was produced by simulating the model of climate change by [63] on a Digital Instruments minicomputer (model PDP 11), an advanced computer at the time. Nowadays accurate digital simulations of either continuous or discrete stochastic processes can be carried out easily on desktop computers. Regardless of the particular algorithm adopted in the diverse cases, digital simulations proved particularly useful in the study of SR in numerous cases.

4.3.4 Analogue Simulation

This type of simulation allows more flexibility than digital simulation and for this reason has been preferred by many researchers as evidenced by the work of [56]. Analogue simulators of stochastic processes are easy to design and assemble [45]. Their results are not as accurate as digital simulations but offer some advantages: (a) a large range of parameter space can be explored rather quickly; and (b) high dimensional systems may be simulated more readily than by computers, though systematic inaccuracies must be estimated and treated carefully. Noise is also not easy to control in analogue systems and their inherent nonlinearities make them difficult to deal with.

4.3.5 Physiological Experiments

To date there are a few experiments where SR has been firmly established in a physiological experiment. [67] report on observing SR in mammalian Hippocampal slices and [50] report on SR being exhibited in the tail fan of a crayfish.

4.3.6 Applications of SR

One of the areas where SR has found application is in the area of speech analysis and recognition. Common sense suggests that noise does not lead to better perception, but rather to interference. Recently, [58] demonstrated that suprathreshold SR improves speech comprehension in patients fitted with cochlear implants. Similar results have been reported in [68]. SR has also been discovered in human vision by [54]. In their study, Mori and Kai shone light signals into the eyes of five students while measuring their electroencephalogram. The researchers shone periodic signals onto the right eyelids and noisy signals onto the left eyelids of the students as they rested, and measured the intensity of their alpha brain waves. They found a sharp peak at 5 Hz, the frequency of the periodic signal. But when they increased the strength of the noise signal relative to the periodic signal, a 'harmonic' peak emerged in the alpha waves at 10 Hz. As the noise signal became stronger, this peak first intensified and then diminished, a feature characteristic of SR.

4.3.7 Summary

Stochastic resonance was loosely defined as a co-operative effect between noise and signal to aid the detection of the signal. It was originally developed to explain the changes in the Earth's climate but has since been extended to explain phenomena in fields such as neuroscience and optics. There are basically two kinds of systems in which SR occurs: bi-stable dynamic systems (systems with two stable states) and excitable systems (systems with a threshold and one stable state). In both cases a clear maximum in the output signal and in the output coherence measure occurs at "tuned" values of the input noise. Neurons are examples of excitable systems. In neuroscience, SR is quantified by interspike interval histograms, power spectrum and signal-to-noise ratio. The tools and techniques used in investigating stochastic resonance in neuroscience range from analogue and digital simulation to actual experimental work. In summary, SR might be a general strategy employed by the central nervous system for the improved detection of weak signals. However, the effects of SR in sensory processing might extend past an improvement in signal detection. As information flows towards progressively more central relay stations, it is handled by systems that might exhibit SR, resulting in improved information processing. This enhancement might start to take place at the earliest stages of processing, as recently suggested by the enhanced vowel coding obtained with the addition of noise to cochlear implants and the amplification of amplitude modulated signals on the auditory nerve fibre by the neurons of the cochlear nucleus. SR seems to take advantage of the natural nonlinearities in speech to give improved hearing to people using cochlear implants.

References

1. Feng, A.S.: Information processing in the auditory brainstem. Current Opinion in Neurobiology. Vol.2. (1992) 511-515
2. Plomp, R. : Auditory handicap of hearing impairment & limited benefit of hearing aids. J. Acoust. Soc. Am. (JASA). Vol.63. (1978) 533-549.
3. Gustaffson, H.A., Arlinger,S.D.: Masking of speech by amplitude modulated noise. J. Acoust. Soc. Am., Vol.95. (1994) 518-529.
4. Darwin C J, McKeown J D, Kirby D.:Compensation for transmission channel & speaker effects on vowel quality. Speech Comm.Vol.8. (1989) 221-234
5. Campbell, D.R.:Binaural Processing for Hearing Aids. In: Ainsworth, W., Greenberg, S. (Eds.): Proceedings of Workshop on Auditory Basis of Speech Perception. Keele University. UK. 15-19 July (1996) 253-256
6. Glasberg, B.R., Moore, B.C.J.: Psychoacoustical abilities of subjects with unilateral and bilateral cochlear hearing impairments and their relationship to the ability to understand speech. Scand. Audio. Suppl. Vol.32. (1989) 1-25.
7. Wightman, F.L., Kistler, D.J.: The dominant role of low-frequency interaural time differences in sound localization, J. Acoust. Soc. Am., Vol.91. (1992) 1648-1661.
8. Carhart, R., Tillman, T.W., Johnson, K.R.: Effects of interaural time delays on masking by two competing signals. J. Acoust. Soc. Am. (JASA). Vol.43. (1968) 1223-1230.
9. Baer, T., Moore, B. C. J., Gatehouse, S.:Spectral contrast enhancement of speech in noise for listeners with sensorineural hearing impairment: effects on intelligibility, quality and response times. J. Rehab. Res. Dev. Vol.30. (1993) 49-72.
10. Bernstein, L.R., Trahiotis,C.: Discrimination of interaural envelope correlation and its relation to binaural unmasking at high frequencies. J. Acoust. Soc. Am. (JASA). Vol.91. (1992) 306-316
11. Culling, J.F., Summerfield, Q.: Perceptual separation of concurrent speech sounds: Absence of cross frequency grouping by common interaural delay. J. Acoust. Soc. Am. (JASA). Vol.98. (1995) 785-797.
12. Durlach, N. : Binaural signal detection: Equalization & cancellation theory. In Foundations of Modern Auditory Theory, Tobias, J.V. (Eds.), Vol.II, Academic Press, London. (1972)
13. Ghitza O.: Auditory models and human performance in tasks related to speech coding and speech recognition. IEEE Trans. Speech & Audio Proc. Vol.2. (1994) 115-132.

14. Cheng, Y. M., O'Shaughnessy D.: Speech-enhancement based conceptually on auditory evidence. IEEE Trans. Sig. Proc. Vol.39. (1991) 1943-1954.
15. Hermansky, H. & Tibrewala, S.: Sub-band Based Recognition of Noisy Speech. In Proc. ICASSP. Munich. 20-24 April. (1997) 1255-1258
16. Bourlard, H., Dupont, S.: Subband-based speech recognition. In Proc. ICASSP. Munich, 20-24 April (1997) 1255-1258
17. Smith, L.S. : Biologically inspired robust onset detection. J. Acoust. Soc. America. Vol.113. (2003)
18. Toner, E. : Speech Enhancement using Digital Signal Processing. PhD thesis. University of Paisley. UK. (1993)
19. Toner, E., Campbell, D. R.: Speech Enhancement using sub-band intermittent adaption. Speech Communication. Vol. 12.(1993) 253-259.
20. Goulding, M. M., Bird, J. S.: Speech enhancement for mobile telephony", IEEE Trans. on Vehicular Technology, 39(4), (1990) 316-326.
21. Hussain. A., Campbell, D.R.: Intelligibility improvements using binaural diverse sub-band processing applied to speech corrupted with automobile noise. IEE Proceedings: Vision, Image & Signal Processing. Vol. 148. (2001) 127-132.
22. Wallace, R.B., Goubran, R.A.: Improved tracking adaptive noise canceller for non-stationary environments. IEEE Trans. on Sig. Proc. Vol.40 (1992) 700-703.
23. Elberling C,Ludvigsen C,Keidser G.: Design &testing of a noise reduction algorithm based on spectral subtraction. Scand. Audiol., Suppl. Vol.38 (1993) 39-48
24. Kollmeier, B., Peissig, J., Hohmann, V.: Binaural noise-reduction hearing aid scheme with real-time processing in the frequency domain. Scand. Audiol., Suppl. Vol.38 (1993) 28-38
25. Moore, B. C. J., Peters, R. W., Stone, M. A.: Benefits of linear amplification and multi-channel compression for speech comprehension in backgrounds with spectral and temporal dips. J. Acoust. Soc. Am. Vol. 105 (1999) 400-411
26. Soede, W., Bilsen, F.A., Berkhout, A.J.: Assessment of a directional microphone array for hearing impaired listeners. J.Acous.Soc.Am., Vol.94 (1993) 799-808
27. Elberling, C., Ludvigsen, C., Keidser, G.: Design &testing of a noise reduction algorithm based on spectral subtraction. Scand.Audiol.Suppl. Vol.38 (1993) 39-49
28. Le Bouquin, R., Azirani, A. A., Faucon, G.: Enhancement of speech degraded by coherent and incoherent noise using a cross-spectral estimator. IEEE Trans. Speech & Audio Proc. Vol. 5 (1997) 484-487.
29. Abutalebi, H.R., Sheikhzadeh, H., Brennan, R.L., Freeman, G.H.: A hybrid sub-band system for speech enhancement in diffused noise fields. IEEE Sig. Process. Letters. (2003)
30. Dabis, H.S., Moir, T.J., Campbell, D.R.: Speech enhancement by recursive estimation of differential transfer functions. In Proceedings of ICSP, Beijing (1990) 345-348.
31. Hussain, A.: A Multi-microphone Sub-band Adaptive Speech Enhancement System employing diverse sub-band processing. International Journal of Robotics & Automation. Vol. 15. (2000) 78-84.
32. Shields, P., Campbell, D. R.: Improvements in intelligibility of noisy reverberant speech using a binaural sub-band adaptive noise-cancellation processing scheme. J. Acous. Soc. Am. Vol.110. (2001) 3232-3242.
33. Hussain, A: Multi-sensor Neural Network processing of Noisy Speech. International Journal of Neural Systems. Vol.9. (1999) 467-472
34. Hussain, A.: Non-linear Speech Processing using Neural Networks based Adaptive Filtering. In Proc. 4th IEEE INMIC. Islamabad. 10-11 Sep (2000)
35. Soraghan, J., Hussain, A., Alkulaibi, A., Durrani, T.S.,: Higher Order Statistics based non-linear speech analysis. Journal of Control and Intelligent Systems. Vol.30. (2002) 11-18
36. Greenwood, D.D.: A cochlear frequency-position function for several species-29 years later. J. Acoustic Soc. Amer. Vol. 86. (1990) 2592-2605.

37. Vaseghi, S.V.: Advanced signal processing and digital noise reduction, John Wiley & Sons. (2000)
38. Ferrara. E.R., Widrow, B.: Multi-channel Adaptive Filtering for signal enhancement. IEEE Trans. on Acoustics, Speech and Signal Proc., Vol. 29. (1981) 766-770
39. Le Bouquin, R., Faucon, G: Study of a voice activity detector and its influence on a noise reduction system. Speech Communication, Vol. 16. (1995) 245-254
40. Yoma, N.B., McInnes F., Jack, M.: Lateral inhibition Net and Weighted Matching Algorithms for speech recognition in noise", Proc. IEE Vision, Image & Signal Processing. Vol. 143 (1996) 324-330
41. Bahoura, M., Rouat, J.: A new approach for wavelet speech enhancement. In Proc. EUROSPEECH. (2001) 1937-2001
42. Bahoura M., Rouat J.: Wavelet speech enhancement based on the Teager Energy Operator. IEEE Signal Proc. Lett. Vol.8 (2001) 10-12
43. Nikias, C., Raghuvers, M. : Bispectrum estimation: A digital signal procession framework. In Proc. IEEE. Vol.75 (1987) 869-891.
44. Lynch M.R, Holden S.B, & Rayner P.J.W.: Complexity Reduction in Volterra Connectionist Networks using a Self-Structuring LMS Algorithm. In Proc. IEE Second Intern. Conf. Artificial Neural Networks. (1991) 44-48.
45. Gammaitoni L., Hanggi, Jung, P., Marchesoni, P.: Stochastic resonance, Review Modern Physics. Vol. 70 (1998) 223-287.
46. Petracchi, D., Gebeshuber I.C., DeFelice L.J., Holden, A.V.: Stochastic resonance in biologocal systems, Chaos, Solutions and Fractals. Vol. 11. (2000) 1819-1822.
47. Douglas J.K., Wilkens, L., E. Pantazelou E., Moss, F: Noise enhancement of information transfer in crayfish mechanoreceptor by stochastic resonance. Nature. vol. 365. (1993) 337-340.
48. Fauve, F. Stochastic resonance in a bistable system, Phys. Lett., vol. 97A. (1983) 5-7.
49. Weisenfeld, Moss F., Stochastic resonance and the benefits of noise: from ice ages to the crayfish and SQUIDs, Nature, Vol. 373. (1995) 33-36.
50. Douglas, K., Wilkens, L., Pantazelou, E., Moss, F.: Noise enhancement of information transfer in crayfish mechanoreceptor by stochastic resonance,.Nature, Vol. 365. (1995) 337-340.
51. Anderson J.S., Lampl I., Gillespie D.C., Ferster, D.: The contribution of noise to contrast invariance of orientation tuning in Cat visual cortex}, Science, Vol. 290. (2000) 1968-1972.
52. Levin, J.E., Miller, J.P.: Broadband neural encoding in the cricket cercal sensory system enhanced by stochastic resonance. Nature. Vol. 380. (1996) 165-168.
53. Usher, M., M. Feingold, M.: Stochastic resonance in the speed of memory retrieval. Biological Cybernetics. Vol. 83. (2000) L11-L16.
54. Mori T., Kai, S.: Noise-induced entrainment and stochastic resonance in human brain waves. Phys. Rev. Lett., 2002, Vol 88. (2002) 1-4.
55. Hohn, N., Burkitt, A.N.: Modelling the neural response to speech: stochastic resonance and coding of vowel-like stimuli. In IEEE EMBS Conference, Monash University (2001)
56. Luchinsky, D.G., Mannella, R., McClintock P.V.E., Stocks, N.G.: Stochastic resonance in electrical circuits {II}. Nonconventional stochastic resonance. IEEE Trans. Circuits and Systems. Vol. 46. (1999) 1215-1224.
57. Stocks, N.G.: Information transmission in parallel arrays of threshold elements: suprathreshold stochastic resonance. Phy. Rev. E. Vol. 63, (2001) 1-9.
58. Stocks, N.G., Allingham, G., Morse, R.P.: The application of suprathreshold stochastic resonance to cochlear implant coding. J. Fluctuation and noise letters, Vol. 2. (2002) 169-181.

59. Gammaitoni, L.: Stochastic resonance and the dithering effect in threshold physical systems. Physical Review E. Vol. 52. (1995) 4691-4698.
60. Longtin, A., Bulsara, A., Moss, F.: Time-interval sequences in bistable systems and noise-induced transmission of information by sensory neurons, Phys. Rev Lett. Vol. 67 (1991) 656-659.
61. Collins, J.J., Chow, C.C., Capela, A.C., Imhoff, T.T.: Aperiodic stochastic resonance, Phys. Rev. E. Vol. 54. (1996) 5575—5584.
62. Stemmler, M., A Single Spike Suffices: the simplest form of stochastic resonance in model neurons, Network: Computation in Neural Systems. Vol. 7. (1996) 687-716.
63. Benzi, R., Sutera, A., Vulpiiani, A.: The mechanism of stochastic resonance, J. Phys. A. Vol. 14. (1981) 453-457.
64. Nicolis, C., Nicolis, G.: Stochastic aspects of climatic transitions - response to periodic forcing. Tellus. Vol. 34. (1982) 1-9.
65. Benzi, R., Parisi, G., Sutera, A., Vulpiani, A.: Stochastic resonance in climatic changes. Tellus. Vol. 34. (1982) 10-16.
66. McNamara, B., Wiesenfeld, K., Roy, R.: Observation of stochastic resonance in a ring laser, Phys. Rev. Lett. Vol 60 (2002) pp 2626-2629.
67. Gluckman, B.J., Netoff, T.I., Neel, E.J., Dittoand, W.L., Spano, M.L., Schiff, S.J.: Stochastic resonance in a neuronal network from a mammalian brain. Physical Review Letters. Vol. 77. (1996) 4098-4101.
68. Morse, R.P., Evans, E.F.: Enhancement of vowel coding for cochlear implants by addition of noise. Nature Medicine, Vol.2, (1996) 928-932.
69. Mtetwa N., Smith, L.S.: Precision constrained stochastic resonance in a feed forward neural network. in press. IEEE Transactions on Neural Networks. (2004)

Perceptive, Non-linear Speech Processing and Spiking Neural Networks

Jean Rouat*, Ramin Pichevar, and Stéphane Loiselle

Université de Sherbrooke
http://www.gel.usherbrooke.ca/rouat/

Abstract. Source separation and speech recognition are very difficult in the context of noisy and corrupted speech. Most conventional techniques need huge databases to estimate speech (or noise) density probabilities to perform separation or recognition. We discuss the potential of perceptive speech analysis and processing in combination with biologically plausible neural network processors. We illustrate the potential of such non-linear processing of speech on a source separation system inspired by an Auditory Scene Analysis paradigm. We also discuss a potential application in speech recognition.

Keywords: Auditory modelling, Source separation, Amplitude Modulation, Auditory Scene Analysis, Spiking Neurones, Temporal Correlation, Multiplicative Synapses, Cochlear Nucleus, Corrupted Speech Processing, Rank Order Coding, Speech recognition.

1 Introduction

Processing of corrupted speech is an important research field with many applications in speech coding, transmission, recognition and audio processing. For example, speech enhancement, auditory modelling and source separation can be used to assist robots in segregating multiple speakers, to ease the automatic transcription of videos via the audio tracks, to segregate musical instruments before automatic transcription, to clean up a signal before performing speech recognition, etc. The ideal instrumental set-up is based on the use of arrays of microphones during recording to obtain many audio channels. In that situation, very good separation can be obtained between noise and the signal of interest [1–3] and experiments with good enhancement have been reported in speech recognition [4, 5] [6, 7] [8]. Applications have been ported on mobile robots [9] [10, 11] and have also been developped to track multiple speakers [12].

In many situations, only one channel is available to the audio engineer that still has to clean the signal and solve the separation problem. The cleaning of

---

* This work has been funded by NSERC, MRST of Québec gvt., Université de Sherbrooke and by Université du Québec à Chicoutimi. Many thanks to Peter Murphy and Daniel Pressnitzer for proofreading this paper and to our COST277 collaborators: Christian Feldbauer and Gernot Kubin from Graz University of Technology for fruitful discussions on analysis/synthesis filterbanks

G. Chollet et al. (Eds.): Nonlinear Speech Modeling, LNAI 3445, pp. 317–337, 2005.
© Springer-Verlag Berlin Heidelberg 2005

corrupted speech is, then, much more difficult. From the scientific literature, most of the proposed monophonic systems perform reasonably well on specific signals (generally voiced speech) but fail to efficiently segregate a broader range of signals. These relatively negative results may be overcome by combining and exchanging expertise and knowledge between engineering, psycho-acoustic, physiology and computer science. Statistical approaches like Bayesian networks, Hidden Markov Models and one microphone ICA perform reasonably well once the training dataset or the probability distributions have been suitably estimated. But these approaches usually require supervised training on huge databases and are designed for specific applications. On the other hand, perceptive and bio-inspired approaches require less training, can be unsupervised and offer strong potential even if they are less mature. In the present work we are interested in monophonic bio-inspired corrupted-speech processing approaches.

2   Perceptive Approach

We propose to combine knowledge from psycho-acoustics, psychology and neurophysiology to propose new non-linear processing systems for corrupted speech. From physiology we learn that the auditory system extracts simultaneous features from the underlying signal, giving birth to simultaneous multi-representation of speech. We also learn that fast and slow efferences can selectively enhance speech representations in relation to the auditory environment. This is in opposition with most conventional speech processing systems that use a systematic analysis[1] that is effective only when speech segments under the analysis window are relatively stationary and stable.

Psychology observes and attempts to explain the auditory sensations by proposing models of hearing. The interaction between sounds and their perception can be interpreted in terms of auditory environment or auditory scene analysis. We also learn from psycho-acoustics that the time structure organisation of speech and sounds is crucial in perception. In combination with physiology, suitable hearing models can also be derived from research in psycho-acoustic.

2.1   Physiology: Multiple Features

Inner and outer hair cells establish synapses with efferent and afferent fibres. The efferent projections to the inner hair cells synapse on the afferent connection, suggesting a modulation of the afferent information by the efferent system. On the contrary, other efferent fibres project directly to the outer hair cells, suggesting a direct control of the outer hair cells by the efferences. It has also been observed that all afferent fibres (inner and outer hair cells) project directly into the cochlear nucleus. The cochlear nucleus has a layered structure that preserves frequency tonotopic organisation. One finds very different neurones that

---

[1] Systematic analysis extracts the same features independently of signal context. Frame by frame extraction of Mel Frequency Cepstrum Coefficients (MFCC) is an example of systematic analysis

respond to various features[2]. Schreiner and Langner [13, 14] have shown that the inferior colliculus of the cat contains a highly systematic topographic representation of AM parameters. Maps showing best modulation frequency have been determined. The pioneering work by Robles, Ruggero and Evans [15] [16][17] reveals the importance of AM-FM[3] coding in the peripheral auditory system along with the role of the efferent system in relation with adaptive tuning of the cochlea. Recently, small neural circuits in relation with *wideband inhibitory input* neurones have been observed by Arnott *et al.* [18] in the cochlear nucleus. These circuits, explain the response of specialised neurones to frequency position of sharp spectral notches. Pressnitzer *et al.* [19] have proposed another use for such networks for auditory scene analysis.

It is also known that the auditory efferent system plays a crucial role in enhancing signals in background noise [20] [21] [22]. Kim *et al.* [22] measure the effect of aging on the medial olivocochlear system and suggest that the functional decline of the medial olivocochlear system with age precedes outer hair cell degeneration.

It is clear from physiology that multiple and simultaneous representations of the same input signal are observed in the cochlear nucleus [23] [24]. In the remaining parts of the paper, we call these representations, *auditory images*. It is interesting to note that Harding and Meyer [25] propose a multi-resolution Auditory Scene Analysis that uses both high- and low- resolution representations of the auditory signal in parallel.

2.2   Cocktail-Party Effect and Auditory Scene Analysis

Humans are able to segregate a desired source in a mixture of sounds (*cocktail-party effect*). Psycho-acoustical experiments have shown that although binaural audition may help to improve segregation performance, human beings are capable of doing the segregation even with one ear or when all sources come from the same spatial location (for instance, when someone listens to a radio broadcast) [26]. Using the knowledge acquired in visual scene analysis and by making an analogy between vision and audition, Bregman developed the key notions of *Auditory Scene Analysis* (ASA)[26]. Two of the most important aspects in ASA are the *segregation* and *grouping (or integration)* of sound sources. The segregation step partitions the auditory scene into fundamental auditory elements and the grouping is the binding of these elements in order to reproduce the initial sound sources. These two stages are influenced by top-down processing (schema-driven). The aim in Computational Auditory Scene Analysis (CASA) is to develop computerised methods for solving the sound segregation problem by using psycho-acoustical cues and physiological characteristics [27, 28]. For a review see [29].

---

[2] onset, chopper, primary-like, etc.

[3] Other features like transients, ON, OFF responses are observed, but are not implemented in this paper

3   Spiking Neural Networks

The previous section introduced the perceptual approach to non-linear speech analysis. In this section we emphasise the computational power of spiking neurones in the context of speech and signal processing. Autonomous bio–inspired and spiking neural networks are an alternative to supervised systems. A good review on bio-inspired spiking neurones can be found in [30] and in books such as [31], [32] and [33].

3.1   Analysis and Perception

In perception, the recognition of stimuli is quasi-instantaneous, even if the information propagation speed in living neurones is slow. This phenomenon is well documented for hearing and visual systems [34] [35, 36]. It implies that neural responses are conditioned by previous events and states of the neural sub-network [37]. The understanding of the underlying mechanisms of perception in combination with that of the peripheral auditory system [38] [39] [40] [41] [42] helps the researcher in designing speech analysis modules.

3.2   Intuitive Notion of Spiking Neurones

In the case of bio-inspired neural networks, temporal sequence processing is done naturally because of the intrinsic dynamic behaviour of neurones. The pioneering work in the field of neural networks has been done by Hodgkin and Huxley (H& H) at the University of Plymouth, who proposed a mathematical description of the behaviour of the giant squid axon. Although this model is complete so far (it can predict most of the behaviours seen in simple biological neurones), it is

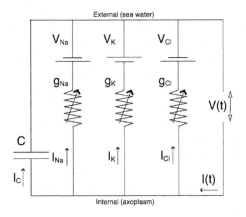

Fig. 1. Equivalent circuit of a membrane section of the giant squid axon (from Hodgkin-Huxley, 1952). g_{Cl}, g_{Na} and g_K are the conductance of the membrane for respective ionic gates. $V(t)$ is the membrane potential when $I(t) = 0$ (no external input)

very complex and difficult to simulate in an artificial neural network paradigm. A very simplified model of the H& H is the Leaky Integrate and Fire model (LIF) as presented in figure 2.

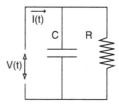

Fig. 2. Equivalent circuit of a leaky integrate and fire neurone. C: membrane capacitance, R: membrane resistance, V: membrane potential

$I(t)$ is the sum of the current going trough the capacitance plus the resistance current. The sub-threshold[4] potential $V(t)$ is given by:

$$I(t) = C(t)\frac{dV(t)}{dt} + \frac{V(t)}{R(t)} \tag{1}$$

$V(t)$ is the output, $I(t)$ is the input. When $V(t)$ crosses a predetermined threshold $\delta(t)$, the neuron fires and emits a spike. Then $V(t)$ is reset to V_r, where V_r is the resting potential.

In this paper we use a non-linear oscillator to reproduce the behaviour of the Integrate and Fire neurone.

In the following subsections, we review some of the studies that are pertinent to speech processing and source separation in spiking neurones.

3.3   Formalisation of Bio-inspired Neural Networks

There are many publications which describe mathematical formalism for spiking neurones. One can cite for example the work by Maass [43] and his team, in which they have shown that networks of spiking neurones are computationally more powerful than the models based on McCulloch Pitts neurones. In [37] the authors have shown that information about the result of the computation is already present in the current neural network state long before the complete spatio-temporal input patterns have been received by the neural network. This suggests that neural networks use the temporal order of the first spikes yielding ultra-rapid computation, according to the observations by [35]. In [44] and [45],

---

[4] Subthreshold potential assumes that the internal potential V(t) is sufficiently small in comparison to the neurone's internal threshold. Supra-threshold potential is the potential of the neurone when it is greater than the internal threshold. The Hodgkin-Huxley model integrates sub-threshold, threshold and supra-threshold activity in the same set of equations. It is not the case with the LIF model

the authors explain how neural networks and dynamic synapses (including facilitation and depression) are equivalent to a given quadratic filter that can, thus, be approximated by a small neural system. The authors also show that any filter that can be characterised by a Volterra series can be approximated with a single layer of spiking neurones.

Mutual Information and Pattern Recognition. Among the many publications in information theory one can cite the works by Fred Rieke *et al.* [46], Sejnowski [47], DeWeese [48] and Chechik and Tishby [49] where it is shown that spike coding in neurones is close to optimal and that plasticity in Hebbian learning rule increases mutual information close to optimal transmission of information.

Novelty Detection. For unsupervised systems, novelty detection is an important property that facilitates autonomy (robots can detect if stimuli is new or already seen). When associated with conditioning, novelty detection can create autonomy of the system [50] [51].

Sequence Classification. Sequence classification is particularly interesting for speech. Recently Panchev and Wermter [52] have shown that synaptic plasticity can be used to perform recognition of sequences. Perrinet [53] and Thorpe [36] discuss the importance of sparse coding and rank order coding for classification of sequences.

3.4 Segregation and Integration with Binding

Neurone assemblies (groups) of spiking neurones can be used to implement segregation and fusion (integration) of objects in an auditory image representation. Usually, in signal processing, correlations (or distances) between signals are implemented with delay lines, products and summation. With spiking neurones, comparison (temporal correlation) between signals can be made without implementation of delay lines. In section 4, page 324, we use that approach by presenting auditory images to spiking neurones with dynamic synapses. Then, a spontaneous organisation appears in the network with sets of neurones firing in synchrony. Neurones with the same firing phase belong to the same auditory objects. In 1976 and 1981, the temporal correlation that performs binding was proposed by Milner [54] and independently by Malsburg [55–57]. Milner and Malsburg have observed that synchrony is a crucial feature to bind neurones that are associated with similar characteristics. Objects belonging to the same entity are bound together in time. In other words, synchronisation between different neurones and de-synchronisation among different regions perform the binding. To a certain extent, this property has been exploited by Bohte [58] to perform unsupervised clustering for recognition on images, by Schwartz [59] for vowel processing with spike synchrony between cochlear channels, by Hopfield [60] to propose pattern recognition with spiking neurones, by Levy *et al.* [61] to perform cell assembly of spiking neurones using Hebbian learning with depression. Wang and Terman [62] have proposed an efficient and robust technique for image segmentation and study its potential in CASA (Computational Auditory Scene Analysis) [28].

3.5   Example of Associative Neural Network

Alkon *et al.* [63] have shown that dendrites can learn associations between input sequences without knowledge about neurone outputs. They derive an image recognition application [64] from this work. The network associatively learns correlation and anti-correlation between time events occurring in pre-synaptic neurones. Those neurones synapse on the same element (same area) of a common post synaptic neurone. A learning rule modifies the cellular excitability at dendritic patches. These synaptic patches are postulated to be formed on branches of the dendritic tree of vertebrate neurones. Weights are associated to patches rather than to incoming connection. After learning, each patch characterises a pattern of activity on the input neurones. In comparison with most commonly used networks, the weights are not used to store the patterns and the comparison between patterns is based on normalised correlation instead of projections between the network input vectors and the neurone weights. Based on this type of network, a prototype vowel recognition system has been designed and preliminary results have shown that the short-time AM structure carries information that can be used for recognition of voiced speech [65]. One of the main drawbacks of that approach is that explicit encoding of reference patterns in dendritic patches of neurones is required.

3.6   Rank Order Coding

Rank Order Coding has been proposed by Simon Thorpe and his team from CERCO, Toulouse to explain the impressive performance of our visual system [53, 66]. The information is distributed through a large population of neurones and is represented by spikes relative timing in a single wave of action potentials. The quantity of information that can be transmitted by this type of code increases with the number of neurones in the population. For a relatively large number of neurones, the code transmission power can satisfy the needs of any visual task [66]. There are advantages in using the relative order and not the exact spike latency: the strategy is easier to implement, the system is less subject to changes in intensity of the stimulus and the information is available as soon as the first spike is generated.

3.7   Summary

Bio-inspired neuronal networks are well adapted to signal processing where time is important. They can be fully unsupervised. Adaptive and unsupervised recognition of sequences is a crucial property of living neurones. Among the many properties we listed in this section, the paper implements the segregation and integration with sets of synchronous neurones. At the moment, this work does not reflect the full potential of spiking neurones and is more or less exploratory.

4   Source Separation

Most monophonic source separation systems require *a priori* knowledge, i.e. expert systems (explicit knowledge) or statistical approaches (implicit knowledge) [29]. Most of these systems perform reasonably well only on specific signals (generally voiced speech or harmonic music) and fail to efficiently segregate a broad range of signals. Sameti [67] uses Hidden Markov Models, while Roweis [68, 69], and Gomez [70] use Factorial Hidden Markov Models. Jang and Lee [71] use Maximum A Posteriori (MAP) estimation. They all require training on huge signal databases to estimate probability models. Wang and Brown [28] proposed an original bio–inspired approach that uses features obtained from correlograms and F0 (pitch frequency) in combination with an oscillatory neural network. Hu and Wang use a pitch tracking technique [72] to segregate harmonic sources. Both systems are limited to harmonic signals.

We propose here to extend the bio-inspired approach to more general situations without training or prior knowledge of underlying signal properties[5].

4.1   Binding of Auditory Sources

Various features of speech are extracted in different areas of the brain[6]. We assume here that sound segregation is a generalised classification problem, in which we want to bind features extracted from the auditory image representations in different regions of our neural network map.

4.2   System Overview

In this work analysis and recognition are integrated. Physiology, psychoacoustic and signal processing are integrated to design a multiple sources separation system when only one audio channel is available (Fig. 3, page 325). It combines a reconstruction analysis/synthesis cochlear filterbank along with auditory image representations of audible signals with a spiking neural network. The segregation and binding of the auditory objects (coming from different sound sources) is performed by the spiking neural network (implementing the *temporal correlation* [54, 55]) that also generates a mask[7] to be used in conjunction with the synthesis filterbank to generate the separated sound sources.

---

[5] Prior knowledge is embodied in the representations of the acoustic signals

[6] AM and FM maps are observed in the colliculus of the cat, onset neurones are present in the cochlear nucleus, etc.

[7] Mask and masking refer here to a binary gain and should not be confused with the conventional definition of masking in psychoacoustics

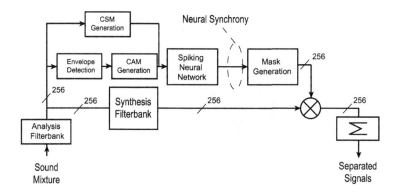

Fig. 3. Source Separation System. Depending on the sources auditory images (CAM or CSM), the spiking neural network generates the mask (binary gain) to switch ON/OFF – in time and across channels – the synthesis filterbank channels before final summation

The neural network uses third generation neural networks, where neurones are usually called *spiking* neurones [43]. In our implementation, neurones firing at the same instants (same firing phase) are characteristic of similar stimuli or comparable input signals[8]. *Spiking* neurones, in opposition to *formal* neurones, have a constant firing amplitude. This coding yields noise and interference robustness while facilitating adaptive and dynamic synapses (links between neurones) for unsupervised and autonomous system design. Numerous spike timing coding schemes are possible (and observable in physiology) [73]. Among them, we decided to use synchronisation and oscillatory coding schemes in combination with a competitive unsupervised framework (obtained with dynamic synapses), where groups of synchronous neurones are observed. This choice has the advantage to allow design of unsupervised systems with no training (or learning) phase. To some extent, the neural network can be viewed as a map where links between neurones are dynamic. In our implementation of the *temporal correlation*, two neurones with similar inputs on their dendrites will increase their soma to soma synaptic weights (dynamic synapses), forcing synchronous response. On the opposite, neurones with dissimilar dendritic inputs will have reduced soma to soma synaptic weights, yielding reduced coupling and asynchronous neural responses.

Figure 4, page 326 illustrates the oscillatory response behavior of the output layer of the proposed neural network for two sources.

While conventional signal processing computation of correlations encounter difficulties in taking simultaneously into account the spatial aspect (multi-step correlation has to be evaluated), the spiking neural network is able to compute a **spatio**-temporal correlation of the input signals in one step.

Compared to conventional approaches, our system does not require a priori knowledge, is not limited to harmonic signals, does not require training and does not need pitch extraction.

---

[8] The information is coded in the firing instants

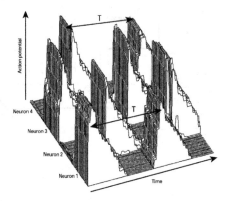

Fig. 4. Dynamic temporal correlation for two simultaneous sources: time evolution of the supra–threshold electrical output potential for four neurones from the second layer (output layer). T is the oscillatory period. Two sets of synchronous neurones appear (neurones 1 & 3 for source 1; neurones 2 & 4 for source 2). Plot degradations are due to JPEG coding

The architecture is also designed to handle continuous input signals (no need to segment the signal into time frames) and is based on the availability of simultaneous auditory representations of signals. Our approach is inspired by knowledge in anthropomorphic systems but is not an attempt to reproduce faithfully physiology or psychoacoustics.

4.3   Proposed System Strategy

Two representations are simultaneously generated: an amplitude modulation map, which we call Cochleotopic/AMtopic (CAM) Map[9] and a Cochleotopic/ Spectrotopic Map (CSM) that encodes the averaged spectral energies of the

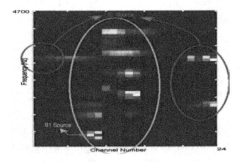

Fig. 5. Example of a twenty–four channels CAM for a mixture of /di/ and /da/ pronounced by two speakers; mixture at $SNR = 0$ dB and frame center at $t = 166$ ms

---

[9] To some extent, it is related to modulation spectrograms. See for example work by [74, 75]

cochlear filterbank output. The first representation somewhat reproduces the AM processing performed by multipolar cells (Chopper-S) from the anteroventral cochlear nucleus [24], while the second representation could be closer to the spherical bushy cell processing from ventral cochlear nucleus [23] areas.

We assume that different sources are disjoint in the auditory image representation space and that masking (binary gain) of the undesired sources is feasible. Speech has a specific structure that is different from that of most noises and perturbations [76]. Also, when dealing with simultaneous speakers, separation is possible when preserving the time structure (the probability at a given instant t to observe overlap in pitch and timbre is relatively low). Therefore, a binary gain can be used to suppress the interference (or separate all sources with adaptive masks).

4.4   Detailed Description

Signal Analysis. Our CAM/CSM generation algorithm is as follows:

1. Down–sampling to 8000 samples/s.
2. Filter the sound source using a 256-filter Bark-scaled cochlear filterbank ranging from 100 Hz to 3.6 kHz.
3. – For CAM: Extract the envelope (AM demodulation) for channels 30-256 (400–3600 Hz); for other low frequency channels (1–29: 100–400 Hz) use raw outputs[10].
    – For CSM: Nothing is done in this step.
4. Compute the STFT of the envelopes (CAM) or of the filterbank outputs (CSM) using a Hamming window[11].
5. To increase the spectro-temporal resolution of the STFT, find the reassigned spectrum of the STFT [78] (this consists of applying an affine transform to the points to re-allocate the spectrum).
6. Compute the logarithm of the magnitude of the STFT. The logarithm enhances the presence of the stronger source in a given 2D frequency bin of the CAM/CSM[12].

For a given instant, depending on the signal, the peripheral auditory system can enhance the AM, the FM, the envelope, or the transient components of the signal.

The Neural Network

First Layer: Image Segmentation. The dynamics of the neurones we use is governed by a modified version of the Van der Pol relaxation oscillator (Wang-Terman oscillators [28]). The state-space equations for these dynamics are as follows:

$$\frac{dx}{dt} = 3x - x^3 + 2 - y + \rho + p + S \qquad (2)$$

---

[10] Low-frequency channels are said to resolve the harmonics while others do not, suggesting a different strategy for low frequency channels [77]

[11] Non-overlapping adjacent windows with 4ms or 32ms lengths have been tested

[12] $\log(e_1 + e_2) \simeq max(\log e_1, \log e_2)$ (unless e_1 and e_2 are both large and almost equal) [69]

$$\frac{dy}{dt} = \epsilon[\gamma(1 + \tanh(x/\beta)) - y] \tag{3}$$

Where x is the membrane potential (output) of the neurone and y is the state for channel activation or inactivation. ρ denotes the amplitude of Gaussian noise, p is the external input to the neurone, and S is the coupling from other neurones (connections through synaptic weights). ϵ, γ, and β are constants[13]. The Euler integration method is used to solve the equations. The first layer is a partially connected network of relaxation oscillators [28]. Each neurone is connected to its four neighbors. The CAM (or the CSM) is applied to the input of the neurones. Since the map is sparse, the original 256 points computed for the FFT are downsampled to 50 points. Therefore, the first layer consists of 256 x 50 neurones. The geometric interpretation of pitch (ray distance criterion) is less clear for the first 29 channels, where harmonics are usually resolved[14]. For this reason, we have also established long-range connections from *clear* (high frequency) zones to *confusion* (low frequency) zones. These connections exist only across the *cochlear channel number* axis in the CAM.

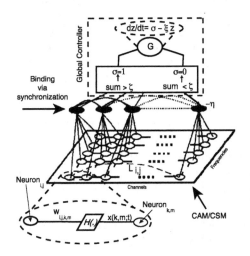

Fig. 6. Architecture of the Two-Layer Bio-inspired Neural Network. G: Stands for global controller (the global controller for the first layer is not shown on the figure). One long range connection is shown. Parameters of the controller and of the input layer are also illustrated in the zoomed areas

The weight, $w_{i,j,k,m}(t)$ (figure 6), between $neurone(i,j)$ and $neurone(k,m)$ of the first layer is:

$$w_{i,j,k,m}(t) = \frac{1}{Card\{N(i,j)\}} \frac{0.25}{e^{\lambda|p(i,j;t)-p(k,m;t)|}} \tag{4}$$

---

[13] In our simulation, $\epsilon = 0.02$, $\gamma = 4$, $\beta = 0.1$ and $\rho = 0.02$
[14] Envelopes of resolved harmonics are nearly constants

here $p(i,j)$ and $p(k,m)$ are respectively external inputs to $neurone(i,j)$ and $neurone(k,m) \in N(i,j)$. $Card\{N(i,j)\}$ is a normalization factor and is equal to the cardinal number (number of elements) of the set $N(i,j)$ containing neighbors connected to the $neurone(i,j)$ (can be equal to 4, 3 or 2 depending on the location of the neurone on the map, i.e. center, corner, etc.). The external input values are normalized. The value of λ depends on the dynamic range of the inputs and is set to $\lambda = 1$ in our case. This same weight adaptation is used for *long range clear to confusion zone* connections (Eq. 8) in the CAM processing case. The coupling $S_{i,j}$ defined in Eq. 2 is:

$$S_{i,j}(t) = \sum_{k,m \in N(i,j)} w_{i,j,k,m}(t)H(x(k,m;t)) - \eta G(t) + \kappa L_{i,j}(t) \tag{5}$$

$H(.)$ is the Heaviside function. The dynamics of $G(t)$ (the global controller) is as follows:

$$G(t) = \alpha H(z - \theta) \tag{6}$$

$$\frac{dz}{dt} = \sigma - \xi z \tag{7}$$

σ is equal to 1 if the global activity of the network is greater than a predefined ζ and is zero otherwise (Figure 6). α and ξ are constants[15].
   $L_{i,j}(t)$ is the long range coupling as follows:

$$L_{i,j}(t) = \begin{cases} 0 & j \geq 30 \\ \sum_{k=225...256} w_{i,j,i,k}(t)H(x(i,k;t)) & j < 30 \end{cases} \tag{8}$$

κ is a binary variable defined as follows:

$$\kappa = \begin{cases} 1 \; for & CAM \\ 0 \; for & CSM \end{cases} \tag{9}$$

Second Layer: Temporal Correlation and Multiplicative Synapses. The second layer is an array of 256 neurones (one for each channel). Each neurone receives the weighted product of the outputs of the first layer neurones along the frequency axis of the CAM/CSM. For the CAM: Since the geometric (Euclidian) distance between rays (spectral maxima) is a function of the pitch of the dominant source in a given channel, the weighted sum of the outputs of the first layers along the frequency axis tells us about the origin of the signal present in that channel. For the CSM: Highly localized energy bursts will be enhanced by that representation. Weights between layer one and layer two are defined as $w_{ll}(i) = \frac{\alpha}{i}$, where i can be related to the frequency bins of the STFT and α is a constant for the CAM case, since we are looking for structured patterns. For the CSM, $w_{ll}(i) = \alpha$ is constant along the frequency bins as we are looking for energy bursts[16].

---

[15] $\zeta = 0.2$, $\alpha = -0.1$, $\xi = 0.4$, $\eta = 0.05$ and $\theta = 0.9$
[16] In our simulation, $\alpha = 1$

Therefore, the input stimulus to $neurone(j)$ in the second layer is defined as follows:

$$\theta(j;t) = \prod_i \overline{w_{II}(i)\Xi\{x(i,j;t)\}} \tag{10}$$

The operator Ξ is defined as:

$$\Xi\{x(i,j;t)\} = \begin{cases} 1 & for \quad x(i,j;t) = 0 \\ x(i,j;t) & elsewhere \end{cases} \tag{11}$$

where $\overline{()}$ is the *averaging over a time window* operator (the duration of the window is on the order of the discharge period). Multiplication is carried out only for non-zero outputs (in which spike is present) [79, 80]. A functional analogue of this behavior has been observed in the integration of ITD (Interaural Time Difference) and ILD (Inter Level Difference) information in the barn owl's auditory system [79] or in the monkey's posterior parietal lobe neurones that show *receptive fields* that can be explained by a multiplication of retinal and eye or head position signals [81].

The synaptic weights inside the second layer are adjusted through the following rule:

$$w'_{ij}(t) = \frac{0.2}{e^{\mu|p(j;t)-p(k;t)|}} \tag{12}$$

μ is chosen to be equal to 2. The *binding* of these features is achieved via this second layer. In fact, the second layer is an array of fully connected neurones along with a global controller. The dynamics of the second layer is given by an equation similar to equation 5 (without long range coupling). The global controller desynchronizes the synchronized neurones for the first and second sources by emitting inhibitory activities whenever there is an activity (spikings) in the network [28].

The selection strategy at the output of the second layer is based on temporal correlation: neurones belonging to the same source synchronize (same spiking phase) and neurones belonging to other sources desynchronize (different spiking phase).

Masking and Synthesis. Time-reversed outputs of the *analysis* filterbank are passed through the *synthesis* filterbank giving birth to $z_i(t)$. Based on an output signal continuity criterion and on the phase synchronisation described in the previous section, a mask is generated by associating zeros and ones to different channels.

$$s(t) = \sum_{i=1}^{256} m_i(t)z_i(t) \tag{13}$$

where $s(N - t)$ is the recovered signal (N is the length of the signal in discrete mode), $z_i(t)$ is the synthesis filterbank output for channel i and $m_i(t)$ is the mask value. Energy is normalised in order to have the same SPL for all frames. Note that two-source mixtures are considered throughout this article but the technique can be potentially used for more sources. In that case, for each time frame n, labeling of individual channels is equivalent to the use of multiple masks (one for each source).

Experiments and Results. Results can be heard and evaluated on one of the authors' web page: [82] [83]. Detailed results and experiments are described in a companion paper by Pichevar and Rouat in the same book where a comparison is made to the work by Hu [72], Wang [28] and Jang [71].

Based on evidences regarding the dynamics of the efferent loops and on the richness of the representations observed in the Cochlear Nucleus, we propose a technique to explore the monophonic source separation problem using a multirepresentation bio-inspired pre-processing stage and a bio-inspired neural network that does not require any a priori knowledge of the signal.

Results obtained from signal synthesis are encouraging and we believe that spiking neural networks in combination with suitable signal representations have a strong potential for use in speech and audio processing. The evaluation scores show that the system yields performance levels roughly comparable with other methods, to which it has been compared. Furthermore, our method does not need any prior knowledge and is not limited to harmonic signals.

5   Exploration in Speech Recognition

We illustrate here another application in speech recognition where perceptive signal analysis combined with non-linear signal processing and spiking neural networks offers a strong potential.

5.1   Auditory Based Features and Pattern Recognisers

Starting in the middle of the '80s, many auditory models have been proposed [84, 85],[86],[87, 88], [89],[90, 91], [92, 93], [94] [95, 96] and have been tested on speech processing systems. At that time, it was objected that auditory models were CPU-intensive and were only useful when speech was noisy.

Furthermore, that first generation of auditory-based models failed to be used by speech recognisers, since recognisers were not able to exploit the great granularity of auditory-inspired model outputs that preserve time structure and generate many simultaneous representations and features suitable to source separation and speech recognition. Furthermore, at that time, pattern recognisers were not able to exploit this information, as they were optimised for parameters (like MFCC) obtained through systematic analysis.

In pattern recognition research, it is well known that signal analysis and recognition are modules that are closely related. For example, very good matching between parameter vector (such as MFCC) distributions and recognition models (such as HMM) yields better performance than systems using auditory cues but with mismatched pattern recognisers. Further discussion is given by M. Hunt in [97, 98].

Since then, research in neuroscience and auditory perception has advanced, yielding greater understanding of the auditory system along with more sophisticated tools for the recognition of time-organised features. See for example the work by Zotkin *et al.* [42].

5.2 Speech Recognition with Ensemble Interval Histograms

Oded Ghitza proposed in 1994 and 1995 the use of an auditory peripheral model for speech recognition [90, 91] that simulates a great number of neurones with different internal threshold values. O. Ghitza introduced the notion of the *Ensemble Interval Histograms* representation (EIH). That representation carries information about the spiking time interval distributions from a population of primary auditory fibres. Experiments were made on the TIMIT database by using a mixture of Gaussian Hidden Markov Models. He observed that the EIH representation is more robust on distorted speech when compared to MFCC. On clean speech there was no gain in using that model.

It is important to note that EIH carries information on averaged spiking intervals, thus specific sequences of spikes can not be identified inside a population of neurones. Furthermore, the representation has to be smoothed to be compatible with the use of a conventional fixed frame pattern recogniser (HMM with multi-Gaussian). Therefore, fine grained information is lost.

We suggest to use a similar front-end as proposed by Ghitza, but to preserve the time structure organisation of spiking sequences across neurones, without computing the histograms. As it prevents the conventional use of HMM, we examine potential techniques to recognise specific spiking sequences. Different coding schemes can be used to perform the recognition. In a collaborative work[17], the Rank Order Coding scheme is explored. The ROC scheme has been proposed for visual categorisation by Thorpe *et al.* [35, 36].

The peripheral auditory system is crudely modelised and it is assumed that the auditory image representation can be processed as images. From preliminary experiments [99], it is observed that bio-inspired approaches could be a good complement to statistical speech recognisers as they might reach very quickly acceptable results on very limited training sets.

6 Conclusion

Conventional speech analysis and recognition techniques can yield good performance levels when correctly trained and when the test conditions match those of the training set. But for real-life situations, the designer has to train the system on huge databases that are very costly to implement. On the other hand, bio-inspired processing schemes can be unsupervised and generalise relatively well from limited data. They could efficiently complement conventional speech processing and recognition techniques. Due to the intrinsic spiking nature of

---

[17] S. Loiselle has been a visiting student in CERCO, Toulouse, France (Simon Thorpe and Daniel Pressnitzer) during his 2003 summer session

neurones, suitable signal representations have to be found to adequately adapt the signal information to the neural networks.

References

1. B. Widrow and al. Adaptive noise cancelling: Principles and applications. *Proceedings of the IEEE*, 63(12), 1975.
2. Y. Kaneda and J. Ohga. Adaptive microphone-array system for noise reduction. *IEEE Tr. on ASSP*, 34(6):1391–1400, 1986.
3. Hyvärinen, Karhunen, and Oja. *Independent Component Analysis*. Wiley, 2001.
4. Dirk Van Compernolle, Weiye Ma, Fei Xie, and Marc Van Diest. Speech recognition in noisy environments with the aid of microphone array. *Speech Communication*, 9(5–6):433–442, 1990.
5. Michael L. Seltzer, Bhiksha Raj, and Richard M. Stern. Speech recognizer-based microphone array processing for robust hands-free speech recognition. In *ICASSP*, volume I, pages 897–900, 2002.
6. M. S. Brandstein and D. B.Ward, editors. *Microphone Arrays: Signal Processing Techniques and Applications*. Springer Verlag, 2001.
7. S. Haykin. *Adaptive Filter Theory*. Prentice Hall, 2002.
8. J.L. Sánchez-Bote, J. González-Rodríguez, and J. Ortega-Garcían. A real-time auditory-based microphone array assessed with E-RASTI evaluation proposal. In *ICASSP*, volume V, pages 447–450, 2003.
9. K. Nakadai, H. G. Okuno, and H. Kitano. Auditory fovea based speech separation and its application to dialog system. In *IEEE/RSJ International Conference on Intelligent Robots and Systems*, pages 1314–1319, Oct. 2002.
10. Jean-Marc Valin, François Michaud, Jean Rouat, and Dominic Létourneau. Robust sound source localization using a microphone array on a mobile robot. In *IEEE/RSJ-Int. Conf. on Intelligent Robots & Systems*, Oct. 2003.
11. J. M. Valin, J. Rouat, and F. Michaud. Microphone array post-filter for separation of simultaneous non-stationary sources. In *IEEE Int. Conf. on Acoustics Speech Signal Processing*, 17–21 May 2004.
12. I. Potamitis, G. Tremoulis, and N. Fakotakis. Multi-speaker DOA tracking using interactive multiple models and probabilistic data association. In *EUROSPEECH*, pages 517–520, September 2003.
13. Cristophe E. Schreiner and John V. Urbas. Representation of amplitude modulation in the auditory cortex of the cat. I.. the anterior auditory filed (AAF). *Hearing research*, 21:227–241, 1986.
14. C.E. Schreiner and G. Langner. Periodicity coding in the inferior colliculus of the cat. II, topographical organization. *Journal of Neurophysiology*, 60:1823–1840, 1988.
15. Luis Robles, Mario A. Ruggero, and Nola C. Rich. Two-tone distortion in the basilar membrane of the cochlea. *Nature*, 349:413, Jan. 1991.
16. E. F. Evans. Auditory processing of complex sounds: An overview. In *Phil. Trans. Royal Society of London*, pages 1–12, Oxford, 1992. Oxford Press.
17. Mario A. Ruggero, Luis Robles, Nola C. Rich, and Alberto Recio. Basilar membrane responses to two-tone and broadband stimuli. In *Phil. Trans. Royal Society of London*, pages 13–21, Oxford, 1992. Oxford Press.
18. Robert H. Arnott, Mark N. Wallace, Trevor M. Shackleton, and Alan R. Palmer. Onset neurones in the anteroventral cochlear nucleus project to the dorsal cochlear nucleus. *JARO*, 5(2):153–170, 2004.

19. D. Pressnitzer, R. Meddis, R. Delahaye and I.M. Winter. Physiological correlates of comodulation masking release in the mammalian VCN. *J. Neuroscience*, 21:6377–6386, 2001.
20. C. Giguere and Philip C. Woodland. A computational model of the auditory periphery for speech and hearing research. *JASA*, pages 331–349, 1994.
21. M.C. Liberman, S. Puria, and J.J. Jr. Guinan. The ipsilaterally evoked olivo-cochlearreflex causes rapid adaptation of the 2f1-f2 distortion product otoacoustic emission. *JASA*, 99:2572–3584, 1996.
22. SungHee Kim, D. Robert Frisina, and Robert D. Frisina. Effects of Age on Contralateral suppression of Distorsion Product Otoacoustic Emissions in Human Listeners with Normal Hearing. *Audiology Neuro Otology*, pages 7:348–357, 2002.
23. C. K. Henkel. The Auditory System. In Duane E. Haines, editor, *Fondamental Neuroscience*. Churchill Livingstone, 1997.
24. Ping Tang and Jean Rouat. Modeling neurons in the anteroventral cochlear nucleus for amplitude modulation (AM) processing: Application to speech sound. In *Proc. Int. Conf. on Spok. Lang. Proc.*, page Th.P.2S2.2, Oct 1996.
25. Sue Harding and Georg Meyer. Multi-resolution auditory scene analysis: Robust speech recognition using pattern-matching from a noisy signal. In *EUROSPEECH*, pages 2109–2112, September 2003.
26. Al Bregman. *Auditory Scene Analysis*. MIT Press, 1994.
27. Michael W. Beauvois and R. Meddis. A computer model of auditory stream segregation. *The Quaterly Journal of Experimental Psychology*, pages 517–541, 1991.
28. D. Wang and G. J. Brown. Separation of speech from interfering sounds based on oscillatory correlation. *IEEE Tr. on Neural Networks*, 10(3):684–697, May 1999.
29. M. Cooke and D. Ellis. The auditory organization of speech and other sources in listeners and computational models. *Speech Communication*, pages 141–177, 2001.
30. *Handbook of Neural Computation*. IOP Publishing Ltd and Oxford University Press, 1997.
31. W. Maass and C. M. Bishop. *Pulsed Neural Networks*. MIT Press, 1998.
32. S. Wermter, J. Austin, and D. Willshaw. *Emergent Neural Computational Architectures Based on Neuroscience, Towards Neuroscience-Inspired Computing*. Springer–Verlag, 2001.
33. W. Gerstner. *Spiking Neuron Models: Single Neurons, Populations, Plasticity*. Cambridge University Press, 2002.
34. Michael R. DeWeese and Anthony M. Zador. Binary coding in auditory cortex. In *NIPS*, December 2002.
35. S. Thorpe, D. Fize, and C. Marlot. Speed of processing in the human visual system. *Nature*, 381(6582):520–522, 1996.
36. S. Thorpe, A. Delorme, and R. Van Rullen. Spike-based strategies for rapid processing. *Neural Networks*, 14(6-7):715–725, 2001.
37. Thomas Natschläger and Wolfgang Maass. Information dynamics and emergent computation in recurrent circuits of spiking. In *NIPS*, December 2003.
38. B. Delgutte. Representation of speech-like sounds in the discharge patterns of auditory nerve fibers. *JASA*, 68:843–857, 1980.
39. R. D. Frisina, R. L. Smith, and S. C. Chamberlain. Differential encoding of rapid changes in sound amplitude by second-order auditory neurons. *Experimental Brain Research*, 60:417–422, 1985.
40. A. N. Popper and R. Fay, editors. *The Mammalian Auditory Pathway: Neurophysiology*. Springer–Verlag, 1992.

41. M. Hewitt and R. Meddis. A computer model of amplitude-modulation sensitivity of single units in the inferior colliculus. *Journal of the Acoustical Society of America*, 95(4):2145–2159, 04 1994.
42. Dmitry N. Zotkin, Shihab A. Shamma, Powen Ru, Ramani Duraiswami, and Larry S. Davis. Pitch and timbre manipulations using cortical representation of sound. In *ICASSP*, volume V, pages 517–520, 2003.
43. W. Maass. Networks of spiking neurons: The third generation of neural network models. *Neural Networks*, 10(9):1659–1671, 1997.
44. Wolfang Maass and Eduardo D. Sontag. Neural systems as nonlinear filters. *Neural Computation*, 12(8):1743–1772, aug 2000.
45. Thomas Natschläger, Wolfgang Maass, and Anthony Zador. Efficient temporal processing with biologically realistic dynamic synapses. *Network: Computation in Neural Systems*, 12(1):75–87, 2001.
46. Fred Rieke, David Warland, Rob de Ruyter van Steveninck, and William Bialek. *SPIKES Exploring the Neural Code*. MIT Press, 1997.
47. Terrence J. Sejnowski. Time for a new neural code? *Nature*, 376:21–22, 1995.
48. Michael DeWeese. Optimization principles for the neural code. *Network: Computation in Neural Systems*, 7(2):325–331, 1996.
49. Gal Chechik and Naftali Tishby. Temporally dependent plasticity: An information theoretic account. In *NIPS*, 2000.
50. Tuong Vinh Ho and Jean Rouat. Novelty detection based on relaxation time of a network of integrate–and–fire neurons. In *Proc. of the IEEE,INNS Int. Joint Conf. on Neural Networks*, volume 2, pages 1524–1529, May 1998.
51. Roman Borisyuk, Mike Denham, Frank Hoppensteadt, Yakov Kazanovich, and Olga Vinogradova. Oscillatory model of novelty detection. *Network: Computation in Neural Systems*, 12(1):1–20, 2001.
52. C. Panchev and S. Wermter. Spiking-time-dependent synaptic plasticity: From single spikes to spike trains. In *Computational Neuroscience Meeting*, pages 494–506. Springer–Verlag, july 2003.
53. Laurent Perrinet. *Comment déchifrer le code impulsionnel de la Vision ? Étude du flux parallèle, asynchrone et épars dans le traitement visuel ultra-rapide*. PhD thesis, Université Paul Sabatier, 2003.
54. P.M. Milner. A model for visual shape recognition. *Psychological Review*, 81:521–535, 1974.
55. Ch. v. d. Malsburg. The correlation theory of brain function. Technical Report Internal Report 81-2, Max-Planck Institute for Biophysical Chemistry, 1981.
56. Ch. v. d. Malsburg and W. Schneider. A neural cocktail-party processor. *Biol. Cybern.*, pages 29–40, 1986.
57. Ch. v. d. Malsburg. The what and why of binding: The modeler's perspective. *Neuron*, pages 95–104, 1999.
58. Sander M. Bohte, Han La Poutré, and Joost N. Kok. Unsupervised clustering with spiking neurons by sparse temporal coding and multilayer RBF networks. *IEEE Tr. on neural networks*, 13(2):426–435, March 2002.
59. J. L. Schwartz and P. Escudier. Auditory processing in a post-cochlear neural network: Vowel spectrum processing based on spike synchrony. *EUROSPEECH*, pages 247–253, 1989.
60. J. Hopfield. Pattern recognition computation using action potential timing for stimulus representation. *Nature*, 376:33–36, 1995.
61. N. Levy, D. Horn, I. Meilijson, and E. Ruppin. Distributed synchrony in a cell assembly of spiking neurons. *Neural Networks*, 14(6–7):815–824, 7 2001.

62. D.L. Wang and D. Terman. Image segmentation based on oscillatory correlation. *Neural Computation*, 9:805–836, 1997.
63. D.L. Alkon and K.T. Blackwell. Pattern recognition by an artificial network derived from biological neuronal systems. *Biological Cybernetics, Spring-Verlag*, 62:363–376, 1990.
64. K. T. Blackwell, T. P. Vogl, S. D. Hyman, G. S. Barbour, and D. L. Alkon. A new approach to hand-written character recognition. *Pattern Recognition Journal*, 25(6):655–666, 06 1992. Implémenté par M. Garcia.
65. J. Rouat and M. Garcia. A prototype speech recogniser based on associative learning and nonlinear speech analysis. In Rosenthal and Okuno, editors, *Computational Auditory Scene Analysis*, pages 13–26. L. Erlbaum, 1998.
66. Rufin VanRullen and Simon J. Thorpe. Surfing a spike wave down the ventral stream. *Vision Research*, 42(23):2593–2615, august 2002.
67. H. Sameti, H. Sheikhzadeh, L. Deng, and R.L. Brennan. HMM based strategies for enhancement of speech signals embedded in nonstationary noise. *IEEE Trans. on Speech and Audio Processing*, pages 445–455, 1998.
68. Sam. T. Roweis. One microphone source seperation. In *NIPS, Denver, USA*, 2000.
69. S.T. Roweis. Factorial models and refiltering for speech separation and denoising. In *Eurospeech*, 2003.
70. M. J. Reyes-Gomez, B. Raj, and D. Ellis. Multi-channel source separation by factorial HMMs. In *ICASSP*, 2003.
71. G. Jang and T. Lee. A maximum likelihood approach to single-channel source separation. *IEEE-SPL*, pages 168–171, 2003.
72. G. Hu and D.L. Wang. Monaural speech segregation based on pitch tracking and amplitude modulation. *IEEE Trans. On Neural Networks*, 1135– 1150, 2004.
73. Duane E. Haines, editor. *Fondamental Neuroscience*. Churchill Livingstone, 1997.
74. Les Atlas and Shihab A. Shamma. Joint acoustic and modulation frequency. *EURASIP J. on Appl. Sig. Proc.*, (7):668–675, 2003.
75. G. Meyer, D. Yang, and W. Ainsworth. Applying a model of concurrent vowel segregation to real speech. *Computational models of auditory function Eds. Greenberg S. and Slaney M.*, pages 297–310, 2001.
76. J. Rouat. Spatio-temporal pattern recognition with neural networks: Application to speech. In *Artificial Neural Networks-ICANN'97*, Lect. Notes in Comp. Sc. 1327, pages 43–48. Springer, 10 1997.
77. J. Rouat, Y. C. Liu, and D. Morissette. A pitch determination and voiced/unvoiced decision algorithm for noisy speech. *Speech Comm.*, 21:191–207, 1997.
78. F. Plante, G. Meyer, and W. Ainsworth. Improvement of speech spectrogram accuracy by the method of reassignment. *IEEE Trans. on Speech and Audio Processing*, pages 282–287, 1998.
79. F. Gabbiani, H. Krapp, C. Koch, and G. Laurent. Multiplicative computation in a visual neuron sensitive to looming. *Nature*, 420:320–324, 2002.
80. JL. Pena and M. Konishi. Auditory spatial receptive fields created by multiplication. *Science*, 292:294–252, 2001.
81. R.A. Andersen, L.H. Snyder, D.C. Bradley, and J. Xing. Multimodal representation of space in the posterior parietal cortex and its use in planning movements. *Ann. Rev. Neurosci.*, page 20:303, 1997.
82. Ramin Pichevar. http://www-edu.gel.usherbrooke.ca/pichevar/, 2004.
83. J. Rouat. http://www.gel.usherb.ca/rouat, 2004.
84. Melvyn J. Hunt and Claude Lefebvre. Speech recognition using an auditory model with pitch-synchronous analysis. In *ICASSP*, pages 813–816, New York, 1987. IEEE.

85. Melvyn J. Hunt and Claude Lefebvre. Speaker dependent and independent speech recognition experiments with an auditory model. In *IEEE ICASSP*, pages 215–218, New York, 04 1988. IEEE.

86. S. Seneff. A joint synchrony/mean-rate model of auditory speech processing. *Journal of Phonetics*, 16(1):55–76, 1988.

87. Robert McEachern. How the ear really works. *IEEE Int. Symp. Time-frequency and Time-Scale Analysis*, 10 1992.

88. Robert McEachern. Hearing it like it is: Audio signal processing the way the ear does it. *DSP Applications*, pages 35–47, 02 1994.

89. Luc Van Immerseel. *Een Functioneel Gehoormodel Voor de Analyse Van Spraak Bij Spraakherkenning*. PhD thesis, 05 1993.

90. Oded Ghitza. Auditory models and human performance in tasks related to speech coding and speech recognition. *IEEE TrSAP*, 2(1):115–132, 1 1994.

91. Sumeet Sandhu and Oded Ghitza. A comparative study of mel cepstra and EIH for phone classification under adverse conditions. *ICASSP*, pages 409–412, 1995.

92. Malcolm Slaney and Richard F. Lyon. A perceptual pitch detector. *ICASSP*, pages 357–360, 03 1990.

93. Malcolm Slaney and Richard F. Lyon. On the importance of time - a temporal representation of sound. In *Visual Representations of Speech Signals*, pages 95–116. John Wiley & Sons, 1993.

94. William Ainsworth and Georg Meyer. Speech analysis by means of a physiologically-based model of the cochlear nerve and cochlear nucleus. In *ESCA ETRW Visual Representations of Speech Signals*, pages 119–124, Sheffield, 1993. John Wiley & Sons.

95. Roy D. Patterson. The sound of a sinusoid I: Spectral models. *JASA*, 96(3):1409–1418, 09 1994.

96. Roy D. Patterson. The sound of a sinusoid II: Spectral models. *JASA*, 96(3):1419–1428, 09 1994.

97. M.J. Hunt and C. Lefèbvre. A comparison of several acoustic representations for speech recognition with degraded and undegraded speech. In *ICASSP*, pages 262–265, May 1989.

98. M.J. Hunt. Spectral signal processing for asr. In *Proc. IEEE International Workshop on Automatic Speech Recognition and Understanding (ASRU)*, Dec. 12-15 1999.

99. Stéphane Loiselle. Exploration de réseaux de neurones à décharges dans un contexte de reconnaissance de parole. Master's thesis, Université du Québec à Chicoutimi, 2004.

An Algorithm to Estimate Anticausal Glottal Flow Component from Speech Signals

Baris Bozkurt, François Severin, and Thierry Dutoit

TCTS Lab. Faculté Polytechnique de Mons, Initialis Sci. Park, B-7000 Mons, Belgium
{baris.bozkurt,francois.severin,thierry.dutoit}@tcts.fpms.ac.be

Abstract. In this paper, we define an algorithm with low complexity which performs a new use of the linear prediction analysis (covariance method) to retrieve the maximum-phase component of speech signals. First, we study the mixed-phase model of speech through a new representation named the Zeros of Z-Transform (ZZT) in the z-plane, which is an all-zero representation of the z-transform of a discrete time signal. Then, based on the properties of the mixed-phase model, we introduce an algorithm to estimate the anticausal glottal flow component from speech signals. LP-covariance analysis is used to estimate a pole pair outside the unit circle corresponding to the anticausal poles of the source signal component in the mixed-phase speech model. Given the pair of anticausal poles, a procedure to resynthesize the anticausal part of the glottal flow, and then an open quotient estimation method, are proposed. Evaluations show that the method is high quality for analyzing synthetic speech but lacks robustness in analysis of natural speech.

1 Introduction

This study targets estimation of the anticausal component in speech due to the first phase of the glottal flow (i.e. the glottal flow signal without the return phase). Our study is based on the mixed-phase speech model, which assumes that the speech signal is produced by convolution of a maximum phase glottal excitation signal with a minimum phase vocal tract filter impulse response [1].

When an all-pole model is studied for such a mixed phase signal, some of the poles fall outside the unit circle. In speech processing, poles outside the unit circle are most of the time (if not all) avoided/reflected due to the minimum-phase assumption. In this study, we follow the inverse path: we try to find outside poles for estimation of glottal flow characteristics.

The minimum-phase assumption relies on two properties: stability and causality. All the poles of a signal that is causal and stable must lie inside the unit circle on the z-plane. However, in the mixed-phase speech model, our assumption is: the speech signal is obtained by convolving an anticausal and stable glottal flow signal with a causal and stable vocal tract filter. The resonances due to the glottal flow signal correspond to poles outside the unit-circle on the z-plane but these poles are anticausal, and therefore still stable. The mathematical background for the glottal flow poles that are outside the unit circle can be found in [2].

In Fig. 1, we present the mixed-phase speech model in the time domain, in the frequency domain through amplitude and group delay spectra, in the z-plane through all-pole representation and zeros of z-transform (ZZT) representation. ZZT repre-

G. Chollet et al. (Eds.): Nonlinear Speech Modeling, LNAI 3445, pp. 338–343, 2005.
© Springer-Verlag Berlin Heidelberg 2005

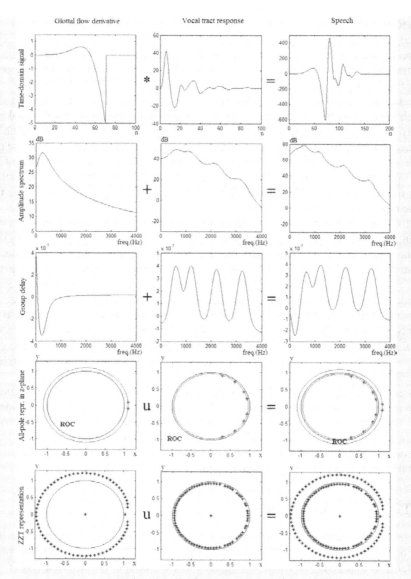

Fig. 1. The mixed-phase speech model

sentation is a new representation that serves as a domain to study z-transform characteristics of an actual discrete time signal. The ZZT representation, is defined as the set
of roots/zeros (which can be found by some numerical method) of the Z-transform
polynomial for a discrete time signal [3]. The last row of Fig. 1 includes the ZZT
representations (roots plotted on the z-plane) of the glottal flow derivative, of the
truncated vocal tract impulse response and of the speech signal obtained by convolution of these two signals (a convolution operation in the time domain corresponds to
the union of ZZT sets). It is necessary to use such a representation in a practical

framework where actual speech signals are to be analyzed, since the existence of the mixed-phase characteristics on speech data (therefore the existence of poles outside the unit circle) depends on the windowing applied. Systematically studying the ZZT of windowed speech signals, we showed that the windowing needs to be properly performed (a Blackman, Gaussian or Hanning-Poisson window of less than two pitch periods size, centered at glottal closure instants) to be able to extract speech data which have the same mixed-phase ZZT structure as that of the theoretical signal presented in Fig. 1 [3]. The ZZT representation is composed of N-1 zeros plotted on the z-plane. It is important to note that the ZZT of glottal flow are located outside the unit circle (with an exception at the origin) surrounding zero-gaps at the location of the poles presented in the all-pole representation. The ZZT of speech signal is organized such that ZZT of glottal flow and ZZT of vocal tract fall on opposite sides of the unit circle in z-plane.

Mixed-phase characteristics are best observed on group delay spectra since causality/anticausality of a resonance cannot be observed on the amplitude spectra. As seen on the third row of Fig. 1, the group delay spectrum of the glottal flow includes a negative peak that also contributes to the speech signal group delay as a negative peak at low frequency part of the spectrum since convolution in time domain corresponds to addition in group delay domain. The anticausal (outside of the unit circle) poles of glottal flow signal which causes negative group delay peak is presented in the all-pole representation on the fourth row of Fig. 1. The region of convergences (ROC) are also indicated on the all-pole representations, which is also linked to causality-stability of the signals. All of the three signals are stable since unit circle is included in the ROC.

Based on the processing of the ZZT of speech signals, we have developed a glottal flow parameter estimation method [4]. However methods including computation of ZZT are computationally heavy since roots of high order polynomials need to be computed, therefore computationally more efficient methods are needed. This study investigates utilization of linear prediction methods to track outside poles due to the glottal flow contribution in the speech signals.

2 The MixLP Algorithm

The proposed Mixed-Phase Linear Prediction (MixLP) algorithm, for detecting a pole pair outside the unit circle corresponding to the contribution of the maximum phase glottal flow signal, is presented in Fig. 2a. First, a glottal closure instant (GCI) synchronous windowing is applied to the speech signal and a single pitch period length signal in-between two consecutive GCI marks is extracted with the method explained in [5]. Obtained speech frame is integrated, to remove the lip radiation contribution. LP-covariance analysis [6] is applied to this signal, which is expected to result in a pole pair outside the unit circle and several other pole pairs inside the unit circle. This is a particular property of the LP covariance analysis, usually considered as a sign of unstability of the estimation algorithm [7].

It is interesting to mention some of the investigations performed during the design of the algorithm. Our first investigation was to find optimum windowing since the existence of poles outside the unit circle heavily depends on the applied windowing. Although we have shown through ZZT representation that mixed-phase characteris-

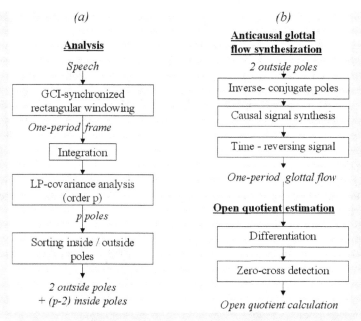

Fig. 2. MixLP algorithm flow diagram

tics can be observed on the Fourier transform of the windowed speech signal when the window is centred at GCI, such windowing is not appropriate for estimation of poles outside the unit circle with LP-covariance. By applying sliding window analysis and checking correctness of estimates on synthetic speech signals, we have observed that the end of the window must be synchronized with the GCI (a few samples before the GCI is a good choice for safety) and including even a few data samples after the GCI results in no poles outside the unit circle most of the time. A second investigation was on the order of the LP analysis, tested in the range [2-32] for 16000Hz synthetic speech signals (for which the LF model was used to synthesize glottal flow excitation and filtered by a four pole-pair all-pole vocal tract filter). The LP degree which provided best estimates is 14 or higher.

3 Analysing Synthetic and Natural Speech

In order to test the MixLP algorithm we have designed a method to estimate the open quotient (Fig. 2b) from poles outside the unit circle. This includes the resynthesis of the glottal flow from the poles, which is achieved by: synthesis of a causal signal by computing the impulse response of a two-pole filter with the inverse-conjugate poles, and time reversion of this signal. A differentiation provides the differentiated glottal flow. In Fig. 3 we present an example of a glottal flow estimate using the MixLP method, together with a glottal flow estimate using a well-known inverse filtering algorithm (PSIAIF [8]). The open quotient is estimated on the differentiated glottal flow with a zero-cross detection method.

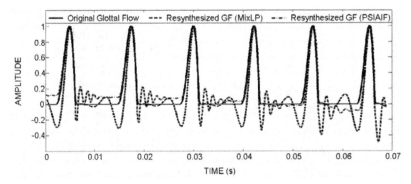

Fig. 3. Resynthesized glottal flow signals obtained with the MixLP and PSIAIF algorithms

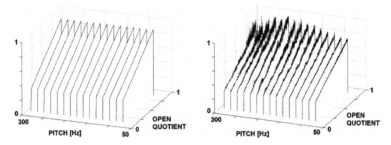

Fig. 4. Real and estimated open quotient, based on synthetic speech (a sustained vowel with constant first formant and return phase) for several values of the pitch

For evaluation of the open quotient estimation method, tests were conducted on synthetic speech signals, in which several parameters (pitch, spectral tilt, first formant frequency and open quotient) were varied systematically and higher formant frequencies are kept constant. Due to space limitations, we only present the output of our test for checking the robustness of estimation to pitch variations in Fig. 4. Some conclusions are: the error is small when the open quotient is higher than 0.7, and otherwise it is negligible. Moreover, the open quotient is better estimated if the return phase is short, and especially if the pitch is high. This open quotient estimation method was also compared to a well-known algorithm ([9]). Both methods provide similar results but the MixLP estimation method is more effective when the first formant frequency is small.

The open quotient estimation on natural speech was also tested. As a reference for the open quotient estimation tests, we used open quotient estimates obtained from differential electro-glotto-graph signals by using a thresholding method. Observations on a few natural utterances showed that the MixLP estimation method is not robust as the estimation error depends on the phonetic context.

4   Conclusions

In this paper, we have discussed the mixed-phase characteristics of windowed speech signals through zeros of z-transform (ZZT) representations which corresponds to the set of roots of the z-transform polynomial for a discrete time signal. ZZT representation appears to be an effective representation for studying mixed-phase characteristics of signals in the Z-domain. For speech signals, the observation of mixed-phase characteristics depends on the applied windowing and GCI synchronous windowing is necessary. A linear method was presented here for estimating the maximum phase glottal flow signal and the open quotient. Tests showed that open quotient estimation can be successfully performed on synthetic signals with LP-covariance analysis but the method lacks robustness when real speech signals are analyzed.

References

1. Bozkurt, B., Dutoit, T.: Mixed-Phase Speech Modeling and Formant Estimation, Using Differential Phase Spectrums. Proc. ISCA ITRW VOQUAL, Geneva, Switzerland (2003) 21–24.
2. Doval, B., d'Alessandro, C., Henrich, N.: The Voice Source As A Causal/Anticausal Linear Filter. Proc. ISCA ITRW VOQUAL, Geneva, Switzerland (2003) 15–19.
3. Bozkurt, B., Doval, B., d'Alessandro, C., Dutoit, T.: Zeros of Z-Transform (ZZT) Decomposition Of Speech For Source-Tract Separation. Proc. ICSLP, Jeju Island, Korea (2004).
4. Bozkurt, B., Doval, B., d'Alessandro, C., Dutoit, T.: A Method For Glottal Formant Frequency Estimation. Proc. ICSLP, Jeju Island, Korea (2004).
5. Kawahara, H., Atake, Y., and Zolfaghari, P.: Accurate vocal event detection method based on a fixed-point to weighted average group delay. Proc. ICSLP, Beijing, (2000) 664–667.
6. Makhoul, J.: Linear Prediction: A Tutorial Review. Proc. IEEE (1975) 561-580.
7. Makhoul, J.: Lattice Methods For Linear Prediction, IEEE Trans. On Acoustics, Speech, And Signal Processing, Vol. ASSP-25 (1977) 423-428.
8. Alku, P.: Glottal Wave Analysis With Pitch Synchronous Iterative Adaptive Inverse Filtering. Speech Communication 11 (1992) 109-118.
9. Hanson, H.M.: Glottal Characteristics Of Female Speakers. Ph.D. Thesis, Harvard University (1995).

Non-linear Speech Feature Extraction for Phoneme Classification and Speaker Recognition

Mohamed Chetouani[1], Marcos Faundez-Zanuy[2],
Bruno Gas[1], and Jean-Luc Zarader[1]

[1] Laboratoire des Instruments et Systèmes d'Ile-De-France
Université Paris VI, Paris, France
[2] Escola Universitària Politècnica de Mataró, Barcelona, Spain

Abstract. In this paper we propose a new feature extraction algorithm based on non-linear prediction: the Neural Predictive Coding (NPC) model which is an extension of the classical LPC one. We apply this model to two significant tasks: phoneme classification and speaker identification. For the first one, the NPC model is trained with a Minimum Classification Error (MCE) criterion. The experiments carried out with the NTIMIT database show an improvement of the classification rates. For speaker identification, we propose a new feature extraction principle based on the NPC model. We also investigate different initialization methods. The new method gives better performances than the traditional ones (LPC, MFCC and PLP).

1 Introduction

The design of speech and speaker recognition systems is commonly based on three stages: signal acquisition, feature extraction and pattern classification. Feature extraction is an important stage in recognition systems. The main objective of this stage is the extraction of relevant characteristics for the next stage which is the classification stage. It is usually done in a same way for phoneme classification and for speaker recognition whereas the final purpose is different. Linear Predictive Coding (LPC) or the Mel Frequency Cepstral Coding (MFCC) are the most used methods.

However, some limits seem to be reached and it is difficult to overcome them with conventional methods. One of the reasons is the great variability of the speech signal. Variations are due to several elements. There are obviously inter-speakers and intra-speakers variabilities. The sound environment as well as the phonetic context (coarticulation) are also elements prone to introduce variability into speech signals. Several authors pointed out the need of specific features for each task [1], [2]: speech transmission, speech, speaker recognition or even language identification.

A good feature extractor must extract the features necessary to the recognition process. The problem is that these features are not really known. A solution consists in the exploitation of knowledge about the human operation. This way is limited by the efficiency of the knowledge for the objective [1]. Some of the

G. Chollet et al. (Eds.): Nonlinear Speech Modeling, LNAI 3445, pp. 344–350, 2005.

phenomena are useful like critical bands (filter banks) or non-linear modelization (Mel and Bark scales) which have been implemented in the MFCC or the PLP. Designing feature extractor by exploiting these knowledge is called data-driven methods [1].

In this paper, we focus on feature extraction for two significant tasks in speech processing: phoneme classification and speaker identification. The proposed work is an investigation on non-linear speech processing in feature extraction. For that, we examine non-linear modelization but also discriminant criteria.

The paper is organized as following. First, we describe our non-linear model called the Neural Predictive Coding (NPC). Then, we discuss on the two different tasks: phoneme classification and speaker identification. For both experiences are carried out and they give significant improvements of the recognition rates.

2   Neural Predictive Coding

The Neural Predictive Coding (NPC) model [3] is a non-linear extension of the well-known LPC encoder. Like in the LPC framework with the AR model, the vector code is estimated by prediction error minimization. The main difference lies in the fact that the model is non-linear and it is a connectionnist model:

$$\hat{y}_k = F(\mathbf{y}_k) = \sum_j a_j \sigma(\mathbf{w}^T \mathbf{y}_k) \tag{1}$$

Where F is the prediction function realized by the neural model. $\hat{y}_k$ is the predicted sample. $\mathbf{y}_k$ the prediction context: $\mathbf{y}_k = [y_{k-1}, y_{k-2}, ..., y_{k-\lambda}]^T$ and λ the length of the prediction window. $\mathbf{w}$ and $\mathbf{a}$ represent the first and the output layer weights. σ is a non-linear activation function, the sigmoid function in our case.

The key idea is to use the NPC model as a non-linear auto-regressive model. As in the LPC framework for the predictor coefficients, the NPC weights are the vector code. It is well-known that the weights can be consider as a representation of the input vector. A drawback of this method is that non-linear models have no clear physical meanings [4]. The solution weights can be very different for a same minimum of the prediction error. In our approach, we impose constraints on weights.

2.1   Description

The NPC model is a Multi-Layer Perceptron (MLP) with one hidden layer. Only the output layer weights are used as coding vector instead of all the neural weights. For that we consider that the function F realized by the model, under convergence assumptions, can be decomposed into two functions: $G_\mathbf{w}$ ($\mathbf{w}$ first layer weights) and $H_\mathbf{a}$ ($\mathbf{a}$ output layer weights):

$$F_{\mathbf{w},\mathbf{a}}(\mathbf{y}_k) = H_\mathbf{a} \circ G_\mathbf{w}(\mathbf{y}_k) \tag{2}$$

With $\hat{y}_k = H_\mathbf{a}(\mathbf{z}_k)$ and $\mathbf{z}_k = G_\mathbf{w}(\mathbf{y}_k)$.

As one can note the NPC structure allows a different prediction window's length independently to the coding vector size contrary to the LPC structure.

For the layers specialization, the learning phase is realized in two times. First, the *parameterization phase* consists in the learning of all the weights by the prediction error minimization criterion:

$$Q = \sum_{k=1}^{K}(y_k - \hat{y}_k)^2 = \sum_{k=1}^{K}(y_k - F(\mathbf{y}_k))^2 \tag{3}$$

With y the speech signal, $\hat{y}$ the predicted speech signal, k the samples index and K the number of samples.

In this phase, only the first layer weights $\mathbf{w}$ which are the NPC encoder parameters are kept. Since the NPC encoder is set up by the parameters defined in the previous phase, the second phase, called the *coding phase*, consists in the computation of the output layer weights $\mathbf{a}$ (vector code). This is done also by prediction error minimization but only the output layer weights are updated. One can note that the output function is linear (cf. equation 1), so it can be done by the Levinson algorithm as for the LPC model. Here, for consistency with the *parameterization phase*, it is done by the backpropagation algorithm.

The result from the layers specialization, the first layer weights $\mathbf{w}$ are common to all the speech signal frames while the second layer weights $\mathbf{a}$ are specific to each frame. For each frame, a feature vector $\mathbf{a}$ is computed by prediction error minimization.

3   Feature Extraction in Phoneme Classification

The purpose of this task is to extract phonetic information from the speech signal. In this section, we investigate the importance of non-linear modelization. First, we compare our non-linear feature extractor (NPC) to traditional methods in order to validate the importance of non-linear modelization. Secondly, we propose a discriminant model with non-linear discrimination.

The discriminant model is based on the simultaneous training of a classifier and the NPC model [5] (see figure 1). For classification, we use the LVQ model (Learning Vector Quantization). The LVQ and the NPC are optimized through the Minimum Classification Error (MCE) criterion and the new model is called the LVQ-NPC model.

3.1   Evaluation and Discussion

The NTIMIT database [6] is used in this experiment and more especially the two first regions (DR1, DR2). By using this database, we carry out speech recognition in telephone quality. We focus on the processing of front vowels (/ih/, /ey/, /eh/, /ae/), voiced plosives (/b/, /d/, /g/) and unvoiced plosives (/p/, /t/, /k/). This choice can be justified by the fact that the classification of these phonemes is known to be difficult and they are also often used. For training and test

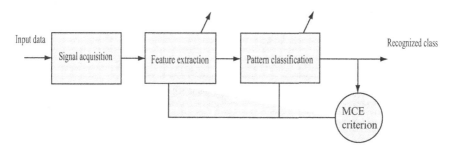

Fig. 1. Discriminative Feature Extraction based on the Minimum Classification Error

databases, we use the division proposed by the database. A part of the training set is used as a cross-validation base, in order to stop the classifiers training but also the LVQ-NPC *parameterization phase*. The classification is carried out by GMM (16 centers, diagonal assumption) and it is a frame by frame classification (32ms with 16ms of overlapping). The dimension of the features is set to 12.

The classification rates for the different methods are presented table 1. For voiced phonemes, the performances are improved by non-linear methods (NPC: 49.03%, LVQ-NPC: 54.81%) even in the case of the plosives.

Table 1. Classification rates: significative improvements by non-linear and discriminant methods

Phoneme	LPC	MFCC	PLP	NPC	LVQ-NPC
/ih/, /ey/, /eh, /ae/	35.22	48.12	45.12	49.03	**54.81**
/b/, /d/, /g/	54.13	59.23	57.21	62.24	**66.33**
/p/, /t/, /k/	44.10	51.45	46.98	49.36	**53.22**

For unvoiced phonemes, the performances are degraded for predictive methods (LPC: 44.10%, NPC: 49.36%) compared to the MFCC (51.45%). However, discrimination makes it possible to overcome this problem and to obtain better results LVQ-NPC: 53.22% (cf. table 1). This result is important because it shows that non-linear approach is obviously needed for modelization but also for discrimination.

4   Feature Extraction in Speaker Identification

This section is devoted to another task: feature extraction for speaker identification. This task consists in the extraction of speaker dependent features and they have to be independent to the phonetic context. As for phoneme classification, these features are not really known even if some efforts have been done [2].

Currently in speaker recognition, feature extraction is carried out in a same way for all the speakers. Most of the efforts have been made in the second

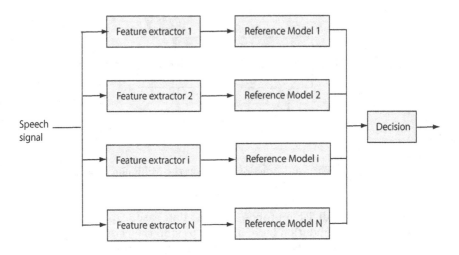

Fig. 2. Speaker dependent feature extraction principle

stage which is the model of the speaker. In our system, the speaker is obviously modelized by the second stage (reference model) but the first stage (feature extractor) is also specialized in the processing of this speaker. The speaker-dependent features are extracted by the NPC model (see figure 2). Each NPC model is specialized in the processing of only one speaker.

4.1   Linear Initialization of Non-linear Models

We also investigate initialization of non-linear models [7]. This initialization is referred as a linear initialization but it differs from conventional neural networks initializations. The proposed initialization exploits speech knowledge. We used the LPC coding method for the initialization of the non-linear coding model. By this way, one can see the NPC as a non-linear feature extractor initialized by a linear model. By neglecting biaises and removing the non-linear activation functions (for linear approximation), one obtains the following equivalence:

$$\Theta = \mathbf{w} \bullet \mathbf{a} \tag{4}$$

Where Θ are the LPC parameters of the speech signal, $\mathbf{w}$ first layer weights (determined in the previous phase: the *parameterization phase*) and $\mathbf{a}$ second layer weights.

If the NPC vector code dimension is ρ and the prediction window is λ then the LPC vector code dimension has to be set to λ. The second layer weights $\mathbf{a}$ are given by:

$$\mathbf{a} = \mathbf{w}^+ \bullet \Theta \tag{5}$$

Where $\mathbf{w}^+$ is the pseudo-inverse of $\mathbf{w}$.

The initialized weights are determined by a simple LPC analysis with an order λ. Once the initialization is accomplished, the coding process (prediction error minimization) proceeds as well as the original NPC *coding phase* by the backpropagation algorithm.

Initialization of non-linear models by linear ones has been already investigated [8] but with matrices decomposition methods (SVD, QR,...). The main limitation relies in the multiplicity of the solution. In this paper, we propose a method which guarantees a single solution.

4.2 Evaluation and Discussion

Our experiments have been computed over 49 speakers from the Gaudi database [9] that has been obtained with a microphone connected to a PC. One minute of read text is used for training, and 5 sentences for testing (each sentence is about 2-3 seconds long). The feature vector dimension is set to 16. A covariance matrix (CM) is computed for each speaker, and an Arithmetic-Harmonic Sphericity (AHS) measure is used in order to compare matrices [10].

Table 2 presents the experimental results. One can see that for the traditional methods, the best performances are obtained for the MFCC (97.55%) and the LPCC (96.73%) coding methods. These methods try to model the phonetic context but also the speaker characteristics. The LPC model has a better score (90.61%) than the PLP (86.12%). This is due to the fact that the PLP method suppresses speaker dependent characteristics. It is why the PLP allows comparable performances with the MFCC in speech recognition task (cf. Section 3).

Table 2. Speaker identification rates

Speech coding method	Identification rate (%)
LPC	90.61
LPCC	96.73
MFCC	97.55
PLP	86.12
NPC (random initialization)	61.63
NPC (linear initialization)	100

Depending on the initialization, the NPC behavior is very different. We obtain 61.63% for the random initialization while for the linear initialization we obtain 100%. This last initialization gives the best results. One of the reasons is that it allows the unicity of the initialization. Another reason is that the LPC is appropriated to the modelization of voiced part which contains more speaker-dependent characteristics.

5 Conclusions

Usually, speech and speaker recognition systems are improved by statistical methods. In this paper, we study the feature extraction stage. This stage can be improved by several methods and among them non-linear processing. Feature extraction in phoneme classification has shown that non-linear processing is needed for modelization but also for discrimination. We proposed another method for feature extraction in speaker identification. In this task, we show that non-linear models can be initialized by linear models and it can be useful.

The proposed work is an investigation on feature extractors. We show that non-linear speech processing can be effective if we use it in a suitable way.

References

1. H. Hermansky: Should Recognizers Have Ears?. Speech Communication. **25** (1998) 3–27
2. L. Mary, K.S. Rama Murty, S.R. Mahadeva Prasanna, B. Yegnanarayana. Features for Speaker and Language Identification. Proc. of ISCA Tutorial and Research Workshop on Speaker and Language Recognition (Odyssey'04). (2004), 323–328
3. B. Gas, J.L. Zarader, C. Chavy, M. Chetouani. Discriminant neural predictive coding applied to phoneme recognition. Neurocomputing. **56**, (2004), 141–166
4. W. B. Kleijn. Signal Processing Representations of Speech. IEICE Trans. Inf. and Syst. **E86-D**, 3, March, (2003), 359–376
5. M. Chetouani, B. Gas, J.L. Zarader. Learning vector quantization and neural predictive coding for nonlinear speech feature extraction. EUSIPCO (2004).
6. C. Jankowski and A. Kalyanswamy and S. Basson and J. Spitz. NTIMIT: A Phonetically Balanced, Continous Speech, Telephone Bandwidth Speech Database. ICASSP, 1, (1990), 109–112.
7. M. Chetouani, M. Faundez-Zanuy, B. Gas, J.L. Zarader. A new nonlinear speaker parameterization algorithm for speaker identification. Proc. of ISCA Tutorial and Research Workshop on Speaker and Language Recognition (Odyssey'04). (2004), 309–314.
8. T. L. Burrows. Speech Processing with Linear and Neural Networks Models. PhD Cambridge, 1996.
9. J. Ortega-Garcia and al. Ahumada: a large speech corpus in Spanish for speaker identification and verification. ICASSP, 2, (1998), 773–776.
10. F. Bimbot and L. Mathan. Text-free speaker recognition using an arithmetic-harmonic sphericity measure. EUROSPEECH, (1991), 169–172

Segmental Scores Fusion for ALISP-Based GMM Text-Independent Speaker Verification

Asmaa El Hannani[1,*] and Dijana Petrovska-Delacrétaz[1,2]

[1] DIVA Group, Informatics Dept., University of Fribourg, Switzerland
asmaa.elhannani@unifr.ch
[2] Institut National des Télécommunications, 91011 Evry, France
dijana.petrovska@int-evry.fr

Abstract. Traditional speaker verification systems are limited to the use of frame-based spectral features that are basically modeled globally via Gaussian Mixture Models (GMM). With such methods the probability density function of the acoustic feature vectors is estimated globally and the linguistic structure of the speech signal is not taken into account. In this paper we study the performance of a speaker verification system based on a combination of a data-driven Automatic Language Independent Speech Processing (ALISP) segmentation and a classical GMM based system. Even though the ALISP classes are not being explicitly modeled by the GMMs and the segmental information is used only during the scoring phase, the proposed segmental approach slightly outperforms the baseline global GMM system. Two techniques are used to combine the segmental scores in order to exploit the different amounts of discrimination provided by the ALISP classes: the Logistic Regression and the Multi-Layer Perceptron. Improvement in performance has been made by using the Multi-Layer Perceptron. The evaluation of the proposed method is done on the NIST 2004 Speaker Recognition Evaluation data.

1 Introduction

Traditional speaker verification systems are limited to the use of frame-based spectral features that are basically modeled globally via Gaussian Mixture Models (GMM). In such systems the linguistic structure of the speech signal is not taken into account and all sounds are represented using a unique model. Hence the phoneme-specific information is ignored. Various studies [1], [2], [3] and [4] have shown that voiced phones and fricatives are the most effective broad speech classes for speaker discrimination.

Among the previous work, [5] used phoneme-specific Hidden Markov Models (HMMs) for modeling the target speakers. [6] and [7] used a speaker verification system based on broad phonetic categories and achieved an improvement over the baseline system. In [8], GMM and HMM were compared, and unlike in the above cited works, phonetic information was used only during the scoring phase.

* Supported by the Swiss National Fund for Scientific Research, No. 2100-067043.01/1.

G. Chollet et al. (Eds.): Nonlinear Speech Modeling, LNAI 3445, pp. 351–356, 2005.
© Springer-Verlag Berlin Heidelberg 2005

[9] introduced a phonetic class-based GMM system based on a tree-like structure, which outperformed the baseline global GMM. Closer to what is presented in [9], are the works done by [10] and [11], where phoneme-adapted GMMs were built for each speaker. [10] and [11] concluded that the phoneme-adapted GMM system outperformed the phoneme independent GMM system. In order to apply such techniques, a phone recognizer is needed. During the training phase of the phone recognizer, transcribed databases are needed. Transcribing databases is an error-prone and expensive task. To avoid this problem, we propose to use Automatic Language Independent Speech Processing (ALISP) tools [12]. The segmentation can be obtained automatically on speech data without any transcriptions.

In the present work we describe an ALISP-based GMM system which is a combination of a GMM system and a data-driven segmentation based on ALISP tools. The ALISP classes are not explicitly modeled by the GMMs and the segmental information is used only during the scoring phase. This paper focuses on the weighted combination of the scores, compared to a baseline system where all the speech classes are being treated in the same way.

The outline of this paper is the following: In Sect. 2 more details about the proposed method are given. Sect. 3 describes the database used and the experimental protocol. The evaluation results are reported in Sect. 4. The conclusions are given in Sect. 5.

2   Systems Description

2.1   Baseline GMM System

The baseline system is based on Gaussian Mixture Models [13] in which the multivariate distribution of the feature vectors is modeled with a weighted sum of Gaussian distributions. Two gender-dependent background models are created and each speaker model is obtained by adaptation of the matching gender background model.

For each frame y_t in the test segment a score is calculated using the log-likelihood ratio of the speaker likelihood to the background likelihood

$$s_{y_t} = log\, p(y_t|X) - log\, p(y_t|\overline{X}) \tag{1}$$

where X and $\overline{X}$ denote the client and the world models respectively. The final score Λ^j is obtained by summing the frames' scores and normalizing by T; the total number of frames in the test utterance j:

$$\Lambda^j = \frac{1}{T} \sum_{t=1}^{T} s_{y_t} \tag{2}$$

2.2   ALISP-Based GMM System

This system is the same as the baseline GMM system except that the scoring corresponds to a combination of scores belonging to the ALISP segments detected in the test speech data. This system is a combination of a traditional GMM system and a data-driven segmentation method.

The data-driven segmentation is achieved using the ALISP tools [12]. This approach is based on units acquired during a data-driven segmentation, where no phonetic transcription of the corpus is needed. The modeling of the set of data-driven speech units, denoted as ALISP units, is achieved through the following stages. After the pre-processing step for the speech data, first Temporal Decomposition is used, followed by Vector Quantization providing a symbolic transcription of the data in an unsupervised manner. Hidden Markov Modeling is further applied for a better coherence of the initial ALISP units.

During the test phase, each test speech data is first segmented with the 64 ALISP HMM models. Then for each ALISP segment found in the test utterance a score is calculated by summing the likelihood estimation of frames present in the segment (see Equation 1) and normalizing by the total number of frames in this segment.

Finally, and after the computation of a score for each ALISP segment, the segmental scores are combined together to generate an overall score for the test utterance.

As described previously, speech classes have different discriminant power for speaker recognition. In this work Logistic Regression [14] and Multi-Layer Perceptrons (MLP) [15] are used to find automatically the different weighs for the ALISP classes from the development set.

3   Experimental Setup

All experiments are done on the NIST'2004 data which is split into two different subsets: the *Development-set* and the *Evaluation-set*, used to test the performance of the proposed system.

The speech parameterization is done with Mel Frequency Cepstral Coefficients (MFCC), calculated on 20 ms windows, with a 10 ms shift. For each frame a 15-element cepstral vector is computed and appended with first order deltas. Cepstral mean substraction is applied to the 15 static coefficients and only bands in the 300-3400 Hz frequency range are used. The energy and delta-energy are used in addition during the ALISP units recognition.

During the preprocessing step, after the speech parametrization, we separated the speech from the non-speech data. The speech activity detector is based on a bi-Gaussian modeling of the energy of the speech data [16]. Only frames higher than a certain threshold are chosen for further processing. Using this method, 56% of the original NIST 2004 data are removed.

In the GMM[1] system two gender-dependent background models are built and for each target speaker, a specific GMM with diagonal covariance matrices is trained via maximum a posteriori (MAP) adaptation of the Gaussian means of the matching gender background model. The two gender-dependent background models (with 512 Gaussians) are trained using 5 iterations of the Expectation Maximization (EM) algorithm.

---

[1] Based on the BECARS package [17]

The gender dependent background models for the GMMs and the gender dependent ALISP recognizers, are trained on a total of about 6 hours of data from (1999 and 2001) NIST data sets.

The MLP and the Logistic Regression are trained on the development set. Since the ALISP units do not always occur in the test data, not all of the ALISP units scores were available for each speaker. For training the MLP, the missing scores were replaced by zero.

4   Experimental Results

We present here results for "8sides-1side" NIST 2004 task on the evaluation data set, as defined in section 3. For this task we dispose of 40 minutes to build the speaker model and 5 minutes for the test data (including silences). Performance is reported in term of the Detection Error Tradeoff (DET) curve [18]. Results are compared via Equal Error Rates (EER): the error at the threshold which gives equal miss and false alarm probabilities.

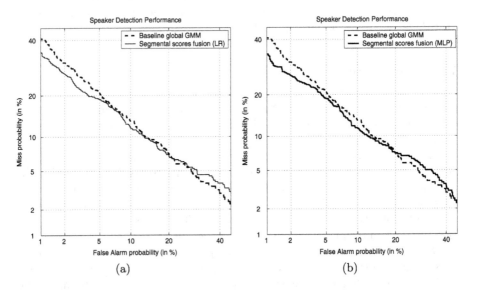

Fig. 1. Speaker verification results for the global GMM system and the ALISP-based system using (a) the Logistic Regression (b) the MLP for the segmental scores fusion on the evaluation data set (subset of NIST'04)

With the ALISP-based system, we can treat each class of segments differently, and give more weights to the speech classes that convey more speaker specific information. We first used the Logistic Regression to determine the optimal weights of the ALISP speech classes for the speaker verification task. Figure 1 (a) shows the speaker verification results for the global and the segmental ALISP-based

GMM systems. The use of the Logistic Regression improves slightly the performances in comparison to the baseline system. The EER is reduced from 11.7% to 11.2%.

As a second trial an MLP is applied to combine the ALISP segmental scores in order to improve the performance of the segmental system. Figure 1 (b) shows that using an MLP instead of the weighted summation brings 12% of improvement in performance over the baseline system. Improvement in the region favoring false alarms is also visible.

Figure 2 summarizes the results of the global GMM system and the results of the combination of the segmental scores for the ALISP-based system using the Logistic Regression and the MLP rules.

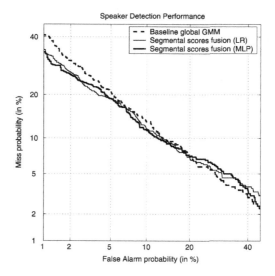

Fig. 2. Speaker verification results for the global GMM system and the two ALISP-based systems (one using the Logistic Regression and the other the MLP for the segmental scores fusion) on the evaluation data set

5   Conclusions

In this paper we have compared three GMM text independent speaker verification systems with identical front end processing, one using global scoring and the two others segmental scoring based on a data-driven segmentation (ALISP). We have also presented two fusion methods of the segmental scores for the ALISP based system. The ALISP-based GMM system provided slightly better performance compared to the global GMM system. We have shown that applying both linear (Logistic Regression) and non linear methods (MLP) to the ALISP segments scores fusion gave an improvement in performance over the baseline system which treats all speech data in the same way. We have concluded that the ALISP segments could capture speaker information.

References

1. Parris, E.S., Carey, M.J.: Discriminative phonemes for speaker identification. In ICLSP (1994) 1843–1846
2. Eatock, J., Mason, J.: A quantitative assessment of the relative speaker discriminant properties of phonemes. Proc. ICASSP 1 (1994) 133–136
3. Olsen, J.: A two-stage procedure for phone based speaker verification. In G. Borgefors J. Bigün, G. Chollet, editor, First International Conference on Audio and Video Based Biometric Person Authentication (1997) 199–226
4. Petrovska-Delacretaz, D., Hennebert, J.: Text-prompted speaker verification experiments with phoneme specific MLP's. In Proc. ICASSP (1998) 777–780
5. Mastui, T., Furui, S.: Concatenated phoneme models for text-variable speaker recognition. Proc. ICASSP (1994) 133–136
6. Koolwaaij, J., de Veth, J.: The use of broad phonetic class models in speaker recognition. Proc. ICSLP (1998)
7. Kajarekar, S.S., Hermanskey, H.: Speaker verification based on broad phonetic categories. 2001: A Speaker Odyssey - The Speaker Recognition Workshop (2001)
8. Auckenthaler, R., Parris, E.S., Carey, M.J.: Improving a GMM speaker verification system by phonetic weighting. Proc. ICASSP (1999)
9. Hébert, M., Heck, L.P.: Phonetic class-based speaker verification. Proc. Eurospeech (2003)
10. Hansen, E.G., Slyh, R.E., Anderson, T.R.: Speaker recognition using phoneme-specific GMMs. Proc. Odyssey (2004)
11. Gutman, D., Bistritz, Y.: Speaker verification using phoneme-adapted gaussian mixture models. Proc. EUSIPCO (2002)
12. Chollet, G., Černocký, J., Constantinescu, A., Deligne, S., Bimbot, F.: Towards ALISP: a proposal for Automatic Language Independent Speech Processing. In Keith Ponting, editor, NATO ASI: Computational models of speech pattern processing Springer Verlag (1999)
13. Reynolds, D., Quatieri, T., Dunn, R.: Speaker verification using adapted gaussian mixture models. DSP, Special Issue on the NIST'99 evaluations 10(1-3) (2000) 19–41
14. Pigeon, S., Druyts, P., Verlinde, P.: Applying logistic regression to the fusion of the nist'99 1-speaker submissions. Digital Signal Processing 10 (2000) 237–248
15. Haykin, S.: Neural Networks: A Comprehensive Foundation. IEEE Computer society Press (1994)
16. Magrin-Chagnolleau, I., Gravier, G., Blouet, R.: Overview of the 2000-2001 elisa consortium research activities. Speaker Odyssey Workshop (2001)
17. Blouet, R., Mokbel, C., Mokbel, H., Sanchez, E., Chollet, G., Greige, H.: Becars: A free software for speaker verification. Proc. Odyssey (2004)
18. Martin, A., Doddington, G., Kamm, T., Ordowski, M., Przybocki, M.: The det curve in assessment of detection task performance. Proc. Eurospeech'97 4 (1997) 1895–1898

On the Usefulness of Almost-Redundant Information for Pattern Recognition

Marcos Faundez-Zanuy

Escola Universitària Politècnica de Mataró
Avda. Puig i Cadafalch 101-111 08303 Mataro (Barcelona), Spain
faundez@eupmt.es
http://www.eupmt.es/veu

Abstract. In this paper we give some pedagogical explanation of those situations where the use of redundant or almost-redundant information can improve the recognition rates of pattern recognition systems. Thus, the main purpose of this paper is to summarize some well-known situations in the pattern recognition field, where the use of "invented", almost-redundant information, etc., can help to improve the results.

1 Introduction

Although common sense says that nothing can be inferred from "invented" information data, this assertion does not state the whole possible situations, or at least those cases where this kind of information can help to overcome other problems.

A well-known problem in the context of pattern recognition [1] is that a pattern recognizer trained with an insufficient number of training samples generalizes poorly when trying to classify input data. Additionally, the higher the number of model's parameters, the higher the number of training data should be. It is generally accepted [2] that using at least ten times as many training samples per class as the number of features ($n/d > 10$) is a good practice to follow in classifier design.

In some situations the use of almost redundant information can help to improve the results. An analogous naïve example easy-to-understand is the polynomial fitting to a given set of points. Figure 1 shows the interpolation of several polynomials to a set of three points. Obviously for a first, second and third degree polynomial fitting the achieved result by means of mean square error minimization can be considered satisfactory. However, for a 17th polynomial degree, the problem is ill-conditioned because the number of parameters to fit is much higher than the number of available training points. Thus, although the fitted polynomial passes through the three training points, strange phenomena take place between points. This result can be considered unsatisfactory taking into account that the range of the "y" axis spreads in a wider range. An important fact to be taken into account is that we cannot try to set up a big model that comprises a lot of parameters if the available number of training data is not enough, because recognition rates will drop instead of improve.

Let us check what happens if the number of training data is artificially extended using randomly generated points, but related to the real data points. For this purpose we work out the standard deviation of the training data set:

$$\sigma_x = \sqrt{\frac{1}{N}\sum_{i=1}^{N}\left(x(i)-\overline{x}\right)^2} \tag{1}$$

G. Chollet et al. (Eds.): Nonlinear Speech Modeling, LNAI 3445, pp. 357–364, 2005.

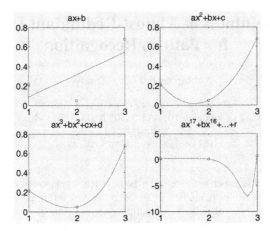

Fig. 1. Example of polynomial fitting to a set of three points

$$\sigma_y = \sqrt{\frac{1}{N}\sum_{i=1}^{N}\left(y(i)-\bar{y}\right)^2} \qquad (2)$$

Where the experimental data set consists of N points in $\mathbb{R}^2$:

$$\left(x(i),y(i)\right) \quad i=1,\cdots,N \qquad (3)$$

And $\bar{x},\bar{y}$ are the mean values of the x and y respectively.

The artificially generated data set $\left(x_{rand}(i),y_{rand}(i)\right)$ $i=1,\cdots,N\times N_2$ is obtained by means of random number generation rand(1), which randomly generates a number on the range $[0,1]$ with a uniform distribution, using the following algorithm:

```
for i=1:N,
    for j=1:N₂,
        x_rand((i-1)*N₂+j)=x(i)+k*σ_x*(rand(1)-0.5);
        y_rand((i-1)*N₂+j)=y(i)+k*σ_y*(rand(1)-0.5);
    end
end
```

Thus, we generate N_2 artificial points for each original one, adding a random perturbation proportional to the standard deviation of the training set.

Figure 2 shows two situations, both of them with $N_2=7$ ($N\times N_2=3\times7=21$). The figure on the top has been obtained with a proportionality constant $k=0.2$, and the bottom one with $k=1$. It is easy to observe that in the first one the generated points are close to the original ones, while in the second case they are better distributed along the original range of signal values.

First case shown on figure 2 on the top reveals the same problem that appeared when we tried to fit the polynomial with a small experimental data set. Thus, this first example is in agreement with the initial statement "we cannot take advantage of redundant information". On the other hand, the almost-invented points on the second example produce a tight response to the original range of values.

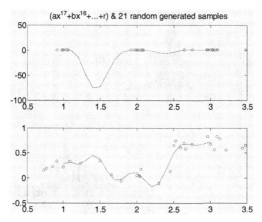

Fig. 2. Example of polynomial fitting to a set of three points plus some random generated data

Unfortunately, pattern recognition problems lie on higher dimensional spaces, where it is not possible to plot the experimental data nor the models, so it is more complicate to understand what is really happening. However, there are experimental evidences of improvements when using redundant or almost-invented information. Next section presents some of them.

2 Examples on Pattern Recognition Field

In this section we summarize several situations where the use of pseudo-random generated data (almost-invented or redundant) can help to improve recognition rates. Described situations include:

a) Pseudo-random training samples generation in order to modify the obtained statistics of the experimental data.
b) Direct modification of obtained statistics from the real experimental data.
c) Replication of the known information (redundant information addition).
d) Systematic generation of new training samples, theoretically "cleaner" than the original ones, and the combination of both sets of data.

2.1 Neural Net Classifier Trained in a Discriminative Mode

Neural nets can be trained as discriminative classifiers in the following fashion: when the input data belongs to a genuine person, the output (target of the nnet) is fixed to 1. When the input is an impostor person, the output is fixed to −1. Figure 3 shows the obtained intra/inter-distance histogram result for a face recognition system (without loss of generality this results would be similar for speaker recognition) using a Multi-Layer Perceptron (MLP) and a database of 40 persons and five training data per person for training. A fitted Gaussian is also plotted to each histogram.

In this example [3], the number of genuine training samples is 40×5, while the number of impostors is 40×40×5−40×5=39×40×5.

It is interesting to observe that there is a preponderance of the negative responses. This is because of the most part of the training vectors are inhibitory. Thus, the MLP

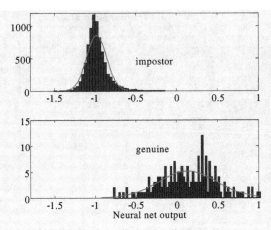

Fig. 3. Inter and intra distance histograms

tends to learn that "all is inhibitory". Although we bounded the MLP to learn +1 or −1, all the values are shifted to negative ones (the mean of the genuine values is close to 0, and far of +1). In general, in patter recognition applications, the number of samples for impostors is always higher than the number of genuine persons, because each person can be considered as impostor for all the other ones. Two solutions [4] have been proposed in order to solve this phenomenon, based on trying to balance both amounts of excitatory (+1) and inhibitory (−1) data:

a) To reduce the number of inhibitory training samples by some kind of data compression such as vector quantization [5].
b) To increase the number of excitatory training samples adding new training data, which consists of genuine users' samples plus some random generated noise.

The second situation corresponds to a solution that consists of adding almost-invented data in order to improve the results.

2.2 GMM Model Estimation

Probably the most accepted model for speaker recognition is the Gaussian Mixture Model (GMM) [6]. When training a nodal variance GMM, it has been observed [6] that variance elements can become quite small in amplitude. This is particularly true for a mixture model with a large (≥ 32) number of mixtures. These small variances produce a singularity in the model's likelihood function and can degrade identification performance by distorting speaker model scores used in the maximum likelihood classifier. These singularities can arise when there is not enough data to sufficiently train a component's variance vector or when using noise-corrupted data. The noisy data can contain outliers in the data that give rise to components with very small variances.

To avoid these spurious singularities, a variance limiting constraint is proposed in [6]. This constraint places a minimum variance value on elements of all variance vectors in a speakers' model. For an arbitrary element of mixture component i's variance vector, σ_i^2, and a minimum variance value, $\sigma_{\min}^2$, the constraint:

$$\overline{\sigma}_i^2 = \begin{cases} \sigma_i^2 & if \ \sigma_i^2 > \sigma_{min}^2 \\ \sigma_{min}^2 & if \ \sigma_i^2 \leq \sigma_{min}^2 \end{cases} \tag{4}$$

is applied to the variance estimates after each expectation-maximization iteration to avoid singularities in the final model. This strategy provides more robust parameter estimates than the unconstrained version.

Care must be taken when setting the minimum variance value. If it is too high, the component variances are masked to the same value which would overly constrain the model and hence degrade identification performance. Setting the value too low may not perform the desired limit at all. The variance limit must be empirically determined for any particular data set, feature set, and model size to optimize performance.

While the example described in section 2.1 tries to modify the statistics by means of a modified training data set, the strategy of this section modifies the statistics itself. Thus, the goal is the same, and equation 4 implies a deviation or distortion from the experimental data extracted from the real data set.

2.3 Bandwidth Extension

In [7-8] we studied the relevance of bandwidth extension for speaker recognition tasks. That is, "what happens if the input voice to a speaker recognizer system has been previously bandwidth extended from a bandwidth of 4 kHz to 8 kHz?". A real example of a bandwidth extension system is the standard named Digital Radio Mondiale (DRM) that can be found in [9-10]. A simple algorithm for bandwidth extension used in DRM consists of the replication of a part of the spectrum, as illustrated on figure 4. For a human being the insertion of the high frequency band (typically from 4 kHz to 8 kHz) produces a more natural speech, but common sense says that neither improvement nor degradation should appear due to this procedure. However, our experimental results revealed some improvement on both identification and verification rates when compared with the narrowband system. Probably in this example a reinforcement of the harmonic structure facilitates the posterior feature extraction, the increase on number of data due to a sampling rate change (which is doubled), etc., are the main reasons.

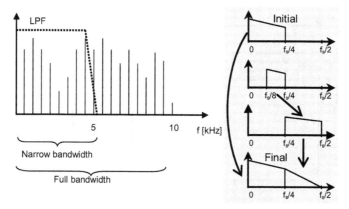

Fig. 4. Bandwidth extension through bandwidth replication

2.4 Blind Inversion of Distortions

In [11-12] we proposed the inversion of nonlinear distortions in order to improve the recognition rates of a speaker recognizer system. This strategy can manage those applications where the training material has been recorded in a controlled situation but the testing signals present some mismatch with the input signal level (saturations).

By means of non-linear channel distortion estimation and compensation, we obtain a new set of feature vectors that theoretically are cleaner than the original ones. The combination of two different recognizers, one working over the original signal and another one with the compensated signal, produces an improvement on recognition rates. Figure 5 shows the proposed scheme. This approach can be interpreted as an increase on the training dataset size, or a data fusion scheme at the score's level [13]. In pattern recognition applications it is well known that a number of differently trained classifiers (that can be considered as "experts"), which share a common input, can produce a better result if their outputs are combined to produce an overall output. This technique is known as committee machine [14], ensemble averaging [15], data fusion, etc. The motivation for its use is twofold [14]:

- If the combination of experts were replaced by a single classifier, the number of equivalent adjustable parameters would be large, and this implies more training time and local minima problems [16].
- The risks of overfitting the data increases when the number of adjustable parameters is large compared to the size of the training data set.

In addition, this strategy improves the vulnerability of biometric systems [17], which is one of the main drawbacks of these systems [18].

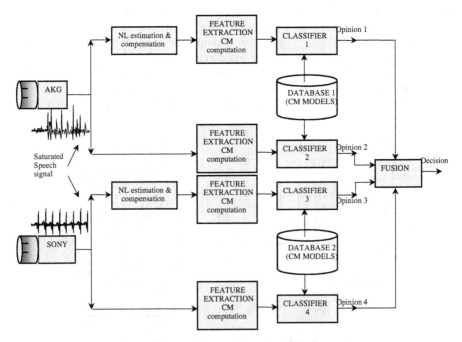

Fig. 5. General Scheme of the recognition system

3   Conclusions

In this paper we have tried to make clear in an easy way some situations where the use of redundant or almost-redundant information can help to improve recognition results on pattern recognition systems. Although common sense says us that nothing can be inferred from redundant or invented information, it must be taken into account that some problems arise when there is an insufficient amount of training data or the model that we are trying to compute is complicated. In these situations, this added information can help to obtain a more accurate statistical result.

Acknowledgement

This work has been supported by FEDER and the Spanish grant MCYT TIC2003-08382-C05-02. It is also motivated by a discussion held in Eusipco'2002 Special session "Nonlinear speech processing" organized for the COST-277 European Project.

References

1. Jain A. K., Duin R. P. W., Mao J., "Statistical pattern recognition: a review". IEEE trans. On Pattern Analysis and Machine Intelligence. Vol.22, No 1, January 2000.
2. Jain A. K., Chandrasekaran B., "Dimensionality and sample size considerations in pattern recognition practice", Handbook of statistics. P. R. Krishnaiah and L. N. Kanal, eds. Vol. 2, pp. 835-855, Amsterdam: North-Holland 1982.
3. Faundez-Zanuy, M. "Face recognition in a transformed domain". 37th IEEE International Carnahan Conference on Security Technology. Pp.290-297. Taipei (Taiwan), ICCST 2003
4. Bishop C.M. "Neural networks for pattern recognition" Ed. Clarendon press. 1995
5. Gersho, A. Gray, R.M. "Vector quantization and signal compression" Kluwer Ed. 1991.
6. Reynolds D. A., Rose R. C., "Robust text-independent speaker identification using gaussian mixture speaker models". IEEE Trans. On speech and audio processing, Vol.3, No 1, pp. 72-83, January 1995
7. Faundez-Zanuy M., Nilsson M., and Kleijn W. B., "On the relevance of bandwidth extension for speaker identification". Vol. III pp.125-128, EUSIPCO'2002, Toulouse
8. Faundez-Zanuy, M., Nilsson M., and Kleijn W. B., "On the relevance of bandwidth extension for speaker verification". Pp. 2317-2320. ICSLP'2002. Denver.
9. Draft new recommendation ITU-R BS. Document 6/63-E, "system for digital sound broadcasting in the broadcasting bands below 30MHz", 25th October 2000
10. http://www.drm.org
11. Faundez-Zanuy M., and Solé-Casals J., "Speaker recognition improvement using blind inversion of distortions". Accepted for publication. European Signal and Image Processing Conference EUSIPCO. September 2004, Vienna (Austria).
12. Solé-Casals J., and Faundez-Zanuy M., "Speaker recognition improvement using blind inversion of distortions". Accepted for publication Independent Component Analysis ICA'2004. Lecture Notes on Computer Science. Granada (Spain).
13. Faundez-Zanuy M., "Data fusion in biometrics" Accepted for publication, IEEE Aerospace and Electronic Systems Magazine. In press, 2004.
14. Haykin S., Chapter 7, Committee Machines. "Neural nets. A comprehensive foundation", 2on edition. Ed. Prentice Hall 1999

15. Perrone M. P., and Cooper L. N. "When networks disagree: ensemble methods for hybrid neural networks" in "neural networks for speech and image processing, R. J. Mammone ed., Chapman-Hall 1993

16. Jain A. K., and Mao J., "Artificial neural networks: a tutorial". IEEE Computer pp.31-44, March 1996

17. Faundez-Zanuy M., "On the vulnerability of biometric security systems". IEEE Aerospace and Electronic Systems Magazine. Vol.19 n° 6, pp.3-8, June de 2004.

18. Faundez-Zanuy M., "Biometric recognition: why not massively adopted yet?" Accepted for publication, IEEE Aerospace and Electronic Systems Magazine. In press, 2004.

An Audio-Visual Imposture Scenario by Talking Face Animation

Walid Karam[1,2], Chafic Mokbel[1], Hanna Greige[1], Guido Aversano[2], Catherine Pelachaud[3], and Gérard Chollet[2]

[1] Computer Science Department, University of Balamand, PO Box 100 Tripoli, Lebanon
{walid,chafic.mokbel,hanna.greige}@balamand.edu.lb
[2] Ecole Nationale Supérieure des Télécommunications, 46 rue Barrault, 75634 Paris, France
{karam,aversano,chollet}@tsi.enst.fr
[3] IUT–Université Paris 8, 140 rue de la Nouvelle France, 93100 Montreuil, France
c.pelachaud@iut.univ-paris8.fr

Abstract. We describe a system that allows an impostor to lead an audio-visual telephone conversation, and sign data electronically on behalf of an authorized client. During the conversation, audio and video of the impostor are altered so as to mimic the client. The voice of an impostor is processed and used to reproduce the voice of the authorized client. Speech segments obtained from client's recordings are used to synthesize new sentences that the client never pronounced. On the visual side, the imposter's talking face is detected and facial features are extracted and used to animate a synthetic talking face. The texture of the impersonated face is mapped onto the talking head and coded for transmission over the phone, along with the synthesized voice. Audio-visual coding and synthesis is realized by indexing in a memory containing audio-visual sequences. Stochastic models (coupled HMM) of characteristic segments are used to drive the memory search.

1 Introduction

With the start of the appearance of PDA's, handheld PC's, and mobile telephones that use biometric recognition for user authentication, there is higher demand for automatic non-intrusive voice and face speaker verification systems. Such systems can be embedded in mobile devices to allow biometrically recognized users to sign and send data electronically, and to give their telephone conversation a legal value. The European project "Secure Contracts Signed by Mobile Phone" (SecurePhone) [1] aims at developing such technology on a 3G/B3G enabled PDA.

One of the risks that a speaker verification system could face is its liability to imposture. With the current communication infrastructure lacking strong user identification, an impostor aware of legal transactions can interfere and be engaged in a telephone conversation so as to alter or replace the true conversation, or even initiate a conversation and impersonate in it another person.

To combat imposture, it is necessary to study imposture techniques and scenarios. In this paper, we describe a system that allows an impostor to start and lead an audio-visual telephone conversation, and sign and exchange data electronically on behalf of another person. During the conversation, audio and video of the impostor are altered in a way as to mimic the other person's voice and face.

G. Chollet et al. (Eds.): Nonlinear Speech Modeling, LNAI 3445, pp. 365–369, 2005.
© Springer-Verlag Berlin Heidelberg 2005

2 The Imposture Model

The SecurePhone project envisions a mobile communication infrastructure that allows speakers on mobile devices to communicate securely via strong biometrical identification techniques. Users will be authenticated in a non-intrusive way with data previously registered on the SIM card of the device. This system is modeled in Fig. 1.

Fig. 1. The SecurePhone project proposes to realize an innovative prototypal 3G/B3G enabled PDA (the "SecurePhone") with biometric identification that allows users to mutually recognize each other, securely authenticate, and e-sign voice statements on the fly

The high level of security and the robustness of the biometric identity authentication system proposed by the SecurePhone project can be verified and improved by the creation of an impostor system that uses the same biometric identification techniques. This scenario is depicted in Fig. 2 and is described as follows.

The impostor maintains a database of face and speech feature vectors of client #1. These feature vectors are used to drive and animate an MPEG-4 compliant face model, Greta [2]. The "altered" SecurePhone captures both the face and the speech features of the impostor and performs the necessary syntheses introduced below and described in the next sections. The impostor is then authenticated as client #1 by face and speech verification.

On the speech side, section 3 below describes a processing technique to reproduce the voice of a client. In particular, speech segments obtained from client's recordings are used to synthesize new sentences pronounced by the impostor. It is shown that a very-low bit-rate speech coding system, such as the ALISP-based one [3], can be adapted to serve forgery purposes, transforming any input speech into client's voice.

On the human face side, the impostor's talking face is detected and facial features are extracted and tracked. Lip movements are used to animate the talking face model, Greta. The facial texture of client #1 is mapped onto Greta and coded for transmission over the phone, along with the synthesized voice. Audio-visual coding and synthesis is realized by indexing in a database containing audio-visual sequences. Stochastic models (coupled HMM) of characteristic segments are used to drive the search in memory. This process is detailed in section 4 below.

3 Speech Synthesis

Data driven approaches have a great relevance in the realization of forgery applications, which can be used to improve the robustness of biometric identity verification systems. For the speaker verification problem, a typical forgery scenario includes automatic voice transformation techniques that an impostor may use to assume the identity of an authorized client.

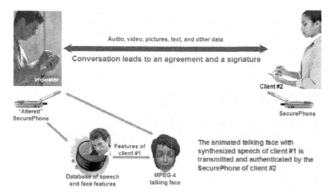

Fig. 2. The imposture model animates an MPEG-4 compliant talking face (Greta) with face and speech feature vectors of the client

For GMM-based speaker verification, in which case the temporal ordering of feature vectors is ignored, it may be sufficient to find a mapping function F between impostor's feature vectors X and client's features Y. Given two sequences composed of the same words, pronounced respectively by the impostor and by the client, F can be found by minimizing the mean square error $\varepsilon_{mse} = E[\|y - F(x)\|^2]$, where E is the expectation. This approach requires a relatively limited amount of client data, but it has the disadvantage of being text, language, and speaker dependent.

Forgery of the above kind is likely to be not so effective in the case of more sophisticated systems that exploit speech recognition in the speaker verification process. To be a real threat for such systems, the impostor should make sure that the linguistic elements present in the source voice are not altered by the voice transformation, so that they can be recognized on the other side as they were for the original voice.

Unfortunately for verification system designers, ALISP-based recognition and synthesis could constitute an interesting forgery tool that is able to transform any arbitrary voice into client's voice, without text or language restrictions. As in the case of phone rate speech coding, a codebook of ALISP units can be built by statistical analysis of client's speech that does not need to be orthographically or phonetically annotated. Then, recognition of impostor's speech in terms of ALISP units allows replacing impostor's voice segments with equivalent representative units taken from the client's codebook. The HMM-based recognition performed in the ALISP processing, assures that a subsequent recognition performed by the verification system will result in a good phonetic matching.

4   Face Synthesis

Realistic face synthesis is one of most difficult problems in computer graphics due to the complexity of its geometric form. Rendering and modeling the human face on a screen has proven to be an extremely challenging task. It is even more challenging to "naturally" animate a synthetic face, since the human brain can effortlessly notice any tiny unnatural deviation from reality. In [4], Pighin et al present a modeling technique to generate realistic texture-mapped 3D face models from face images and videos. Speech-driven facial animation has also been investigated in the literature [5]–[12].

In this study, an MPEG-4 compliant talking head, Greta, is used for facial animation. Facial animation in MPEG-4 is controlled by the Facial Definition Parameters (FDPs) and Facial Animation Parameters (FAPs), which describe the face shape, and movement, respectively [13].

5   The Audio-Visual Imposture System

Fig. 3 below describes the complete audio-visual imposture system. In the synthesis phase, a texture-mapped 3D face model of the client is used on Greta, along with the FAP's and the synthesized voice.

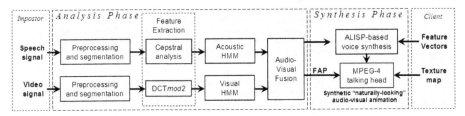

Fig. 3. The imposture system

In the analysis phase, the video signal of the impostor is preprocessed and then face features are extracted using a DCT-*mod2* technique that uses polynomial coefficients derived from 2-D DCT coefficients of spatially neighboring blocks [14]. A hidden Markov model (HMM) classifier is used to model the stochastic behavior of the speech and visual facial features. Visual and acoustic information are integrated in an audio-visual fusion classifier so as to create a complete audio-visual model of the impostor [15].

6   Experiments and Conclusions

Preliminary experiments were conducted on speech imposture using the BECARS [16] automatic speech recognition system. The equal error rate (EER) found for verification tests on non-forged speech data was 16%. After voice transformation, the equal error rate was increased to 26%. The statistical uncertainty for the above results is 2%, corresponding to a 95% confidence interval.

To conclude, this paper describes an audio-visual imposture system that can be used to test the robustness of a multimodal biometric authentication system embedded on a PDA. Features of a speaker are used to train an HMM system and to drive an MPEG-4 talking head. The question of how "realistic" face and audio synthesis is still to be answered by experiments underway.

References

1. The SecurePhone project, Sixth Framework Programme, Proposal/Contract No. IST-2002-506883
2. Pasquariello, S., Pelachaud, C.: Greta: A Simple Facial Animation Engine. 6th Online World Conference on Soft Computing in Industrial Applications, Session on Soft Computing for Intelligent 3D Agents, September 2001

3. Chollet, G., Cernocky J., Constantinescu, A., Deligne S., Bimbot, F.: Toward ALISP: a proposal for Automatic Language Independent Speech Processing. Computational Models of Speech Processing, NATO ASI Series, 1997
4. Pighin, F., Szeliski, R., Salesin, D.: Modeling and Animating Realistic Faces from Images. International Journal of Computer Vision, Volume 50, 143-169
5. Simons, A., Cox, S.: Generation of mouth shapes for a synthetic talking head. Proc. Inst. Acoust., vol. 12, 1990, pp. 475–482
6. Bregler, C., Covell, M., Slaney, M.: Video Rewrite: Driving Visual Speech with Audio. Proc. ACM SIGGRAPH 97, 1997
7. Yamamoto, E., Nakamura, S., Shikano, K.: Lip movement synthesis from speech based on hidden Markov models. Speech Commun., vol. 26, no. 1–2, pp. 105–115, 1998
8. Tamura, M., Masuko, T., Kobayashi, T., Tokuda, K,: Visual Speech Synthesis Based on Parameter Generation from HMM: Speech-Driven and Text-and-Speech-Driven Approaches. Proc. Auditory-Visual Speech Processing 1998, Dec. 1998
9. Schroeter, J., Graf, H.P., Beutnagel, M., Cosatto, E., Syrdal, A., Conkie, A., Stylianou, Y.: Multimodal speech synthesis, IEEE International Conference on Multimedia and Expo (I) 2000: 571-578
10. Nakamura, S.: Fusion of Audio-Visual Information for Integrated Speech Processing. Audio- and Video-Based Biometric Person Authentication (AVBPA), pp. 127-143, Halmstad, Sweden, June 2001
11. Williams, J., Katsaggelos A.: An HMM-Based Speech-to-Video Synthesizer. IEEE Tran Neural Networks, vol. 13, no, 4, Jul. 2002
12. Aleksic, P., Williams, J., Katsaggelos A.: Speech-To-Video Synthesis Using MPEG-4 Compliant Visual Features. IEEE Trans. circuits and systems for video technology, vol. 14, no. 5, May 2004
13. Text for ISO/IEC FDIS 14496-2 Visual, ISO/IEC JTC1/SC29/WG11 N2502, Nov. 1998.
14. Sanderson, C., Paliwal, K.K.: Polynomial Features for Robust Face Authentication. Proc. International Conf. on Image Processing, Rochester, NY, 2002, pp. 997-1000 (Vol. 3)
15. A. Ross, A. K. Jain, and J. Z. Qian, "Information Fusion in Biometrics", Proc. 3rd International Conference on Audio- and Video-Based Biometric Person Authentication, pp. 354-359, Sweden, June 6-8, 2001
16. R. Blouet, C. Mokbel, G. Chollet, "BECARS: a free software for speaker recognition," ODYSSEY 2004, Toledo, 2004

Cryptographic-Speech-Key Generation Using the SVM Technique over the lp-Cepstral Speech Space

Paola L. García-Perera, Carlos Mex-Perera, and Juan A. Nolazco-Flores

Computer Science Department, ITESM, Campus Monterrey
Av. Eugenio Garza Sada 2501 Sur, Col. Tecnológico
Monterrey, N.L., México, C.P. 64849
{paola.garcia,carlosmex,jnolazco}@itesm.mx

Abstract. In this research we propose a new scheme for generating binary vectors, which can be used as keys for cryptographic purposes. These vectors are obtained from the speech signal and from the spoken user passphrase. The key bits are built using the Automatic Speech Recognition Technology to detect the phoneme limits in the speech utterance and the Support Vector Machines technique for classification. Linear prediction cepstral coefficients, (first and second derivatives) of the speech signal are calculated to create a 39-dimensional hyperspace. Then a hyperplane is created using an RBF kernel, and the SVM classifies the user's phonemes. Applying our method to a set of 10, 20, 30 and 50 speakers from the YOHO database, the results show that this method is sufficiently robust to reliably regenerate the cryptographic key.

1 Introduction

The goal of cryptographic-speech-key generation is to obtain a password using the intrinsic attributes of the user's voice. Voice was chosen among other biometrics because it has the flexibility that by the changing the sentence, the cryptographic key will change.

The main challenge of this research is to produce a cryptographic-speech-key that should repeatedly be equal every time a user produces the same utterance under certain conditions. Monrose *et. al* [6] showed a method in which a partition plane for the feature vector space was suggested to generate binary biometric keys. The key is unknown until the plane is chosen. However, a plane that can produce the same key is difficult to find due to the fact that infinite planes are possible. A more flexible way to produce a key – in which the exact control of the assignation of the key values is available – is always attractive.

Therefore, the objective of this proposal is to generate a cryptographic-speech-key from the attributes of the voice signal and the spoken user passphrase. The main challenge of this research is to find a suitable set of planes that can significantly partition the handled data and give a key as a result. In the first stage, *speech processing* and *recognition* techniques are used to get the model

G. Chollet et al. (Eds.): Nonlinear Speech Modeling, LNAI 3445, pp. 370–374, 2005.

parameters and the segments of phonemes in each user utterance. Afterwards, using the model parameters and the segments the feature sets are formed. Next, the *Support Vector Machine* classifier (SVM) produces a new model according to a specific kernel and bit specifications. Finally, using the SVM model the key is generated. Each part as depicted in Figure 1 will be discussed in the following sections.

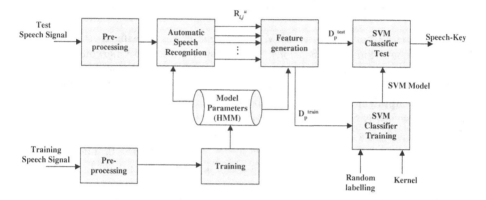

Fig. 1. System Architecture

2   Speech Processing and Phoneme Feature Generation

Firstly, the speech signal is divided into short windows and the *linear prediction coefficients* (LPC) are obtained. The LPC are then transformed into the cepstral coefficients, resulting in a 13-dimension vector, 12-dimension lp-cepstral coefficients followed by one energy coefficient. To emphasize the dynamic features of the speech in time, the time-derivative (Δ) and the time-acceleration (Δ^2) of each parameter are calculated [9].

Afterwards, the phoneme segments are obtained using a forced-alignment ASR. The ASR is based on a 3 state, left-right, Gaussian-based continuous Hidden Markov Model (HMM). Instead of words, the phonemes were selected because it is possible to generate larger keys with shorter length sentences. Assuming the phonemes are modelled with a three-state left-to-right HMM, and assuming the middle state is the most stable part of the phoneme representation, let, $C_P = \{C_i\}$ denote the set of mean vectors of the central gaussian of the middle states, where P is the set of all the phonemes and i is the index associated to each phoneme.

Given the phonemes' segments, the lp-cepstral coefficients for each phoneme in the utterances can be arranged forming the sets $R_{i,j}^u$, where i is the index associated to each phoneme, j is the j-th user, and u is an index that starts in zero and increments every time the user utters the phoneme i. Then, the feature vector is defined as $\psi_{i,j}^u = \mu(R_{i,j}^u) - C_i$ where $\mu(R_{i,j}^u)$ is the mean vector of the data in the lp-cepstral coefficient set $R_{i,j}^u$, and $C_i \in C_P$ is known as the matching phoneme mean vector of the model. Let us denote the set of vectors, $D_p = \{\psi_{p,j}^u \mid \forall\ u, j\}$ where p is a specific phoneme. Afterwards, this set is divided in subsets: D_p^{tr} and D_p^{test}. 80% of the total D_p are elements of D_p^{tr} and the remaining 20% form D_p^{test}. Then, $D_p^{train} = \{[\psi_{p,j}^u, b_{p,j}] \mid \forall\ u, j\}$ where $b_{p,j} \in \{-1, 1\}$ is the key bit or class assigned to the phoneme p of the j-th user.

3   Support Vector Machine

The *Support Vector Machine* (SVM) *Technique* is a promising method used for pattern recognition (classification), derived by Vapnik and Chervonenkis [1, 3]. Given the observation inputs and a function-based model, the goal of basic SVM is to classify these inputs into one of two classes. Although SVM has been used for several applications, it has also been employed in biometrics [7, 8]. In this research, we study SVM with radial basis function (RBF) kernel to transform a feature, based on a lpc-vector, to a binary number (key bit) assigned randomly. The RBF is denoted as $K(x_i, x_j) = e^{(-\gamma||x_i - x_j||^2)}$, where $\gamma > 0$. The SVM uses also a decision criteria, which depends on C, a tradeoff parameter between error and margin.

For our research, the methodology used to implement the SVM training is as follows. Firstly, the training set for each phoneme (D_p^{train}) is formed by assigning a one-bit random label ($b_{p,j}$) to each user. Since a random generator of the values (-1 or 1) is used, the assignation is different for each user. The advantage of this random assignation is that the key entropy grows significantly. Afterwards, by employing a grid search the parameters C and γ are tuned. Finally, a testing stage is performed using D_p^{test}s.

This research considers just binary classes. The final key could be obtained by concatenating the bits produced by each phoneme. For instance, if a user utters two phonemes: /F/ and /AH/, the final key is $K = \{f(D_{/F/}), f(D_{/AH/})\}$, thus, the output is formed by two bits.

4   Experimental Methodology and Results

The experiments were performed using the YOHO database [2, 4]. YOHO contains clean voice utterances of 138 speakers of different nationalities. It is a combination lock phrases (for instance, "Thirty-Two, Forty-One, Twenty-Five") with 4 enrollment sessions per subject and 24 phrases per enrollment session; 10 verification sessions per subject and 4 phrases per verification session. Given 18768 sentences, 13248 sentences were used for training and 5520 sentences for testing.

The utterances are processed using the Hidden Markov Models Toolkit (HTK) by Cambridge University Engineering Department [5] configured as a forced-alignment automatic speech recogniser. The important results of the speech processing stage are the twenty mean vectors of the phonemes given by the HMM and the phoneme segmentation of the utterances. The phonemes used are: /AH/, /AX/, /AY/, /EH/, /ER/, /EY/, /F/, /IH/, /IY/,/K/, /N/, /R/, /S/, /T/, /TH/, /UW/, /V/, /W/. Following the method already described, the D_p sets are formed. It is important to note that the cardinality of each D_p set can be different since the number of equal phoneme utterances can vary from user to user. Next, subsets D_p^{train} and D_p^{test} are constructed. For training, the number of vectors picked per user and per phoneme for generating the model is the same. Each user has the same probability to produce the correct bit per phoneme. However, the number of testing vectors that each user provided can be different.

For this work, the key bit assignation is arbitrary. Thus, the keys have liberty of assignation, therefore the keys entropy can be easily maximised if they are given in a random fashion with a uniform probability distribution.

SVMlight [10] was used to perform the classification of D_p vectors. The training and the testing stage needed the selection of the parameters γ and C. The behaviour of the SVM is given in terms of the average classification accuracy on test data for a given number of users and is computed by the ratio

$$\eta = \frac{\text{classification matches on test data}}{\text{total number of vectors in test data}}. \tag{1}$$

From several experiments was concluded that a suitable values of C and γ are 9 and 0.01 respectively. Those parameters were adjusted in order to maximise η.

Table 1 shows the values for η for several number of users. The statistics were computed as follows: 500 trials were performed for 10 and 20 users, and 1000 trails were performed for 30 and 50 users.

Table 1. Value of η for different number of users

number of users	global average η	variance
10	.8854	.00554731
20	.8577	.00644144
30	.8424	.007316
50	.8189	.00841168

Results in Table 1 shows that the SVM using the RBF kernel generates proper separating hyperplanes that allow key regeneration.

5 Conclusion

We have presented a method to produce a cryptographic key from voice based on a phoneme segmentation, where one key bit was assigned to each user's phoneme. The main advantage of our approach is that key bits can be selected and assigned for each user before the partition plane is computed. Thus, key bits are freely assigned regardless of the parameter values for the algorithms used in our method. From the experiments conducted on several groups of users, it is concluded that the feasibility of using the SVM to classify data vectors derived from users voice where the classes are labelled arbitrarily.

However, error correction mechanisms have to be considered in future research since the key bits must not present any error, although the number of users increment. Adding extra bits for error correction demands more phonemes in the passphrase but it might reduce the possibility of wrong key production. Besides, future studies on a M-ary key may be useful to increase the number of different keys available for each user given a fixed number of phonemes in the passphrase.

Acknowledgments

The authors would like to acknowledge the Cátedra de Seguridad, ITESM, Campus Monterrey and the CONACyT project CONACyT-2002-C01-41372 who partially supported this work.

References

1. Boser, B., I. Guyon, and V. Vapnik. A training algorithm for optimal margin classifiers. In Proceedings of the Fifth Annual Workshop on Computational Learning Theory, 1992.
2. Campbell, J. P., Jr. Features and Measures for Speaker Recognition. Ph.D. Dissertation, Oklahoma State University, 1992.
3. Cortes, C. and V. Vapnik. Support-vector network. Machine Learning 20, 273–297, 1995.
4. Higgins, A., J. Porter and L. Bahler. YOHO Speaker Authentication Final Report. ITT Defense Communications Division, 1989.
5. Young,S., P. Woodland HTK Hidden Markov Model Toolkit home page. http://htk.eng.cam.ac.uk/
6. F. Monrose, M. K. Reiter, Q. Li , S. Wetzel. Cryptographic Key Generation From Voice. Proceedings of the IEEE Conference on Security and Privacy, Oakland, CA. May, 2001.
7. E. Osuna, R. Freund, and F. Girosi. Support vector machines: Training and applications. Technical Report AIM-1602, MIT A.I. Lab., 1996.
8. E. Osuna, R. Freund, and F. Girosi, Training Support Vector Machines: An Application to Face Recognition, in IEEE Conference on Computer Vision and Pattern Recognition, pp. 130-136, 1997.
9. L.R. Rabiner and B.-H. Juang. Fundamentals of speech recognition. Prentice-Hall, New-Jersey, 1993.
10. T. Joachims, SVMLight: Support Vector Machine, SVM-Light Support Vector Machine http://svmlight.joachims.org/, University of Dortmund, November 1999.

Nonlinear Speech Features
for the Objective Detection of Discontinuities
in Concatenative Speech Synthesis

Yannis Pantazis and Yannis Stylianou

University of Crete, Computer Science Department, 71110 Heraklion Crete, Greece
{pantazis,yannis}@csd.uoc.gr

Abstract. An objective distance measure which is able to predict audible discontinuities in concatenative speech synthesis systems is very important. Previous results showed that linear approaches are not very effective to detect audible discontinuities. The best result was obtained by using the Kullback-Leibler distance on power spectra with the rate of 37%. In this paper, we present two nonlinear approaches for the detection of discontinuities. The first method is based on a nonlinear harmonic model for speech while the second method is based on the demodulation of speech in an amplitude and a frequency component using the Teager energy operator. Results show that detection rate can exceed 70%, which is an improvement of about 95% over previous published results.

1 Introduction

Many modern speech synthesis systems based on non-uniform unit concatenation are quite popular due to their ability to procude high quality and natural-sounding synthetic speech signals [1], [2], [3], [4]. These systems make use of large databases containing many instances of each speech unit (e.g, diphones). In an attempt to minimize audible discontinuities at the concatenation point, these systems try to select the optimum unit from the database. This is done by assigning a target and a concatenation cost to each candidate unit. Target cost, which express the closeness between the context of the target and that of the candidate unit, is evaluated as a weighted sum of differences between prosodic and phonetic parameters. Concatenation cost, which refers to how well adjacent units can be joined, is calculated as a weighted sum of differences between F0, mismatches in spectral features, energy, etc. Total cost is the sum of target and concatenation cost. Optimum unit selection is then achieved by a Viterbi search for the lowest total cost path through the lattice of candidate units. Among these two costs, the concatenation cost is the most important for the selection of two successive acoustic units. Recent studies attempted to specify which concatenation distance measures are able to predict audible discontinuities. Thus, units that are identified to produce audible discontinuities will have less chances of being selected.

Concentrating on concatenation cost, researchers put a lot of effort looking for an objective distance measure which highly correlates with human perception of

G. Chollet et al. (Eds.): Nonlinear Speech Modeling, LNAI 3445, pp. 375–383, 2005.
© Springer-Verlag Berlin Heidelberg 2005

discontinuity at unit concatenation point. Klabbers and Veldhuis [5] found that the best predictor of discontinuities was the Kullback-Leibler distance on LPC power spectra. Wouters and Macon [6] found that the Euclidean distance on mel-scale LPC-based cepstral coefficients performed well. Stylianou and Syrdal [7] showed that Kullback-Leibler distance on FFT-based power spectra was the best predictor. Donovan [8] proposed Mahalanobis distance between perceptual cepstral parameters employing decision trees. Since these studies were conducted on different databases, it is not possible to make direct comparisons between features and methods that were used and draw useful conclusions from them. Despite this fact, most of them showed that Kullback-Leibler distance was on the right track. However, the scores were not very high.

In this paper, we introduce two new sets of features for detecting discontinuities and a new discrimination function in order to increase detection rate. The first set of features are obtained by modeling the speech signal as a sum of harmonics with time varying complex amplitude [9]. The second set of features is based on a technique which tries to decompose speech signals into AM and FM components [10]. Speech signals pass through a filterbank which covers the most important frequencies of the speech spectrum, and then an algorithm referred to as DESA is applied for the separation of the AM and FM component. In contrast with the previous reported studies, we work with vectors instead of scalars which make the discrimination procedure more intricate. We further suggest using Fisher's linear discriminant as a discrimination function.

The paper is organized as follows. In section 2 the extraction of the two sets of parameters is presented while in section 3 Fisher's linear discriminant is quickly reviewed. Section 4 describes the database used and how we construct it. Results from the evaluation of various distance measures are presented in section 5. A summary on the derived results as well as future work concludes the paper.

2   New Set of Features

In previous work, speech signals were considered stationary around the concatenation point. Hence, the techniques used for the extraction of the feature set did not take into account any dynamic information of the speech signal. But experimental work provided evidence that speech resonances can change rapidly within few – even a single – speech periods [11], [12]. Therefore, in an attempt to incorporate dynamic information in the decision whether or not there is an audible discontinuity, we introduce two techniques for the extraction of nonlinear as well as of linear features. Linear features are estimated for comparison purposes only.

2.1   Nonlinear Harmonic Model

The first technique for analysing speech signals is through a nonlinear harmonic model [9]. The model assumes the speech signal to be composed as a periodic signal, h[n], which is designated as sums of harmonically related sinusoids

$$h[n] = \sum_{k=-L(n_i)}^{L(n_i)} A_k[n]e^{j2\pi k f_0(n_i)(n-n_i)} \tag{1}$$

where $L(n_i)$ denotes the number of harmonics at $n = n_i$, $f_0(n_i)$ denotes the fundamental frequency at n $= n_i$, while $A_k[n]$ can take one of the following forms:

$$A_k[n] = a_k(n_i) \tag{2}$$

$$A_k[n] = a_k(n_i) + (n - n_i)b_k(n_i) \tag{3}$$

where $a_k(n_i)$ and $b_k(n_i)$ are assumed to be complex numbers which denote the amplitude of the kth harmonic and the first derivative(slope) respectively. The first method, which leads to a linear harmonic model, is only evaluated for comparison purposes.

The size of analysis window is two pitch periods and it is centered at the concatenation point. It is important to make the analysis at the concatenation point because in our decisions, as explained above, we use dynamic information which may change rapidly within few pitch periods. Therefore, n_i denotes the time instant of the concatenation point. First, the current fundamental frequency, $f_0(n_i)$, is evaluated from the autocorrelation function of the speech signal around the concatenation point. Then, in order to consider the whole spectrum, the number of harmonics, $L(n_i)$, is computed by $L(n_i) = \lfloor \frac{f_s}{2f_0(n_i)} \rfloor$ where f_s denotes the sampling frequency and $\lfloor \rfloor$ denotes the floor operator.

The unknown complex amplitudes (eq. (2) & eq. (3)) are estimated by minimizing a weighted time-domain least-squares criterion with respect to $a_k(n_i)$ or to $a_k(n_i)$ and $b_k(n_i)$,

$$\epsilon = \sum_{n=n_i-T_0}^{n=n_i+T_0} w^2[n](s[n] - h[n])^2 \tag{4}$$

where s[n] denotes the original speech signal, h[n] denotes the harmonic signal to estimate, w[n] denotes the weighted window (which is typically a Hanning window) and T_0 denotes the local fundamental period $(f_s/f_0(n_i))$, in samples. Using Simple Harmonic Model(SHM, eq. (2)) a mean squared error in the order of 5dB is achieved, while using Harmonic Model With Slopes(HMWS, eq. (3)) mean squared error is about 25dB. Obviously, the nonlinear approach models speech signals better.

2.2   AM-FM Decomposition

Teager [11], [12], in his work on nonlinear modeling of speech production, used the nonlinear operator

$$\Psi\{x[n]\} = x^2[n] - x[n-1]x[n+1] \tag{5}$$

on speech signals x[n]. This operator, also known as Teager energy operator, was used by Maragos et al. [10] for the separation of amplitude from frequency modulations of a AM-FM signal. The core of the Discrete Energy Separation Algorithm(DESA) are the following equations:

$$G[n] = 1 - \frac{\Psi\{y[n]\} + \Psi\{y[n+1]\}}{4\Psi\{x[n]\}} \tag{6}$$

$$\Omega[n] \approx \arccos(G[n]) \tag{7}$$

$$|a[n]| \approx \sqrt{\frac{\Psi\{x[n]\}}{1 - G^2[n]}} \tag{8}$$

where $y[n] = x[n] - x[n-1]$, $\Omega[n]$ is the instantaneous frequency and $a[n]$ is the instantaneous amplitude.

One application of DESA in speech analysis is the separation of a signal around a resonance in an amplitude and a frequency component [13]. The extraction of a single resonance is done by bandpass filtering the speech signal with a Gabor filter with impulse response defined by

$$h_G[n] = \exp(-b^2 n^2)\cos(\Omega_c n) \tag{9}$$

where b controls the bandwidth of the filter and Ω_c is the central frequency of the resonance.

In our case, we decided to construct a filterbank of twenty Gabor filters. In our filter design the value of b was selected to be 250, hence the bandwidth of each filter was approximately 425Hz. Mel-frequencies were the central frequencies of the filterbank. This choice was motivated by the importance of these frequencies (as this has repeatedly shown in speech literature) in the perception of speech sounds. The size of analysis window was 300 samples (approximately 20msec) centered at the concatenation point.

3   Discrimination Functions and Features

Up to now, research on predicting audible discontinuities in concatenative speech synthesis was concentrated on finding the right features and on finding a distance measure to be applied on these features. In our approach, we construct a feature vector – hence a feature space – for each speech signal instead of finding a distance measure. Then, we define two classes, one for perceptually audible discontinuous signals and another for signals that were detected to be continuous and try to separate the two classes with statistical methods. An advantage of using Fisher's linear discriminant for the separation of the two classes is its simplicity, as well as, its direct comparison with distances used so far.

3.1 l_p Norms

A well known category of norms are l_p norms, where p can take real positive values. They are defined by

$$l_p\{\mathbf{x}\} = ||\mathbf{x}||_p = (\sum_{i=1}^{d} |x_i|^p)^{1/p} \tag{10}$$

where $\mathbf{x} = [x_1, x_2, ..., x_d]^T$, donotes a real or a complex valued vector. For $p = 2$, (l_2) the well known Euclidean distance is obtained, while for $p = 1$ (l_1) is the absolute sum of the elements of the vector. Both norms have used for measuring the differences between spectral amplitude features, in previous work [7], [14]. Euclidean distance on mel-scaled LPC had given the best results at [6].

Apart from these well known norms, we suggest $l_{1/2}$ for measuring differences. Despite this norm's not satisfying the triangular inequality, it has other useful mathematical properties. Intuitively, $l_{1/2}$ norm favors smaller differences than larger ones. This property makes $l_{1/2}$ norm attractive for measuring differences between frequency parameters.

3.2 Fisher's Linear Discriminant

Suppose that we have a set of N d-dimensional samples $\mathbf{x_1},...,\mathbf{x_N}$, N_0 samples be in the subset D_0 and N_1 samples be in the subset D_1. If we form a linear combination of the elements of $\mathbf{x}$, we obtain the scalar dot product

$$y = \mathbf{w}^T\mathbf{x} \tag{11}$$

and a corresponding set of N samples $y_1,...,y_N$ that is divided into the subsets Y_0 and Y_1. This is equivalent to form a hyperplane in d-space which is orthogonal to $\mathbf{w}$ (Fig. 1).

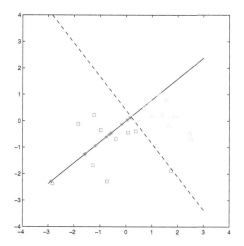

Fig. 1. Example of Fisher's Linear Discriminant

The direction of $\mathbf{w}$ is important for adequate separation and is given by

$$\mathbf{w} = \mathbf{S_W^{-1}}(\mathbf{m_0} - \mathbf{m_1}) \tag{12}$$

where

$$\mathbf{S_W} = \sum_{i=0}^{1} \sum_{\mathbf{x} \in D_i} (\mathbf{x} - \mathbf{m_i})(\mathbf{x} - \mathbf{m_i})^T \tag{13}$$

and

$$\mathbf{m_i} = \frac{1}{N_i} \sum_{\mathbf{x} \in D_i} \mathbf{x} \,, \qquad i = 0, 1. \tag{14}$$

Since Fisher's linear discriminant projects feature vectors to a line it can also be viewed as an operator(FLD) which is defined by

$$FLD\{\mathbf{x}\} = \sum_{i=1}^{d} w_i x_i \tag{15}$$

where w_i are the elements of $\mathbf{w}$. If x_i are real positive numbers, this is a kind of weighted version of l_1 norm (weights can be negative numbers). Now, we are able to combine features which are in different scale.

3.3   Detection Scenario

In distance measures as well as in vector projection we deal with scalars. The evaluation of the distance measures was based on the detection rate, P_D, given a false alarm rate, P_{FA}. In our experiments, false alarm was set to 5%. For each measure, y, two probability density functions, $p(y|0)$ and $p(y|1)$ were computed depending on the results from the perceptual test; if the synthetic sentence was perceived as continuous (0), and (1) if it was perceived as discontinuous by the listeners. Then the detection rate for that measure, y, is computed as:

$$P_D(\gamma) = \int_{\gamma}^{\infty} p(y|1) \, dy \tag{16}$$

where γ is defined by:

$$P_{FA}(\gamma) = \int_{\gamma}^{\infty} p(y|0) \, dy \tag{17}$$

3.4   Features

Synthetic test words, as this will be explained in the next section, consist of two parts; a left part and a right one. For both parts, features are computed at the concatenation point. Many options may be considered for the comparison of these features. We present those that gave high detection rates while at the same time, they have an intuitive meaning. For instance, the features of the harmonic models are complex numbers, hence the absolute of their complex difference is considered the same as Euclidean distance between two points on the complex plane. For the second set of parameters, the AM features are defined as the l_1 norm between the AM components estimated for the left and right part for each filter of the filterbank. Similarly, the FM features are estimated as the $l_{1/2}$ norm of the corresponding FM components.

4 Listening Test

Database used for our research was consisted of 2016 monosyllabic words which were generated by concatenative synthesis using an acoustic inventory of recordings from a native American female speaker. The sampling frequency of these recording was 16kHz. The context of the inventory contained 336 monosyllabic test words that constitute the Modified Rhyme Test(MRT)[15]. Synthetic words were obtained by simple concatenation of raw waveforms using each time two halves of original words. The concatenation point was approximately obtained in the middle of the vowel. In order to avoid linear phase mismatches between the concatenated parts, a cross correlation function was used. From listening tests we may say that, in general, pitch continuation was preserved. The 336 spoken words were separated into 56 groups of 6 words. Each group had words with same vowel nucleus but different initial or final consonant(s). Therefore, for each group 36 synthetic words (test stimuli) were constructed (all possible combinations of the 6 recorded words). These 36 synthetic words constitute a subtest. Every subtest contained 6 "synthesized" words which actually were human spoken words and we used them for validation purposes.

The listening task was conducted in a quiet office room using headphones. Listeners were presented with a test stimulus along with a decision in order to familiarize themselves with the listening test. After this training period, listeners started to hear the test words followed by a single interval of forced choice (Yes/No) depending on whether or not they had heard a concatenation discontinuity. The number of subtests listened by the participants was 386.

Twelve listeners participated in the perceptual test. Four of them were native Americans while the others were Greeks with satisfactory knowledge of English language. Five of the participants had experience in listening to synthetic speech. As a validation check, we tested how many of the continuous words were considered as discontinuous. A subtest was rejected if more than one continuous word was considered as discontinuous. This way, 62 subtests were rejected from the database while 324 subtests remained.

Finally, two numbers were assigned to each test stimulus. First number counted how many listeners perceived test stimulus discontinuous while second number counted how many listeners perceived test stimulus continuous. A synthetic speech signal was considered discontinuous(or continuous) if the first number was greater(or less) to the second number. Rarely, when a tie occured synthetic signal was considered as discontinuous.

5 Results

In Table 1, detection rate of various measure distances are presented. We remind that the false alarm was set to 5%.

The parameters of the harmonic models are complex numbers and as mentioned before we use as a difference between complex numbers the absolute of the complex difference. In order to keep the size of the measured vectors small while

Table 1. Detection Rates

Distance	Detection Rate (%)
l_1 on a_k of SHM	32.34
l_2 on a_k of SHM	39.77
l_1 on a_k of HMWS	40.83
l_2 on a_k of HMWS	43.92
Fisher on a_k of SHM	45.46
Fisher on a_k of HMWS	44.50
Fisher on a_k & b_k of HMWS	54.63
Fisher on AM	28.86
Fisher on FM	29.92
Fisher on AM & FM	39.29
Fisher on a_k & b_k & AM & FM	70.46

preserving the important information from a speech frame, we have decided to prune the size vector of complex amplitudes to the twenty first frequencies. Indeed, given that the average fundamental frequency of the voice is about 200Hz we cover most of the time the first 4000Hz of a speech frame. We have considered l_1 norm, l_2 norm and Fisher linear discriminant for both harmonic models. Fisher's linear discriminant on a_k & b_k from the nonlinear harmonic model has given the best score(54.63%).

The second feature set composed by features of the AM & FM model performed poorer than harmonic models. However, these results were higher than previous reported work. Detection rate with the use of Fisher's linear discriminant on the FM components performed slightly better than the AM components. A simple combination of these two components has resulted in a higher detection rate(39.29%). Finally, by applying Fisher's linear discriminant on the whole set of features(Harmonic parameters, AM, FM) an impressive detection rate of 70.46% has been obtained.

6   Conclusion and Future Work

This paper introduced two new feature sets for the problem of detecting audible discontinuities in concatenative speech synthesis. The first set of features, which gave the best result, were extracted from a nonlinear speech model which assumes speech signals as a sum of harmonic sinusoids. The second set of features was based on a method that decomposes speech signals into AM and FM components. Signals with audible discontinuities were separated from those without audible discontinuities by a hyperplane which was determined by Fisher's linear discriminant.

A remarkable detection rate(compared to previous published results) was obtained when the above features were combined. However, we expect that better results can be obtained if we use more sophisticated discrimination functions. Moreover, the number of parameters used in this experiment is quite large. Therefore, data reduction is necessary for a feasible implementation of the suggested approach in the concatenative speech synthesis systems. These two observations draw the line of our future research work.

References

1. A. Hunt and A. Black. Unit selection in a concatenative speech synthesis system using large speech database. *Proc. IEEE Int. Conf. Acoust., Speech, Signal Processing*, pages 373–376, 1996.
2. W. N. Campbell and A. Black. Prosody and the selection of source units for concatenative synthesis. In R. Van Santen, R.Sproat, J.Hirschberg, and J.Olive, editors, *Progress in Speech Synthesis*, pages 279–292. Springer Verlag, 1996.
3. M. Beutnagel, A. Conkie, J. Schroeter, Y. Stylianou, and A. Syrdal. The AT&T Next-Gen TTS System. *137th meeting of the Acoustical Society of America*, 1999. http://www.research.att.com/projects/tts.
4. G. Coorman J. Fachrell P. Rutten and B.Van-Coile. Segment selection in the l&h realspeak laboratory tts system. *Proc. ICSLP 2000*, 2000.
5. E. Klabbers and R. Veldhuis. On the reduction of concatenation artefacts in diphone synthesis. *International Conference on Spoken Language Processing ICSLP 98*, pages 1983–1986, 1998.
6. J. Wouters and M. Macon. Perceptual evaluation of distance measures for concatenative speech synthesis. *International Conference on Spoken Language Processing ICSLP 98*, pages 2747–2750, 1998.
7. Y. Stylianou and A. Syrdal. Perceptual and objective detection of discontinuities in concatenative speech synthesis. *Proc. IEEE Int. Conf. Acoust., Speech, Signal Processing*, 2001.
8. Robert E. Donovan. A new distance measure for costing spectral discontinuities in concatenative speech synthesis. *The 4th ISCA Tutorial and Research Workshop on Speech Synthesis*, 2001.
9. Yannis Stylianou. *Harmonic plus Noise Models for Speech, combined with Statistical Methods, for Speech and Speaker Modification*. PhD thesis, Ecole Nationale Supèrieure des Télécommunications, 1996.
10. P. Maragos J. Kaiser and T. Quatieri. On separating amplitude from frequency modulations using energy operators. *Proc. IEEE Int. Conf. Acoust., Speech, Signal Processing*, Mar 1992.
11. H. M. Teager. Some observations on oral air flow during phonation. *IEEE Trans. Acoust., Speech, Signal Processing*, Oct 1980.
12. H. M. Teager and S. M. Teager. Evidence for nonlinear sound production mechanism in the vocal tract. *Speech Production and Speech Modelling*, 55, Jul 1990.
13. P. Maragos T. F. Quatieri and J. F. Kaiser. Speech nonlinearities, modulations and energy operators. *Proc. IEEE ICASSP-91*, May 1991.
14. J. Vepa S. King and P. Taylor. Objective distance measures for spectal discontinuities in concatenative speech synthesis. *ICSLP 2002*, pages 2605–2608, 2002.
15. A. S. House C. E. Williams M.H. L. Hecker and K. D. Kryter. Phycoacoustic speech test: A modified rhyme test. *Tech. Doc. Rept. ESD-TDR-63-403*, Jun 1963.

Signal Sparsity Enhancement Through Wavelet Transforms in Underdetermined BSS

Eraldo Pomponi, Stefano Squartini, and Francesco Piazza

Universitá Politecnica delle Marche, Dipartimento di Elettronica, Intelligenza
Artificiale e Telecomunicazioni,
Via Brecce Bianche, 60131, Ancona, Italy

Abstract. Source sparsity is a common assumption in many solutions proposed in literature to the problem of blind source separation with more sources than mixtures. As shown in this work, representation of signals in different wavelet domains can be efficiently applied in order to get improved sparsity. Moreover, the approach here presented allows to directly perform a de-noising operation after the separation algorithm, at a very low computational cost, resulting in a further improvement of source recovering when noise is present at mixture level. Experimental results confirm the effectiveness of developed idea.

1 Introduction

The present work faces the problem of blind source separation (BSS), widely studied in literature. The goal of techniques attempting to solve such a problem consists of recovering the original N sources vector $\mathbf{s}(t)$ mixed by a non-singular $M \times N$ matrix $\mathbf{A}$, the mixing matrix, when both are unknown and the only available information is the mixed N signals vector $\mathbf{x}(t)$. Such a task is called under-determined when the number of mixture M is less than the number of sources N: in such a case the usual algorithms addressed in square and over-determined BSS problems can not be directly applied and different assumptions are usually made. Indeed, several approaches in literature make use of source sparsity, according to which only a small number of sources are contemporarily present in the mixture at a certain instant. Some works [1]-[3] have been pointed out that such sparsity can be enhanced through a suitable representation of signals, as by means of Short Time Fourier Transform. Wavelet transform has also been used for sparse representation of signals in BSS problem in [4], but not in the under-determined case yet. As authors show in [4], this kind of transform allow to achieve a better sparsity than STFT: this is the reason why we have chosen it in substitution to STFT in the two-step algorithm proposed in [1] to recover the mixing matrix and sources. This has been developed in case of discrete wavelet transform (DWT), discrete wavelet packet transform (DWPT), and best discrete wavelet packet transform where a criterium is defined to determine the best tree in DWPT. Experimental results show that the developed idea allows to get improved source separability. A de-noising operation has been easily added

G. Chollet et al. (Eds.): Nonlinear Speech Modeling, LNAI 3445, pp. 384–391, 2005.

after the source separation algorithm, by exploiting widely used thresholding techniques on wavelet coefficients, to address the case when noise is taken into account in the mixing model.

2   The Existing Approach

The existing underdetermined blind source separation algorithm we are referring to is that one presented in [1]. Let $\mathbf{x}(t)$ (namely the data point) and $\mathbf{s}(t)$ be the M-dimensional mixture and the N-dimensional source vectors respectively at the discrete time instants t for $t = t_0, .., T$: our goal consists in finding the solution of the following system:

$$\mathbf{x}(t) = \mathbf{A}\mathbf{s}(t) \tag{1}$$

without having specific information on the mixing matrix $\mathbf{A}$. The only assumptions we make are the sparsity and independence of sources The approach is divided into two separate steps: the blind mixing model recovery (BMMR) step (the mixing matrix has to be reconstructed from the mixtures) and the blind source recovery (BSR) step (the sources have to be reconstructed given the mixing matrix, previously estimated, and the mixtures. The same approach is used in [5], with the only difference that a geometric method is employed to face the BMMR step, while a clustering algorithm is described here. It must be observed that also another two-step approach is present in literature [6], with the relevant difference that they are performed separately at each time instant.

The BMMR algorithm is based on the definition of a potential function describing the directions along which the data points occurr. This can be easily visualized in the case $M = 2$, when the mixture space is a plane and the directions are characterized by one parameter, the angle Θ.

After have been performed such an estimation of the mixing matrix, we can go further to the BSR step: since the system in 2 is underdetermined, its solution is not unique and a suitable algorithm must be defined to extract the sources. The approach for the source reconstruction is the maximum likelihood algorithm, which means maximizing the posterior probability of $\mathbf{s}$ by means of its prior probability. In other words:

$$\hat{\mathbf{s}} = \arg \max_{\mathbf{x}=\mathbf{A}\mathbf{s}} P(\mathbf{s}|\mathbf{x},\mathbf{A}) \tag{2}$$

Using the Bayes Theorem, the source sparsity property (modeled as a Laplacian distribution, i.e. $P(s_i) \propto \exp(-\lambda|s_i|)$) and the independence of the sources, we can say that the ML problem to solve turns to be a linear programming one. In formula:

$$\hat{\mathbf{s}} = \arg \max_{\mathbf{x}=\mathbf{A}\mathbf{s}} \|\mathbf{s}\|_1 \tag{3}$$

where $\|\mathbf{s}\|_1$ is the ℓ_1-norm of source vector $\mathbf{s}$. In case $M = 2$ this means that for a given data point we select the closest two columns $\mathbf{a}_j, \mathbf{a}_k$ of $\mathbf{A}$ to it.

This algorithm is usually addressed as the shortest path algorithm.

These two steps are carried out in the time-frequency plan in [1], after having applied the STFT to the mixtures. As aforementioned, this operation allows us to get an improved source sparsity in the new domain. Then, taking into account the linearity ($F(\mathbf{x}) = F(\mathbf{As}) = \mathbf{A}F(\mathbf{s})$) and invertibility of the operator, we can easily applied the BMMR and BSR algorithms to the sequences obtained by concatenation of all windowed and transformed mixture frames. Finally, the recovered sources are converted to the time domain through the $STFT^{-1}$.

3   The New Wavelet-Based Approach

In this section we describe the innovative contributions to the existing approach: the application of different wavelet transforms on the the mixture signals instead of the STFT and the denoising operation occurring after the separation algorithm.

3.1   Sparse Representation in Different Wavelet Domains

As aforementioned, three are the diverse wavelet transforms here considered: DWT, DWPT and B.DWPT [7]. The Discrete Wavelet Transform can be seen as an octave band filter bank where the filters are selected to ensure perfect reconstruction. Such a filter bank has a recursive structure: at each step the input signal is low-pass and high-pass filtered to yield two sequences that are so decimated by a 2 factor. The result is a set of sequences, namely wavelet coefficient sequences, each one corresponding to a different part of the spectrum of the signal transformed, at different time and frequency resolutions: lower frequencies are sampled with a larger time step than the higher ones. This means that we can represent a signal with resolution that is inversely proportional to the frequency, resulting in a more accurate analysis of signals under inspection. Indeed information contained in the signal under study is generally not uniformly distributed all over the spectrum, but localized only in particular zones of it (low frequencies, in case of speech). In formulas, we can express such a transform as follows:

$$\{x(t)\} \rightarrow DWT \rightarrow \{w_1(n), .., w_i(n), .., w_{2^{J-1}}(n), v_{2^{J-1}}(n)\} \tag{4}$$

where $n = 1, .., T/2^{i-1}$, and J is the decomposition level. The overall number of wavelet coefficients is equal to the number of samples in the original signal, that means we deal with a critically sampling based transform. The same happens in the case of discrete Wavelet Packet Transform, that generalizes the previous one since the user can fix the shape of the decomposition tree, resulting in a more specific examination of the original spectrum and enhanced versatility on handling signals in comparison to STFT. The selection of optimal decomposition tree from the global wavelet packet tree one (corresponding to uniform resolution all over the spectrum) can be performed by means of heuristic methods or maximization or minimization of suitable indexes. Here, we have employed a variation of Shannon entropy as cost function, by which we select the tree bands in order to maximize the information carried therein:

$$\text{cost}_{shannon} = -\sum_n w[n]^2 \ln(w[n]^2) \tag{5}$$

where $w[n]$ is the coefficient of wavelet decomposition. The node selection for the best WP tree is carried out according to the following algorithm:

- The tree is analysed from the leaf-nodes towards the root.
- A leaf-node return its cost.
- If the node addressed has some son-nodes, we name the cost of the node V_1 and the sum of costs of son-nodes V_2.
- If $V_1 \leq V_2$, we label the nodes belonging to the best decomposition tree and we remove all the labels from the nodes of the sub-tree starting from this node; else if $V_1 > V_2$, the cost is replaced by V_2.
- Repeat the procedure until the tree root is reached and every leaf-node considered.
- Labeled nodes are the nodes of the decomposition tree, optimal in the sense of the cost function used for entropy maximization.

3.2   The Denoising Operation

The usage of wavelet transform allowed us to perform a denoising operation with a very low computational cost directly on the coefficient sequences available at the output of the separation algorithm described in the previous section. Such an operation describes how we have addressed the problem of the noise presence in the mixing model:

$$\mathbf{x} = \mathbf{As} + \mathbf{v} \tag{6}$$

where $\mathbf{v}$ is the additive noise M-vector. Such an operation consists in thresholding the detail wavelet coefficients, in order to get significant reduction of background noise. This enhanced quality of final recovered sources has been specially underlined by several informal subjective tests made by the authors. It must be noted that the choice of threshold value is fundamental for the efficacy of the operation. Different solutions are available in the literature: in our case the threshold has been chosen minimizing a quadratic function that estimate the loss of information obtained limiting those coefficients that exceed it (Stein's Unbiased Estimate of Risk) [8]. It is relevant to observe that an operation like this, in the representation domain addressed in [1], would require more complex operations than a mere threshold as done here, leading to significantly increasing the computational cost.

3.3   The Overall Algorithm

The separation procedure is summarized as follows:

- Each mixture is transformed through one of these methods: DWT, DWPT or B.DWPT.

- The coefficients of the transform are concatenated for each mixture and used as the actual input vector. In terms of the previous sections, the set of those coefficients play the role of $\mathbf{x}$.
- An estimation of mixing matrix is yielded by means of the BMMR algorithm.
- The source wavelet coefficient sequences are estimated following the BSR procedure.
- For each estimated source, the coefficient vector is reverse-transformed into the time-domain representation (notice that, in the case of B.DWPT, the selected best tree shape is stored and, in this step, filled with the suitable coefficients, to perform a correct reconstruction).

4 Experimental Results

Speech signals obtained from TIMIT database (different sentences and different male/female speakers, sampling rate=16kHz, coding scheme=PCM-16bit) have been employed in the experimental session. This is the followed mixing procedure:

- In order to achieve a balanced mix, all source are normalized: $\mathbf{s}' = \mathbf{s}/\|\mathbf{s}\|$.
- The $2 \times N$ mixing matrix $\mathbf{A}$ is defined by imposing the basis vectors $\mathbf{a}_j$ to have unit length and equally spaced angles.
- The mixtures are re-scaled into (-1,1) range: $\mathbf{x}' = \mathbf{x}/\max_{i,t} |x_i(t)|$.
- In case of noisy signals, pink noise (band limited: 10 Hz -1,5 KHz, amplitude adjusted to have equal to 20 dB) is added to the mixture signals.

Experiments have been carried out in different cases: two, three, four and five speech source signals, with and without noise. Performances of the implemented algorithm have been estimated by means of the following indexes:

1. Differences between the angles of the estimated and the original basis vectors (i.e., columns of the mixing matrix).
2. Reconstruction index, defined in [1] as:

$$R = 10 \log \frac{\|\hat{\mathbf{s}} - \mathbf{s}\|^2}{\|\mathbf{s}\|}^2 \tag{7}$$

where $\hat{\mathbf{s}}$ is the recovered source matrix.

First, we can observe the differences between the scatter plots for three mixed sources obtained in the time domain and in two transformed domains, the standard and the B.DWPT ones (Figure 2 and 1): in the latter case, the data point distribution allows us to detect the matrix directions easier than the former. This aspect influences the shape of respective potential functions resulting in improved separation performances. Such an improvement is confirmed by results in Table 1, reporting the reconstruction index values for different transforms adopted and in the case study of $M = 2$, $N = 4$. Concerning the noisy case, informal acoustical tests confirmed the superior enhancement achieved through the

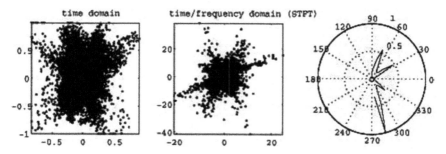

Fig. 1. Scatter plot of two mixtures (4 sources) in the time domain and in the time-frequency domain (STFT). The relative potential function is also depicted

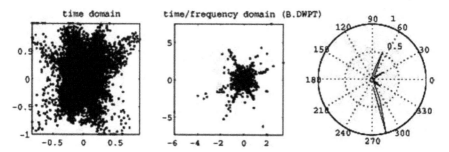

Fig. 2. Scatter plot of two mixtures (4 sources) in the time domain and in the time-frequency domain (best-DWPT). The relative potential function is also depicted

Table 1. Reconstruction index values for 4 different transforms used in $M = 2$, $N = 4$ in noiseless *(a)* and noisy case study *(b)*

(a)	standard	DWT	DWPT	B.DWPT
source 1	3.04	4.53	4.27	3.98
source 2	8.96	13.1	-10.22	10.37
source 3	5.74	-14.83	-19.72	-19.72
source 4	8.94	-2.41	-6.08	-5.88

(b)		standard	DWT	DWPT	B.DWPT
source 1	noisy	2.94	5.33	5.59	4.49
	denoised	2.26	5.33	5.23	4.46
source 2	noisy	9.91	14.16	13.84	13.53
	denoised	9.80	13.97	13.65	13.53
source 3	noisy	5.89	-11.52	-15.35	-15.33
	denoised	5.84	-11.52	-15.52	-15.51
source 4	noisy	9.15	0.94	-0.19	-0.93
	denoised	8.7	0.94	-1.12	-1.58

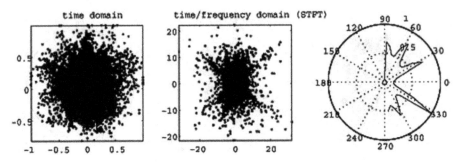

Fig. 3. Scatter plot of two mixtures (5 sources) in the time domain and in the time-frequency domain (STFT). The relative potential function is also depicted

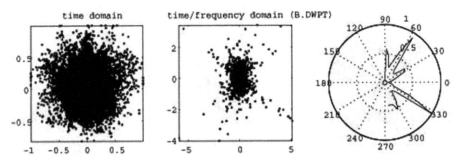

Fig. 4. Scatter plot of two mixtures (5 sources) in the time domain and in the time-frequency domain (best-DWPT). The relative potential function is also depicted

wavelet based method. Other case studies corresponding to different N values have been considered, leading to the same conclusions. In particular a relevant difference between the two approaches can be detected when $N = 2$, $N = 3$, while it decreases (but still existing) when we deal with more than 4 sources. This can be explained looking at the scatterplots reported in Figure 4 and 3: now the potential functions do not allow us to recover the mixing directions as well as before, and this results in a remarkable reduction of separation performances.

5   Conclusions

The wavelet approach to the blind sources separation problem in the under-determined case with sparse representation has been here presented and experimental results let us conclude that superior performances can be achieved than in common STFT approach. Moreover an adjunctive source de-noising operation at a very low computational cost has been implemented, ensuring an improvement of intelligibility of extracted sources even in the noisy case.

Further developments, actually under study, concern the optimization of the de-noising step and the introduction of a priori knowledge on the nature of signals involved (as speech), to improve the overall source recovering quality. An interesting issue to be investigated is to perform the de-noising operation directly at the mixture level rather than separated sources, resulting in a non-linear operation before the separation algorithm: its feasibility should be studied and proved from a theoretical point of view.

References

1. Bofill, P., Zibulevsky, M.: Underdetermined blind source separation using sparse representation. Signal Processing **81** (20001) 2353–2362.
2. Jourjine, A., Rickard S., and Yilmaz, O.: Blind separation of disjoint orthogonal signals: demixing N sources from 2 mixtures. Proc. ICASSP 2000 (2000) 2985–2988.
3. Casey, M.A.: Separation of mixed audio sources by independent subspace analysis. Proc. International Computer Music Conference (2000).
4. P.Kisilev, M. Zibulevsky, Y. Zeevi, and B.A. Pearlmutter, Blind source separation via multimode sparse representation. Advances in Neural Information Processing Systems (2002) 1049–1056.
5. Theis, F.J., and Lang, E.W.: Formalization of the two-step approach to overcomplete BSS. SIP (2002).
6. Lewicki, M.S. and Sejnowski, T.J.: Learning overcomplete representation. Neural Computation (1988).
7. Vetterli, M., and Kovacevic, J.: Wavelet and subband coding. Prentice Hall (1995).
8. Donoho, D.L., Johnstone, I.M., Kerkyacharian G. and Picard, D.: Wavelet shrinkage: asymptopia. Jour. Roy. Stat. Soc., series B, **57** (1995) 301–369.

A Quantitative Evaluation
of a Bio-inspired Sound Segregation Technique
for Two- and Three-Source Mixtures

Ramin Pichevar and Jean Rouat

Dept. of Elect. Eng., University of Sherbrooke, QC, Canada
{Ramin.Pichevar,Jean.Rouat}@usherbrooke.ca

Abstract. A sound source separation technique based on a bio-inspired neural network, capable of functioning in more than two-source mixtures, is proposed. Separation results are compared with other proposed techniques in the literature using quantitative evaluation criteria.

1   The Sound Source Separation Problem

In our life we are confronted to situation in which a mixture of sound sources is present in the environment and our goal is to extract one of the sources among others. While the auditory system may not always succeed in this goal, the range of situations in which recognition is possible in the presence of competing sources highlights the flexibility and robustness of human in speech perception. Here we propose a technique that roughly simulates the behavior of the auditory pathway. Our separation technique uses the Computational Auditory Scene Analysis [1].

2   The Proposed Model

An enhanced FIR Gammatone filterbank is used to mimic the behavior of the cochlea [2]. From the output of the cochlear channels two different anthropomorphic maps are generated. The Cochleotopic/ AMtopic and Cochleotopic/ Spectrotopic Maps, which try to mimic partially the behavior of the peripheral auditory pathway are generated. These maps are based on the reassigned FFT (Fast Fourier Transform) and envelope detection [3]. A two-layered network of spiking neurons is used to perform cochlear channel selection (Fig. 2) based on temporal correlation: neurons associated to those channels belonging to the same sound source synchronize.

2.1   Three-Source Sound Source Separation

In our previous works, we applied our proposed model to two-source sound source separation [3] [2]. Most of other proposed models in the literature for ASA-based sound source separation deal only with two-source sound source separation (see [4] [5] [6] [7] [8]). One of the exceptions to this general tendency is the work by

G. Chollet et al. (Eds.): Nonlinear Speech Modeling, LNAI 3445, pp. 392–396, 2005.

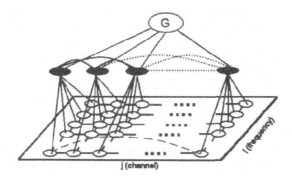

Fig. 1. The Two-Layer Neural Network. G: Stands for global controller. One long range connection is shown in the figure. The first layer segregates the CAM/CSM maps and the second layer binds the information

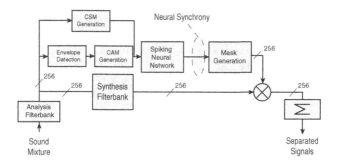

Fig. 2. Proposed source separation system: the CAM & CSM are generated in two different paths. Based on neural synchrony, a binary mask is generated, which mutes certain cochlear channel that don't belong to the desired source

Yilmaz & Rickard [9]. For some of the two-source separation techniques proposed in the literature, it seems that the extension to higher number of sources is not straightforward, or at least not explored. For instance, architectures based on factorial models as proposed in [7] [8] inherently deal with two rows of Markov chains, each of which corresponding to one of the sources. Hence, in order to separate a three-source mixture the whole architecture must be revised by adding additional Markov chains. It is also unclear how the pitch tracking technique proposed by Hu & Wang [4] can be used for higher number of sources. In the temporal correlation based technique proposed by Wang & Brown [5] some synaptic connections in the second layer are established according to the pitch of the voiced source in the two-source mixture. This architecture cannot be used as proposed for higher number of sources unless some modifications are done. However, no conceptual modifications are required to our proposed architecture in [2] [3]. Ideally, the only constraints on the number of sources that can be separated by our work is the number of distinct synchronization phase the neural architecture can have, which is equal to 4-5 in the analog Wang-Terman oscillator case and ideally infinity in the algorithmic version [5].

3   Evaluation Criteria

Three different criteria are considered and evaluated in this section.

3.1   PEL and PNR

Let us consider that the mixture is processed by a sound separation system and segregated speech is obtained. The target is the ideal desired extracted sound. The intrusion is the sound from other sources in the mixture that has been mistakenly associated to the desired source by the segregation technique. The PEL (Percentage of Energy Loss) is defined as the percentage of target speech excluded from segregated speech. The PNR (Percentage of Noise Residue) is the percentage of intrusion included in the synthesized speech. Although the PEL and PNR are used in the literature as performance criteria, our perceptive tests have shown that these criteria do not reflect exactly the real performance of a given sound separation system at least for the middle to high performance range and the perceptive quality can be very different for two different approaches with equal PELs and PNRs. For totally different extracted signals we can obtain similar PEL and PNR.

3.2   Log Spectral Distortion (LSD)

Another criterion used in the literature is the LSD [10] given by:

$$LSD = \frac{1}{L} \sum_{l=0}^{L-1} \sqrt{\frac{1}{K} \sum_{k=0}^{K-1} (20 \, log_{10} \frac{|I(k,l)| + \epsilon}{|O(k,l)| + \epsilon})^2} \qquad (1)$$

Where $I(k,l)$ and $O(k,l)$ are the FFT of the desired and original signals respectively. L is the number of frames, K is the number of frequency bins and ϵ is meant to prevent extreme values. In table 1 separation results for Cooke's database [11] are given for our technique and compared with techniques given in [4] and [5].

However, this criteria doesn't reflect some temporal aspects like the phase distortion. The result of the LSD would be the same, if a separation technique had phase distortion. On the other hand, some authors have shown that phase discrepancies have slight impact on the perceptive quality of sound.

3.3   PESQ

Another quantitative performance criterion used in speech coding is the PESQ (Perceptual Evaluation of Speech Quality). We propose here to use this criterion for sound source separation[1].

---

[1] Many thanks to Vijay Parsa from the University of Western Ontario for fruitful discussions on PESQ

Table 1. The log spectral distortion for three different methods: P-R (our proposed approach), W-B ([5]), and H-W ([4]). The intrusion noises are: 1 kHz pure tone, FM Siren, telephone ring, white noise, the male intrusion (/di/) for the French /di//da/ mixture, and the female intrusion (/da/) for the French /di//da/ mixture. Lower values mean better performance

Intrusion	SNR of the initial mixture(dB)	P-R LSD	W-B LSD	H-W LSD
Tone	-2 dB	7.1	23.2	16.5
Siren	-5 dB	8.7	17.3	8.5
Tel. ring	3 dB	15.4	16.6	10.1
White noise	-5 dB	15.3	18.4	12.8
Male (da)	0 dB	23.7	N/A	N/A
Female (di)	0 dB	17.9	N/A	N/A

The PESQ is an objective method for end-to-end speech quality assessment of narrow-band telephone networks and speech codecs, which is applicable to any end-to-end measurement. This evaluation method has been proposed by the ITU (International Telecommunication Union) under the recommendation P.862. The code and documentation for PESQ can be downloaded at [12].

Table 2. The PESQ of three different methods: P-R (our proposed approach), W-B ([5]), and H-W ([4]) (see caption of Table 1). Higher values mean better performance

Intrusion (noise)	ini. SNR mixture	P-R (PESQ)	W-B (PESQ)	H-W (PESQ)
Tone	-2 dB	0.4	0.2	0.4
Siren	-5 dB	2.1	1.6	1.2
Tel. ring	3 dB	0.9	0.7	0.9
White	-5 dB	0.9	0.2	0.3
Male (da)	0 dB	2.1	N/A	N/A
Female (di)	0 dB	0.7	N/A	N/A

Our technique gives better result compared with [4] [5] based on the PESQ for all mixtures tested (except for telephone ring, in which case performance is comparable). However, according to LSD, our technique performs better than Wang & Brown [5] and performs either better or worse (depending on the mixture used) compared with Hu & Wang [4]. Compared with a statistical approach proposed in [6] our approach performs better for the extraction of music and performs slightly worse for the extraction of speech. However, the technique proposed in [6] had been statistically trained with speech before the separation phase.

Table 3. PESQ for two different methods: P-R (our proposed approach) and J-L ([6]). The mixture comprises a female voice with musical rock background

Mixture	Separated sources	P-R (PESQ)	J-L (PESQ)
Music & female	music	1.70	0.35
(AF)	voice	0.55	0.63

4 Conclusion

A sound separation technique based on a two-layered neural network of spiking neuron has been proposed. Different quantitative criteria have been studied and we have found that the PESQ and the LSD are more close to the perceptual quality of sound. Our proposed technique is then compared with other techniques proposed in the literature based on these two criteria. Evaluation based on PESQ or LSD doesn't always favor the same separation technique.

References

1. A.S. Bregman. *Auditory Scene Analysis*. MIT Press, 1990.
2. R. Pichevar, J. Rouat, C. Feldbauer, and G. Kubin. A bio-inspired sound source separation technique in combination with an enhanced FIR gammatone Analysis/Synthesis filterbank. In *EUSIPCO Vienna*, 2004.
3. R. Pichevar and J. Rouat. Cochleotopic/AMtopic (CAM) and Cochleotopic/Spectrotopic (CSM) map based sound source separation using relaxation oscillatory neurons. In *IEEE Neural Networks for Signal Processing Workshop, Toulouse, France*, 2003.
4. G. Hu and D.L. Wang. Monaural speech segregation based on pitch tracking and amplitude modulation. *IEEE Trans. On Neural Networks*, pages 1135– 1150, Sept. 2004.
5. D. Wang and G. J. Brown. Separation of speech from interfering sounds based on oscillatory correlation. *IEEE Transactions on Neural Networks*, 10(3):684–697, May 1999.
6. G. Jang and T. Lee. Single-channel signal separation using time-domain basis functions. *Signal Processing Letters*, pages 168–171, June 2003.
7. M.R. Gomez, D. Ellis, and N. Jojic. Multiband audio modeling for single-channel acoustic source separation. In *ICASSP 2004*, 2004.
8. S.T. Roweis. Factorial models and refiltering for speech separation and denoising. In *Eurospeech 2003*, 2003.
9. O. Yilmaz and S. Rickard. Blind separation of speech mixtures via time-frequency masking. *IEEE Trans. On Signal Processing*, pages 1830 – 1847, July 2004.
10. J.-M. Valin, J. Rouat, and F. Michaud. Microphone array post-filter for separation of simultaneous non-stationary sources. In *ICASSP, Montreal, Canada*, 2004.
11. Martin Cooke. http://www.dcs.shef.ac.uk/~martin/.
12. http://www.itu.int/home/.

Application of Symbolic Machine Learning to Audio Signal Segmentation

Arimantas Raškinis and Gailius Raškinis

Vytautas Magnus University, Center of Computational Linguistics,
Donelaičio 52, LT-3000 Kaunas, Lithuania
{Arimantas_Raskinis,Gailius_Raskinis}@fc.vdu.lt

Abstract. In this paper, we address a data-driven approach to the problem of automatic segmentation of speech and music into phones and notes respectively that makes use of symbolic machine learning techniques. The whole segmentation process is subdivided into four steps: series of non-linear transformations are used for building first-order features that allow easy detection of segmentation candidates, second-order features that describe sound properties in the neighborhood of a segmentation candidate are developed, the set of segmentation candidates is transformed into machine learning data set by labeling candidates in accordance to the annotated speech corpus, and supervised symbolic machine learning methods are applied resulting in segmentation rules[1].

1 Introduction

In this paper, we address the problem of segmentation of speech and music (monodic singing) into phones and notes respectively assuming that the transcription of an audio signal is not available. We argue that in both cases segmentation can be achieved by means of the same data-driven processing architecture that incorporates symbolic machine learning (ML) techniques.

Presently, speech recognition research (including speech segmentation) is dominated by Hidden Markov modeling (HMM) which is a kind of statistical machine learning [1, 2]. HMM favor features that show best average performance for all acoustic classes as HMM is bound to find statistical regularities no matter how much overlapping are training instances of different acoustic classes in the feature space.

1.1 Symbolic Learning

Symbolic learning techniques understand regularities as laws that manifest themselves through training instances but do not depend on them. Let F be the set of features describing training instances, and let C be the set of possible classes. Symbolic ML induces a set of rules of prepositional logic of the type:

if p_{i1} and p_{i2} and ... and p_{in_i} then class = c_i, $i = 1, ..., m$.

Here $c_i \in C$, and p_{ij} is the preposition of the form "$f_k \in [v_1, v_2]$", $f_k \in F$, $v_1, v_2 \in R$.

---

[1] This research was partially supported by Lithuanian State Science and Studies Foundation

G. Chollet et al. (Eds.): Nonlinear Speech Modeling, LNAI 3445, pp. 397–403, 2005.

Rules within a set may be ordered or unordered, may cover overlapping or non-overlapping areas in a feature space. Rules are usually obtained by generating and testing all hypotheses within a hypothesis space in an exhaustive manner [4] or using some hill climbing search strategies, for instance, incrementally adding/removing rule conjuncts [3]. Top-down decision tree induction techniques [5] belong to the symbolic ML as well.

Symbolic rules are able to separate hyper-rectangular areas in the multidimensional feature space. Due to this constraint, symbolic ML may fail if sets of segmentation instances belonging to different classes significantly overlap. This is especially true, if zero inconsistency with the training instances is required during rule set induction. Thus, the extraction of good features is of extreme importance to symbolic ML. Symbolic machine learning favors features that may be useful for discriminating just a single class but useless for the remaining classes.

2   Data-Driven Architecture for Audio Signal Segmentation

We have constructed a data-driven processing scheme that incorporated supervised symbolic learning (fig. 1). This scheme is discussed in more detail below.

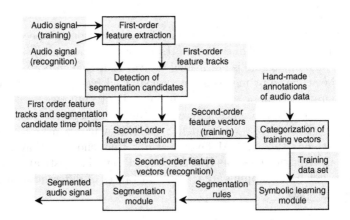

Fig. 1. The data-driven processing scheme used for automatic segmentation

Initially, training audio signals are transformed into the first-order feature tracks, where each transformation consists of an application of a sequence of basic signal processing procedures called *operators*. Certain first-order feature tracks are scanned for *cues* or *segmentation candidates* that are known to be related to the presence of transitions in acoustic events. Then, various feature characteristics called *the second order features* are measured in the neighborhood of the segmentation candidate. The step of the second-order feature extraction results in a set of vectors each describing one particular candidate. During categorization of training vectors each vector is labeled as positive or negative segmentation instance. Class labels are extracted from human-made annotations of the same audio data. Thereafter training data set is supplied to one of the supervised symbolic learning methods which outputs segmentation rules stated in the language of prepositional logic. These rules are then passed to the recognition module which uses them for deciding the class of segmentation candidates of unknown test data.

2.1   First-Order Feature Extraction

Feature extraction has been an intensive field of study for a few decades. Both empirically stated and perceptually inspired signal transformations [7] have been proposed for finding the most appropriate features for discriminating various types of speech sounds. Our approach was different from the previous ones as we were using a combinatorial search to solve the problem.

Speech segmentation task was split into a set of complementary tasks of spotting particular phone transitions. The set of basic signal processing operators, their parameters and their chaining rules were defined thus defining the space of possible first-order features. Finally, this space was sought for the best first-order features for each particular transition spotting task. Search criterion measured the degree of correspondence between maxima of an automatically generated feature track and phone transition instants indicated by annotation data. Thus, each first-order feature track was the result of a complex non-linear signal transformations. Our basic operator set included: arithmetical operators (ABS, LOG, SQR, MIN, MAX, AVG), derivation operator (DER), standard deviation operator (STD), pitch, intensity, envelope and zero crossing rate extractors (PITCH, INT, ENV, ZCR), filter bank analysis (FB), normalization operator (NORM), thresholding operator (THR), and others. A few examples of such operators are given by formulas (1- 6) and some of their feature tracks are shown in fig. 2.

$$f_A(i) = NORM(\alpha_A, \beta_A, THR(\gamma_A, PITCH(ABS(s(t))))) . \qquad (1)$$

$$f_B(i) = NORM(\alpha_B, \beta_B, THR(\gamma_B, ENV(ABS(s(t))))) . \qquad (2)$$

$$f_C(i) = NORM(\alpha_C, \beta_C, THR(\gamma_C, STD(ZCR(s(t))))) . \qquad (3)$$

$$f_2(i) = NORM(\alpha_2, \beta_2, THR(\gamma_2, ENV(ABS(FB(3500, 5000, s(t)))))) . \qquad (4)$$

$$f_3(i) = NORM(\alpha_3, \beta_3, THR(\gamma_3, ENV(ABS(FB(0, 800, s(t)))))) . \qquad (5)$$

$$f_4(i) = f_2(i) - f_3(i) . \qquad (6)$$

Here $s(t)$ represents an audio signal and $\alpha_j, \beta_j, \gamma_j, j = A, B, C, 1, 2$ are various normalisation and thresholding constants.

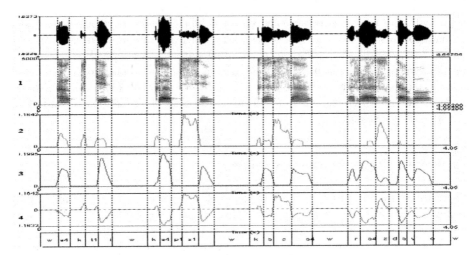

Fig. 2. The first-order feature tracks 2, 3 and 4 obtained through the transformations (4), (5) and (6) respectively. Vertical dotted lines indicate phone boundaries

2.2   Detection of Segmentation Candidates

The first order feature tracks are useful to the extent they provide cues for "noticing" that a desired type of change/transition occurred within an audio signal. Cues gives no guarantee of transitions actually having place but simply state that some particular signal portions should be considered as segmentation candidates and that further deliberation is necessary in order to take the final segmentation decision. Cues are feature-specific. Some first-order features tracks often exhibit maxima exceeding some threshold near phone transition points. Others exhibit certain evolution patterns in time (ex. "increase for at least 100 ms then decrease by at least 3dB"). Finding and registering the set of cues that is both informative and complete is a human-labor intensive task. An ideal set of cues is such that it assures that no desired type of transition is left unnoticed.

We have determined about 10 types of cues that were informative for music segmentation [6]. The most useful one was the so called "intensity gap" cue (fig. 3) that was present at $\widetilde{4}1\%$ of all note onsets. Procedures that scanned for each particular cue within an appropriate feature track were also constructed.

Detection of segmentation candidates for speech is more complicated. For instance, sharp changes within feature tracks $f_A(i), f_B(i), f_C(i)$ seem to provide cues for detecting transitions between vowels, fricatives and silent portions of a signal. Our work of determining cue sets for spotting particular phone transitions is still in progress.

2.3   Second-Order Feature Construction and Symbolic Learning

Segmentation system still needs to be trained to take the final decision about every segmentation candidate (time instant or time interval). In our approach,

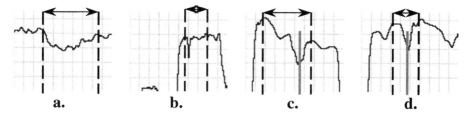

Fig. 3. Intervals of an intensity track spotted by the "intensity gap" cue. Dashed lines indicate interval boundaries, vertical solid lines indicate actual note-to-note transitions in the training corpus. Segmentation candidates are grouped into classes of negative (*a, b*) and positive (*c, d*) instances with respect to the presence of actual note-to-note transitions. Vertical gradation is in 3dB. Horizontal gradation is in 100 ms

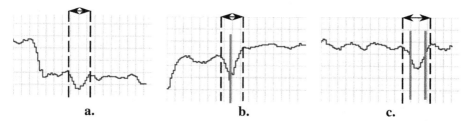

Fig. 4. Intervals of a pitch track spotted by the "stable-drop-rise-stable" cue. Dashed lines indicate interval boundaries, vertical solid lines indicate actual note-to-note transitions in the training corpus. Segmentation candidates are grouped into three classes with respect to the number of note-to-note transitions they contain. Vertical gradation is in semitones. Horizontal gradation is in 50 ms

every cue generates segmentation candidates that can be regarded as training instances belonging at least two distinct classes (fig. 3, 4). This results in as much ML tasks as there were different cues defined. Let the segmentation candidate X_i^j be spotted by the cue c_j at the time instant t_i. Segmentation candidate represents a vector $X_i^j = \{x_1, ..., x_n, class\}_i^j$ where each value x_k is the result of some specific computation at the neighborhood of the time instant t_i. Those computations extract information about a larger context of a segmentation candidate and are called the second-order features. The value of the *class* component is automatically extracted from annotation data.

The second-order features are cue-specific. They are picked by humans after a careful inspection of the first-order feature tracks. For instance, one of the most useful features for distinguishing negative and positive segmentation cases in the case of "intensity gap" ML task (fig. 3) is the gap size. Other typical measurements that are common to many other ML tasks include maximum, minimum or averaged values of the first-order features in the neighborhood of a segmentation candidate as well as ratios, slopes, distances, durations, transitions, etc.

```
if gapsize_10 >= 7.3 then class = positive [602,2]
else if pitch_dif_avg_10 >= 90 then class = positive [67,3]
        else if left_slope_len <= 20 then class = positive [13,3]
            else if sllavgrge_10 <= 1.6 and
                    left_slope_unvoiced_ratio <= 0.03
                        then class = positive [7,0]
                        else class = negative [4,28].
```

(The rule set obtained for the ML task shown in fig. 3. Numbers in square brackets indicate the number of positive and of negative training instances covered by each rule)

3   Results

The data-driven segmentation scheme described in this paper was applied to the problem of segmentation of monodic folk songs into notes [6]. Our experiments were based on 4h corpus of sung data. A small part of this corpus (5%) was manually annotated and used for training.

We have defined 10 machine learning tasks for discriminating between particular sets of positive and negative segmentation candidates. Ripper [3] and Charade [4] symbolic machine learning algorithms were used. Automatically induced rule sets achieved 90-95% recall and precision during 10-fold cross validation experiments for each of the 10 of the machine learning tasks. The combined accuracy of all sets of rules yielded 5% split notes and 18% missed notes with respect to segmentation performed by humans. The presence of missed notes is explained by the fact that segmentation system lacked some usefull cues for spotting specific types of note-to-note transitions. Addition of complementary cues and of corresponding ML tasks would solve the problem.

We have also performed some preliminary experiments by trying to detect voiced/unvoiced, vowel/fricative/plosive phone transitions that are the most "visible" in a speech signal. These experiments have given promising results. Voiced/unvoiced transitions, for instance, were detected with over 90% accuracy in a speech databese containing 16000 Lithuanian phones.

4   Discussion

In this paper, we present an approach to audio signal segmentation that is highly flexible. An acoustic front-end is no longer constrained to use a uniform parametrisation of a signal. It can choose different parametrisations (the first-order features) for detecting different types of transitions. Moreover, the most appropriate parametrisations are found automatically as a result of an off-line search procedure. This approach makes no assumptions about the frame independence. Desired aspects of sound dynamics can be explicitly included into the model and captured by the second-order features. It is also advantageous to be able to track causes of segmentation errors to some particular decision making step.

Nevertheless, the proposed approach has some drawbacks too. First of all, it is human labor-intensive. It requires phonetically labeled speech copora and hours of manual work for designing sets of the second order features. Second, it is not backed by mathematical theories. In contrast, we have a guarantee that an optimum solution will be found as the result of exhaustive search over the space of possible segmentations in HMM case.

This approach has been successfully applied to music. Whether it can be carried to speech remains an open question even if preliminary results are encouraging.

References

1. Bahl, L.R., et al.: Speech Recognition with Continuous-Parameter Hidden Markov Models. Computer Speech and Language, **2** (1987) 219–234
2. Baum, L.E., Eagon, J.A.: An Inequality with Applications to Statistical Estimation for Probabilistic Functions of Markov Processes and to a Model for Ecology. Bulletin of American Mathematical Society, **73** (1967) 360–363
3. Cohen, W.W.: Fast effective rule induction. Proceedings of the 12th International Conference on Machine Learning. (1995)
4. Ganascia, J.-G.: CHARADE: A Rule System Learning System. International Joint Conference on artificial Intelligence. (1987) 345–347
5. Quinlan, J.R., Rivest, R.L: Inferring decision trees using the minimum description length principle. Information and Computation, **80** (1989) 227–248
6. Raškinis, G.: Automatic Transcription of Lithuanian Folk Songs. PhD. Thesis. Vytautas Magnus University (2000)
7. Vorstermans, A., Martens, J.-P., Van Coile, B.: Automatic Segmentation and Labeling of Multi-Lingual Speech Data. Speech Communications, Vol. 19 (4). North-Holland (1996) 271–293

Analysis of an Infant Cry Recognizer for the Early Identification of Pathologies

Orion F. Reyes-Galaviz[1], Antonio Verduzco[2],
Emilio Arch-Tirado[2], and Carlos A. Reyes-García[3]

[1] Instituto Tecnológico de Apizaco, Av. Tecnológico S/N, Apizaco, Tlaxcala, 90400, Mexico
orionfrg@yahoo.com
[2] Instituto Nacional de la Comunicación Humana, Mexico, D.F, Mexico
[3] Instituto Nacional de Astrofísica Óptica y Electrónica,
Luis E. Erro 1, Tonantzintla, Puebla, 72840, Mexico
kargaxxi@inaoep.mx

Abstract. This work presents the development and analysis of an automatic recognizer of infant cry, with the objective of classifying three classes, normal, hypo acoustics and asphyxia. We use acoustic feature extraction techniques like MFCC, for the acoustic processing of the cry's sound wave, and a Feed Forward Input Delay neural network with training based on Gradient Descent with Adaptive Back-Propagation for classification. We also use principal component analysis (PCA) in order to reduce vector's size and to improve training time. The complete infant cry database is represented by plain text vector files, which allows the files to be easily processed in any programming environment. The paper describes the design, implementation as well as experimentation processes, and the analysis of results of each type of experiment performed.

1 Introduction

Almost all of the pathological diseases in babies are commonly detected several months, and sometimes even years after the infant is born. If any of these diseases would have been detected earlier, they could have been treated or maybe even avoided by the application of opportune treatments and therapies. Some past studies show that the infant's cry carries plenty of useful information on its sound wave [6]. For small children this is the first form of communication, a very limited one, but similar to the way a fully talking human communicates. Using the infant's cry sound wave information we can detect the infant's physical or psychological state, on the first stages of the infant's life. If there exists this kind of relevant information inside the cry of an infant, the extraction of acoustical features, recognition and classification of the cry can be possible through automatic means. This work presents the design of a system that classifies three different kinds of cries. They are recordings of normal, deaf and asphyxiating infants, of ages from 1 day up to 6 months old. For the acoustic processing we used Praat [1]. Additionally, to classify the infant's cry information, we used Matlab to build an input delay neural network. In the model here presented, we classify the input vectors, after reduction, in three corresponding classes, normal cry, hypoacoustic (deaf) and asphyxiating cries. We train the neural network using a randomly selected set of infant's cry samples, and we test the system using a separate set of infants's cry samples. Here we show scores that go from 96.08% up to 97.39% in precision on the classification.

G. Chollet et al. (Eds.): Nonlinear Speech Modeling, LNAI 3445, pp. 404–409, 2005.
© Springer-Verlag Berlin Heidelberg 2005

2   The Infant Cry Automatic Recognition Process

The infant cry automatic classification process is simply a pattern recognition problem, similar to Automatic Speech Recognition (ASR). For doing this we basically have to take the wave from the infant's cry as the input pattern, and at the end obtain the type of cry or pathology detected on the baby. Generally, the process of Automatic Cry Recognition is done in two steps; the first step is known as signal processing, or feature extraction, whereas the second is known as pattern classification. In the acoustical analysis phase, the cry signal is first normalized and cleaned, next it is analyzed to extract the most important characteristics in function of time. Some of the more popular techniques for the acoustic processing are those to extract: linear prediction coefficients, cepstral coefficients, pitch, intensity, spectral analysis, and Holmes banks among others. The set of obtained characteristics can be represented like a vector, and each vector can be taken like a pattern. The feature vector is compared with the knowledge that the computer has to obtain the classified output. Four main pattern recognition approaches have been traditionally used: pattern comparison, stochastic models, knowledge based systems, and connectionist models. In the present work we are focused in the last approach.

3   Acoustic Processing

A cry signal is very complex and codifies more information than the one needed to be analyzed and processed in real time applications. For that reason, in our cry recognition system we use a feature extraction function as a first plane processor. Its input is a cry signal, and its output is a vector of features that characterizes key elements of the cry's sound wave. All the vectors obtained this way are later fed to a recognition model, first to train it, and later to classify the type of cry or pathology. We have been experimenting with diverse types of acoustic characteristics, emphasizing by their utility the Mel Frequency Cepstral Coefficients.

3.1   MFCC (Mel Frequency Cepstral Coefficients)

The low order cepstral coefficients are sensitive to overall spectral slope and the high-order cepstral coefficients are susceptible to noise. This property of the speech spectrum is captured by the Mel spectrum. The Mel spectrum operates on the basis of selective weighing of the frequencies in the power spectrum. High order frequencies are weighed on a logarithmic scale where as lower order frequencies are weighed on a linear scale. The Mel scale filter bank is a series of L triangular bandpass filters that have been designed to simulate the bandpass filtering believed to occur in the auditory system. This corresponds to series of bandpass filters with constant bandwidth and spacing on a Mel frequency scale. On a linear frequency scale, this spacing is approximately linear up to 1KHz and logarithmic at higher frequencies. Many speech recognition systems are based on the MFCC technique [2].

3.2   Principal Component Analysis (PCA)

The basic goal in PCA is to reduce the dimension of the data. Thus one usually chooses $n<<m$. Indeed, it can be proven that the representation given by PCA is an

optimal linear dimension reduction technique in the mean-square sense. Such a reduction in dimension has important benefits. First, the computational overhead of the subsequent processing stages is reduced. Second, noise may be reduced, as the data not contained in the n first components may be mostly due to noise. Third, a projection into a subspace of a very low dimension, for example two, is useful for visualizing the data. Note that often it is not necessary to use the n principal components themselves, since any other orthonormal basis of the subspace spanned by the principal components (called the PCA subspace) has the same data compression or denoising capabilities [3].

4 Cry Patterns Classification

The acoustic characteristics set obtained in the extraction stage, is generally represented as a vector, and each vector can be taken as a pattern. These vectors are later used to make the classification process. For the present work we are using a classifier corresponding to the type of connectionist models known as neural networks. We have selected this kind of model, in principle, because of its adaptation, simplicity and learning capacity. Besides, one of its main functions is pattern recognition.

4.1 Neural Networks

The neural networks are defined as systems composed of many simple processing elements, that operate in parallel and whose function is determined by the network's structure, the strength of its connections, and the processing carried out by the processing elements or nodes. We can train a neural network to execute a function in particular, adjusting the values of the connections (weights) between the elements. Generally, the neural networks are adjusted or trained so that an input in particular leads to a specified or desired output. The training of a neural network can be supervised or not supervised. The methods of supervised training are those used when labeled samples are available.

4.2 Feed Forward Input (Time) Delay Neural Networks

Cry data are not static, and any cry sample at any instance in time is dependent on crying patterns before and after that instance in time. A common flaw in the traditional Back-Propagation algorithm is that it does not take this into account. Waibel et al. set out to remedy this problem in [4] by proposing a new network architecture called the ``Time-Delay-Neural Network'' or TDNN. The primary feature of TDNNs is the time-delayed inputs to the nodes. Each time delay is connected to the node via its own weight, and represents input values in past instances in time. TDNNs are also known as Input Delay Neural Networks because the inputs to the neural network are the ones delayed in time. If we delay the input signal by one time unit and let the network receive both the original and the delayed signals, we have a simple time-delay neural network. Of course, we can build a more complicated one by delaying the signal at various lengths. If the input signal is n bits and delayed for m different lengths, then there should be nm input units to encode the total input [5]. In this work we tested the network with delays that go from 1 to 10.

4.3 Training by Gradient Descent
with Adaptive Learning Rate Backpropagation

The training by gradient descent with adaptive learning rate backpropagation, proposed for this project, can train any network as long as its weight, net input, and transfer functions have derivative functions. Back-propagation is used to calculate derivatives of performance with respect to the weight and bias variables. Each variable is adjusted according to gradient descent. At each training epoch, if the performance decreases toward the goal, then the learning rate is increased. If the performance increases, the learning rate is adjusted by a decrement factor and the change, which increased the performance, is not made [5].

5 System Implementation for the Crying Classification

On the first stage, the infant's cries are collected by recordings obtained directly from doctors of the Mexican National Institute of the Human Communication (INCH) and the IMSS Puebla (Mexican Institute of Social Security). This is done using SONY (ICD-67) digital recorders. Each signal wave is divided in segments of 1 second, each one constituting a sample. For the present experiments we have a corpus made up of 1049 samples of normal infant cry, 879 of hypo acoustics, and 340 with asphyxia. At the following step the samples are processed extracting their acoustic characteristics, MFCC in the present case, by the use of the freeware program Praat 4.0 [1]. The acoustic characteristics are extracted as follows: for every second we extract 16 coefficients from each 50-millisecond frame, generating with this vectors with 304 coefficients by sample. In order to reduce the vector dimensions, next we apply Principal Component Analysis (PCA), obtaining in this way vectors made up, in the reported experiments, of 35 components. In order to make the training and recognition test, we select 340 samples randomly on each class. The number of asphyxiating cry samples available determines this number. From them, 238 samples (70%) of each class are randomly selected for training. The training is made up until 2000 epochs are completed or a 1×10^{-6} error is reached. After the network is trained, we test it with the 102 samples (30%) of each class set apart from the original 340 samples. The neural network's architecture consists of 35 neurons on the input layer, 20 neurons in the hidden layer, and 3 in the output layer. The neural network was tested with delays from 1 to 10. The recognition accuracy percentage, from each experiment, is presented in a confusion matrix. Due to space restrictions, we show only two of those matrices, the one with lowest and the one with the highest accuracy, in Table 2 and Table 3 respectively.

Table 1. Results of each delay

1: 96.40%	6: 97.05%
2: 96.08%	7: 97.05%
3: 97.05%	8: 96.40%
4: 97.39%	9: 97.05%
5: 96.41%	10: 96.40%

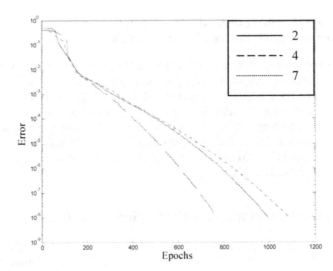

Fig. 1. Graphic showing 3 delays, one with the lowest accuracy (2), one with the highest accuracy (4), and one with the highest epochs (7)

Table 2. Confusion matrix for the classification of Infant Cry with a delay of 2, showing a total recognition accuracy of 96.08 %

Class	Normal	Deaf	Asphyxia
Normal	94	4	4
Deaf	0	102	0
Asphyxia	3	1	98

Table 3. Confusion matrix for the classification of Infant Cry with a delay of 4, showing a total recognition accuracy of 97.39 %

Class	Normal	Deaf	Asphyxia
Normal	98	1	3
Deaf	1	101	0
Asphyxia	3	0	99

6 Conclusions and Future Work

This work demonstrates the efficiency of the feed forward input (time) delay neural network, when using the Mel Frequency Cepstral Coefficients. As we can see in the graphic, when we obtained the highest accuracy of the network, we also obtained the lowest number of epochs to train that network. Nevertheless, the results are very consistent in the range of the delays tested, and the training graphics are very much alike. This means that the infant cry is very time invariant. Among the works in progress of this project, we are in the process of testing new neural networks, and also testing new kinds of hybrid models, combining neural networks with genetic algorithms and fuzzy logic, or other complementary models.

References

1. Boersma, P., Weenink, D. Praat v. 4.0.8. A system for doing phonetics by computer. Institute of Phonetic Sciences of the University of Amsterdam. February, 2002
2. Gold, B., Morgan, N. (2000), Speech and Audio Signal Processing. Processing and Perception of Speech and Music. John Wiley & Sons, Inc.
3. Hyvarinen, Aapo. http://www.cis.hut.fi/aapo/papers/NCS99web/node5.html. April 23 de 1999.
4. Waibel A., Hanazawa T., Hinton G., Shikano K., Lang K., Phoneme Recognition Using Time-Delay Neural Networks, IEEE Transactions on Acoustics, Speech and Signal Processing, Vol 37, No 3, March 1989, pp 328 - 339.
5. Limin Fu., Neural Networks in Computer Intelligence. McGraw-Hill International Editions, Computer Science Series, 1994.
6. O. Wasz-Hockert, J. Lind, V. Vuorenkoski, T. Partanen y E. Valanne, El Llanto en el Lactante y su Significación Diagnóstica, Cientifico-Medica, Barcelona, 1970.

Graphical Models
for Text-Independent Speaker Verification

Eduardo Sánchez-Soto, Marc Sigelle, and Gérard Chollet

École Nationale Supérieure des Télécommunications,
Département de Traitement du Signal et des Images, CNRS UMR LTCI
46, rue Barrault 75634 Paris Cedex 13, France
{esanchez,sigelle,chollet}@tsi.enst.fr
http://www.tsi.enst.fr/~esanchez

Abstract. Our approach in text independent Speaker Verification (SV) proposes to integrate different aspects of the speech signal which convey information about the speaker's identity using Graphical Models (GM). Prosodic, spectral and source information obtained from the residue of linear prediction analysis are modeled in a probabilistic framework with a system based on Bayesian Networks (BN). The structure, or conditional independencies between the variables, is learned directly from the data using two different algorithms. In particular, the interpretation and comparison of the structures is presented. Some experiments conducted on the NIST 2003 one speaker text-independent data base have been conducted to demonstrate the feasibility of this approach.

1   Introduction

The performance of speech processing systems in some cases is still far from that of humans. At the decision step, a difference between those systems and humans is in one hand the used information quantity and in the other hand the relationships made between those informations. The spectral and prosodic aspects of speech signal are an abundant source of knowledge, but a joint representation of those aspects is until now a problem. The state-of-the-art SV systems use Gaussian Mixture Models (GMM) [7] in order to represent the data distribution. All the data are represented in a single space where no difference is made between the data that comes from one source or another. To overcome this problem GM can be used. GM are naturally modular and can represent in a visual way the relations between different variables in a given problem. Particularly, a BN [6] is a GM which represents in an optimal way conditional independencies between a set of random variables. Then, various aspects of speech signal can be jointly represented in a formal mathematical way using different variables which are related in a BN.

The relationship among the variables can be defined by an expert using some knowledge about the variables or by a learning technique that is applied directly to the data. The first work done in automatic learning of the structure in a BN [1] was able to obtain a simple tree structure from a database. Later an alternate approach [2] which works also with multiply-connected networks was proposed. This technique is based on a Bayesian approach which assumes a prior uniform distribution over all the structures. Another approach is based on the principle of Minimal Description Length (MDL). From the Bayesian point of view the MDL approach assumes a prior distribution over the models which is inversely proportional to their encoding length.

However, finding the best structure, the conditional independencies which best represent the present relationships into the database, is a research field very important. Then we propose a technique to score the structure based on the MDL principle and its comparison with another structure obtained using other quality measure.

The organization of the paper is as follows. In section 2, we will first introduce Bayesian Networks. Section 3 reviews briefly some ideas about structure learning in BNs specially the proposed MDL technique, section 3.2. In section 4, we will present the experiments, results and its probabilistic interpretation. Finally we will give our conclusions in section 5.

2   Bayesian Networks

A BN [6] makes a representation of a joint probability distribution defined on a finite set of random variables. The nodes in a Directed Acyclic Graph (DAG) represent random variables and arcs represent conditional probabilistic dependencies among those variables. Nodes have relative names by its position and relation with others nodes in the graph. Each edge points from one node, called parent, to another, called child.

In a BN, a Conditional Probability Distribution (CPD) is associated with each node X_i. It describes the dependency between this node and its parents. In general, each node is conditionally independent from its non-descendants given its parents. Those dependence relations induces a factorization in the joint distribution function expressed as:

$$P(X_1, \ldots, X_N) = \prod_{i=1}^{N} P(X_i | Pa(X_i)), \tag{1}$$

where $Pa(X_i)$ is the set of X_i's parents.

Each Conditional Probability Distribution or Conditional Probability Tables represented by a factor in (1) describes the interaction between a node and its immediate predecessors.

3   Structure Learning

Learning Bayesian Network from data consists in automatically building the network structure and compute the parameters, from information in data. Some aspects must be considered in the process of finding the best structure, even if the space of variables is fully observable. The amount of possible structures is very large. This quantity depend on the number of variables in an exponential way. To manage this problem two different approaches exists. One searches in all the structure space and the other starts with a specific connected graph which can be place to put some prior knowledge about the variables relation. Then it searches for independence relations in the data S, putting in or taking away arcs.

The algorithm used in this work, K2 [2], belongs to the second approach. It uses a greedy search method to construct the structure. It starts with the simplest structure, i.e. a graph without arcs. Given an ordering, or prior knowledge about relationship between the variables, the nodes considered as candidate for the set of parents $Pa(X_i)$ for each variable X_i are restricted to those nodes with smaller order numbers than X_i. All possible structures have to be scored to know which one has the highest quality.

3.1 Bayesian Information Criterion

Since a fully connected graph has the greatest number of parameters the maximum likelihood is not an adequate quality measure. Thus, a prior knowledge on the model can be used to overcome this problem. Let G be the structure and S the database or sequence of N samples for all the nodes of G. The posterior probability of data is:

$$P(G|S) \propto P(S|G)P(G), \qquad (2)$$

where $P(G)$ is the prior probability of structure. Now, the likelihood of data obtained by integration on the possible values of parameters θ is:

$$P(S|G) = \int P(S|G,\theta)P(\theta|G)d\theta. \qquad (3)$$

The marginal likelihood can be approximated [4] with a Laplace method, and finally get the Bayesian Information Criterion (BIC):

$$\log P(S|G) \approx \log P(S|G,\hat{\theta}) - \frac{d}{2}\log M, \qquad (4)$$

where M is the number of samples, $\hat{\theta}$ is the estimate of the parameters and d is the dimension (number of free parameters) of the model.

3.2 MDL

MDL [8] is used for the encoding of the data given a model. From equation (3) and from its limited expansion up to the second order one has:

$$P(S|G) \approx L(\hat{\theta}) \int exp - \frac{1}{2}(\theta - \hat{\theta})^t \mathbf{A}(\theta - \hat{\theta})d\theta \approx L(\hat{\theta})(\frac{1}{2\pi})^{\frac{d(G)}{2}} \frac{1}{\sqrt{det\ \mathbf{A}}}, \qquad (5)$$

where $d(G)$ is the number of parameters specifying the model G. At the lowest order if N is the number of observations the MDL equation is obtained:

$$\mathcal{L} = \log P(S|G) \approx L(\hat{\theta}) - \frac{d(G)}{2} \log N. \tag{6}$$

Now, for a tree structure and in particular when all the nodes are independents it can be written:

$$\log P(S|G) \approx \sum_{s \in G} \{ [\sum_{i \in \Omega^s} (N_i^s) + \frac{1}{2} \log N_i^s] - (N + |\Omega^s| - \frac{1}{2}) \log N + (|\Omega^s| - 1) \log \sqrt{2\pi} \}, \tag{7}$$

where Ω^s is the set of observable states at generic node s, and N_i^s is the observed number of times of the variable s in the state i.

3.3 Modelisation

The training and test parameter vectors consist of a set of four types of parameters. The first vector is a 24-dimensional LP Cepstral Coefficients obtained as follow: 12-dimensional LPCC, with sliding CMS and augmented with their first derivatives, $SLPCC$, for Signal Linear Prediction Cepstral Coefficients. The second vector, 24-dimensional LP Cepstral Coefficients has been obtained as before from the LP-residual signal $RLPCC$, and finally the frame pitch F_0 and the frame energy E. A gender-dependent Universal Background Models (UBM) have been created using part of the 2001 cellular development and evaluation datasets (similar to the database described in section 4).

First, those data had been used with K2 algorithm to find the best structure for the four variables. It has worked with all the possible orders and used the BIC score [4]. From this analysis we have obtained the conditional independence relations that define the first network structure which is set to be speaker independent, Figure 1.

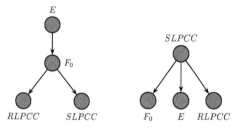

Fig. 1. Structure for the four variables (energy, pitch, signal lpcc and residual lpcc) issue of the K2 algorithm with BIC (left) and issue of the MDL analysis (right)

From this graph we can write the joint probability distribution for these four variables $U = \{E, F_0, RLPCC, SLPCC\}$ as:

$$P(U) = P(E)\, P(F_0|E)\, P(RLPCC|F_0)\, P(SLPCC|F_0). \tag{8}$$

The terms $P(RLPC|F_0)P(SLPC|F_0)$ can be interpreted as $I(RLPC \perp SLPC|F_0)$, that is, the $RLPC$ and $SLPC$ are independent given F_0. The second term $P(F_0|E)$ reflects the close relation between energy and voicing in speech.

In a second part the MDL algorithm was performed using discrete data in order to simplify the probabilistic scheme. Those data were obtained using Vector Quantization (VQ) of variables initialized with the k-means algorithm. $SLPCC$ and $RLPCC$ variables were discretized using 32 values, E with two values and F_0 with three values (one value corresponding to the unvoiced parts). The obtained structure is shown in Figure 1. The conditional probability density for the four variables given the structure is:

$$P(U) = P(SLPCC) \, P(E|SLPCC) \, P(F_0|SLPCC) \, P(E|SLPCC). \quad (9)$$

Thinking about the SLPCC coefficients computation it is easy to see that those coefficients contain a lot of information which depend on the p number used in the autocorrelation function computation. In these coefficients one can find the excitation, the energy and then also the pitch characteristics since the LP model is not perfect.

Once the structure has been learned, the final world model uses a Gaussian Mixture (GM) implemented with BN to represent each variable (32 Gaussians for RLPCC and SLPCC, five for the pitch and two for the energy). The parameters were then learned with EM [3]. *LBG* algorithm was used to determine the initial setting. Target Speaker Models have been obtained by adaptation of the means in the world model by three iterations of the EM algorithm initialized with the world model.

4   Experiments and Results

The data are taken from the second release of the Cellular Switchboard Corpus of the Linguistic Data Consortium (LDC) [5]. The experiments were done using a half part of the male test database, 751 files. Each test file is tested against 11 speaker models. Then there are 8261 tests in total.

The decision score is directly based on the log-likelihood ratio between the target speaker and the world model over all the frames without any kind of normalization. The results in the Figure 2 show the influence of the structure in the final results. The structure obtained with MDL perform better than the structure obtained with K2 and BIC if the arcs between the continuous variables that model the mixture of gaussians are used. With the discrete relations the best performance is obtained with the K2 and BIC structure. The used relations to relate the variables (discrete or continuous) does not affect to much to the MDL structure, but it is not the case for the other structure which change in more than 2%.

5   Conclusions

In this paper, a system achieving SV based on BNs is presented. This system infers the BN structure automatically from the data using two different quality

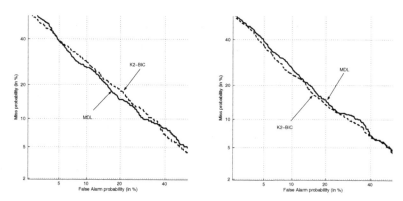

Fig. 2. Results obtained using the continuous relation (left) and discrete relation (right)

measure functions. The obtained structures are compared and used for integrate all the information presented on the speech signal in a single probability distribution. Results reflect the influence of conditional independencies used in each model. It also shows that BNs are a flexible mathematical tool that can help to model information from different aspects of the speech signal. The physical interpretation given to the equations describing the structures suggests that the learning algorithms for BN are able to adequately infer the relations present in data.

References

1. C. K. Chow and C. N. Liu. Approximating discrete probability distributions with dependence trees. *IEEE Transactions on Information Theory*, 14(3):462–467, 1968.
2. G. F. Cooper and E. Herskovits. A Bayesian Method for the Induction of Probabilistic Networks from Data. *Machine Learning*, 9:309–347, 1992.
3. A. P. Dempster, N. M. Laird, and D. B. Rubin. Maximum Likelihood from Incomplete Data via the EM Algorithm. *Journal of the Royal Statistical Society*, 34:1–38, 1997.
4. D. Heckerman. *A tutorial on Learning with Bayesian Network Structures. Lerning in Graphical Models*. MIT Press, Cambridge, 1998.
5. Switchboard Corpora LDC. http://www.ldc.upenn.edu/.
6. J. Pearl. *Probabilistic Reasoning in Intelligent Systems: Networks of Plausible Inference*. Morgan Kaufmann, San Diego, 1988.
7. D. A. Reynolds. *A Gaussian Mixture Modeling Approach to Text-Independent Speaker Identification*. PhD thesis, Georgia Institute of Technology, 1992.
8. J. Rissanen. Modeling by shortest data description. *Automatica*, 14:465–471, 1978.

An Application to Acquire Audio Signals with ChicoPlus Hardware

Antonio Satué-Villar[1] and Juan Fernández-Rubio[2]

[1] Escuela Universitaria Politécnica de Mataró (EUPMT), Universidad Politécnica de Cataluña, Av. Puig i Cadafalch 101-111, 08303 Mataró, Spain
satue@eupmt.es
[2] Escuela Técnica Superior de Ingenieros de Telecomunicación de Barcelona (ETSETB), Universidad Politécnica de Cataluña, C. Jordi Girona 1-3, 08034 Barcelona, Spain
juan@gps.tsc.upc.es

Abstract. In this paper we present a method to acquire the overall signal (signal of interest plus interferences plus noise) impinging upon an array of 4 microphones. This is achieved by using the "Chico Plus" audio recorder card, by Innovative Integration, a Borland C++ Builder 5 program to develop an application for the user communicating with the card, an array of microphones, and some filtering algorithms implemented with MatLab. We also want to compare the results obtained using these real signals with those ones got with simulated signals described in previous work.

1 Introduction

It has been shown in the literature that microphone arrays are useful both to clean noisy signals [1], [2] and for speaker recognition purposes [3]. The first goal of this paper is to present a method to simultaneously capture four signals, based on a specific hardware that we have programmed. With these signals, we will be able to prove algorithms that minimize the interferences and the noise when a person speaks in a noisy environment.

To capture the signals, an audio card capturer is used, and we create an interface between the card and the user, which allows this user to communicate with the card. This can be achieved with the program Borland C++ Builder 5.

As it has been mentioned, the main hardware is the audio card capturer ChicoPlus [4] of Innovative Integration [5] along with a SD16 module that connects the card with the microphones by means of a bus. This OMNIBUS SD16 module allows us to capture up to sixteen audio signals of sixteen possible microphones connected to this module.

The software used to carry out the capture of the signals is the Borland C++ Builder 5 program [6]. This program, along with the Armada software of the card allows designing an application for acquiring the signals. Once the Armada and the C++Builder are installed, the necessary tools to manage the ChicoPlus card appear in the menu of the C++ program.

G. Chollet et al. (Eds.): Nonlinear Speech Modeling, LNAI 3445, pp. 416–420, 2005.

The overall application consists of the following phases:

- Card configuration that enables acquisition.
- Storage of the data in the disk.
- Application of an algorithm to reduce the noise and the interferences.

In the first phase the software of the acquisition card is configured and loaded, as well as the Borland C++ Builder in order to enable the interaction between the card and the person capturing the signals.

In the second one, the signals captured by the different microphones, from different angles and in different environments are stored in the hard disk of the PC, as they are in a real environment and in an anechoic chamber.

In the third phase, the signals are processed by a simple "Average algorithm" as our efforts are mainly devoted to the signals acquisition. The objective is to apply this algorithm to establish preliminary comparisons between the captured multichannel real signals and monochannel signals.

This paper is organized as follows. In the following section we describe practical considerations of signal capture. Section 3 gathers some methodological considerations on how results have been achieved. We conclude the paper in section 4 with a final discussion on the results of the experiments.

2   Practical Realization

The application is the communication interface between the user and the capturer card. This application has been developed with the support of the libraries installed in C++ Builder 5.

This application allows to select the number of channels, the sampling frequency, auto scale option, a figure where the maximum and minimum values can be seen, a button to get out of the application and a button to start the data capture (stream) among other things.

2.1   Connection of the Equipment Before the Captures

First, we connect the ChicoPlus card installed in the computer with the Breakout module. A second connection is that of each channel of Breakout module with each microphone of the array.

The number of each channel in the card of the Breakout module is serigraphied in order to know in which microphone the connections have to be done.

The signal coming out of each microphone is amplified by a pre-amplifier module. These amplifiers are made of operational amplifiers with integrated circuits and they are fed by a ± 5 V power supply source.

2.2   Signal Capture

Signal acquisition takes place in two environments:

- A rectangular room (a University Laboratory)
- An anechoic chamber

In the experiment, three speakers (named A, B and C) are placed at the 0°, 50° and -30° angles. We want to maximize the signal arriving at 0° and minimize the other ones. There is not a special reason for choosing 50° and –30° so that we could take other values.

Each speaker reads two sentences and the signal capture is made by 4 microphones. The microphones used are very cheap but good enough for our purposes. They are arranged in a millimetered space.

Acquisitions were made in 3 sessions; the speakers' positions were different in each session.

Prior to these acquisitions, each speaker was placed at 0 degrees and read a text with a duration of 30 seconds. The files obtained after this capture will be useful for speaker recognition techniques of further work.

In the first session, speaker A is at 0 degrees, speaker B at -30° and speaker C at 50°. Seven different situations are taken into account, and each of them generates 4 files (4 microphones):

> First situation: speaker A reads sentences at 0°.
> Second situation: speaker A reads sentences at 0°; speaker B reads at –30°.
> Third situation: speaker A reads sentences at 0°; speaker C reads at 50°.
> Fourth situation: speaker A reads sentences at 0°; B at -30°; C at 50°.
> Fifth situation: speaker B reads sentences at -30° (only speaker B).
> Sixth situation: speaker C reads sentences at 50° (only speaker C).
> Seventh situation: speaker B reads sentences at -30°; speaker C reads at 50°.

In session 2, speaker A is at 50 degrees, user B at 0° and user C at -30°. Again, seven situations are considered.

In session 3, speaker A is at -30 degrees, user B at 50° and user C at 0°. Finally, seven more layouts are envisaged.

3   Results

As mentioned above, captured signals are processed by the "averaged algorithm". The N signals (in our case 4 signals) are summed up and the result is divided by N.

This algorithm is equivalent to realizing a beamforming with the look direction pointing to zero degrees [7]. The noise and part of the interference signal are reduced at the beamformer output.

In order to evaluate the speaker recognition capacity a Merit Factor is defined in equation (2). It implies the computation of a covariance matrix for each speaker (target and interferers in our case), and the following arithmetic-harmonic sphericity measure distance [8]:

$$\mu(C_j, C_{test}) = \log[tr(C_{test} \cdot C_j^{-1}) \cdot tr(C_j \cdot C_{test}^{-1})] - 2 \cdot \log(m) \tag{1}$$

where C_{test} is the covariance matrix of the array output, C_j is the covariance matrix of the speaker to be tested and m is the matrix dimension (20 in all the experiments, as suggested in [9]).

The Merit Factor is defined as follows:

$$Merit\_Factor = (\mu_{IS} / \mu_{DS}) / (\mu_{IE} / \mu_{DE}) \tag{2}$$

where $\mu_{DE} = \mu$ (C_j target, array input), $\mu_{IE} = \mu$ (C_j interferer, array input), $\mu_{DS} = \mu$ (C_j target, array output), $\mu_{IS} = \mu$ (C_j interferer, array output)

In tables 1, 2 and 3 some results are presented. These are the Merit Factor (MF), which is non-negative. MF=1 means that the input is equal to the output (the array does not operate properly). Table 1 corresponds to session 1 (user A is at 0 degrees), table 2 to session 2 (user B at 0 degrees) and table 3 to session 3 (user C at 0 degrees).

Results between brackets correspond to monochannel signals. In this case, the delays between the taps of structures are simulated and the effects of reverberations are considered using the image method [10] (only in a rectangular room)

Table 1. Some results for session 1 (Merit Factor)

Rectangular room	1st	0,833 (0,973)	3rd	0,877 (0,907)
Anechoic chamber	comb.	1,021 (1,000)	comb.	0,914 (1,162)
Rectangular room	2nd	0,901 (0,966)	4th	0,940 (0,911)
Anechoic chamber	comb.	0,903 (0,922)	comb.	0,911 (0,952)

Table 2. Some results for session 2 (Merit Factor)

Rectangular room	1st	1,040 (1,005)	3rd	1,154 (1,176)
Anechoic chamber	comb.	0,947 (1,000)	comb.	1,153 (1,296)
Rectangular room	2nd	0,986 (1,001)	4th	0,948 (0,974)
Anechoic chamber	comb.	1,016 (1,260)	comb.	1,035 (1,247)

Table 3. Some results for session 3 (Merit Factor)

Rectangular room	1st	1,086 (1,054)	3rd	0,975 (0,901)
Anechoic chamber	comb.	1,193 (1,000)	comb.	1,012 (1,068)
Rectangular room	2nd	1,066 (1,090)	4th	1,128 (1,127)
Anechoic chamber	comb.	1,113 (1,198)	comb.	1,107 (1,249)

4   Conclusions

After capturing the signals with 4 microphones separated 4,25 cm from each other in two different environments (a typical room and an anechoic chamber), the proper operation of ChicoPlus audio acquisition card has been verified by means of a program that we have developed. The separation between microphones corresponds to half wave-length at the array central frequency (4 KHz).

Using monochannel signals, MF=1 in an anechoic environment when only one speaker is present (first situation). This is logical, as the array only reduces the noise (not the interference). Preliminary measurements prove that with monochannel signals the results are better than with real signals. For example, if the results of the second combination are considered, MF in anechoic chamber is better than in rectangular room. Moreover, MF with monochannel signals (data between brackets) is better than MF with real data.

With the application developed (C++ over Chico Plus card), real-signal acquisition and simulation closer to real world are possible. In future work we will be able to apply more sophisticated algorithms with capabilities of reducing interferences (GSC, wavelet-GSC,...) and validate the methods that simulate the delays between the taps of the structures and the effects of reverberations due to room geometry.

Acknowledgements

This work has been supported by MCYT under contracts TIC2003-08382-C05-02 and TIC2001-2356-C02-01.

References

1. Satué, Fernández, "Time-frequency transforms and beamforming for speaker recognition", *Internat. Conf. Speech Language Processing (ICSLP) vol.4 pp.2533-2536*. Denver, 2002
2. Wauters, Eneman, Delaet, Lauwereins, Adaptive Speech Beamforming Using the TMS320C40 Multi-DSP. *Texas Instr. Application Note SPRA305*, EFRIE, France,1995
3. McCowan, Pelecanos, Sridharan, "Robust speaker recognition using microphone arrays", *Speaker Recognition Workshop (Crete, Greece, june 2001)*
4. Reference Handbook of ChicoPlus, Omnibus, and Armada software. Innovative Integration.
5. www.innovative-dsp.com Web of Innovative Integration enterprise
6. Borland C++ Builder 5, *Charte*, ISBN 84-415-1046-6, Editorial Anaya, 2000
7. Griffiths, Jim, "An alternative approach to linearly constrained adaptive beamforming", *IEEE Trans. Antenna Prop. vol AP.30 núm. 1 pp 27-34, aug. 1982*
8. Bimbot, Mathan, "Text-free speaker recognition using an arithmetic-harmonic sphericity measure" *pp.169-172, Eurospeech 1993*
9. Satué, Faundez, "On the relevance of language in speaker recognition", *Eurospeech 1999*
10. Allen, Berkley, "Image method for efficiently simulating small-room acoustics", *Journal of the Acoustical Society of America vol 65 núm. 4 pp.943-950, april 1979*

Speech Identity Conversion

Martin Vondra[1] and Robert Vích[2]

[1] Brno University of Technology, Purkyňova 118, 61200 Brno, Czech Republic
vondra@feec.vutbr.cz
[2] Institute of Radio Engineering and Electronics, Academy of Sciences of the Czech Republic, Chaberská 57, 182 51 Prague 8, Czech Republic
vich@ure.cas.cz

Abstract. In this paper a new voice conversion algorithm will be presented, which transforms the utterance of a source speaker into the utterance of a target speaker or into the utterance of a new unknown speaker. Presented voice conversion algorithm is based on spectral speech analysis, spectral envelope warping, spectrum interpolation and parametrical high quality IIR or FIR cepstral speech synthesis. Several approaches to frequency warping of the speech spectrum are compared, e.g. linear frequency transformation, piecewise linear frequency modification and nonlinear frequency low-pass to low-pass transformation. Prosodic transformation i.e. fundamental frequency, time and intensity scale modifications are not mentioned.

1   Introduction

In these days there are many different approaches and algorithms for voice conversion [1], [2]. Voice conversion is also several years in the centre of interest in the Institute of Radio Engineering and Electronics of the Czech Academy of Sciences in Prague. Different approaches have been studied, e.g. using spline interpolation and harmonic speech modeling [3], by decimation and interpolation of the speech signal and cepstral speech synthesis [4] and last but not least using PSOLA and resampling [5]. In [6] a nonlinear frequency scale mapping for voice conversion combined with spline interpolation and implemented in the harmonic speech model was presented.

In this paper a new comp-utionaly effective and efficient voice conversion algorithm is presented. It is based on the application of the cepstral vocoder. The whole voice conversion system is shown in Fig. 1. There are the speech analysis and speech synthesis blocks. Speech analysis is performed pitch-asynchronous. Speech spectrum envelope is estimated using cepstral deconvolution. The fundamental frequency is determined by looking for the location of the main peak of the autocorrelation and of the real cepstrum. For speech reconstruction the composite cepstral model is applied excited for voiced speech by an impulse generator and for unvoiced speech by a white noise generator [7] [8].

G. Chollet et al. (Eds.): Nonlinear Speech Modeling, LNAI 3445, pp. 421–426, 2005.

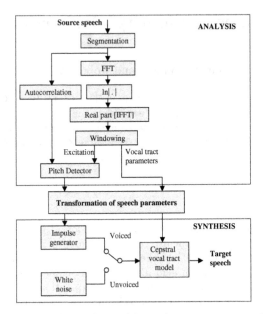

Fig. 1. The cepstral vocoder with speech parameter transformation

2 Transformation of the Speech Spectrum Envelope

The short-time speech spectrum envelope is the basic segmental characteristic in the voice conversion point of view [1]. The shape of the short-time speech spectrum depends on the dimension and on the adjustment of the vocal tract. Great differences in the vocal tract are first of all between male, female and childish, but differences exist also between these classes. It can be stated that the formant frequencies for female voices are approximately 16-20 % higher than that for male voices. In Fig. 2. the short-time LPC speech spectrums corresponding to the vowel "e" for a male and female speaker are shown.

Frequency warping has the greatest influence on the voice change. The frequency tilt given by the relative amplitudes of formants will not be modified.

The warping of the speech spectrum envelope is given by requirement:

$$|S_T(f)| = |S_S(F)|, \tag{1}$$

where $|S_T(f)|$ and $|S_S(F)|$ are the short time spectrum envelopes of the *target* speaker and the *source* speakers respectively. The variables f and F are the corresponding frequency variables. In speech spectrum analysis using DFT the source spectrum $|S_S(F)|$ is given equidistantly for:

$$F_k = k\frac{F_S}{N_F}, \quad k = 0, 1, 2, \ldots (N_F - 1). \tag{2}$$

where F_S is the sampling frequency and N_F is the dimension of the applied DFT. The transformation of the source speaker spectrum $|S_S(F)|$ into the target

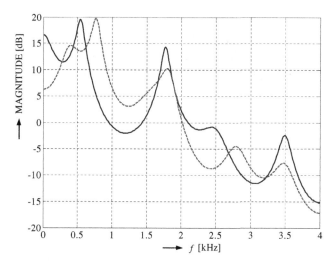

Fig. 2. Short-time spectrum envelope of the stationary part of the vowel "e" for male (solid line) and female(dashed line) voice

speaker spectrum $|S_T(f)|$ is accomplished by mapping of the variable F into the variable f; i.e.:

$$f = Q(F). \tag{3}$$

This function may be given numerically by a table or analytically and generally it is nonlinear. That means that even if F is equidistantly sampled, f is not equidistantly sampled. Therefore the transformed $|S_T(f)|$ must be interpolated for further application at points:

$$f_k = k \frac{F_S}{N_F}, \quad k = 0, 1, 2 \ldots (N_F - 1). \tag{4}$$

2.1 Piecewise Linear Frequency Warping

Let us suppose that the mapping function $f = Q(F)$ is given, for example, by some chosen formant frequencies of the source and target speaker. We shall call these points as significant frequencies. The number of significant frequencies is $M + 1$ and is equal for the source and the target speaker. Further we shall assume that the boundary significant frequencies $F = 0$ and $F = F_M = F_S/2$ are mapped into $f = 0$ and $f = f_M = F_S/2$, respectively.

Let the sequence of significant frequencies for the source speaker be $\{F_l\} = \{0, F_1, F_2, \ldots F_l \ldots F_M\}$ and for the target speaker $\{f_l\} = \{0, f_1, f_2, \ldots f_l \ldots f_M\}$, $l = 0, \ldots M$. Then, between the significant frequencies F_l and F_{l+1} of the source speaker the transformed frequency f can be linearly interpolated using the relation:

$$f = \frac{f_{l+1} - f_l}{F_{l+1} - F_l}(F - F_l) + f_l. \tag{5}$$

The index l changes in the interval $l = 0 \ldots M-1$. The complete frequency mapping $f = Q(f)$ is given by composition of the individual interpolated frequency intervals f. This piecewise frequency warping together with the corresponding spectrum transformation is shown in Fig. 3 for $M = 5$.

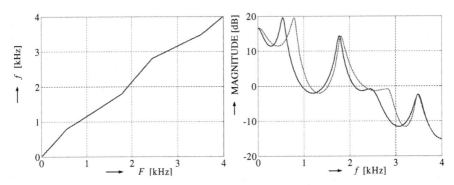

Fig. 3. Piecewise frequency warping for $M = 5$ together with the corresponding spectrum transformation. Source spectrum is shown by solid line, target spectrum by dashed line

2.2 Nonlinear Frequency Warping

In general frequency transformations of digital filters can be obtained by using transformations similar to the bilinear transformation [9]. In our case of voice conversion we need not to transform the transfer function of the digital vocal tract model, we may apply only the frequency warping corresponding to the allpass transfer function:

$$Z = \frac{z - \alpha}{1 - \alpha z}. \tag{6}$$

This transfer function transforms a lowpass filter with the cutoff frequency $F = F_C < F_S/2$ – the source filter – into a new lowpass filter – the target filter – with the cutoff frequency $f = f_C < F_S/2$. Setting e.g. the cutoff frequency F_C equal to the 1st formant frequency of the source speaker, i.e. $F_C = F_1$ and the cutoff frequency f_C equal to the 1st formant frequency of the target speaker, i.e. $f_C = f_1$, then the transformation parameter α is given by:

$$\alpha = \frac{\sin(\pi(F_1 - f_1)/F_S)}{\sin(\pi(F_1 + f_1)/F_S)}. \tag{7}$$

The frequency warping function $f = Q(F)$ follows after some manipulation:

$$f = F + \frac{F_S}{\pi} \arctan \frac{\alpha \sin(2\pi F/F_S)}{1 - \alpha \cos(2\pi F/F_S)}. \tag{8}$$

This lowpass-to-lowpass nonlinear frequency warping together with the corresponding spectrum transformation is depicted in Fig. 4.

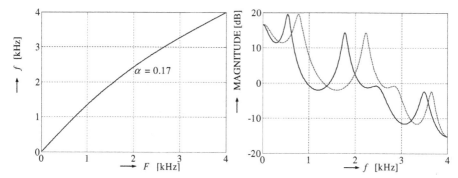

Fig. 4. Nonlinear frequency warping using lowpass-to-lowpass frequency transformation together with the corresponding spectrum transformation. Source spectrum is shown by solid line, target spectrum by dashed line

3 Experiments

Experiments have been performed with voice conversion from male to female and to childish voices and vice versa. Records of identical utterances of several male and female voices have been analyzed and the fundamental frequency F_0 have been estimated. From the stationary parts of vowels the formant frequencies have been estimated and used for transformation of the speech spectrum envelope. The fundamental frequency modification matching the F_0 variances and mean values for the target and the source speakers described in [10] has been applied. The experiments have been realized using the cepstral vocoder combined with voice conversion for 16 kHz sampling frequency.

4 Conclusion

In all solved examples only one transforming function for all phonemes in the utterance has been used without respect to the phonetic content. The subjective voice conversion quality has been judged quite well. The algorithm is, in contrary to other approaches, numerically modest and does not require a training phase. The total similarity of the transformed speech to that of the target speaker is not achieved because the transformation parameters approach the optimal parameter set only in the mean. The evaluation of speech conversion was performed by subjective listening tests. The differences between the described approaches of speech spectrum envelope transformation are very subtle. Nevertheless, better results have been achieved by piecewise linear and nonlinear spectrum envelope transformation than with linear frequency scaling. The identity of the transformed voice is perceived as different from that of the source speaker and close to that of the target speaker. Generally, better results have been obtained with female-male voice conversion than in the reverse direction.

Acknowledgements

This research has been supported by the Grant Agency of the Czech Republic (GA102/04/1097 "Enhancement of speech signal hidden in noise" and GA102/02/0124 "Voice Technologies for Support of Information Society") and by the Ministry of Education, Youth and Sports of the Czech Republic (OC 277.001 "Transformation of Segmental and Suprasegmental Speech Models").

References

1. Moulines, E., Sagisaka, Y (Eds.): Voice Conversion: State of the Art and Perspectives. Special issue of Speech Communication, Vol. 16, No. 2, February 1995.
2. Kain, A. B.: High Resolution Voice Transformation. Ph.D. thesis, Oregon Graduate Institute of Science and Technology, October 2001.
3. Přibilová, A.: Speech Spectrum Envelope Modification. In: R. Vích (Ed.): Proc. of the 13th Czech-German Workshop on Speech Pwrocessing, Prague, September 15-17, 2003, pp. 30-37.
4. Vondra, M.: Voice Transformation in Parametric Speech Synthesis. In: R. Vích (Ed.): Proc. of the 13th Czech-German Workshop on Speech Processing, Prague, September 15-17, 2003, pp. 35-37.
5. Nemšák, S.: Pitch Shifting and Voice Transformation Using PSOLA. In: R. Vích (Ed.): Proc. of the 13th Czech-German Workshop on Speech Processing, Prague, September 15-17, 2003, pp. 38-41.
6. Přibilová, A., Vích, R.: Non-Linear Frequency Scale Mapping for Voice Conversion. In: Proc. of the 14th International Czech-Slovak Scientific Conference Radioelektronika 2004, Bratislava, Slovak Republic, April 27-28, 2004, pp. 100-103.
7. Vondra, M., Smékal, Z.: Composite Cepstral Models for TTS Synthesis. In: R. Vích (Ed.): Speech Processing, Proc. of the 11th Czech-German Workshop on Speech Processing, Prague, September 17-19, 2001, pp. 76-78.
8. Vích, R.: Cepstrales Sprachmodell, Kettenbrüche und Anregungsanpassung in der Sprachsynthese. Wissenschaftliche Zeitschrift der Technischen Universität Dresden, Vol. 49, No. 4/5, 2000, pp. 116 -121.
9. Oppenheim, A. V., Schafer, R. W: Discrete-Time Signal Processing. Prentice-Hall, 1989.
10. Arslan, L. M.: Speaker Transformation Algorithm using Segmental Codebooks (STASC). Speech Communication, vol. 28, pp. 211-229, 1999.

Robust Speech Enhancement
Based on NPHMM Under Unknown Noise

Ki Yong Lee[1] and Jae Yeol Rheem[2]

[1] School of Electronic Engineering, Soongsil University, Korea
kylee@ssu.ac.kr
[2] School of Information and Technology, Korea Univ. of Technology and Education, Korea
rheem@kut.ac.kr

Abstract. In this paper, a new speech enhancement based on the nonlinear H_∞ filtering and neural predictive HMM (NPHMM) is presented. In H_∞ filtering, no *a prior* knowledge of the noise source statistics is required. Speech is modeled as the output of a neural predictive HMM combining MLP neural network and HMM. The proposed enhancement method consists of multiple nonlinear H_∞ filters with parameter of the NPHMM. The switching between the nonlinear H_∞ filters is governed by a finite state Markov chain according to the transition probabilities. An approximate improvement of 0.4-1.8dB in output SNR is achieved at various input SNRs compared with conventional Kalman method.

1 Introduction

Speech enhancement techniques based on autoregressive hidden Markov models (ARHMM) have been proposed [1]. In most of these methods, the speech signal is modeled by linear predictive model. The model of the vocal tract must consider the time variation of the vocal tract shape, the nonlinear of vocal tract due to heat conduction and viscous friction at the vocal tract walls, softness of the vocal tract walls, radiation of sound at the lips, and nasal coupling. Thus, the conventional speech enhancement based on linear ARHMM cannot capture accurately the nonlinear nature of speech. Recently, to overcome these problems, an approach based on neural predictive HMM (NPHMM) is suggested for speech enhancement [2]. However, basic issue of ARHMM and NPHMM arise when only noisy speech signals are available. It is an estimation problem of unknown noise and a matching problem of the energy contour of the signal to a model for the same signal.

In this paper, a new approach based on the nonlinear H_∞ filtering and HMM is presented for speech enhancement. In H_∞ filtering, no a priori knowledge of the noise source statistics is required and the estimation criterion is to minimize the worst possible effects of the disturbances on the signal estimation errors [3]. In this method, speech is modeled as the output of a neural predictive HMM combining MLP neural network and HMM. This proposed enhancement method consists of multiple nonlinear H_∞ filters with parameter of the NPHMM. The switching between the nonlinear H_∞ filters is governed by a finite state Markov chain according to the transition probabilities. An improvement of approximately 0.6dB in output SNR is achieved at input SNR with 10 and 15 dB. A performance comparison between the proposed and conventional method will be accomplished in terms of SNR.

G. Chollet et al. (Eds.): Nonlinear Speech Modeling, LNAI 3445, pp. 427–431, 2005.
© Springer-Verlag Berlin Heidelberg 2005

2   Neural Predictive Hidden Markov Model of Speech

The NPHMM is a nonlinear predictive model with its parameters associated with Markov chain states. Consider a first-order Markov chain with L-states and a state transition matrix $A = [a_{ij}]$, $i, j = 1, \cdots, L$, where element a_{ij} is the transition probability from the state i to the state j. At time t, the speech data conditioned on state i is described by a neural network based predictor as follow;

$$y(t) = h_i(\mathbf{Y}(t-1)) + e_i(t) \tag{1}$$

where $\mathbf{Y}(t-1) = [y(t-1) \cdots y(t-p)]^T$ is sequence of the past p observations, and the driving sequence $e_i(t)$ is assumed to be Gaussian and i.i.d. with zero mean and variance σ_i^2. The term $h_i(\cdot)$ is a feed forward neural network based predictor associated with state i and can be written as

$$h_i(\mathbf{Y}(t-1)) = \sum_{k=1}^{K} w_{k|i} f\left(\sum_{j=1}^{p} w_{k,j|i} y(t-j) \right) \tag{2}$$

where $w_{k|i}$ is the weight coefficient between the output unit and the hidden layer, and $w_{k,j|i}$ is the weight matrix between the hidden layer and input layer, and $f(\cdot)$ is a differential nonlinear function such as the sigmoid function. Here, we choose the MLP neural network for nonlinear predictor of NPHMM.

In this case, the parameter set to determine an NPHMM is $\lambda = \{A, \sigma, \mathbf{W}\}$, where $\sigma = [\sigma_1^2, \sigma_2^2, \cdots, \sigma_L^2]$, $\mathbf{W} = [W_1 \ W_2 \ \cdots \ W_L]$ and $W_i = [w_{1|i}, \cdots, w_{K|i}, w_{1,1|i}, \cdots, w_{L,p|i}]$. The parameter set λ of the model is estimated by the Baum-Welch algorithm as [2].

3   Robust Speech Enhancement Based on Extended H_∞ Filter

We assume that only the noisy speech sequence $\mathbf{Z}(t) = \{z(1), z(2), \cdots, z(t)\}$ contaminated by the additive noise is available for speech enhancement. Then $z(t)$ is presented by $z(t) = y(t) + v(t)$, where $v(t)$ is noise with variance V. To develop the speech enhancement algorithm, we write nonlinear state-space models with Markov states sequence $s(t) \in \{1, \cdots, L\}$ at time t, of the form

$$\mathbf{Y}(t) = f(\mathbf{Y}(t\text{-}1) \mid s(t)) + Ge_{s(t)}(t), \ z(t) = H^T \mathbf{Y}(t) + v(t), \tag{3}$$

where $f(\mathbf{Y}(t\text{-}1) \mid s(t)) = h_{s(t)}(\mathbf{Y}(t\text{-}1))$, $G = [1 \ 0 \ \cdots \ 0]^T$ and $H = [1 \ 0 \ \cdots \ 0]^T$. In Eq. (3), the parameter of NPHMM for $f(\mathbf{Y}(t\text{-}1) \mid s(t))$ is given from the learning algorithm in Section 2. We assume that $e_{s(t)}(t)$ and $v(t)$ are uncorrelated. Given the noisy speech $\mathbf{Z}(t)$, the estimate $\hat{\mathbf{Y}}(t)$ is obtained by

$$\hat{\mathbf{Y}}(t) = \sum_{j=1}^{L} \hat{\mathbf{Y}}_j(t) p(s(t) = j \mid \mathbf{Z}(t)) \tag{4}$$

where $\hat{\mathbf{Y}}_j(t)$ is the conditional mean estimate of $\mathbf{Y}(t)$ given $s(t) = j$. The estimate $\hat{\mathbf{Y}}(t)$ of Eq. (4) is a weighted sum of the L individual estimates $\hat{\mathbf{Y}}_j(t)$. The weighting factor $p(s(t)=j|\mathbf{Z}(t))$ is the probability that the individual estimators are correct ones for the given noisy speech $\mathbf{Z}(t)$. At $s(t)=j$, the extended state equations are derived by expanding the nonlinear function $f(\mathbf{Y}(t\text{-}1)|s(t))$ around the current estimate vector $\hat{\mathbf{Y}}(t-1)$;

$$f(\mathbf{Y}(t\text{-}1)|s(t)=j)\approx f\left(\hat{\mathbf{Y}}(t\text{-}1)|s(t)=j\right)+F\left(\hat{\mathbf{Y}}(t\text{-}1)|s(t)=j\right)\!\left(\mathbf{Y}_j(t\text{-}1)-\hat{\mathbf{Y}}_j(t\text{-}1)\right),\tag{5}$$

where $F(\cdot)$ is the $p\times p$ matrix of the partial derivatives of $f(\cdot)$ evaluated at $\hat{\mathbf{Y}}(t-1)$. Specifically,

$$F(\cdot\,|\,s(t)=j)=\begin{bmatrix} F_j^1(t) & \cdots & F_j^p(t) \\ 10 & \cdots & 0 \\ 0 & \ddots & 01 \end{bmatrix},$$

where $F_j^i=\dfrac{\partial}{\partial \mathbf{Y}^i(t)}f(\mathbf{u})\big|_{\mathbf{u}=f(\hat{\mathbf{Y}}(t\text{-}1)s(t)=j)}$ for $i=1,\cdots,p$, and $\mathbf{Y}^i(t)$ is i-th element of vector $\mathbf{Y}(t)$. Then, in Eq. (4) each estimate $\hat{\mathbf{Y}}_j(t)$ is found from an extended H_∞ filter. H_∞ filter is interested the estimation of some arbitrary linear combination of $\mathbf{Y}_j(t)$, i.e. $o_j(t)=\mathbf{U}\mathbf{Y}_j(t)$ where $\mathbf{U}\in R^{l\times p}$. The optimal estimate of $o_j(t)$ among all possible $\hat{o}_j(t)$ should satisfy

$$\sup J=\sup\frac{\sum\limits_{t=1}^{T}\left|o_j(t)-\hat{o}_j(t)\right|_Q^2}{\left|\mathbf{Y}_j(0)-\hat{\mathbf{Y}}_j(0)\right|_{P_j^{-1}(0)}^{-1}+\sum\limits_{t=1}^{T}\left\{\left|e_j\right|_{W_j^{-1}}^2+\left|v(t)\right|_{V^{-1}}^2\right\}}\le\gamma^2,\tag{6}$$

where "sup" stands for supremum and is $\gamma>0$ a prescribed level of noise attenuation.

The discrete filtering H_∞ can be interpreted as a minimax problem where plays against the exogenous inputs $e_{s(t)}(t)$, $v(t)$ and the uncertainty of the initial state $\mathbf{Y}_j(0)$, so the performance criterion can be write from using $o_j(t)=\mathbf{U}\mathbf{Y}_j(t)$ and $\hat{o}_j(t)=\mathbf{U}\hat{\mathbf{Y}}_j(t)$,

as $\min\max J=-\dfrac{1}{2}\gamma^2\left|\mathbf{Y}_j(0)-\hat{\mathbf{Y}}_j(0)\right|_{P_j^{-1}(0)}^{-1}+\dfrac{1}{2}\sum\limits_{t=1}^{T}\left[\left|\mathbf{Y}_j(t)-\hat{\mathbf{Y}}_j(t)\right|_{\bar{Q}}^2-\gamma^2\left\{\left|e_j\right|_{W_j^{-1}}^2+\left|z(t)-H\mathbf{Y}_j(t)\right|_{V^{-1}}^2\right\}\right]$

where $\bar{Q}=U^TQU$.

From [4, 5], the nonlinear H_∞ filter for $\hat{\mathbf{Y}}_j(t)$ is given by

$$\hat{\mathbf{Y}}_j(t)=f\left(\hat{\mathbf{Y}}_j(t-1)|s_t=j\right)+K_j(t)\!\left\{z(t)-H^TF\!\left(\hat{\mathbf{Y}}_j(t-1)|s(t)=j\right)\right\},\tag{7}$$

$$L_j(t)=\left(I-r^{-2}\bar{Q}P_j(t)+HV^{-1}H^TP_j(t)\right)^{-1},\tag{8}$$

$$K_j(t)=F\left(\hat{\mathbf{Y}}_j(t-1)|s(t)=j\right)P_j(t)L_j(t)HV^{-1},\tag{9}$$

$$P_j(t)=F\left(\hat{\mathbf{Y}}_j(t-1)|s(t)=j\right)P_j(t-1)L_j(t)F^T\left(\hat{\mathbf{Y}}_j(t-1)|s(t)=j\right)+GW_jG^T,\tag{10}$$

where $W_j=\sigma_j^2\cdot I$. The weighting factor $p(s(t)=j|\mathbf{Z}(t))$ becomes

$$p(s(t)=j|\mathbf{Z}(t))=\frac{p(z(t)|s(t)=j,\mathbf{Z}(t-1))\cdot p(s(t)=j|\mathbf{Z}(t-1))}{p(z(t)|\mathbf{Z}(t-1))},\tag{11}$$

using $\mathbf{Z}(t)=\{z(t),\mathbf{Z}(t-1)\}$ and Bayes rule.

The first term of the numerator of Eq. (11) can then be approximated by

$$p(z(t)|s(t)=j, \mathbf{Z}(t-1)) \approx N\left[H^T F(\hat{\mathbf{Y}}_j(t-1)|s(t)=j), HP_j(t)H^T + V\right], \tag{12}$$

where $N[\cdot,\cdot]$ denotes a normal distribution. The second term of the numerator of Eq. (11) is the predicted probability given by $p(s(t)=j|\mathbf{Z}(t-1))$

$\approx \sum_{i=1}^{L} a_{ij} p(s(t-1)=i|\mathbf{Z}(t-1))$. Since the denominator term of Eq. (11) is independent of

j, it becomes a scale factor.

Therefore, $p(s(t)=j|\mathbf{Z}(t))$ can be efficiently calculated using the previous weight-

ing factor by $p(s(t)=j|\mathbf{Z}(t))=D_t \cdot p(z(t)|s(t)=j, \mathbf{Z}(t-1)) \times \sum_{i=1}^{L} a_{ij} p(s(t-1)=i|\mathbf{Z}(t-1))$,

where D_t is scale factor determined at time t guaranteeing that the sum of all the

weighting factor is equal to one: $\sum_{j=1}^{L} p(s(t)=j|\mathbf{Z}(t))=1$. The enhanced speech signal

$\hat{y}(t)$ can be obtained from the first element of the estimated vector
$\hat{\mathbf{Y}}(t)=[\hat{y}(t)\,\hat{y}(t-1)\cdots\hat{y}(t-p+1)]^T$ or the p-th component of the estimated
$\hat{\mathbf{Y}}(t-p+1)=[\hat{y}(t-p+1)\,\hat{y}(t-p+2)\cdots\hat{y}(t)]^T$ at time $t-p+1$.

4   Experimental Results

The proposed enhancement approach was examined in enhancing speech signals which have been degraded by additive white noise at input signal-to-noise ratio (SNR) values of 0, 5, 10, 15, 20 dB. The parameter γ is chosen to be 2.5. Training of the NPHMM for speech production was performed using 8 min clean Korean speech data spoken by four male and four female speakers. In the enhancement test, neither the speakers nor the speech material used for testing were in the training set. Enhancement tests were performed on 4 test sentences spoken by different two male and two female speakers. The objective distortion measure used is the output SNR defined by

$$\text{output SNR} = 10\log\frac{(1/T)\sum_{t=1}^{T} y^2(t)}{(1/T)\sum_{t=1}^{T}[y(t)-\hat{y}(t)]^2},$$

where T is the total number of samples in the utterance, and $y(t)$ and $\hat{y}(t)$ are clean and enhanced speech sequence, respectively.

In the experiment, speech is sampled at 12kHz, the nonlinear predictor using neural network based on MLP is a single hidden-layer feed forward neural net with 1, 2 and 12 units in its output, hidden and input layers, respectively and the number of states of the NPHMM is 8. Then, the successive layers in neural network are fully interconnected. Their activation function is the commonly used sigmoid function.

Table 1 shows performance of proposed method and the conventional method based on Kalman filter [2]. In the conventional Kalman filtering method, the variance of the noise is estimated from an initial segment of noisy signal which is known to contain noise only. While in the proposed method, the information on the noise variance is unknown, i.e., it is not estimated and not given. An approximate improvement of 0.4-1.8dB in output SNR is achieved at various input SNRs. In informal listening tests at an input SNR 10dB, the enhanced speech had good intelligibility.

Comparing with the NPHMM without H_∞ filtering [2], the performance of the NPHMM with known noise variance is slightly better than that of the proposed method. But when the variance of the noise is not given to the NPHMM method, the performance is less than that of the proposed method. So, the proposed method based on H_∞ filtering shows more robust performance than the NPHMM method considering the information of the noise variance given or not.

Table 1. SNR performance of the H_∞ and Kalman filter

SNR[dB]	0	5	10	15	20
Kalman filter	5.42	10.05	14.20	17.93	21.50
NPHMM+H_∞	7.21	10.70	14.80	18.40	21.90

5   Conclusions

A new speech enhancement based on the nonlinear H_∞ filtering and neural predictive HMM (NPHMM) is presented. In H_∞ filtering, no a priori knowledge of the noise source statistics is required. In this method, speech is modeled as the output of a neural predictive HMM combining MLP neural network and HMM. This proposed enhancement method consists of multiple nonlinear H_∞ filters with parameter of the NPHMM. The switching between the nonlinear H_∞ filters is governed by a finite state Markov chain according to the transition probabilities. Comparing with the conventional Kalman filtering method where the variance of the noise is given, an approximate improvement of 0.4-1.8dB in output SNR is achieved at various input SNRs in the proposed method where the variance of the noise is not given.

Acknowledgement

This work was supported by Korea Research Foundation (KRF-2003-041-D00456).

References

1. Ephraim, Y.: A Bayesian estimation approach for speech enhancement using HMM, IEEE Trans. Signal Proc., 41, (1993) 725-735
2. Lee, K.Y. et al.: Speech enhancement based on neural predictive hidden Markov model, Signal Processing, 65, (1998) 373-381
3. Shen, X. and Deng, L.: A dynamic system approach to speech enhancement using the H_∞ filtering algorithm, IEEE Trans. Speech and Audio Proc., 7, (1999) 391-399
4. Banavar, R.N. and Speyer, J.L.: A linear quadratic game theory approach to estimation and smoothing, Proc. IEEE ACC, (1991) 2818-2822
5. Nishiyama, K. and Suzuki, K.: H_∞ -learning of layered neural networks, IEEE Trans. Neural Networks, 12, (2001) 1265-1277

Author Index

Lecture Notes in Artificial Intelligence (LNAI)

Vol. 3339: G.I. Webb, X. Yu (Eds.), AI 2004: Advances in Artificial Intelligence. XXII, 1272 pages. 2004.

Vol. 3336: D. Karagiannis, U. Reimer (Eds.), Practical Aspects of Knowledge Management. X, 523 pages. 2004.

Vol. 3327: Y. Shi, W. Xu, Z. Chen (Eds.), Data Mining and Knowledge Management. XIII, 263 pages. 2005.

Vol. 3315: C. Lemaître, C.A. Reyes, J.A. González (Eds.), Advances in Artificial Intelligence – IBERAMIA 2004. XX, 987 pages. 2004.

Vol. 3303: J.A. López, E. Benfenati, W. Dubitzky (Eds.), Knowledge Exploration in Life Science Informatics. X, 249 pages. 2004.

Vol. 3301: G. Kern-Isberner, W. Rödder, F. Kulmann (Eds.), Conditionals, Information, and Inference. XII, 219 pages. 2005.

Vol. 3276: D. Nardi, M. Riedmiller, C. Sammut, J. Santos-Victor (Eds.), RoboCup 2004: Robot Soccer World Cup VIII. XVIII, 678 pages. 2005.

Vol. 3275: P. Perner (Ed.), Advances in Data Mining. VIII, 173 pages. 2004.

Vol. 3265: R.E. Frederking, K.B. Taylor (Eds.), Machine Translation: From Real Users to Research. XI, 392 pages. 2004.

Vol. 3264: G. Paliouras, Y. Sakakibara (Eds.), Grammatical Inference: Algorithms and Applications. XI, 291 pages. 2004.

Vol. 3259: J. Dix, J. Leite (Eds.), Computational Logic in Multi-Agent Systems. XII, 251 pages. 2004.

Vol. 3257: E. Motta, N.R. Shadbolt, A. Stutt, N. Gibbins (Eds.), Engineering Knowledge in the Age of the Semantic Web. XVII, 517 pages. 2004.

Vol. 3249: B. Buchberger, J.A. Campbell (Eds.), Artificial Intelligence and Symbolic Computation. X, 285 pages. 2004.

Vol. 3248: K.-Y. Su, J. Tsujii, J.-H. Lee, O.Y. Kwong (Eds.), Natural Language Processing – IJCNLP 2004. XVIII, 817 pages. 2005.

Vol. 3245: E. Suzuki, S. Arikawa (Eds.), Discovery Science. XIV, 430 pages. 2004.

Vol. 3244: S. Ben-David, J. Case, A. Maruoka (Eds.), Algorithmic Learning Theory. XIV, 505 pages. 2004.

Vol. 3238: S. Biundo, T. Frühwirth, G. Palm (Eds.), KI 2004: Advances in Artificial Intelligence. XI, 467 pages. 2004.

Vol. 3230: J.L. Vicedo, P. Martínez-Barco, R. Muñoz, M. Saiz Noeda (Eds.), Advances in Natural Language Processing. XII, 488 pages. 2004.

Vol. 3229: J.J. Alferes, J. Leite (Eds.), Logics in Artificial Intelligence. XIV, 744 pages. 2004.

Vol. 3228: M.G. Hinchey, J.L. Rash, W.F. Truszkowski, C.A. Rouff (Eds.), Formal Approaches to Agent-Based Systems. VIII, 290 pages. 2004.

Vol. 3215: M.G.. Negoita, R.J. Howlett, L.C. Jain (Eds.), Knowledge-Based Intelligent Information and Engineering Systems, Part III. LVII, 906 pages. 2004.

Vol. 3214: M.G.. Negoita, R.J. Howlett, L.C. Jain (Eds.), Knowledge-Based Intelligent Information and Engineering Systems, Part II. LVIII, 1302 pages. 2004.

Vol. 3213: M.G.. Negoita, R.J. Howlett, L.C. Jain (Eds.), Knowledge-Based Intelligent Information and Engineering Systems, Part I. LVIII, 1280 pages. 2004.

Vol. 3209: B. Berendt, A. Hotho, D. Mladenic, M. van Someren, M. Spiliopoulou, G. Stumme (Eds.), Web Mining: From Web to Semantic Web. IX, 201 pages. 2004.

Vol. 3206: P. Sojka, I. Kopecek, K. Pala (Eds.), Text, Speech and Dialogue. XIII, 667 pages. 2004.

Vol. 3202: J.-F. Boulicaut, F. Esposito, F. Giannotti, D. Pedreschi (Eds.), Knowledge Discovery in Databases: PKDD 2004. XIX, 560 pages. 2004.

Vol. 3201: J.-F. Boulicaut, F. Esposito, F. Giannotti, D. Pedreschi (Eds.), Machine Learning: ECML 2004. XVIII, 580 pages. 2004.

Vol. 3194: R. Camacho, R. King, A. Srinivasan (Eds.), Inductive Logic Programming. XI, 361 pages. 2004.

Vol. 3192: C. Bussler, D. Fensel (Eds.), Artificial Intelligence: Methodology, Systems, and Applications. XIII, 522 pages. 2004.

Vol. 3191: M. Klusch, S. Ossowski, V. Kashyap, R. Unland (Eds.), Cooperative Information Agents VIII. XI, 303 pages. 2004.

Vol. 3187: G. Lindemann, J. Denzinger, I.J. Timm, R. Unland (Eds.), Multiagent System Technologies. XIII, 341 pages. 2004.

Vol. 3176: O. Bousquet, U. von Luxburg, G. Rätsch (Eds.), Advanced Lectures on Machine Learning. IX, 241 pages. 2004.

Vol. 3171: A.L.C. Bazzan, S. Labidi (Eds.), Advances in Artificial Intelligence – SBIA 2004. XVII, 548 pages. 2004.

Vol. 3159: U. Visser, Intelligent Information Integration for the Semantic Web. XIV, 150 pages. 2004.

Vol. 3157: C. Zhang, H. W. Guesgen, W.K. Yeap (Eds.), PRICAI 2004: Trends in Artificial Intelligence. XX, 1023 pages. 2004.

Vol. 3155: P. Funk, P.A. González Calero (Eds.), Advances in Case-Based Reasoning. XIII, 822 pages. 2004.

Vol. 3139: F. Iida, R. Pfeifer, L. Steels, Y. Kuniyoshi (Eds.), Embodied Artificial Intelligence. IX, 331 pages. 2004.

Vol. 3131: V. Torra, Y. Narukawa (Eds.), Modeling Decisions for Artificial Intelligence. XI, 327 pages. 2004.

Vol. 3127: K.E. Wolff, H.D. Pfeiffer, H.S. Delugach (Eds.), Conceptual Structures at Work. XI, 403 pages. 2004.

Vol. 3123: A. Belz, R. Evans, P. Piwek (Eds.), Natural Language Generation. X, 219 pages. 2004.

Vol. 3120: J. Shawe-Taylor, Y. Singer (Eds.), Learning Theory. X, 648 pages. 2004.

Vol. 3097: D. Basin, M. Rusinowitch (Eds.), Automated Reasoning. XII, 493 pages. 2004.

Vol. 3071: A. Omicini, P. Petta, J. Pitt (Eds.), Engineering Societies in the Agents World. XIII, 409 pages. 2004.

Vol. 3070: L. Rutkowski, J. Siekmann, R. Tadeusiewicz, L.A. Zadeh (Eds.), Artificial Intelligence and Soft Computing - ICAISC 2004. XXV, 1208 pages. 2004.

Vol. 3068: E. André, L. Dybkjær, W. Minker, P. Heisterkamp (Eds.), Affective Dialogue Systems. XII, 324 pages. 2004.